Visual Basic® and GUI Applications

PEARSON
Custom
Publishing

Printed in the United States of America

10 9 8 7 6 5 4 3 2 1

ISBN 0-536-90421-9

2004200355

AG

Please visit our web site at *www.pearsoncustom.com*

PEARSON CUSTOM PUBLISHING
75 Arlington Street, Suite 300, Boston, MA 02116
A Pearson Education Company

TABLE OF CONTENTS

Chapter 3—Working with Forms and Controls

Chapter 4—Working with Menus and Windows

Chapter 5—Working with Databases

Chapter 6—Using Advanced ActiveX Controls with Databases

Chapter 7—Classes and Collections

Chapter 8—Distributing VB Applications

Glossary

Bibliography

Index

About the Book

The VB and GUI applications book deals with the role of Visual Basics 6 for designing the graphical user interface. This book shows the importance of GUI factors for designing an application. It presents the principles, methodologies, and processes related to the user interface design in an easy and comprehensive way. It provides details for creating applications using Visual Basics by showing the step-by-step process of developing applications.

Chapter 1 introduces the concept of an interface. It also discusses the concept and techniques related to the user interface design. In addition, the chapter identifies the factors affecting the user interface design and the principles involved in the design phase of a user interface.

Chapter 2 introduces the design process of the user interface. It explains the design methodology and the design models required to design a graphical user interface. This chapter discusses different types of users and also explains the design cycle involved in the user interface design process. In addition, the chapter deals with VB 6 IDE as a Rapid Application Development (RAD) tool, used for designing the prototype of an application.

Chapter 3 discusses how to use forms and controls in Visual Basic 6 to design the user interface. The chapter also explains the interface styles that can be used to present the user interface applications.

Chapter 4 highlights the creation and implementation of menu-driven applications. It discusses the types of interface designs, Single Document Interface (SDI) and Multiple Document Interface (MDI). The chapter also explains how to create the SDI and MDI applications in Visual Basic 6 IDE.

Chapter 5 defines the concept of databases, their design, and database providers. It discusses the SQL statement for manipulating databases. In addition, the chapter explains how to create databases using MS Access and Visual Data Manager.

Chapter 6 introduces the ActiveX controls used for designing an interface. It discusses how to use ActiveX controls with databases to represent data in a visual form. The ActiveX controls discussed in the chapter are DataList, DataCombo, DataGrid, and Microsoft Hierarchical FlexGrid.

Chapter 7 discusses classes, collations, and their use in Visual Basic 6. It also discusses object-oriented programming and how it is implemented in the class modules created in Visual Basic 6.

Chapter 8 lists the steps to develop and install packages using the Package and Deployment Wizard. The chapter also discusses the requirements for the Visual Basic 6 project and how to include them in the installation package.

Conventions Used in the Book

This book contains features, such as notes, tips, warnings, and references, identified by various icons. Each of these icons presents a different type of information. Following is the list of icons that will be used in the book.

 A note provides information about the topic in context. This is additional information related to the topic.

 A tip provides an alternative method for performing a task. It can also contain a simplified, although unconventional, method of doing a task.

 Just-a-Minute presents nice-to-know information or a quick question that checks the learners' understanding of the current topic.

 A warning informs you about the dire effects of an action. Focusing on these warnings reduces the likelihood that learners will make the same errors.

 A reference provides links to Web sites or relevant books and white papers for further study on a particular topic.

 Each topic begins with objectives that inform learners about the learning outcome of a topic.

In addition, you will come across *italicized text* that represents newly introduced terms.

An Introduction to User Interface Design

This chapter discusses the concept of an interface. It explains the meaning, functions, importance, and advantages of an interface. It discusses how the concept and techniques related to user interface design have evolved over the years. It also identifies the factors that affect a user interface design. Finally, it discusses the principles that are crucial in the design phase of a user interface.

At the end of this chapter, you will be able to:

- Explain the concept of an interface.

- Explain the components of a user interface.

- Explain the evolution of the graphical user interface.

- Explain the factors affecting a user interface design.

- Explain the importance of a user interface design.

- Explain the principles of a user interface design.

1.1 Concept of a User Interface

The term "interface" means a boundary or an edge. An interface is a layer that bridges the gap between the internal operations of an entity and the activities of the users using the entity. It serves as the boundary between the user and the entity.

In daily life, you may come across a number of interfaces. For instance, a circuit breaker panel acts as an interface between you and the electrical connections in your home. The circuit breaker panel makes it easy (and safe) for you to work on these electrical connections. Although most people do not know the intricacies of electrical circuits, they can easily manipulate the switches on the circuit breaker panel and then perform any needed work on a circuit.

An interface is designed to simplify the use of an entity, to protect the user from any harm caused by the entity, and to protect the entity from misuse by the user. In terms of software engineering, an interface is a medium of interaction between the end users and the computer. The interface is what a user sees while working with software. A user interface is used to:

- Enter the data, present output, and guide the user.

- Simplify the task of executing applications on the computer.

- Protect the computer from any intentional or unintentional damage caused due to user interaction.

- Present understandable information to the user.

A graphical user interface (GUI) uses pictures rather than text to provide information and perform tasks. A GUI is a more expressive, accessible, and pleasing way of presenting information to the user, which is a benefit for computer novices. Moreover, a GUI supports a variety of input devices in contrast to textual interfaces. GUIs such as Microsoft Windows provide interactive content with the help of icons, tool tips, menus, and assistance with errors and other actions that need to be taken by the user.

Figure 1.1 illustrates the functions of a user interface.

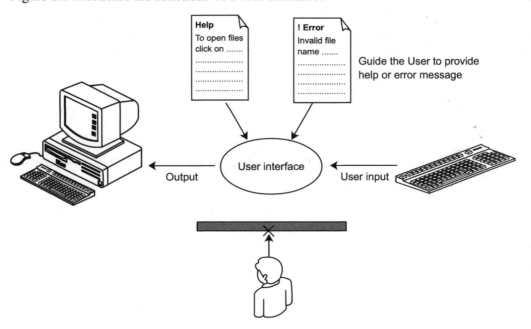

Figure 1.1: Functions of a User Interface

1.1.1 Components of a GUI and Object-Action Interface Model

 Explain the components of a GUI and the object-action interface model.

The two main components of a GUI are:

- The screen area and the graphical objects on the screen.
- The events associated with user actions.

The user interacts and performs tasks with the graphical objects on the screen. These graphical objects are designed to represent real world items so that the user can easily map real-world tasks to the graphical objects that they represent.

Another component of an interface is an event. An event is triggered when a user interacts with a graphical object. The event leads to the completion of a task that the user wants to perform.

The most important task of interface design is to apply an object-action interface model. This model represents how direct interaction or manipulation of each object leads to some sequence of events and forms the basis of interface design. Figure 1.2 shows an object-action interface model for an icon that inserts tables in an active window.

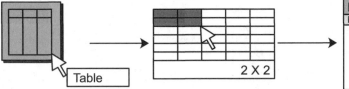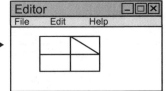

Click the table icon to insert a table.	Drag the mouse to select the dimensions of the table. The highlighted part shows the dimensions.	Draw the table at the current position in the window.

Figure 1.2: Object-Action Interface Model

In Figure 1.2, the "Table" icon (graphical object) is clicked (event). The result is that a second object is now displayed. The user can now drag the mouse over the grid (another event) to select the dimensions of the table. When the user completes this action, the table is inserted in the active window.

As an end user, you must have used different software, some with good interfaces, and others with bad interfaces. What parameters helped you categorize them as good or bad?

1.1.2 Good and Bad Interfaces

 Analyze the factors that determine the qualities of well-designed interfaces.

A well-designed interface gives preference to users and their needs and wants. A GUI designer must understand the user's needs and wants so that they are matched up with the capabilities of the hardware and software of a computer. Good interfaces are also designed to meet the needs of a variety of user experience levels. For instance, most modern GUIs have consistent keyboard shortcuts, as shown in Table 1.1. Suppose a designer develops an interface that does not use these shortcuts. It may not make any difference to a novice user, but it may be frustrating to a user who is accustomed to working on computers and uses these shortcuts frequently.

Task	Description	Keyboard Shortcut
Cut	Remove selected or highlighted text or graphics.	Ctrl + X
Copy	Copy the selected text or graphics.	Ctrl + C
Paste	Paste the cut or copied text or graphics.	Ctrl + V
Undo	Undo the most recent action.	Ctrl + Z
Close	Close or terminate the application having the input focus.	Alt + F4

Table 1.1: Commonly Used Keyboard Shortcuts

One of the earliest user interfaces was MS-DOS. Many users do not like the MS-DOS interface because:

- It is cumbersome to memorize commands.
- It is a completely textual interface and does not support mouse or other input devices other than the keyboard.
- It is not visually pleasing.

In contrast, users find the Microsoft Windows user interface to be exceptional. The interface of Windows-based software is not only visually pleasing, but also functionally efficient. For example:

- It allows users to use either the keyboard or mouse.
- It displays helpful descriptive messages and text.
- It provides immediate and reversible actions and feedback.
- It provides meaningful paths and exits.
- It accommodates users with different skill levels.
- It allows users to customize the interface.
- It allows users to directly manipulate interface objects.

Therefore, users are allowed to control the interface in order to complete the tasks and events they wish to accomplish.

Figure 1.3 shows the directories and files in the hard disk drive of a computer.

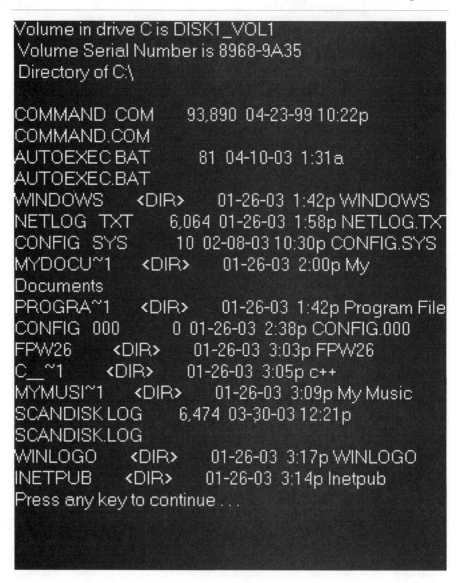

```
Volume in drive C is DISK1_VOL1
 Volume Serial Number is 8968-9A35
 Directory of C:\

COMMAND  COM       93,890  04-23-99 10:22p
COMMAND.COM
AUTOEXEC BAT          81  04-10-03 1:31a
AUTOEXEC.BAT
WINDOWS     <DIR>        01-26-03 1:42p WINDOWS
NETLOG  TXT      6,064 01-26-03 1:58p NETLOG.TX
CONFIG  SYS        10 02-08-03 10:30p CONFIG.SYS
MYDOCU~1     <DIR>        01-26-03 2:00p My
Documents
PROGRA~1     <DIR>        01-26-03 1:42p Program File
CONFIG  000        0 01-26-03 2:38p CONFIG.000
FPW26     <DIR>        01-26-03 3:03p FPW26
C__~1      <DIR>        01-26-03 3:05p c++
MYMUSI~1     <DIR>        01-26-03 3:09p My Music
SCANDISK LOG      6,474 03-30-03 12:21p
SCANDISK.LOG
WINLOGO     <DIR>        01-26-03 3:17p WINLOGO
INETPUB     <DIR>        01-26-03 3:14p Inetpub
Press any key to continue . . .
```

Figure 1.3: Directories and Files in a Hard Disk Drive Using MS-DOS

Figure 1.4 shows the drives and folders of a computer in Windows.

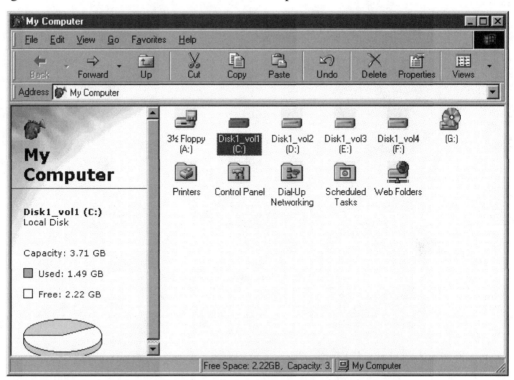

Figure 1.4: Drives and Folders of a Computer Using Windows

Figure 1.5 shows the folders and files in Windows after Drive C is double-clicked.

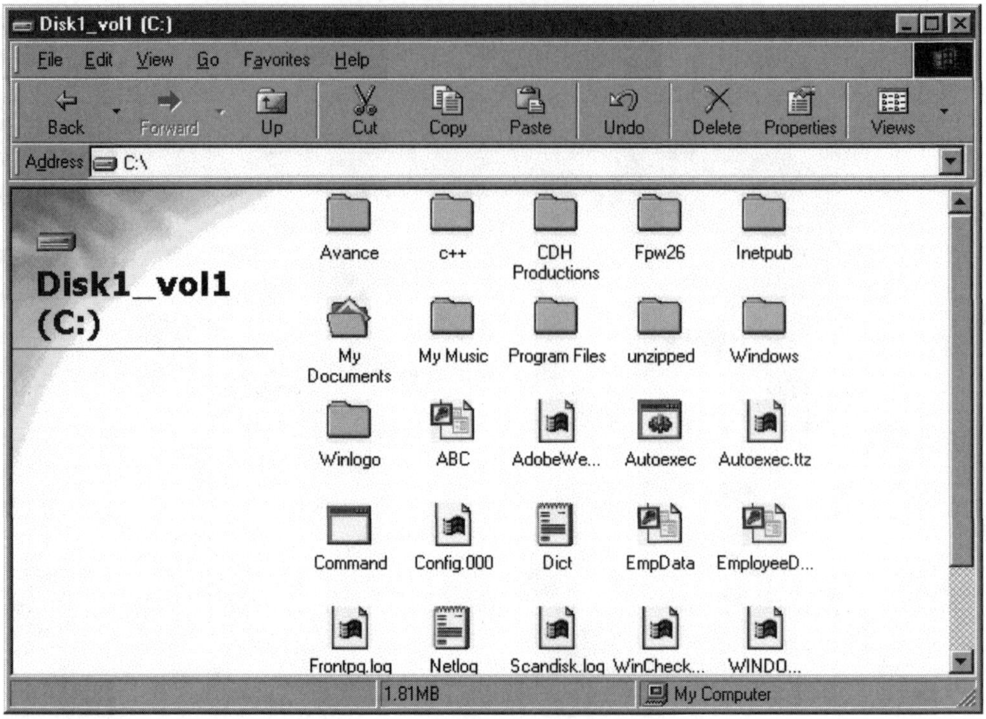

![Windows Explorer window titled Disk1_vol1 (C:) showing folders and files]

Disk1_vol1 [C:]	_ □ ✕

File   Edit   View   Go   Favorites   Help

Back   Forward   Up   Cut   Copy   Paste   Undo   Delete   Properties   Views

Address 💾 C:\

Disk1_vol1
(C:)

Avance   c++   CDH Productions   Fpw26   Inetpub

My Documents   My Music   Program Files   unzipped   Windows

Winlogo   ABC   AdobeWe...   Autoexec   Autoexec.ttz

Command   Config.000   Dict   EmpData   EmployeeD...

Frontpg.log   Netlog   Scandisk.log   WinCheck...   WINDO...

1.81MB   💻 My Computer

Figure 1.5: Folders and Files in a Drive in Windows

The **dir** command in MS-DOS lists all the files in a directory as well as the capacity of the drive. In Windows, accessing the drive is as easy as double-clicking the **My Computer** icon and then the **drive** icon. All the files are listed, as shown in Figure 1.5. You can perform file operations such as deleting, copying, and moving by using the appropriate menus. However, in MS-DOS you have to explicitly type a command for each of these operations.

The strategy behind designing good GUIs is using graphics in a sensible and intuitive manner.

Some key points to remember when creating a good interface are:

- Graphics should be used to accurately portray data. Overusing graphics in GUIs defeats the purpose behind using pictures instead of plain text.

- Color can be effectively used to improve performance. It should portray meaningful information in the interface, and not just be used as a decorative element.

- Menus are effective because they use the more powerful human capability of recognition rather than depending on the user's memory to recall. However, menus are not without their problems, and so the type of menu style used must be carefully considered.

- A good interface must follow the WYSIWYG (What You See Is What You Get) principle. On performing an action, a user should get the expected outcome.

With the advent of technically superior, visually appealing, and user-friendly GUIs, computers have gained a foothold in the everyday lives of the public. Electronic documents have replaced printed and handwritten documents while postal services have given way to electronic mail. Similarly, manual accounting has been replaced by powerful and efficient software packages, such as QuickBooks or Peachtree.

In the next topic, you will learn about how it all started.

1.1.3 Evolution of GUIs

 Explain the evolution of GUIs.

Until the early 1980s, interfaces similar to MS-DOS were common. These interfaces supported only text-based, keyboard entries. Interface technology was in its initial stages of development, and resources were expensive. As a result, graphics were not used extensively.

In those days, the approach to designing interfaces was problem-centric rather than user-centric. Software was not designed for homes and offices. It was designed for people who knew the internal details of computers. The emphasis was only on efficiency. The evolution of GUIs saw the focus of design shifting from problem-centric issues such as hardware concerns and software issues to user-centric issues such as user perception and user demands. The user-centric approach concentrated on the human-computer interface: how human psychology works, and how to make software user friendly, visually appealing, and efficient.

Figure 1.6 illustrates the evolution of GUIs.

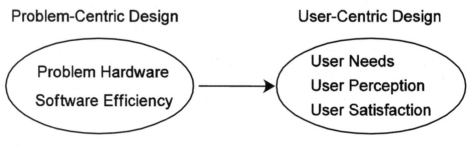

Figure 1.6: Evolution of GUIs

The Apple Macintosh, introduced in 1984, is commonly thought of as the product that brought the GUI to life as a commercially successful personal computer desktop. Much of its success can be attributed to the work done by Ivan Sutherland at the Massachusetts Institute of Technology and the Xerox Palo Alto Research Center (PARC). In 1985, Microsoft released Windows 1.0 followed by several enhanced versions, ultimately resulting in Windows 95. In 1989, UNIX-based GUIs were released, and these interfaces were later incorporated into the Linux environment. Today, GUIs are widely available for any situation; yet they all generally subscribe to the same features.

1.1.4 Factors Affecting Interface Design

 Explain the factors affecting an interface design.

Designing an interface is not merely a software engineering concept. It includes creative and artistic activity. By combining software engineering principles and methodologies with an artistic outlook, you can create a good GUI.

The three main factors that affect the design of a user interface are:

- Human factors
- Software factors
- Hardware factors

Figure 1.7 illustrates these three factors.

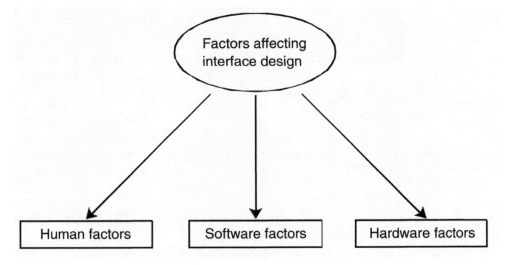

Figure 1.7: Factors Affecting an Interface Design

All these factors are important while designing an interface. Ignoring any one of these factors can reduce its effectiveness and value.

Human Factors

Human factors are the foundation on which an interface is designed. A user-centric approach to designing an interface has a higher chance of satisfying the user, because it gives highest priority to user demands. An interface designer must remember that the user perceives the interface as the entire software. Therefore, it is very important to understand the requirements of the user. The interface designer must find the answers to the following questions to analyze human factors during the interface design process.

- Who are the end users of the software?
- How knowledgeable are they about computers, and what is their comfort level with computers?
- What are the working environments of the users?
- How do the users perceive the interface in their minds?

- How willing are the users to adjust to a new, computerized working environment?
- How motivated are the users to change their old style of working and learn new concepts?

If the design team understands the perspective, likes, and dislikes of users, they can easily generate a successful interface design.

Some users understand computers well and are willing to computerize or upgrade their working environment. These users can easily perform tasks on the computer and take the associated changes in stride. Other users want to computerize or upgrade their working environment just for the sake of efficiency but have no prior knowledge of computers. These set of users require a lot more time to get used to computers. They also need extensive training to learn new software.

Usability testing is particularly important in interface design. In usability testing, the user tests a prototype of the interface in the appropriate working environment, and provides feedback to the design team. Based on the feedback, the team can incorporate changes in the initial design. Frequent usability testing helps in designing better interfaces.

Figure 1.8 shows a user-centric design process that places the user in the crucial position while designing the interface.

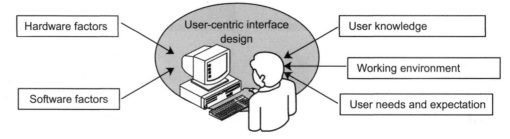

Figure 1.8: A User-Centric Interface Design

Software Factors

Software factors usually apply to basic user interface characteristics. Standards have been developed to make information processing equipment easier and safer for people to use by eliminating unnecessary inconsistencies and variations in the user interfaces. Thus, interface design becomes a series of tradeoffs, a series of conflicts among principles, and these concepts are sometimes difficult to incorporate into guidelines.

Effective design and development requires very diverse talents. No one person possesses all the skills to perform all the necessary tasks. A balanced design team with very different talents must be established. Design specialists are needed to define requirements, human factors specialists to define behavioral requirements and apply behavioral considerations, and people with good visual design skills. Also needed are people skilled in testing and usability assessment.

Hardware Factors

Screen design is affected by the physical characteristics of the display device itself. The design must be compatible with the following hardware capabilities:

- Processor power: A slow processing speed and limited memory may inhibit the effective use of Windows. In addition, slow responses can be error-prone, grossly inefficient, and very aggravating.

- Screen size: Some screens are not large enough in size to take full advantage of windowing capabilities. In this case, users prefer to see one window rather than small parts of many windows. On the other hand, as larger screen sizes become more prolific, a larger screen size will require longer control movements to reach all locations on the screen, and more head and eye movement. There are also situations where multiple screens may be employed, which further impact users and control movement.

- Screen resolution and graphics capability: Poor screen resolution and graphics capability may deter effective use of a graphical system by not displaying sharp and realistic drawings and shapes. Adequate screen resolution and graphics capability is a necessity to achieve meaningful representations.

- Displayable colors: The color palette must be large enough to display a family of discriminating colors. The colors must be accurately and clearly presented in all situations.

1.1.5 Importance of a User Interface Design

 Explain the importance of a user interface design.

Greatly improved technology has eliminated many of the barriers to good interface design and unleashed a variety of new display and interaction techniques wrapped into a package called the GUI. The amount of programming code of an operating system devoted to the user interface now exceeds 50 percent.

A well-designed interface is terribly important to users. It is their window to view the capabilities of their computer system. To many, *it is the system*, being one of the few visible components of the product software designers create. It is also the vehicle through which many critical tasks are presented. These tasks often have a direct impact on an organization's relations with its customers and its profitability.

An interface's layout and appearance affects a person in a variety of ways. If they are confusing and inefficient, people will have greater difficulty in doing their jobs and will make more mistakes. Poor design may permanently discourage some people from using a system. It can also lead to aggravation, frustration, and increased stress.

Practice Questions

1. How is a GUI better than textual interfaces if both have the same basic functionality?

2. Give an example of an object-action interface model as described in the chapter.

3. Which GUI popularized the use of graphics in applications and is considered as a standard among other GUIs?

4. List the costs involved in interface design. Briefly explain the importance of each cost and its effect on the design process.

5. "Bulk of the code in software is due to interface design." Is this statement true?

1.2 Principles of User Interface Design

User perceptions often determine whether an interface is good or bad. An interface may be acceptable to one user and unacceptable to another. However, certain guidelines specify basic qualities of a good interface. Adhering to these principles while designing an interface may increase the probability of its acceptance by the user. These basic principles, known as the golden rules of interface design, are essential for every interface, regardless of the operating environment for which the interface is designed.

1.2.1 The Three Golden Rules of Interface Design

 Explain the three golden rules for designing interfaces.

The following rules of interface design help create well-designed interfaces:

- Provide control of the interface to the user
- Design a consistent interface
- Place the least amount of burden on system memory

Figure 1.9 illustrates the three golden rules of interface design.

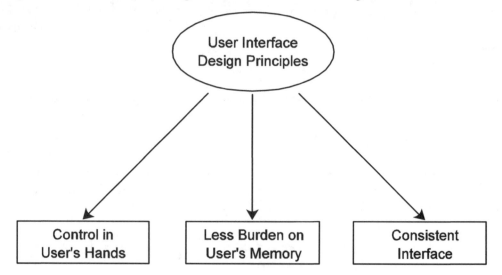

Figure 1.9: The Three Golden Rules of Interface Design

Placing the User in Control

A good interface is always placed under the user's control. The user should be able to manipulate the interface in a variety of possible ways. At the same time, there should be a balance between user control and misuse. For example, the user should not be able to destroy the interface or system data.

In addition, users should not be compelled to perform tasks in a particular sequence. As far as possible, users should be capable of performing tasks in their own desired order. However, there are unavoidable situations, such as system errors, that should get the focus before any further actions are performed.

Recall from IT104 that a modal dialog box requires the user to close the dialog box before activating another window in the application. Thus, avoid using modal dialog boxes for tasks that are lengthy. Use them only when it is mandatory for a task to be executed before any other task. For instance, the **Save As** dialog box in various interfaces is modal because one must provide a file name before any further processing can occur.

It is important to remember that the user is typically not an interface designer. The user is curious to explore the interface, although the user may not be clear on how to perform certain tasks. Therefore, the interface must be robust enough to handle any possible errors arising out of such user behavior. This makes the user feel safe. Also, some user tasks should be confirmed before they are carried out. For instance, confirming a file deletion operation, or warning the user against a potentially dangerous action gives complete control to the user over the interface and simultaneously protects the system from damage.

An interface may have a number of users. A good interface provides a list of predefined modes and schemes. A wide range of options, such as different screen resolutions, variety of input devices, and different fonts should be provided to suit the preferences of the individual users. The users should also be able to customize the interface depending on their working environments and needs. In a good interface, objects provided on the desktop are analogous to objects placed on the users' desks. The users choose or select objects to manipulate. The objects are moved around and placed as desired. This gives the users a sense of control and familiarity with the interface.

Early versions of Windows allowed users to tile windows when more than one window was open. This was counter-intuitive to the idea of a desktop. In later versions, documents on a desktop could be layered on top of one another.

Designing a Consistent Interface

A good interface should be consistent in terms of visual appearance as well as actions performed. All option (radio) buttons, for instance, must be of a fixed shape. Usually, these buttons are small circles and clicking on them changes the appearance of the interface, which indicates its selection. If an interface is designed to show an option button as a square (commonly used for check boxes) instead of a circle, then the users may confuse them with check boxes. Thus, controls and other interface objects should not only be consistent in their appearance but also in their function. For instance, an icon with an exclamation mark is used for showing error messages in most interfaces. If you use it in your interface, it helps the user to understand that an error has occurred. Do not use an exclamation mark for an error notification at one place, and something else at another place in your interface.

Placing the Least Amount of Burden on System Memory

A consistent interface places few burdens on the system memory. The sequence of actions defined for accomplishing tasks should be intuitive. Commands and their shortcuts must be consistent. For instance, having the same keyboard accelerators for cut, copy, and paste options make the interface consistent and prevent the need for memorizing them. An interface should be suggestive of real world objects so that the user can relate it to everyday chores. The human mind can remember things more easily if they are in context to other common things. The use of terminology, such as desktop, folders, and recycle bins in computers is indicative of the importance of this factor.

1.2.2 Principles of Data Entry and Display in an Interface

 Explain the principles pertaining to data entry and display.

It is very important to display information and input data in an organized fashion. A chaotic screen layout can confuse the user. The principles for displaying and typing data are:

- Use graphics, sound, and animation. A good interface uses a variety of techniques to display data. However, colors and sounds should not irritate the user. Fonts must be legible and visually pleasing. No unnecessary graphics or animation should be introduced in the interface. Every object and method used in the interface must make sense to the user. Do not use graphics where only text is necessary. The text used in an interface should be clear and concise. Choose the color, font, size, and background of the text very carefully.

Figure 1.10 shows help files opened in two different interfaces. The first uses a font and color scheme that is artistic but not legible. The language used in the first file is very confusing and unimpressive. The second uses a simple font and color scheme that is clear, readable, and easy to understand.

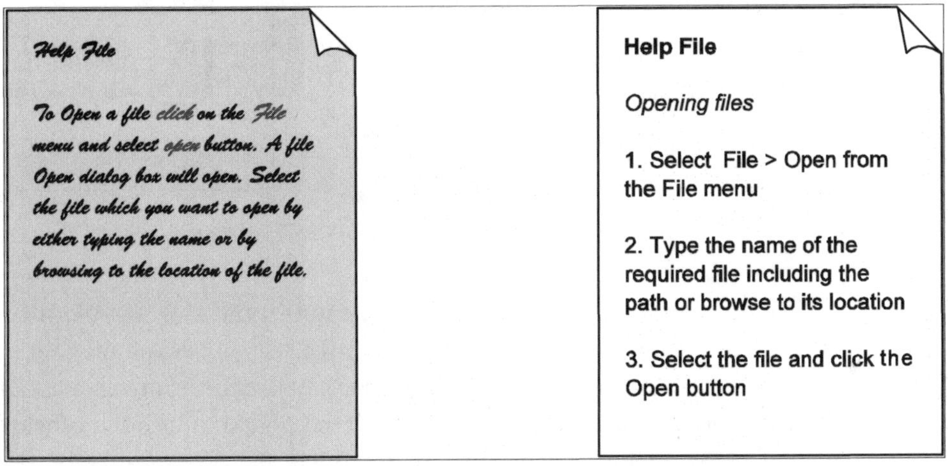

Figure 1.10: Using Legible Text in Interfaces

- Use minimal direct input from the user. An interface should let the user choose from a predefined list of possible inputs. For instance, when a user enters a date, it is better to use a predesignated list of formats for the day, month, and year, rather than having the user type it from a keyboard. If the user must perform the typing, provide hints that show how the user should type it in.

- Provide consistent feedback to the user. A good interface provides consistent feedback to the user, making the interface closer to the real world. The user should be able to see that input via a pointing device or keyboard has been accepted, and the corresponding tasks are being performed. Another common practice is to change the pointer when the user performs different operations. For instance, an hourglass shaped pointer indicates that the application is busy.

- Use descriptive interfaces. A good interface should provide explanatory messages to guide the user, particularly when an error has occurred.

Figure 1.11 shows two error messages pertaining to data being copied to a floppy disk with no capacity.

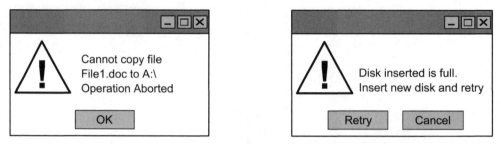

Figure 1.11: Displaying Descriptive Error Messages

The first error message in Figure 1.11 informs the user that the file cannot be copied to the disk, but does not specify the reason, and simply aborts the operation. The second error message, on the other hand, informs the user about the reason for the error. It also provides the user with the option to insert another disk, retry, or cancel the operation. The success of the interface does not lie in the method of presentation of errors but in avoiding errors as much as possible. Descriptive and efficient interfaces reduce the probability of errors. Nevertheless, users are bound to make mistakes and there should be provisions to rectify them.

■ Use real world descriptions for depicting applications with the help of icons. This makes the interface intuitive, easy to use, and easy to learn. Remain consistent in the use of descriptions in the interface. For instance, you may use a phone icon for depicting a dial-up connection to the Internet on the main page of your application. If you switch to an icon with a computer connected to a phone on some other part of the interface, the user may get confused. Though the functionality is clear in both the icons, it is a very confusing practice to use separate icons for the same application. Using metaphors is a descriptive way to present information, but do not use them where they are not necessary. You must also try not to use any offensive symbols or graphics.

■ Use keyboard support for the interfaces. Even though support for multiple input devices in a GUI is its strength, you must try to emulate every action of other input devices with keystrokes. Using a particular input device is a matter of preference. Some users prefer to work with the keyboard. In some cases, using keyboard shortcuts saves time.

A good interface is easy to use, is visually appealing, intuitive, requires minimal effort from the user, and is efficient. It does not lead to errors, yet supports recovery from errors. The user should not require a help system, yet the interface should support one. Overall, an interface which is complete in itself is considered a good interface.

Practice Questions

1. How does a designer's personal preference affect an interface?

2. State principles important to you in a good GUI design (other than the ones explained in the chapter).

3. An interface designer plans to use different fonts for different parts of the interface. Which principles is the designer violating and how?

4. In a text editor interface, the **Font** command for changing the font of the text is arranged in the menu hierarchy as follows:

   View → Toolbox → Text Editing & Formatting → Font

   Is this a satisfactory way of arranging a menu item? If not, which principles are being violated? How would you correct them?

Case Study

XYZ is a popular library for Information Technology books. The management has identified the need for an automated system to keep track of the books in the library, members, and issue and receipt of books. The requirement specification of the system states that the system should allow the addition and deletion of book details as well as have an interface to add and modify member accounts. The system should ensure that only one book is issued to a member at a time and the maximum time for possession of the book is one week. There will be a late fine of $5 for each extra day beyond the deadline. The books are identified by their ISBN number and members are identified by their registration number. The books are classified into categories based on subjects.

Summary

- A computer interface is a medium of communication between the user and the computer's hardware and software. A GUI presents information using graphics, sound, and animation.

- An interface simplifies the task of processing the software, guides the user, and protects the computer from damage due to user misuse.

- A GUI consists of two main components: the graphical objects and events. Creating the object-action model is the primary job of an interface design team.

- Earlier interfaces were mainly textual in nature. With improvement in technology and a shift in focus from a problem-centric to a user-centric approach, designing GUIs has become an integral part of the software design process.

- Three factors affect interface design: human factors, software factors, and hardware factors. User-centric designs give the highest priority to human factors.

- Human factors deal with the user's psychology, working environment, and demands.

- Software factors deal with designing, making assumptions, assessing the limitations of a design, and coding an efficient interface.

- Hardware factors deal with the financial and performance constraints related to the hardware that will be used with the interface.

- Interface design is very important to software development because it incurs a great amount of cost, effort, and hardware and software resources. The success of the software lies in the acceptance of the interface by the user.

- The golden rules of interface design are: place the interface under the user's control, place the least amount of burden on the system memory, and design consistent interfaces.

- Never overuse graphics, sound, and animation in GUIs.

- Keep direct input from the user to a minimum.

- A good interface provides timely, effective response to the user.

- A good interface supports keyboard shortcuts.

- A good interface uses real world examples to represent graphical objects, such as icons and buttons.

- An intuitive interface design has the least probability of errors yet provides detailed support for tackling errors. The user should not be dependent on the help facility.

References

- http://www.library.itt-tech.edu/periodicals.asp> FindArticles.com (Accessed on Aug. 12, 2004)
- http://www.library.itt-tech.edu/periodicals.asp> MSDN Magazine (Accessed on Aug. 12, 2004)

Homework Exercises

1. Give an example of an object-action interface model as given in the chapter.

2. How is the interface affected if the designer's personal preferences are incorporated into the design of an interface?

3. Which GUI, considered as a standard for other GUIs, popularized the use of graphics in applications?

4. What is an interface in terms of software engineering? State the functions of an interface.

5. Give an example (other than the one in the chapter) of an interface that you encounter in your daily life. In your own opinion, what is the importance of interface design?

6. Determine if the interfaces in Figures 1.12 and 1.13 are acceptable GUI designs. Give reasons for your answers. The interface in Figure 1.12 below makes the user type in all the fields and has an **Add** button to insert records into a database. The interface in Figure 1.13 presents a menu-driven database management system. The figure shows the first menu option. A help file is also open.

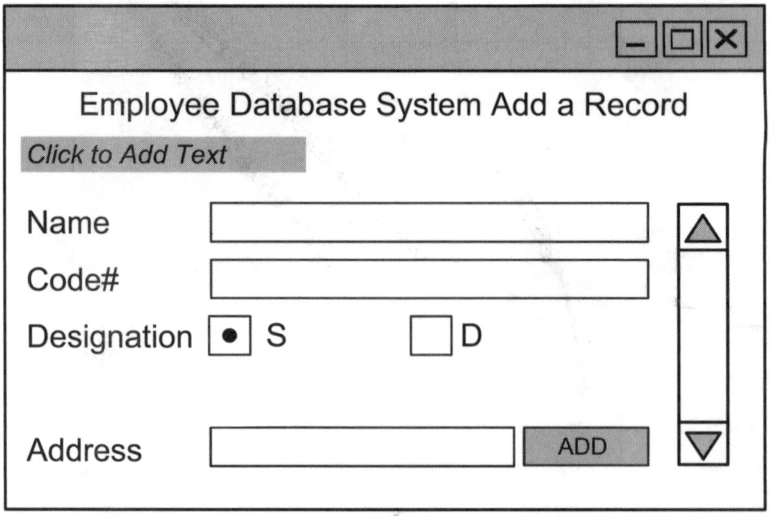

Figure 1.12: First Menu Option

Figure 1.13 shows a menu-driven database management system.

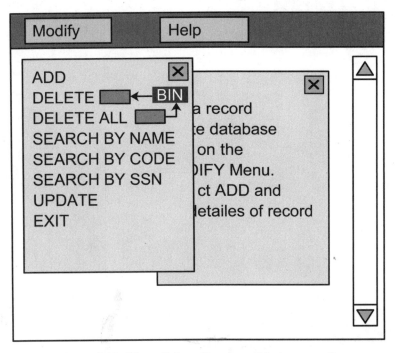

Figure 1.13: Menu-Driven Database Management System

a. State the principles that should be followed to improve the GUIs shown in Figures 1.12 and 1.13.

b. What is the importance of designing interfaces for users?

c. If you had to design the interface for a car race game, what software and hardware factors would you consider?

Lab Exercises

Exercise 1

Objective

- The objective of this assignment is to familiarize the students with the principles that are important to user interface design.

Problem Statement

Give a rough design view, using Microsoft Visual Basic or any drawing package, of a simple interface for inventory management software. The first page of the interface includes two modes, **Customer** and **Owner**. The **Owner** mode allows the owner to modify the contents, and the **Customer** mode simply shows a list of items to the customer along with their price and item codes. Design the first page of this interface showing the two modes. List the design principles applied.

Lab Setup

Computer Requirements:

- Microsoft Windows operating system
- Pentium III or later processors
- 128-MB RAM
- 3-GB hard disk
- CD-ROM drives
- Floppy disk drives
- LAN connections
- Microsoft Visual Basic 6.0
- Microsoft Paint or some other graphics package

Procedure

The procedure for this lab assignment begins with understanding the requirements of the interface to be designed. Decide on the use of graphics, colors, fonts, interface layout, and other details beforehand to maintain consistency while designing the interface. You may use Visual Basic, Microsoft Paint or any other painting package with which you are familiar. Paper and pencil can be used, but this approach often requires additional notes and details regarding colors, fonts, etc. Design the interface as you have visualized it, and list the principles applied while designing it.

The inventory interface can be designed as shown in Figure 1.14.

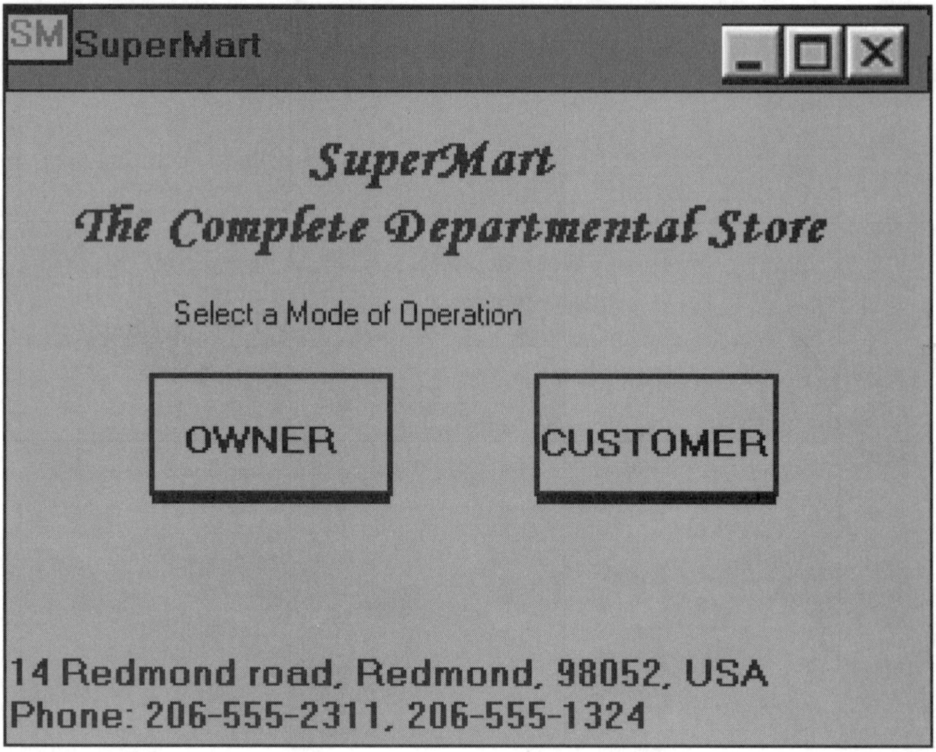

Figure 1.14: Inventory Interface

The principles applied to the design shown in Figure 1.14 are:

- Use of legible text.

- No overuse of graphics. The interface colors are simple and not distracting. No unnecessary pictures or graphical objects have been used.

- Minimal direct input from the user. This has been achieved by using command buttons to specify the mode that the user wants to work in.

- Self-descriptive interface. The user can instantly understand the functionality provided by the interface.

Conclusion/Observation

The assignment clarifies the importance of applying good design principles while designing an interface. The art of designing a good interface is examined in closer detail in the next lab assignment.

Lab Activity Checklist

S. No.	Tasks	Completed	
		Yes	No
· 1.	Applied the principle of placing the least amount of burden on the user		
2.	Applied the principle of placing the user in control		
3.	Applied the principle of consistency		
4.	Avoided the overuse of graphics		
5.	Minimal direct input from the user required		
6.	Legible text, graphics, and layout		
7.	Self-descriptive interface design		
8.	Followed factors affecting the interface design while designing		

Exercise 2

Objective

- Familiarize the students with the principles that are important to user interface design by applying them in practice.

Problem Statement

Continue to design the interface you began in Exercise 1 by developing the interface that appears when the user clicks on the **Owner** option button. Use Microsoft Visual Basic or other paint program. This page shows a price list of the inventory items, and buttons for modifying the price list. List the principles applied in the design.

Lab Setup

Computer Requirements:

- Microsoft Windows operating system
- Pentium III or later processors
- 128-MB RAM
- 3-GB hard disk
- CD-ROM drives
- Floppy disk drives
- LAN connections
- Visual Basic 6.0
- Microsoft Paint or some other paint package

Procedure

The procedure for this lab assignment begins with getting a clear idea of the requirements of the interface to be designed. The requirements for this part of the interface must be decided by keeping in mind the interface designed in Exercise 1. Design the interface as you have visualized it, and list the principles applied while designing it.

The interface can be designed as shown in the Figure 1.15.

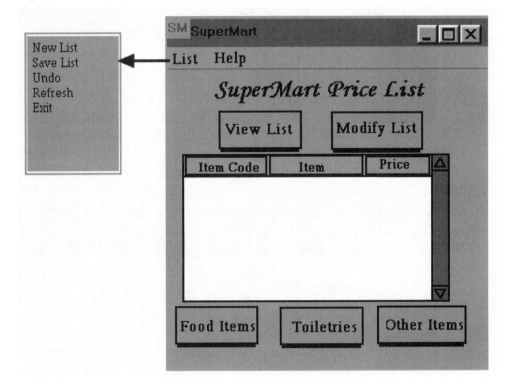

Figure 1.15: Interface Design

The interface shows two main features, a **View List** command button, and a **Modify List** command button. Since these are frequently used options, they have been shown clearly on the interface and not hidden.

The interface in Figure 1.15 currently shows the **View List** display. The **View List** display can also be of three forms shown by the command buttons at the bottom of the interface. These features have been included as command buttons so that the user can quickly and easily switch between them. If they were put in a menu, the user would have to use additional mouse clicks to change between these options. Other features that are not used as frequently have been put in the **List** menu. A **Help** menu has also been included in the interface.

The design principles that have been applied to the interface are:

- Consistency is maintained for colors, graphics, and layout.
- The burden on the system's memory is minimized because all the features have been arranged in a visible and practical way.

- Direct input from the user is reduced.

- The interface is controlled by the user. The list changes can be saved; the changes can be undone if the user desires; and the user can exit from this part of the interface.

Conclusion/Observation

This exercise clarifies the importance of applying good design principles while designing an interface. The art of designing a good interface is further examined in the next lab exercise.

Lab Activity Checklist

S. No.	Tasks	Completed	
		Yes	No
1.	The principle of placing the least amount of burden on the user is applied		
2.	The principle of placing the user in control is applied		
3.	The principle of consistency is applied		
4.	Overuse of graphics is avoided		
5.	Direct input from the user is kept minimal		
6.	Text, graphics, and layout are legible		
7.	Interface design is self-descriptive		
8.	Factors affecting interface design are followed while designing		

Exercise 3

Objective

■ Familiarize the students with the principles that are important to user interface design by applying them in practice.

Problem Statement

Answer the following questions for each of the interfaces shown.

1. Suppose the **Owner** mode of the inventory software discussed in the previous lab exercise is being run. The objective is to add, delete, modify, or view the list of items in the inventory. Figures 1.16 and 1.17 show two interfaces. Which is a better interface for the desired operations and why?

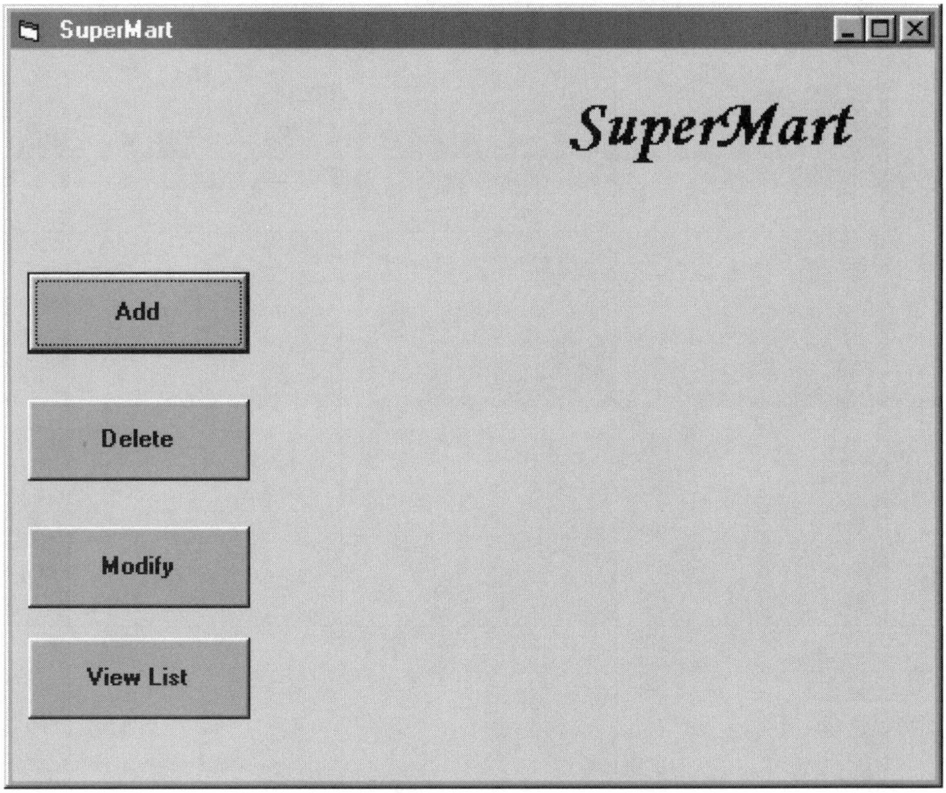

Figure 1.16: Interface with Buttons

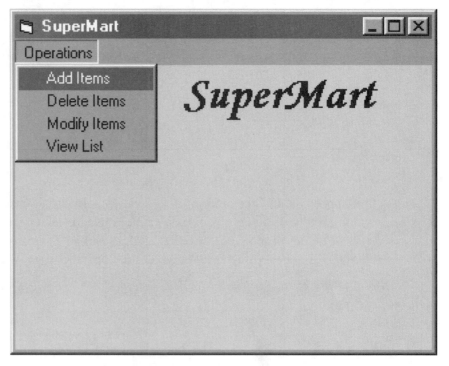

Figure1.17: Interface with Menu Options

2.   Identify any flaws in the interface shown in Figure 1.18.

Figure 1.18: Enter Password Dialog Box

3.   A part of an interface for a game is shown in Figures 1.19 and 1.20. Identify any flaws that you find with the interface.

Figure 1.19: Play Menu

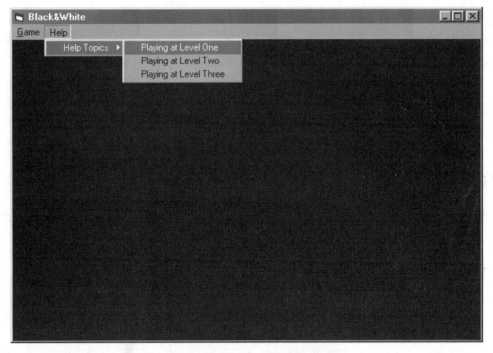

Figure 1.20: Help Topics Menu

Lab Setup

Computer Requirements:

- Microsoft Windows operating system
- Pentium III or higher processors
- 128-MB RAM
- 3-GB hard disk
- CD-ROM drives
- Floppy disk drives
- LAN connections
- Visual Basic 6.0
- Microsoft Paint or some other paint package

Procedure

The procedure for this lab exercise begins with getting a clear idea of what the interface represents. This helps you to understand the problems with the interface. Next, list all the possible flaws with the interface. The flaws must map to the design principles.

1. The interface in Figure 1.16 is better than the interface in Figure 1.17 because the operations to be performed are primary operations. Putting them in a menu hides them and requires extra clicks to perform the operations. Since these operations form the basis of the interface, they are frequently required. Thus, an extra click means wasting time and effort for the user. However, the buttons used in the first interface can be made more appealing by using icons. They can also be arranged in a toolbox to enhance the look of the interface as well as to organize screen elements.

2. The interface in Figure 1.18 overuses graphics. It requires a user to click on a command button to type a password in the text box. This wastes the user's time and effort by requiring an unnecessary click on the command button.

3. The menus used in Figures 1.19 and 1.20 are badly organized. They include unnecessary levels of depth. Submenus have been used without any actual requirements. The items placed in the menus and submenus have not been worked out properly. For instance, the **Help** menu can include a single option called **Help Topics**. In this way, it will maintain consistency with other software encountered by users and also have a more organized menu structure.

Conclusion/Observation

The lab exercise clarifies the importance of applying good design principles while designing an interface.

Lab Activity Checklist

S. No.	Tasks	Completed	
		Yes	No
1.	All the flaws pointed out in the questions		
2.	Flaws pointed out do not reflect personal opinion		
3.	Flaws pointed out map to the design principles studied		

Project

XYZ Inc. has five departments: Administration, Marketing, Finance, Research, and Store. Each department has several employees. Management has developed system requirements for a new application that will manage employee information. Employees are grouped into five grades: A, B, C, D, and E. The salary of an employee depends on his grade. The user interface should include features to input, modify, or delete the employee details and search for employee records based on department, grade, and employee code.

User Interface Models and Design Processes

2

This chapter describes the process of designing a user interface. It discusses design models and methodologies used for interface design. The chapter also focuses on the attributes of different types of users. It then explains the user interface design cycle. In addition, it describes the use of Microsoft Visual Basic as a Rapid Application Development (RAD) tool for designing user interfaces.

At the end of this chapter, you will be able to:

- Explain user interface models.
- Explain the methodologies used in designing user interfaces.
- Explain the design cycle of user interfaces.
- Analyze the role of Microsoft Visual Basic as an RAD tool.

2.1 User Interface Models

2.2 Designing an Interface

2.1 User Interface Models

A user interface is a communication medium between a user and an application. The effectiveness of an application depends on its ease of use. You may develop an efficient application but if its interface is disorganized, the application may not function as expected.

The user interface of an application needs to be intuitive. While working on an application, a user should have full control over the application. The user must be able to recover from erroneous actions without causing harm to the computer or the application. For example, when the user clicks the **Delete** command on the **File** menu, the application must confirm the deletion before deleting the file. The user may have accidentally clicked the **Delete** command. It is, therefore, essential to help the user recover from the mistake.

The user should not find it difficult to learn the conventions and procedures for using the application interface. Despite being a good operating system in terms of functionality, MS-DOS lost in popularity to the Microsoft Windows operating system because of the lack of a graphical user interface (GUI). Unlike the graphical interface of Microsoft Windows, MS-DOS required users to type commands, which was tedious. Today, a consistent, visually attractive, and easy-to-use interface is the key to the success of a well-developed application.

A GUI conveys information using icons instead of plain text. The study of human psychology has revealed that the human mind is more receptive and responsive to a pictorial representation of data. Moreover, graphical interfaces use pointing devices more than the keyboard, which eases the user's workload.

The process of designing a user interface begins with modeling. A model represents the task flow as it exists in the real world. Four models that form the basis of the GUI design are:

- User's model: This model represents the expectations and levels of knowledge of the user. Typically, this includes the tasks to be performed and the business objectives that are to be achieved.

- Designer's model: This model is the intermediary between the user's model and the programmer's model. The gap between the user's environment and the programmer's world is bridged by the interface designer and others on the design team.

- Programmer's model: Usually explicit and more formally defined, the programmer model is the functional specification for a software product.

■ Prototype model: This model is used to quickly and easily visualize design alternatives and ideas.

2.1.1 User's Model

 Explain the features of the user's model.

Interface designing must be a user-centric activity. All users have their own perceptions of an interface. An interface designer who understands user requirements has a higher probability of satisfying users by providing a well-designed interface than a designer who is not well versed with the user's requirements. The interface is not designed to prove the technical capability of the designer or the coding skills of the programmer. On the contrary, it is designed to satisfy the needs of the user. However, users may not explicitly state all their requirements. Thus, it is also essential for the designer to understand and implement implicit user requirements. Suppose a user owns a fast food business. The user wants the software to display a menu that accepts orders from customers. The software issues a check with a unique customer number and the details of the order. The receipt is presented at the counter for the ordered items. As far as the owner of the fast food business is concerned, the software is the interface, and he may not be aware of the technical process of developing the software.

The model shown in Figure 2.1 is a model of the interface in the user's mind that the designer has to interpret.

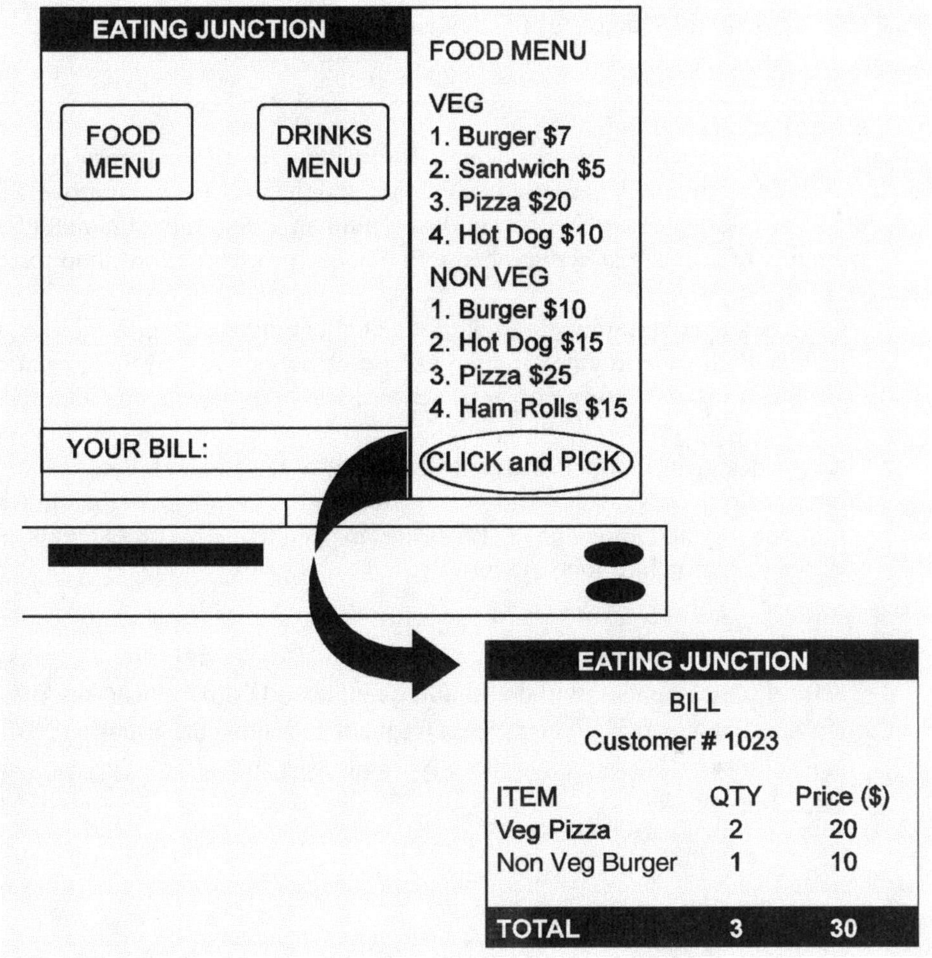

Figure 2.1: User's Model for a Fast Food Business

2.1.2 Designer's Model

 Explain the features of the designer's model.

The designer's model is a conceptual framework that forms a bridge between the model of the system that is held by the designer and the user's mental model. The designer has a responsibility to aid the user in developing an accurate mental model. Thus, as tasks are identified, they are developed into objects, process actions, and relationships.

Objects are anything involved with the application, and their attributes. Process actions include both the computer and the user; each action has certain attributes. Finally, there are relationships between objects, actions, and both objects and actions.

As the designer's model evolves, a blueprint of the screen layout is created. Graphical interface objects such as windows, menus, and icons are described in terms of functionality and appearance. Tasks are mapped to events and actions and implemented as object-action interface models.

Primary and secondary tasks should be identified clearly. Primary tasks are those activities that the user will do on a frequent basis. Primary tasks are often located on the main screen. Secondary tasks (less frequent activities) are usually organized in menus and submenus. Nevertheless, both types of tasks should be easily accessible. Never hide a secondary task.

Figure 2.2 shows the activities involved in creating the designer's model.

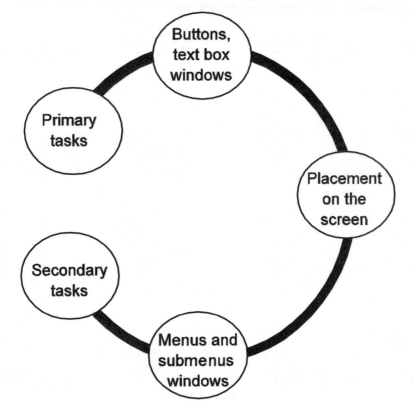

Figure 2.2: Designer's Model (High Level of Abstraction)

2.1.3 Programmer's Model

Explain the features of the programmer's model.

The designer understands the profile, requirements, constraints, business aspects, and the working environment of the user. This is translated into a conceptualized designer's model as shown in Figure 2.2 above. Tasks and other actions are further refined into a flow that can be used to generate a programmer's model. Figure 2.3 shows one aspect of a programmer's model generated from the designer's model in Figure 2.2 and based on the user's model shown in Figure 2.1.

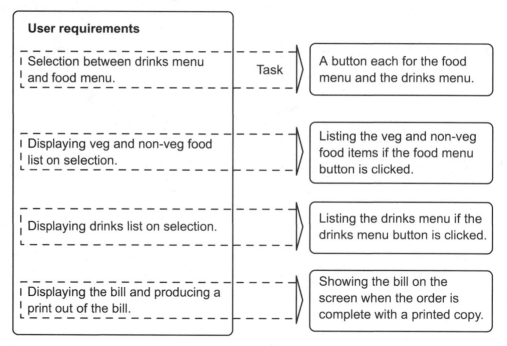

Figure 2.3: One Aspect of the Programmer's Model

As the user's and designer's models are further developed, the programmer is able to refine the coding requirements of each object, process action, and relationship. It is these refined details that form the basis of the programmer's model. These details are defined using a prescribed set of coding standards, naming conventions, and other specific programming requirements.

2.1.4 Prototype Model

Explain the features of the prototype model.

The designer's model is implemented as a working prototype of the interface using various tools. Rapid application tools such as Microsoft Visual Basic facilitate the quick construction of a prototype. This model is then presented to the user for validation and testing. The prototype can then be modified, or even discarded and started over, depending on the results of usability testing and other user inputs.

Practice Questions

1. Identify the four interface design models and explain their functions.
2. How do design models simplify the task of designing interfaces?

1.

2. The design model simplify the
task of designing because, you have
all the ideas that the user would like.
You're directly brain storming with the
user, and for relationships between actions,
objects and ideas.

2.2 Designing an Interface

There are various methodologies that can be used to design an interface. In addition, user interface design, just like other software design, goes through a complete life cycle to meet user requirements. Fortunately, there are a number of tools available to make the design effort more efficient and productive. Microsoft Visual Basic is one such tool that provides features that enable you to swiftly develop applications.

2.2.1 Design Methodologies

 Explain design methodologies and the importance of user participation.

As the various models are developed, interface design methodologies map these models to design objects. These design objects are then transformed into the GUI entities that the user will manipulate.

The design methodology that is used by the design team depends on the workload and the team chosen to perform the tasks. The team should be a balanced blend of analysts, designers, and programmers. Professional relationships between members of the team should be well defined. There should not be any conflict between the team members. A bad team structure is reflected in the quality of the product.

The interface should be designed to strike a balance between software engineering concepts and real-life requirements. The chosen design methodology can depend on the experience level of the user; user involvement can be very helpful in software development.

A user can be classified as:

- Novice: These users do not have any syntactic or semantic knowledge of computer systems or applications. Such users cannot express their requirements to the engineer using technical terminology.

- Occasional user: These users have an idea about the basic working of computers but are not experienced as far as applications are concerned.

- Experienced user: These users are knowledgeable and are always on the look out for better ways of using applications.

Three design methodologies are possible:

- Ethnographic methodology: This approach requires an understanding of the working environment as well as the psychological and social aspects of the user. The designer helps the user to state his or her requirements more clearly with the help of discussions and interviews. The user states the requirements in crude terminology and the designer interprets them. The analysis leads to prototyping, testing, and then repeating the whole process in order to build a better product.

- Structured methodology: This methodology is used when the requirements have been stated clearly. It uses a top-down approach for design. Design begins with the main structure and is decomposed into logical modules. Each module leads to a more detailed design at a lower level of abstraction.

- Use Case methodology: This methodology uses scenarios that describe how the software is used in a particular environment. It is employed when the user is experienced and knowledgeable about computer working environments. Based on use cases, which are described using the language of the user and provide an external view of the interface, the main tasks and requirements are analyzed and a design is constructed.

Each design methodology rests on the following three pillars of software design:

- Guidelines, documentation, and tasks: Standards have been developed that consider every aspect of user interface design. Armed with these standards, a designer can define specific guidelines and documentation for a particular user interface design project. Guidelines are specified for the user interface layout, images used in the application, and event sequences. Documentation is developed for creating technical help for the user as well as the designer. It contains a list of features provided, goals of the user, screen shots, notes on the designing process, and explanations using various scenarios. Guidelines and user goals included in the documentation help the designer to focus on the user demands and design principles. Identifying tasks clearly further simplifies the design process.

- User interface design tools: These are the tools used to create and develop a prototype of the user interface design. The design tools facilitate quick and easy design of the interface.

- Expert reviews and usability tests: These tests are used to assess the effectiveness of the user interface on real users. They provide scope for improvement and more satisfaction to the user.

Using these three pillars, regardless of the design methodology taken, leads to a common design cycle that must be followed in order to develop the software efficiently.

2.2.2 Design Cycle

 Explain the steps in the design cycle such as analysis, requirements gathering, and prototyping.

The GUI design process presented in this text employs the prototyping paradigm technique in which quick models, called prototypes, are iteratively developed and assessed. The prototyping paradigm technique begins with gathering information about the requirements and the working environment of the user. This is followed by a design phase. Next, a prototype or a trial product is developed from this design. The prototype of the GUI is presented to the user, which is subsequently tested. At this phase, the user may give more input for refinement. The whole process is repeated to build a prototype that is very similar to the final product.

The design process cycle is shown in Figure 2.4.

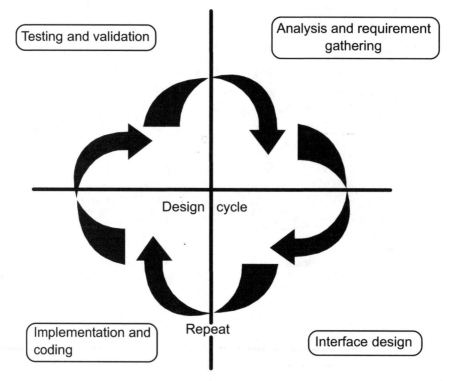

Figure 2.4: The Design Cycle

Designing a user interface is an iterative process that comprises:

- Gathering Requirements and Analyzing Design
- Designing
- Coding
- Testing and Validating

Gathering Requirements and Analyzing Design

The first step in the design process is gathering requirements and analyzing design. Detailed discussions and interviews are carried out to determine what is expected of the interface design. When designing an interface, it is essential to understand that an interface is not just a software engineering concept. It has more to do with the psychology of the user.

A user profile is also generated at this time. This profile contains the specific requirements, intellectual level, psyche, and an analysis of the working environment of the user. The tasks performed by the user are examined carefully. Each of the tasks has to be interpreted in the design either directly or by further decomposition into simpler elements. The requirements gathering and task analysis lead to the construction of the designer's model from the user model.

Designing

The second step is designing, which is the detailed representation of the interface that is to be built. The design analysis previously done is at a higher level of abstraction compared to the design that is accomplished at this step.

Each of the tasks identified in the first step is mapped to a set of actions that would be performed in response to user interaction. Interface objects, such as icons, are defined. Icons represent tasks to the user on the screen. A workflow corresponding to the task flow of the first step is defined. The appearance of the screen at each stage of the workflow is described.

A few additional issues that need to be addressed at the design stage are error handling and the help feature. Error handling should be done appropriately. It must explain to the user, in simple and explanatory language, the error that has occurred, along with an appropriate recovery option. Further, many times users require a help feature to be provided with the product. While the help feature can take various forms, the design issues for providing help deal with the presentation of the help feature and how to move between the application and the help feature.

Coding

The third step is coding, which is the implementation of the design into a working model of the interface. This prototype can be tested and validated by the user. Various implementation tools, such as Microsoft Visual Basic, are available for the rapid development of the prototype. These tools provide objects and controls that help to handle windows, appearance, placement of the interface, handle user input (mouse or keyboard), provide error handling, and a help feature.

The code should be clear and efficient. It should have an appropriate number of comments and should be self-explanatory. Good code speeds up modifications when required and is beneficial to the design team. At the same time, it is important that the resulting application should not only be technically efficient but also pleasing to the user.

Testing and Validating

The fourth step is testing and validating the developed prototype. The prototype is tested in the working environment of the user. The results of this step depend on the answers to a variety of questions, such as:

■ Is the look and feel of the interface visually appealing?

■ How easy is it for the user to adapt to the new interface?

■ Are interface objects self-explanatory?

■ Is the memory load less on the system?

■ How accessible are objects in the interface?

The validating phase involves testing the interface. It also involves providing training to the user for the new interface.

 The user may like the prototype and compel the designer to accept the prototype as the final product. It is vital for the user and the designer to understand that the prototype is just a "quick look" and not software that conforms to predefined programming and coding standards.

2.2.3 Microsoft Visual Basic as an RAD Tool

 Analyze the role of Microsoft Visual Basic as an RAD tool.

Microsoft Visual Basic is a development tool that can be used to design the prototype quickly and efficiently. It provides an environment in which designing the interface is as easy as picking up objects, putting them on a form, and coding the actions to be taken in response to user actions. Visual Basic offers a considerable number of features that facilitate prototype design. Some of these features are:

■ Various graphical objects that aid in manually drawing or designing the interface

■ Handling responses to mouse and keyboard input

■ A number of icons, pictures, and cursors in a range of colors

■ Many built-in mathematical, string, and graphical functions

■ Database connectivity and access

■ Sequential as well as random file access

■ Clipboard and printer support

■ A debugger, error handling routines, and help facilities

■ ActiveX support

■ A tool that helps to create application installation packages

Thus, Visual Basic helps develop prototypes of the interface with maximum functionality. It also allows you to work with multiple projects at one time with easy access to each one of them. Developing a prototype in Visual Basic requires the following steps:

■ Designing a visually pleasing and self-explanatory prototype of the interface, using a variety of objects and their properties.

■ Writing code for identified tasks as event procedures.

■ Running and debugging the application.

The Visual Basic Integrated Development Environment (IDE) is the work space where applications are developed. It provides all the tools required for designing an application.

Figure 2.5 shows the Microsoft Visual Basic IDE.

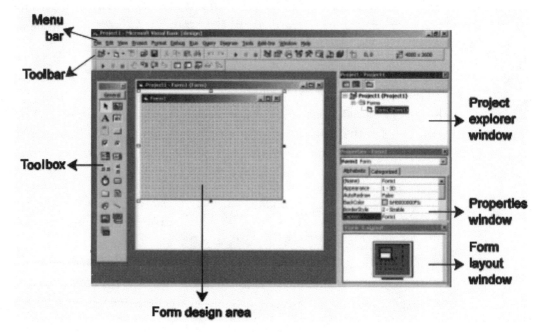

Figure 2.5: Visual Basic IDE

The following are the main components of the Microsoft Visual Basic IDE:

■ Menu bar: The menu bar is the rectangular object that contains text representing menu options. Clicking these menu options provides drop-down menus that reveal more options. Some of the important options on the main menu are:

- **File**: This option allows you to open, close, save, and print the files.

- **View**: This option handles the layout of the screen. You select those components of the IDE that are to be displayed on the screen.

- **Project**: This option allows you to add or remove forms, code modules, user controls, data reports, DHTML pages, ActiveX designers, and other files.

- **Format**: This option deals with the formatting of a form. It has options for aligning and placing controls on forms in various ways.

- **Query**: This option is used for database access.

- **Tools**: This option allows you to set IDE options, access the menu editor for inserting menus in your application, and add and set procedures.

- **Add-Ins**: This has two options, the Visual Data Manager that allows designing of databases in formats, such as Microsoft Access, and the Add-In Manager that allows you to add more options to the add-in menu.

- Toolbar: The toolbar is placed below the menu bar in the Visual Basic IDE. It has a number of small icons that represent the commonly accessed options of the menu bar. Whenever the cursor is placed over any of these icons, a small text box, called a tool tip, is displayed. The tool tip specifies the function of the icon. The toolbar can be customized for the user's needs. The icons can be moved from their positions on the toolbar and placed elsewhere on it by selecting the **Customize** option and dragging the icon to the desired position.

- Toolbox: The toolbox is a rectangular box that contains a number of small icons. Each icon represents a control that can be placed on the form. The controls include command buttons, check boxes, option boxes, list boxes, and text boxes that participate in user interaction.

- Form: The form is the main window where the interface designing is done. A form lies over another window called the form designer. All controls are placed on a form. A form is the window that appears on the screen as the interface when the application is executed. Double-clicking the form opens the Code Window.

 A form can be resized. The scroll bars of the form designer can be used to scroll through the form.

- Properties Window: This window contains a list of properties for an object in a project. The object could be a form or any of the controls placed on the form from the toolbox. The properties deal with the visual and behavioral aspect of these objects. By modifying these properties, the programmer can have complete control over the design and behavior of the GUI. Though most of the properties are self-explanatory, a brief definition of the property can be seen by selecting the required property in the Properties Window. The Properties Window shows the properties of an object, which has the focus (object that has been clicked). Properties can be set in the Properties Window as well as in the code.

- Project Explorer Window: This window contains the various elements that make up the current project. These elements include forms and code modules. The details of an object within the project can be viewed by clicking on the Project Explorer, and then on the **View Object** icon in the left side of the window. The Code Window can be viewed by clicking on the small icon named **View Code**, on the top left of the project explorer. Right-clicking on the Project Explorer presents a pop-up menu. This menu has options for adding objects to the project, saving them, setting properties related to the project, and positioning the Project Explorer window. An object can be removed by selecting the **Remove** option from the **Project** menu. The object can also be removed by right-clicking the object in the Project Explorer and clicking the **Remove** option on the menu.

■ Form Layout Window: This window gives a thumbnail view of the placement of the form on the screen. Dragging the form shown on the screen thumbnail view and placing it elsewhere changes the position of the actual form on the screen.

■ Object Browser: The Object Browser is a collection of all available objects, methods, and events. It specifies their functions and gives information on the proper syntax to use with the object. The Object Browser is shown in Figure 2.6.

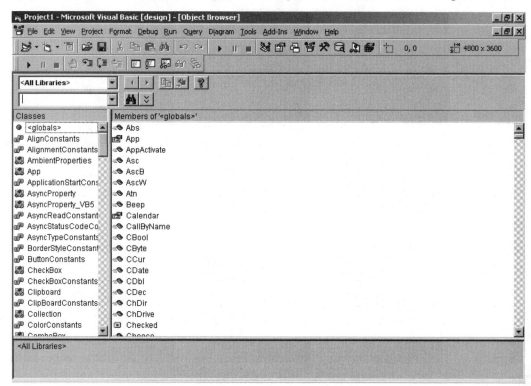

Figure 2.6: Microsoft Visual Basic Object Browser

- Code Window: The Code Window is where the actual coding action takes place. Visual Basic is an event-driven language and thus code is required to define how and under what circumstances the events will take place, and the results of the events.

The IDE is an efficient and complete tool. It is adaptable to any user's preferences and working style, which enhances the interface designing process.

Practice Questions

1. How can users be classified?
2. What is an IDE? How does it reduce the workload?
3. Library database management software is to be developed. Explain the steps of the design cycle that you will follow to develop the software.

1. A user can be classified By the information gathered by the designer. INfo that leads to what some idea that users would like to have done to the interface. Also they are classified by their Knowledge of computers, Novice, Occasional and Experienced User.

2. IDE is Intergrated Development Environment, and it where applications are made. It reduces workload because it has all to tools required to design or application. It enhances the designing process in production of apps & interfaces.

3.

Case Study

The analysis and design of a Library Management System is carried out. System design is based on two entities, books and members of the library. The system will be a menu-driven application providing an interface to access and manipulate the data stored in the database. The database design is done at this stage. Once the database design is being finalized, the interface design phase can be carried out.

The interface will allow users to perform the following tasks:

- Add a book to the library.
- Delete a book from the library.
- Add a new member.
- Edit and delete member information.
- Search for a member.
- Issue a book to a member.
- Update the database about the return of an issued book.

The database will consist of the information related to the books, issue of the books and their return, and members of the library. This information is separated into the following four groups:

- Books: ISBN number, book name, author name, price, publication date, category ID, and availability
- Categories: Category ID and category name
- Book Issue: ISBN number, registration number of the member being issued to, date of issue, estimated date of return, and actual date of return
- Members: Member registration number, first name, last name, addresses, city, state, country, and phone number

Summary

- A user interface is a medium of communication between a user and the application on a computer.

- The types of user interface models are:
  - User's model
  - Designer's model
  - Programmer's model
  - Prototype model

- Designing an interface requires that the design team understand:
  - Various classes of users
  - Design methodologies
  - Steps in the software design life cycle
  - Tools that can be used to develop a prototype of the interface, such as Microsoft Visual Basic

References

- http://www.library.itt-tech.edu/periodicals.asp > FindArticles.com (Accessed on Aug. 12, 2004)
- http://www.library.itt-tech.edu/periodicals.asp > MSDN Magazine (Accessed on Aug. 12, 2004)
- http://www.microsoft.com

Homework Exercises

1.   What are the phases in the design cycle of an interface? Briefly explain the importance of each phase.

2.   Why is documentation important in interface design methodologies?

3.   Can you directly start coding and skip the design phase after gathering information from the user? Why or why not?

4.   Discuss the importance of usability testing in an interface design.

5.   How efficient is Microsoft Visual Basic as an RAD tool?

Lab Exercise

Exercise 1

Objective

- Perform the tasks of designing an interface starting from requirement gathering to preparing the GUI using Microsoft Visual Basic.

Problem Statement

Design an interface using Visual Basic for student information management software. The software has provisions for listing the details of all the students, adding students to a database, updating the information of students in the database, deleting students from the database, and finding a particular student's details by name, class, or admission number. You can assume that you are connected to a database and all operations are being performed free of errors. Code only the actions that take place in response to the graphical objects used in the interface. You must follow the complete design cycle. Record the requirements gathering and analysis phase in a text document. Show a diagram of the programmer's and designer's models. Code the interface and perform usability testing.

Lab Setup

Computer Requirements:

- Microsoft Windows Operating System
- Pentium III or later processors
- 128-MB RAM
- 3-GB of hard disk space
- CD-ROM drives
- Floppy disk drives
- LAN connections
- Visual Basic 6.0

Procedure

1. Perform requirements gathering and analysis. A sample requirements gathering session is shown in Figure 2.7 below. Questions are asked by the design team developing the interface and users answer the questions. List the exact procedures for carrying out the user's tasks. Support the steps with relevant screen shots/sketches.

Requirements gathering

Q1. What are your basic requirements?

A1. The software should replace the current handwritten record-keeping system, and it should be reliable. There should be provisions for storing details about all the students, adding more student details with time, deleting existing student details when students leave or graduate, and changing the student details when necessary. It should include additional features, such as a calculator, to simplify work. There should be one central copy available to all concerned personnel. Any changes made in one copy should be automatically reflected in all other copies.

Q2. What details about each student do you want to store?

A2. The details for each student should contain name, date of birth, address, phone number, year of enrollment, and current grade, as well as father's name, mother's name, father's occupation, mother's occupation, their work addresses, and their home and work phone numbers.

Figure 2.7: Requirements Gathering

2. The sample requirements gathering session shown in Figure 2.7 is followed by analysis to prepare the designer's model.

Figure 2.8 below shows a portion of the designer's model.

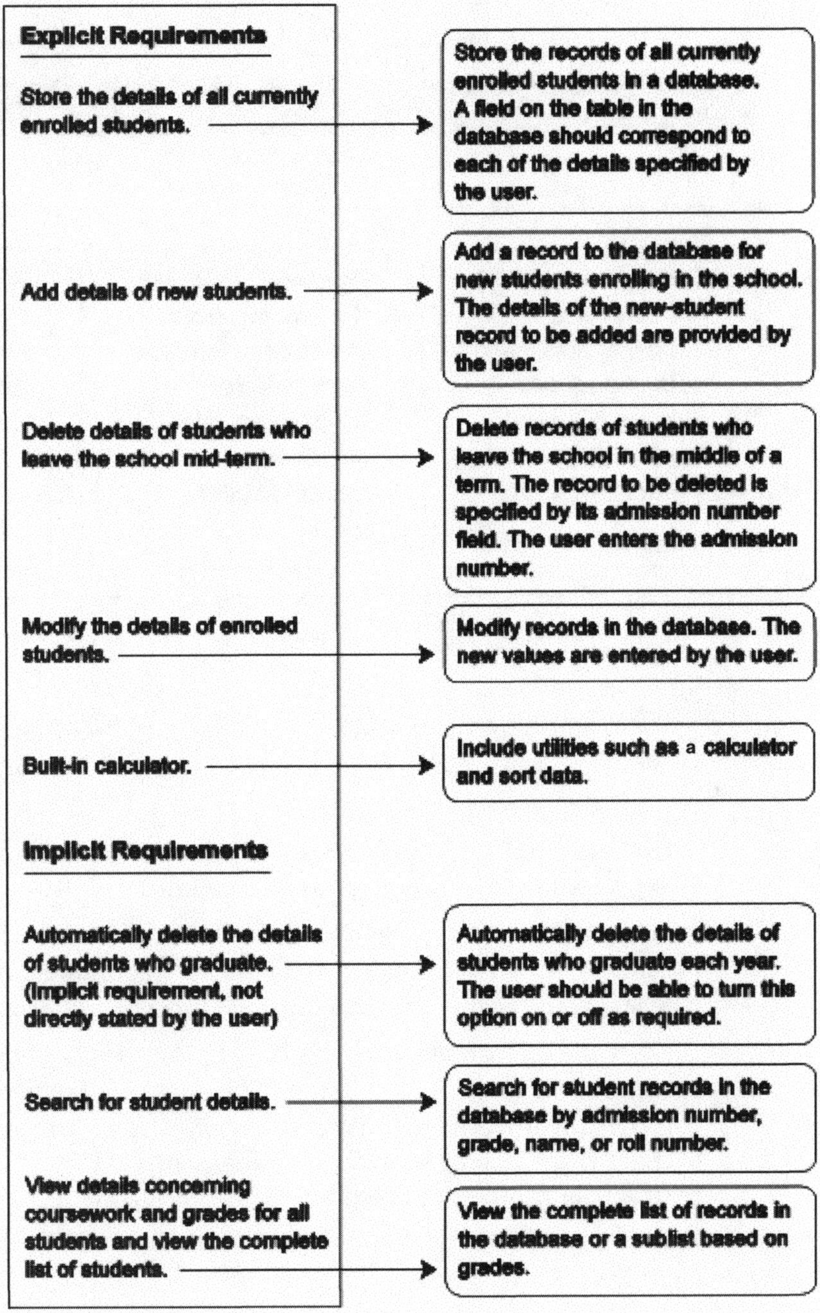

Explicit Requirements

Store the details of all currently enrolled students. ⟶ Store the records of all currently enrolled students in a database. A field on the table in the database should correspond to each of the details specified by the user.

Add details of new students. ⟶ Add a record to the database for new students enrolling in the school. The details of the new-student record to be added are provided by the user.

Delete details of students who leave the school mid-term. ⟶ Delete records of students who leave the school in the middle of a term. The record to be deleted is specified by its admission number field. The user enters the admission number.

Modify the details of enrolled students. ⟶ Modify records in the database. The new values are entered by the user.

Built-in calculator. ⟶ Include utilities such as a calculator and sort data.

Implicit Requirements

Automatically delete the details of students who graduate. (Implicit requirement, not directly stated by the user) ⟶ Automatically delete the details of students who graduate each year. The user should be able to turn this option on or off as required.

Search for student details. ⟶ Search for student records in the database by admission number, grade, name, or roll number.

View details concerning coursework and grades for all students and view the complete list of students. ⟶ View the complete list of records in the database or a sublist based on grades.

Figure 2.8: One Aspect of the Designer's Model

3.   The next phase is the design phase. The designer's model is used to build the programmer's model. Figure 2.9 below shows a high-level abstraction of the programmer's model, in this case, a layout of the opening screen.

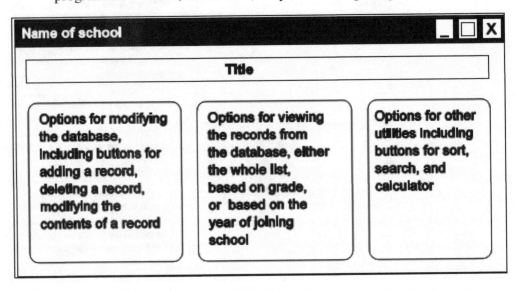

Figure 2.9: Programmer's Model (High Level Abstraction of Opening Screen)

4.   Next is the implementation and coding phase. Open Microsoft Visual Basic and select a Standard Exe project. Name the project **Students**.

5.   Set the name property of the form to **frmstd** and its caption to **Horizon International**. Set an appropriate background color (preferably a light color). Set the **Show Window** property to **Maximized**.

6.   Add a Label control to the form for displaying the title of the software. Set the name of the label to **labelstd** and its caption to **Students Record Keeping System**. Select an appropriate font and fore color property to display the title.

7.   Next, add three frames to the form and place them evenly spaced across the width of the form. Set the names of the frames to **framemodi**, **frameview**, and **frameutil**, each for one of the options shown in the design view of the above figure. Set the caption of **framemodi** to **Make Changes**, **frameview** to **View** and **frameutil** to **Utilities**. Select the appropriate font and colors.

8. Next, add three command buttons to each of the frames and set their names and captions as shown in Table 2.1 below.

Command Button Name	Command Button Caption	Name of the Frame
cmdAdd	ADD STUDENT	framemodi
cmdDel	DELETE STUDENT	framemodi
cmdModi	MODIFY DETAILS	framemodi
cmdViewAll	VIEW ALL	frameview
cmdViewGr	VIEW BY GRADE	frameview
cmdViewYr	VIEW BY YEAR OF JOINING	frameview
cmdSearch	SEARCH	frameutil
cmdSor	SORT	frameutil
cmdCalc	CALCULATOR	frameutil

Table 2.1: Names and Captions

9.   Figure 2.10 shows the form in the design view after all the controls have been added.

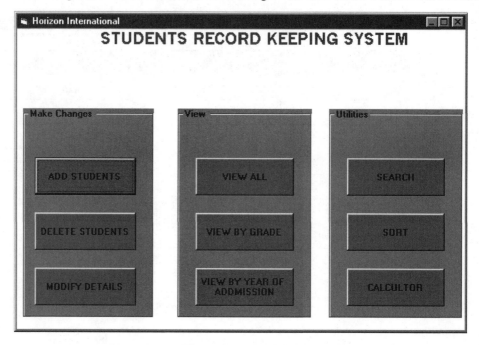

Figure 2.10: Design View

10.   The run-time view of the form is shown in Figure 2.11 below.

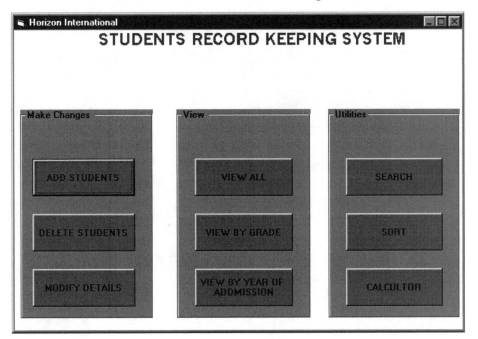

Figure 2.11: Run-time View

11.   You should now add code for the **Click** events of each of the command buttons. For example, Code 2.1, shown below, displays the code for the Click event of the Search command button.

```
Private Sub Search_Click()
  frmsrch.Show
  frmstd.Hide
End Sub
```

Code 2.1: Code for the Click Event of the Search Command Button

In the above code, the **Click** event of the **Search** command button displays the search form (discussed below) and hides the opening form.

12.   The window that opens on clicking the **Search** button is shown in Figure 2.12 below. Open a new form. Set the name property of the form to **frmsrch** and its caption to **Horizon International**. Set an appropriate background color (preferably a light color). Set the **Show Window** property to **Maximized**. Add a label control to the form for displaying the title of the software. Set the name

of the label to **labelsrch** and its caption to **Students Record Keeping System**.
Use the same font and fore color property to display the title that was used in
the first form.

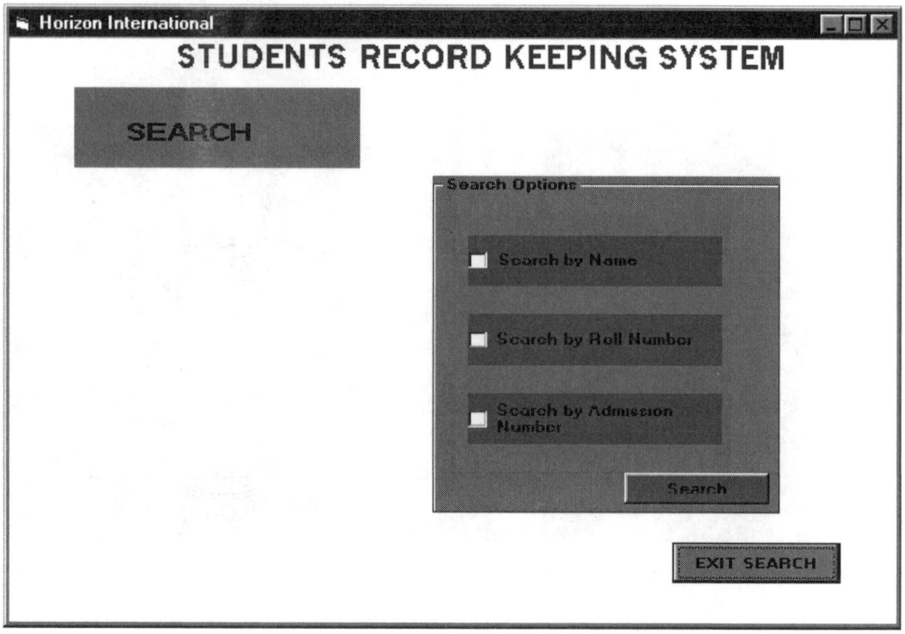

Figure 2.12: Search Form

13.   Add another label named **labelsrch**. Set its caption to **Search**. Use an
        appropriate font and forecolor property. Add another frame named
        framesrch. Set its caption to **Search Options** and add three check boxes to
        this frame. Their names and captions are shown in Table 2.2 below.

Checkbox Position in the Frame	Checkbox Name	Checkbox Caption
1	chkname	Search by Name
2	chkrno	Search by Roll Number
3	chkadno	Search by Admission Number

Table 2.2: Names and Captions

14. Add a command button to the frame. Name it **donesel** and set its caption to **Search**. This button is clicked after one or more options have been selected.

15. Finally, add a command button named **back** at the bottom of the window. Set its caption to **Exit Search.**

16. The following Code 2.2 is added to the **Click** event of the **Search** button (**donesel**) of the form shown in Figure 2.12.

```
Private Sub donesel_Click()
  Dim stri
  stri = " SEARCHING FOR RECORD BY
  If chkname.Value = vbChecked Then
        stri = stri & "Name"
  End If
  If chkrno.Value = vbChecked Then
     stri = stri & ", Roll Number"
  End If
  If chkadno.Value = vbChecked Then
     stri = stri & ", Admission Number"
  End If
  MsgBox stri, vbOKOnly
  ' other lines of code to perform the search would be added
here
  End Sub
```

Code 2.2: Code for Click Event of the Search Button

In the **Click** event of the **donesel** command button, the values of the check boxes are tested to see if they are checked and a message is generated to indicate the options selected for the search. No search is actually performed here as additional components are required that have not been developed at this stage in the project.

Figure 2.13 below shows the sample output.

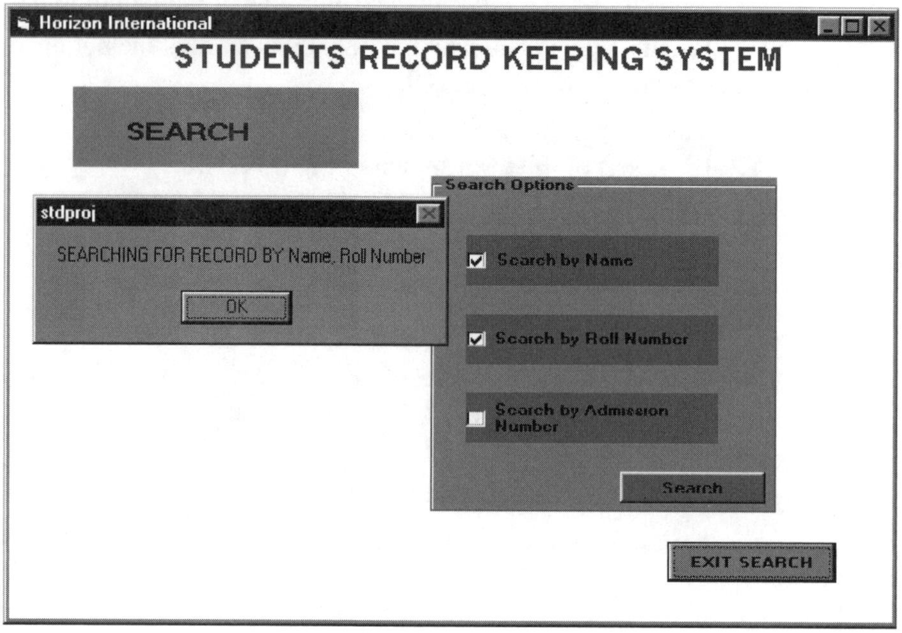

Figure 2.13: Sample Output

17.   Save the project and close it.

18.   Schedule a time with the users to perform usability testing.

Lab Activity Checklist

S. No.	Tasks	Completed	
		Yes	No
1.	Requirement gathering to create the user model being performed		
2.	Design of the interface provided in the designer's model		
3.	Programmers' model developed based on designer's model		
4.	Prototype model created using forms in Visual Basic		
5.	Sample code provided to perform basic tasks		

Conclusion/Observation

The various phases of designing an interface are a continuous process. The final outcome is just a physical representation of the data being collected in the user's model and the way the data was conceptualized in the designer's model. The more significant the data being collected, the more efficient the programmer's model that leads to a perfect interface.

Project

The analysis and design of the Employee Information System is based on the requirements of XYZ Inc. The system will be a menu-driven application providing an appropriate interface to perform the required tasks.

The information to be stored in the database is classified into three groups: Departments, Grades, and Employees. The Departments group will contain the department name and information. The Grades group will contain the grade and its respective salary. The Employees group will contain the employee code, first name, last name, date of joining, department number, and grade.

The system will provide a menu containing the options to handle all the information related to these three groups. However, emphasis will be on the design and development of the interface related to the treatment of the employee information. The information of the departments and the groups will be stored in the database manually as they are already predefined and fixed. The system will mainly handle the following tasks:

- Provide a menu-driven application.
- Add a new employee record.
- Modify an existing employee record.
- Delete employee information.
- Search for employee record(s) based on department number, grade, and employee code.

Working with Forms and Controls

3

This chapter describes forms and controls, the basic components in a Microsoft Visual Basic application. It teaches the fundamental concepts of object properties, methods, events, and the order in which events occur. The section on controls discusses techniques involved in using standard and non-standard controls. The section on interface styles explains the importance of presenting an attractive interface to the user.

At the end of this chapter, you will be able to:

- Explain the concept of forms in Microsoft Visual Basic.
- Set the properties of forms, and compare the different types of properties.
- Apply form methods in developing applications.
- Explain the sequence of form events and their order of execution.
- Create applications using intrinsic controls.
- Create applications using Label, TextBox, and CommandButton controls.
- Distinguish between a CheckBox and an OptionButton control.
- Apply ListBox and ComboBox controls in applications.
- Use ScrollBar, Timer, Shape, and Line controls.
- Use the DriveListBox, DiListBox, and FileListBox controls.
- Create applications using the Tabbed Dialog (SSTab) control and the Microsoft Multimedia control (MMControl).
- Apply screen resolution techniques in applications.
- Explain features and policies of interface style.
- Apply color and design techniques in applications.

3.1 Using Forms

Forms are objects that are visible to the users. They are the windows that you see and use in a Graphical User Interface (GUI). At runtime, the form represents the window occupied by the application. At design time, the form represents the building block that is used to create the user interface for an application. The three important features of forms are:

- Properties or attributes
- Methods or actions
- Events

For example, a motorbike has different characteristics associated with it, such as the type (Sports or Cruiser), horsepower (10, 15, or 30), mileage (80 miles/gallon), and color. It also has certain functions such as acceleration and brakes that are meant for use by everyone, and certain others, such as energy conversion that are used internally. A motorbike also has certain events, which you can trigger with your actions. For example, a rider can apply the brakes, which slows down the bike. There may be a chain of events triggered by your actions, each resulting in a different kind of response. Similar to a motorbike, a form also has certain properties, methods, and events.

A form also serves as a container for controls. Controls are graphical objects that the user uses to interact with the application. Forms cannot do much by themselves; they always need controls on them to provide functionality to the user.

 You have learned in detail about some of the controls in IT104, Introduction to Computer Programming.

3.1.1 Creating a Form

 Create a form in Visual Basic.

The first thing that is visible to the user on opening the Microsoft Visual Basic IDE is a form. This view is called the Design Time view of the application. The manner in which you manipulate the form will directly affect the way the application behaves at runtime. A form looks like the GUI window of applications you use on the computer. It has **Maximize**, **Minimize**, and **Close** buttons.

Figure 3.1 shows the Design Time view of a project and a form in Visual Basic.

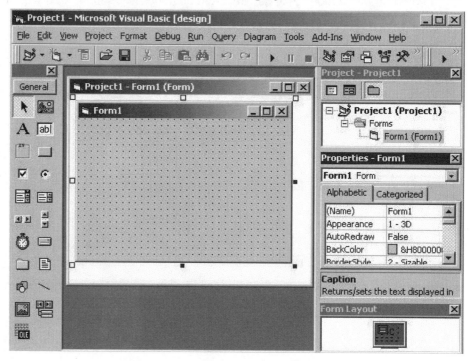

Figure 3.1: The Design Time View of a Form

To create a new form in Visual Basic, follow these steps:

1. Open the Visual Basic IDE and click **File** and then **New**.

2. The **New Project** dialog box appears on the screen. Select **Standard EXE** and click **OK**.

3. A window as shown in Figure 3.1 is displayed. A default form named **Form1** is opened. This form is created in a default project named **Project1**.

You can change the names of the project and the form to suit your needs. You can optionally add prefixes "prj" and "frm" to each object, respectively.

3.1.2 Form Properties

Evaluate the properties of a form and their significance.

You can set form properties either during design or runtime. Most of the form properties have default values. In the Properties window, you can see a list of the properties that you can change during design time. There are 13 more properties available to you during the application's run time. Traditionally, the syntax for setting a form's property is:

```
<FormName.Property>
```

This format is referred to as the **dot notation**. There is the name of the object, then a dot (.), and finally the property of that object.

Figure 3.2 shows some of the contents of the Properties window of a form:

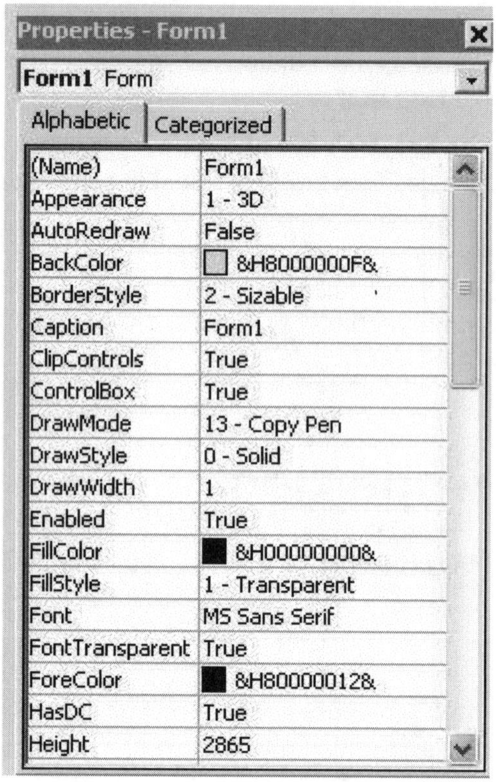

Figure 3.2: Properties Window of a Form

Form properties can be classified as:

- Appearance properties
- Behavior properties
- Positional properties
- Runtime properties
- Other important properties

Appearance Properties

Appearance properties affect the way a form looks, such as its colors and fonts. Table 3.1 lists some of the 51 properties along with their descriptions.

Property	Description
Caption	The text that appears in the form's title bar. The default caption is same as the Name property.
Appearance	The look of the form at runtime. Can be set to Flat or 3D.
BackColor	The background color of the form. You can select a color from the color palette or set a hexadecimal color value.
BorderStyle	The style of the form's border. You can set six values ranging from 0 to 5. The default value is 2, which means a Sizeable Border.
FillColor	The color used to fill shapes or boxes drawn on the form.
FillStyle	Contains eight different styles that determine the patterns used in shapes drawn on the form.
FontTransparent	Determines whether background text or graphics on a form are displayed.
ForeColor	The foreground color of the form. You can set a color from the color palette or assign a hexadecimal color value.
Picture	Returns/sets a graphic to be displayed in a control.
Palette	Returns/sets an image that contains the palette to use on an object when the PaletteMode property is set to Custom.

Table 3.1: Appearance Properties of the Form

The examples in Code 3.1 through Code 3.3 show how to change some of the appearance properties of a form during run time. The program sets the caption, appearance, and colors during the Form Loading event. Then it draws an ellipse in the center of the form during the Paint event. To create this form, perform the following steps:

1.   Open a new project in Visual Basic and double-click the empty form on your screen.

2.   The Code window appears showing the form's **Load** event.

3. Now enter the code found in Code 3.1. Notice that in the General Declarations section, two variables are declared that will be used while drawing the ellipse. These two variables will be used to specify the radius and the aspect ratio of the ellipse, respectively.

```
Option Explicit
Dim rad As Integer
Dim aspect As Double
```

Code 3.1: General Declarations Section

4. Now, in the form's **Load** event, add Code 3.2. The code specifies the required values for the radius and the aspect ratio and sets the various properties of the form to prepare for the display of the ellipse.

```
Private Sub Form_Load()
   rad = 1500                  'radius of the ellipse
   aspect = 1 / 3              'ratio of the ellipse's radii a and b
   FillColor = vbRed           'color to fill graphic
   FillStyle = vbSolid          'solid filling style
   Appearance = 1               'allow 3D effects in the form
   BackColor = vbBlue           'Blue Background
   ForeColor = vbYellow         'Color used to draw the graphic
   BorderStyle = vbFixedSingle  'Fixed border (no resizing)
   Caption = "Changing Form's Appearance Properties"
End Sub
```

Code 3.2: Code for the Load Event

5. Finally, add Code 3.3 to the form's **Paint** event. The code invokes the **Circle** method of the form to display an ellipse at the center of the form.

```
Private Sub Form_Paint()
 'rad is the radius and aspect is the aspect ratio
 'an aspect equal to 1 will draw a circle
 'Note that the circle is painted with a yellow outline and
 'filled in with red
 Circle (ScaleWidth / 2, ScaleHeight / 2), rad, , , , aspect
End Sub
```

Code 3.3: Code for the Paint Event

Code 3.3 does not use any control. It uses the form's properties and the **Circle** method to draw the ellipse. Notice that instead of using the syntax as `FormName.Property`, a different coding arrangement is used. This is a relatively new Visual Basic construct that can improve both the readability and efficiency of your code—and save you quite a few keystrokes in the process. That construct is the **With...End With** statement. The **With...End With** statement allows you to "bundle" Property and Method calls to a single object within the **With...End With** block. Not only are the number of keystrokes reduced in the procedure, using the **With...End With** construct also produces a more efficient code.

Each reference to an object's property or method requires a Registry "look up" to execute the code statement—by using the **With...End With** statement. VB is able to "pool" this lookup into a single input/output (I/O) operation—thereby making your program run faster.

The bottom line—whenever you find yourself coding multiple operations against an Object, use the **With...End With** statement.

TiP

- If you try to set a form's property from another form, always mention the form's name followed by the property.

- You can use the **Me** keyword to refer the currently active form. For example, you can use Me.BackColor = vbBlack to set the form's **BackColor** property from within its code.

---

6. Run the application by pressing **F5**. The output is shown in Figure 3.3.

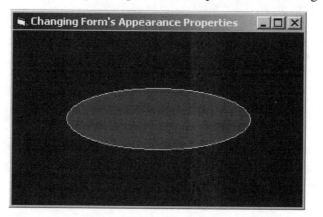

Figure 3.3: Changing a Form's Appearance Properties During Run Time

Behavior Properties

Behavior properties determine how the form is displayed on a user's screen. Some of the 11 properties are listed in Table 3.2.

Property	Description
DrawMode	Contains 16 settings that you can use to set the drawing mode of graphic objects. They are basically raster operations. The default value of this property is **Copy Pen**.
DrawStyle	Contains seven advanced settings that determine the appearance of lines that you draw.
AutoRedraw	If **True**, Visual Basic automatically redraws graphic images that reside on the form when another window hides the image or when the user resizes the object. If **False**, which is the default value, Visual Basic does not automatically redraw.
Enabled	If **True**, the form can respond to events generated by the user.
Visible	Determines whether the form is visible or hidden.
PaletteMode	Determines the palette to be used to draw controls. This property is used by the palette.
ClipControls	If **True**, the **Paint** event redraws the entire graphics. If **False**, only newly exposed areas of the graphics are repainted.
RightToLeft	Determines whether text is displayed from right to left or in the opposite direction. Note that the system has to be bidirectional to use this property.

Table 3.2: Behavior Properties of a Form

You can disable the **Maximize**, **Minimize**, and **Close** buttons of the form by setting its **Enabled** property to **False**.

You can also change the drawing mode in a form by changing the **DrawMode** property. Let us consider the previous example of displaying an ellipse, and enhancing it so as to display the ellipse with different **DrawMode** values.

Perform the following steps to do this:

1. In the General Declarations section of Code 3.1, add the shown in Code 3.4, to declare a variable, which will be used to specify the value for the **DrawMode** property of the form.

```
Dim modeindex As Integer
```

Code 3.4: Declaring the Indexing Variable

2. In the code for the form's **Load** event, initialize this variable to the value **1**, as shown in Code 3.5. This will specify the initial value for the **DrawMode** property.

```
modeindex = 1
```

Code 3.5: Initializing the Variable

3. In the code for the form's **Click** event, add the code example given in Code 3.6. The code allows the user to change from one **DrawMode** to another whenever the user clicks the form. Each time the user clicks the form, the **DrawMode** property is set to the value stored in the variable **modeindex,** and the value of the variable **modeindex** is incremented to get the next value for the **DrawMode** property. Since there are only 16 possible values ranging from one to 16 for the DrawMode property of the form, the variable is reinitialized to one if it exceeds 16. The effect of the change in the **DrawMode** property of the form cannot be seen until the form is refreshed, which is done by calling the **Refresh** method of the form.

```
Private Sub Form_Click()
    DrawMode = modeindex
    modeindex = modeindex + 1
    If modeindex > 16 Then
        modeindex = 1
    End If
    Me.Refresh
End Sub
```

Code 3.6: Code for Click Event

Upon running the application, the ellipse is painted in a different mode whenever you click on the screen. The **Click** event assigns the value of the **DrawMode** property to the value of the integer variable **modeindex**. As a result, every time you click the form the **DrawMode** is changed. The **IF** condition checks whether the variable has exceeded the maximum value, the property can take, which is 16.

Positional Properties

Positional properties are useful in determining the location of a form on the screen. Table 3.3 lists the positional properties of a form.

Property	Description
Top	Distance between the top edges of the form and the screen.
Left	Distance between the left edges of the form and the screen.
Height	Height of the form in twips (1440 twips = 1 inch).
Width	Width of the form in twips.
StartUpPosition	Determines the position of the form during initial display. Default value is "Manual."
Moveable	Determines whether the form can be moved around on the screen.

Table 3.3: Positional Properties of a Form Object

Code 3.7 shows how to display a form at the center of the screen. It also sets the height and width of the form to half of that of the screen. Instead of using any constant value to specify the form properties, the code manipulates the **Width** and **Height** properties of the **Screen** object so that the code has the same output irrespective of the resolution of the user screen.

```
Private Sub Form_Load()
    Caption = "Changing Form's Positional Properties"
    Width = Screen.Width / 2    'uses the screen object
    Height = Screen.Height / 2
    Left = Screen.Width / 2 - Width / 2
    Top = Screen.Height / 2 - Height / 2
End Sub
```

Code 3.7: Setting a Form's Position

Run Time Properties

Run time properties of a form are not available during design time. They can be set only through code. Some of the important run time properties are listed in Table 3.4.

Run Time Property	Description
hWnd	The operating system returns a handle to the form's window.
hDC	The operating system returns a handle to the form's device context.
Controls	A collection object, which contains all the control elements on a form. This includes the elements of control arrays.
ActiveControl	Returns the control object in the form that has focus.
FontName	Specifies the name of the font that appears using the **Print** command.
FontSize	Specifies the size (in points) of the font that appears using the **Print** command.
CurrentX	Determines the horizontal coordinate for the next **Print** or **Draw** method.
CurrentY	Determines the vertical coordinates for the next **Print** or **Draw** method.
Count	Returns the number of objects in a collection.

Table 3.4: Important Run Time Properties of a Form

Using the **ActiveControl** property in the form's **Load** event, will generate a run time error because there is no valid reference to the object at that time.

While using these run time properties, the Forms and Controls collection objects are automatically created.

Collections

In Visual Basic, a collection is a way of grouping a set of related items. Collections are used in Visual Basic to keep track of many things, such as the loaded forms in your program (the Forms collection), or all the controls on a form (the Controls collection).

Visual Basic provides the generic **Collection** class to give you the ability to define your own collections. You can create as many **Collection** objects—that is, instances of the Collection class—as you need.

- Forms Collection: Consists of all the Visual Basic forms that are loaded into the memory. It consists of MDI parent forms, MDI child forms, and regular forms. You can refer to each form using an index starting from 0, for example, Forms(0), and Forms(1). The **Count** property of the collection gives the total number of forms in the Collection object. As the indexing starts from 0, the highest index is (Forms.Count – 1).

- Controls Collection: Consists of all the controls that are present in a form. It also includes all the elements of control arrays. The **Count** property of a collection returns the total number of objects in the collection. In addition, the collection object has the following methods:

  - **Add**: Adds an item to the collection.

  - **Remove**: Removes an item from the collection, by key or index.

  - **Item**: Returns an item, by key or index.

 You will learn more about classes and collections in Chapter 7, "Classes and Collections."

Using Run Time Properties

To demonstrate the use of run time properties of a form object, follow these steps:

1. Open a new project and rename the default form as **frmRT**.

2. In the Toolbox, double-click the CommandButton control to add it to the form. Set the name to **cmdButton**.

3. In the Toolbox, double-click on the TextBox control to add it to the form. Set its name to **txtTextBox**.

4. Add Code 3.8 to the **Load** event of **frmRT**. The purpose of the code is to retrieve the names of the controls in the form and print them (using

Debug.Print) in the **Immediate** window. It also displays the number of forms displayed and the number of controls in the current form.

```
Private Sub Form_Load()
 Debug.Print " Number of forms = " & Forms.Count
 Debug.Print " Number of controls = " & Controls.Count
 Debug.Print Controls(0).Name
 Debug.Print Controls(1).Name
End Sub
```

Code 3.8: Using the Controls Collection

5.   Add Code 3.9 to the form's **Click** Event. The given code displays the name of the active control in the **Immediate** window. The **ActiveControl** property is available only during run time.

```
Private Sub Form_Click()
    Debug.Print ActiveControl.Name 'cannot use in form's Load
                                   'event
End Sub
```

Code 3.9: Using the ActiveControl Property

6.   Press **F5** to run the application.

7.   Click on the text box. Then click on the form.

8.   Now, click on the command button and then click on the form.

9.   The output in the **Immediate** window will be as shown in Figure 3.4.

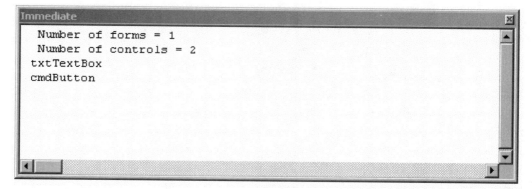

Figure 3.4: Output in Immediate Window

You can directly access form and control collections as shown in Code 3.8. To access the controls that you have added, refer to them with an index, like Controls(0), Controls(1) and so on. You can access the name of the first control with Controls(0).Name.

The **ActiveControl** property refers to the control object that is active in the form. Code 3.9 uses this property to view the name of the active control in the form. When you click on the textBox, it becomes active. Therefore, the **Click** event prints the active command button's name.

Code 3.10 displays the use of the Controls collection of the Form object. While developing a user interface that accepts user input through a variety of controls, there might be a need to reset the values in all these controls. Attempting to reset these values by referring to the controls separately might result in a long sequence of code. Here we can make the use of the Controls collection within a loop. Code 3.10 also makes use of the **TypeOf** operator to determine the type of the control because different controls provide different properties to refer to their values. For example, the value of a text box is referred to by the **Text** property while the value of the option button is referred to by the **Value** property.

To implement the code, create a form with many text boxes, option buttons, check boxes, and list boxes. Provide a command button named **cmdReset** and add Code 3.10 to its **Click** event. During run time, change the values of the controls and click the **Reset** button.

```
Private Sub cmdReset_Click()
  Dim varObj As Variant
  For Each varObj In Me.Controls
    If TypeOf varObj Is TextBox Then
      varObj.Text = " "
    ElseIf TypeOf varObj Is CheckBox Then
      varObj.Value = 0
    ElseIf TypeOf varObj Is OptionButton Then
      varObj.Value = False
    ElseIf TypeOf varObj Is ListBox Then
      varObj.Clear
    End If
  Next
End Sub
```

Code 3.10: Using the Controls Collection to Clear the Values in All the Controls

In order to understand the significance of Code 3.10, write the code to perform the same task by referring to all the controls separately.

Other Important Form Properties

Some of the other important form properties are listed in Table 3.5.

Property	Description
Name	Used to identify the form. Cannot change at runtime.
ControlBox	Determines whether the control menu box is displayed.
MaxButton	If enabled (default), the form displays a **Maximize** button.
MinButton	If enabled (default), the form displays a **Minimize** button.
MDIChild	Determines whether a form is a standalone form or a child form of another Multiple Document Interface (MDI) form.
MousePointer	Sets the type of pointer displayed on the form.
WindowState	Determines whether the application window is displayed as maximized, minimized, or normal.
MouseIcon	Allows the user to display a custom pointer on the form.

Table 3.5: Other Important Properties of a Form Object

By setting the MaxButton and MinButton to **False** and BorderStyle to 0, 1, or 3, you can make your window behave like a dialog box.

Another important property of the form is the **ScaleMode** property. This property sets the measuring system that is used by the various graphics methods available in Visual Basic. The default unit of measurement is twips.

Table 3.6 describes the other available units of measurement.

Value	Description
0	User customized values
1	Twips (the default)
2	Points
3	Pixels
4	A standard character (120 twips wide and 240 twips high)
5	Inches
6	Millimeters
7	Centimeters

Table 3.6: Options for the ScaleMode Property

3.1.3 Form Methods

Explain the methods available in the Form object.

Form methods are built-in procedures that perform various actions related to the form. Table 3.7 lists some of the common methods of a form.

Method	Description
Move	Moves the form on the screen.
Refresh	Forces a complete repaint of the form.
Show	Displays the form object.
Hide	Hides a form object from the screen. This does not unload it from memory. You have to explicitly call **Unload** to do so.
SetFocus	Moves the focus to the specified form.
ValidateControls	Validates the contents of the last control on the form before exiting. Can be used to force the user to enter data in a form before continuing.
Circle	Draws a circle, ellipse, or arc (depending on the parameters) on the form.

Line	Draws lines and rectangles on a form.
ZOrder	Places a form at the specified position of the zorder. This property determines whether the form is placed in front or behind other objects at that level.

Table 3.7: Form Methods

Move Method

The **Move** method moves the form on the screen. The syntax for the method is:

> <Formname>.Move *left, top, width, height*

In the syntax, the **Left** field is the only required field. The other fields are optional. However, to specify any of the optional arguments, you have to specify the arguments before it. For example, to change the height, you must specify *left, top,* and *width* parameters.

Code 3.11 demonstrates the use of the **Move** method. If you have a command button named **cmdExpand** in your form, clicking the button will expand the form by half the value given in the variable **intAmount**.

```
Private Sub cmdExpand_Click()
Dim intAmount As Integer
intAmount = 40        'value in twips


Move Left - intAmount/2, Top - intAmount/2, Width + intAmount, _
Height + intAmount
End Sub
```

Code 3.11: The Move Method

Avoid giving numerical values for the arguments in the **Move** method unless you are sure of the measurement system. This will prevent unpredictable window behavior.

Refresh Method

The **Refresh** method triggers the **Paint** event and forces the form to repaint itself. For example, if you change the value of any form property related to graphic objects, you have to refresh the form in order to view the particular change. Code 3.12 shows an instance where you have to refresh the form to update the changes. After changing the **DrawMode** property of the form to vbMergeNotPen, you have to explicitly refresh the form to view the change in any graphic object present on the form.

Also, you should have some graphic object in the form (such as a circle or a line) to view the changes.

```
Private Sub Form_Click()
    DrawMode = vbMergeNotPen
    Me.Refresh
End Sub
```

Code 3.12: Using the Refresh Method

 The Refresh method does not work with MDI forms. It only works with regular Visual Basic forms and MDI child forms. You will learn about MDI forms later in this chapter.

Show Method

The **Show** method displays a hidden form on the screen. The syntax for the method is:

```
<Formname>.Show style, formowner
```

In this syntax, both the arguments are optional. The `style` argument can take two values, 0 for modeless and 1 for modal form. The `formOwner` argument is a string that represents the component, which is the owner of the form.

If the form is not loaded into memory and the **Show** method is called, it automatically triggers the **Load** event and loads it into the memory. For example, if you have two forms in an application, named, **frmMain** and **frmSub**, where **frmMain** is the main form, then to display **frmSub** on the screen, you need to execute Code 3.13 from within the **frmMain** form's code.

```
Private Sub Form_Load()
  Dim newform As New frmSub
  newform.Show
End Sub
```

Code 3.13: Using the Show Method

If you mention a form's name as the startup object, the form is automatically shown on the screen after the **Load** event. You do not need to explicitly call the **Show** method. For any other forms in the application, you have to invoke formName.Show to display the form.

Hide Method

The **Hide** method hides a form from the screen but does not unload it from memory. The form is removed from the screen and its **Visible** property is set to **False**. None of the controls in the form are accessible to the user directly. You can only interact with them in code.

The syntax for the Hide method is:

    <Formname>.Hide

Continuing with the previous example of the two forms, adding Code 3.14 to **frmMain** will hide the form **frmSub** on clicking the main form.

```
Dim newform As New frmSub
Private Sub Form_Load()
 newform.Show
End Sub
Private Sub Form_Click()
 newform.Hide
End Sub
```

Code 3.14: Using the Hide Method

If you call the **Hide** method and the form is not yet loaded into memory, the method will call the **Load** event to load the form but will not display it.

SetFocus Method

The **SetFocus** method moves the focus to the specified form. The syntax for the SetFocus method is:

    <Formobject>.SetFocus

If the Formobject is not a valid object, you get a run time error stating that an invalid object reference has occurred.

Modifying Code 3.14 to Code 3.15 will make **frmSub** show up every time you click on **frmMain**.

```
Private Sub Form_Load()
  Dim newform As New frmSub
  Set newform = frmSub
  newform.Show
End Sub


Private Sub Form_Click()
  frmSub.SetFocus              'or use Forms(1).SetFocus
End Sub
```

Code 3.15: Using the SetFocus Method

Circle Method

The **Circle** method is used to draw a circle, ellipse, or an arc on the form. The syntax for the Circle method is:

```
<Formobject>.Circle (x,y), radius, color, startAngle,
endAngle, aspectRatio
```

In this syntax, the x and y arguments are the coordinates of the center of the graphic object. **Radius** determines the radius of the circle. The rest of the fields are optional. **Color** is the outline color of the object. The **startAngle** and **endAngle** fields can be used to draw arcs, specifying the angles in radians. Their values range from $(-2*pi)$ to $(2*pi)$ radians and the **aspectRatio** can be used to draw an ellipse with its value being the ratio between the major and minor axis.

Code 3.16 shows some of the methods used to draw circles, ellipses, and arcs.

```
Private Sub Form_Paint()
  ScaleMode = 5 'measure in inches

  'draw a circle at the center with radius of 3 inches
  Circle(ScaleWidth/2, ScaleHeight/2), 3

  'draw an ellipse at center with radius 2 inches where aspect
  'is (a=2b)
  Circle(ScaleWidth/2, ScaleHeight/2), 2, , , , 1 / 2
```

```
'draw an elliptic arc at origin with radius 2 from 180 to 360
'degrees
'color is specified as Green with RGB value
Circle(0,0), 2, RGB(0,255,0), 3.14,2*3.14, 1/2
End Sub
```

Code 3.16: Using the Circle Method

3.1.4 Form Events

Explain form events and their order of execution.

A form passes through four phases during its life cycle:

- Created, but not loaded
- Loaded, but not displayed
- Displayed
- Destroyed, where memory and resources are completely reclaimed

Various form events lead to these phases. These events are generated in a certain order and comprise the stages of a form's lifetime.

To understand the concept of an event-driven program and implement it, you need to know the order in which these events are triggered. These events can be programmed according to the end user's requirements to make your application flexible and versatile. The following procedure explains the order of the events generated by a form object, when you create, activate, minimize, maximize, and destroy it.

1.   Click **File** menu and then select **New Project** and select **Standard EXE**. Now click OK.

2.   Open the Code window of the form by selecting, **Code** from the **View** menu.

3.   Enter Code 3.17 in the Code window. The code displays the name of the form event in the **Immediate** window whenever the event is triggered. The purpose of the code is to demonstrate the sequence and occurrence of the events depending on the actions being performed on the form.

```vb
Option Explicit
Private Sub Form_Activate()
  Debug.Print "Form_Activate Event"
End Sub
Private Sub Form_Deactivate()
  Debug.Print "Form_Deactivate Event"
End Sub
Private Sub Form_GotFocus()
  Debug.Print "Form_GotFocus Event"
End Sub
Private Sub Form_Initialize()
  Debug.Print "Form_Initialize Event"
End Sub
Private Sub Form_Load()
  Debug.Print "Form_Load Event"
End Sub
Private Sub Form_LostFocus()
  Debug.Print "Form_LostFocus Event"
End Sub
Private Sub Form_Paint()
  Debug.Print "Form_Paint Event"
End Sub
Private Sub Form_QueryUnload(Cancel As Integer, UnloadMode As Integer)
  Debug.Print "Form_QueryUnload Event"
End Sub
Private Sub Form_Resize()
  Debug.Print "Form_Resize Event"
End Sub
Private Sub Form_Terminate()
  Debug.Print "Form_Terminate Event"
```

```
End Sub
Private Sub Form_Unload(Cancel As Integer)
 Debug.Print "Form_Unload Event"
End Sub
```

Code 3.17: Form Events

4.   Save the project as **prjEvent.vbp** and the form as **frmTest**. Press **F5** to run the application.

5.   You can view the **Immediate** window to see the output of the **Debug.Print** statements. If the **Immediate** window is not visible, press **Ctrl** and **G** or click **View** and then **Immediate** window.

6.   Press the **Maximize** button twice, and then click the **Minimize** button. Now restore the form from the taskbar. Now resize the form using the **Resize** handles, and finally close the window by clicking the **Close** button.

7.   Check the contents of the **Immediate** window. They should resemble the sample given in the following list, as shown in Code 3.18. The text within parentheses is not displayed in the **Immediate** window. It is given just to explain when the succeeding events are triggered.

```
(Until the point the form is displayed)
 Form_Initialize Event
 Form_Load Event
 Form_Resize Event
 Form_Activate Event
 Form_GotFocus Event
 Form_Paint Event
(During maximize)
 Form_Resize Event
 Form_Paint Event
(During restore down)
 Form_Resize Event
(During minimize)
  Form_Resize Event
(During restore from the taskbar)
 Form_Resize Event
 Form_Paint Event
```

```
(During resize)
 Form_Resize Event
 Form_Paint Event
(During the closing of the application)
 Form_QueryUnload Event
 Form_Unload Event
 Form_Terminate Event
```

Code 3.18: Output in the Immediate Window

Initialize() Event

The beginning of the Created, But Not Loaded state is marked by the **Initialize** event. The code you place in the Form_Initialize() event procedure is therefore the first code that gets executed when a form is created.

In this state, the form exists as an object, but it has no window. None of its controls exist yet. A form always passes through this state, although its stay there may be brief.

For example, if you execute Form1.Show, the form will be created, and Form_Initialize() will be executed; as soon as Form_Initialize() is completed, the form will be loaded, which is the next state.

The same thing happens if you specify a form as your Startup Object, on the **General** tab of the **Project Properties** dialog box (which is available from the **Project** menu). A form specified as the Startup Object is created as soon as the project starts, and is then immediately loaded and shown. Once Form_Initialize() has ended, the only procedures you can execute without forcing the form to load are Sub, Function, and Property procedures you have added to the form's Code window.

You can execute as many custom properties and methods as you like without forcing the form to load. However, the moment you access one of the form's built-in properties, or any control on the form, the form enters the next state.

You may find it helpful to think of a form as having two parts, a code part and a visual part. Before the form is loaded, only the code part is in memory. You can call as many procedures as you like in the code part without loading the visual part of the form.

Created, But Not Loaded is the only state *all* forms pass through. However, you can destroy a form before it is loaded into memory. To do this, perform the following steps:

1.   Add a new form to project **prjEvent** by clicking **Project**. Then select **Add Form** and click **Form.**

2.	Name the form **frmKill** and save it. Now you have two forms in the Event project.

3.	Add the same Form event procedures given in Code 3.17 to **frmKill**.

4.	Modify the event procedure for **frmTest's Form_Load** event as shown in Code 3.19. The given code creates a new object from frmKill, named **Test** and executes the procedure **Prn** on the object without displaying the form.

```
Private Sub Form_Load()
    Dim Test As New frmKill      'creating the new form frmTest
    Test.Prn              'call the procedure Hello in form frmTest
    Set Test = Nothing    'destroy the object instance
End Sub
```

Code 3.19: Code for the frmTest Load Event

5.	Add Code 3.20 to **frmKill**.

```
Public Sub Prn()
 Debug.Print "Hello!"
End Sub
```

Code 3.20: Code for the Procedure Prn

6.	Click **Project** and then select **prjEvent** properties.

prjEvent is the name of the current project.

7.	Select **frmTest** as the StartUp object.

8.	Press **F5** to run the application.

9. Code 3.21 is an extract of the contents in the **Immediate** window, which shows the output displayed for the object Test.

```
form_Initialize Event
Hello!
form_Terminate Event
```

Code 3.21: Code for Object Test

Notice that only the **Initialize** event and the **Terminate** event have occurred. Without generating a **Form_Load()** event, the form immediately generates the **Form_Terminate()** event.

Load() Event

The event that marks the beginning of the Loaded, But Not Shown state, is the familiar Load event. The code you place in the Form_Load() event procedure is executed as soon as the form enters the Loaded, But Not Shown state.

When the Form_Load() event procedure begins, the controls on the form have all been created and loaded, and the form has a window—complete with window handle (hWnd) and device context (hDC)—although that window has not yet been shown.

Any form that becomes visible must first be loaded.

Many forms pass automatically from the Created, But Not Loaded state into the Loaded, But Not Shown state. A form will be loaded automatically if:

- The form has been specified as the Startup Object, on the General tab of the Project Properties dialog box.

- The Show method is the first property or method of the form to be invoked, for example Form1.Show.

- The first property or method of the form to be invoked is one of the form's built-in members, for example, the Move method. This case includes any controls on the form, because each control defines a property of the form; that is, in order to access the Caption property of Command1, you must go through the form's Command1 property: Command1.Caption.

Forms return from the visible state to the loaded state whenever they are hidden. However, returning to the loaded state does not re-execute the Load event. Form_Load() is executed only once in a form's life.

Replace the code in the Form_Load event of the form frmTest with Code 3.22.

```
Option Explicit
Private Sub Form_Load()
    Dim Test As New frmKill
    Test.Prn              'calling a user-defined procedure
    Debug.Print Test.Name 'calling an built-in property of the
                                'form
    Unload Test              'unload the form from memory


    Set Test = Nothing
End Sub
```

Code 3.22: Testing the Load Event

In Code 3.22, following the **Initialize** event, the **Load** event occurs as referred to in the **Name** property. This loads the form into memory, creating a window handle for internal handling by windows. You can put all initialization code in this event. Any variables you want to initialize must be in the **Load** event before the form is displayed.

 Without the "Unload Test" statement in the code, the application will not end. Since the form Test was loaded into memory with the reference of the Name property, it also must be unloaded. Otherwise setting Test to Nothing will not unload it from memory or terminate the form. This will result in an error.

The output will be as shown in Code 3.23.

```
form_Initialize Event
Hello!
form_load Event
frmKill
form_QueryUnload Event
form_Unload Event
form_Terminate Event
```

Code 3.23: Output of the Load Event

Resize() Event

The form is ready to enter the Displayed state. Before the form is displayed, the Resize event is called, and it resizes the form appropriately and makes it ready for display. After that, every time you resize the form by dragging its corners, minimize it, or maximize it, the **Resize** event is called. In addition, you can generate the **Resize** event by writing code that changes the size properties of a form. Modify the code in the form frmTest to Code 3.24.

```
Private Sub Form_Load()
    Dim Test As New frmKill
    Test.Prn
    Debug.Print Test.Name
    Test.Height = 2000    'setting this property forces a call to
                          'Resize
    Unload Test
    Set Test = Nothing
End Sub
```

Code 3.24: Triggering Resize

In the output, you will see the reference to the **Form_Resize** event when you set the **Height** property of the form Test, as shown in Code 3.25.

```
form_Initialize Event
 Hello!
 form_load Event
frmKill
 form_Resize Event (induced by the setting of the Height
 property)
 form_QueryUnload Event
 form_Unload Event
 form_Terminate Event
```

Code 3.25: Output of Code 3.24

The form is still not visible on the screen. It was unloaded from the memory even before it was displayed.

You can trace a program execution by using the **Step Into** option in the **Debug** menu (press F8) and figure out exactly which lines of code are executed in every step.

Activate() Event

Any code that you want to run after loading the form into memory, and before displaying, should be included in the **Activate** event. Every time the form becomes active in the application, it generates the **Activate** event. Modify the code for the frmTest form as shown in Code 3.26.

```
Private Sub Form_Load()
    Dim Test As New frmKill
    Test.Prn
    Debug.Print Test.Name
    Test.Show
End Sub
```

Code 3.26: Triggering the Activate Event

You will see both the forms on your screen. The form **frmKill** is activated and **frmTest** is deactivated as shown in Figure 3.5.

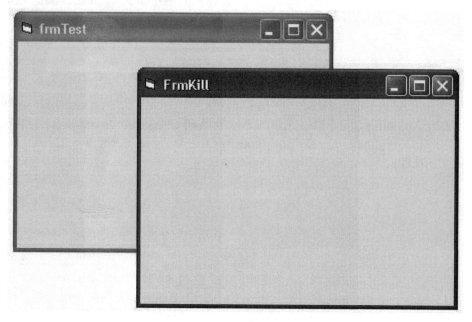

Figure 3.5: Activating a Form

If you close **frmKill** and **frmTest**, and check the output in the window, you can see Code 3.27.

```
form_Initialize Event
 Hello!
 form_load Event
 frmKill
 form_Resize Event
 form_Activate Event   (called by Show procedure)
 form_GotFocus Event
 form_LostFocus Event
 form_Deactivate Event
 form_paint Event
 form_Activate Event   (after you click on the frmTest window)
 form_GotFocus Event
 form_paint Event
 form_QueryUnload Event
```

```
form_Unload Event
form_Terminate Event
```

Code 3.27: Output of Activating and Deactivating a Form

The **Activate** event is generated upon clicking the frmKill window. You can also generate the **Activate** event by setting the **Visible** property of the form. For example, the following statement generates a Form_Activate event:

```
frmKill.Visible = True
```

GetFocus() Event

This event occurs only when no other control on the form can get the focus. In the project **prjEvent**, you have not included any controls on the forms. Therefore, the **GetFocus** event is generated every time after the **Activate** event. You can add a command button to **frmKill** and run the sample code written in the previous example. Close both the windows. The sample output is shown in Code 3.28.

```
form_Initialize Event
Hello!
 form_load Event
frmKill
 form_Resize Event
 form_Activate Event
 form_Deactivate Event
 form_paint Event
 form_Activate Event
 form_paint Event
 form_QueryUnload Event
 form_Unload Event
 form_Terminate Event
```

Code 3.28: Sample Output

You can see that there is no statement with **form_GotFocus** or **form_LostFocus** because the control you added gets the focus instead of the form. As a result, no GotFocus or LostFocus event occurs on the form.

QueryUnload() Event

Before a form enters the Destroyed state, the Form_QueryUnload() event procedure occurs, followed by the Form_Unload() event procedure. The user can cancel the unloading of the form from memory by returning a **True** value to the *Cancel* argument. The format for the event is:

Form_QueryUnload(*Cancel As Integer, UnloadMode As Integer*)

In this format, if *Cancel* is set to a non-zero value, it will cancel the **Unload** event, giving a user the opportunity to recover from a wrong decision. You can see the use of this event in almost all applications nowadays.

If you try to close an editor program and your data is not saved, you are offered a last chance to save the data.

If you write the following statement, the **QueryUnload** event is triggered first:

```
Unload Test
```

Code 3.29 demonstrates the use of the **QueryUnload** event.

```
Private Sub Form_QueryUnload(Cancel As Integer, UnloadMode As
Integer)
    Dim result As Integer
    result = MsgBox("Are you sure ?", vbOKCancel, "Save
Changes")
    Cancel = result - 1    'result is 1 for OK and 2 for cancel
End Sub
```

Code 3.29: Using the QueryUnload Event

 If you press **OK**, when the message box is displayed, the variable **Cancel** gets the value 0, and the form unloads. However, if you press the option **Cancel**, the variable **Cancel** gets the value 1, and the Unload event does not occur.

Unload() Event

The only way to enter the Memory and Resources Completely Reclaimed state is to unload the form and then set all references to Nothing. The **Unload** event removes the form from the screen and unloads it from memory. Even if the form is not visible, it is unloaded from memory. The forms collection removes its entry for the particular form whose **Unload** event is called.

The memory resources used up by the form during its lifetime are retrieved by the system after the **Unload** event. If you keep a reference to the form in some variable before unloading, the form returns to its unloaded state. You can then load the form again into memory by using this reference.

Code 3.30 shows that after the **QueryUnload** event, the **Unload** event occurs, which unloads the form from memory. To see the step-by-step execution of the application press **F8** and observe how the form receives the **Unload** event right after the **QueryUnload** event. To prevent the form from unloading, you can return a positive value for the Cancel argument in the **QueryUnload** event.

```
Private Sub Form_Load()
    Dim Test As New frmKill
  Test.Show
    Unload Test
    Set Test = Nothing
End Sub
```

Code 3.30: Testing Unload

The output of Code 3.30 is given in Code 3.31.

```
form_Initialize Event
 form_load Event
 form_Resize Event
    (after the line "Unload Test" the following events occur →)
 form_QueryUnload Event
 form_Unload Event
 form_Terminate Event
```

Code 3.31: Output of Testing Unload Event

Other Form Events

Some of the other important events of a form are listed below:

- Text.LostFocus: Occurs when the object has lost focus. Remember that the object first has to get focus to lose it. Therefore, if an object does not have the focus until a point, it cannot lose focus. You can use LostFocus to reverse conditions you create in the GotFocus event.

- Paint: Occurs when any portion of the form requires a repaint. For example, when you move or enlarge a form at run time, it generates the **Paint** event. In addition, when another window overlaps some part of a form, a paint event occurs. Calling the **Refresh** method also triggers this event. You should be careful not to add a call to **Refresh** the **Paint** event as it will recursively call the paint event.

- Deactivate: When the form is not an active window any more, it generates a **Deactivate** event. If the form is still visible after it is deactivated, another **Paint** event is generated to paint the form showing it as a deactivated window.

- Terminate: When you use the syntax Set <formname> = Nothing, the form generates a **Terminate** event and all references to the form are removed. All resources occupied by the form are released after this event.

The **End** statement in your code will prevent the form from getting the **QueryUnload**, **Unload**, and **Terminate** events. Therefore, you should be careful while using the **End** statement.

Mouse Events

The form object receives certain events when the user clicks the mouse buttons. These are called mouse events. A form can only receive these events when there are no controls on the particular area where the user has clicked the mouse button. These mouse events are:

- Click: Occurs when the user clicks a mouse button over the form. If the user clicks over any control in a form, the control receives the **Click** event instead of the form.

- DblClick: Occurs when the user double-clicks on the form. The system sends a double-click message to the application only when the time interval between the two click events is less than or equal to the user-defined mouse setting on the system.

- MouseMove: This event occurs when the user moves the mouse over the form. The syntax for the event is:

  Private Sub Form_MouseMove(*button As Integer, shift As Integer, x As Single, y As Single*)

In this syntax, the **button** argument represents the left, right, or middle button of the mouse. This argument represents an integer that corresponds to the state of the mouse buttons in which a bit is set if the button is down. The argument uses bits corresponding to the left button (bit 0), right button (bit 1), and middle button (bit 2). These bits correspond to the values 1, 2, and 4, respectively. The argument indicates the complete state of the mouse buttons; some, all, or none of these three bits can be set, indicating that some, all, or none of the buttons are pressed.

The **shift** argument is also a bit field that has the state of the SHIFT, CTRL, and ALT keys. They represent bit 0, bit 1, and bit 2, respectively. Their integer values are 1, 2, and 4. The arguments x and y specify the location of the mouse pointer on the form.

- MouseUp and MouseDown: The **MouseUp** event occurs when the user releases a mouse button and the **MouseDown** event occurs when the user presses a mouse button. The syntaxes for the two events are:

  Private Sub Form_MouseUp(*button As Integer, shift As Integer, x As Single, y As Single*)

  Private Sub Form_MouseDown(*button As Integer, shift As Integer, x As Single, y As Single*)

In these syntaxes, the **button** argument is the same as that of the **MouseMove** event except that it indicates which button is pressed or released. The rest of the arguments are the same. Code 3.32 demonstrates how to paint on the form with a mouse using the mouse events. Create a new project and add Code 3.32 to the default form named **Form1**.

```
Private Sub Form_Load()
    ForeColor = RGB(120, 120, 120)
    BackColor = vbWhite
    DrawWidth = 5
End Sub
Private Sub Form_MouseMove(Button As Integer, Shift As Integer,
X As Single, Y As Single)
    If Button = 1 Then
        Line (CurrentX, CurrentY)-(X, Y)
    End If
End Sub
```

```
Private Sub Form_MouseDown(Button As Integer, Shift As Integer,
X As Single, Y As Single)
    PSet (X, Y)        ' Draws a point when the user presses any
button
End Sub
```

Code 3.32: Mouse Events

In Code 3.32, the fore color and back color are changed to shades of gray and white, respectively. The width of the line is set to 5 to get a thicker line. The **MouseDown** event draws a point at the location where the user has clicked the mouse. The **MouseMove** button event checks whether the left button is pressed or not. If it is pressed, it draws a line from the point denoted by (CurrentX, CurrentY) to the point (X, Y). Figure 3.6 shows the output of mouse events.

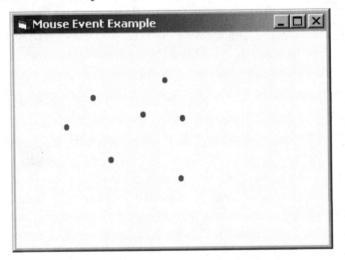

Figure 3.6: Mouse Events

1. What are three characteristics of objects in Visual Basic?

2. Name the two built-in collections in Visual Basic.

3. What types of shapes can the **Circle** method draw?

4. Name the stages in a form's life cycle.

5. Which event creates all the controls in a form?

6. What happens when you refer to any built-in form property or procedure of a form that is not loaded?

7. Which event is called when you use a statement like **Unload Me** in a form?

8. What happens when you call the **Refresh** method in a form's **Paint** event?

3.2 Using Controls

Controls are objects designed to provide functionality to forms. They are an integral part of every application. All controls are created within forms. They have their own set of properties, methods, and events. Controls help you to interact with an application. The interaction can be data input or display, accessing remote applications or databases, or simply using the application's features.

Microsoft Visual Basic provides a basic set of controls called standard or intrinsic controls that are always present in the toolbar. They provide most of the common functionality to applications. You have learned to use most of them in the previous course, "Introduction to Computer Programming."

The standard, or *intrinsic*, controls present in Visual Basic are listed in Table 3.8 along with their description and toolbar icons.

Control	Description	Icon
Label	Displays text that cannot be modified by the user.	A
TextBox	Displays or obtains text for interaction with the user.	abl
Frame	Behaves as a container for controls and groups them together.	
CommandButton	Executes a command when clicked by the user.	
CheckBox	Provides a True/False or Yes/No option to the user.	
OptionButton	Lets the user select an option from a group of similar controls. Only one button can be selected from a group.	
ListBox	Provides a user with a scrollable list of items to select.	
ComboBox	Combination of a list box and a text box. Can be displayed as a list or a drop-down list.	
HScrollBar and VScrollBar	Provides scrolling functionality to controls which do not have scroll bars.	
Timer	Executes events after specified time intervals.	

DriveListBox	Displays a list of drives present on the user's hard disk from which the user is allowed to select.	
DirListBox	Displays a list of directories on the current drive from which the user is allowed to select.	
FileListBox	Displays a list of files in the current directory and from which the user is allowed to select.	
Shape	Displays various shapes (circle, rectangle, oval, square, etc.) on a form or picture box.	
Line	Draws a line on the form.	
PictureBox	Displays graphical objects. Can also be used as a container for other controls.	
Image	Displays clickable graphical images similar to the Picture Box but uses less resources.	
Data	Provides connectivity to a database. Can be used by data bound controls to display data.	
OLE	OLE (Object Linking and Embedding) container provides the facility to embed data in an application.	

Table 3.8: Intrinsic Controls in Visual Basic

For further functionality, you can add other controls by clicking **Components** under the **Project** menu. These controls reside in .dll or .ocx files that can be easily added to an application.

Figure 3.7 shows controls that you can add to your project from the **Components** menu.

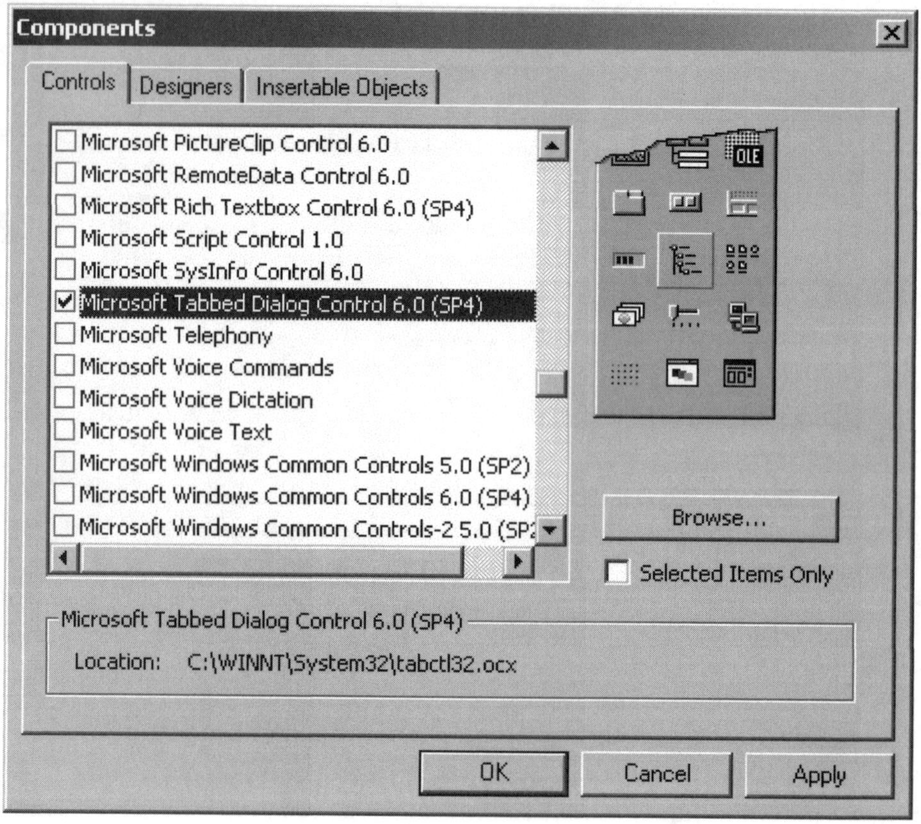

Figure 3.7: Adding Controls

After you select a control, it is added to the controls toolbar where you can double-click on it to add it to your form.

There are also custom controls designed by third party component vendors that provide many other options to programmers. While developing custom applications, if none of the available VB controls provide the needed functionality to the application, you can search for third party controls or develop them on your own.

3.2.1 Label Control

 Apply features of the Label control.

The Label control is a graphical control used to display text on a form. You can also use it as a status bar to display messages. The Label control is not directly editable, but you can write code to change the displayed contents or properties of a label control. The important properties of the Label control are:

- AutoSize: If **True**, allows the label control to automatically adjust to the size of its contents. The label control will expand horizontally to fit the entire contents of the Caption property.
- Caption: Specifies the text that appears on the label.
- Enabled: Determines whether the label can generate events.
- Alignment: Determines the alignment of the label's contents. The text can be left justified, right justified, or centered.
- DataSource: Specifies the name of the Data control from which the label gets its data.
- DataField: Binds the label to the specified data field.
- WordWrap: If **True**, allows the contents to wrap and expand vertically.

Code 3.33 displays how to change the caption of a Label on certain events. Add a Label control to a form. Then, enter Code 3.33 in the form's Code Editor.

```
Private Sub Form_Click()
    lblHeader.Caption = "You Just Clicked the Form"
    lblHeader.BackColor = vbGreen
End Sub

Private Sub Form_Load()
    With lblHeader
        .Alignment = vbCenter
        .WordWrap = True
        .AutoSize = True
```

```
      End With
End Sub
Private Sub lblHeader_Click()
    lblHeader.BackColor = vbWhite
    lblHeader.Caption = "You Clicked Me"
End Sub
```

Code 3.33: Changing a Label's Caption

Every time you click on the Label control or the form, the caption of the label changes. The **Alignment**, **WordWrap**, and **AutoSize** properties are set during the **Load** event. You can also do the same at design time.

If the **AutoSize** property is set to **False** and **WordWrap** to **True**, the text in the label will not be fully visible if it is lengthy.

3.2.2 TextBox Control

Evaluate the uses of the TextBox control.

The TextBox control is used to collect information from the user at run time. This control can display multi-line text and has both horizontal and vertical scroll bars. Some of the important properties of the text box are:

- Enabled: Determines whether the text box can respond to events generated by the user.

- Text: Is the default property of the control.

- Alignment: Justifies the text in the text box.

- MaxLength: Determines the maximum number of characters you can enter in the text box. The default setting of this property is **0**, which means you can enter 2048 characters in a text box. If you set the **MultiLine** property to **True**, you can enter up to 32 KB of text.

- PasswordChar: Displays the password character in the text box instead of the actual text that is typed in by the user. The control takes a string as the parameter. The default value is the empty string (" "). Additional characters are ignored, and only the first character of the string is set as the password character.

- MultiLine: Determines whether the contents of the text box are displayed in a single line or several lines. Text wraps automatically if the property is set to **True**.

- Locked: The user cannot edit the text in the text box if you set this property to **True**. However, the user can still scroll and select text.

- ScrollBars: Determine whether the text box has horizontal or vertical scroll bars. The default value is **vbSBNone** (0), which means that there are no scroll bars.

- SelText: Determines the string in the text box that is selected.

- SelLength: Determines the number of characters selected.

- SelStart: Determines the starting point of the selected text.

Some of the useful events of the TextBox control are:

- Change: Indicates that the contents of the text box have changed.

- KeyDown and KeyUp: Report the exact physical state of the keyboard itself: A key is pressed down (KeyDown) and a key is released (KeyUp).

- KeyPress: Supplies the character that the key represents. Occurs only for ANSI characters.

- Click: Occurs when the user has clicked the mouse on the TextBox control.

Code 3.34 shows how to code the **KeyPress** event of the TextBox control to force the user to enter only digits between 0 and 9. When any other character is typed, a message box prompts the user to enter only numbers. The **Asc()** function is used to specify character code values. Character codes that are outside the desired range (in this case, numbers) will be intercepted (KeyAscii = 0) and ignored.

```
Private Sub txtTest_KeyPress(KeyAscii As Integer)
  If KeyAscii < Asc(0) Or KeyAscii > Asc(9) Then
       MsgBox "Please enter digits between 0-9", _
                vbOKOnly, "Error Message"
       KeyAscii = 0
  End If
End Sub
```

Code 3.34: KeyPress Event of a TextBox Control

3.2.3 Frame Control

 Apply the Frame control in applications.

The Frame control acts as a container for other controls. The Frame control is usually used to group together a set of option buttons or check boxes. For example, if you want more than one set of option buttons in your form, you have to use a frame. The option buttons in the frame will behave separately from the other option buttons in the form. However, the Frame control can also be used as a container for other controls within a form.

The only property of the Frame control you are required to set is the **Caption** property. This property helps the user to recognize the meaning of the controls inside the frame.

When using the Frame control to group other controls, first draw the Frame control, and then draw the controls inside it. This enables you to move the frame and the controls it contains together.

To add other controls to the frame, draw them inside the frame. If you draw a control outside the frame, or use the double-click method to add a control to a form, and then try to move it inside the frame control, the control will be on top of the frame and you will have to move the frame and controls separately.

Figure 3.8 shows two sets of option buttons in a form, one set is drawn in the form, and the other set is restricted within a frame. The two sets are logically separated and you can use them for different purposes.

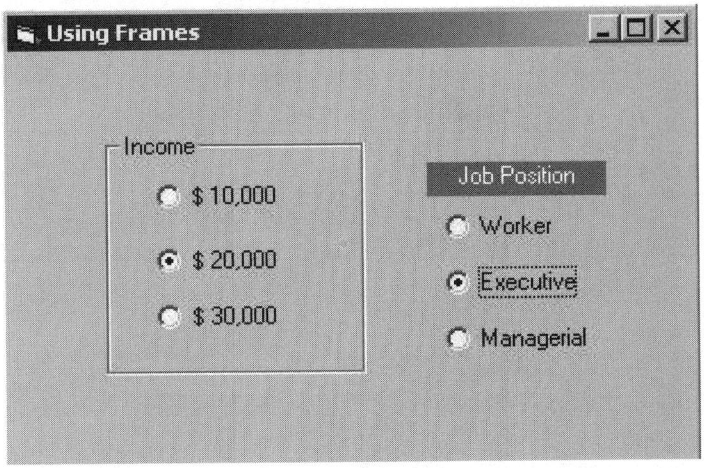

Figure 3.8: Using Frames in a Form

3.2.4 Command Button Control

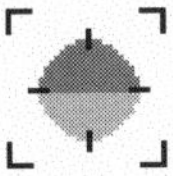

Evaluate the properties and uses of the command button.

The command button or push button is used to initiate, interrupt, or terminate a process. It is one of the most commonly used controls in Microsoft Visual Basic. Some of the important properties of this control are:

■ Name: Returns the name of the command button. It is a read-only property at run time.

■ Caption: Sets the text displayed on the button. You can associate an access key to the command button by adding an ampersand (&) before the character you want to use as a shortcut. For example, setting the caption to "E&xit" will enable you to access the command button by pressing the Alt +X key.

■ Default: Determines the default button on a form. If set to true, the button is set as the default button for the form and the default properties of all the other buttons are automatically set to false. The user can press ENTER to select a default command button.

- Cancel: Sets a button as the cancel button for a form. If set to true, pressing the ESC key selects the particular command button.

- Value: Sets or returns a value indicating whether the button is selected. The default value is **False**. This property is not available at design time.

- Style: Determines whether the button is a standard or a graphical button.

Code 3.35 shows the use of a Command Button control.

```
Private Sub Form_Load()
  cmdTest.Caption = "E&xit"
  cmdTest.Enabled = False
End Sub


Private Sub Form_Click()
  cmdTest.Enabled = True
End Sub


Private Sub cmdTest_Click()
  Unload Me
End Sub
```

Code 3.35: Using the Command Button Control

In the Code 3.35, the caption of the command button **cmdTest** is set to "E&xit" so that the user can press Alt +X to select this control. The button is initially disabled. On clicking the form, the button gets enabled. When the user clicks on the button or presses the access key combination, the form unloads from the memory.

3.2.5 CheckBox and OptionButton Controls

 Analyze the features of CheckBox and OptionButton controls.

The CheckBox and OptionButton controls are somewhat similar in their functionality. They both offer the user a choice of **Yes/No** or **True/False** option. The major difference between them is that the CheckBox control functions independently while the OptionButton control functions in a group. This means that you can select several

CheckBox controls in a form simultaneously but can select only one OptionButton from a group.

To group several OptionButton controls together, put them within a container like a form or a frame. Some of the common properties of the CheckBox and OptionButton controls are:

- Value: In a CheckBox control, the Value property can be 0 or Unchecked (default), 1 or Checked, and 2 or Grayed. In an OptionButton control, **True** means the button is selected and **False** means it is not selected.

- Style: When the Style is set to 0 (vbButtonStandard), the control is displayed like a normal window CheckBox or OptionButton. When the Style is set to 1 (vbButtonGraphical), the control is displayed like a push button, and the user can add a graphic to the control.

- Caption: The message displayed on the control.

- Enabled: If set to **True**, the control can respond to user-generated events.

- TabStop: Determines whether the user can use the TAB button to set focus on the control.

Code 3.36 shows how to change properties of a CheckBox control. Add two CheckBox controls to a form and name them **chkComp** and **chkSubscribe**. Then add the Code 3.36.

```
Private Sub chkComp_Click()
  If chkComp.Value = vbChecked Then
      chkSubscribe.Enabled = True
  Else
      chkSubscribe.Enabled = False
  End If
End Sub


Private Sub Form_Load()
    chkSubscribe.Enabled = False
    chkComp.Caption = "Computer Professional"
    chkSubscribe.Caption = "Subscribe Dr. Dobb's"
End Sub
```

Code 3.36: Changing Properties of a CheckBox Control

On executing Code 3.36, the check box **chkSubscribe** is initially disabled. When you select the **chkComp** check box, the button is enabled.

A sample output is shown in Figure 3.9.

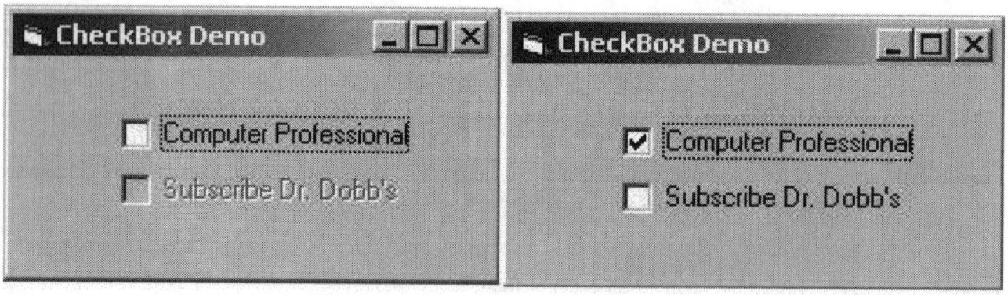

Figure 3.9: The Use of the Check Box in a Code

To use OptionButton controls in a form, perform the following steps. The example displays an interface displaying two sets of option buttons to accept the type of Linux desktop and boot loader from the user, and displays the selection being made by the user.

1.   Open a new form and name it **OptionButton Demo**.

2.   Add a command button and name it **cmdConfirm**.

3.   Add a frame and change its caption to **Choose Desktop**.

4.   Add two option buttons to the frame and change their **Name** and **Caption** property to:

      a. Name: optKDE   Caption: "KDE 3.0"

      b. Name: optGNOME   Caption: "GNOME 4.0"

5.   Add another frame and change its caption to **Choose BootLoader**.

6.   Add three option buttons to the frame and change the following properties:

      a. Name: optGRUB   Caption: "GRUB"

      b. Name: optLILO   Caption: "LILO"

      c. Name: optXOSL   Caption: "XOSL"

7.   Add a Label control named **lblSelection** and change its Caption to **Selected Items**.

8.   Add a Label control for the header and change its caption to **Customizing Your OS**.

9.   Add Code 3.37. The code checks the value of the option buttons in both the groups. Depending on these values, the code constructs a string containing the selected type of desktop and boot loader, and updates the Label control named **lblSelection** with the string.

```vb
Private Sub cmdConfirm_Click()
Dim strSel As String
strSel = "DESKTOP: "
If optKDE.Value = True Then
    strSel = strSel & " KDE "
ElseIf optGNOME.Value = True Then
        strSel = strSel & " GNOME "
End If
strSel = strSel & "     BOOTLOADER: "
If optGRUB.Value = True Then
    strSel = strSel & "GRUB"
ElseIf optLILO.Value = True Then
    strSel = strSel & "LILO"
ElseIf optXOSL.Value = True Then
    strSel = strSel & "XOSL"
End If
lblSelection.Caption = strSel
End Sub
```

Code 3.37: Using OptionButton Control

10.   Press **F5** to run the application. Select any options from the two frames and click the **cmdConfirm** button.

A sample output is given in Figure 3.10.

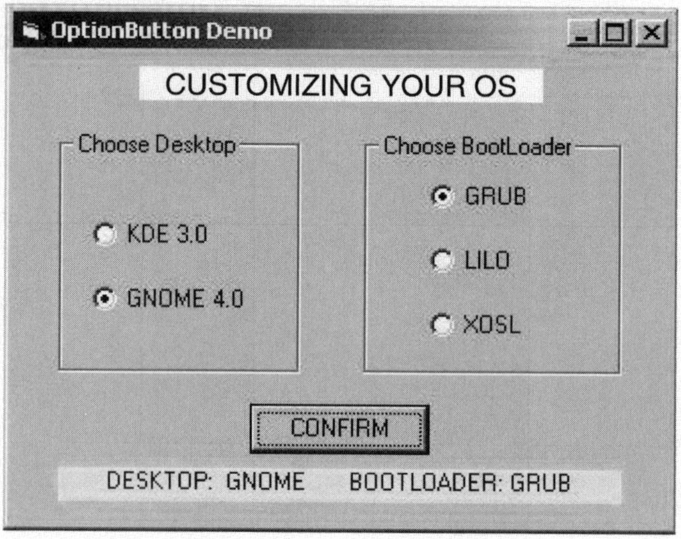

Figure 3.10: Using Option Buttons

The code for the application is a bit lengthy because you have to check each button's status. The string variable **strSel** keeps track of the options you have selected. It adds the chosen option to the end of the string and finally displays the resultant string in the label **lblSelection**.

3.2.6 ListBox and ComboBox Controls

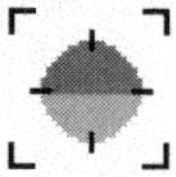

Apply the features of the ListBox and ComboBox controls.

The ListBox and ComboBox controls let the end user choose one or more items from a list. The combo box integrates the features of a list box and a text box. It provides the user with the option of using a text box to type data, or selecting an item from the list. A scroll bar is automatically added when the number of items is more than what the list can display on the screen.

The common properties of the ListBox and ComboBox controls are listed below:

- Enabled: Determines whether the ListBox or ComboBox control can respond to events generated by the user.
- ItemData: Modifies a specific number for each item in a ListBox or ComboBox control. Can be used as an index to the items in the list.
- List: Used to access or modify list items by their index. Returns (-1) when the index specified is out of range.
- ListCount: Returns the number of items present in the list box.
- ListIndex: Returns the index of the item selected from the list.
- NewIndex: Returns the last item that was included in the list.
- Style: Determines whether a check box is added to every list item in the ListBox control. The default value is 0 (Standard), and no check box is displayed. A value of one adds a check box to every entry. For ComboBox controls, the **Style** property determines whether it is a Dropdown combo box, Simple combo box with text box, or a Dropdown list.
- Sorted: Determines whether the list items are sorted or not.
- Text: Returns the text contained in the selected item in the list.

Some of the properties of a ListBox control that are not found in a ComboBox control are:

- Columns: Determines whether the list items are displayed in a single column with a vertical scroll bar, or multiple columns with a horizontal scroll bar.
- MultiSelect: Determines whether the user can select several items from the list.
- Selected: Determines whether the item given in the index is selected.
- SelCount: Returns the number of items selected in the list.

Some of the properties of a ComboBox control not present in a ListBox control are mentioned below. Note that these properties also belong to a TextBox control.

- SelText: Determines the string in the text currently selected in the text box portion.
- SelLength: Determines the number of characters selected.
- SelStart: Determines the starting point of the selected text.

The important methods of the ListBox and ComboBox controls are:

- AddItem: Adds an item to the list box or combo box. Returns the index for that item in NewIndex.

- RemoveItem: Removes an item from the ListBox or ComboBox control.

- Clear: Clears all the contents of the control.

To use ListBox and ComboBox controls, perform the following steps. The given example displays an interface enabling the user to add values to a list box and a combo box during run time. It also provides a command button to clear all the values in the list box and the combo box.

1.   Open a new form and name it **frmComboList**.

2.   Add a list box to the form and set the following properties:

      a. Name: lstNames

      b. Columns: 2

      c. Sorted: True

      d. Style: (1) CheckBox

3.   Add a combo box to your form and set the following properties:

      a. Name: cmbNames

      b. Sorted: True

      c. Style: (0) DropDownCombo

4.   Add a text box and name it **txtNewItem**.

5.   Add two command buttons and set the following properties:

      a. Name: cmdAdd   Caption: Add Entry

      b. Name: cmdClear   Caption: Clear All

6.   Your form should look like the form shown in Figure 3.11.

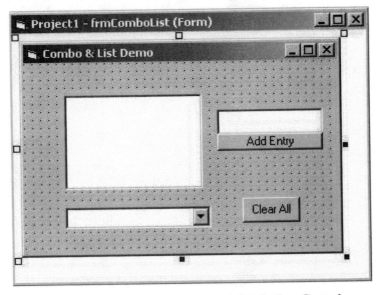

Figure 3.11: Form Using ListBox and ComboBox Controls

7.   Add Code 3.38 to the form's **Load** event. This code fills the list box and the combo box with some sample data. It also sets the **Add** button's **Enabled** property to **False**.

```
Private Sub Form_Load()
  lstNames.AddItem "Ralph"
  lstNames.AddItem "Amelia"
  lstNames.AddItem "Adam"
  lstNames.AddItem "Steve"
  lstNames.AddItem "Eddie"
  cmbNames.AddItem "Robert"
  cmbNames.AddItem "Candy"
  cmbNames.AddItem "Sharon"
  cmbNames.AddItem "Edward"
  cmbNames.AddItem "Michito"


   cmdAdd.Enabled = False
End Sub
```

Code 3.38: Filling the List Box and Combo Box

8. Add Code 3.39 to the **cmdAdd** button's **Click** event. On clicking the **Add** button, the item is added to the list box and combo box. This code also displays the last item in the combo box (given by ListCount – 1) in the text portion of the combo box.

```
Private Sub cmdAdd_Click()
    lstNames.AddItem txtNewItem.Text
    cmbNames.AddItem txtNewItem.Text
    cmbNames.ListIndex = cmbNames.ListCount - 1
End Sub
```

Code 3.39: Code for the Add Button

9. Add Code 3.40 to the **cmdClear** button's **Click** event. This code example clears both the list box and combo box by calling their **Clear** methods.

```
Private Sub cmdClear_Click()
    lstNames.Clear
    cmbNames.Clear
End Sub
```

Code 3.40: Code for the Clear Button

10. Add Code 3.41 to the txtNewItem's **Change** event. It monitors any change in the content of the text box. If you enter any character, it enables the **Add** button. This ensures that only non-empty strings are added to the list box and the combo box, because the value in the text box can be added only if the **Add** command button is enabled.

```
Private Sub txtNewItem_Change()
    If Trim(txtNewItem.Text) <> "" Then
        cmdAdd.Enabled = True
    Else
        cmdAdd.Enabled = False
    End If
End Sub
```

Code 3.41: Code for Change Event of the TextBox Control

11. Press **F5** to run the application. Figure 3.12 gives a run time view of the application.

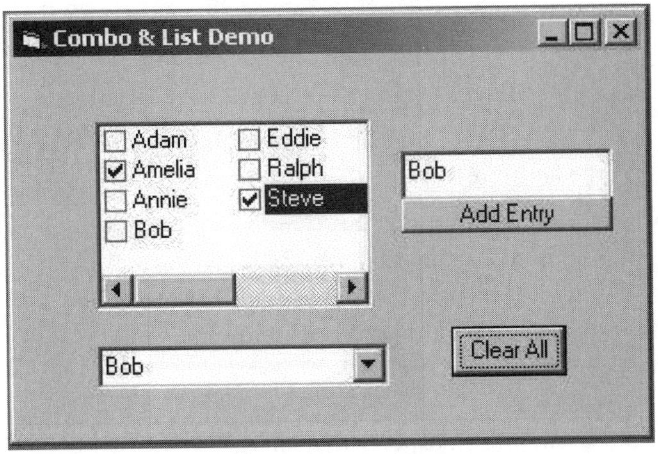

Figure 3.12: Using the ComboBox and ListBox Controls

3.2.7 HScrollBar and VScrollBar Controls

Evaluate the uses of the HScrollBar and VScrollBar controls.

Scrollbars are basically used as tools for navigation. They help you browse through a large amount of data. They are also used as a measure of quantity. You can use scroll bars to magnify an image, increase the volume of your speakers, and so on. The HScrollBar and VScrollBar controls are used to provide such functionality to controls that do not have built-in scrollbars. They are also useful when the normal scrollbars do not suffice for the kind of function you want to provide in your applications.

Some of the important properties of scrollbars are:

■ Value: Determines the current position of the scroll bar. Its value is always between the maximum and minimum values of the scroll bar.

■ Max: Determines a scroll bar's maximum value for the Value property. This occurs when the HScrollBar is at the rightmost position and the VScrollBar is at the bottom position.

- Min: Determines a scroll bar's minimum value for the Value property. This occurs when the HScrollBar is at the leftmost position and the VScrollBar is at the top position.

- LargeChange: Determines the amount by which Value changes when the user clicks in the area of the scroll bar excluding the arrows.

- SmallChange: Determines the amount by which Value changes when the user clicks the scroll arrows.

The most important event for the scroll bars is the **Change** event, which determines the kind of action to take when the user clicks on the scrollbar and changes the **Value** property. You can also use the KeyPress, KeyDown, and KeyUp events to allow the user to use key combinations to control the scrolling.

If you set the Max property to a value less than that of Min, the maximum value of a horizontal scroll bar is set at the leftmost position and that of a vertical scroll bar at the top position.

To use scroll bars to change the color of a Shape control, perform the following steps:

1. Add a new form to your project and name it **frmScroll**.

2. Add a Shape control, shpOval to your form and set the following properties:

   a. BorderStyle: Solid

   b. BorderWidth: 3

   c. DrawMode: 13 – Copy Pen

   d. FillStyle: Solid

   e. Shape: 2 – Oval

   f. BorderColor: vbBlue

The BorderColor property is selected and set though the palette.

3. Add three labels and set their **Caption** property to Red, Green, and Blue, respectively. You may change the BackColor to the colors Red, Green, and Blue to indicate the function of the scroll bars they label.

4. Add a label to indicate the current RGB values and set the following properties:

   a. Name: lblRGB

   b. AutoSize: True

   c. Alignment: Center

   d. Caption: " "

5. Add three horizontal scroll bars to the form and name them hsbRed, hsbGreen, and hsbBlue. Place them along the labels as shown in Figure 3.13.

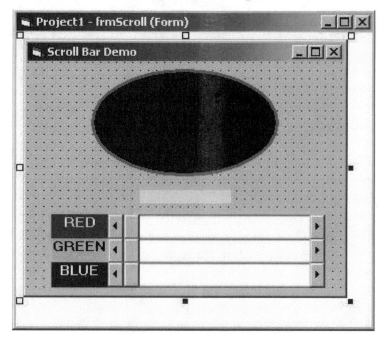

Figure 3.13: Form for Scroll Bar Demo

6.   Add Code 3.42 to the form's Load event. In the form's Load event, you change the Max, LargeChange, and SmallChange properties of the three scrollbars. The Max value assigned is 255, as that is the maximum RGB value for a color. LargeChange is set to 10 so that clicking in the area inside the scroll bar will change the value by 10. The SmallChange value assigned is 2, but you may change it as you desire.

```
Private Sub Form_Load()
    hsbRed.Max = 255
    hsbRed.LargeChange = 10
    hsbRed.SmallChange = 2
    hsbGreen.Max = 255
    hsbGreen.LargeChange = 10
    hsbGreen.SmallChange = 2
    hsbBlue.Max = 255
    hsbBlue.LargeChange = 10
    hsbBlue.SmallChange = 2
    shpOval.FillColor = RGB(0, 0, 0)
    Debug.Print shpOval.FillColor
    prnRGB
End Sub
```

Code 3.42: Code for the Form's Load Event

7.   Add Code 3.43 to the scroll bar's **Change** events. All the events call the same procedure prnRGB that changes the color of the Shape control.

```
Private Sub hsbRed_Change()
    prnRGB
End Sub
Private Sub hsbGreen_Change()
    prnRGB
End Sub

Private Sub hsbBlue_Change()
    prnRGB
End Sub
```

Code 3.43: Code for Change Events of Scroll Bars

8. Add Code 3.44 for the procedure prnRGB.

```
Private Sub prnRGB()
    shpOval.FillColor = hsbRed.value + _
        (256 * CLng(hsbGreen.value)) + _
        (65536 * CLng(hsbBlue.value))
    lblRGB.Caption = "RGB = (" & Str(hsbRed.value) & ", " & _
                        Str(hsbGreen.value) & ", " & _
                        Str(hsbBlue.value) & " )"
End Sub
```

Code 3.44: Code for Procedure prnRGB

Here the FillColor of the shape changes according to the value obtained from the position of the scroll bars. The factors 256 and 65536 shift the Green value in RGB by 8 bits and the Blue value by 16 bits. The function CLng converts the intermediate product to a long value so that any potential overflow problem is avoided. After the color of the shape is set, the label lblRGB prints the current RGB value.

Figure 3.14 shows the output of the application.

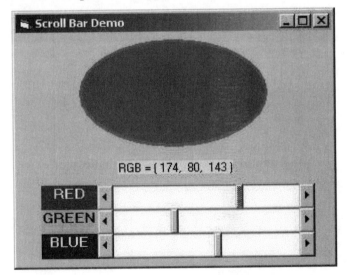

Figure 3.14: Using Scroll Bars

3.2.8 The Timer Control

 Explain the uses of the Timer control.

The Timer control causes a Timer event at regular intervals. The user can execute any code when a Timer event occurs. Generally, the control is used for processing events in the background. Some of the important properties of the Timer control are:

- Name: Determines the name of the control (Read-only at run time).
- Enabled: Determines whether the control can respond to the passage of time.
- Interval: Determines the gap (in milliseconds) after which the Timer event is triggered. Default value is 0, which means the Timer is disabled. The maximum value for this property is 65,535.

There are no built-in methods for this control. The only event associated with a Timer is the **Timer** event. It occurs only if the **Enabled** property is set to **True** and the Interval is greater than 0. After every interval specified by the **Interval** property, the system causes a **Timer** event.

To use a Timer control, perform the following steps:

1.   Add a form to your project and name it frmTimer.
2.   Add a Timer control to the form and set the following properties:
    a. Name: tmrEllipse
    b. Enabled: True
    c. Interval: 200 (milliseconds)
3.   Add Code 3.45 to the control's Timer event.

```
Private Sub tmrEllipse_Timer()
    FillStyle = vbSolid
    FillColor = RGB(255 * Rnd, 255 * Rnd, 255 * Rnd)
    Circle (Width * Rnd, Height * Rnd), 200 + 1000 * Rnd, , , ,_
1 / 3
End Sub
```

Code 3.45: Code for Timer Event

---

4. Press **F5** to run the application. You can see random ellipses all over your screen being drawn after the specified timer interval as shown in Figure 3.15.

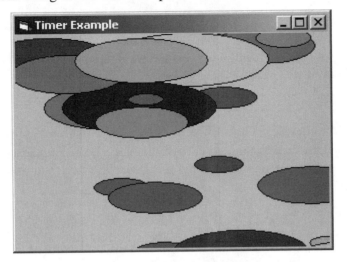

Figure 3.15: Drawing Ellipse Using Timer Control

The **Timer** event draws an ellipse every 200 milliseconds. The color for the ellipse is set to a random value by using the Rnd() function. The center of the ellipse is also set to a random value ranging from 0 to the width or height of the form. The radius is set to a random value ranging from 200 to 1200 twips. Finally, the aspect ratio is set to 1/3.

This example only demonstrates the use of the properties and the Timer event. You can write code for the timer event that can perform important tasks for an application. For example, if you design a text editor, you can save the currently open files within certain intervals of time in the background, without bothering the end user (a feature called autosave). This will ensure that even if the user forgets to save the file and the program crashes, file recovery is possible. You can also display time in the status bar through a Timer control.

3.2.9 DriveListBox, DirListBox, and FileListBox

 Apply the DriveListBox, DirListBox, and FileListBox controls in file system browsing.

The DriveListBox, DirListBox, and FileListBox controls provide the user access to the disk drives, directories, and files in the file system. They are similar in function and have several common properties and methods. These controls must be added in applications that browse files. They must be synchronized to work together.

DriveListBox

The DriveListBox provides a drop-down list consisting of the valid drives in the system. The user can select a drive from the list at run time to perform operations like directory browsing. The important properties of this control are:

- Drive: Determines the drive selected at run time.
- List: Returns the array of items in the drive list (read-only at run time). It takes an index as a parameter that ranges from 0 to (ListCount – 1).
- ListCount: Number of drives in the user's system.
- ListIndex: Gives the index of the currently selected drive.

The important event processed by the DriveListBox is the Change event. It is generated when the user selects a different drive from the list or a change occurs in the Drive property of the control through code.

DirListBox

The DirListBox displays paths and directories in a list box. The list is displayed in a hierarchical fashion similar to file managers. The important properties of the control are:

- List: Determines the List items in the DirListBox. The index argument ranges from $(-n)$ to (ListCount – 1) where n is the depth of the concerned directory from the currently expanded directory. For example, if the currently expanded directory is "C:\Visual Studio\VB" then its depth is –1, and "C:\Visual Studio" has a depth of –2 and this process goes on as you go higher up the hierarchy. Sub-directories of the current directory have index values ranging from 1 to (ListCount − 1).

- ListCount: Returns the count of number of subdirectories in the current directory.
- ListIndex: Index of the currently selected item in the list. Default value is 0, meaning no item is selected.
- Path: Determines the current path. Takes a string as an argument, consisting of a relative or absolute path. Changing its value triggers a Change event for a DirListBox.

The Change event of the DirListBox occurs when you change the Path through code or double-click a different directory from the list items.

FileListBox

This control lists the files in a directory specified by the value present in property Path. The important properties of this control are:

- FileName: Determines the path and the filename of a selected file. If you set the FileName property to "C:\windows\win.ini"; then the path of the control will be "C:\windows" and the FileName will be "win.ini." If you specify a path, then FileName will return an empty string.
- Normal: Determines whether files with their Normal attributes are displayed.
- Hidden: Determines whether files with their Hidden attributes are displayed.
- Archive: Determines if the control displays the files with their Archive attributes set.
- System: Determines whether files with their System attributes are displayed.
- ReadOnly: Determines whether the control displays read-only files in the list box.
- ListCount: Returns the number of files present in the current directory matching the pattern.
- List: The array of list items in the control's list box that match the pattern string.
- ListIndex: Determines the index of the selected item in the FileListBox.
- Pattern: Determines the patterns used to display files in the list. Can have multiple patterns, like "*.jpg; *.png."
- MultiSelect: Determines whether the user can select several files together.
- Selected: Determines whether an item is selected in the list.
- Path: Specifies the path of the selected file.

Important events of the FileListBox are:

- Click: Occurs when the user clicks the left mouse button on an item in the FileListBox.
- DoubleClick: Occurs when the user double-clicks the mouse button on a list entry.
- PatternChange: Occurs when the user changes the pattern used for file listing. This can happen when the FileName or Pattern properties are changed.
- PathChange: Occurs when the current path is changed through the Path or FileName property.

Code 3.46 demonstrates the use of the DriveListBox, DirListBox and the FileListBox controls. Perform the following procedure to create this application:

1. Add a form named frmFileBrowser to your Visual Basic project.
2. Add a DriveListBox control and name it drvTest.
3. Add a DirListBox and name it dirTest.
4. Add a FileListBox control and name it filTest.
5. Add a label above the FileListBox and name it lblTotFiles.
6. Add a text box and name it txtPattern.
7. Add a label to the text box and name it lblPattern.
8. Enter Code 3.46 to the Declarations section of your Code window.

```vb
Private Sub dirTest_Change()
    filTest.Path = dirTest.Path
    lblTotFiles.Caption = "Total Files: " & filTest.ListCount
End Sub

Private Sub drvTest_Change()
    dirTest.Path = drvTest.Drive
    filTest.Path = drvTest.Drive
End Sub

Private Sub Form_Load()
    lblTotFiles.Caption = "Total Files: " & filTest.ListCount
End Sub

Private Sub txtPattern_KeyPress(KeyAscii As Integer)
    If KeyAscii = 13 Then' user has pressed ENTER
```

```
        filTest.Pattern = txtPattern.Text
    End If
End Sub
```

Code 3.46: File System Browsing

In Code 3.46, code for the DirListBox's Change event assigns the new path set by changing the current directory to the Path property of the FileTextBox. In the DriveListBox's Change event, the path values of both the DirListBox and the FileTextBox are modified to reflect the current drive selected by the user.

The form's Load event assigns the caption of the label lblTotFiles to the number of files present in the current directory. This value is obtained from the ListCount property of the FileTextBox.

The user is given the facility of viewing files matching patterns in the FileListBox. The **KeyPress** event of the text box txtPattern is monitored and whenever ENTER is pressed, the pattern in the text box, which is stored in the Text property, is assigned to the FileListBox's Pattern property.

Figure 3.16 shows the output of the application.

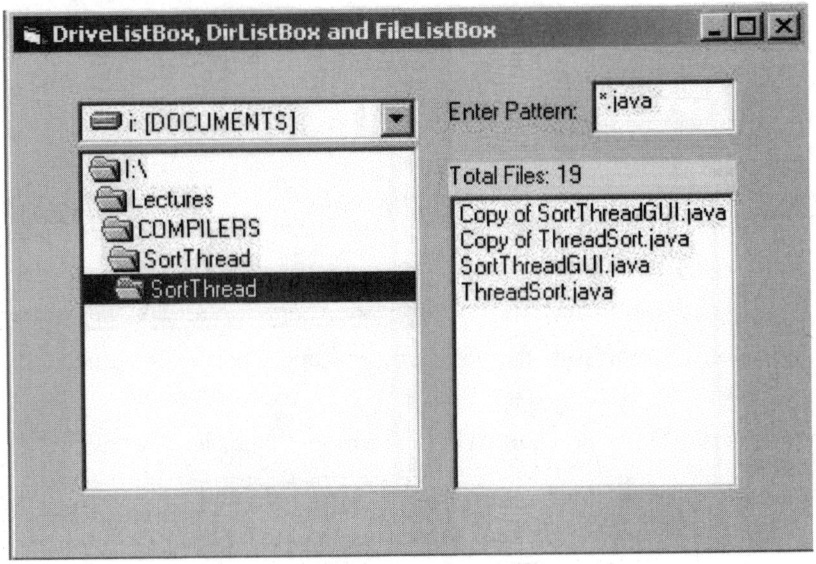

Figure 3.16: Displaying Files in a Directory

3.2.10 Shape and Line Controls

 Evaluate uses of Shape and Line controls.

These controls are used to add different shapes and lines on a form, respectively.

Shape Control

The Shape control is a graphical control which provides you with shape objects such as circle, oval, rectangle, rounded rectangle, square, or rounded square. You can have shapes with varying borders and fill them with different colors and patterns.

The important properties of the Shape control are:

■ Shape: Determines the shape of the control. Can take six values ranging from 0 to 5. Default shape is a rectangle. The six types of shapes are:

- Rectangle
- Square
- Oval
- Circle
- Rounded rectangle
- Rounded square

■ FillStyle: Determines the style or pattern with which the Shape is filled. Default is Transparent (value = 1).

■ BackStyle: Determines whether the shape has an opaque or transparent background.

■ BorderColor: Sets the color of the shape's border. You need to have a positive value for BorderSize property to view the border color.

■ BorderStyle: Sets the style of the object's border. Default value is Solid.

■ FillColor: Sets the color that fills the Shape object.

■ DrawMode: Determines the mode of the graphic's output. These modes are the result of raster operations between the object's color and the background's color. Values range from 1 to 16 with default set as CopyPen (13).

If you set the BorderSize of a Shape to a value greater than one, the BorderStyles Dash, Dot, Dash-Dot, and Dash-Dot-Dot (2,3,4,5) are not available.

Code 3.47 displays various shapes and fill styles in a Shape Object. To create this application, perform the following steps:

1.   Add a form to your project and name it frmShapes.

2.   Add a Shape control to the form and set the following properties (you can set these properties through code by adding them in the Load event).

      a. BorderColor: Brown (select from palette)

      b. BorderStyle: Solid

      c. BorderWidth: 5

      d. DrawMode: CopyPen

      e. FillColor: vbBlue

      f. FillStyle: Solid

TheFillColor property is selected and set through the palette.

3.   Add a command button and name it cmdShape.

4.   Add another command button and name it cmdfillstyle.

5.   Add Code 3.47. In this code, the variables shapeval and fill_style are used to store the current value of the Shape and FillStyle properties. On clicking the cmdShape button, the shapeval variable is increased by 1 if its value is less than 5; otherwise the value is reset to 0. Similarly, on clicking the cmdfillstyle button, the FillStyle property is increased from 0 to 7. The Shape control redraws itself every time one of the properties is modified.

```vb
Option Explicit
Dim intShapeval As Integer       'keeps track of current shape
Dim intFill_style As Integer     'keeps track of current fill
style


Private Sub cmdshape_Click()
    If intShapeval < 5 Then
        intShapeval = intShapeval + 1
    Else
        intShapeval = 0             'reset shape to lowest value
possible
    End If
    Shape1.Shape = intShapeval
End Sub


Private Sub cmdfillstyle_Click()
    If intFill_style < 7 Then
        intFill_style = intFill_style + 1
    Else
        intFill_style = 0
    End If
    Shape1.FillStyle = intFill_style
End Sub
```

Code 3.47: Using the Shape Control

Line Control

The Line control is another graphic control that draws a vertical, horizontal, or diagonal line on a Form, Frame, or a PictureBox control. The important properties of the Line control are:

- BorderColor: Sets the color of the line's border.
- BorderStyle: Sets the Line's border style. Default value is Solid. Other styles are Transparent, Dash, Dot, Dash-Dot, Dash-Dot-Dot, and Inside Solid.
- DrawMode: Determines the mode for output of the line. Same as DrawMode in Shape control.
- X1: The x coordinate of the line control's starting point.
- X2: The x coordinate of the line control's ending point.
- Y1: The y coordinate of the line control's starting point.
- Y2: The y coordinate of the line control's ending point.

Code 3.48 shows the use of properties of a line. Add a Line control to a form and name it linDiag. Add the code in the form's Click event. Every time you click the form, the line will toggle its visibility. Assigning the BorderStyle property to toggle between 0 and 1 does this. The line is drawn diagonally from the top-left to the bottom-right of the form.

```
Private Sub Form_Click()
    With linDiag
      .BorderStyle = .BorderStyle Xor 1
      .BorderWidth = 5
      .X1 = 0
      .Y1 = 0
      .X2 = ScaleWidth
      .Y2 = ScaleHeight
    End With
End Sub
```

Code 3.48: Using the Line Control

3.2.11 Other Useful Controls

 Explain the uses of other common controls.

There are a number of other controls available to create professional applications. Microsoft provides some of these and the rest are from third-party vendors. You can add these controls to your project by selecting the control from the Components menu under Project. Some of these are explained in detailed in this topic.

Tabbed Dialog Control (SSTab)

SSTab is a very useful control with which you can put a lot of related information in a single form. All the property settings are spread across several tabs instead of forms; this provides easy and quick access to the user. It results in less confusion on the part of the user.

To add a SSTab control to your project, click on the **Components** menu under **Project** and select **Microsoft Tabbed Dialog Control 6.0 (tabctl32.ocx)**. The icon for the control is added to your toolbar, to add it to your application.

Some of the important properties of the SSTab control are:

- Style: Determines the style of the tabs, whether they should look like standard tabs or property page tabs. The two values are:
  - ssStyleTabbedDialog
  - ssStylePropertyPage
- TabMaxWidth: The maximum width of each tab in the control.
- TabOrientation: Determines the side of the control on which the tabs appear. It can take four values, representing the four sides of the control's rectangle. These values are:
  - ssTabOrientationTop
  - ssTabOrientationBottom
  - ssTabOrientationLeft
  - ssTabOrientationRight
- Tabs: Number of tabs displayed by the control.

- Tab: The active tabs number. It takes values from 0 to (Tabs-1).
- TabsPerRow: Number of tabs displayed per row.

If you set the tab orientation to right or left, the IDE warns that you should have True Type fonts that support rotation. Change the Font property of the tab control to a True Type font for proper display of tab captions.

Adding Controls

There are two ways to add controls to tabs. If you want a control to appear on a single tab, select that tab and place the control. To display a control on all the tabs, add the control to your form and drag it over to the tab. This will display the common control on all the tabs. For example, you might want the user to click an OK button from any of the tabs to submit the information contained in them. Instead of adding separate OK buttons on all the tabs, add a single control to the form and drag it to the preferred position on the tab control.

Working with Tabs

Code 3.49 shows how to display a particular tab every time the form gets activated. Add a SSTab control to a form and name it tabProperties. To display tab 2 when the form gets an activate event, add Code 3.49.

```
Private Sub Form_Activate()
tabProperties.tab = 2
End Sub
```

Code 3.49: Activating a Tab

To add a tab to the control at run time, if you have a command button on tab 2 with the name cmdAddTab use Code 3.50.

```
Private Sub cmdAddTab_Click()
  With tabProperties
      .Tabs = .Tabs + 1
      .Tab = .Tabs - 1
      .Caption = "Property " & Str(.Tabs - 1)
```

```
      .Tab = 2
  End With
End Sub
```

Code 3.50: Adding Tabs Via Code

In Code snippet 3.50, the Tabs property is incremented by 1 to add a new tab to the control. Then the newly added tab is selected by setting the Tab property to the value returned by (Tabs – 1). Then the caption of the tab is changed to <"Property" + current tab number>. The last statement sets the focus back to the tab with the command button, which is tab 2.

Figure 3.17 shows the state of the form after adding six new tabs.

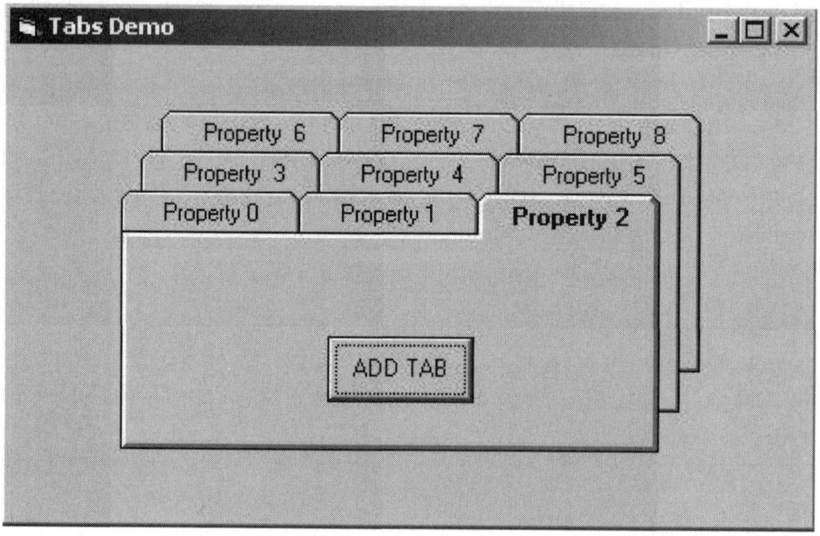

Figure 3.17: Adding Tabs at Run Time

Tab order should be set properly throughout a form. This results in users having the flexibility of using your application. Controls that can interact with the end users have two important properties: TabStop and TabIndex. These two properties determine whether pressing the tab key brings focus to a control and in what order. The TabStop property can either be true or false. If true, the user can press the tab to move to the control instead of using the mouse. This makes it easier for the user to continue with the keyboard to interact with the application. The TabIndex takes values beginning from 0. You should set TabIndex as 0 for the first object you want the user to begin with. Keep the continuity of the tab order throughout the form. However in case of OptionButton controls, it is considered as one tab stop. The one with the lowest TabIndex gets the focus and arrow keys can access the rest of the controls in the group. Whenever you have dialog boxes, you should set the Default and Cancel properties of the CommandButtons.

Microsoft Chart Control (MSChart)

The MSChart control is a graphical control that displays data graphically in 2D and 3D charts. It supports display in Bar, Area, Line, Step, and Combination chart types in 2D and 3D, and Pie chart and XY chart in 2D. You can use the chart control to make data representations in a very effective and attractive manner.

To add a MSChart control to your project, perform the following steps:

1.   Select **Projects** and then select **Components**.

2.   Click Microsoft Chart Control 6.0 (SP4) (OLEDB).

3.   Select Apply and the control is added to your toolbar. The icon for the MSChart control is shown in Figure 3.18.

Figure 3.18: Chart Control Icon

Some of the important properties of the MSChart control are:

- Allow Dynamic Rotation: Determines whether the user can rotate the chart.

- ChartType: Determines the type of the chart displayed.

- Column: Determines the current column in the chart.

- ColumnCount: Specifies the number of columns in the chart.

- ColumnLabel: Specifies the label of the current column given by Column property.

- RandomFill: Determines whether the chart is filled with random samples.
- ShowLegend: Determines whether the chart control displays the legend.
- Row: Specifies the current row in the chart.
- RowCount: Specifies the number of rows in the chart.
- RowLabel: Specifies the label of the current row given by row property.
- TitleText: Specifies the title of the chart.

Figure 3.19 shows a form with a MSChart control.

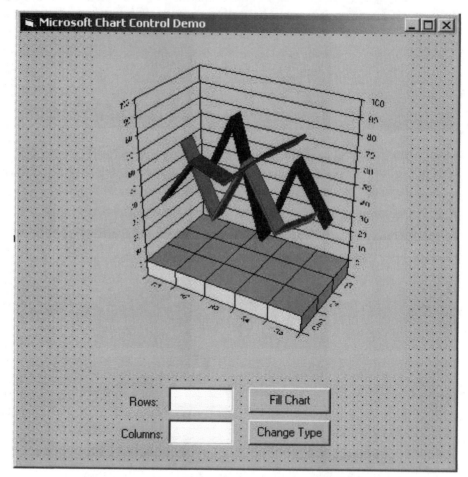

Figure 3.19: Form Showing the Chart Control

Code 3.51 shows how to display data in different chart types. It sets the row and column numbers dynamically and fills the chart with some random values. You can also change the chart type by clicking the button labeled "Change Type."

The procedure to create the application is as follows:

1. Add a MSChart control to your form and name it chMarks.

2. Add two TextBox controls named txtRows and txtCols.

3. Add two CommandButtons named cmdFill and and cmdType.

4. Add Code 3.51 to the Code editor.

```
Dim intChtype As Integer 'determines the type of chart displayed
Dim intRowcnt As Integer 'indexes the row
Dim intColcnt As Integer 'indexes the column
Dim intColnum As Integer 'indexes Column property to set legend

Private Sub Form_Load()
    intChtype = 0
    With chMarks
        .chartType = intChtype 'set ChartType to 0
        .ShowLegend = True      'display legend
        .TitleText = "Semester Marks"
    End With
    setlegend        'call function Setlegend
End Sub
Private Sub setlegend()
    intColnum = 0
    With chMarks
    For intColnum = 1 To .ColumnCount
        .Column = intColnum
        .ColumnLabel = "Semester " & Str(.Column)
    Next intColnum
    End With
End Sub
Private Suzb cmdType_Click()
    If intChtype < 9 Then
        chMarks.chartType = intChtype
        intChtype = intChtype + 1
```

```
      Else
            intChtype = 0
      End If
End Sub
Private Sub cmdFill_Click()
   With chMarks
      chMarks.RowCount = Val(txtRows.Text)
      chMarks.ColumnCount = Val(txtCols.Text)

      For intRowcnt = 1 To .RowCount
          For intColcnt = 1 To .ColumnCount
              .Row = intRowcnt
              .Column = intColcnt
              .Data = Rnd * 10 + .Row * .Column
          Next intColcnt
      Next intRowcnt
   End With
   setlegend
End Sub
```

Code 3.51: Using the Chart Control

In Code 3.51, in the form's Load event, the chart's title is set to "Semester Marks" and ShowLegend is set to true. The current chart type is set to 0 (3D bar chart). The Sub Setlegend is called to fill the column legends to the names of the semesters.

In the Setlegend Sub, the variable column indexes the current column of the chart (the Column property). The For…Next loop sets the label of the current column to the name of the current semester. You can also write another loop to set the label of the rows to the names of subjects.

In the **Click** event of the **cmdType** button, the code changes the **ChartType** property of the control chMarks from 0 to 9 and back to 0.

The code for the **cmdFill** button, takes the value of rows and columns entered by the user in the text box, txtRows, and txtCols respectively, and sets them to the number of rows and columns in the chart control. The two For…Next loops fills up every item in the chart with a random value that depends on the current row and column property. Setlegend is called to show the modified legend.

Figure 3.20 shows a snapshot of the application at run time.

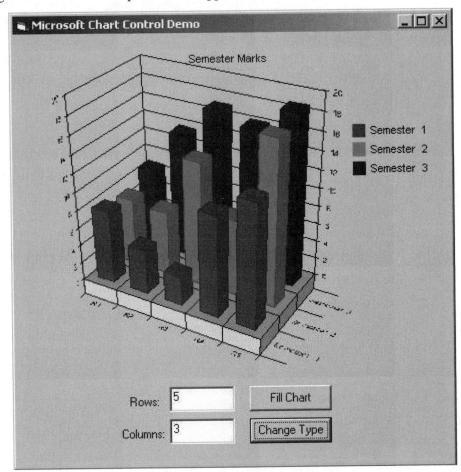

Figure 3.20: Chart Control Application

Microsoft Multimedia Control (MMControl)

The MMControl is another control that you can add to your applications to provide a simple and easy interface to play audio and video files. This control is contained in the MCI32.OCX file that you can add to the project from the Components menu under Project by clicking on Microsoft Multimedia control 6.0. Figure 3.21 shows a MMControl.

The buttons from left to right are shown in Figure 3.21.

Figure 3.21: MCI Control Buttons

The MMControl uses the Media Control Interface to provide support to the audio and video devices. The type of device is set through the DeviceType property. The different devices this control supports are:

- WaveAudio: Wave Device; files with extension ".wav"
- Sequencer: MIDI device
- CDAudio: Compact Disc audio player
- Overlay: Overlay devices
- DigitalVideo: Digital video
- AVIVideo: Audio Video Interleaved Video
- DAT: Digital Audio Tape player
- VideoDisc: VideoDisc player
- Scanner: Image Scanner
- VCR: Video Cassette Recorder
- Other: Any other MCI capable device

The Control commands for the MMControl are:

- Seek: Seeks a position in the current file.
- Prev: Moves to the beginning of the current track.
- Next: Moves to the beginning of the next track.
- Play: Plays the device mentioned in DeviceType property.
- Pause: Pauses or resumes playing.
- Back: Steps backward.
- Step: Steps forward.
- Stop: Stops playing or recording.
- Record: Enables recording.
- Eject: Ejects the media device.

- Save: Saves an open file.
- Open: Opens an MCI device.
- Close: Closes an MCI device.
- Sound: Plays a sound.

Code 3.52 shows how to open a ".wav" file with a MMControl named mciMusic.

```
Private Sub Form_Load()
    mciMusic.DeviceType = "WaveAudio"
    mciMusic.FileName = "hello.wav"
    mciMusic.Command = "Open"
End Sub
```

Code 3.52: Loading a WAV Device

Code 3.53 shows a procedure named CloseDevice, which you can call from a command button or the Unload event of a form to close the MCI device.

```
Private Sub CloseDevice()
   With mciMusic
     .Command = "Stop"
     .Command = "Close"
   End With
End Sub
```

Code 3.53: Closing a Multimedia Control

If you want to call the procedure from another form, declare the procedure as Public (in a module) and qualify the name of the Multimedia control with the name of the form. For example, if the control is in a form named frmWAV, replace the statement "mciMusic" with "With frmWAV.mciMusic."

 By default, the buttons on the mciMusic control are disabled. You can enable them by setting the properties, such as PlayEnabled and PauseEnabled, to true.

Example 3.1

Let us consider an interface to accept the official information of a student. The information to be accepted from the user are as follows:

- Registration number of the student—a numeric value.
- First name of the student.
- Last name of the student.
- Date of admission.
- Name of the course enrolled. The available courses are—MCA (Master in Computer Application), DCA (Diploma in Computer Application), BCA (Bachelor in Computer Application) and PGDCA (Post Graduate Diploma in Computer Application).
- Mode of payment—installments or a lump sum.
- Mode of installments—monthly, quarterly or yearly. This should be specified only if the mode of payment is in installments.
- Details of additional facilities available to the student. This includes certain predefined facilities like accommodation, conveyance, library, personal Web space which are available to the students. The student can select any or none of these facilities.

While designing the interface for the above requirement, the following points should be taken into consideration:

- There should be proper controls for the input of the above information.
- Since certain information like the course name will be one of the available options, it will be more appropriate to display them in a list box or a combo box so that the user can select the required value, rather than allowing the user to type in the name of the course. For better presentation we will use a combo box to display the available name of the courses.
- As in the above case, the mode of payment may also be

displayed in a list box or combo box. But instead of using the same control we can present option buttons thus improving the look and feel of the interface. This has become possible because there are just two possible values for the mode of payment. Had it been a bigger number, we would have no other option but a list box or a combo box. Using too many option buttons in an interface could affect the appearance of the interface.

- The input for the additional facilities of the student can be accepted through a set of check boxes so the student can select none or any combination of the available facilities. However, the same information can also be obtained using a list box with multiple selections instead of check boxes.Check boxes provide a better presentation than the selected and deselected options together, compared to the list box where the user has to scroll through the list to confirm the selected and deselected values.

- The date of admission can be accepted with the help of three combo boxes for month, day and year respectively. This will allow the user to provide the proper date without getting confused about the format of the required date.

- Appropriate code to verify the user input should be provided in order to maintain validity. We will discuss the possible ways of validation after creating the interface.

Complete the following steps to create the interface for the above mentioned requirement:

1. Create a new project in Visual Basic and name it as StudentInfo.

2. Name the default form as frmStudentInfo and add controls to the form as shown in Figure 3.22.

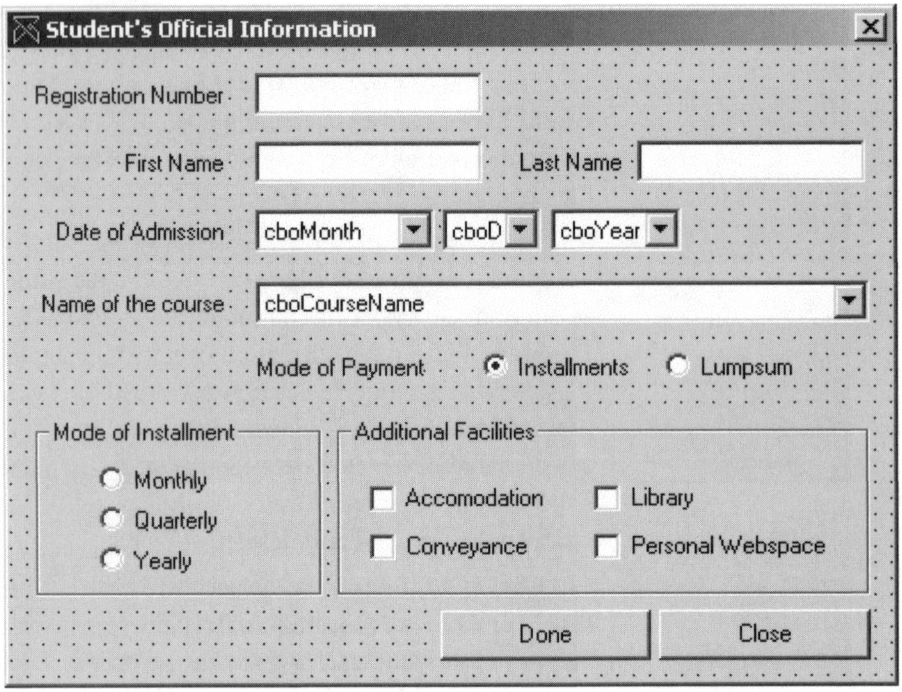

Figure 3.22: Design View of the Required Interface

Name the controls as mentioned in the Table 3.9.

Control	Name
Label for Registration Number	lblRegNo
TextBox for Registration Number	txtRegNo
Label for First Name	lblFirstName
TextBox for First Name	txtFirstName
Label for Last Name	lblLastName
TextBox for Last Name	txtLastName
Label for Date of admission	lblAdmDate
ComboBox for month	cboMonth
ComboBox for day	cboDay

ComboBox for year	cboYear
Label for Name of the course	lblCourseName
ComboBox for name of the course	cboCourseName
Label for mode of payment	lblPaymentMode
Option buttons for mode of payment (control array)	optPaymentMode
Frame for installment modes	fraInstallment
Option buttons for installment modes (control array)	optInstallments
Frame for additional facilities	fraFacilities
CheckBoxes for additional facilities (control array)	chkFacilities
CommandButton (Done)	cmdDone
CommandButton (Close)	cmdCloseForm

Table 3.9: Naming the Controls

3.   Write Code 3.54 for the Form load event.

```
Private Sub Form_Load()
  With Me.cboCourseName
    .AddItem "MCA - Master in Computer Application"
    .AddItem "BCA - Bachelor in Computer Application"
    .AddItem "DCA - Diploma in Computer Application"
    .AddItem "PGDCA - Post Graduate Diploma in " + _
      "Computer Application"
  End With
  Me.cboCourseName.ListIndex = 0

  With Me.cboMonth
    Dim intMonth As Integer
    For intMonth = 1 To 12
      .AddItem MonthName(intMonth)
    Next
    .ListIndex = Month(Date) - 1
```

```
    End With

    With Me.cboDay
      Dim intDay As Byte
      For intDay = 1 To 31
        .AddItem intDay
      Next
      .Text = Day(Date)
    End With

    With Me.cboYear
      Dim intYear As Integer
      For intYear = Year(Date) - 35 To Year(Date)
        .AddItem intYear
      Next
      .Text = Year(Date)
    End With
End Sub
```

Code 3.54: Populating the ComboBox Controls with Appropriate Values
During Form Load

Code 3.54 performs the initialization tasks mainly populating the various combo boxes
and setting the initial value for each of them. The combo box for month is filled with
the name of the months instead of numbers in order to improve presentation. The
current date is displayed as the default admission date so that the user does not have to
mention the admission date separately as the data will mostly be entered on the same
date. This will reduce the time required to fill in the various information.

The form in Figure 3.23 displays the form during run time.

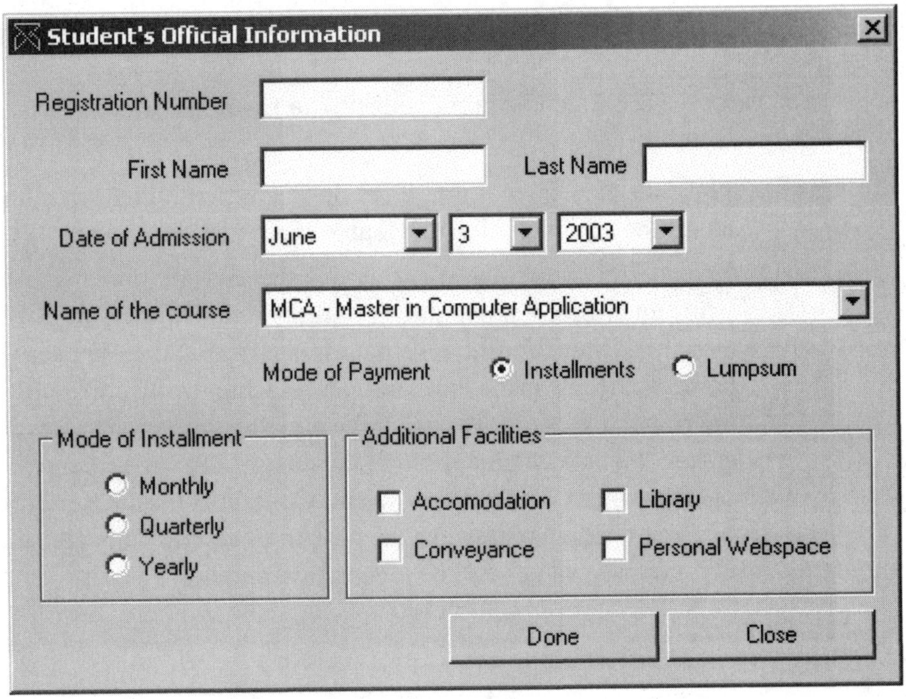

Figure 3.23: Run Time View of the Required Interface with Filled Combo Boxes

4. As per the requirement, the mode of installments should be specified, only if the mode of payment is in installments. This can be controlled at the interface level by disabling the frame containing the various modes of payments if the user selects the mode of payment as a lump sum. Disabling the frame will disable the controls, preventing the user from selecting any of them. Code 3.55 performs this task. The code is written for the click event of the option buttons control array optPaymentMode.

```
Private Sub optPaymentMode_Click(Index As Integer)
  If Index = 0 Then
    Me.fraInstallment.Enabled = True
  Else
    Me.fraInstallment.Enabled = False
    Dim varInstallment As Variant
    For Each varInstallment In Me.optInstallments
      varInstallment.Value = False
```

```
      Next
    End If
End Sub
```

Code 3.55: Enabling and Disabling the Frame for Mode of Installments

The code also ensures that if the option button for a lump sum is selected, it clears the selection of the available modes of payments.

5.   The interface should also ensure that the user does not make any mistakes while entering data, intentional or unintentional, such as providing an alphabetic value for the registration number, a numeric value for the first name or the last name etc. This can be achieved by preventing such values in the respective text boxes using the KeyPress event of the text box. This will ensure the data entered through the controls are free from errors, making the interface more robust and efficient. Code 3.56 for the KeyPress event of the text box txtRegNo prevents the user from entering any alphabetic or non-numeric values for the registration number.

```
Private Sub txtRegNo_KeyPress(KeyAscii As Integer)
  If Not IsNumeric(Chr(KeyAscii)) And _
        KeyAscii <> vbKeyBack Then
     KeyAscii = 0
  End If
End Sub
```

Code 3.56: Disabling the Non-numeric Values for Registration Number

Code 3.56 disables any keystrokes that are not a numeric value or a backspace. The backspace key is excluded to allow the user to correct the value being entered. Similarly the following two procedures for the KeyPress event of the text boxes txtFirstName and txtLastName ensure that the user can enter only letters for the first name and the last name of the student.

```
Private Sub txtFirstName_KeyPress(KeyAscii As Integer)
  If Not (KeyAscii >= Asc("a") And KeyAscii <= Asc("z")) And _
       Not (KeyAscii >= Asc("A") And KeyAscii <= Asc("Z")) And _
        KeyAscii <> vbKeyBack Then
     KeyAscii = 0
  End If
```

```
End Sub

Private Sub txtLastName_KeyPress(KeyAscii As Integer)
   If Not (KeyAscii >= Asc("a") And KeyAscii <= Asc("z")) And _
      Not (KeyAscii >= Asc("A") And KeyAscii <= Asc("Z")) And _
      KeyAscii <> vbKeyBack Then
      KeyAscii = 0
   End If
End Sub
```

Code 3.57: Disabling the Values Other than Letters for First Name and Last Name

6.   The above validations are performed if the user presses any key in the control. But what if the user does not press any key? In fact, the above codes cannot restrict the user from specifying blank values in the text boxes. This might lead to erroneous data storage. For instance, maintaining a student's record without a registration number or a record with the admission date mentioned as 30th of February, will not be acceptable. This can be prevented in the interface level. There are two ways to implement this preventive measure.

The first is to write the validation codes for the Validate event of the control. The Validate event of a control takes place when the control loses the focus. The validate event procedure provides a Cancel argument which can be used to cancel the requested action if the value is not valid and forces the control to retain the focus. This method is mainly used when it is certain that the user cannot skip the control. If the user can skip the control the user might complete the task without having the focus in the control which implies that the control would lose the focus that is essential to raise the Validate event for the control.

Code 3.58 explains how to validate the value for the text box txtRegNo using the Validate event of the text box.

```
Private Sub txtRegNo_Validate(Cancel As Boolean)
  If Trim(Me.txtRegNo) = "" Then
    MsgBox "Please enter a valid Registration Number", _
        vbCritical, "Student Information"
    Cancel = True
  End If
End Sub
```

Code 3.58: Check If the Registration Number Is Empty in the Validate Event

The above procedure is executed when the text box **txtRegNo** loses the focus. It checks if the value for the registration number is blank. If it is, the requested action is cancelled and the focus is transferred back to txtRegNo. We can write similar code for the Validate events of the text boxes txtFirstName and txtLastName or the other controls.

The second method of performing validation provides a remedy to the uncertainty of the previous method. Here we can write a procedure or function to check the validity of the values in all the controls all at the same time. The validation can then be performed simply by calling the appropriate procedure or function and proceeding with the rest of the task based on the outcome of the call.

Code 3.59 is a function named IsValidData() which checks for the validity of the values of the controls. The function returns true if all controls contain valid values and False if any of the controls has an invalid value.

```
Private Function IsValidData() As Boolean
  IsValidData = True
  If Trim(Me.txtRegNo) = "" Then
    MsgBox "Please enter a valid Registration Number", _
        vbCritical, "Student Information"
    IsValidData = False
    Me.txtRegNo.SetFocus
    Exit Function
  End If


  If Trim(Me.txtFirstName) = "" Then
```

```
MsgBox "The First Name of the student cannot be left blank",
vbCritical, "Student Information"
    IsValidData = False
    Me.txtFirstName.SetFocus
    Exit Function
  End If


  If Trim(Me.txtLastName) = "" Then
    MsgBox "The Last Name of the student cannot be left blank",
        vbCritical, "Student Information"
    IsValidData = False
    Me.txtLastName.SetFocus
    Exit Function
  End If


  Dim strAdmDate As String
  strAdmDate = (Me.cboMonth.ListIndex + 1) & "/" & _
      Me.cboDay.Text & "/" & Me.cboYear.Text
  If Not IsDate(strAdmDate) Then
    MsgBox "The specified admission date is not a valid date", _
        vbCritical, "Student Information"
    IsValidData = False
    Me.cboMonth.SetFocus
    Exit Function
  End If


  If Me.optPaymentMode(0).Value = True Then
    If Me.optInstallments(0).Value = False And _
        Me.optInstallments(1).Value = False And _
        Me.optInstallments(2).Value = False Then

      MsgBox "Please specify an appropriate Installment mode", _
        vbCritical, "Student Information"
      IsValidData = False
      Me.txtLastName.SetFocus
```

```
        Exit Function
      End If
   End If
End Function
```

Code 3.59: Function to Perform Validation of the Data in the Form

Once the function has been defined, it can be called whenever the validation needs to be performed. Code 3.60 displays the use of the above mentioned function in the click event of the command button cmdDone. Here it displays a message box showing successful registration if the result of the function is True.

```
Private Sub cmdDone_Click()
  If IsValidData Then
    MsgBox "Specified student has successfully been registered",
        vbExclamation, "Student Information"
  End If
End Sub
```

Code 3.60: Code to Call the Above Function for Validation

7.   Code 3.61 for the click event of the command button cmdCloseForm to unload the current form.

```
Private Sub frmCloseForm_Click()
  Unload Me
End Sub
```

Code 3.61: Code to Unload the Form

8.   Code 3.62 for the QueryUnload event of the form that displays a confirmation message box asking for the user's confirmation before unloading the form from memory. It cancels the unloading of the form if the user chooses No in the message box.

```
Private Sub Form_QueryUnload(Cancel As Integer, UnloadMode As
Integer)
  If MsgBox("Are you sure to exit the application", _
        vbQuestion + vbYesNo, "Confirm Exit") = vbNo Then
    Cancel = 1
  End If
```

```
End Sub
```

Code 3.62: Code to Ask for Confirmation Before Unloading the Form

The above example illustrates how to provide functionality to an interface as far as ease, efficiency and robustness of the interface is concerned. Save and run the project. Figure 3.24 displays the form during run time with some sample data as input.

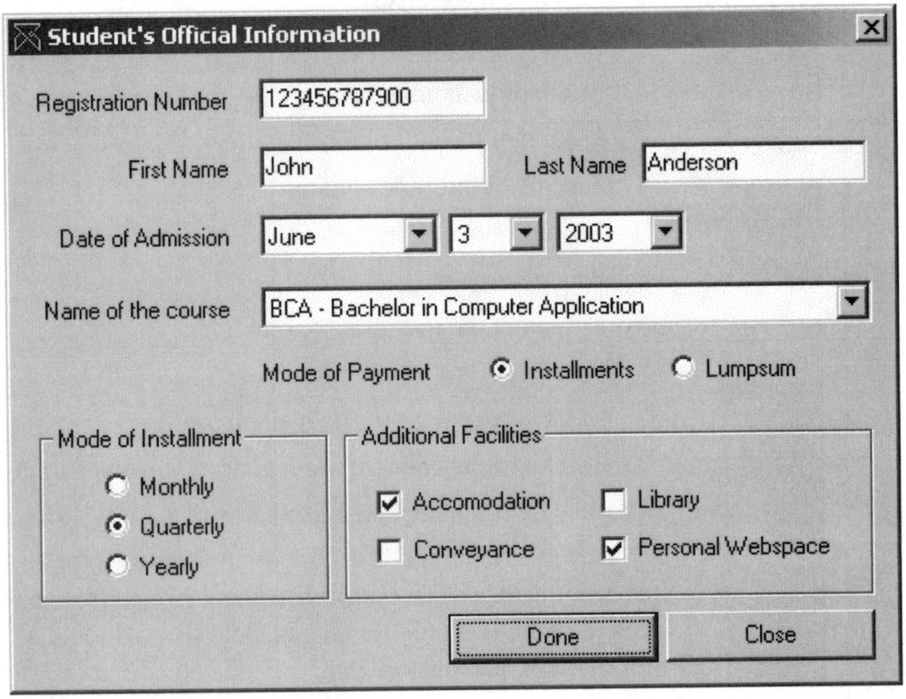

Figure 3.24: Run Time View of the Required Interface Filled with Sample Data

Example 3.2

The case mentioned in the previous example was related to an interface to accept minimal information during the registration of a student. However, there may be situations when the amount of data to be accepted from the user is too large. The following example is a representation of such a situation. Here the data to be accepted from the user is larger than the previous example. Here we will discuss about designing the appearance of the GUI. The way of writing the code to provide certain functionality of the GUI is the same as that in the previous example.

The various information to be accepted from the user are as follows:

- Registration number of the student
- First name of the student
- Last name of the student
- Date of admission
- Name of the course enrolled
- Mode of payment
- Mode of installments
- Details of the additional facilities
- Date of birth of the student
- Correspondence address of the student
- Phone number
- Details of the interests of the student
- Amount of the registration fees
- Mode of payment of the registration fees
- Details of the check if the registration fee is paid by check
- Date of commencement of the course

In order to avoid a GUI with too many controls, the above pieces of data are accepted from the user in parts. For this, the data required is divided in three categories—official information, personal information and other details. These three categories could be accepted in three different forms. However, the user might not be aware that the task is completed after filling in three different forms. Instead of using three different forms to accept this information, a single form using the Tabbed Dialog control is used.

Figures 3.25, 3.26, and 3.27 display the contents of the three tabs of a Tabbed Dialog control which accepts the three different above mentioned categories.

Figure 3.25 depicts the required interface to accept the official information of the student.

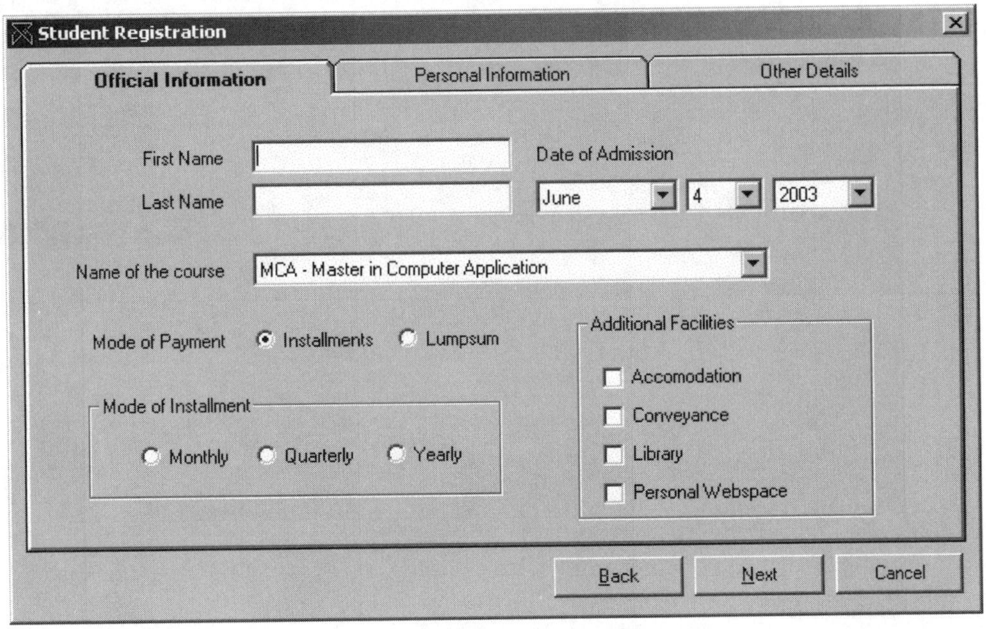

Figure 3.25: Required Interface to Accept the Official Information of the Student

Figure 3.26 depicts the required interface to accept the personal information of the student.

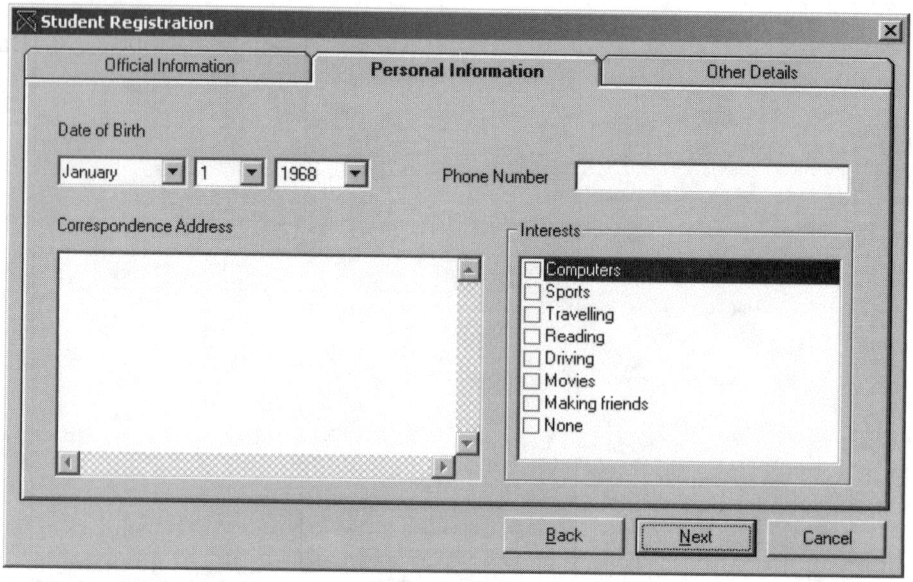

Figure 3.26: Required Interface to Accept the Personal Information of the Student

Figure 3.27 depicts the required interface to accept the other details of the student.

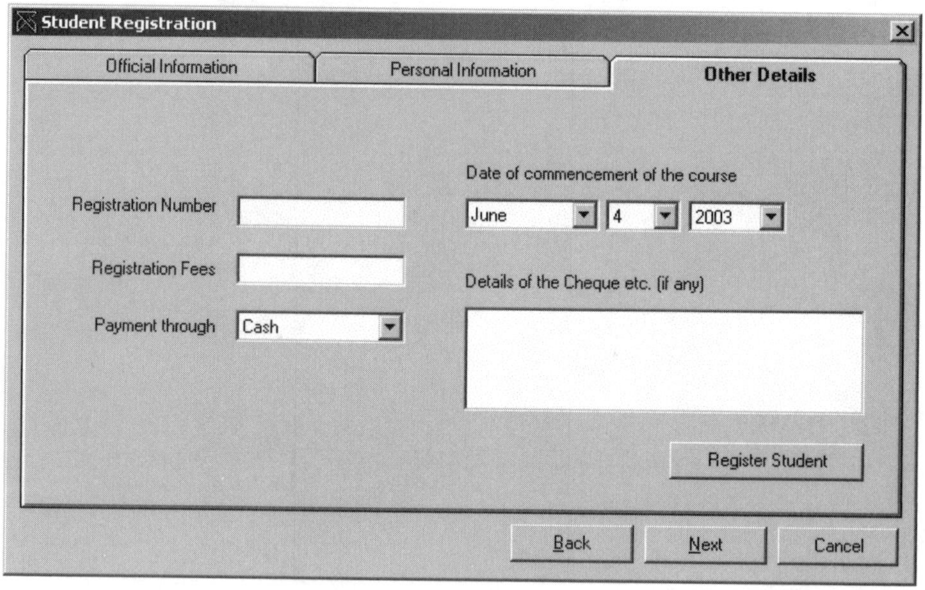

Figure 3.27: Required Interface to Accept the Other Details of the Student

The task of performing the validation for the controls in the form or populating the combo boxes with the required values can be done in a similar manner as it is done in the previous example. The previous GUI has two navigation buttons—Back and Next—in order to provide a way to navigate through the tabs of the Tabbed Dialog control. This approach not only improves the presentation of the GUI but also makes the data entry process appear less tedious than it would have appeared if all the controls were placed together in the same form without using the Tabbed Dialog control.

Practice Questions

1. What are the two types of controls in Visual Basic?
2. Name the two properties of the Label control that are used to fit and display lengthy captions.
3. How do you use a text box as a simple editor?
4. When is the Frame control used?
5. How do you use a command button by pressing a key combination?
6. Which properties of a command button are set to select the button, using ESC or ENTER keys?
7. Name the controls that provide easy access to the file system.
8. Which properties of the Line control denote the end points of the line?

3.3 Interface Style

Interface style is an essential part of designing useful applications in Visual Basic. Applications designed for the MS Windows platform should have the standard look and feel. Therefore, while developing applications in Visual Basic for Windows 98, NT, or XP, you should follow Microsoft's guidelines for design. There are several guidelines for the development of toolbars, menus, controls, and form design. You can take the example of standard industry applications to get consistency in your applications.

In a RAD environment, effort should be placed on interface design. Having an interface with too many colors and controls placed at random gives the impression of poor design. Follow the techniques to make your application attractive to the user, keeping it simple at the same time.

3.3.1 Screen Resolution

 Apply screen resolution techniques for better display.

You should design your applications to suit the screen resolution for all users. Most users have their screen resolution set at (640×480) or (800×600). Create forms for the lowest resolution (640×480) so that users are not inconvenienced. Forms you create on a large screen will be too large for a smaller screen or a screen with lower resolution.

You can see the form's appearance at (640×480) or (800×600) resolution using the Form Layout window. Perform the following procedure:

1. Right-click the **Form Layout** window at the bottom-right of the Visual Basic IDE. If the window is not visible, select **Form Layout** window from **View** in the main menu.

2. Select **Resolution Guides** from the pop-up menu.

3.   The window shows the position of your form with respect to different screen resolutions. Figure 3.28 shows the **Form Layout** window.

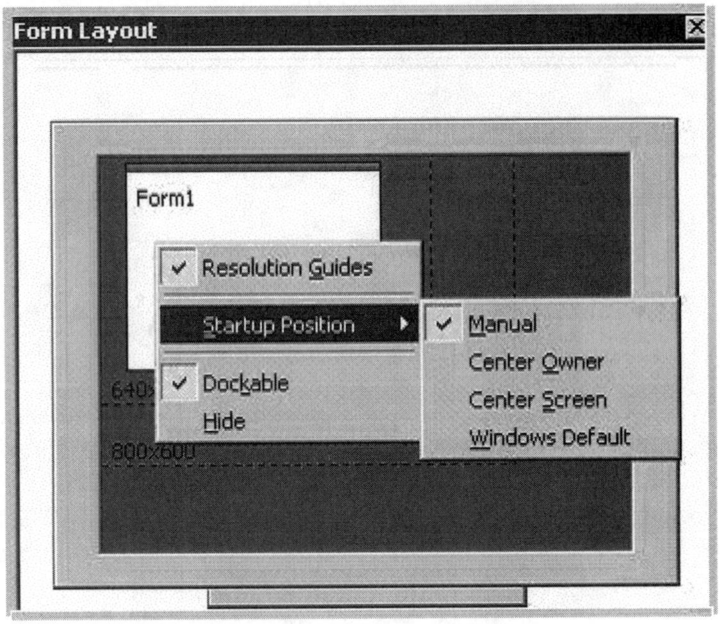

Figure 3.28: Form Layout Window

4.   You can set the startup position of the form by right-clicking on the form in the Layout window and selecting an option.

- Form.Width
- Screen.TwipsPerPixelX
- Form.Height
- Screen.TwipsPerPixelY

To ensure that your application window shows completely in a 640×480 display, use Code 3.63. You should not set the width and height properties during design time as it reduces the flexibility of the application.

```vb
Private Sub Form_Load()
    Width = Screen.TwipsPerPixelX * 640
    Height = Screen.TwipsPerPixelY * 480
End Sub
```

Code 3.63: Setting a Form's Width and Height

You can also use a relative window size by using Code 3.64. The code sets the size of the application window to half the size of the screen and places the window at the center of the screen.

```
Private Sub Form_Load()
    Width = Screen.Width / 2
    Height = Screen.Height / 2
    Top = (Screen.Height - Height) / 2
    Left = (Screen.Width - Width) / 2
End Sub
```

Code 3.64: Sizing the Form According to the Screen

 When your controls get out of sight, choose that particular control which you cannot see in the Object List in the Properties window and change the Left and Top properties to 0. The control appears at the top-left position. Drag it to your preferred location.

3.3.2 Features of a Good Interface

 Explain the features and design policies of a good user interface.

A good interface should have the following features:

- It should be able to perform the task it is designed for effectively.
- It should be flexible to use.
- The transition from a beginner to an expert should be fast and smooth.
- There should be minimal requirement of training.
- Error recovery should be easy for the user. The system should not halt on simple errors.
- The features of the application should be easy to identify.
- There should be less errors and the system should be predictable.

Some design policies that you should follow while designing your applications:

- Do not keep unnecessary controls in your application. Overusing controls makes your application look complex and ugly. Keep only those controls that are absolutely necessary.

- Do not expect the user to remember too many details. Make things look obvious to the user. The application should be predictable.

- There should be consistency in your application. Design menus and controls that look familiar to users.

- Design from a user's point of view, not a designer's or programmer's point of view. Unless you consider what the user wants, your application will always lack certain features. Right from the beginning, take the user's perspective. This will prevent the need for changes at the time of delivery of the software.

3.3.3 Using Graphics and Colors

 Evaluate methods of using graphics and colors effectively.

The importance of color and graphics in computer applications cannot be ignored because color monitors and printers are common these days. Every application's interface should be designed to utilize graphics and colors effectively. The developer should not abuse the use of colors and graphics in their application.

Colors are used for aesthetics as well as for realism. Careless use of color makes an application look less attractive than a monochrome application. The developer should always use color conservatively. Random colors give a brash and untidy look. Use colors with uniformity. Using gray in the background is soothing to the eyes; it is pleasant as well as inconspicuous. To separate bright colors, use a dark border between them. The color contrast between the background and foreground is essential.

Be careful while using colors as codes in your application. Users might associate colors like red with trouble. Do not try to convey wrong meanings through color codes. Avoid colors in dialog boxes, menus, and status bars. Keep their color the same as that of the background. Use color combinations that contrast. Using yellow text on a white background will strain the user's eyes. Use black on a white background or yellow on a dark blue background. In particular, do not use red or green colors in screen elements, as most color-blind people are not sensitive to these two colors.

Basic techniques that you should apply in your applications to use graphics effectively are:

- Group related objects together in a form. Use frames to hold related items.
- You should align your controls properly. Putting your controls everywhere around the form haphazardly will only confuse the user.
- Direct the user's attention to the relevant parts of the application. For example, if you are designing a text editor, ensure that the text box is of good size and other features of your application do not overshadow it.
- Keep a proper balance of white space in the form.
- Use few fonts. Stick to the default fonts of the system. Use the Sans Serif font wherever possible for consistency.
- Do not use boldface type unless necessary. Keep the font size regular. Use a large font size where you really need to catch the user's attention.
- Do not use too many colors. The predominant color to use is gray. It is pleasant and looks professional.
- Do not use colors for identification purposes. Keep in mind that some users are color-blind.
- Labels that you use as a caption should be transparent with no borders. Only those labels that are used to output messages should have borders to differentiate them from other labels.

Practice Questions

1. What are the main features of a good interface?
2. How can I preselect an entry in a combo box?
3. How do you change the default font for all controls in a form without changing the font of each control?

Case Study

Once the design of the database for the Library Management System has been completed, it's time to start designing the interfaces to interact with the database. In this section, the VB application will be created and some forms will be added to the VB project with the basic controls to the used in the forms. This section will also provide codes to the forms in order to prevent incorrect data entry by the user.

1. Open a new Standard Exe project in Visual Basic 6.0. Set the name of the project to LibraryMgmt.

2. Set the name of the default form to frmBooks. Set the caption of the form to Books Information. This form will be used to add and delete book(s) from the library. Set the properties of the form as shown in Table 3.10.

Property	Value
Name	frmBooks
Caption	Books Information
BorderStyle	Fixed Single

Table 3.10: Properties to Be Set for the Form

3. Add a Tabbed Dialog (SSTab) control named tabBooks to the form with the properties, as shown in Table 3.11.

Property	Value
Name	TabBooks
Tabs	2
TabsPerRow	3
Caption of the first tab	Add New Book
Caption of the second tab	Existing Books

Table 3.11: Properties of the Form

4. Add controls to the first tab of the SSTab control, as shown in Figure 3.29.

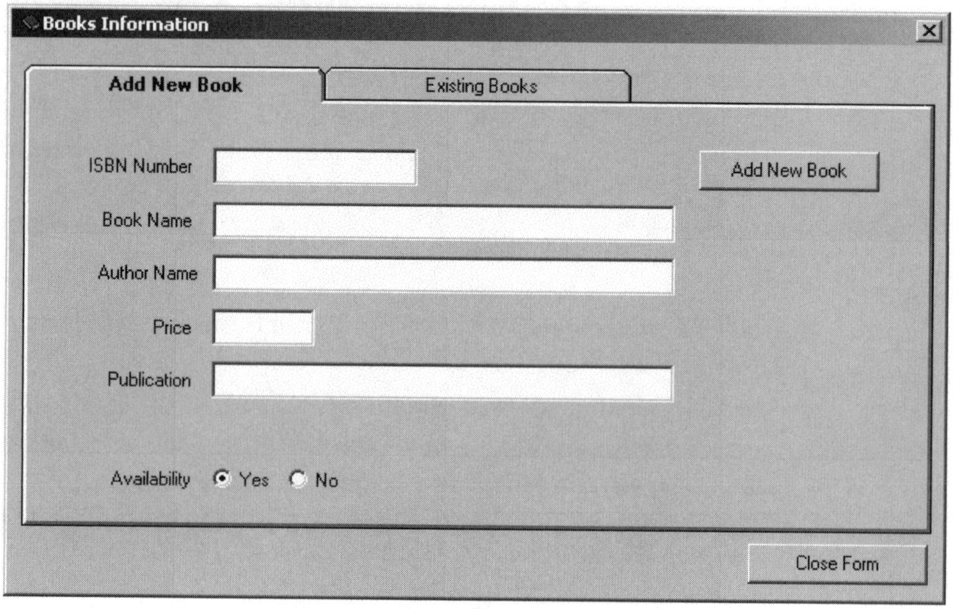

Figure 3.29: Books Information

Set the properties of the controls in the form as given in Table 3.12.

Control Type	Name	Caption / MaxLength Property	Index
Label control	lblISBN	ISBN Number	Text
Label control	lblBookName	Book Name	Text
Label control	lblAuthorName	Author Name	Text
Label control	lblPrice	Price	Text
Label control	lblPublication	Publication	
Label control	lblAvailability	Availability	
TextBox control	txtISBN	15	
TextBox control	txtBookName	50	
TextBox control	txtAuthorName	50	
TextBox control	txtPrice	50	
TextBox control	txtPublication	50	
OptionButton control	optAvailability	Yes	0

OptionButton control	optAvailability	No	1
CommandButton control	cmdAddBook	Add New Book	
CommandButton control	cmdClose	Close Form	

Table 3.12: Properties of the Controls

6.   Add Code 3.65 for the Form Load event of the form. This code sets the Top and Left property of the form to make sure that the form is always displayed in the same location. It also ensures that the form displays the first tab whenever it is loaded and sets the value of the first option button to True.

```
Private Sub Form_Load()

  Me.Left = 120
  Me.Top = 120
  Me.tabBooks.Tab = 0
  Me.optAvailability(0).Value = True

End Sub
```

Code 3.65: Code for the Form Load Event

7.   Add Code 3.66 for the Click event of the command button cmdClose.

```
Private Sub cmdClose_Click()
  Unload Me
End Sub
```

Code 3.66: Code for the Click Event of the Command Button cmdClose

8.   Add Code 3.67 to the KeyPress event of the TextBox controls for Author name, price, and ISBN to provide validation to the value being entered in the text box. The text box for author can have only alphabetical characters, the ISBN number can be numbers and hyphens (-), and the price can only be numbers and a decimal. The KeyPress event is invoked when the user presses a key in a TextBox control. The event procedure for the KeyPress event provides an argument named KeyAscii which stores the ASCII code of the key being pressed. The following code makes use of this argument to check if the pressed key is a valid character or not. If not, the key press is canceled by

assigning 0 (zero) to the KeyAscii argument. The value in the KeyAscii argument is compared with the ASCII code of the required character or range of characters.

```
Private Sub txtAuthorName_KeyPress(KeyAscii As Integer)
  If Not (KeyAscii >= Asc("A") And KeyAscii <= Asc("Z")) And _
      Not (KeyAscii >= Asc("a") And KeyAscii <= Asc("z")) And _
      Not KeyAscii = vbKeyBack And KeyAscii <> vbKeySpace Then

    KeyAscii = 0
  End If
End Sub


Private Sub txtISBN_KeyPress(KeyAscii As Integer)
  If Not IsNumeric(Chr(KeyAscii)) And KeyAscii <> vbKeyBack _
      And KeyAscii <> Asc("-") Then

    KeyAscii = 0
  End If
End Sub


Private Sub txtPrice_KeyPress(KeyAscii As Integer)
  If Not IsNumeric(Chr(KeyAscii)) And KeyAscii <> vbKeyBack _
      And KeyAscii <> Asc(".") Then

    KeyAscii = 0
  End If
End Sub
```

Code 3.67: Code for the KeyPress Event of the TextBox Controls

9.   Add the procedure Reset, as given in Code 3.68 to the form which uses the Controls collection of the form to clear all the values in the TextBox controls and set the value of the first option button control to True.

```
Private Sub Reset()
  Dim varControl As Variant
  For Each varControl In Me.Controls
```

```
      If TypeOf varControl Is TextBox Then
        varControl.Text = ""
      End If
    Next
    Me.optAvailability(0).Value = True
  End Sub
```

Code 3.68: Code for Reset Procedure

10.   Add the function IsValidData, as given in Code 3.69 to the form which checks
        if the user has entered all the required values in the form. If the user has
        specified all the values the function returns True, otherwise it returns False.

```
Private Function IsValidData() As Boolean
  IsValidData = True
  If Trim(Me.txtISBN) = "" Then
    MsgBox "ISBN number cannot be blank", vbCritical, "Input
Error"
    Me.txtISBN.SetFocus
    IsValidData = False
    Exit Function
  End If
  If Trim(Me.txtBookName) = "" Then
    MsgBox "Book Name cannot be blank", vbCritical, "Input
Error"
    Me.txtBookName.SetFocus
    IsValidData = False
    Exit Function
  End If
  If Trim(Me.txtAuthorName) = "" Then
    MsgBox "Author Name cannot be blank", vbCritical, "Input
Error"
    Me.txtAuthorName.SetFocus
    IsValidData = False
    Exit Function
  End If
  If Val(Me.txtPrice) = 0 Then
```

```
      MsgBox "Price cannot be blank or zero", vbCritical, "Input
Error"
      Me.txtPrice.SetFocus
      IsValidData = False
      Exit Function
   End If
   If Trim(Me.txtPublication) = "" Then
      MsgBox "Publication Name cannot be blank", vbCritical,
"Input Error"
      Me.txtPublication.SetFocus
      IsValidData = False
      Exit Function
   End If
End Function
```

Code 3.69: Code for Function IsValidData

11.   Write Code 3.70 for the Click event of the command button cmdAddBook which calls the above function IsValidData().

```
Private Sub cmdAddBook_Click()
   If IsValidData = False Then
      Exit Sub
   End If
   'rest of the codes
End Sub
```

Code 3.70: Code for the Click Event of the Command Button cmdAddBook

12. Add a new form to the project and name it frmAddMember. This form will be used to enter the details of a new member of the library. Set the properties of the form as given in Table 3.13.

Property	Value
Name	frmAddMember
Caption	Add New Member
BorderStyle	Fixed Single

Table 3.13: Properties of the New Form

13. Add controls to the form as shown in Figure 3.30.

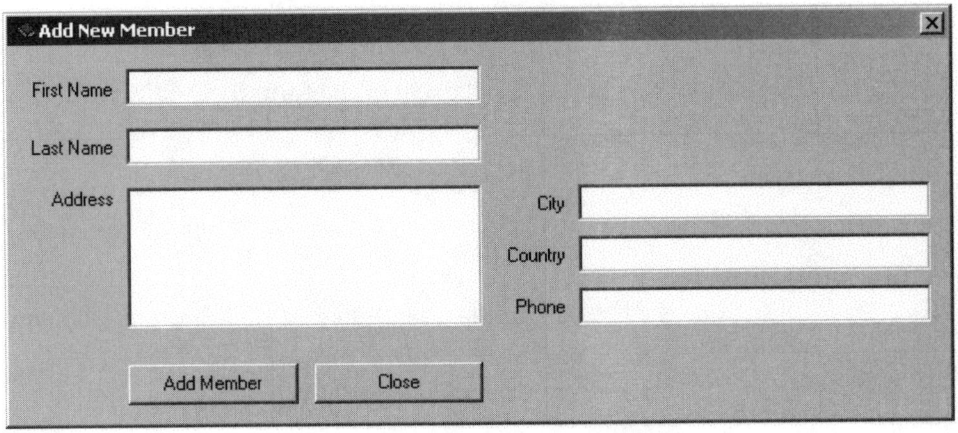

Figure 3.30: Form Layout Window

14. Set the properties of the controls in the form as given in Table 3.14.

Control Type	Name	Caption / MaxLength Property	Index
Label	lblFieldLabel	First Name	1
Label	lblFieldLabel	Last Name	2
Label	lblFieldLabel	Address	3
Label	lblFieldLabel	City	4
Label	lblFieldLabel	Country	5
Label	lblFieldLabel	Phone	6

TextBox	txtFirstName	20	
TextBox	txtLastName	20	
TextBox	txtAddress	100	
TextBox	txtCity	30	
TextBox	txtCountry	20	
TextBox	txtPhone	20	
CommandButton	cmdAddMember	Add Member	
CommandButton	cmdCloseForm	Close	

Table 3.14: Different Properties of the Controls

15.   Set the MultiLine property of the Text Box txtAddress to True.

16.   Add Code 3.71 for the Load event of the form frmAddMember.

```
Private Sub Form_Load()
  Me.Top = 120
  Me.Left = 120
End Sub
```

Code 3.71: Code for the Load Event of the Form frmAddMember

17.   Add Code 3.72 for the Click event of the command button cmdCloseForm to unload the form.

```
Private Sub cmdCloseForm_Click()
  Unload Me
End Sub
```

Code 3.72: Code for the Click Event of the Command Buton cmdCloseForm

18.   Add Code 3.73 for the KeyPress event of the TextBox controls to restrict invalid characters. This code follows the same logic as in step 8.

```
Private Sub txtCity_KeyPress(KeyAscii As Integer)
  If Not (KeyAscii >= Asc("A") And KeyAscii <= Asc("Z")) And _
      Not (KeyAscii >= Asc("a") And KeyAscii <= Asc("z")) And _
      Not KeyAscii = vbKeyBack And KeyAscii <> vbKeySpace Then
```

```vb
      KeyAscii = 0
   End If
End Sub


Private Sub txtCountry_KeyPress(KeyAscii As Integer)
   If Not (KeyAscii >= Asc("A") And KeyAscii <= Asc("Z")) And _
      Not (KeyAscii >= Asc("a") And KeyAscii <= Asc("z")) And _
      Not KeyAscii = vbKeyBack And KeyAscii <> vbKeySpace Then

     KeyAscii = 0
   End If
End Sub


Private Sub txtFirstName_KeyPress(KeyAscii As Integer)
   If Not (KeyAscii >= Asc("A") And KeyAscii <= Asc("Z")) And _
      Not (KeyAscii >= Asc("a") And KeyAscii <= Asc("z")) And _
      Not KeyAscii = vbKeyBack And KeyAscii <> vbKeySpace Then

     KeyAscii = 0
   End If
End Sub


Private Sub txtLastName_KeyPress(KeyAscii As Integer)
   If Not (KeyAscii >= Asc("A") And KeyAscii <= Asc("Z")) And _
      Not (KeyAscii >= Asc("a") And KeyAscii <= Asc("z")) And _
      Not KeyAscii = vbKeyBack And KeyAscii <> vbKeySpace Then

     KeyAscii = 0
   End If
End Sub


Private Sub txtPhone_KeyPress(KeyAscii As Integer)
   If Not IsNumeric(Chr(KeyAscii)) And KeyAscii <> vbKeyBack _
        And KeyAscii <> Asc("-") Then
```

```
      KeyAscii = 0
   End If
End Sub
```

Code 3.73: Code for the KeyPress Event of the TextBox controls

19.   Add the function IsValidData, as given in Code 3.74 to check if the user has
       entered all the required values in the form. The function returns True if the
       values are correct.

```
Private Function IsValidData() As Boolean
  IsValidData = True
  If Trim(Me.txtFirstName) = "" Then
    MsgBox "First Name cannot be blank", vbCritical, "Input
Error"
    Me.txtFirstName.SetFocus
    IsValidData = False
    Exit Function
  End If
  If Trim(Me.txtLastName) = "" Then
    MsgBox "Last Name cannot be blank", vbCritical, "Input
Error"
    Me.txtLastName.SetFocus
    IsValidData = False
    Exit Function
  End If
  If Trim(Me.txtAddress) = "" Then
    MsgBox "Address cannot be blank", vbCritical, "Input Error"
    Me.txtAddress.SetFocus
    IsValidData = False
    Exit Function
  End If
  If Trim(Me.txtCity) = "" Then
    MsgBox "City name cannot be blank", vbCritical, "Input
Error"
    Me.txtCity.SetFocus
    IsValidData = False
```

```
     Exit Function
  End If
  If Trim(Me.txtCountry) = "" Then
     MsgBox "Country name cannot be blank", vbCritical, "Input
Error"
     Me.txtCountry.SetFocus
     IsValidData = False
     Exit Function
  End If
End Function
```

Code 3.74: Code for the Function IsValidData

20. Add a new form to the project and name it frmSearchMember. Set the properties of the form as specified in Table 3.15.

Property	Value
Name	frmSearchMember
Caption	Search Member
BorderStyle	Fixed Single
Height	3150

Table 3.15: Properties of the frmSearchMember Form

21. Add controls to the form as shown in Figure 3.31.

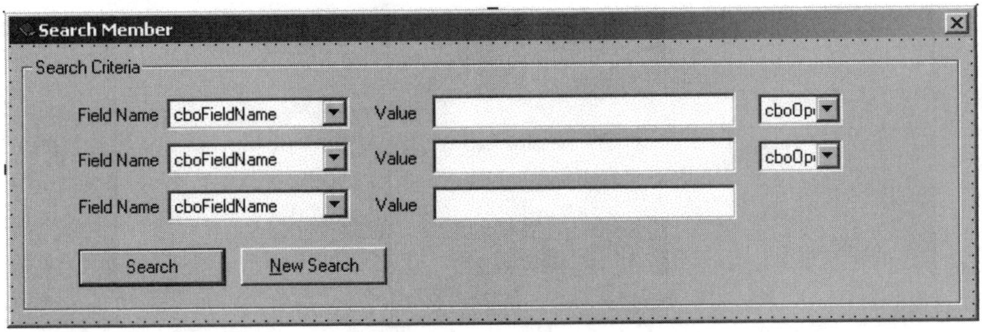

Figure 3.31: Search Criteria

22. Set the properties of the controls in the form as given in Table 3.16. The properties are specified for the respective controls from left to right across the form.

Control Type	Name	Caption Property	Index
Frame	fraCriteria	Search Criteria	
Label	lblFieldName	Field Name	0
ComboBox	cboFieldName		0
Label	lblValue	Value	0
TextBox	txtValue		0
ComboBox	cboOperator		0
Label	lblFieldName	Field Name	1
ComboBox	cboFieldName		1
Label	lblValue		1
TextBox	txtValue	Value	1
ComboBox	cboOperator		1
Label	lblFieldName	Field Name	2
ComboBox	cboFieldName		2
Label	blValue	Value	2
TextBox	txtValue		2
CommandButton	cmdSearch	Search	
CommandButton	cmdNewSearch	&New Search	

Table 3.16: Properties from Left to Right

23. Set the List property of the ComboBox control named cboFieldName with the values: RegNo, FirstName, LastName, Address, City, Country, and Phone. Press Ctrl+Enter to specify all the values in the Properties window and press Enter to confirm the list.

24. Set the List property of all the ComboBox control named cboOperator with the values AND and OR.

25. Add Code 3.75 for the Click event of the command button cmdNewSearch. It sets the first item in all the ComboBox controls as the default selection, clears the TextBox controls, and sets the focus to the first ComboBox control.

```
Private Sub cmdNewSearch_Click()
  Me.cboFieldName(0).ListIndex = 0
  Me.cboFieldName(1).ListIndex = 0
  Me.cboFieldName(2).ListIndex = 0
  Me.cboOperator(0).ListIndex = 0
  Me.cboOperator(1).ListIndex = 0
  Me.txtValue(0) = ""
  Me.txtValue(1) = ""
  Me.txtValue(2) = ""
  Me.Height = 3150
  If Me.cboFieldName(0).Visible Then Me.cboFieldName(0).SetFocus
End Sub
```

Code 3.75: Code for the Click Event of the Command Button cmdNewSearch

26. Add Code 3.76 for the Form Load event of the form. It sets the top-left location to display the form and calls the Click event procedure of the command button cmdNewSearch.

```
Private Sub Form_Load()
  Me.Top = 120
  Me.Left = 120
  cmdNewSearch_Click
End Sub
```

Code 3.76: Code for the Form Load Event

27. Save the project. It is preferable to save the project and the forms in a new folder relevant to the project.

Summary

- Forms are objects which have properties or attributes, perform functions called methods, and respond to events.

- Different types of properties of forms can be grouped as:
  - Appearance properties
  - Behavior properties
  - Positional properties
  - Run time properties
  - Additional properties

- There are two built-in collections in Visual Basic:
  - Forms collection
  - Controls collection

- Some important form methods are:
  - Move
  - Refresh
  - Show
  - Hide

- A form passes through four phases during its life cycle:
  - Created, but not not loaded
  - Loaded, but not displayed
  - Displayed
  - Destroyed, where memory and resources are completely reclaimed

- The Load event is one of the most important form events.

- The Resize event occurs every time a form is resized, minimized or maximized.

- The QueryUnload event gives a last chance to the user to prevent a form from being unloaded from memory.

- Setting a form object to "Nothing" removes all references of a form.

- The types of controls available in Visual Basic:
  - Intrinsic (standard) controls

- ActiveX controls

■ The Label control can be used to label various controls as well as display messages to the user.

■ The TextBox control takes input from the user and it can be multi-line and have scrollbars.

■ Frames group control objects in a form. They also act as containers for OptionButton controls.

■ The CommandButton is one of the most useful standard controls, and can initiate, interrupt, or terminate processes.

■ CheckBox and OptionButton controls provide options to the user. CheckBox controls can be used on their own while OptionButtons work in groups.

■ The ListBox and ComboBox controls let the user select one or more items from a list. The combo box has an optional text box where the user can directly enter data. It takes less space than a list box when used as a dropdown combo box.

■ Scroll bars provide navigation to controls and are used to measure quantity.

■ The Timer control triggers Timer events at certain intervals of time. These events can be used to perform background tasks in an application.

■ DriveListBox, DirListBox, and FileListBox controls provide easy access to the file system.

■ Shape and Line are graphical controls used to draw various geometrical shapes and lines on objects.

■ The Tabbed Dialog (SSTab) control can display a lot of information in a small space. Related information should be stored in tabs instead of several forms.

■ The MSChart control is a graphical control that displays data graphically in 2D and 3D charts. You can use the chart control to make data representations in a very effective and attractive manner.

■ The Multimedia control (MMControl) provides easy access to various MCI audio and video devices.

■ Design forms to work at low resolution to prevent inconvenience to users who have low-resolution screens.

■ A good interface should be efficient, flexible, attractive, easy to use, and error-free.

■ There should be consistency in menus, dialog boxes, and toolbars. Users should not be confused while using these controls.

- Colors should be used in uniformity in applications. You should use industry-standards while designing forms. Keep color usage to a minimum.
- Fonts should not be overused and controls should be in an organized manner.

References

- http://www.library.itt-tech.edu/periodicals.asp> Programming Tutorials (Accessed on Aug. 12, 2004)
- http://www.library.itt-tech.edu/periodicals.asp> MSDN Magazine (Accessed on Aug. 12, 2004)

Homework Exercises

1. What is the RightToLeft property?

2. Define Point and Twips.

3. Write code to pass a control array to a Sub.

4. Explain the difference between the ListBox and ComboBox controls.

5. Create the form in Figure 3.32 that validates the Login procedure in a system. If the user name field is empty, the application should prompt for the user name and set focus to the text box. If the password is wrong, notify the user that the password is wrong and ask for re-entry. If the user fails after three attempts, tell the user that no more attempts are allowed and close the application.

   Add access keys to all the buttons and make the button labeled "Cancel" as the Cancel button and the OK button as the Default button.

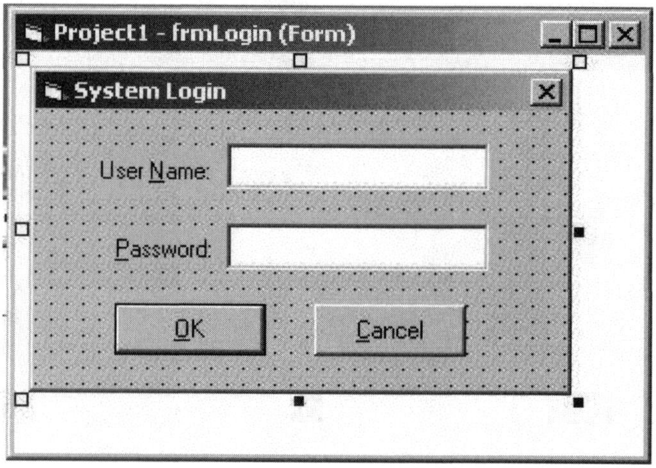

Figure 3.32: Form That Validates the Login Procedure in a System

6. What is the range of the Tab property in a Tabbed Dialog (SSTab) control?

7. Write code to create a moving marquee out of two label controls. Create a control array of two labels and put one on top of the other. Their background should be black and the color of the text should change every millisecond to a random color. The caption should move from right to left in a steady manner similar to the marquee controls.

8. What are the control commands for the Microsoft Multimedia control (MMControl)?

Lab Exercises

Exercise 1

Objective

■ Create a form using ListBox, ComboBox, CommandButton, TextBox, and Label controls.

Problem Statement

Create the form shown in Figure 3.33 using the ListBox, combo box, CommandButton, text box, and Label controls:

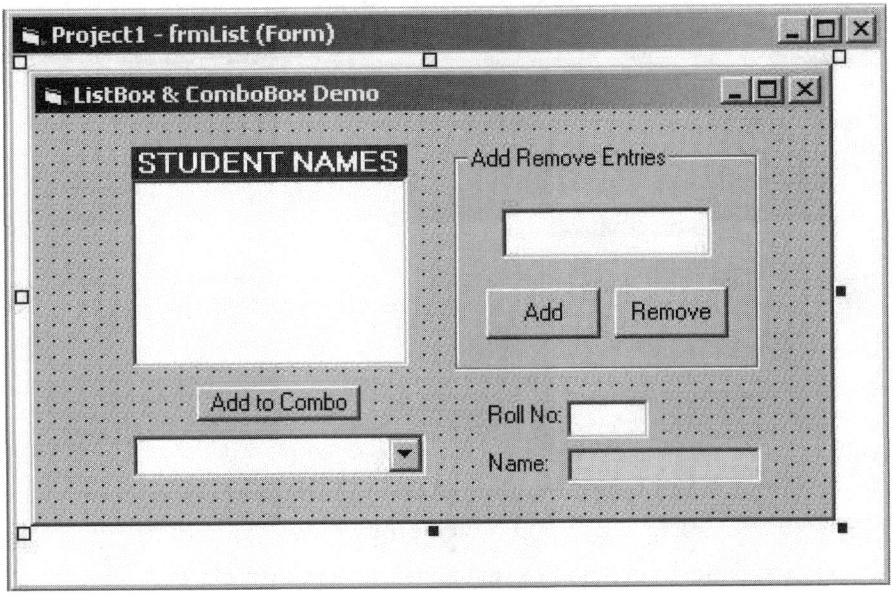

Figure 3.33: Sample Form with Controls for Exercise 1

Add the following features to the form:

1. Fill the List box with some sample data. The list box should be CheckBox style.

2. Add a button addCombo which should add the selected items in the List box to a ComboBox control.

3.   Add a TextBox control in which the user can enter a name. On clicking the Add button the text in the text box should get added to the List box.

4.   Clicking Remove should delete the entry from the List box. Add proper message boxes to inform the user whether deletion was successful.

5.   Also add code to keep the Add and Remove buttons disabled if there is no text in the text box.

6.   In the text box labeled Roll No (which is the ListIndex in this case), when the user enters a Roll No, the corresponding value stored at that index should be displayed on the label below the Roll No text box.

Lab Setup

Computer Requirements:

- Microsoft Windows Operating System
- Pentium III or higher processors
- 128-MB RAM
- 3-GB of hard disk space
- CD-ROM drives
- Floppy disk drives
- LAN connections
- Visual Basic 6.0

Procedure

Perform the following procedure to create the form:

1.   Create a new project and set the name of the default form as frmList.

2.   Add a ListBox control. Name it lstNames. Set the Style property to 1 - CheckBox and Sorted property to True.

3.   Add a combo box and name it cboNames.

4.   Add a command button below the List box and name it cmdaddCombo.

5.   Add a frame and set its caption to "Add Remove Entries."

6.   Add a text box to the frame and name it txtNewItem.

7.   Add two command buttons to the frame named cmdAdd and cmdRemove.

8.   Add a text box named txtItemNo and label it "Roll No."

9.   Add a label named lblItemNo to display the searched name corresponding to the index in txtItemNo. Label it "Name."

10.   Add Code 3.77 to the Load event of the form. It adds items to the List box lstNames. The Add and Remove buttons are disabled initially.

```
Private Sub Form_Load()
  lstNames.AddItem "Ralph"
  lstNames.AddItem "Amelia"
  lstNames.AddItem "Adam"
  lstNames.AddItem "Steve"
  lstNames.AddItem "Robert"
  lstNames.AddItem "Candy"
  lstNames.AddItem "Sharon"


  cmdAdd.Enabled = False
    cmdRemove.Enabled = False
End Sub
```

Code 3.77: Code for the Form Load Event for Exercise 1

11.   Add Code 3.78 to the Click event of the command button cmdaddCombo. The For…Next loop runs for all the elements in the list box. The If-Then-Else statement checks if an item is selected and adds it to the combo box if the item is chosen. After the loop finishes, the combo box is set to display the last item in the control.

```
Private Sub cmdaddCombo_Click()
    Dim i as Integer
    For i = 0 To lstNames.ListCount - 1
        If lstNames.Selected(i) = True Then
            cmbNames.AddItem lstNames.List(i)
        End If
    Next
      cboNames.ListIndex = cboNames.ListCount - 1
End Sub
```

Code 3.78: Code for the Click Event of the Command Button cmdaddCombo

12. Add Code 3.79 to the KeyPress event of the Combo Box cboNames. If the user presses enter (ASCII value is 13) the item is added to the combo box.

```
Private Sub cboNames_KeyPress(KeyAscii As Integer)
    If KeyAscii = 13 Then
        cboNames.AddItem cmbNames.Text
    End If
End Sub
```

Code 3.79: Code for the KeyPress Event of the Combo Box cboNames

13. Add Code 3.80 to the Click event of the command button cmdAdd. It adds the item to the list box.

```
Private Sub cmdAdd_Click()
        lstNames.AddItem txtNewItem.Text
End Sub
```

Code 3.80: Code for to Click Event of the Command Button cmdAdd

14. Add Code 3.81 to the Click event of the command button cmdRemove. It declares an integer variable named index, which keeps track of the current item being matched. The Boolean variable deleted is set to true if a matching record has been deleted from the list. It displays a message stating whether a matching record was found in the list box items, according to the value of the deleted variable.

```
Private Sub cmdRemove_Click()
        Dim index As Integer
        Dim deleted As Boolean
        deleted = False
        For index = 0 To lstNames.ListCount - 1
            If lstNames.List(index) = txtNewItem.Text Then
                lstNames.RemoveItem index
                deleted = True
            End If
        Next
        If deleted = False Then
            MsgBox "Record for " & txtNewItem.Text & _
            " does not exist!", , "Item not Found"
```

```
        Else: MsgBox "Record for " & txtNewItem.Text _
             & " has been deleted!", , "Record Deleted"
        End If
End Sub
```

Code 3.81: Code for the Click Event of the Command Button cmdRemove

15.   Add Code 3.82 to the Change event of the text box txtItemNo. It converts the
       data entered in the text box to its numeric value. The corresponding record is
       displayed in the label lblItemNo.

```
Private Sub txtItemNo_Change()
    Dim value As Integer
    value = Val(txtItemNo.Text)
    lblItemNo.Caption = lstNames.List(value - 1)
End Sub
```

Code 3.82: Code for the Change Event of the Text Box txtItemNo

16.   Add Code 3.83 to the Change event of the text box txtNewItem. It enables the
       two buttons below it (Add and Remove buttons) if the text box is not empty.

```
Private Sub txtNewItem_Change()
    If txtNewItem.Text <> "" Then
        cmdAdd.Enabled = True
        cmdRemove.Enabled = True
    Else
        cmdAdd.Enabled = False
        cmdRemove.Enabled = False
    End If
End Sub
```

Code 3.83: Code for the Change Event of the Text Box txtNewItem

Lab Activity Checklist

S. No.	Tasks	Completed	
		Yes	No
1.	Added a form to the project		
2.	Added all the required controls		
3.	Set the appropriate properties for all the codes		
4.	Added all the required codes for different methods and events of the controls		

Conclusion/Observation

1. The list box is filled with some sample data and is in CheckBox style.
2. An addCombo command button adds the selected items in the ListBox to a ComboBox control.
3. A TextBox control accepts the user name. On clicking the Add button the text in the text box is added to the list box.
4. Clicking Remove deletes the entry from the list box. Message boxes inform the user whether deletion was successful.
5. Add and Remove buttons are disabled if there is no text in the text box.
6. When the user enters a Roll No, the corresponding value stored at that index is displayed on the label below the Roll No text box.

Exercise 2

Objective

■ Use FileListBox, DirListBox, and DriveListBox controls in a form.

Problem Statement

Create the form frmFiles shown in Figure 3.34 with the FileListBox, DirListBox, and DriveListBox controls.

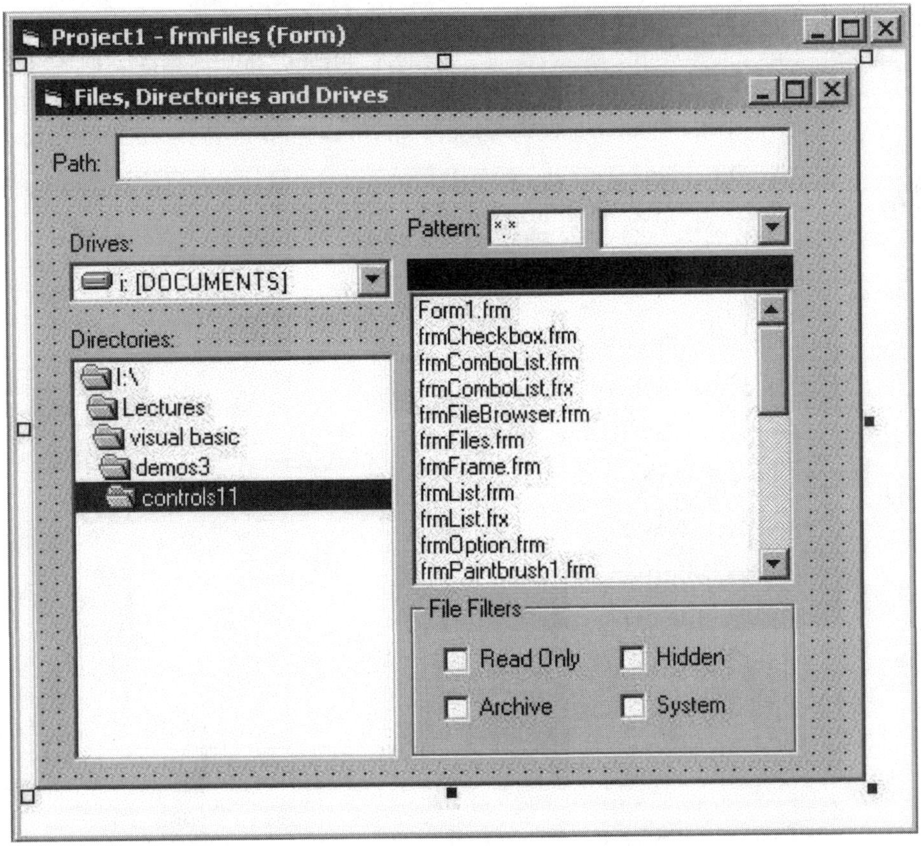

Figure 3.34: Form with the FileListBox, DirListBox, and DriveListBox Controls

The application should have the following features:

1. In the text box labeled Path, the complete path for a file along with filename should be displayed when the user clicks on a file name in the FileListBox control.

2. On top of the FileListBox, a label should display the total number of files in the current directory.

3. The text box labeled Pattern should take a pattern string and on pressing ENTER, the FileListBox should display results according to the new pattern.

4. The combo box next to the text box should allow the user to select common patterns from a list.

5. The frame labeled "File Filters" should have 4 CheckBoxes that provide the option of displaying Read-only, Hidden, Archive, and System files. These CheckBox controls should be initialized to their default values.

6. On changing the drive, the contents of both the DirListBox and the FileListBox controls should reflect changes.

Lab Setup

Computer Requirements:

- Microsoft Windows Operating System
- Pentium III or higher processors
- 128-MB RAM
- 3-GB of hard disk space
- CD-ROM drives
- Floppy disk drives
- LAN connections
- Visual Basic 6.0

Procedure

Perform the following procedure to create the form:

1. Create a new project and set the name of the default form as frmFiles.
2. Add a DriveListBox control. Set name to drvTest.
3. Add a DirListBox control and name it dirTest.
4. Add a FileListBox and name it filTest.

5.   Add a text box named txtPath and label it Path.

6.   Add a text box txtPattern and set its Text to "*.*". Add a Label control to label the text box as Pattern.

7.   Add a combo box and name it cboPattern.

8.   Add a label lblTotFiles above the FileListBox which will display the total files in the current directory.

9.   Add a frame fraFilter and set its Caption to "File Filters."

10.   Add four CheckBox controls to the frame for the file filters and name them chkReadOnly, chkArchive, chkHidden and chkSystem. Set their caption appropriately.

11.   Add Code 3.84 to the Form Load event of the form. lblTotFiles displays the total number of files in the current directory from the ListCount property. Some common patterns are added to the combo box. The filter properties are checked and the CheckBox controls are checked accordingly.

```
Private Sub Form_Load()
    lblTotFiles.Caption = "Total Files: " & filTest.ListCount
    txtPath.Text = filTest.Path
    cboPattern.AddItem "*.*"
    cboPattern.AddItem "*.exe; *.com; *.bat"
    cboPattern.AddItem "*.jpg; *.bmp; *.gif; *.png"
    cboPattern.AddItem "*.doc; *.txt; *.rtf"
    cboPattern.AddItem "*.htm; *.html; *.mht"
    cboPattern.AddItem "*.c; *.cpp; *.java; *.py"
    cboPattern.ListIndex = 0    'show the first item in the list

If filTest.ReadOnly Then
        chkReadOnly.value = vbChecked
    End If
If filTest.System Then
        chkSystem.value = vbChecked
    End If
    If filTest.Archive Then
        chkArchive.value = vbChecked
    End If
    If filTest.Hidden Then
```

```
        chkHidden.value = vbChecked
    End If
End Sub
```

Code 3.84: Code for the Form Load Event of Exercise 2

12.   Add Code 3.85 to the KeyPress event of txtPattern. When the user presses
       ENTER, it assigns the new pattern to the Pattern property of the FileListBox
       control.

```
Private Sub txtPattern_KeyPress(KeyAscii As Integer)
    If KeyAscii = 13 Then
        filTest.Pattern = txtPattern.Text
    End If
End Sub
```

Code 3.85: Code for the KeyPress Event of txtPattern

13.   Add Code 3.86 to the Click event of the FilTest control. It sets the text box
       txtPath's Text property to the complete Path of the clicked file with file name.
       When the current path is a drive's root folder, the Path contains a "\" with it,
       like "C:\". But in other cases, the Path doesn't have a forward slash character.
       So the right-most character of the path is checked using Right and then the
       FileName is appended to the Path with or without a "\".

```
Private Sub filTest_Click()
    If Right(filTest.Path, 1) = "\" Then
        txtPath.Text = filTest.Path & filTest.FileName
    Else
        txtPath.Text = filTest.Path & "\" & filTest.FileName
    End If
End Sub
```

Code 3.86: Code for the Click Event of the FilTest Control

14. Add Code 3.87 to the Change property of the DriveListBox control. The current path of both the DirListBox and the FileListBox are updated.

```
Private Sub drvTest_Change()
    dirTest.Path = drvTest.Drive
    filTest.Path = drvTest.Drive
End Sub
```

Code 3.87: Code for the Change Property of the DriveListBox Control

15. Add Code 3.88 to the Change event of dirTest. On changing the current directory, the contents of the FileListBox are updated. Also lblTotFiles shows the count of the new directory.

```
Private Sub dirTest_Change()
    filTest.Path = dirTest.Path
    lblTotFiles.Caption = "Total Files: " & filTest.ListCount
End Sub
```

Code 3.88: Code for the Change Event of dirTest

16. Add Code 3.89 to the Change event of the combo box cmbPattern. It assigns the new pattern selected to filTest's Pattern property.

```
Private Sub cmbPattern_Change()
    filTest.Pattern = cboPattern.Text
End Sub
```

Code 3.89: Code for the Change Event of the Combo Box cmbPattern

17. Add Code 3.90 to the Click event of the combo box cmbPattern. It assigns the new pattern to filTest's Pattern property.

```
Private Sub cmbPattern_Click()
    filTest.Pattern = cboPattern.Text
End Sub
```

Code 3.90: Code for the Click Event of the Combo Box cmbPattern

18. Add Code 3.91 to the Click event of all the CheckBox controls. It checks the value of the CheckBox and sets or unsets the corresponding properties of the filTest control.

```vb
Private Sub chkSystem_Click()
    If chkSystem.value = vbChecked Then
        filTest.System = True
    Else
            filTest.System = False
    End If
End Sub


Private Sub chkReadOnly_Click()
    If chkReadOnly.value = vbChecked Then
    filTest.ReadOnly = True
    Else
        filTest.ReadOnly = False
    End If
End Sub


Private Sub chkHidden_Click()
    If chkHidden.value = vbChecked Then
        filTest.Hidden = True
    Else
        filTest.Hidden = False
    End If
End Sub


Private Sub chkArchive_Click()
    If chkArchive.value = vbChecked Then
        filTest.Archive = True
    Else
        filTest.Archive = False
    End If
End Sub
```

Code 3.91: Code for the Click Event of All the CheckBox Controls

Lab Activity Checklist

S. No.	Tasks	Completed	
		Yes	No
1.	Added a form to the project		
2.	Added all the required controls		
3.	Set the appropriate properties for all the codes		
4.	Added all the required codes for different methods and events of the controls		

Conclusion/Observation

1. In the Path text box, the complete path for a file along with the file name is displayed when the user clicks on a file name in the FileListBox control.

2. On top of the FileListBox, a label displays the total number of files in the current directory.

3. The text box labeled Pattern takes a pattern string and on pressing ENTER, the FileListBox displays results according to the new pattern.

4. The combo box next to the text box allows the user to select common patterns from a list.

5. The frame labeled "File Filters" has 4 CheckBoxes that provide the option of displaying Read-only, Hidden, Archive, and System files. These CheckBox controls are initialized to their default values.

6. On changing the drive, the contents of both the DirListBox and the FileListBox controls reflect changes.

Exercise 3

Objective

◾ Use the Shape control in forms.

◾ Set different properties of the Shape control.

Problem Statement

Create the form shown in Figure 3.35.

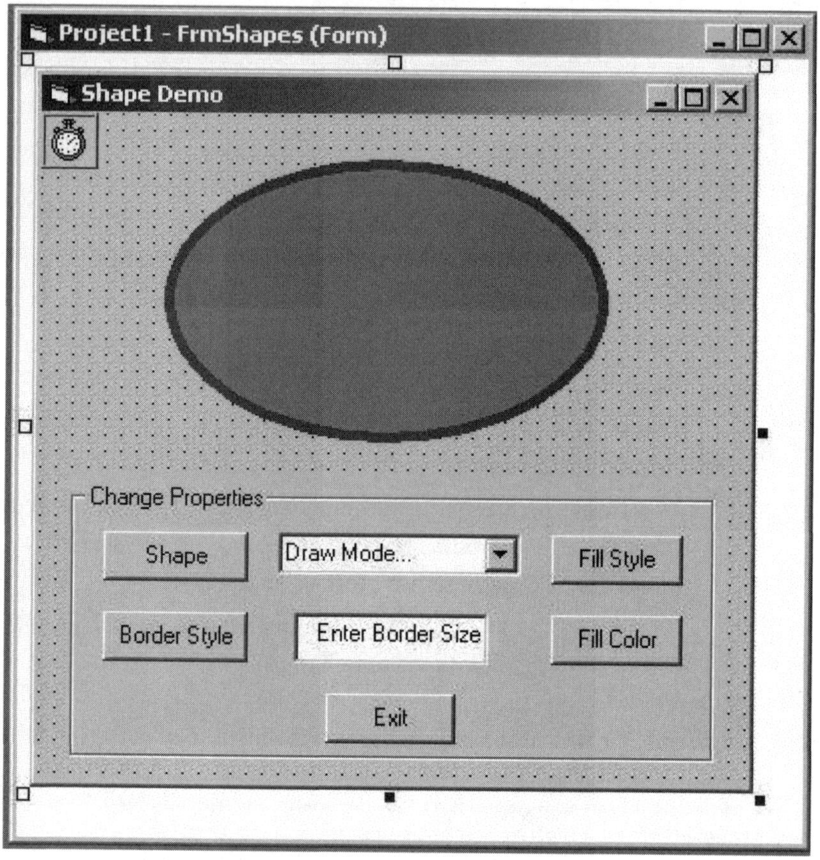

Figure 3.35: Shape Demo Form

Add the following features to the application:

1. Add a Shape control and add command buttons to cycle through different values of properties Shape, BorderStyle, FillStyle, and FillColor. Write loops that take different valid values for the properties. For FillColor, use a random color every time the user clicks the button.

2. Add a combo box from which the user can select any of the 16 valid Draw Modes.

3. Add a text box in which the user can enter the BorderWidth. Take values ranging from 1 to 30 only. Display a message if the input is beyond limits. On pressing Enter, the BorderWidth should be set to the new value.

4. The text box should display the text "Enter Border Size" and when the user clicks on the text box, it should clear the text. After pressing Enter, the text Enter Border Size" should be shown again and the focus from the control should be removed to the button labeled "Shape."

5. Add an Exit button that unloads the form.

Lab Setup

Computer Requirements:

- Microsoft Windows Operating System
- Pentium III or higher processors
- 128-MB RAM
- 3-GB of hard disk space
- CD-ROM drives
- Floppy disk drives
- LAN connections
- Visual Basic 6.0

Procedure

Perform the following procedure to create the form:

1. Add a frame with caption "Change Properties" where you will add all the controls.

2. Add five CommandButton controls and name them cmdBorderstyle, cmdColor, cmdShape, cmdFillstyle and cmdExit.

3. Add a text box and set the name to txtBorder.

4.   Add a combo box and name it cboDrawmode. Set the Text property to "Draw Mode…".

5.   Add a Shape control. Set the name to Shape1, BorderStyle and FillStyle to Solid.

6.   Add a timer to the form named Timer1 and set Enabled to true and Interval to 5000.

7.   Save the form as frmShapes.

8.   Add Code 3.92 to the General Declarations section to declare variables:

```
Option Explicit
Dim shapeval As Integer
Dim fill_style As Integer
Dim border As Integer
```

Code 3.92: Code for Declaring Variables in the General Declaration Section

9.   Add Code 3.93 to the Form Load event of the form.

```
Private Sub Form_Load()
  shapeval = 0
  border = 0
  fillcombo     'calls function to fill up the ComboBox
End Sub
```

Code 3.93: Code for the Form Load Event of Exercise 3

10.   Code 3.94 is a Sub that fills up the combo box with the values taken by DrawMode property.

```
Private Sub fillcombo()
    CboDrawmode.AddItem ("1, Blackness")
    CboDrawmode.AddItem ("2, Not Merge Pen")
    CboDrawmode.AddItem ("3, Mask Not Pen")
    CboDrawmode.AddItem ("4, Not Copy Pen")
    CboDrawmode.AddItem ("5, Mask Pen Not")
    CboDrawmode.AddItem ("6, Invert")
    CboDrawmode.AddItem ("7, Xor Pen")
    CboDrawmode.AddItem ("8, Not Mask Pen")
    CboDrawmode.AddItem ("9, Mask Pen")
```

```
    CboDrawmode.AddItem ("10, Not Xor Pen")
    CboDrawmode.AddItem ("11, Nop")
    CboDrawmode.AddItem ("12, Merge Not")
    CboDrawmode.AddItem ("13, Copy Pen")
    CboDrawmode.AddItem ("14, Merge Pen Not")
    CboDrawmode.AddItem ("15, Merge Pen")
    CboDrawmode.AddItem ("16, Whiteness")
End Sub
```

Code 3.94: Code to Add Items to the Combo Box Control

11.   Add Code 3.95 to the Timer event of the timer control.

```
Private Sub Timer1_Timer()
  BackColor = RGB(Rnd * 255, Rnd * 255, Rnd * 255)
End Sub
```

Code 3.95: Code for the Timer Event of the Timer Control

12.   Add Code 3.96 to the Click event of the text box control TxtBorder.

```
Private Sub Txtborder_Click()
 Txtborder.Text = ""
End Sub
```

Code 3.96: Code for the Click Event of the Text Box Control TxtBorder

13.   Add Code 3.97 to the KeyPress event of the text box control TxtBorder.

```
Private Sub txtBorder_KeyPress(KeyAscii As Integer)
    'you may use IsNumeric(txtBorder.Text) to check for valid
values
    Dim value As Integer
    value = Val(Txtborder.Text)
    If KeyAscii = 13 Then
        If value < 1 Or value > 30 Then
            MsgBox "Wrong Entry! Please enter between
1-30",,"Error!"
            txtborder.Text = ""
        Else
```

```
        Shape1.BorderWidth = Val(Txtborder.Text)
        txtBorder.Text = "Enter Border Width"
        cmdShape.SetFocus
    End If
  End If
End Sub
```

Code 3.97: Code for the KeyPress Event of the Text Box Control TxtBorder

14.   Add Code 3.98 to the Click event of the command buttons CmdShape and CmdFillStyle.

```
Private Sub cmdShape_Click()
    If shapeval < 5 Then
        shapeval = shapeval + 1
    Else
        shapeval = 0
    End If
    Shape1.Shape = shapeval
End Sub
Private Sub cmdFillstyle_Click()
    If fill_style < 7 Then
        fill_style = fill_style + 1
    Else
        fill_style = 0
    End If
    Shape1.FillStyle = fill_style
End Sub
```

Code 3.98: Code for the Click Event of the Command Buttons CmdShape and CmdFillStyle

15. Add Code 3.99 for the combo box CboDrawmode.

```
Private Sub CboDrawmode_Click()
    Debug.Print CboDrawmode.ListIndex
    'list index starts from 0, so you add 1 to get actual index
    Shape1.DrawMode = CboDrawmode.ListIndex + 1
End Sub
```

Code 3.99: Code the Combo Box CboDrawmode

16. Add Code 3.100 for the command buttons CmdColor and CmdExit.

```
Private Sub cmdColor_Click()
    Shape1.FillColor = RGB(255 * Rnd, 255 * Rnd, 255 * Rnd)
End Sub


Private Sub cmdExit_Click()
  Unload frmShapes
End Sub
```

Code 3.100: Code for the Command Buttons CmdColor and CmdExit

17. Add Code 3.101 for the Click event of the command button cmdBorderstyle.

```
Private Sub cmdBorderstyle_Click()
    If border < 5 Then
        border = border + 1
    Else
        border = 0
    End If
    Shape1.BorderStyle = border
End Sub
```

Code 3.101: Code for the Click Event of the Command Button cmdBorderstyle

Lab Activity Checklist

S. No.	Tasks	Completed	
		Yes	No
1.	Added a frame with caption "Change Properties" to the form		
2.	Added five CommandButton controls to the form		
3.	Added a text box and a combo box to the form that named them properly		
4.	Added a Shape control and a timer to the form and set the appropriate properties		
5.	Saved the form as frmShapes		
6.	Added all the codes correctly		
7.	Added a form to the project		

Conclusion/Observation

1. A Shape control and CommandButtons to cycle through different values of properties Shape, BorderStyle, FillStyle, and FillColor have been added. Loops have been written that take different valid values for the properties. For FillColor, a random color is used every time the user clicks the button.

2. A combo box from which the user can select any of the 16 valid Draw Modes is included.

3. A text box in which the user can enter the BorderWidth is included. This takes values ranging from 1 to 30 only. A message is displayed if the input is beyond limits. On pressing Enter, the BorderWidth is set to the new value.

4. The text box displays the text "Enter Border Size" and when the user clicks on the text box, it clears the text. After pressing Enter, the text "Enter Border Size" is shown again and the focus from the control is removed to the button labeled "Shape."

5. An Exit button is included that unloads the form.

Project

1.   Create a new Visual Basic project named EmpInfo.

2.   Add the following three forms to the project as shown in the following figures.

         Form named frmAddEmp, as shown in Figure 3.36 will be used to add the records of a new employee.

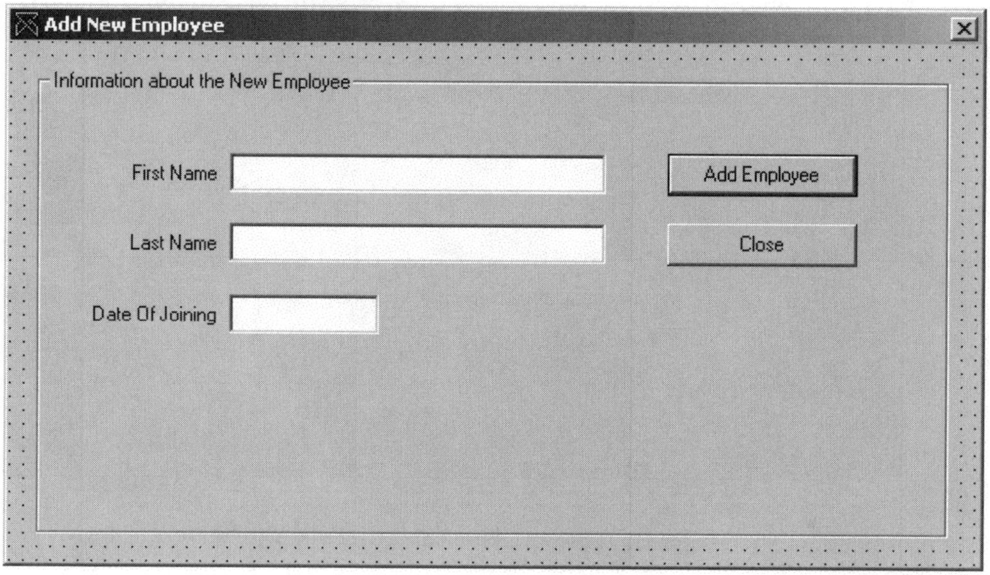

Figure 3.36: frmAddEmp Form

Form named frmEditEmp, as shown in Figure 3.37 will be used to modify the records of the existing employees.

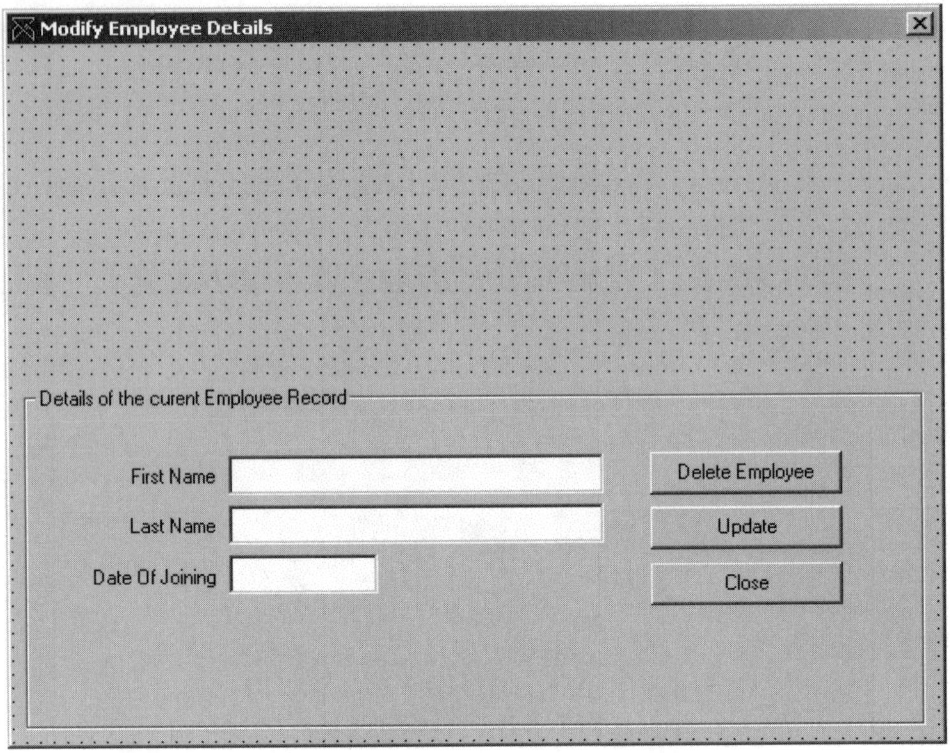

Figure 3.37: frmEditEmp Form

Form named frmSearchEmp, as shown in Figure 3.38, will be used to search for employee records based on certain criteria.

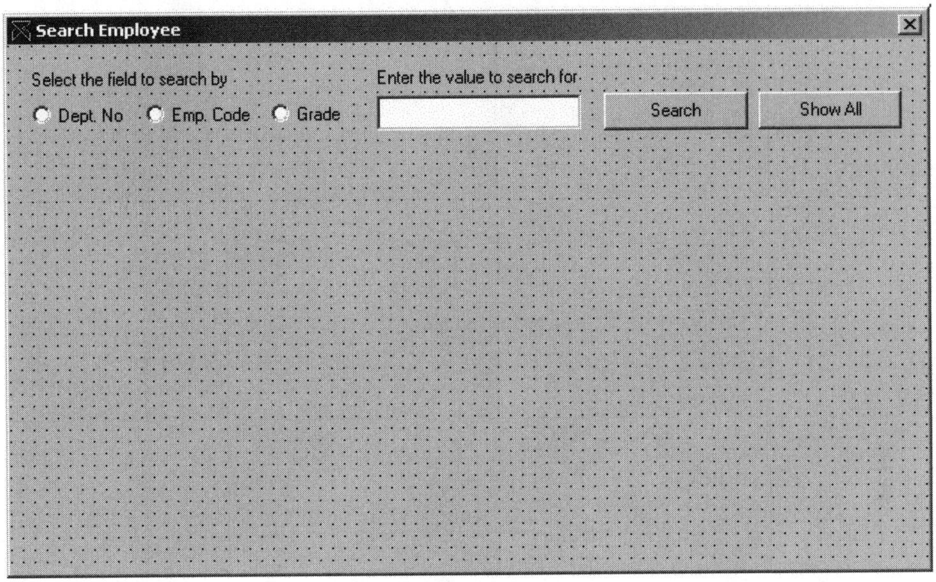

Figure 3.38: frmEditEmp Form

3. Open the form frmAddEmp. Write proper code to prevent invalid characters in the TextBox controls. For instance, the first and the last names should not accept numeric characters and the date should only accept numeric and date separator characters (- or /). Write a sub-procedure named Reset to clear all the TextBox controls. Add another function named IsValidData to check if the user has entered a valid value for each of the text boxes. The function should return a Boolean value depending on the validity of the values being entered. Write the code to close the form on the Click event of the Close button.

4. Open the form frmEditEmp. Write the code to close the form when the user clicks the Close button. Write the code to prevent invalid characters in the TextBox controls as mentioned for the form frmAddEmp in the previous question. Implement the Validate event of the TextBox controls to prevent the transfer of the focus if the text box does not have a valid value.

5. Save the project.

Working with Menus and Windows

4

This chapter explains how to create menu-driven applications. It demonstrates how to create menus quickly using the Menu Editor in Microsoft Visual Basic. It also describes two types of interfaces: The Single Document Interface (SDI) and the Multiple Document Interface (MDI). It also demonstrates how Visual Basic may be used as a Rapid Application Development (RAD) tool to create such interfaces. At the end of this chapter, you will be able to:

- Explain the advantages of menus in graphical user interface (GUI) applications.

- Explain the structure of a menu.

- Explain the features of the Menu Editor.

- Design menus using the Menu Editor.

- Create an SDI application using the Application Wizard.

- Create an MDI application using the Application Wizard.

4.1 Menus

4.2 Windows

4.1 Menus

In a GUI application, you can choose items and execute programs by pointing and clicking a mouse. For example, consider the interface of Microsoft Excel, a spreadsheet application. You can create or open a spreadsheet by clicking the menu items in the GUI of the application.

You have learned to create forms and controls in Visual Basic. In addition to these interface components, Visual Basic allows you to create menus and windows. A menu offers a convenient and consistent way to group commands so that users can easily access them. For example, in Microsoft Word, commands for carrying out similar types of actions are grouped together under one menu, such as the **Copy**, **Paste**, and **Cut** commands under the **Edit** menu. This feature makes the application user-friendly and interactive.

Visual Basic provides two main tools to create menus in an application:

- Menu Editor: This tool allows you to create new menus or modify existing menus in an application.

- Visual Basic (VB) Application Wizard: This tool helps you to create applications with customized menus.

In this chapter, you will learn to create menus in a Visual Basic application by using the Menu Editor and the VB Application Wizard.

4.1.1 Advantages of Menus

 Explain the advantages of menus in GUI applications.

Menus in GUI applications have been popular for many years. Menus provide the following advantages:

- Menus reduce the load on the system's memory. For example, in Microsoft Word, the **Edit** menu contains all commands meant for editing a document. You are not required to remember the actual command to perform any action because the commands are grouped under the title **Edit**.

- Compared to the command-line interface, the use of menus reduces the number of actions required to perform a specific task.
- Menus help the user navigate an application. In a GUI application, you can provide menu items so that the user may select the appropriate command to navigate further in the application.
- Menus increase the accessibility of an application.

4.1.2 Designing Menus

- Explain the structure of a menu.
- Design menus using the Menu Editor in Visual Basic.

Before you begin designing a menu, you need to define its structure. This involves identifying the features that will be provided by each menu item. After identifying all the functions on the menu bar, you need to group these functions under relevant headings. For example, if you are providing a **File** menu, include **New File**, **Open File**, and **Save File** options in this menu.

Figure 4.1 displays the structure of a Notepad menu bar.

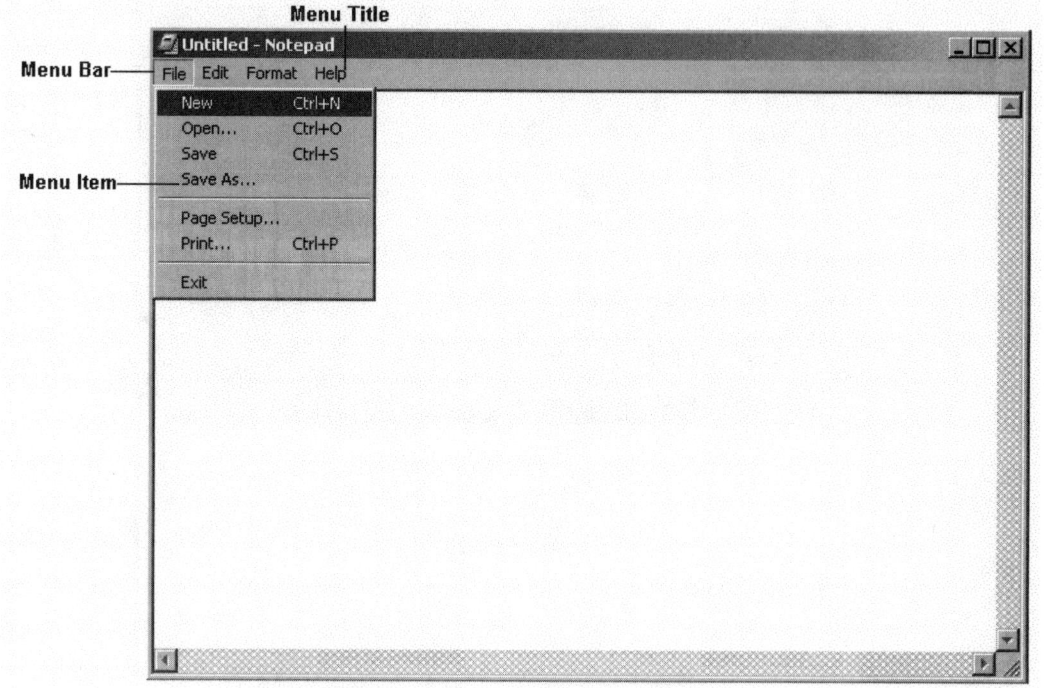

Figure 4.1: Structure of Notepad Menu Bar

Microsoft Visual Basic's Menu Editor helps you to design menus for your applications. The Menu Editor lets you assign names to the menu controls, use captions to display control titles, and define submenu options.

Figure 4.2 displays the Menu Editor window in Visual Basic.

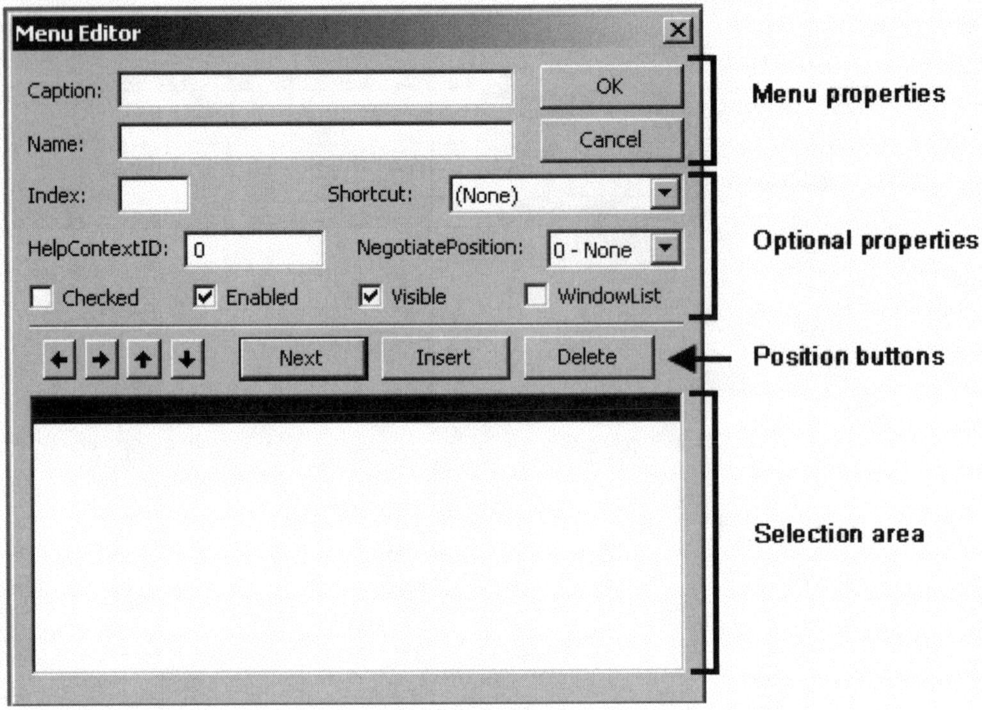

Figure 4.2: Menu Editor Window in Visual Basic

To add a menu to a form, perform the following steps:

1.   Select **Menu Editor** from the **Tools** menu. The Menu Editor is displayed.

 On the form window, you can also use the Ctrl + E shortcut to display the Menu Editor.

2.   In the **Menu Editor** dialog box, specify the caption to be displayed on the menu bar in the Caption text box, as shown in Figure 4.3.

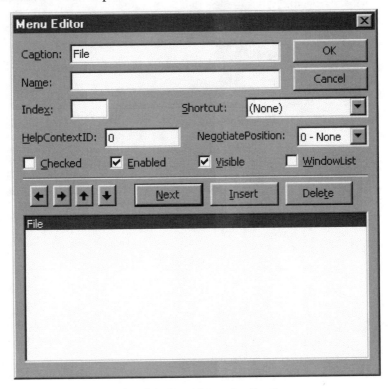

Figure 4.3: Specifying the Caption

3.   In the Name text box, specify the name of the menu item, as shown in Figure 4.4.

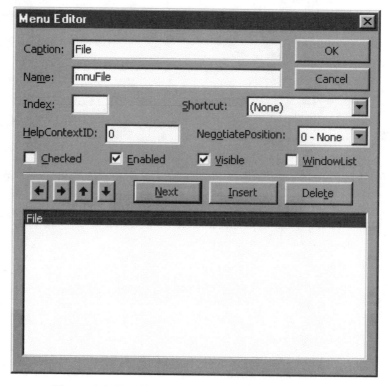

Figure 4.4: Specifying the Name of the Menu Item

4.   To move the menu items up or down in the command list, use the arrow buttons.

The Menu Control list box (the lower portion of the Menu Editor that is called the Selection Area in Figure 4.2), lists all of the menu controls in the current form. When you type a menu item in the Caption text box, that item also appears in the Menu Control list box. Selecting an existing menu control from the list box allows you to edit the properties for that control.

The position of a menu control in the **Menu Control** list box determines if the control is a menu title, menu item, or a submenu item.

▪ A menu control that appears flush left in the list box is displayed as a menu title. In Figure 4.4, **File** is a menu title.

▪ A menu control that is indented once in the list box is displayed on the menu as a menu item when the user clicks the menu title.

To add a menu item in a form, perform the following steps:

1.   In the Menu Editor, add a menu title **Edit** as shown in Figure 4.5.

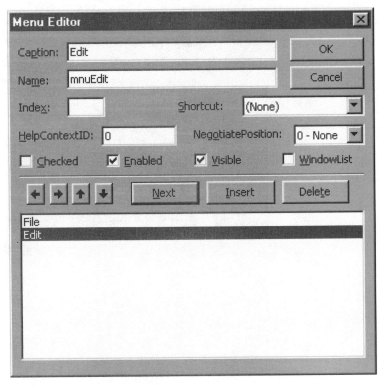

Figure 4.5: Creating the Edit Menu Title

2.   Click **Insert** to create a new item above the Edit item. Click the right arrow button to indent the new item. This indicates that the menu item is related to the **File** menu title, as shown in Figure 4.6.

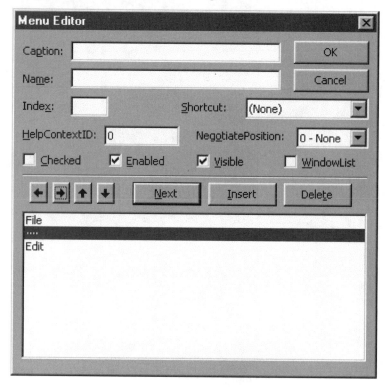

Figure 4.6: Creating a Menu Item

3.   In the Caption text box, specify the name of the menu item that will be displayed in the **File** menu.

4.   In the Name text box, specify the **Object** name for the menu item, as shown in Figure 4.7. This name will be used to reference the object in the application's code.

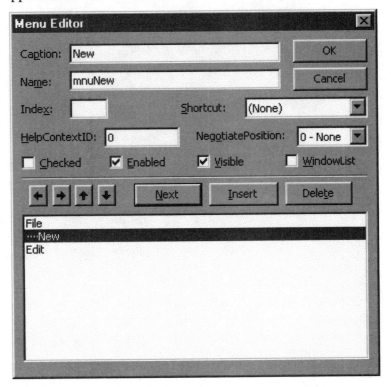

Figure 4.7: Specifying Object Name for the Menu Item

5.   Click **OK** in the Menu Editor to accept the changes.

6.   Run the project. The output is shown in Figure 4.8.

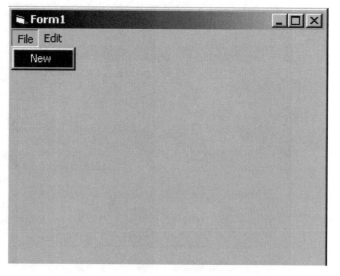

Figure 4.8: Displaying the New Menu Item

 You can also associate keyboard shortcuts with menu items. For example, in Microsoft Word, you can use the **Edit** menu or Ctrl + C, to copy the contents of the document. To assign a shortcut key for a menu item in Visual Basic, specify the shortcut property in the Menu Editor.

An indented menu control followed by further indented menu control is a submenu item.

To add a submenu item in a form, perform the following steps:

1.   In the Menu Editor, select the **Edit** menu title, as shown in Figure 4.9.

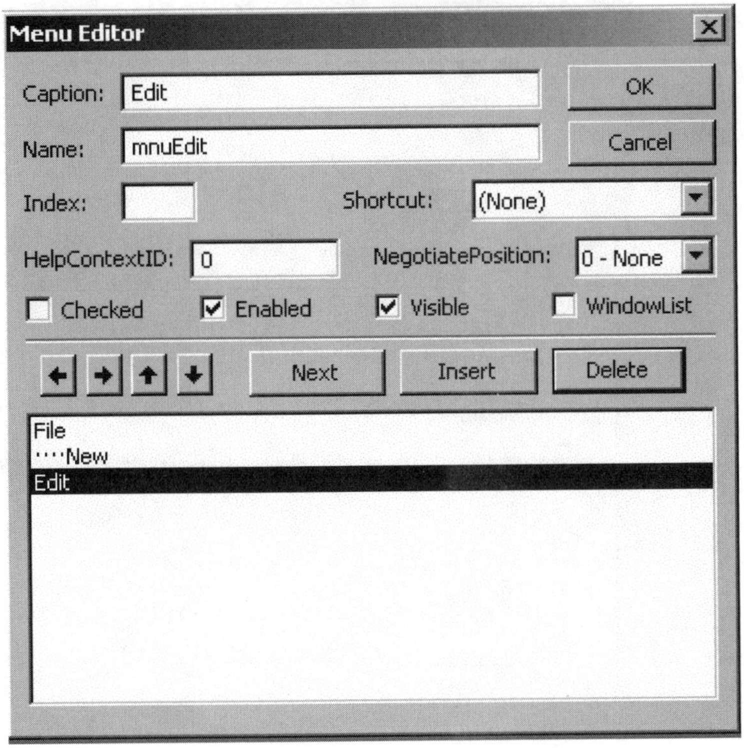

Figure 4.9 Selecting the Edit Menu Item

2.   Click **Insert** to create a new menu item above **Edit**. Click the right arrow button to indent the new item. Click the right arrow button again.

This indicates that the menu item is related to the **New** menu item, as shown in Figure 4.10.

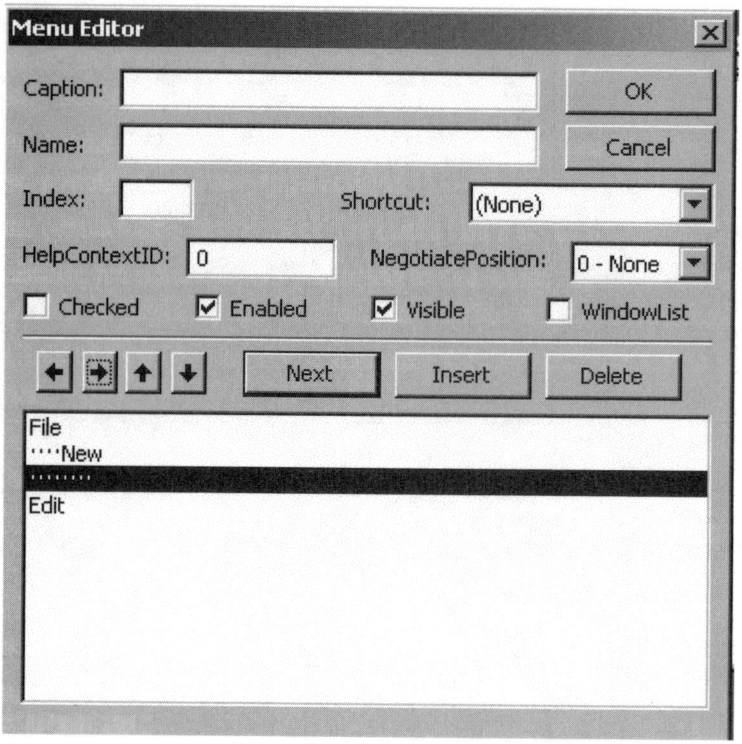

Figure 4.10: Creating a Submenu

3.   In the Caption and Name text boxes, type appropriate entries for this submenu item, as shown in Figure 4.11.

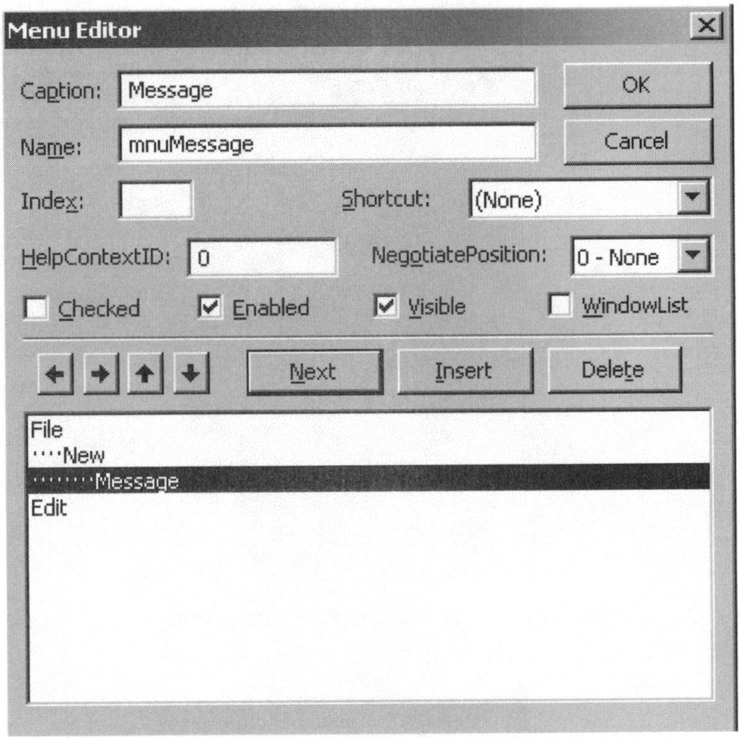

Figure 4.11: Naming the Submenu Item

4.   Click **OK** in the Menu Editor to accept the changes.

5.   Run the project. The output is shown in Figure 4.12.

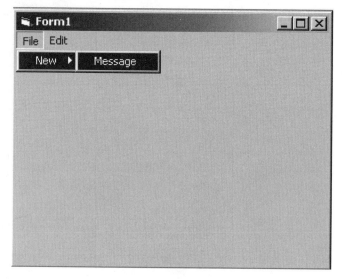

Figure 4.12: Completed Submenu Item

You can also place a Separator line between menu items. This allows you to further organize your menu configuration.

To insert a Separator line, perform the following steps:

1.   In the Menu Editor, select the **Edit** menu title, as shown in Figure 4.13.

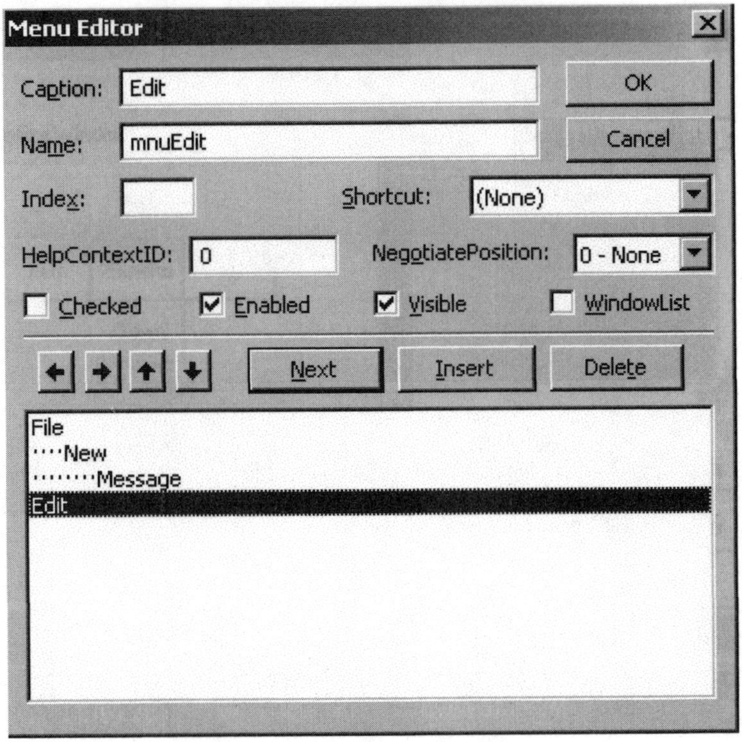

Figure 4.13: Preparing to Add a Separator Line

2.   Click **Insert** to create a new menu item above **Edit**. Click the right arrow button once.

3.   Enter **View** in the Caption text box and **mnuView** in the Name text box, as shown in Figure 4.14.

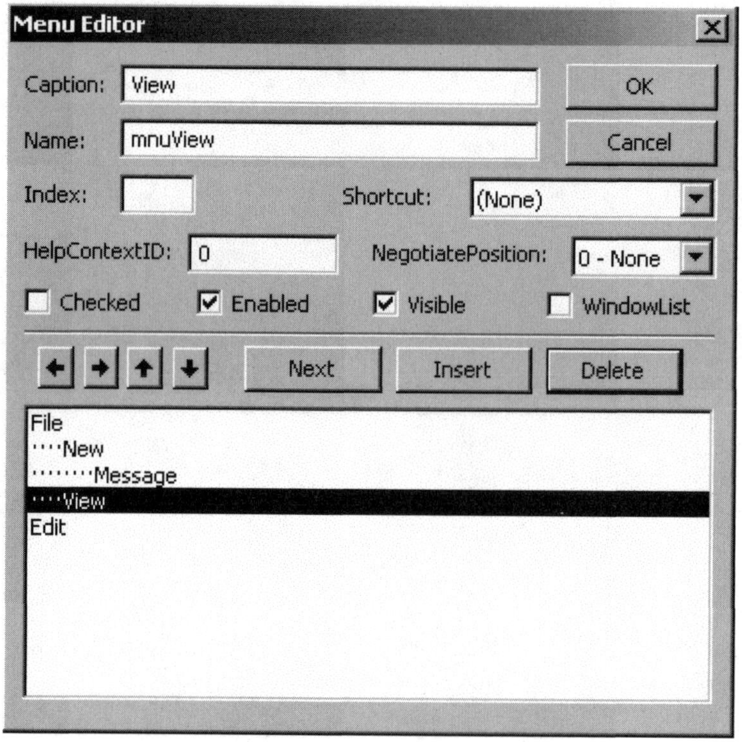

Figure 4.14: Creating a New Menu Item Using Menu Editor

4.   Click **Insert** to create a Separator line between **View** and **Message**. Click the right arrow button once. Then, in the Caption text box, enter a single dash (-) and in the Name text box enter **mnuSeparator**.

It should look like Figure 4.15.

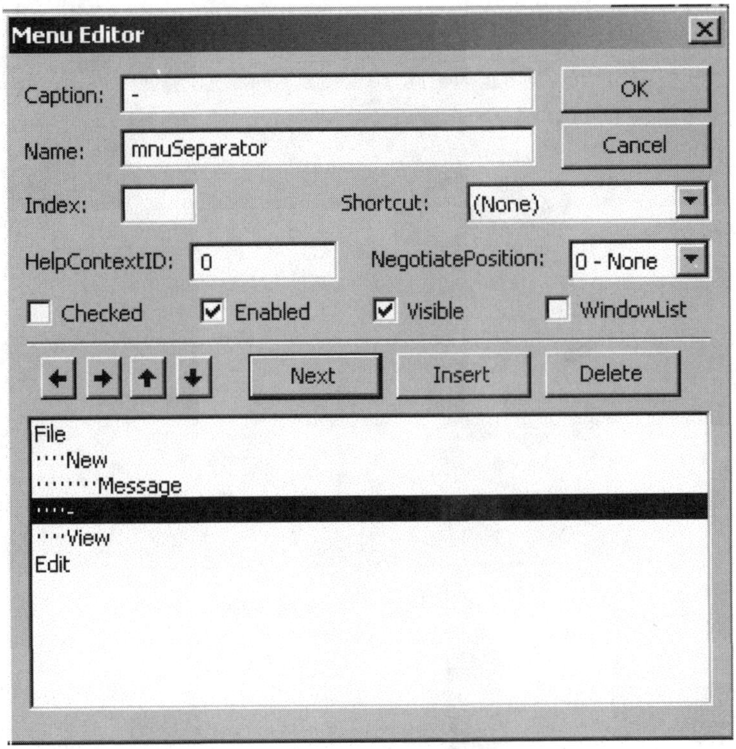

Figure 4.15: Creating the Separator Line

5.   Click **OK** in the Menu Editor to accept the changes.

6.   Run the project. The output is shown in Figure 4.16.

Notice that the separator line is between the **New** and **View** menu items.

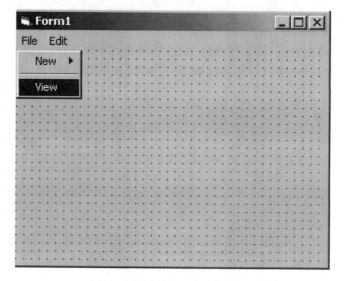

Figure 4.16: Completed Menu

Suppose that you are designing an editor called **ScriptEditor**. This editor is similar to Notepad in its usage and has many menu items.

Figure 4.17 displays the tree structure of the menu items in the ScriptEditor application.

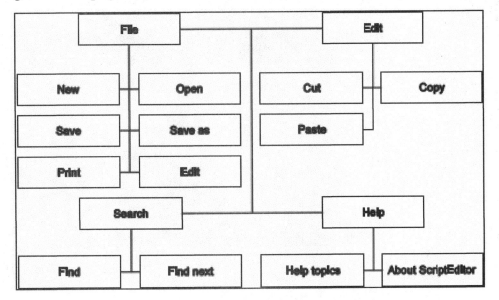

Figure 4.17: Tree Structure of Menu Items

In Figure 4.17, File, Edit, Search, and Help are the menu titles.

This menu structure can be created using the Menu Editor in Microsoft Visual Basic, as displayed in Figure 4.18.

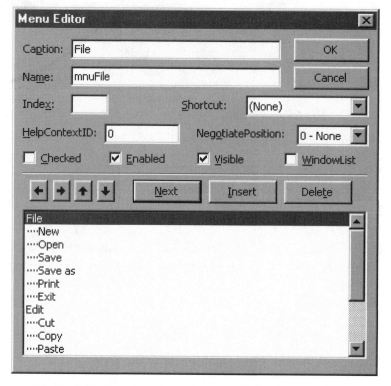

Figure 4.18: Creating Menu Structure Using Menu Editor

The complete ScriptEditor application is displayed in Figure 4.19.

Figure 4.19: ScriptEditor Application

Practice Questions

1. List the advantages of menus in a GUI application.
2. Differentiate between a menu bar and a menu item.
3. Create the tree structure of the **Tools** menu in the Microsoft Word application.

1. GUI reduces the mem load, they held navigate a user through the application, and it increases the accesibility of an app.

2. A menu bar include many menu items, and a menu item is a single function going to be executed.

3.

4.2 Windows

Most of your work with Visual Basic has involved creating a form that contained all the user interface controls and menu items needed by the user. If you used multiple forms, you would usually first open one form and hide the other. Such applications are called *Single Document Interface* (SDI) applications, in that only one window (and form) is open at a time.

Visual Basic also allows you to display multiple forms at the same time. Each form is displayed in a separate window. For example, you can create an application in which new forms are displayed within the main form. Such applications are called *Multiple Document Interface* (MDI) applications. This interface allows you to create complex applications. Almost all software applications, such as Microsoft Word and Microsoft Excel, have multiple document interfaces.

In this section, you will learn to create SDI and MDI applications in Visual Basic using the VB Application Wizard.

4.2.1 SDI Applications

Create an SDI application using the Application Wizard in Visual Basic.

An SDI application contains a single document window. For example, WordPad is an SDI application in which you can open only one document at a time. In such an application, when you want to open a new window, the contents of the earlier window are replaced by the new window.

The VB Application Wizard helps you to create an application using one of the predefined interfaces, SDI or MDI. The VB Application Wizard allows you to:

- Create fully customized menu bars, toolbars, and status bars in your application without specifying each of them in the Menu Editor.

- Create menus with standard Windows features and layout. This provides a consistent look and feel to the applications created using the VB Application Wizard.

You cannot use the VB Application Wizard to modify previously created projects. To modify the menus in an existing application, you can use the Menu Editor.

To create an SDI application, perform the following steps:

1. Click **New** on the **File** menu. The **New Project** dialog box is displayed, as shown in Figure 4.20.

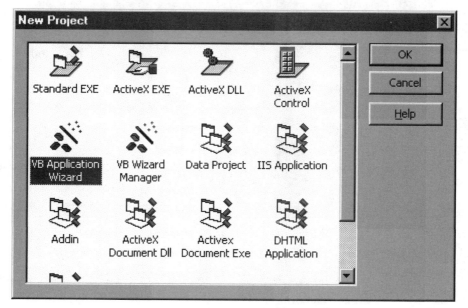

Figure 4.20: New Project Dialog Box

2. In the **New Project** dialog box, select **VB Application Wizard** and click **OK.**

The **Introduction** dialog box is displayed, as show in Figure 4.21.

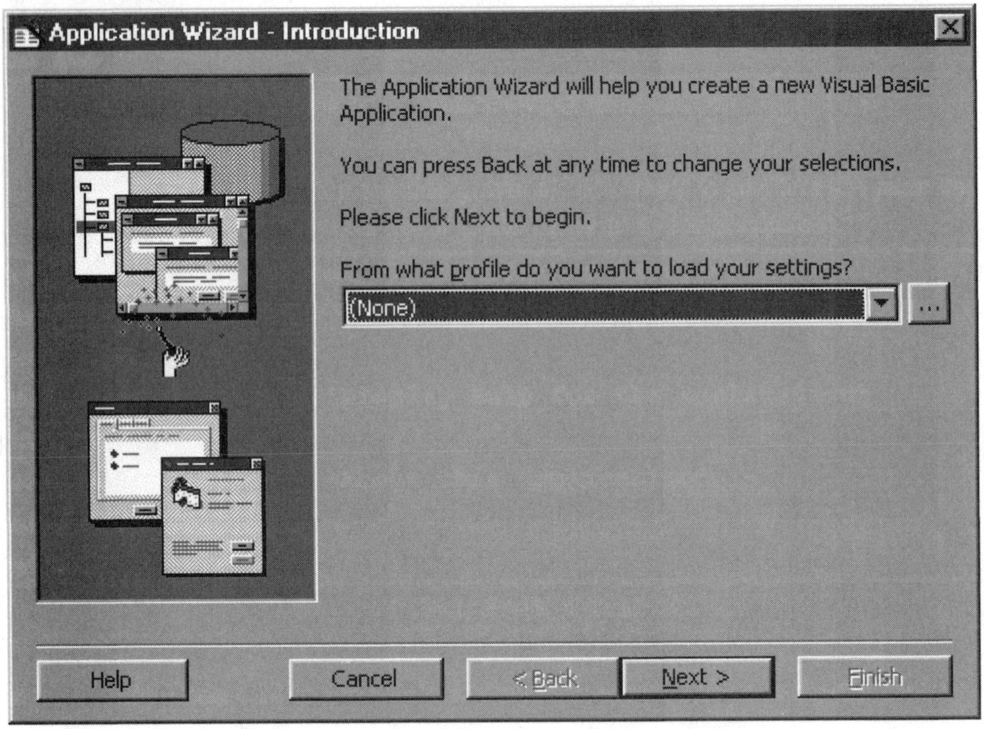

Figure 4.21: The Introduction Dialog Box

3.   Select the profile from the **Application Wizard** dialog box. A profile
         describes a previously saved configuration. Click **Next.**

4.   Select **Single Document Interface (SDI)** from the Interface Type dialog box. Specify the name of the application, and click **Next**, as shown in Figure 4.22.

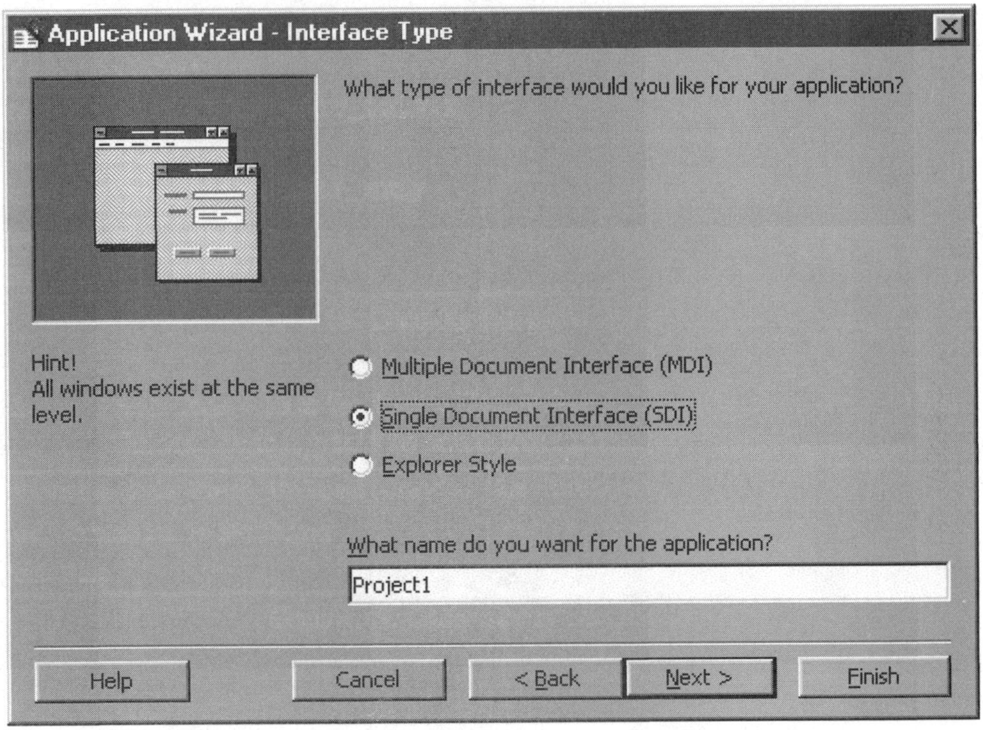

Figure 4.22: Interface Type Dialog Box

The Menus dialog box is displayed.

5. Select the menus from the **Menus** list, and the submenus from the **Sub Menus** list, and click **Next**, as shown in Figure 4.23.

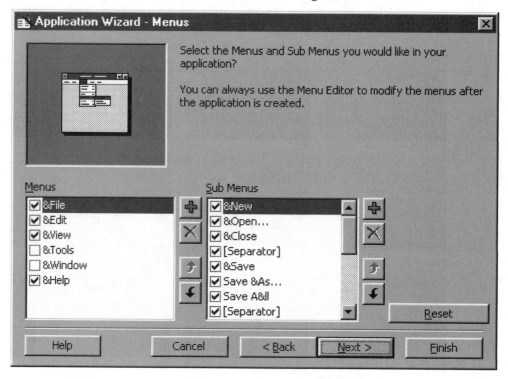

Figure 4.23: Menus Dialog Box

6. In the **Customize Toolbar** dialog box, select the buttons to be displayed on the toolbar of your application. Toolbars contain buttons that provide easy access to commonly used commands. On this page, you need to select the buttons from the list on the right and move it to the list on the left as shown in Figure 4.24.

Figure 4.24: Customize Toolbar Dialog Box

7. Click **Next**.

On the **Customize Toolbar** dialog box, you can also specify your own icon by clicking the **Load an External bitmap or Icon** button. You can include any bitmap in the toolbar of your application.

---

8. The next screen shows the **Resources** dialog box. On this page, select **Yes** if you would like to use a resources file in your application; or select No, as shown in Figure 4.25.

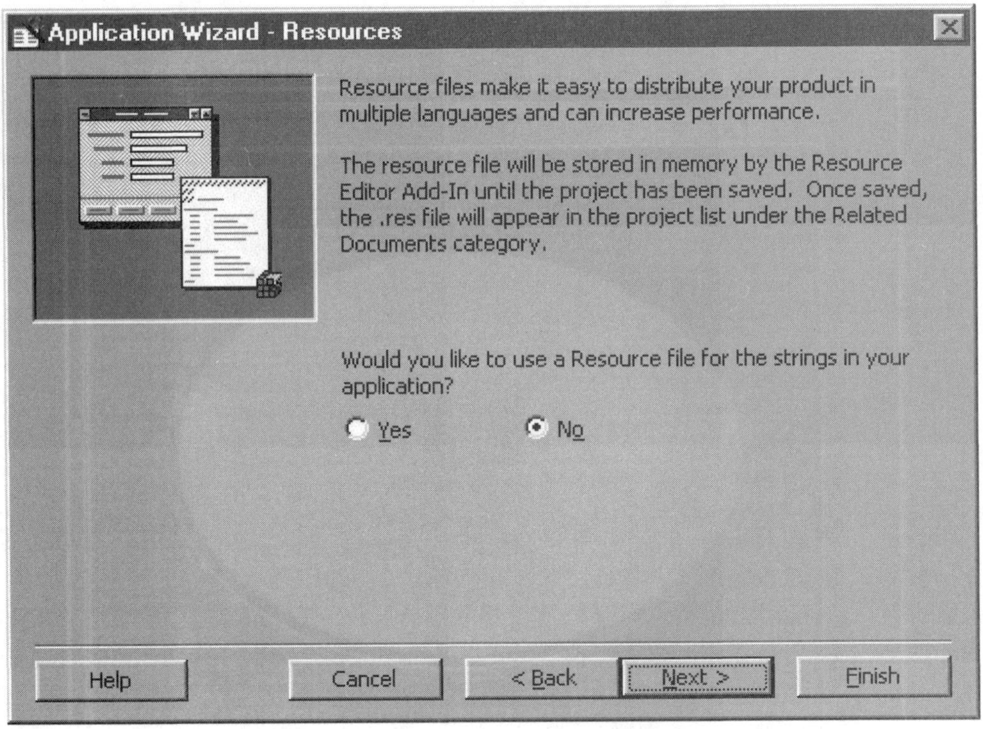

Figure 4.25: Resources Dialog Box

9. On the **Internet Connectivity** dialog box, you can specify the URL that you want included in your SDI application. Select **No** if your application does not support Internet connectivity, as shown in Figure 4.26. Click **Next**.

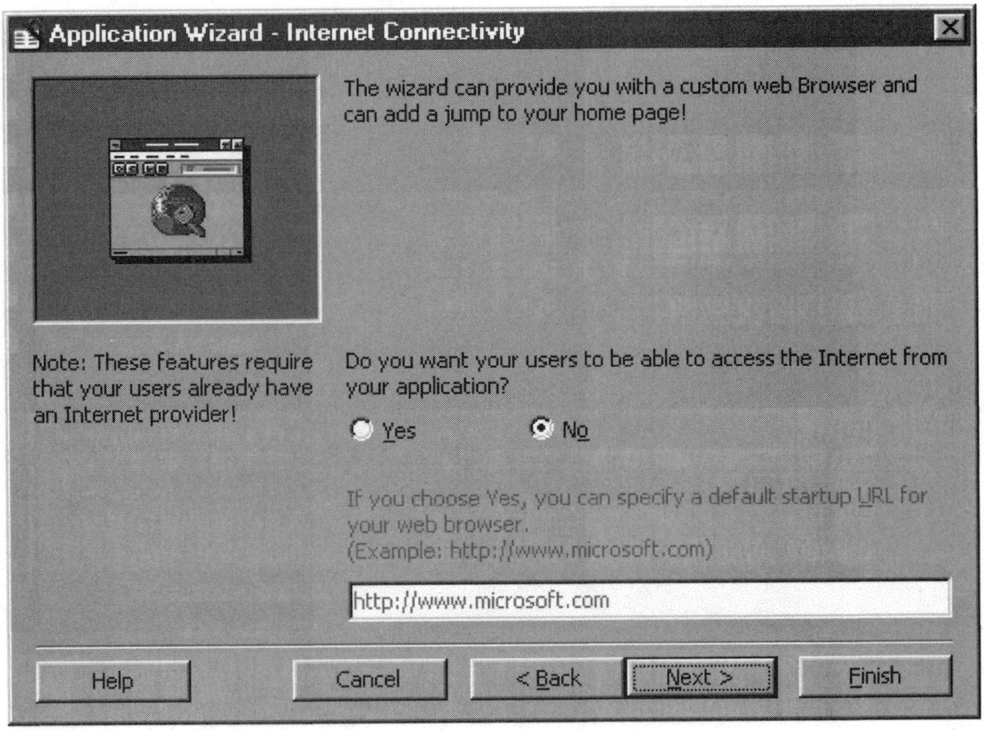

Figure 4.26: Internet Connectivity Dialog Box

The **Standard Forms** dialog box is displayed.

10. Select the form you want to include in your application from the **Standard Forms** dialog box. For example, if you want a logon screen when the application starts, select **Login dialog to accept an ID and password**, as shown in Figure 4.27. Click **Next.**

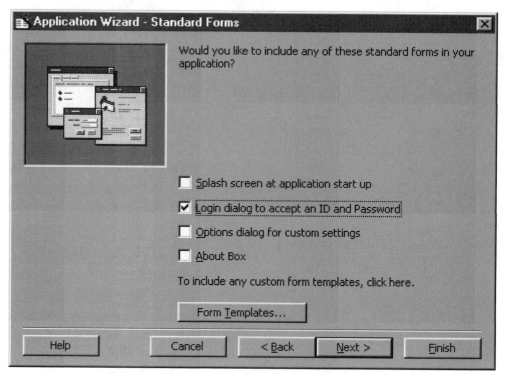

Figure 4.27: The Standard Forms Dialog Box

The **Data Access Forms** dialog box is displayed.

11. On the **Data Access Forms** dialog box, click the **Create New Form** button to specify that the form in the SDI application can use data from an existing database. You may skip this page by clicking **Next,** as shown in Figure 4.28.

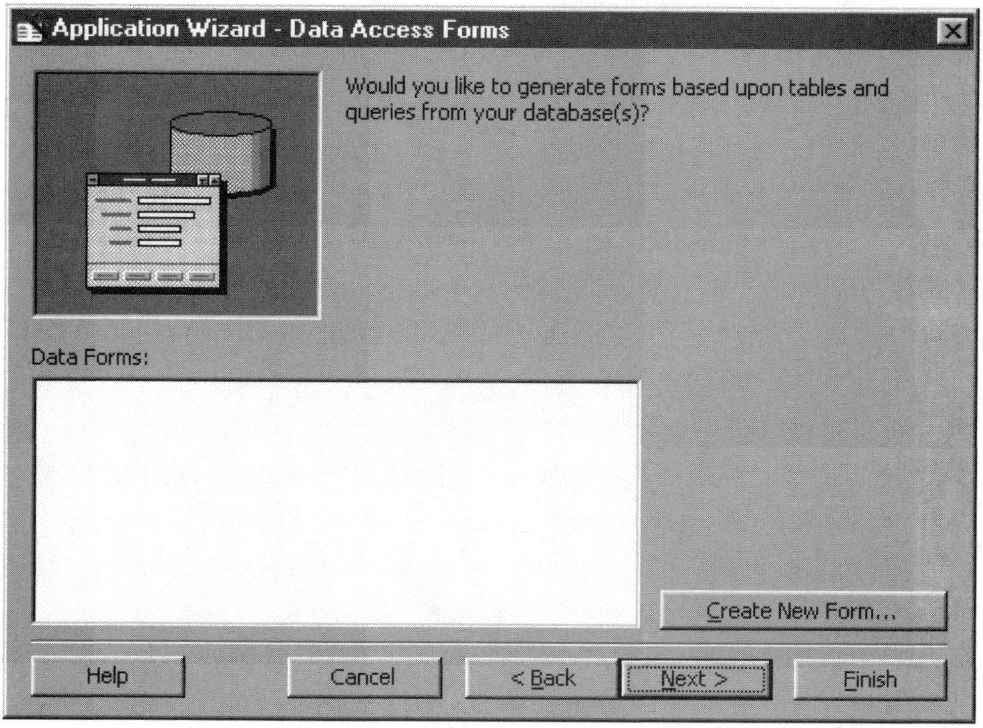

Figure 4.28: Data Access Forms Dialog Box

12. The **Application Wizard - Finished!** dialog box is displayed. Here, you can save the settings specified in the Wizard for your project, as a profile. You can also see a summary report of the project by clicking **View Report**, as shown in Figure 4.29.

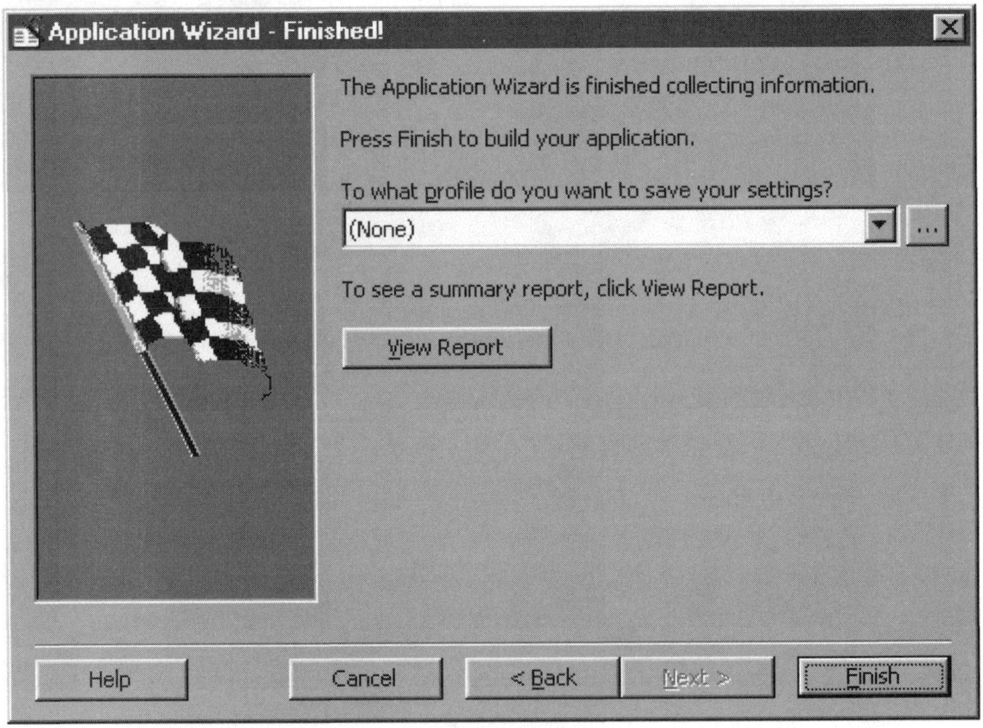

Figure 4.29: Application Wizard - Finished Dialog Box

The report is displayed, as shown in Figure 4.30.

Figure 4.30: The Summary Report

13.   You can save the report by clicking **Save**. Click **Close** to close the report window.

14.   Click **Finish** to accept the settings in the Wizard.

15.   Run the project.

The SDI application has been created. Notice that a **Login** screen is displayed, as shown in Figure 4.31.

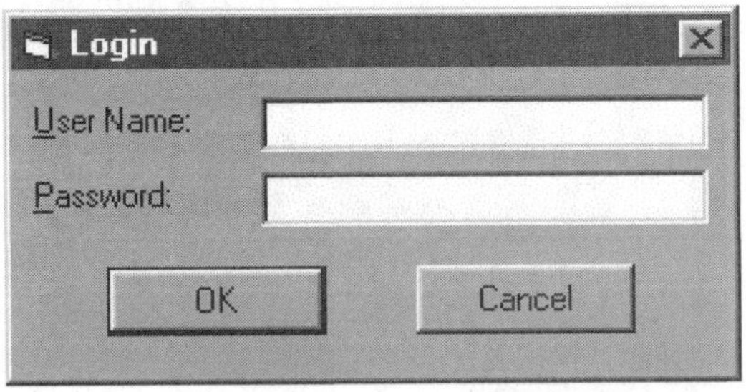

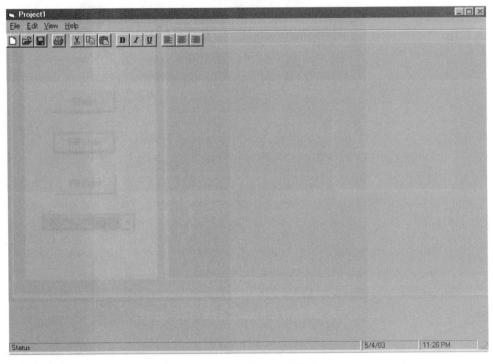

Figure 4.31: Login Screen of the SDI Application

16.   Specify the User Name and Password, and click **OK** on the **Login** dialog box. The application will be displayed, as shown in Figure 4.32.

Figure 4.32: An SDI Application

In the previous example, you created an SDI application using the Application Wizard. However, you can also create an SDI application without using the Wizard. For example, assume that you need to create an SDI application with three forms: **frmMain**, **frmModal**, and **frmModeless**.

The main form should be as shown in Figure 4.33.

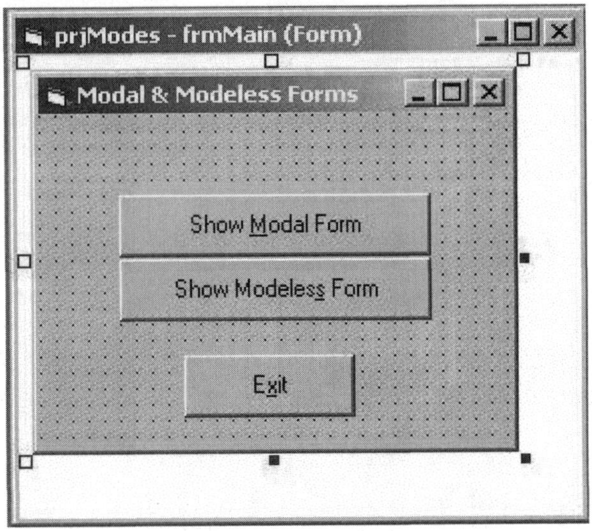

Figure 4.33: The Main Form

Add three command buttons to the main form, as shown in Figure 4.33. When the user clicks the **Show Modal Form** button, a modal form should be shown. Similarly, a modeless form should be displayed when the user clicks the **Show Modeless Form** button. The modal form should only have the **Close** button (no **Maximize** or **Minimize** buttons) and should not be sizeable. Add **Close** buttons to the two forms. In addition, you need to add code to unload all the forms when the user clicks the **Exit** button in the main form.

To create the SDI application, perform the following steps:

1.   Open a new project and name it **FormModes.vbp**.

2.   Add a new form **frmMain** to the project.

3.   Add three command buttons named **cmdModal**, **cmdModeless**, and **cmdExit** to the form.

4.   Set the **Cancel** property of the **cmdExit** button to true.

5.   Add a form named **frmModal**.

6.   Set the **Borderstyle** property of the form to 3 (Fixed Dialog).

7.   Add a command button named **cmdClose**.

8.   Add another form named **frmModeless**.

9.   Set its **Borderstyle** property to 2 (Sizable).

10.   Add a button named **cmdClose**.

11.   Add Code 4.1 to **frmMain's** Code window:

```
Private Sub cmdExit_Click()
Unload Me
End Sub
Private Sub cmdModal_Click()
   frmModal.Show vbModal
End Sub
Private Sub cmdModeless_Click()
   frmModeless.Show vbModeless
End Sub
Private Sub Form_Load()
    Top = (Screen.Height - Height) / 2
    Left = (Screen.Width - Width) / 2
End Sub
Private Sub Form_Unload(Cancel As Integer)
    Dim frm As Form
    For Each frm In Forms
Unload frm
    Next
End Sub
```

Code 4.1: The Code for frmMain

Code 4.1 handles the **Click** event of the three command buttons in frmMain, to display the modal and modeless forms and to unload itself. The **Load** event of the form is used to display the form in the middle of the screen and the unload event loops through all the forms in the Forms collection and unloads each of the forms loaded in memory.

12.   Add Code 4.2 to **frmModal's** Code window to hide it.

```
Private Sub cmdClose_Click()
    Me.Hide
End Sub
```

Code 4.2: The Code for the Close Button in frmModal

13.   Add Code 4.3 to the **frmModeless's** Code window to hide it.

```
Private Sub cmdClose_Click()
  Me.Hide
End Sub
```

Code 4.3: Code for the Close Button in frmModeless

14.   Run the application.

4.2.2 MDI Applications

Create an MDI application using the VB Application Wizard.

Unlike an SDI application, an MDI application can display multiple forms or documents at the same time. For example, in Microsoft Office applications such as Microsoft Word or Microsoft Excel, you can open more that one document at the same time.

You can also navigate between the two documents, as shown in Figure 4.34.

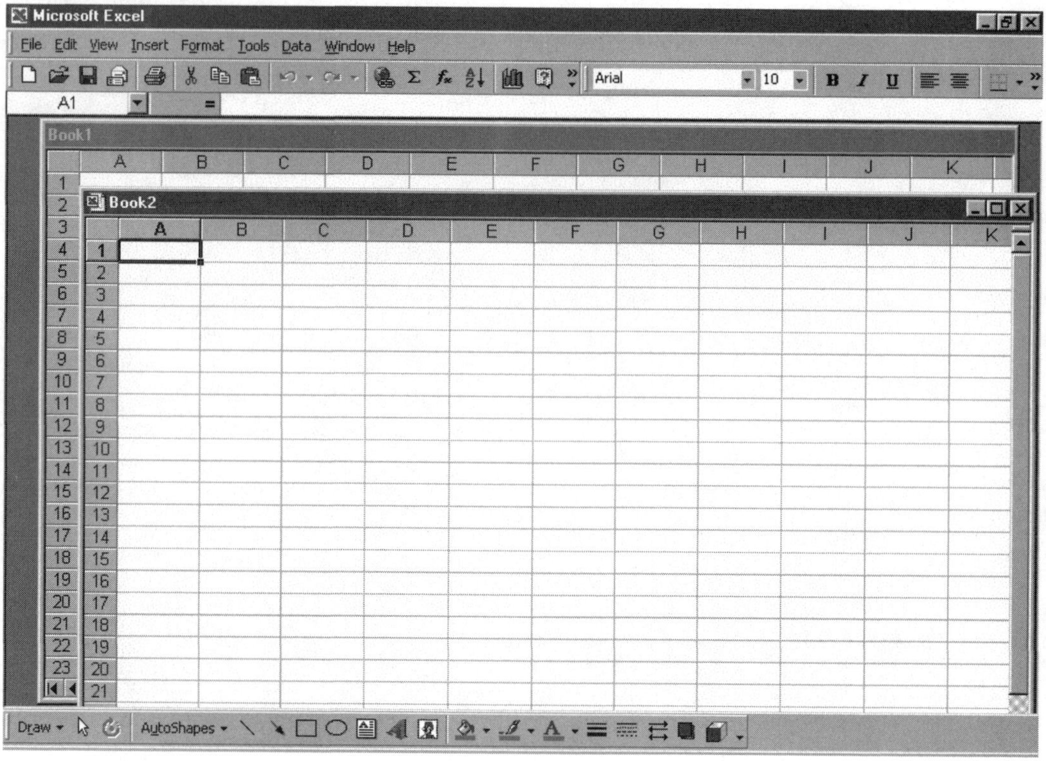

Figure 4.34: MS Excel - An MDI Application

In an MDI application, the main window is called the *parent window*. The rest of the windows, which are displayed within the main window, are called *child windows*.

You can create an MDI application using the VB Application Wizard. The steps to create MDI application using the wizard are similar to those that are involved in creating SDI applications, but you need to select the **Multiple Document Interface (MDI)** option from the **Interface Type** dialog box, as shown in Figure 4.35.

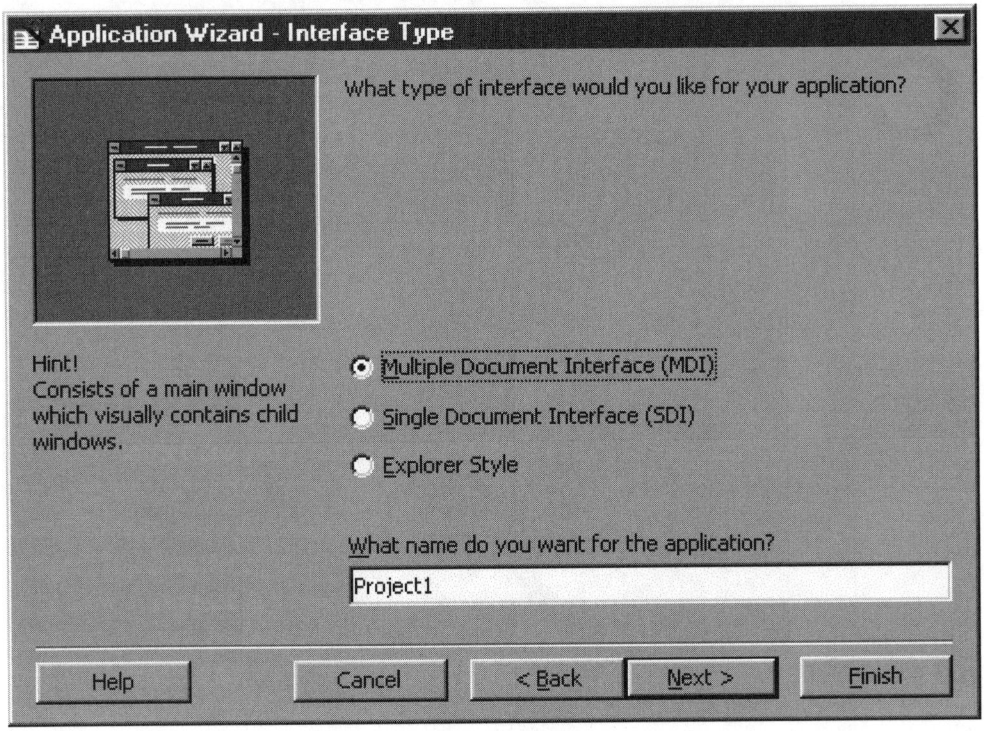

Figure 4.35: Selecting MDI from the Interface Type Dialog Box

In addition, the menus in an MDI application are displayed on the parent window and not on the child windows.

Figure 4.36 displays an MDI application created using the VB Application Wizard.

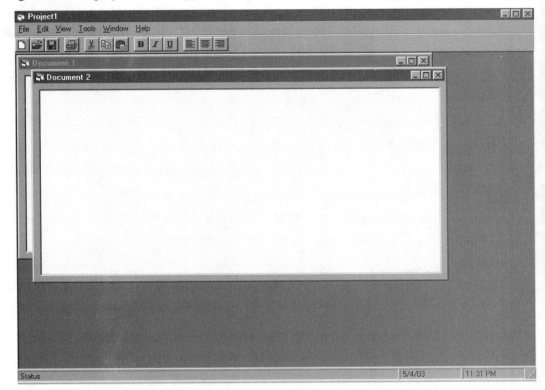

Figure 4.36: An MDI Application Created Using VB Application Wizard

You can also create an MDI application without using the VB Application Wizard.

For example, suppose you need to create an MDI application with four forms: **frmMain** (MDI parent form), **frmMainChild** (MDI child form), **frmChild** (MDI child form), and **frmModal** (non-child form).

The **frmMainChild** form should look as shown in Figure 4.37.

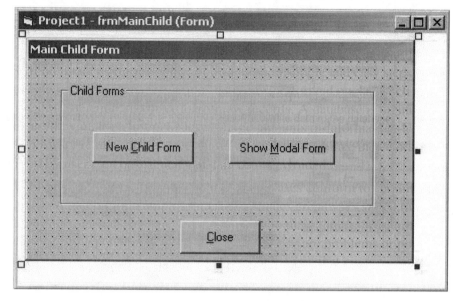

Figure 4.37: frmMainChild Form

On clicking the **New Child Form** button, a new instance of **frmChild** should be created (same as the menu option). The form should display a caption **Untitled #** (where "#" is the form's index value). The **frmChild** form should display a random shape in its body. The **Show Modal Form** button should display a modal form. Add a **Close** button to the modal form. Note that the modal form cannot be an MDI child.

The **frmModal** form should look as shown in Figure 4.38.

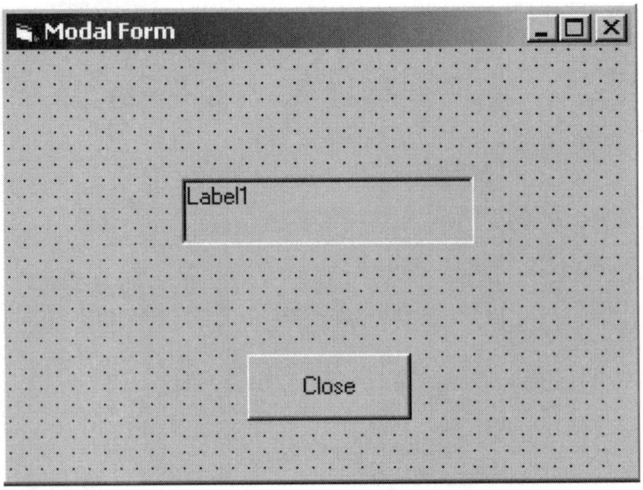

Figure 4.38: frmModal Form

To create the MDI application, perform the following steps:

1.   Open a new project and name it **MDI.vbp**.

2. Click on **Project** → **Add MDI form** to add a new MDI form **frmMain** to the project, as shown in Figure 4.39. Set its caption to "MDI Parent Form."

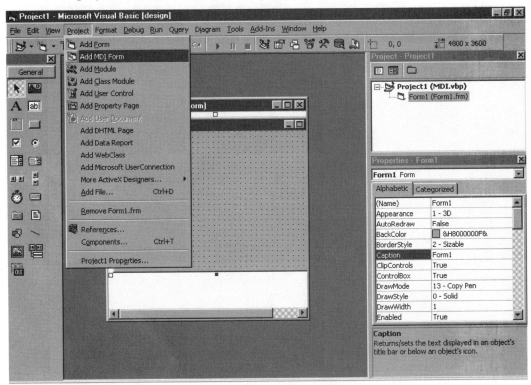

Figure 4.39: Adding a New MDI Form to the Project

3. Add two more forms named **frmMainChild** and **frmModal**. Set the **MDIChild** property of **frmMainChild** to **True**.

4.   Open the menu editor of **frmMain** and add the following menu items, as shown in Table 4.1.

Menu Title (Caption)	Menu Item (Caption)	Name	Shortcut
&File		mnuFile	(None)
	&Main Window	mnuMainChild	
	&New Child	mnuNew	Ctrl+N
	Show Modal	mnuModal	
	E&xit	mnuExit	Ctrl+Q
&Window		mnuWindow	
	Tile &Horizontally	mnuWindowTileHorizontal	
	Tile &Vertically	mnuWindowTileVertical	
	&Cascade	mnuWindowCascade	

Table 4.1: Structure of the Menu Bar in the MDI Form

5.   Add Code 4.4 to **frmMain**.

```
Option Explicit
Private Sub MDIForm_Load()
frmMainChild.Move (Me.Width - frmMainChild.Width) / 2, _
                  (Me.Height - frmMainChild.Height) / 2
   frmMainChild.Show
End Sub
Private Sub MDIForm_Unload(Cancel As Integer)
    Dim frm As Form
    For Each frm In Forms
        Unload frm
    Next
End Sub
Private Sub mnuExit_Click()
    Unload Me
End Sub
Private Sub mnuMainChild_Click()
```

```
    frmMainChild.Show
    frmMainChild.SetFocus
End Sub
Private Sub mnuModal_Click()
    frmMainChild.cmdModal_Click
End Sub
Private Sub mnuNew_Click()
    frmMainChild.cmdChild_Click
End Sub
Private Sub mnuWindowCascade_Click()
    Me.Arrange vbCascade
End Sub
Private Sub mnuWindowTileHorizontal_Click()
    Me.Arrange vbTileHorizontal
End Sub
Private Sub mnuWindowTileVertical_Click()
    Me.Arrange vbTileVertical
End Sub
```

Code 4.4: frmMain Code

In Code 4.4, the **Load** event of **frmMain** moves the form **frmMainChild** to the middle of the MDI form and displays it. The **Unload** event of **frmMain** loops through all the forms in the Forms collection and ensures that all the forms loaded in the memory are unloaded. The **Click** event of the menu item **mnuExit** is used to unload the MDI form. The **Click** event of **mnuMainChild** is used to display **frmMainChild** and make it active. The Click event of **mnuModal** is used to execute the Click event procedure of the command button, **cmdModal**, in the form **frmMainChild**. The Click event of the menu item **mnuNew** is used to execute the Click event of **cmdChild** in the **frmMainChild** form. The menu items **mnuWindowCascade**, **mnuWindowTileHorizontal**, and **mnuWindowTileVertical** are used to arrange the displayed MDI child windows on the screen.

6.	Open **frmMainChild** and add a frame with caption "Child Forms." Add two command buttons to the frame named **cmdChild** and **cmdModal**. Add a button named **cmdExit** to the form. Write the code as given in Code 4.5. The output of Code 4.5 will be as shown in Figure 4.37.

```
Option Explicit
Private Sub cmdExit_Click()
   Me.Hide
End Sub
Public Sub cmdModal_Click()
   frmModal.Show vbModal
End Sub
Public Sub cmdChild_Click()
   Static intFormIndex As Integer
   Dim frmChildForm As New frmMainChild
   intFormIndex = intFormIndex + 1
   With frmChildForm
      .Caption = "Untitled " & intFormIndex
      .Shape1.Shape = Int(Rnd * 7)
      .Show
   End With
End Sub
```

Code 4.5: Code for the Form frmMainChild

Code 4.5 handles the **Click** event of the command buttons in **frmMainChild**. The Click event of **cmdExit** is used to hide the form. The button **cmdModal** displays **frmModal** as a modal window. Displaying a form as a modal window means that while the modal form is visible, no other windows in your application can get the focus. The command button **cmdChild** maintains a static variable named **intFormIndex** in order to keep track of the number of child forms that have been displayed. Each time the **cmdChild** is clicked, it increments the value of the variable and displays a newly created instance of the form **frmChild**. The code also sets a random shape of the shape control in the newly created form.

Open **frmChild** and add a command button **cmdClose**. Add a Shape control and set its **FillStyle** property to Solid.

The form should look like Figure 4.40.

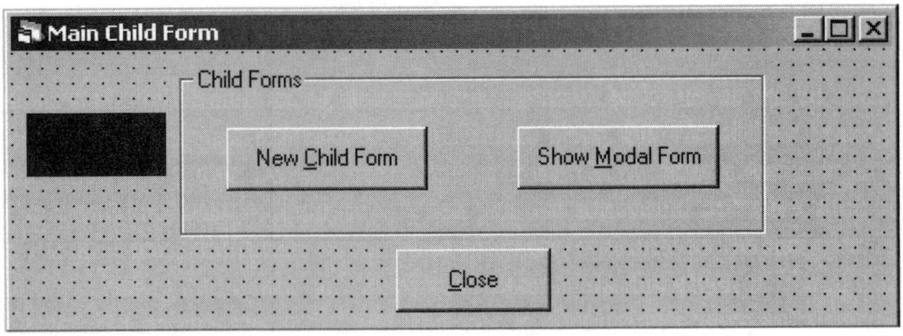

Figure 4.40: frmMainChild

Add Code 4.6 in the form's code window. The code is used to hide the form in the
Click event of the command button **cmdClose**.

```
Private Sub cmdClose_Click()
  Me.Hide
End Sub
```

Code 4.6: Code for Click Event of the Command Button cmdClose

7. Open **frmModal**. Add a button **cmdClose** and a label control **Label1** to the
    form. Set the **BorderStyle** property of Label1 to **Fixed Single**. Add Code 4.7
    to the form. The code sets the properties of the Label control during the
    form's **Load** event and hides the form whenever the **Close** button is clicked.

```
Private Sub cmdClose_Click()
  Me.Hide
End Sub
Private Sub Form_Load()
    With Label1
        .Caption = " This is a Modal Child Form "
        .AutoSize = True
        .WordWrap = True
    End With
End Sub
```

Code 4.7: The Code for frmModal

8.   Run the application.

Now, let us consider an example involving the design of the main interface of an inventory control system for a department store. The department store procures items from various suppliers and then sells them to its customers. The activities of the Store, Sales, and Admin departments are:

- The Store department enters the details of the items being sold on a daily basis. It also maintains the details of items in stock, tracks the reorder level and reorder details, creates purchase orders for various items, and tracks the supply of items from the suppliers.

- The Sales department enters details of sales, tracks available items including their rates and quantities available, and prints invoices.

- The Admin department monitors all the activities of the department store. It handles the details regarding the inclusion and the exclusion of items from the store, rates of the items, registration of the suppliers, manages the details of the various registered suppliers, sales being made during specific intervals, generates administrative reports, and keeps track of payments.

Thus, there will be at least three different interfaces to enable automation to all store departments, Admin, Store, and Sales. Since the Store and Sales departments manage simple and limited tasks, an SDI interface is appropriate for both these departments. This will help the sales and the store personnel, who are usually novice computer users, to utilize the application efficiently. The Admin department interface can be implemented as an MDI interface. This will make the software appear more organized with the help of menus and toolbars. At the same time, the details can be displayed in appropriate child windows allowing the user to have a comprehensive comparison of the output.

This approach is applicable in the present example, while it may not be applicable for an inventory control system with more complex functionality. The design of an interface is completely customized per the requirement of the system and the profile of the user.

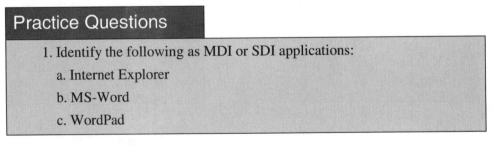

Practice Questions

1. Identify the following as MDI or SDI applications:

    a. Internet Explorer

    b. MS-Word

    c. WordPad

d. Visual Basic

2. List the differences between an SDI and an MDI application.

3. What are the steps to create an SDI application using the Visual Basic Application wizard?

4. Explain the advantages of using MDI applications.

Case Study

Continuing the design and development of the Library Management System created in the previous chapters, the following section provides the main interface and menu of the system. The Library Management System will be a menu-driven MDI application. This section explains the development of the MDI form and some child forms.

1. Open the project named **LibraryMgmt,** created in Chapter 3 "Working with Forms and Controls."

2. Add an MDI form to the project by clicking **Project → Add MDI Form**. Set the properties of the MDI form as given in Table 4.2.

Property	Value
Name	frmMain
Caption	Library Management System

Table 4.2: Properties of the MDI Form

3. Set the **MDIChild** property of **frmBooks**, **frmAddMember**, and **frmSearchMember** to **True**.

4. Use the Menu Editor to create the menu system in **frmMain** as given in Table 4.3.

Caption		Name	Shortcut Key
Menu Title	Menu Item		
Library		mnuLibrary	
	Book Details	mnuBooks	
-		mnuSep1	
	Issue Book	mnuIssueBook	Ctrl+N
	Book Return Info	mnuBookReturn	
-		mnuSep2	
	Exit	mnuExit	Ctrl+Q
Members		mnuMembers	
	Add New Member	mnuAddMember	Ctrl+M
	Modify Member Details	mnuModifyMember	
-		mnuSep3	
	Search Member	mnuSearchMember	Ctrl+F
Reports		mnuReports	
	Book List	mnuBookList	
	Currently Issued Books	mnuCurrentlyIssuedBooks	
	Member List	mnuMemberList	
	Defaulter's List	mnuDefaulters	
Users		mnuUsers	
Add New User		mnuAddUser	
-		mnuSep4	
	Change Password	mnuChangePassword	
Window		mnuWindow	
	Cascade	mnuCascade	
	Tile Horizontally	mnuTileHorizontally	
	Tile Vertically	mnuTileVertically	

Help		mnuHelp	
	About Library Management System	mnuAboutSystem	F4
	-	mnuSep5	
	About Us	mnuAboutUs	

Table 4.3: Details of Menu Titles and Menu Items to Create the Menu System

5.   In the Menu Editor, select the menu named **mnuWindow** and select the check box for **WindowList** property as shown in Figure 4.41. It enables this menu to display the names of all opened windows during run time.

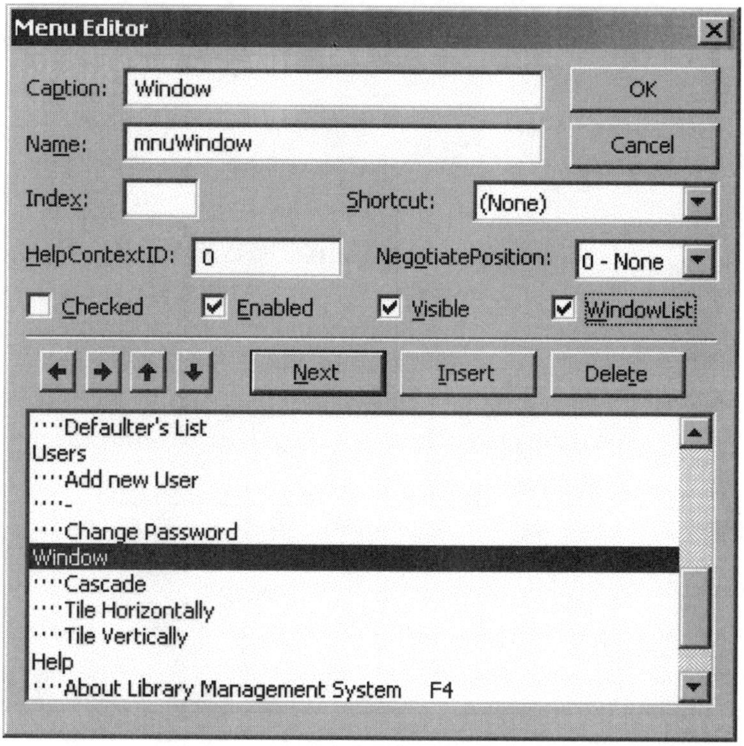

Figure 4.41: Selecting the Check Box for WindowList Property

Figure 4.42 displays the run time view of **frmMain**.

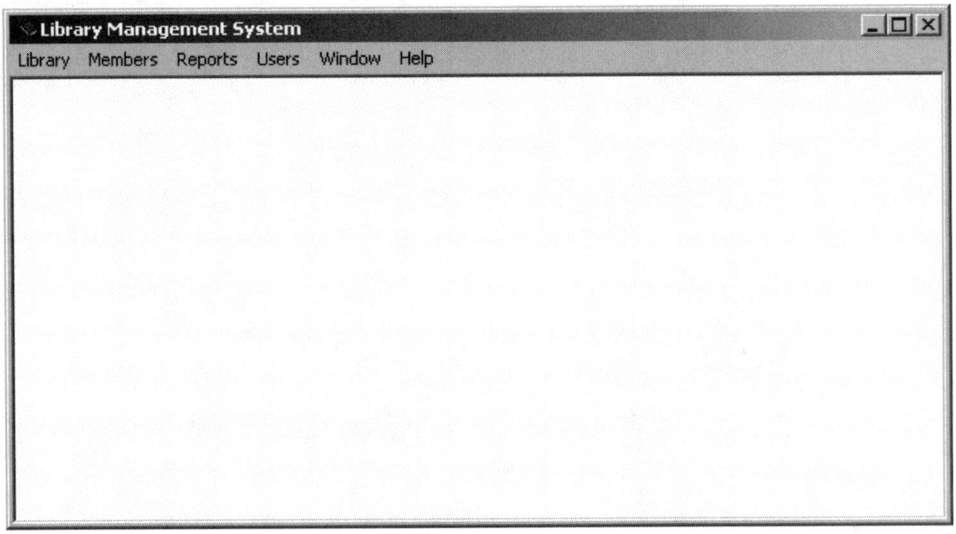

Figure 4.42: Run Time View of frmMain

6.   Add Code 4.8 to **frmMain**. The code implements the **Click** event of the menu items **mnuAddMember**, **mnuBooks**, and **mnuSearchMember** to display the respective forms. It also provides the implementation of the **Click** event of the menu items **mnuCascade**, **mnuTileHorizontally**, and **mnuTileVertically** to arrange the child windows of **frmMain**. The **Unload** event of the form is also implemented to prompt for the user's confirmation before exiting the application.

```
Private Sub MDIForm_Unload(Cancel As Integer)
  If MsgBox("Are you sure to exit the application", _
        vbQuestion + vbYesNo, "Confirm Exit") = vbNo Then
    Cancel = 1
  End If
End Sub
Private Sub mnuAddMember_Click()
  frmAddMember.Show
  frmAddMember.SetFocus
End Sub
Private Sub mnuBooks_Click()
  frmBooks.Show
```

```
        frmBooks.SetFocus
End Sub


Private Sub mnuSearchMember_Click()
   frmSearchMember.Show
   frmSearchMember.SetFocus
End Sub


Private Sub mnuCascade_Click()
   Me.Arrange vbCascade
End Sub


Private Sub mnuExit_Click()
   Unload Me
End Sub


Private Sub mnuTileHorizontally_Click()
   Me.Arrange vbTileHorizontal
End Sub
Private Sub mnuTileVertically_Click()
   Me.Arrange vbTileVertical
End Sub
```

Code 4.8: Click Event of the Menu Items

7.   Add a new form to the project and set the properties as given in Table 4.4.
      This form will be used to accept the information regarding the issue of a
      book.

Property	Value
Name	frmIssueBook
Caption	Issue Book
BorderStyle	Fixed Single
MDIChild	True

Table 4.4: Properties of the Project

8.　　　Add controls to the form, **frmIssueBook**, as shown in Figure 4.43.

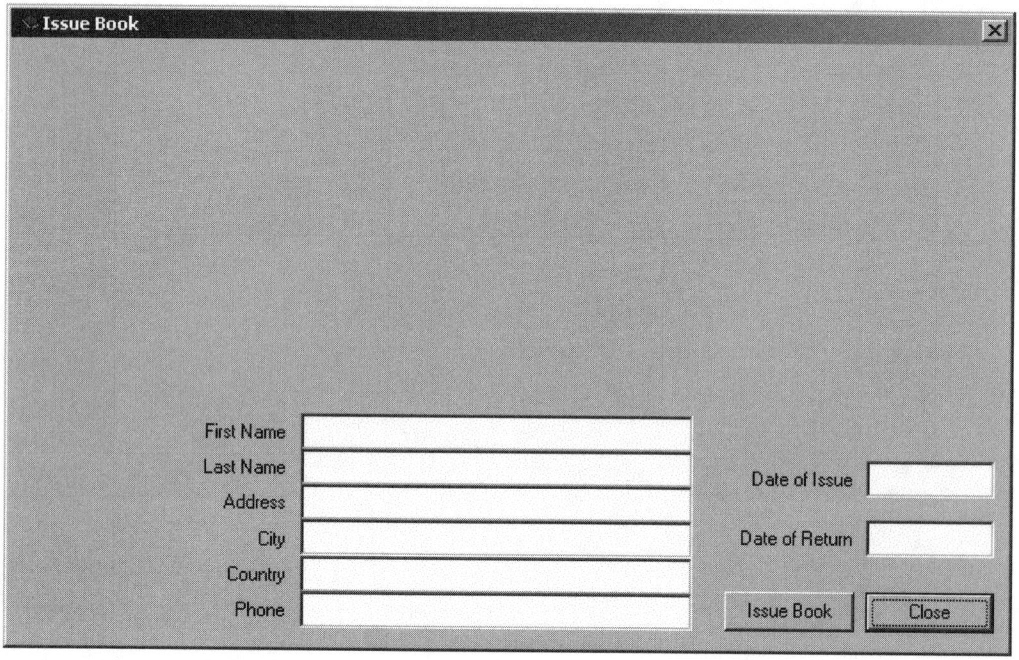

Figure 4.43: Run Time View of frmIssueBook

9.　　　Set the properties of the controls in the form as given in the Table 4.5.

Control Type	Name	Caption Property	Index
Label control	lblFieldLabel	First Name	1
Label control	lblFieldLabel	Last Name	2
Label control	lblFieldLabel	Address	3
Label control	lblFieldLabel	City	4
Label control	lblFieldLabel	Country	5
Label control	lblFieldLabel	Phone	6
Label control	lblIssueDate	Date of Issue	
Label control	lblReturnDate	Date of Return	
TextBox control	txtFirstName		
TextBox control	txtLastName		
TextBox control	txtAddress		

TextBox control	txtCity		
TextBox control	txtCountry		
TextBox control	txtPhone		
TextBox control	txtIssueDate		
TextBox control	txtReturnDate		
CommandButton control	cmdIssueBook		
CommandButton control	cmdClose		

Table 4.5: Properties of the Controls in the Form

10. Make all the text box controls read-only by setting their **Locked** properties to **True**.

11. Add Code 4.9 for the **Form Load** event of the form. It sets the top-left position of the form for display and fills the text box controls for **issue date** and **date of return**. The **issue date** is set to the current date and the **return date** is set to the date seven days after the current date. A book is issued for a period of one week.

```
Private Sub Form_Load()
  Me.Top = 120
  Me.Left = 120
  Me.txtIssueDate = Date
  Me.txtReturnDate = Date + 7
End Sub
```

Code 4.9: Code for Form Load Event

12. Add Code 4.10 for the Click event of the command button **cmdClose**.

```
Private Sub cmdClose_Click()
  Unload Me
End Sub
```

Code 4.10: Click Event of the Command Button cmdClose

13.   Add another form to the project and set its properties as given in Table 4.6. This form will be used to modify the details of the existing members of the Library.

Property	Value
Name	frmModifyMember
Caption	Modify Member Details
BorderStyle	Fixed Single
MDIChild	True

Table 4.6: Project Properties of the New Form

14.   Add controls to **frmModifyMember**, as shown in Figure 4.44.

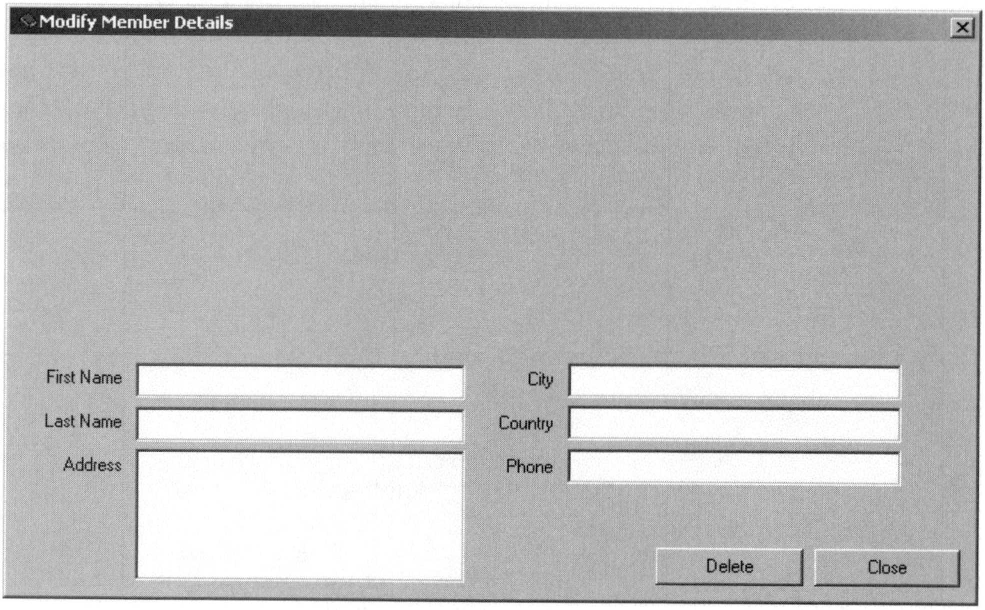

Figure 4.44: Form frmModifyMember with Controls

15.   Set the properties of the controls in the form as specified in Table 4.7.

Control Type	Name	Caption / MaxLength Property	Index
Label control	lblFieldLabel	First Name	1
Label control	lblFieldLabel	Last Name	2
Label control	lblFieldLabel	Address	3
Label control	lblFieldLabel	City	4
Label control	lblFieldLabel	Country	5
Label control	lblFieldLabel	Phone	6
Label control	lblIssueDate	Date of Issue	
Label control	lblReturnDate	Date of Return	
TextBox control	txtFirstName	20	
TextBox control	txtLastName	20	
TextBox control	txtAddress	100	
TextBox control	txtCity	30	
TextBox control	txtCountry	20	
TextBox control	txtPhone	20	
CommandButton control	cmdDelete	Delete	
CommandButton control	cmdCloseForm	Close	

Table 4.7: Properties of the Controls in the Form

16.   Set the **MultiLine** property of **txtAddress** to **True**.

17.   Add Code 4.11 for the **Load** event of the form.

```
Private Sub Form_Load()
  Me.Top = 120
  Me.Left = 120
End Sub
```

Code 4.11: Load Event of the Form

18.   Add Code 4.12 for the **Click** event of **cmdCloseForm**.

```
Private Sub cmdCloseForm_Click()
  Unload Me
End Sub
```

Code 4.12: Click Event of cmdCloseForm

19.   Add Code 4.13 for the **KeyPress** event of the TextBox controls to
        prevent invalid input.

```
Private Sub txtFirstName_KeyPress(KeyAscii As Integer)
  If Not (KeyAscii >= Asc("A") And KeyAscii <= Asc("Z")) And _
      Not (KeyAscii >= Asc("a") And KeyAscii <= Asc("z")) And _
      Not KeyAscii = vbKeyBack And KeyAscii <> vbKeySpace Then

    KeyAscii = 0
  End If
End Sub


Private Sub txtLastName_KeyPress(KeyAscii As Integer)
  If Not (KeyAscii >= Asc("A") And KeyAscii <= Asc("Z")) And _
      Not (KeyAscii >= Asc("a") And KeyAscii <= Asc("z")) And _
      Not KeyAscii = vbKeyBack And KeyAscii <> vbKeySpace Then

    KeyAscii = 0
  End If
End Sub


Private Sub txtCity_KeyPress(KeyAscii As Integer)
  If Not (KeyAscii >= Asc("A") And KeyAscii <= Asc("Z")) And _
      Not (KeyAscii >= Asc("a") And KeyAscii <= Asc("z")) And _
      Not KeyAscii = vbKeyBack And KeyAscii <> vbKeySpace Then

    KeyAscii = 0
  End If
End Sub
```

```
Private Sub txtCountry_KeyPress(KeyAscii As Integer)
  If Not (KeyAscii >= Asc("A") And KeyAscii <= Asc("Z")) And _
     Not (KeyAscii >= Asc("a") And KeyAscii <= Asc("z")) And _
     Not KeyAscii = vbKeyBack And KeyAscii <> vbKeySpace Then

    KeyAscii = 0
  End If
End Sub


Private Sub txtPhone_KeyPress(KeyAscii As Integer)
  If Not IsNumeric(Chr(KeyAscii)) And KeyAscii <> vbKeyBack _
    And KeyAscii <> Asc("-") Then

    KeyAscii = 0
  End If
End Sub
```

Code 4.13: Code for the KeyPress Event of the TextBox Controls

20.   Save the project.

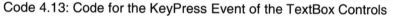

Summary

- A menu offers a convenient and consistent way to group commands so that users can easily access them.

- You can create a menu for a form. Visual Basic provides the Menu Editor that helps you design menus for your applications.

- You can create a tree structure of the menu items in an application.

- Menu Editor provides the user interface to designate names to the menu controls, use captions to display those controls, and define submenu options.

- Visual Basic allows you to simultaneously display multiple forms in separate windows.

- There are two types of interfaces for an application, the Single Document Interface (SDI) and the Multiple Document Interface (MDI).

- An SDI application contains a single document window. For example, WordPad is an SDI application in which you can open only one document at a time.

- Visual Basic's Application Wizard helps you to create an application using one of the predefined interfaces; namely SDI and MDI.

- You can also create SDI and MDI applications without using the VB Application Wizard.

- An MDI application can display multiple forms or documents at the same time.

- In an MDI application, the main window is called the parent window. The rest of the windows are called child windows.

References

- http://www.library.itt-tech.edu/periodicals.asp > FindArticles.com (Accessed on Aug. 12, 2004)
- http://www.library.itt-tech.edu/periodicals.asp > MSDN Magazine (Accessed on Aug. 12, 2004)
- http://www.microsoft.com

Homework Exercises

1. Write a code snippet for the Unload event to unload all forms present in a project from a main form.

2. Add the following features to the Text Editor you create in Lab Exercise 1:

    - Add code for the **Cut, Copy, Paste, and Delete** menu items. (Use the Clipboard methods).

    - Disable the **Cut** and **Delete** button in the toolbar when the form is loaded. Check for any text in the clipboard and enable or disable the **Paste** button accordingly.

    - Add an **About** Dialog box to the project.

    - Add code for the text box control. When the user selects the text, the **Cut** and **Delete** buttons must be enabled, at all other times, they should be disabled.

3. Create an SDI application with the following two forms:

    - The first form should be a **Login** form that asks the user's name and password. On authenticating them, the user must be allowed to continue. Only three attempts should be given to the user to enter the correct password. Exit the application on login failure.

    - The second form should open when the user logs in. The Resize buttons should resize or move the window by a certain amount (around 50 twips). The **Open Command Prompt** button should open the Command Prompt window. The six buttons below the textbox should change the properties of the text in the textbox according to their captions.

The second form is displayed in Figure 4.45.

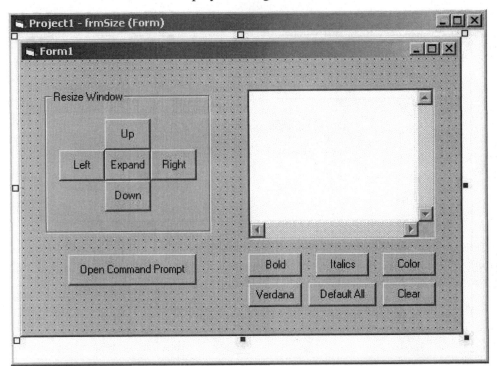

Figure 4.45: View of Second Form

4. Create an MDI application with three forms. **frmMDI** is the parent MDI form. **frmFreehand** and **frmPrefs** are two child forms. The MDI form's menu should have two items to open the child windows and an exit option. The window menu should have options to tile the windows vertically, horizontally, or cascade them. It should also have a window list.

- The **frmFreehand** form should have a picture box in which the user can draw freehand drawings. Add a **Clear** button to clear the picture box, and a **Close** button to close the window. Figure 4.46 shows a sample of the application. Display the current mouse coordinates in a label.

Figure 4.46 Freehand Drawing

- The **frmPrefs** form, as shown below, should have a tabbed dialog control with two tabs, **Style** and **Orientation**. The user should be able to change these properties of the control by selecting the option buttons, as shown in Figure 4.47. Use true-type fonts for proper display and use an array of control buttons for the **Orientation** property.

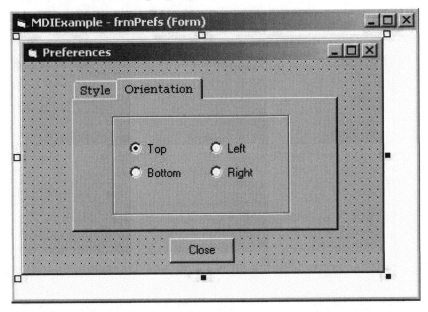

Figure 4.47: Form with Array of Option Buttons

Lab Exercises

Exercise 1

Objective

■ Add menus to a form by using the Menu Editor.

Problem Statement

Create a menu for a simple text editor application. The menu should have the following features:

■ File
- New
- Open
- Save
- Print
- Exit

■ Edit
- Cut
- Copy
- Paste
- Delete

■ View
- Show Toolbar (checked when toolbar is visible, unchecked otherwise)

■ Help
- Help On
- About

Add proper keyboard shortcuts for the menu items and index the subitems of each menu.

Add a module to store the index constants used by the menu items. For example, if you set the **File→New** option's index to 10, add the following line to the module:

Public Const FILE_NEW = 10

Add a **Multiline** textbox with scrollbars, which can be used as a text editor. Add a label below the textbox that displays messages to the user when a menu item is selected. Add a toolbar with buttons corresponding to the menu items and an image list control to store the toolbar icons. Add handlers for the menus' **Click** events (Hint: Use "Select Case Index" for each menu's handler) and display the information of the button clicked in the label below the textbox. Your form should look like the one in Figure 4.48.

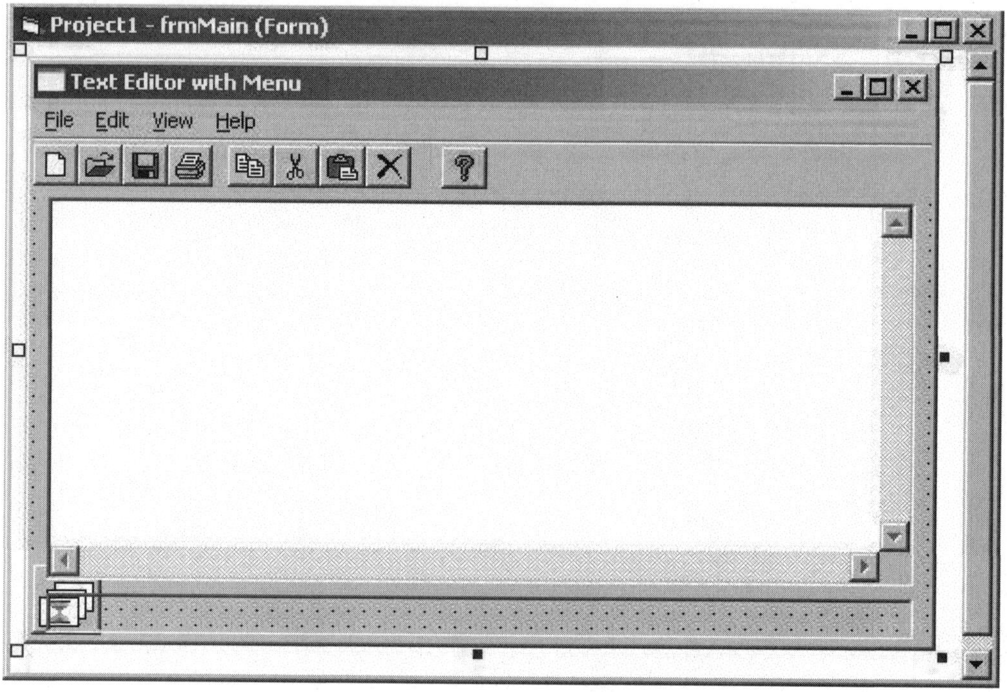

Figure 4.48: Text Editor with Menu

Lab Setup

Computer Requirements:

- Microsoft Windows Operating System
- Pentium III or higher processors
- 128-MB RAM
- 3-GB of hard disk space
- CD-ROM drives

- Floppy disk drives
- LAN connections
- Visual Basic 6.0
- Microsoft Access

Procedure

1. Open a new project and name it Menu.vbp.
2. Add a new form **frmMain** to the project.
3. Add a module modMenuConst.bas to the project.
4. Right-click on the form and select "Menu Editor...."
5. Add menu items and set their properties as shown in Table 4.8.

Caption	Name	Name of the Parent Menu	Index	Shortcut
&File	mnuFile	(None)		(None)
&New...	mnuFileItem	mnuFile	10	Ctrl+N
&Open...	mnuFileItem	mnuFile	20	Ctrl+O
&Save	mnuFileItem	mnuFile	30	Ctrl+S
-	mnuFileItem	mnuFile	35	
&Print...	mnuFileItem	mnuFile	40	Ctrl+P
-	mnuFileItem	mnuFile	45	
E&xit	mnuFileItem	mnuFile	50	Ctrl+Q
&Edit	mnuEdit	(none)		(None)
Cu&t	mnuEditItem	mnuEdit	10	Ctrl+X
&Copy	mnuEditItem	mnuEdit	20	Ctrl+C
&Paste	mnuEditItem	mnuEdit	30	Ctrl+V
&Delete	mnuEditItem	mnuEdit	40	Del
&View	mnuView	(none)		(None)
&Show Toolbar	mnuViewItem	mnuView	10	Ctrl+T
&Help	mnuHelp	(none)		(None)
&Help on...	mnuHelpItem	mnuHelp	10	F1

-	mnuHelpItem	mnuHelp	15	
&About	mnuHelpItem	mnuHelp	20	Ctrl+A

Table 4.8: Properties of the Menu Items

6. Ensure you have added the MS Windows Common Controls 6.0 (SP6) to your Toolbox. Then, add an image list control named **imlToolbar** and add nine, 16 X 16 icons as shown in the form's figure.

7. Add a toolbar control and name it **tbrMain**. Set its image list property to **imlToolbar** and add nine buttons with their key values set as **New, Open, Save, Print, Cut, Copy, Paste, Delete, and Help**. Set corresponding icons from the imagelist. Ensure you are using Bitmap graphics. These key values are used to identify the clicked item in the toolbar's **Click** event.

8. Add Code 4.14 to the module modMenuConst.bas. It declares constants associated with the index value of the appropriate menu items as shown in the table in Step 5. These constants are used in the Click event procedure of the respective menu arrays.

```
Option Explicit


Public Const VIEW_TOOLBAR = 10


Public Const FILE_NEW = 10
Public Const FILE_OPEN = 20
Public Const FILE_SAVE = 30
Public Const FILE_PRINT = 40
Public Const FILE_EXIT = 50


Public Const EDIT_CUT = 10
Public Const EDIT_COPY = 20
Public Const EDIT_PASTE = 30
Public Const EDIT_DELETE = 40


Public Const HELP_HELP = 10
Public Const HELP_ABOUT = 20
```

Code 4.14: Code for the Module modMenuConst

9. Add Code 4.15 to the mnuFileItem's **Click** event. The code checks the index of the menu item being clicked in the menu array mnuFileItem against the constants declared in Step 8 and updates the label control named **lblMessage** displaying the description of the task that can be performed by clicking the menu item.

```
Private Sub mnuFileItem_Click(Index As Integer)


Select Case Index
Case FILE_NEW
lblMessage.Caption = "Open a New File"
Case FILE_OPEN


lblMessage.Caption = "Open an Existing File"
Case FILE_SAVE
lblMessage.Caption = "Save the Current File"
Case FILE_PRINT
lblMessage.Caption = "Print the Current File"
Case FILE_EXIT
Unload Me
End Select
End Sub
```

Code 4.15: Click Event of mnuFileItem

10. Add Code 4.16 to the mnuEditItem's **Click** event. The code performs the same task as in Step 9 for the menu items in the menu array mnuEditItem.

```
Private Sub mnuEditItem_Click(Index As Integer)
On Error Resume Next
Select Case Index
Case EDIT_COPY
lblMessage.Caption = "Text Copied to Clipboard"
Case EDIT_CUT
lblMessage.Caption = "Text Stored in Clipboard"
Case EDIT_PASTE
lblMessage.Caption = "Text Pasted from Clipboard"
Case EDIT_DELETE
```

```
lblMessage.Caption = "Selected Text Deleted"
End Select
End Sub
```

Code 4.16: Click Event of mnuEditItem

11.   Add Code 4.17 to the mnuHelpItem's Click event to perform the same task as in Step 10 for the menu items in the menu array mnuHelpItem.

```
Private Sub mnuHelpItem_Click(Index As Integer)
 Select Case Index
Case HELP_HELPON
lblMessage.Caption = "Display Help for the Application"
Case HELP_ABOUT
lblMessage.Caption = "About this Application"
End Select
End Sub
```

Code 4.17: Click Event of mnuHelpItem

12.   Add Code 4.18 to tbrMain's ButtonClick event. The code checks the key of the button to determine the button being clicked. Since the buttons in the toolbar are just a representation of certain commands in the menu bar, instead of rewriting the code to perform the tasks, it executes the **Click** event procedure of the respective menu item based on the button being clicked.

```
Private Sub tbrMain_ButtonClick(ByVal Button As
ComctlLib.Button)
Select Case Button.Key
Case "New"
mnuFileItem_Click FILE_NEW
Case "Open"
mnuFileItem_Click FILE_OPEN
Case "Save"
mnuFileItem_Click FILE_SAVE
Case "Print"
mnuFileItem_Click FILE_PRINT
Case "Copy"'
mnuEditItem_Click EDIT_COPY
```

```
Case "Cut"
mnuEditItem_Click EDIT_CUT
Case "Paste"
mnuEditItem_Click EDIT_PASTE
Case "Delete"
mnuEditItem_Click EDIT_DELETE
Case "Help"
mnuHelpItem_Click HELP_HELP
End Select
End Sub
```

Code 4.18: Code for tbrMain's ButtonClick event

13.   Add Code 4.19 to the form's Unload event. Here you do not need to call
        Unload Me as it would be called from the menu's Exit button.

```
Private Sub Form_Unload(Cancel As Integer)
Set frmMain = Nothing
End Sub
```

Code 4.19: Code for Form's Unload Event

Conclusion/Observation

In this exercise, you learned how to create menus by using the Menu Editor in Visual
Basic. This exercise helped you learn how to add keyboard shortcuts for menu items
and index submenus. You also learned how to add a toolbar to a form that contains
certain commands used in a menu bar.

Lab Activity Checklist

S. No.	Tasks	Completed	
		Yes	No
1.	The menu bar is added to the application as specified in the Problem Statement		
2.	A toolbar is provided for the common options of the menu bar		
3.	Appropriate code is implemented to provide the functionality		

Exercise 2

Objective

▪ Create an MDI application.

Problem Statement

Create an MDI application with three forms: a new MDI parent form named MDIShapes, and two MDI child forms named frmTools and frmShape. The form frmTools should look as shown in Figure 4.49.

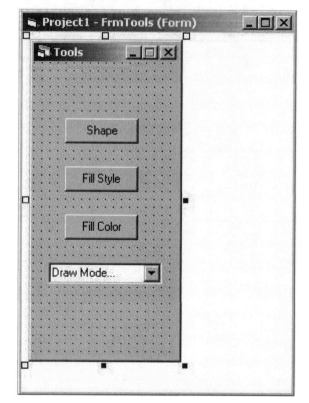

Figure 4.49: frmTools Form

The user should be able to change the Shape, FillStyle, FillColor, and DrawMode of the Shape control in the form frmShape, as shown in Figure 4.50. (Give a few colors to the FillColor button). The DrawMode ComboBox should display all the available draw modes of the shape control.

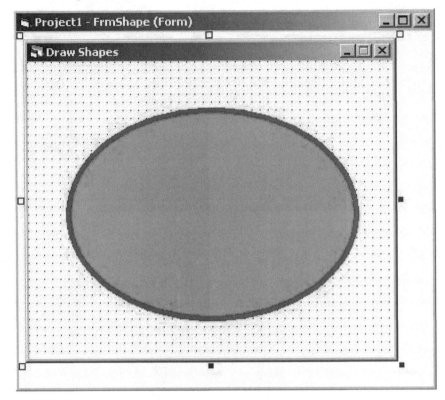

Figure 4.50: Shape Control in the Form frmShape

Add code to adjust both the child forms in the parent window properly. Remove their maximize buttons. When the user clicks on the frmShape form and drags the mouse, the shape should be sized accordingly (Hint: Use the MouseDown and MouseMove events to achieve the elastic nature of the shape).

In the MDI parent form:

- Add a File menu with an Exit button to unload all forms.
- Add a Tools menu to change Shape, FillStyle, and Fillcolor of the shape control.
- Add a Help menu with About and Help Contents.

Lab Setup

Computer Requirements:

- Microsoft Windows Operating System
- Pentium III or higher processors
- 128-MB RAM
- 3-GB of hard disk space
- CD-ROM drives
- Floppy disk drives
- LAN connections
- Visual Basic 6.0
- Microsoft Access

Procedure

1. Open a new project and name it MDIDemo.vbp.

2. Add a new module to the form and add Code 4.20 in the General Declaration section to declare two objects from the two MDI child forms frmTools and frmShape.

```
Public Toolbar As New FrmTools
Public Shapes As New FrmShape
```

Code 4.20: Code for General Declaration

3. Create the menu system as given Table 4.9:

Caption	Name
&File	mnuFile
E&xit	mnuExit
&Tools	mnuTools
Change &Shape	mnuShape
Change &Fillstyle	mnuFillstyle
Change &Color	mnuColor
&Help	mnuHelp

&About MDIApp	mnuAboutMDIApp
&Help Contents	mnuHelpContents

Table 4.9: Details of Menu Titles for Exercise 2

4.   Add Code 4.21 to the MDI parent form MDIShapes.

```
Private Sub MDIForm_Load( )
MDIShapes.Width = Screen.Width * (5 / 8)
Toolbar.Show
Shapes.Show
End Sub
Private Sub mnuColor_Click()
Toolbar.CmdColor_Click
End Sub
Private Sub mnuExit_Click()
For Each frm In Forms
Unload frm
Next
End Sub
Private Sub mnuExit_Click()
For Each frm In Forms
Unload frm
Next
End Sub
Private Sub mnuFillstyle_Click()
Toolbar.Cmdfillstyle_Click
End Sub
Private Sub mnuShape_Click()
Toolbar.Cmdshape_Click
End Sub
```

Code 4.21: Code for MDI Parent Form MDIShapes

In Code 4.21, the Form Load event of the MDIForm manipulates the width of the screen to set the width of the MDI form. It then displays its two child windows using the two objects declared in Step 2. The Unload event loops through all the forms in the Forms collection and unloads the currently loaded forms from memory. The code also handles the Click event of the menu items mnuColor, mnuFillStyle, and mnuShape.

5.   Add Code 4.22 to the form frmShape.

```
Private Sub Form_Load()
Left = MDIShapes.Left + MDIShapes.Width / 4
Width = MDIShapes.Width * (3 / 5)
    Top = MDIShapes.Top
    Height = MDIShapes.Height * (3 / 4)
    MousePointer = vbCrosshair
End Sub
Private Sub Form_MouseDown(Button As Integer, Shift As Integer,
X As Single, Y As Single)
    Shape1.Height = 0
    Shape1.Width = 0
    Shape1.Left = X
    Shape1.Top = Y
End Sub
Private Sub Form_MouseMove(Button As Integer, Shift As Integer,
X As Single, Y As Single)
    If Button = vbLeftButton Then
      If X > Shape1.Left And Y > Shape1.Top Then
        Shape1.Width = X - Shape1.Left
        Shape1.Height = Y - Shape1.Top
      End If
    End If
End Sub
```

Code 4.22: Code for Form frmShape

In Code 4.22, the Form Load event sets the position along with the width and height of the form with respect to the dimension of the MDI form and sets the mouse pointer of the form.

6. Add Code 4.23 to the form frmTools.

```
Option Explicit
Dim intShapeval As Integer
Dim intFill_style As Integer
Dim intBorder As Integer
Private Sub CmbDrawmode_Click()
Debug.Print CmbDrawmode.ListIndex
' list index starts from 0, so you add 1 to get actual index
Shapes.Shape1.DrawMode = CmbDrawmode.ListIndex + 1
End Sub
Private Sub Form_Load()
Top = MDIShapes.Top
Left = MDIShapes.Left
Width = MDIShapes.Width / 4
Height = MDIShapes.Height * (3 / 4)
intShapeval = 0
intFillcol = 1
intBorder = 0
fillcombo
End Sub
Private Sub fillcombo()
CmbDrawmode.AddItem ("1,   Blackness      ")
CmbDrawmode.AddItem ("2,   Not Merge Pen ")
CmbDrawmode.AddItem ("3,   Mask Not Pen   ")
CmbDrawmode.AddItem ("4,   Not Copy Pen   ")
CmbDrawmode.AddItem ("5,   Mask Pen Not   ")
CmbDrawmode.AddItem ("6,   Invert         ")
CmbDrawmode.AddItem ("7,   Xor Pen        ")
CmbDrawmode.AddItem ("8,   Not Mask Pen   ")
CmbDrawmode.AddItem ("9,   Mask Pen       ")
CmbDrawmode.AddItem ("10, Not Xor Pen    ")
CmbDrawmode.AddItem ("11, Nop            ")
CmbDrawmode.AddItem ("12, Merge Not      ")
CmbDrawmode.AddItem ("13, Copy Pen       ")
CmbDrawmode.AddItem ("14, Merge Pen Not ")
```

```
CmbDrawmode.AddItem ("15, Merge Pen     ")
CmbDrawmode.AddItem ("16,  Whiteness     ")
End Sub
Public Sub CmdColor_Click()
If intFillcol = 1 Then
Shapes.Shape1.FillColor = &HFF00&
ElseIf intFillcol = 2 Then
Shapes.Shape1.FillColor = &HF0F0&
ElseIf intFillcol = 3 Then
Shapes.Shape1.FillColor = &HFFFF80
ElseIf intFillcol = 4 Then
Shapes.Shape1.FillColor = &HFF&
ElseIf intFillcol = 5 Then
Shapes.Shape1.FillColor = &HF&
intFillcol = 0
End If
intFillcol = intFillcol + 1
End Sub
Public Sub Cmdshape_Click()
If intShapeval < 5 Then
intShapeval = intShapeval + 1
Else
intShapeval = 0
End If
Shapes.Shape1.Shape = intShapeval
 End Sub
Public Sub Cmdfillstyle_Click()
If intFill_style < 7 Then
intFill_style = intFill_style + 1
Else
intFill_style = 0
 End If
Shapes.Shape1.FillStyle = intFill_style
End Sub
```

Code 4.23: Code for Form frmTools

Code 4.23 controls the display of the Shape control in the form frmShape. The four variables at the beginning keep track of the shape type, fill color, fill style, and border style. The Form Load event sets the dimension and position of the form, initializes the variables, and calls the procedure fillcombo to populate the combo box for DrawMode. The Click event of the DrawMode combo box has been implemented so that the shape control in the form frmShape is updated with the selected DrawMode value. The command button cmdColor is used to change the FillColor property of the shape control in the form frmShapes with five different values. The command button cmdShape is used to change the shape displayed in the form frmShape. The Click event of the command button cmdfillstyle is used to change the FillStyle property of the shape control.

A run time view of the application is shown in Figure 4.51.

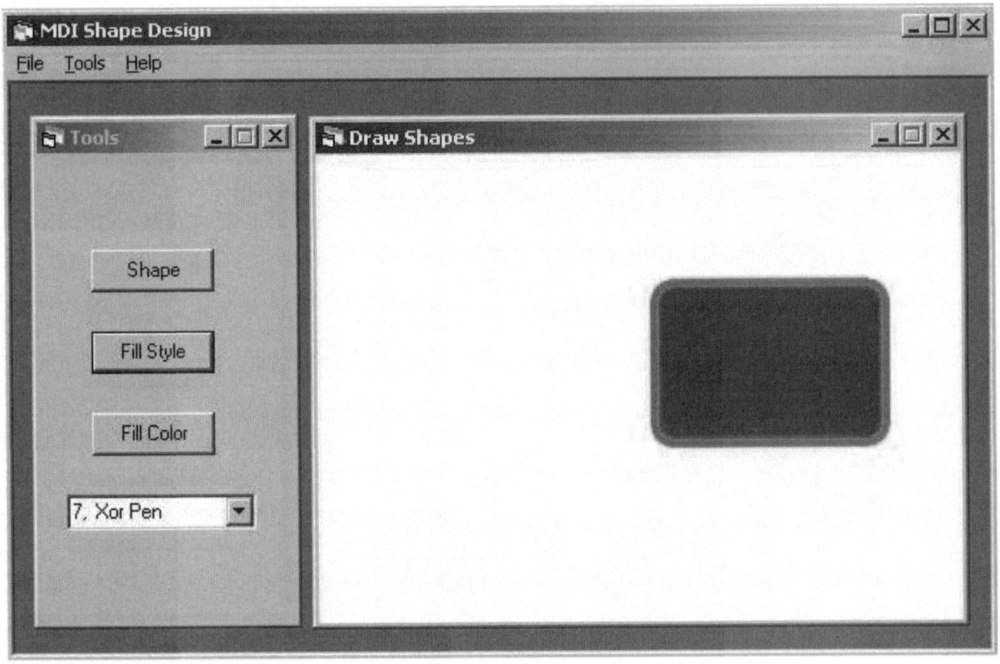

Figure 4.51: Run Time View of the Application

Conclusion/Observation

In this exercise, you learned how to create MDI forms. You also learned how to add child forms to the main form in an application. This exercise helped you learn the steps to create a realtime MDI application with parent and child forms.

Lab Activity Checklist

S. No.	Tasks	Completed	
		Yes	No
1.	Application created as MDI type		
2.	Menu bar is added to the MDI form		
3.	The two other forms are added as MDI child		
4.	Appropriate code is provided to perform the required task		

Project

1. Open the VB project named **EmpInfo**.
2. Add a MDI form to the project named **frmMain**.
3. Ensure that all the forms created in the previous section are set as the child of **frmMain**.
4. Create the following menu, given in tables 4.10 to 4.14 **frmMain**. The following tree displays the structure of the menu identified by the captions of the menu items and their respective names.

■ Menu Title: Company (mnuCompany), as given in Table 4.10.

Caption	Name
Add New Department	mnuAddDept
Edit Department Info	mnuEditDept
Delete Department	mnuDeleteDept
–	mnuSep1
Grades Information	mnuGrades
–	mnuSep2
Exit	mnuExit

Table 4.10: Details of Menu Title Company for Project

■ Menu Title: Employee (mnuEmployee) , as given in Table 4.11.

Caption	Name
Add Employee	mnuAddEmp
Modify Employee Details	mnuModifyEmp
–	mnuSep3
Search Employee	mnuSearchEmp

Table 4.11: Details of Menu Title Employee for Project

■ Menu Title: Tools (mnuTools), as given in Table 4.12.

Caption	Name
Company Information	mnuCompanyInfo
–	mnuSep4
Holiday List	mnuHolidayList
Birthday Reminder	mnuBdayReminder

Table 4.12: Details of Menu Title Tools for Project

■ Menu Title: Windows (mnuWindow), as given in Table 4.13.

Caption	Name
Cascade	mnuCascade
Tile Horizontally	mnuTileHorizontally
Tile Vertically	mnuTileVertically

Table 4.13: Details of Menu Title Windows for Project

■ Menu Title: Help (mnuHelp), as given in Table 4.14.

Caption	Name
About the System	mnuAboutSystem
–	mnuSep5
About Us	mnuAboutUs

Table 4.14: Details of Menu Title Help for Project

5.   Set the appropriate property to ensure that the Windows menu title displays the names of all the open windows during run time. Figure 4.52 displays the design view of the form **frmMain** after adding the menu bar.

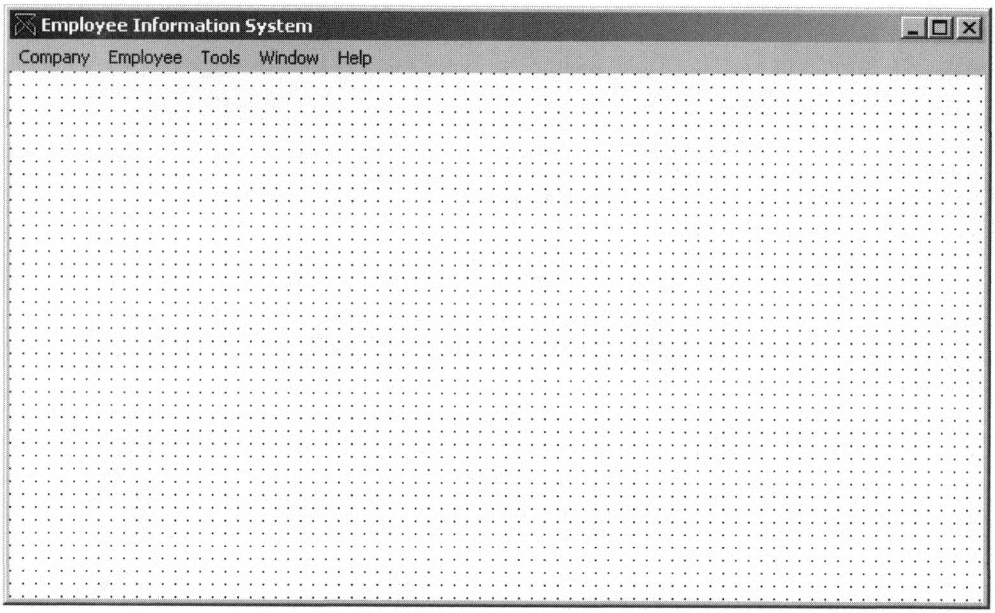

Figure 4.52: Design View of the Form frmMain

6.   Write appropriate code to display the forms **frmAddEmp**, **frmEditEmp**, and **frmSearchEmp** when the user clicks the menu items mnuAddEmp, mnuModifyEmp, and mnuSearchEmp respectively.

7.   Write the code to implement the menu items mnuCascade, mnuTileHorizontally, and mnuTileVertically.

8.   Write the code for the menu item mnuExit. Also ensure that proper code is added to ask for the user's confirmation before exiting the application.

9.   Save the project.

Working with Databases

5

This chapter covers the basic concepts of database design. The chapter also provides information on tables, primary keys, and foreign keys and explains Structured Query Language (SQL) statements for manipulating databases. It explains how databases are created in Microsoft Access, and in Microsoft Visual Basic using the Visual Data Manager. Further, it elaborates how the Visual Data Manager is used to access and modify databases. Finally, it explains the concept of ActiveX Data Objects (ADO) in Visual Basic, including connection objects, Recodset objects and field objects.

At the end of this chapter, you will be able to:

- Explain the concepts and functions of a database.

- Explain specific database operations.

- Explain specific SQL commands.

- Explain how the Visual Data Manager in Microsoft Visual Basic works.

- Explain how to use ADO in Microsoft Visual Basic.

5.1 Database Concepts

5.2 Creating Databases

5.3 Manipulating Databases in Visual Basic

5.1 Database Concepts

A database is essentially a collection of data. Databases are used to store data in a way that will facilitate its retrieval and modification in simple and easy steps. A database management system manages various activities performed on data such as its retrieval, modification, deletion and insertion of new records. A database is organized so that it can be used by multiple users to access large amounts of information. Using a central data repository reduces the chances of data redundancy. Since the central repository is modified by users, inconsistencies in data can be avoided.

Standards have been developed that ensure databases conform to certain ways to store data in a computer. For example, data such as dates are always stored in a standard format. Databases must also be secure and able to maintain a consistent, stable state. Databases handle potential cataclysms such as hardware problems or power failures in such a way that data is not lost altogether. Transactions that are not completed due to such problems can be rolled back; that is the database is brought back to the state before the transaction was initiated.

Database management software such as Microsoft SQL Server 2000, Oracle, and Microsoft Access manipulate databases for various operations. Such software makes storing and retrieving data easy, secure, reliable, and fast.

Although sequential files can be used to store and retrieve related data, they are highly inefficient owing to their sequential nature. Sequential files cannot be accessed randomly. This has major consequences in terms of speed at which the data is accessed, especially for large amounts of data. You can write to sequential files only at the end of the file. It is also difficult to store and retrieve related data as rows and fields. Delimiters such as commas are used to differentiate between fields in a row, which is cumbersome. The size of fields is also fixed. If any one field has to be modified, then it could result in overwriting or loss of data. Thus, sequential files are not reliable.

Databases have the functionality of random access files and indexed sequential files. Records are stored as tables in databases. Each table has rows representing records and columns representing fields. Records can be accessed randomly. The concept of primary key indexes allows you to sort databases and retrieve data in any order that you desire. Databases employ queries to retrieve data from the database. Queries are special commands that are executed to manipulate the data stored in databases. Structured Query Language (SQL) is a query language that is used to perform these (and other) operations.

Figure 5.1 shows the advantages of using databases to store data.

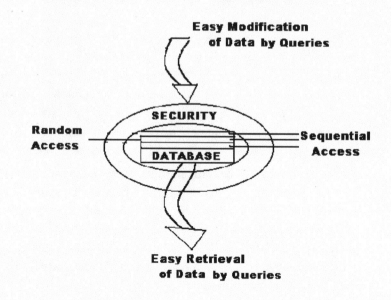

Figure 5.1: Advantages of Using Databases to Store Data

Visual Basic provides database access through a variety of methods. One of the more recent methods added to Visual Basic are ActiveX Data Objects (ADO). An ADO data control establishes a connection to a database and then works with it. In addition, Visual Basic's Visual Data Manager enables you to create database, queries, and manage all other aspects of database management. Methods like these support Visual Basic as a Rapid Application Development (RAD) tool.

5.1.1 Database Connection Providers

 Explain how different database connection providers work.

Database connection providers are the interfaces for applications that need to access databases. You can connect to any database using the provider, which makes the necessary adaptations.

Three commonly used database connection providers are:

- ODBC—Open Database Connectivity
- OLE DB—Object Linking and Embedding Database
- JDBC—Java Database Connectivity

These database drivers provide an interface for the software to access different databases:

- ODBC is the oldest of all the three drivers and works with many databases. All the references are made to the ODBC interface regardless of the type of database used (provided the driver is installed for that type of database). ODBC is very stable. New drivers that have been introduced since ODBC continue to support ODBC features because of its widespread usage.

- OLE DB is Microsoft's new database driver designed similar to that of ODBC. It has excellent support for accessing large databases. Its most beneficial feature is interoperability. It supports complete integration with all Microsoft databases such as Access and Exchange. It is based on the Component Object Model (COM) technology, and provides simple and flexible components to manipulate databases. It also offers full support for ODBC.

- JDBC is Sun's database driver designed specifically for Java applets and servlets. ODBC and OLE DB use SQL commands whereas JDBC supports Java commands. It can work with large data sets without migrating them from the server to the client. JDBC performs better than other drivers in certain cases. For instance, it performs better when multiple records are updated as a batch. Batch updates cause multiple records to be updated in a single operation. Using JDBC also makes the code portable.

5.1.2 Database Tables

 Identify the concept of tables in a database.

Databases store data in the form of tables consisting of rows and columns. This eases the retrieval and modification of data. Microsoft Access and SQL Server 2000 store data in tables. These tables are stored as part of a parent database. Thus, a single database can have many tables in it.

In a table, each row represents a record. A record is a set of related data representing one entity. For example, in an employee table, each record represents the information of one particular employee. Each column of the table represents a field in each row. A field stores a value that describes an attribute or property of a record.

Table 5.1 shows a table of the **Employee** table.

ID	FirstName	LastName	Designation
100001	John	Brown	Sales Representative
100002	Steve	Moore	Sales Manager
100003	Martha	Jones	Sales Representative

Table 5.1: Employee Table

Each row of Table 5.1 represents the data of a single employee. For example, the first record stores the data for an employee named John Brown. The ID column stores the identification number of John Brown. All of the identification numbers in the ID column have the same data type for all the records in the table. Another column, such as FirstName, can be a different data type.

5.1.3 Constraints

Identify database constraints such as primary keys, foreign keys, and indexes.

In order for a database to function properly, certain limitations can be placed on database objects, such as fields and tables. These constraints help to:

- Counter redundancy of data in the database.
- Minimize inconsistency of data in the database.
- Merge different tables semantically.
- Quickly retrieve and manipulate data types.

Index

An index is a special object that is used to quickly access or mark rows in a table so that they can be retrieved quickly. All the fields that a user wants to use to sort data, such as primary or foreign keys, may be indexed. It is always preferable to sort a single index column than the whole table. The sorted index is then used to sort the rows in the table. Indexes do not need to be single values. If they comprise multiple columns they are known as composite indexes.

Primary Key

A primary key is a column that uniquely identifies a row. A primary key never has the same value in more than one row. A primary key is also typically used to automatically create an index but, remember, all indexes are not necessarily primary keys. For example, the **FirstName** field of the database table shown in Table 5.1 could be considered as a primary key. In this situation, the **FirstName** field would be called a **candidate key**. However, this field cannot be an ideal primary key because two employees may have the same first name. On the other hand, the ID field would probably make an ideal primary key because it is unique for each employee. Apart from providing uniqueness to the records in a table, a primary key plays an important role in maintaining relationships between the tables.

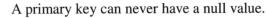

A primary key can never have a null value.

If there are no fields in the database fields that may be qualified as a primary key, then an additional value such as a record number or serial number can be used as the primary key.

Foreign Key

A foreign key is a field that is used to maintain the referential integrity among tables. This means that the foreign key in a table always corresponds to the primary key values in another table. The foreign key ensures that the table contains only those records that have a corresponding primary key value in the table being referred to. This relieves the user from the task of checking the master table every time they enter a record in the details table. Also, the foreign key does not have to be unique, compared to a primary key. That is, a foreign key value may exist in more than one record in a table.

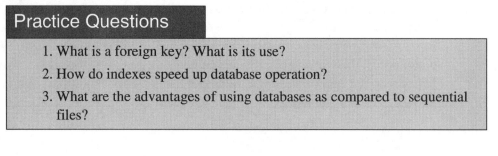

Practice Questions

1. What is a foreign key? What is its use?
2. How do indexes speed up database operation?
3. What are the advantages of using databases as compared to sequential files?

5.2 Creating Databases

Databases can be created using database management software or can be built using the Visual Data Manager in Microsoft Visual Basic. Thus, the Visual Data Manager and the Visual Basic Integrated Development Environment (IDE) offer a designer an integrated way to create database applications. When you use additional software, such as Access, with Visual Basic, additional capabilities are made available to the designer. However, manually creating databases outside Visual Basic ruins the effect of Visual Basic as a RAD tool. It also requires additional finances to obtain the Access software, and there are file management needs that must be considered. So, to make an easy and interactive GUI through Visual Basic you can create databases using the Visual Data Manager. It not only creates databases but also builds queries to manipulate the databases. It saves the developer a lot of time and effort.

5.2.1 Using the Visual Data Manager

 Explain the steps involved in creating databases using the Visual Data Manager.

Let us create a database to store information related to the employees in an organization. First, a database is created and then other components such as tables are added to the database.

To create the database:

1.   Select **Add-Ins → Visual Data Manager** to start the Visual Data Manager as shown in Figure 5.2.

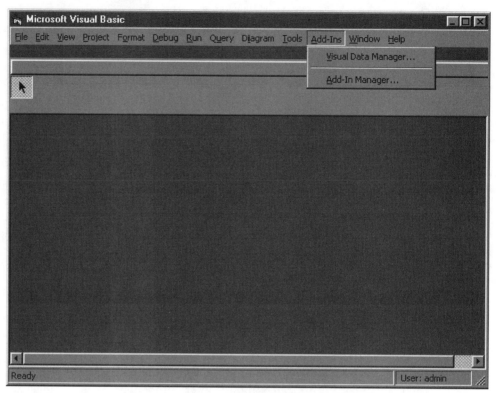

Figure 5.2: Starting the Visual Data Manager

2.   A new window opens for the Visual Data Manger. Select **File →New →Microsoft Access →Version 7.0 MDB** to create a database in Access as shown in Figure 5.3. Any other option, such as Excel or Dbase can be selected depending on your choice.

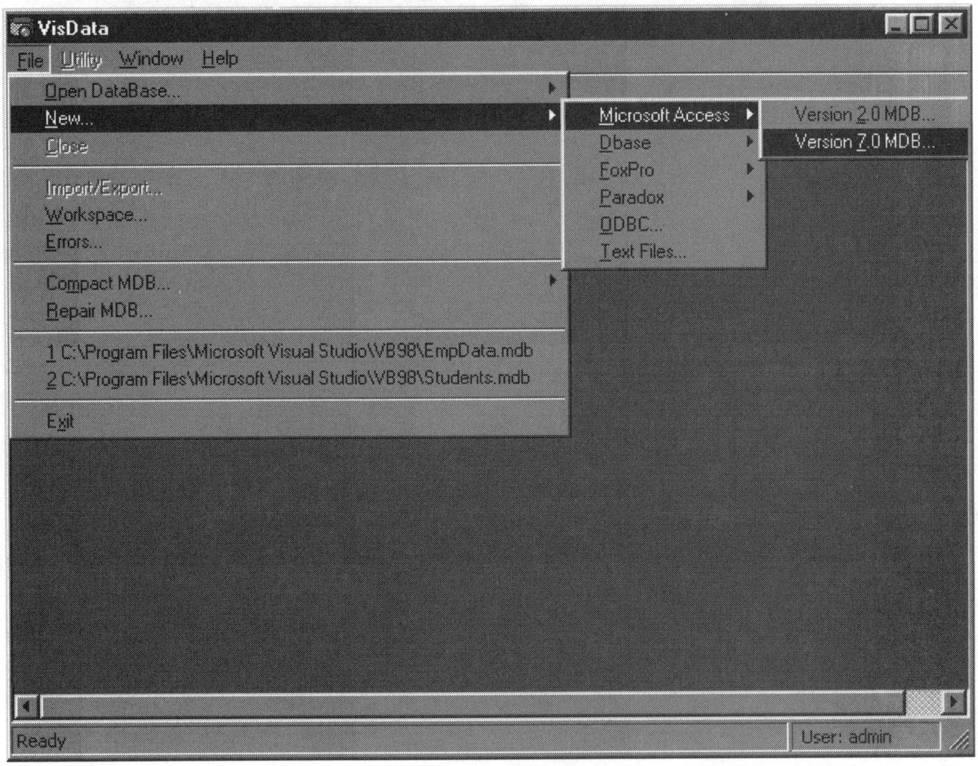

Figure 5.3: Creating a Database in Access

3.　　　　The **Select Microsoft Access Database to Create** dialog box opens as shown in Figure 5.4. Type a name of the database, for example **EmpData**, and click **Save**. The database is automatically saved as EmpData.mdb.

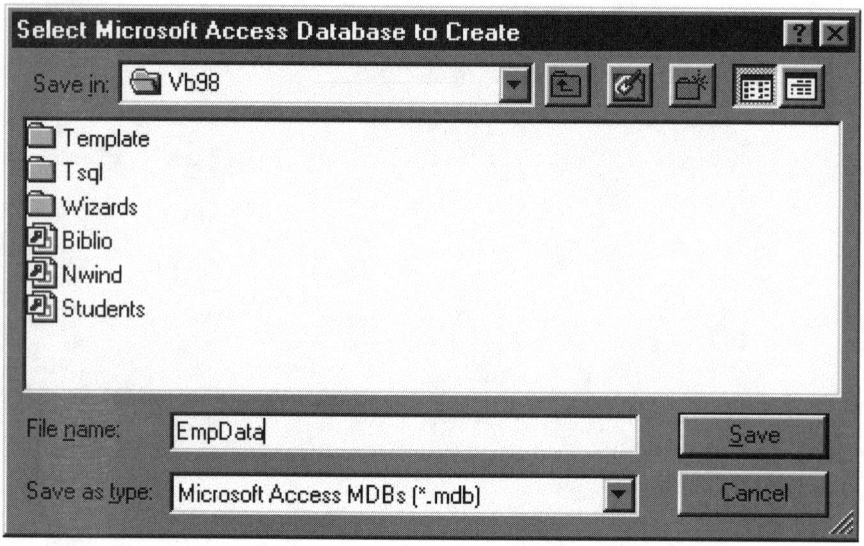

Figure 5.4: Saving the Database

After you create EmpData, two windows are displayed: a database window with the name of your database in the title bar, and an SQL Statement window. The database window shows a list of properties of the database that you created.

Figure 5.5 shows the database window on the left and the SQL Statement window on the right.

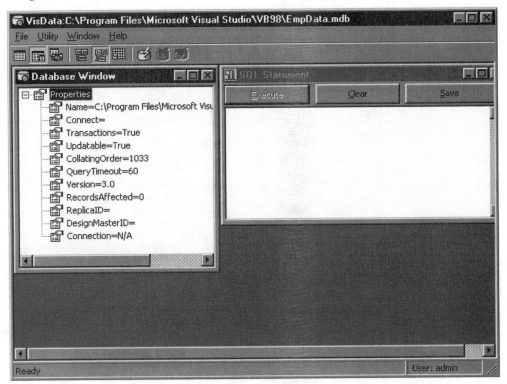

Figure 5.5: Database Window and SQL Statement Window

When the database is newly created, it contains no tables or queries. You need to add tables and queries to it.

Creating Database Tables

The **EmpData** database will have two tables:

- A table named **Employee** that contains the personal information of all the employees having the following fields:

    - Id: A unique identification number for every employee. This field is the primary key of the **Employee** table. It is a Long data type, and stores a six-digit number.

    - FirstName: Stores the first name of an employee. It is a Text data type, which has a maximum length of twenty characters.

- LastName: Stores the last name of an employee. It is a Text data type, which has a maximum length of twenty characters.

- Address: Stores the local address of an employee. It is a Text data type, which has a maximum length of seventy characters.

- ZipCode: Stores the zip code of an employee's address. It is a Text data type, which has a maximum length of ten characters.

- Country: Stores the name of the country in which an employee resides. It is a Text data type, which has a maximum length of twenty characters.

- Phone: Stores the phone number of an employee. It is a Text data type, which has a maximum length of thirty characters.

- Age: Stores the age of an employee. It stores an Integer data type.

- Dependents: Stores the number of non-working family members of an employee. It is an Integer data type.

- A table named **Company** that stores professional information of all the employees having the following fields:

  - Id: A unique identification number for every employee. This field is the primary key of the **Company** table. It is a Long data type and stores a six-digit number. This key also acts as a foreign key in operations involving both the **Employee** table and the **Company** table.

  - Designation: Stores the designation of an employee. It is a Text data type with a maximum length of thirty characters.

  - Salary: Stores the salary in dollars of an employee. It is a Currency data type.

Follow these steps to create the **Employee** table:

1.　　Right-click on the database window and select **New Table** from the menu. A
Table Structure dialog box appears. You design the table in this window
specifying the fields and their data types. Figure 5.6 shows the **Table
Structure** dialog box.

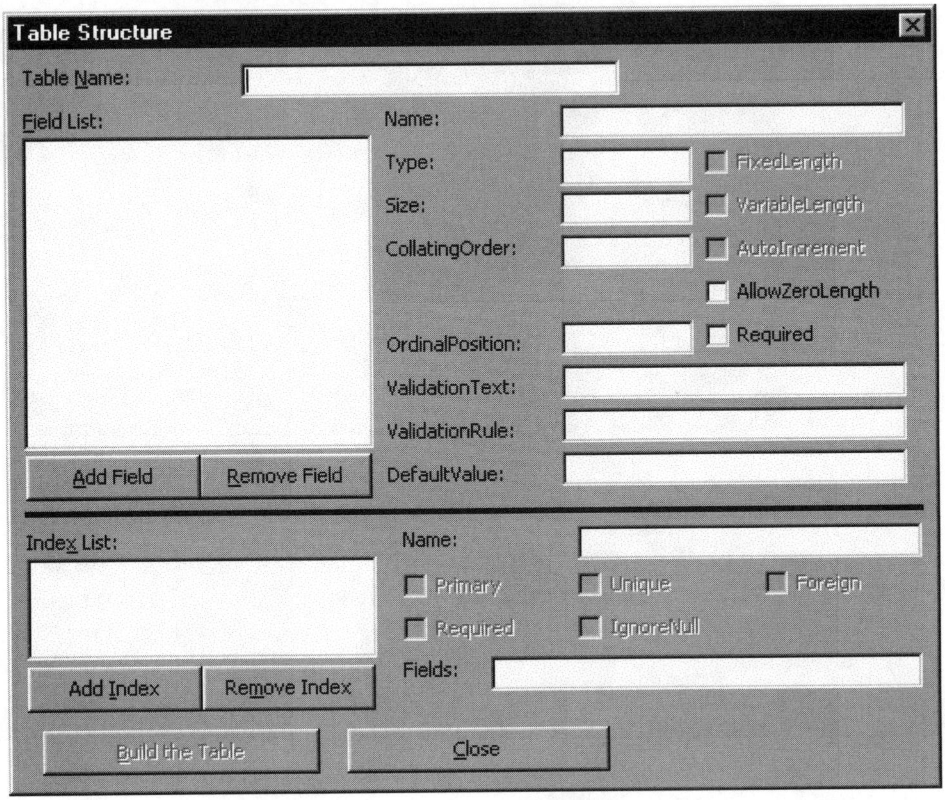

Figure 5.6: Designing a Table in the Table Structure Dialog Box

2.　　Enter the name of the table in the Table Name text box of the **Table
Structure** dialog box. The Field List on the left side of the Table Structure
dialog box contains the list of all the fields defined for the table. In Figure 5.6,
this list is empty because no fields have been added to the table. On the right
of the Field List are other text boxes that contain the description of fields of
the table.

3.   To add fields to the table, click on the **Add Field** button. An **Add Field** dialog box appears, as shown in Figure 5.7.

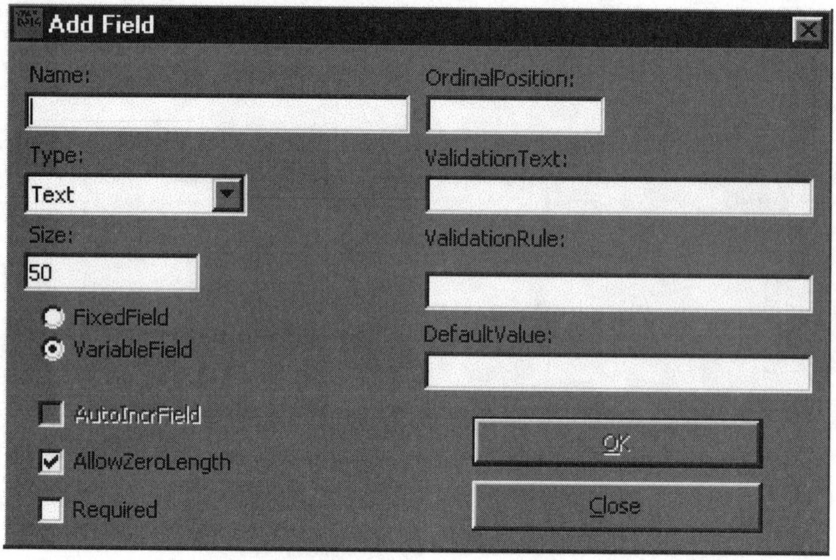

Figure 5.7: Add Field Dialog Box

4.   Type the name of a field in the Name text box of the **Add Field** dialog box. The first field of the **Employee** table is Id. Type **Id** in the Name text box to start adding fields. The **Type** drop-down box sets the data type of your field to Text.

The different types of data types available are shown in Table 5.2.

Type	Range/Description	Size (Bytes)	Decimal Places
Byte	0 – 255	1	0
Integer	–32,768 – 32,767	2	0
Long	–2,147,483,648 – 2,147,483,647	4	0
Single	$-3.4 \times 10^{38} - 3.4 \times 10^{38}$	4	7
Double	$-1,797 \times 10^{308} - 1,797 \times 10^{308}$	8	15
Boolean	For storing Yes/No or True /False values	–	–
Currency	For holding currency value, prefixed with the default currency symbol, automatically show two decimal places for cents; require as much storage as Double type	8	15
Text	For holding characters	255	–
Memo	For holding free form text, such as notes	64,000	–
Date/Time	For holding date and/or time values	–	–

Table 5.2: Data Types for Table Field

Change the data type to **Long**. The **Add Field** dialog box for the **Id** field is shown in Figure 5.8. Click **OK** to add the field to your table. The field is added to the Field List in the **Table Structure** dialog box.

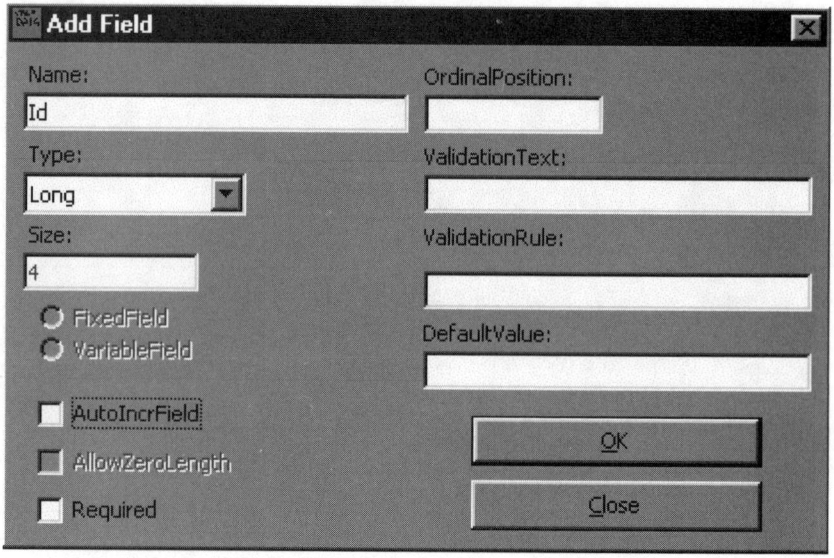

Figure 5.8: Adding the Id Field to the Table

5. Similarly, add the other fields to the **Employee** table. After you add all the fields of the **Employee** table, the **Table Structure** dialog box appears as shown in Figure 5.9. The selected field's details are shown in the text boxes on the right side.

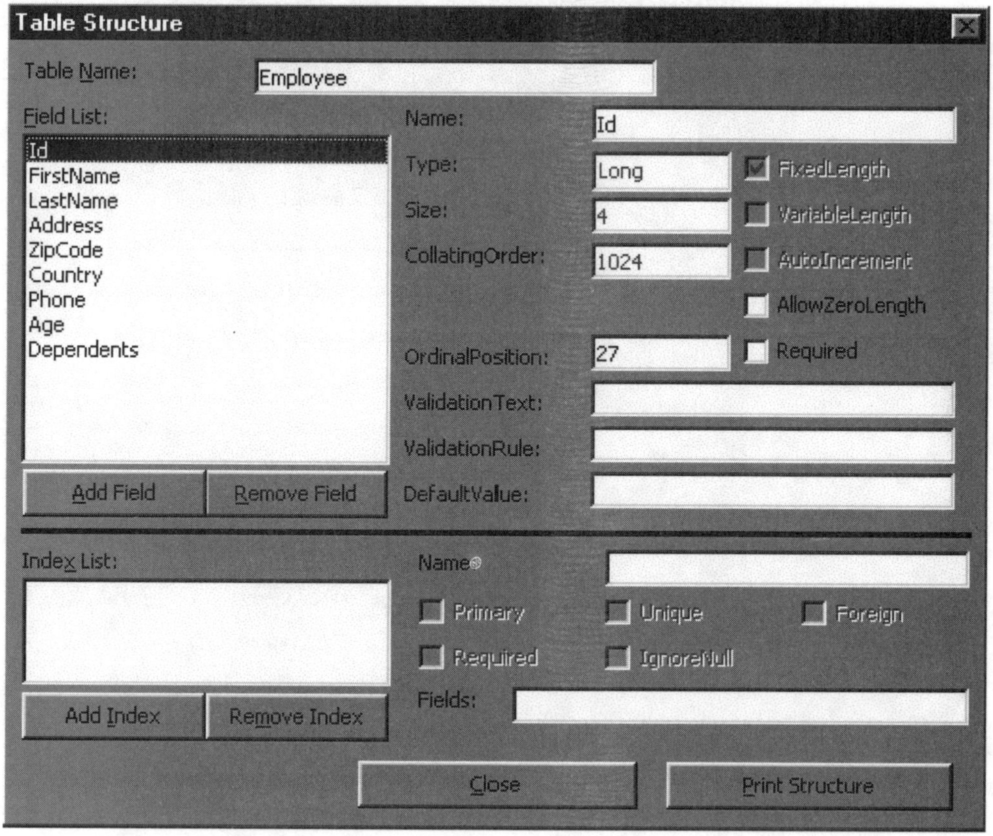

Figure 5.9: Table Structure Dialog Box after All the Fields Have Been Added

6. To add the table you have designed to the database, click on the **Build Table** button in the **Table Structure** dialog box. The table appears in the database window.

7. To manipulate the table, right-click on the **Employee** table in the database window and select the desired option.

8.   To add, delete, edit, find, or sort records, right-click on the **Employee** table and select **Open**. The **Dynaset:Employee** dialog box appears, as shown in Figure 5.10.

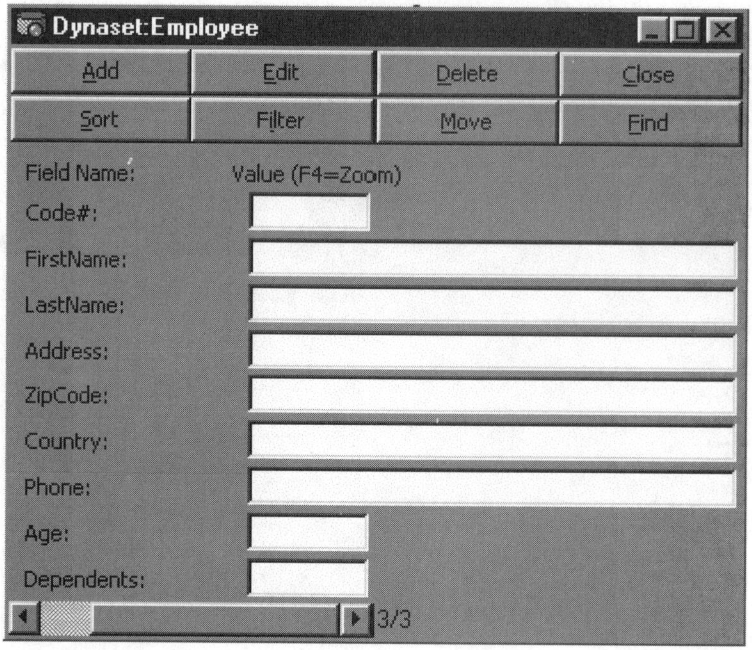

Figure 5.10: Dynaset:Employee Dialog Box for Manipulating Records in the Table

9.   To add a new record to the table, click the **Add** button. A **Dynaset:Employee** dialog box for adding records appears, as shown in Figure 5.11.

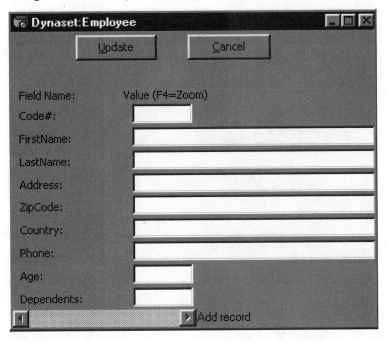

Figure 5.11: Adding a Record to the Table

Type the values for all the fields and click **Update** to add the record to the table. Repeat the process to add more records. You can move from one record to another by using the scroll bars at the bottom of the **Dynaset:Employee** dialog box.

To enter the date, 29 March 2002, in a field storing a Date/Time data type, use any of the following formats: 3 29 02, 29 March, March 29, or 03/29/2002. If you do not specify the year, then the current year is selected by default.

Primary keys are unique value fields for each record. Primary keys are used to create indexes and help in efficient and quick retrieval of records. To add a primary key to the **Employee** table:

1.   In the Database Window of the Visual Data Manager, right-click the **Employee** table and select Design. (If you have the **Table Structure** dialog box already open, click on the **Add Index** button.) The **Add Index to Employee** dialog box appears, as shown in Figure 5.12.

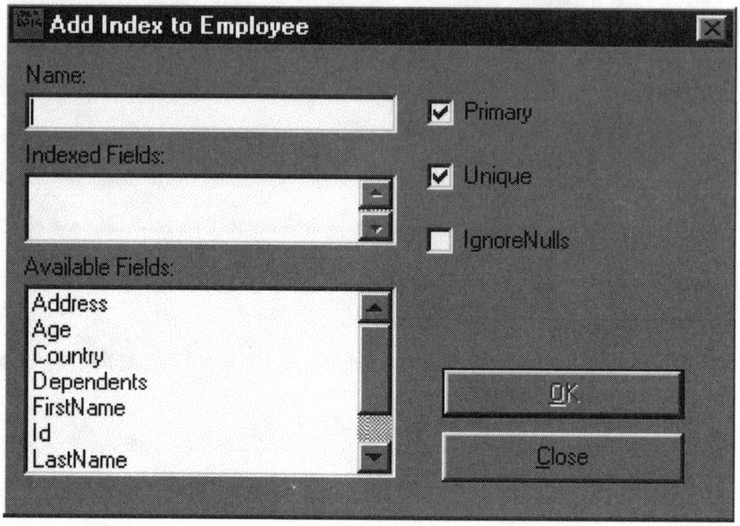

Figure 5.12: Add Index Dialog Box

2.   Type a name for the index and select the fields comprising the index. You can select more than one field if you want a composite index. Check the **Primary** and **Unique** check boxes to make the index a primary key. Figure 5.13 shows the Id field as the primary key in the **Add Index** dialog box.

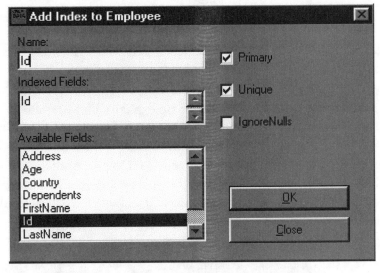

Figure 5.13: Making the Id Field the Primary Key

In some cases, the table has no primary key. In such a situation, a Counter field can be used to perform as the primary key. A Counter field stores data that automatically increments by one for every record that is added to the table. Thus, each record has a field that contains a unique value for that record. To incorporate a counter field in your table:

1.   Add a field as you added other fields to the table and give it an appropriate name.

2.   Set the data type for the field as **Long**.

3.   Check the Auto Increment Option in the **Add Field** dialog box.

4.   Make the field a primary key by clicking the **Add Index** button and selecting the field in the **Add Index** dialog box.

After the **Employee** table is created, you can repeat the same procedure to create the **Company** table and add it to the database.

5.2.2 Creating Databases Using Microsoft Access

 Explain the creation of databases in Microsoft Access.

Despite the numerous benefits of the Visual Data Manager GUI in creating a database you might consider creating a database explicitly in Microsoft Access. The Visual Data Manager in Visual Basic is an add-on tool for creating basic databases and does not provide the advanced features needed to create robust databases. Microsoft Access is a database management system that helps you to create additional database objects such as queries and macros. Moreover, the relationships between the tables cannot be established using Visual Data Manager. To create the database in Microsoft Access:

1. Open Microsoft Access. The **Microsoft Access** dialog box opens as shown in Figure 5.14.

Figure 5.14: Microsoft Access Dialog Box

2. Select the **Blank Access** database option from the **Microsoft Access** dialog box. The **File New Database** dialog box opens as shown in Figure 5.15. Type a name for the database in the File Name field, and click the **Create** button.

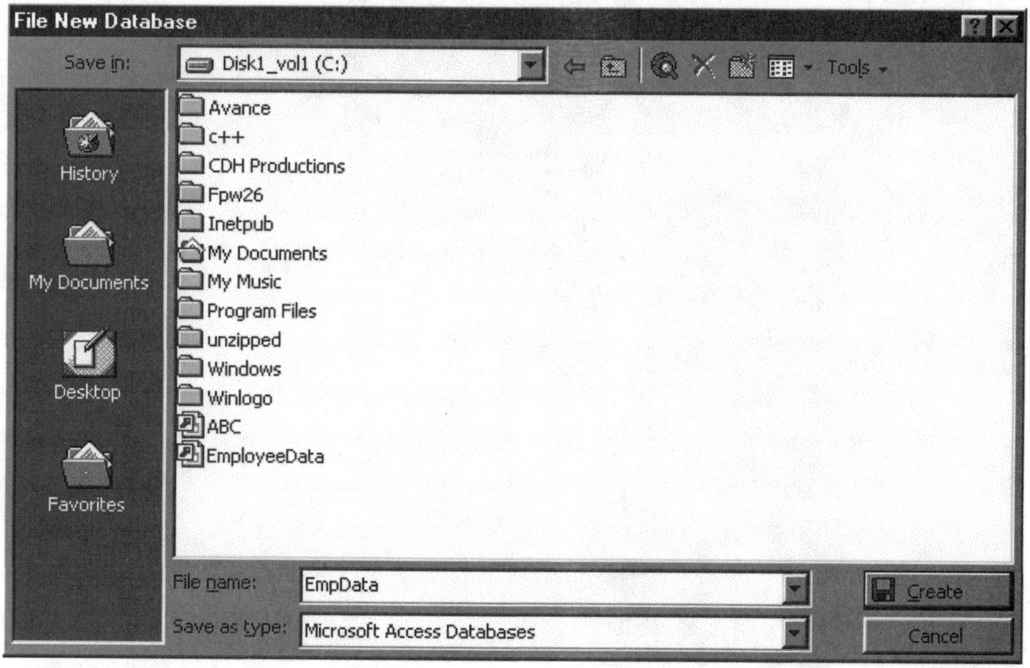

Figure 5.15: File New Database Dialog Box

3.   A database window opens, as shown in Figure 5.16. The name of your database appears in the title bar of the window (db2 is shown in Figure 5.16). Click on the **Tables** tab if it is not already selected. Select the **Create table by entering data** option and click **Open**.

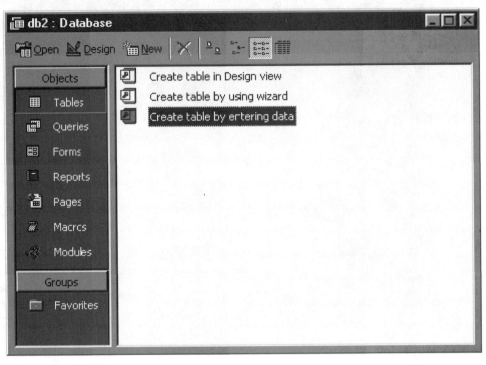

Figure 5.16: Database Window

4.   A window with a blank table is opened. The field captions are initially named Field1, Field2, etc. To change the names of the fields according to your database requirements, double-click on the field caption and type the desired name of the field. Figure 5.17 shows a blank table with the field names set to the fields of the **Employee** table.

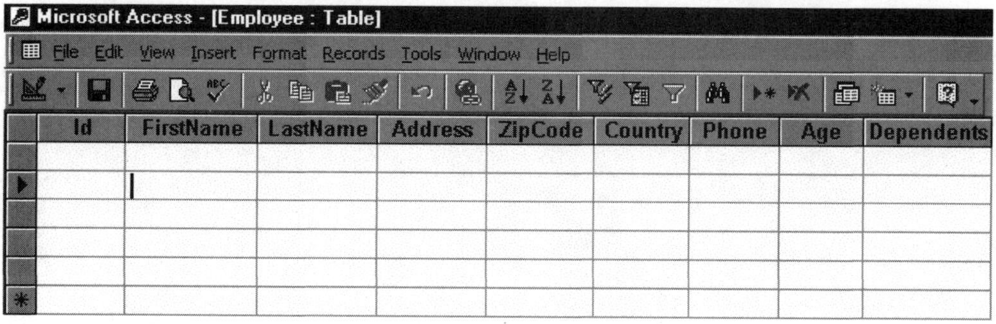

Figure 5.17: Blank Access Database Table

5.   Change the captions for all the fields appropriately and fill in the data in the fields.

6.   Save the table by selecting **File → Save** from the Access window menu. If you click the **Close** button without saving the table, you will be prompted to save the table. Enter a name for the table and click **OK**. Figure 5.18 shows the **Save As** dialog box.

Figure 5.18: Saving the Table

After the database and all the tables are created, you can create queries to access and modify the data in the database.

1. What are the advantages of the Visual Data Manager?

2. Explain the various methods of creating a table in Microsoft Access.

3. Read about other database packages, such as SQL Server 2000 or MySQL. Write a brief summary about available features, limitations, etc.

5.3 Manipulating Databases in Visual Basic

Databases store data to provide information to multiple users. Databases allow you to retrieve, insert, delete, and modify existing data, and perform other data utilization operations.

Retrieving data from a database does not change the database. However, update, insert, and delete operations modify the data stored in a database. These modifying operations are called transactions. A transaction is either completed successfully, or it fails. If the transaction fails, the database must be restored to its initial state. If any errors occur during the course of a transaction, then the transaction is not committed (changes are not reflected in the database). In this case, the transaction is rolled back, that is, the database is restored to its initial state. Only transactions that are logged (whose details and the data affected are saved) can be rolled back. Some transactions, such as deletion of all the records of a database, are not logged. These transactions cannot be rolled back. Thus, they should be used carefully because once data is lost, it cannot be recovered.

Databases hold large amounts of data so that they can be easily and efficiently accessed. Queries are specialized commands that extract data from the database or write data to the database. SQL queries can be created in Visual Data Manager to access the data stored in databases. The main advantage of using the Visual Data Manager for accessing the database is the GUI, which makes creating and executing queries very easy and quick.

Another way to access databases in Visual Basic is to use ADO data control. This technique is a benefit for commercial software that needs to access large databases. Using ADO, you can create an efficient database access code. ADO is particularly suitable for Web-based and client/server applications. It has several features that enable it to place the least amount of burden on the server.

5.3.1 Using SQL

 Explain different database operations using SQL queries.

Using SQL, you can write specialized queries to manipulate the database. Common SQL commands are listed in Table 5.3.

Database Operation	SQL Query
Retrieving Data	SELECT
Adding Data	INSERT
Deleting Data	DELETE
Updating Data	UPDATE

Table 5.3: Some Common SQL Queries

Although SQL is not case-sensitive, the following section uses uppercase to depict SQL commands. The following section uses a database named **EmpData** that stores the personal and professional details of employees working in an organization. This database was created in the previous topic. It has two tables, **Employee** and **Company**.

These databases can also be created in any database management software such as SQL Server 2000 or Oracle.

SQL Statements and Clauses

SQL statements and clauses create queries that access and manipulate databases. Clauses impose conditions on the data being retrieved or modified. You can also sort and group data, based on one or more fields.

SELECT Statement and the WHERE Clause

The SELECT statement retrieves data from the database. The syntax for the SELECT statement is:

```
SELECT <field1, field2,…>
FROM <tablename>
[WHERE <condition>]
[ORDER BY <field1 [ASC|DESC]>[, <field2 [ASC|DESC]>,…]
```

Only the field list following SELECT and the **tablename** following the FROM clause are mandatory in the query. All other clauses of the SELECT statement are optional.

To select all the records in a table, the following statement is used:

```
SELECT * FROM tablename
```

Using an asterisk (*) in a SELECT statement is an easy way to select all the fields from the table. It retrieves the fields in their physical order; that is, the way they are stored in the database. By specifying the names of the fields, you can choose the order in which you want the fields to be retrieved. The fields are always retrieved in the order of the query.

To select the **Id number**, **first names**, **last names**, and **phone numbers** of all the employees from the table **Employee**, the following query is executed:

```
SELECT Id, FirstName, LastName, Phone
FROM Employee
```

To conditionally select records from a database, you can use the WHERE clause with the SELECT statement. The SELECT statement can retrieve records in a specified order using the ORDER BY clause. This clause arranges the retrieved records in ascending or descending order by the field specified. If ASC or DESC is not specified in the ORDER BY clause, then by default the records are sorted in ascending order.

```
SELECT FirstName, LastName, Dependents
FROM Employee
WHERE Dependents<3
ORDER BY FirstName
```

This query lists the **FirstName**, **LastName**, and **Dependents** of all employees whose number of dependents is less than 3, sorted in ascending order by their first names.

INSERT Statement

The INSERT statement is used to add records to a database. The syntax of the INSERT statement is:

```
INSERT INTO <tablename> [(field list)]
VALUES (value list)
```

The INSERT statement inserts all the values in the *value list*, corresponding to the fields in the field list of the table. The number of values specified in the value list should be the same as the number of fields mentioned in the field list. If the field list is not specified, the INSERT statement considers all the fields in the table. Thus, the field list is normally specified only during partial data insertion.

You should be very careful about the order in which you specify the field list and value list.

The INSERT statement for inserting a record into the **Employee** table is:

```
INSERT INTO
Employee (Id, FirstName, LastName, Address, ZipCode,
Country, Phone, Age, Dependents)
VALUES (100005, 'Ben', 'Mark', '28 Garette Hills London',
'SW1 8JR', 'UK', '71-555-4848', 25, 3)
```

The INSERT query inserts a new record for the employee named **Ben Mark** in the **Employee** table.

Values to be inserted in the table may not be explicitly specified. They can also be retrieved from another table (or even the same table) using the SELECT statement and then inserted into the first table as:

```
INSERT INTO tablename (field list)
SELECT statement
```

The values retrieved by the SELECT statement are inserted in the table corresponding to the field list. The name of the table in which the values are inserted is specified after the INSERT INTO keywords. The name of the table from which values are retrieved will be specified in the FROM clause of the SELECT statement.

DELETE Statement

The DELETE statement is used to delete one or more records from a database. The syntax of the DELETE statement is:

```
DELETE
FROM <tablename>
[WHERE <condition>]
```

A DELETE statement without a WHERE clause deletes all the records from the specified table. If the WHERE clause is specified, it deletes only those records where the condition following the WHERE clause is satisfied.

To delete a record from the **Employee** table where the first name of the employee is John, the following query is executed:

```
DELETE
FROM Employee
WHERE FirstName LIKE 'John'
```

The DELETE query deletes all the records in which the **FirstName** is John. The comparison of the names is performed using the LIKE keyword.

The **Employee** table and the **Company** table store the personal and professional information for the employees working in an organization. If an employee resigns from an organization and the employee's record is deleted from the **Company** table, then the following query deletes the corresponding record from the **Employee** table.

```
DELETE
FROM Employee
WHERE Id NOT IN (SELECT DISTINCT Id FROM Company)
```

This query deletes all records for which there is no matching Id number in the **Company** table. The **IN** keyword tests the presence of values in a query that is a part of another query. The **NOT** operator here is used to reverse the result of the **IN** operator. The **DISTINCT** keyword selects only distinct values from the table. No repeated values are selected.

The DELETE statement deletes data without prompting. It must be used very carefully or you could lose important data.

Avoid using a DELETE statement without a WHERE clause.

To delete all the records from a table, you can also use the TRUNCATE statement instead of DELETE. The TRUNCATE statement is a faster way to delete all the records because it is not a logged transaction. At the same time, you cannot recover data deleted by the truncate statement.

UPDATE Statement

The UPDATE statement modifies existing data in a table. It changes data in one or more fields or records. The WHERE clause is generally used with an UPDATE statement to specify which record or field is to be updated. An UPDATE statement without a WHERE clause updates all the records in the table. The syntax for the UPDATE statement is:

```
UPDATE <tablename>
SET <field1>=<Value or Expression> [, <field2>=<Value or
Expression>, … ]
[WHERE <condition>]
```

The UPDATE statement updates the record specified by the WHERE clause in the table. The field names (field1, field2, …) following the SET clause are the fields whose value is to be changed. The new value of the field is specified by a value or expression following the field name.

For instance, if the salaries of employees earning $10,000 are raised to $12,000, then the following query is executed to update the records.

```
UPDATE Company
SET Salary = 12000
WHERE Salary = 10000
```

The following statement updates the designation to **Team Leader** and salary to $15,000 of all the employees whose Id is between 15 and 18,

```
UPDATE Company
SET designation='Team Leader', salary=15000
WHERE Id>=15 and id<=18
```

JOIN Operator

You can manipulate more than one table simultaneously using the JOIN operator. The JOIN operator joins two tables on a common field (usually a primary key in one table and a foreign key in the other). The INNER JOIN is performed to retrieve records that have matching values in the common field. The LEFT OUTER and the RIGHT OUTER joins are used to retrieve the records with a common value in both the tables along with those that do not have any common value.

For example, retrieve the Ids of all the employees whose:

- Number of dependents are more than three
- Salary is less than $10,000

Here you need to perform a JOIN operation on the **Employee** table and the **Company** table as the information for the number of dependents is stored in the **Employee** table while the salary details are stored in the **Company** table. The two tables have the Id field in common. The query is as follows:

```
SELECT Id
FROM Employee INNER JOIN Company
ON Employee.Id = Company.Id
WHERE Employee.Dependents > 3 AND Company.Salary < 10000
```

The query retrieves all the records from the **Employee** table that have a corresponding record in the **Company** table with similar values in the **Id** field. The fields of the tables are referred to by the table name followed by a period (.), and then the field name. This prevents any errors due to ambiguity in case there are fields with similar names in both the tables. You can use multiple JOIN statements within one another to retrieve more data from multiple tables simultaneously.

GROUP BY Clause

The GROUP BY clause is generally used to retrieve certain aggregate values like the maximum, minimum, count, average, and sum for a subset of records. These aggregate values are retrieved using certain functions provided by SQL such as MAX(), MIN(), COUNT(), AVG(), and SUM(), respectively. For instance, the following query retrieves the average age of the employees of different countries.

```
SELECT country, AVG(age)
FROM Employee
GROUP BY country
```

The query groups all the records in the **Employee** table based on the country name and calculates the average age in each of these groups. The fields retrieved by the query have the name of the country and the respective average age of the employees.

The COUNT function is used for counting the total number of records. You can obtain the count of a subset of the records in the table by grouping them over a value. For example, to count the number of employees with equal salaries of more than $10,000 in the **Company** table, the following query is executed.

```
SELECT Salary, COUNT(Salary) As NumEmp
FROM Company
GROUP BY Salary
HAVING Salary >= 10000
```

The query groups all the records of the **Company** table based on the **Salary** field having similar values, and retrieves the salary and the number (count) of records of only those groups whose salary is more than $10,000. The COUNT function is used to find the number of records retrieved in the query for each group. The column representing the number of employees in the query is named **NumEmp** using the AS clause, and the grouping of the records is specified by the name of the field mentioned with the GROUP BY clause. The HAVING clause specifies a condition as the WHERE clause, but is used only when the GROUP BY clause is specified. Unlike the WHERE clause, the condition specified with the HAVING clause is applied to the groups rather than on the individual records.

Table 5.4 shows that the sample output of the query might vary, depending on the data being stored in the Company table:

Salary	NumEmp
10000	2
15000	3
18000	2

Table 5.4: Salary Details of Employees

The first column displays the salary amount and the second column displays the number of employees who earn it.

5.3.2 Creating Queries in Visual Data Manager

 Identify the steps involved in manipulating a database by creating queries in the Visual Data Manager.

The **Employee** table created using the Visual Data Manager can be queried for data by creating queries using the Query Builder.

To create a query that selects all the employees aged 25 years:

1. Right-click on the database window shown in Figure 5.5, and select **New Query** from the pop-up menu. The **Query Builder** dialog box opens, as shown in Figure 5.19. You can also open the query builder by selecting **Utility → Query Builder** from the Visual Data Manager menu.

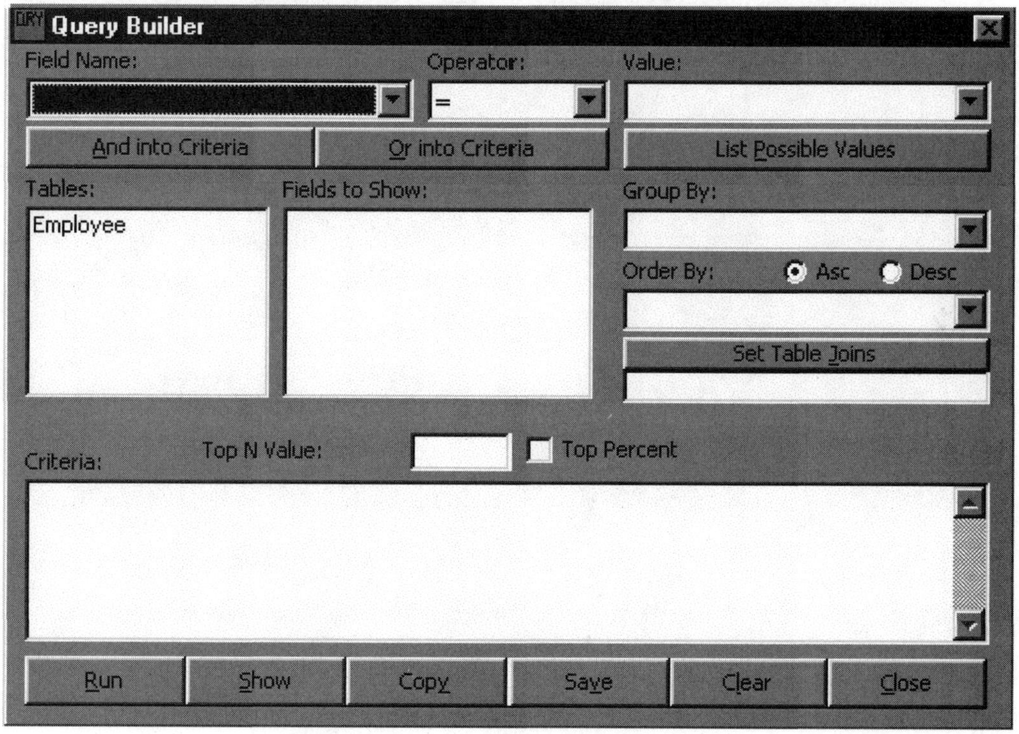

Figure 5.19: Query Builder Dialog Box

2. The **Tables** list specifies the name of the table to be queried. Select the **Employee** table from the **Tables** list. All the fields in the table appear in the **Fields to Show** list. The fields in this list can be selected. The values of the selected fields are retrieved from the database table when a query is executed.

3. The **Field Name** list is used to specify the condition in the query, if any. By default, the **Field Name** list is set to the first field in the table (Id field in the case of **Employee** table). You can select any other field to appear in place of the first field from the list. Select the **Employee.Age** field from the drop-down list. All fields appear qualified with the table name to resolve ambiguities when you are working with multiple tables.

4. The **Operator** list in the query builder lists various relational operators and the SQL LIKE operator. Set the operator to "=".

5. The **Value** list contains the value with which the field chosen in the **Field Name** list is to be compared. Initially this list is empty. To use the list, click on the **List Possible Values** button. The possible values for field specified in the Field Name list are added to the list. Select 25 from the list, or type 25. Click the **And into Criteria** button to add the criteria to the query. This will display the line "Employee.Age = 25" in the Criteria text box as shown in Figure 5.20.

6. Select Employee.FirstName and Employee.LastName from the Fields to Show list, as shown in Figure 5.20.

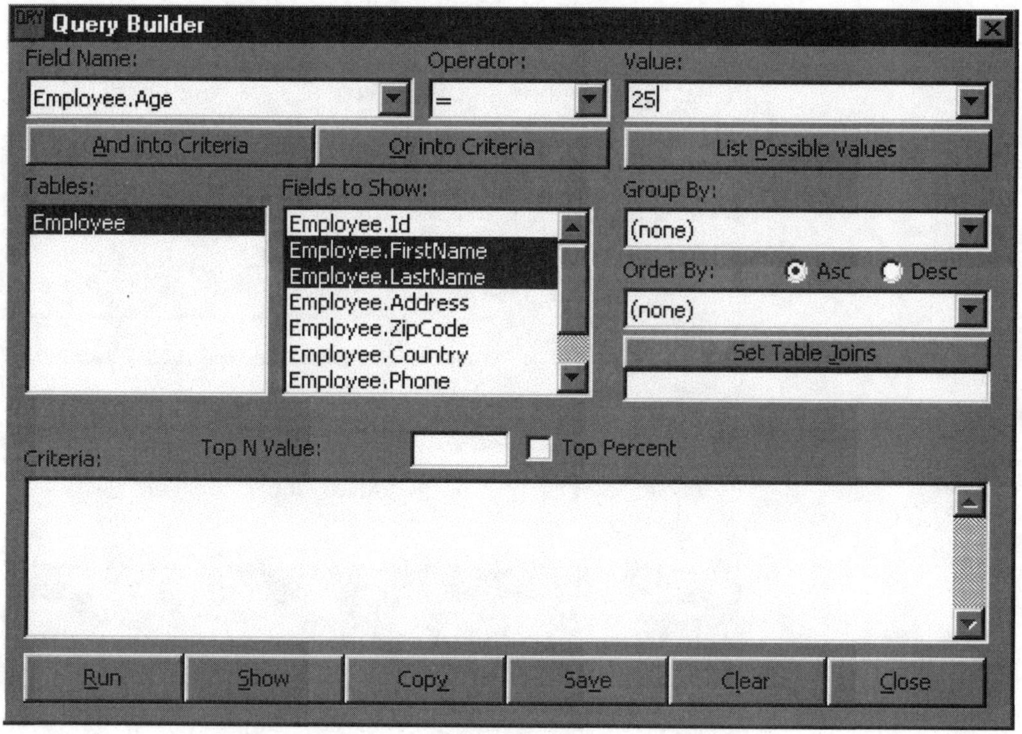

Figure 5.20: Creating a Query in the Query Builder

7. You can see the query in SQL by clicking the **Show** button at the bottom of the query builder.

8. To execute the query, click the **Run** button. If a dialog box appears asking whether the query is a SQL pass through query, click **No**. Assuming that the query retrieves two records from the table, the retrieved records appear as shown in Figure 5.21 and Figure 5.22 in the **SQL Statement** dialog box. Close the dialog box and click **Save** to save your query.

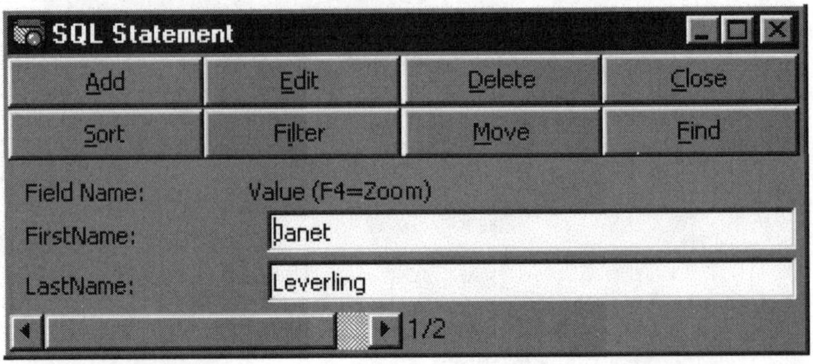

Figure 5.21: First Record Retrieved on Executing the Query

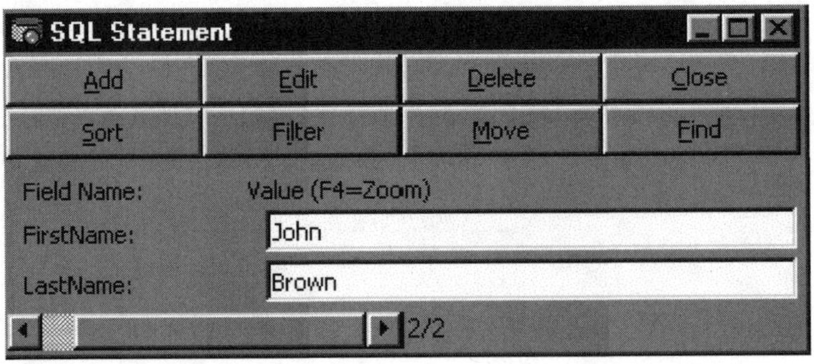

Figure 5.22: Second Record Retrieved on Executing the Query

You can execute more complex queries that test for multiple values before retrieving records by using either the **And into Criteria**, or the **Or into Criteria** buttons. To execute a query that retrieves the names of employees who are 25 years old with two or less dependents, perform the following steps:

1. Select the Employee.Age field from the **Field Name** list, and set the operator to the "=" operator. Type 25 in the Value field.

2. Click the **And into Criteria** button. The "Employee.Age = 25" condition is added to the Criteria box at the bottom of the Query Builder.

3.   Select "Employee.Dependents" from the Field Name list. Set the operator to the "<=" operator. Set Value field to 2. Click the **And into Criteria** button. This condition is also added to the Criteria box as shown in Figure 5.23.

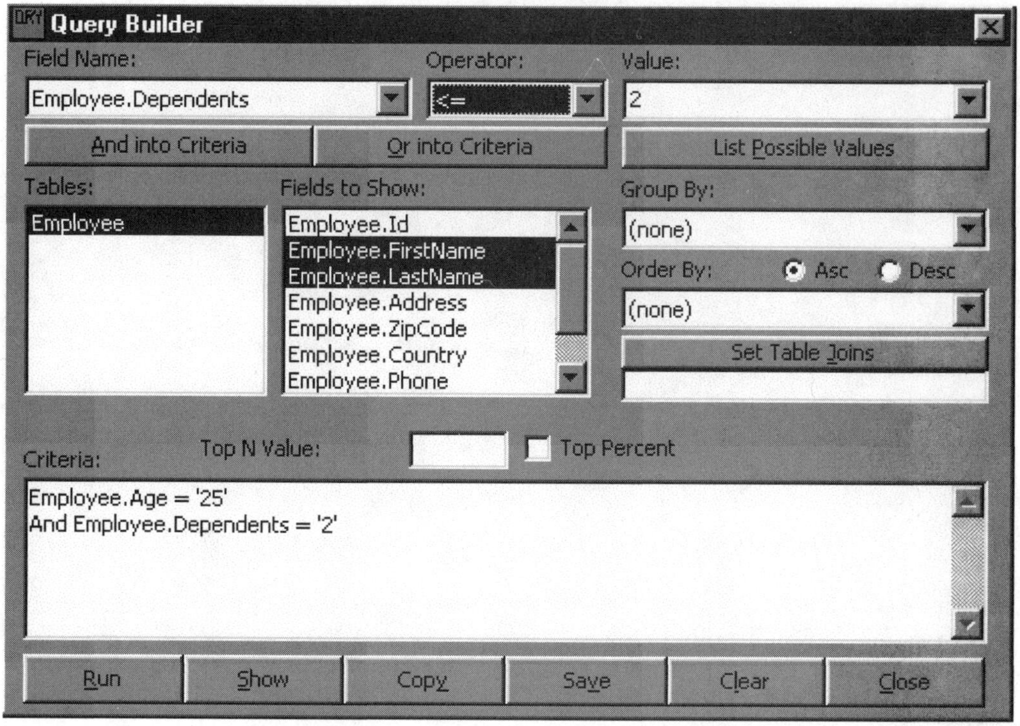

Figure 5.23: Adding Multiple Criteria to a Query

4. Run the query to retrieve records. The record retrieved is shown in Figure 5.24. The **And** operator between the two conditions enables the retrieval of records that satisfy both conditions at the same time. Clicking the **Or into Criteria** button in step 3 creates a place for an **Or** operator instead of **And**. This will retrieve records that satisfy either of the two specified conditions.

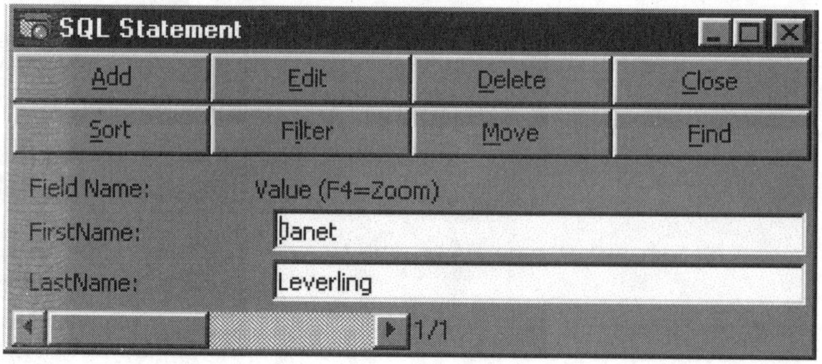

Figure 5.24: Record Retrieved on Running the Query

5.3.3 Using ADO in Visual Basic

Explain the benefits of ADO in Visual Basic.

Large-scale software applications often have to access large amounts of information stored in databases. ADO provides a platform to access and manipulate databases in a simple, quick, and easy way. ADO is particularly useful for client/server and Web-based applications, because it is extremely fast. It can perform multiple operations even when disconnected, as it keeps an account of the database name, server name, user, and password details. You can update recordsets offline and return them to the database when reconnected. In this way, it puts the least amount of load on the server, as shown in Figure 5.25.

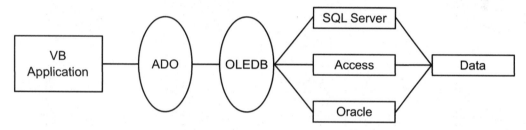

Figure 5.25: Working of ADO

ADO is implemented through a simple object model. The five main objects comprising ADO are:

- The Connection Object
- The Recordset Object
- The Field Object
- The Command Object
- The Error Object

All the ADO objects are contained in an ADO Library that must be referenced in a project so that the objects can be accessed. The ADO Object Model is shown in Figure 5.26.

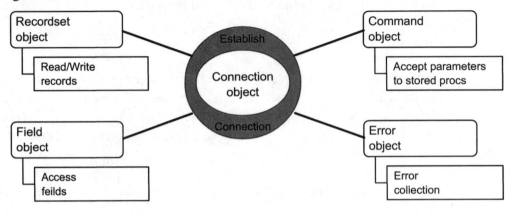

Figure 5.26: ADO Object Model

The Connection object is central to the ADO object model. All other objects require a connection before accessing the database. The connection object establishes a connection that provides a platform for all the other objects to function.

To access the ADO Objects in your Visual Basic code:

1.   Select **Project → References** from the Visual Basic menu. The **References** dialog box opens, as shown in Figure 5.27.

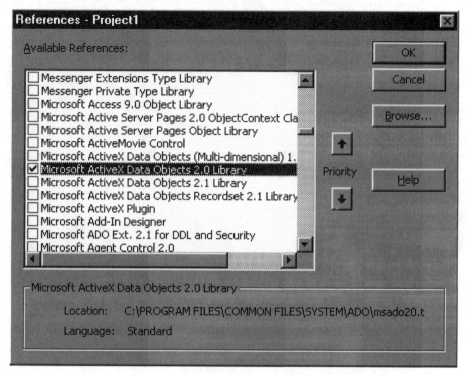

Figure 5.27: Setting Reference for the ADO Objects in Visual Basic

2.   Check the **Microsoft ActiveX Data Objects 2.0** Library in the list of references, and click **OK**.

ADO Connection Object

The ADO Connection object is the basis of the ADO object model. It establishes a connection to a database. A connection to the database is used to access the database, execute queries, and retrieve or modify data. Connection objects have several properties and methods that make them flexible and efficient for connecting to a database. A Connection object is instantiated by using the **New** keyword that allocates memory to a variable of type ADODB.Connection. The syntax for instantiating a Connection object is:

```
Dim Con As ADODB.Connection
Set Con = New ADODB.Connection
```

Connection Object Properties

The most essential property of the Connection Object is the **Connection string** property. The Connection object connects to a database using this property. The connection string consists of the following parts:

- Provider name
- Name of database server
- Name of database
- User ID and password

Depending on the provider and database that you want to connect to, all or some of the parts of the connection string are used.

Code 5.1 shows a function `ConnectToDb()` that uses the **connection string** property to connect to an Access database, EmpData.mdb, created in the previous section.

```
Dim ConStr As String
Dim Con as As ADODB.Connection


Private Sub ConnectToDb()
    ConStr = "Provider=microsoft.jet.OLEDB.3.51;" _
    & "Data Source=C:\EmpData.mdb"


    Set Con = New ADODB.Connection 'Establish a new connection
    Con.ConnectionString = ConStr
    'Other lines of code
End Sub
```

Code 5.1: Connecting to an Access Database Using OLE DB

In Code 5.1, the variable **ConStr** is set to the provider name (OLE DB), and Data source of the Access database. A new connection variable, **Con**, is defined to establish a connection to the database.

To use ODBC you have to create a Data Source Name (DSN). To create a DSN:

1. Open your computer's Control Panel and double-click on the **ODBC** icon.

2.   The **ODBC Data Source Administrator** dialog box opens, as shown in Figure 5.28.

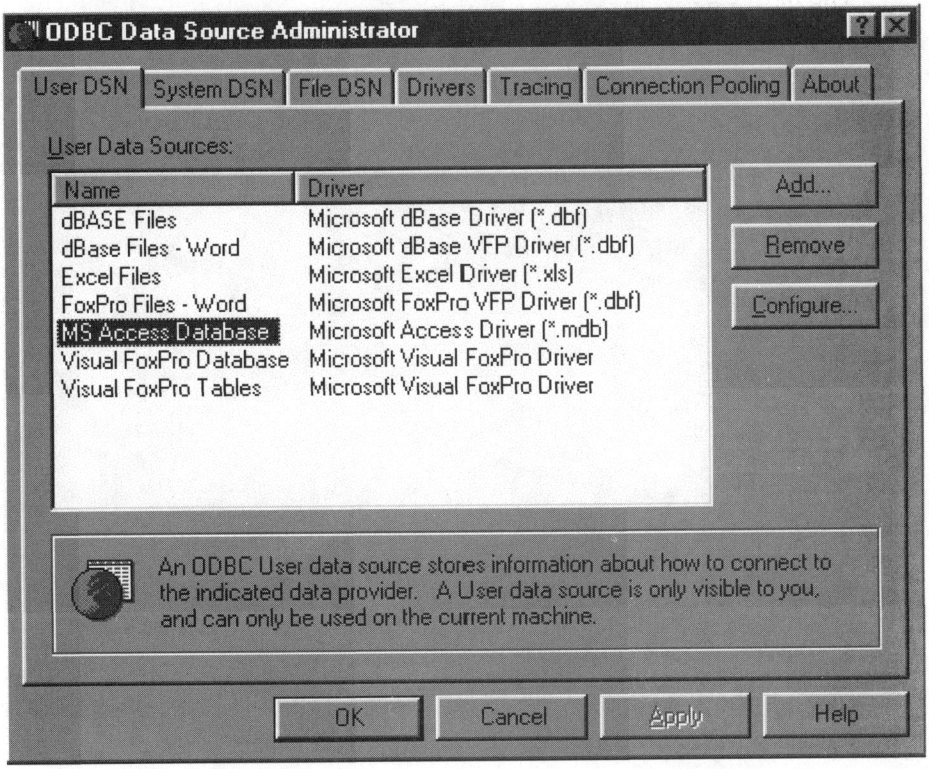

Figure 5.28: ODBC Data Source Administrator Dialog Box

3.	Double-click on the type of database you want to create, for example, Microsoft Access Database. The ODBC Microsoft Access Setup dialog box opens, as shown in Figure 5.29.

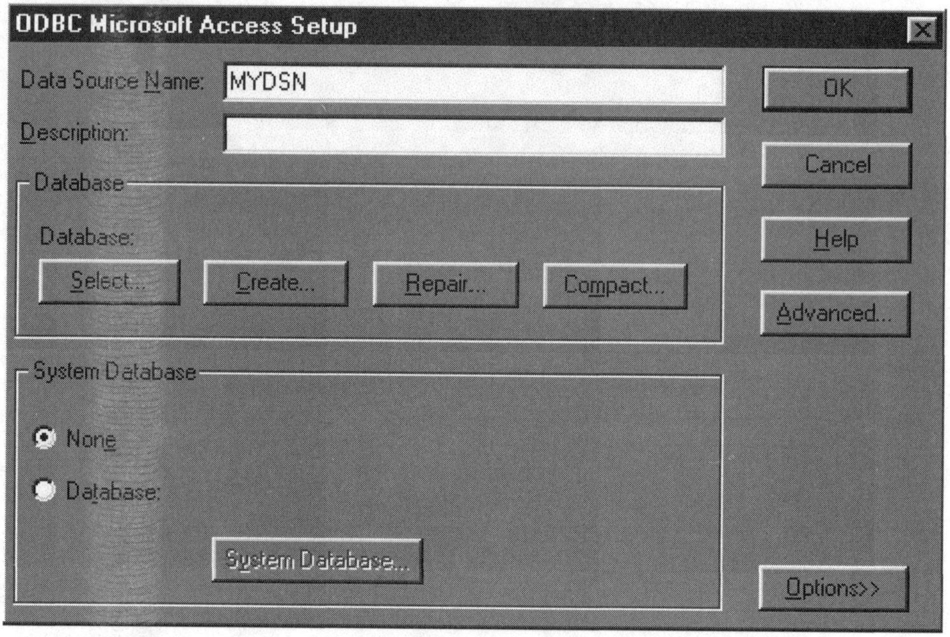

Figure 5.29: ODBC Microsoft Access Setup Dialog Box

4.	Type a name for the DSN in the Data Source Name field. Click **Select** to select a database from the existing databases, or click **Create** to create a database.

5. To set the username and password for security purposes, click the **Advanced** button. The **Set Advanced Options** dialog box opens, as shown in Figure 5.30.

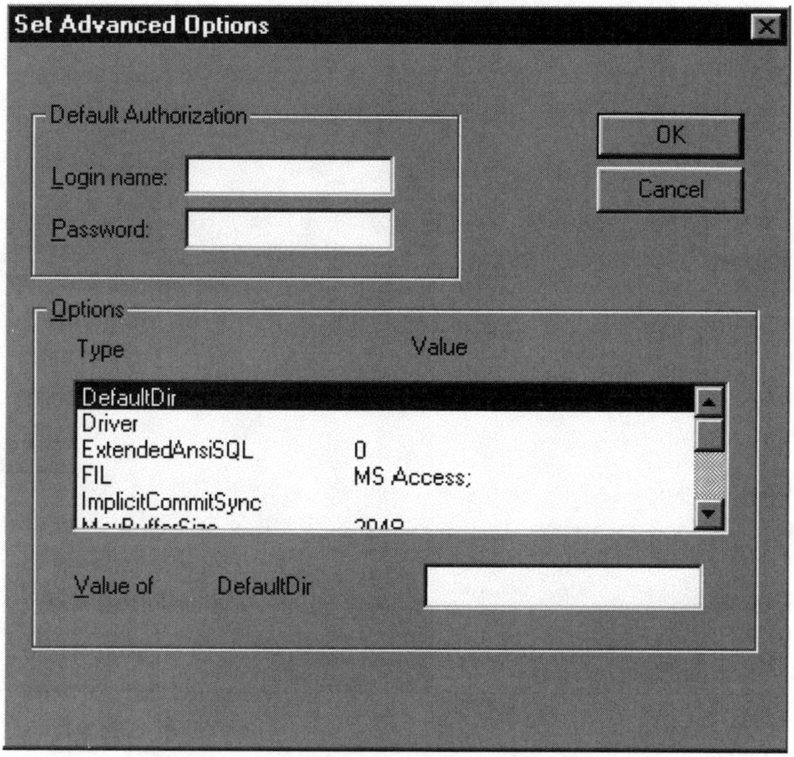

Figure 5.30: Set Advanced Options Dialog Box

You can leave the password and user name fields blank in the **Set Advanced Options** dialog box.

Code 5.2 shows a function, **ConnectToDb()**, for connecting to a database using an ODBC provider. The **connection string** property contains the DSN, a user ID, and a password.

```
Dim ConStr As String
Dim Con as As ADODB.Connection
Private Sub ConnectToDb()
    ConStr = "DSN = MYDSN;UID =;PWD="


    Set Con = New ADODB.Connection 'Establish a new connection
    Con.ConnectionString = ConStr
    'Other lines of code
End Sub
```

Code 5.2: Connecting to a Database Supporting ODBC

In Code 5.2, a connection is established to an ODBC database by specifying the DSN, user ID, and password.

It is a good programming practice to pass the value of the connection string as an argument to the function establishing a connection to the database. This makes the code independent of the database provider and enables you to connect to ODBC or OLE DB database using the same function.

By default, connections are established in a read-only mode; you can only read from the database but you can't write to it. You can change the mode of the database connection by setting the **Mode** property of the connection object.

The possible values for the mode property are shown in Table 5.5.

Value	Constant	Description
AdModeUnknown	0	Unknown mode
AdModeRead	1	Only read data from the database
AdModeWrite	2	Only write data to the database
AdModeReadWrite	3	Read and write data to the database
AdModeShareDenyRead	4	Prevent other connections from reading the database
AdModeShareDenyWrite	8	Prevent other connections from writing to the database, but allow them to read from the database
AdModeShareExclusive	&Hc	Prevent other connections from opening the database
AdModeShareDenyNone	&H10	Allow other connections to access the database without any permissions
AdModeRecursive	&H400000	Used in conjunction with other share type modes to apply the settings of those share modes to a subset of records in the database

Table 5.5: Possible Values for the Mode Property

The **adModeRead**, **adModeWrite**, and **adModeReadWrite** are the most commonly used modes. The share type modes are used for Web-based applications.

When a query is executed, you need to navigate through the result, called a Recordset. A cursor lets you control the navigation through the Recordset. Cursors can be created for the client as well as the server. Using a server-side cursor is resource intensive because the connection has to be open until the cursor is in use. In addition, only one server-side cursor is supported at a time. Nevertheless, using cursors enables your application to access data almost instantly. Client-side cursors are slower. Multiple client-side cursors may be maintained at a time. The location of cursors is controlled by the **CursorLocation** property.

You can create a client cursor by setting the value of the **CursorLocation** property to adUseClient. Setting the value of the **CursorLocation** property to adUseServer creates a server-side cursor. Code Snippet 5.3 shows the function **ConnectToDb()** to connect to a database modified to set the mode and cursor location.

```
Dim ConStr As String
Dim Con as As ADODB.Connection
Dim mode
Dim cursorloc
Private Sub ConnectToDb(ConStr, mode, cursorloc)
    Set Con = New ADODB.Connection 'Establish a new connection
    Con.Mode = mode
    Con.CursorLocation = cursorloc
    Con.ConnectionString = ConStr
    'Other lines of code
End Sub
```

Code 5.3: Function ConnectToDb()

In Code 5.3, the function **ConnectToDb( )** establishes a connection to the database. The mode, cursor location, and connection string are passed as arguments to the function.

Another property of the Connection object is the **Errors** property that stores an **Error** type object. It is used to retrieve information about errors that occur while using an ADO connection to a database.

Connection Object Methods

A connection is opened using the Open method of the Connection object. The Open method has the following four optional arguments:

- Connection string
- User ID
- Password
- Options argument having any one of the values from the ConnectOptionEnum constants

If you have set the connection string, user ID, or password using the **ConnectionString** property of the connection object, then the arguments to the Open method are omitted.

An open connection must be closed when it is not required using the **Close** method of the Connection object.

Code Snippet 5.4 shows a connection being established and closed.

```
Dim ConStr As String
Dim Con as As ADODB.Connection

Private Sub ConnectToDb(ConStr, mode, cursor)
    Set Con = New ADODB.Connection 'Establish a new connection
    Con.ConnectionString = ConStr
    Con.Mode = mode
    Con.CursorLocation = cursorloc
    Con.Open 'Open a connection
    'Other lines of code
End Sub


Private Sub DisConDb()
    Con.Close 'Close the connection
    Set Con = Nothing
End Sub
```

Code 5.4: Opening and Closing a Connection

In Code 5.4 a connection is established in the function **ConnectToDb()**, as explained in Code 5.3.

The **Open** method can be executed without any arguments. You can also pass user name and password to the **Open** method. Finally the **Close** method is executed to close the connection in the **DisConDb()** function. Invoking the **Close** method when the connection is not open will result in an error. This situation can be avoided by checking the **State** property of the connection object.

The **Execute** method of the connection object is used to execute certain SQL commands or stored procedures in the database. It has three arguments:

■ **CommandText**: An SQL statement, table, view, or stored procedure name.

■ **RecordsAffected**: A variable containing the number of records affected after the Execute method finishes executing. This argument is optional.

- **Options**: CommandTypeEnum constant that specifies the type of query and whether to return a Recordset object. The possible values for this argument are adCmdText, adCmdTable, adCmdTableDirect, adCmdStoredProc, adCmdFile, or adCmdUnknown depending on the CommandText argument. This argument is optional.

The **Execute** method manipulates the database based on its first argument called ComandText. By default, the Execute method returns a Recordset object (discussed later). The Recordset object stores the result of the query that is executed. If your query does not require the Execute method to return a Recordset, then you can add the **adExecuteNoRecords** constant to the Options argument.

Although most of the arguments passed to methods in ADO are optional, it is advisable to set their values explicitly in your code. This makes the code more flexible. If you do not provide values for optional arguments, they are set by ADO. This reduces your control on the application and the speed of the application.

Once the database has been created, the next step is to create the interfaces to provide access, and to manipulate the data stored in the database. Let us consider the interface, which enables the user to delete the record of an employee. The interface accepts the ID of the employee whose record is to be deleted, and deletes the record when the user clicks the **Delete** button. The GUI asks for the user's confirmation before proceeding with the record deletion task.

Create a new project and modify the default form as shown in Figure 5.31 to provide the interface for deleting an employee record. Name the form as frmDeleteEmp, the text box to accept the ID as txtEmpID, and the command button for the delete option as cmdDeleteEmp.

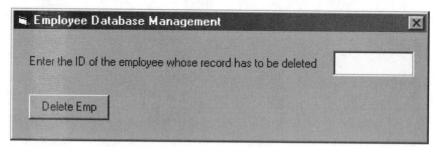

Figure 5.31: Form to Delete the Record of an Employee Based on a Specified Employee ID

Following are the steps to provide the required functionality to the form:

1.   Click **Project → References** on the menu bar to include the reference of Microsoft ActiveX Data Objects 2.0 Library in the project.

2.   Enter Code 5.5 in the code window of the form.

The code declares a module level variable named dbCon to store the database connection object. The **Form Load** event opens the database connection for the EmpData database created above. The **Form Unload** event is used to close the connection object.

```
Option Explicit
Dim dbCon As ADODB.Connection

Private Sub Form_Load()
  Set dbCon = New ADODB.Connection
  dbCon.ConnectionString = "Provider=Microsoft.Jet.OLEDB.3.51;" _
+ _
    "Data Source=C:\EmpData.mdb"
  dbCon.Mode = adModeReadWrite
  dbCon.CursorLocation = adUseClient
  dbCon.Open
End Sub


Private Sub Form_Unload(Cancel As Integer)
  If dbCon.State = adStateOpen Then dbCon.Close
End Sub
```

Code 5.5: Opening and Closing the Connection Object

3. In order to ensure that the user enters only numeric values for the employee ID, enter the Code 5.6 for the **KeyPress** event of the text box txtEmpID. The code allows only numeric values as input in the text box.

```
Private Sub txtEmpID_KeyPress(KeyAscii As Integer)
  If Not IsNumeric(Chr(KeyAscii)) Then
    KeyAscii = 0
  End If
End Sub
```

Code 5.6: Preventing Non-Numeric Values as Input

4. Write Code 5.7 to perform the actual task of deleting the record of the desired employee.

The code first checks if the text box for the employee ID is empty. If it is empty, the user is asked to enter a valid employee ID. If the user has entered an employee ID, it asks for the confirmation of the user to delete the employee record. If the user approves it, the desired record is deleted by executing the appropriate DELETE statement on the connection object. Appropriate messages are displayed at the end to inform the user about the task being performed.

```
Private Sub cmdDeleteEmp_Click()
  If Trim(Me.txtEmpID) = "" Then
    MsgBox "Please enter a valid Employee ID", vbCritical, _
      "Employee Database Management"
  Else
    If MsgBox("Are you sure to delete the record", _
      vbQuestion + vbYesNo, "Confirm Delete") = vbYes Then

      dbCon.Execute "DELETE FROM employee WHERE id=" & _
        Trim(Me.txtEmpID)

      MsgBox "Record deleted", vbExclamation, _
        "Employee Database Management"
    Else
      MsgBox "Record Deletion cancelled", _
        vbExclamation, "Employee Database Management"
```

```
     End If
   End If
End Sub
```

Code 5.7: Deleting an Employee Record Based on the Employee ID

5.   Save and run the project.

Figure 5.32 displays the record deletion form during run time.

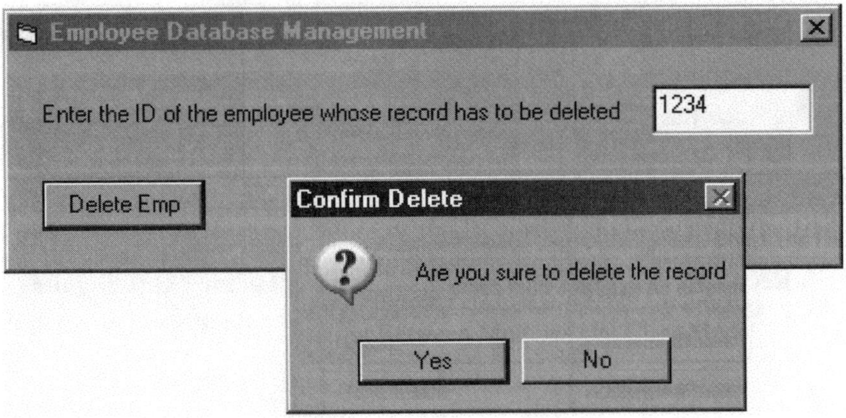

Figure 5.32: Time View of the Form to Delete the Record of an Employee

Recordset Object

A Recordset is similar to a table in structure. It contains records returned when a query is executed. The values in the Recordset may belong to different tables (JOIN Query) or they may be calculated from other values. You can search and sort a Recordset, convert them into strings or arrays, read/write them to a disk or display the values in list boxes. A Recordset object is instantiated by using the **New** keyword as:

```
Dim rs As ADODB.Recordset
Set rs = New ADODB.Recordset
```

Recordset Object Properties

The most commonly used properties of the Recordset object are Sort, EOF, BOF, and RecordCount. The Number of records in a Recordset can be obtained from the value of the RecordCount property. The RecordCount property is a read-only property. You cannot alter the value of this property.

You can sort a Recordset based on one or more fields. The name of the field on which the Recordset is sorted is set as the value of the **Sort** property of the Recodset object. If the sorting is done on more than one field, then the Sort property is set to the string containing all the field names separated by commas. The string assigned to the Sort property is called the sorting string. By default, sorting is done in ascending order. You can specify the order add ASC or DESC to the end of the sorting string.

You can check the end or beginning of a Recordset using the EOF or BOF properties. When the cursor is at the end of the Recordset the EOF property is set to **True**. The BOF property is set to true when the cursor is at the beginning of a Recordset. Both the properties are read-only. In the case of an empty Recordset, both the BOF and EOF properties are set to True.

The Recordset object also has a Fields property that stores a Field Object Type value. It is used for accessing the fields of records in the Recordset. It is a read-only property.

Recordset Object Methods

A Recordset is opened before it is used, except while executing the Execute Method of the Connection object. The Open method of the Recordset object opens a Recordset. It takes the following arguments:

- **CommandText**: The query to be executed.
- **Connection/ConnectionString**: A ConnectionString or reference to a Connection Object.
- **CursorType**: One of the adCursorTypeEnum constants. The possible values for the type of cursor used in the Recordset are shown in Table 5.6.

Value	Constant	Description
AdOpenForwardOnly	0	Returns a cursor that can traverse the Recordset only in the forward direction. This is the default and fastest cursor type.
AdOpenKeyset	1	Returns a cursor that can move forward, backward, to the first record, to the last record, and to bookmarks. Changes made to records in the Recordset by other users are visible but the records added after you opened a Recordset are not accessible. Records deleted by others are not accessible. Preferred cursor for a large Recordset.
AdOpenDynamic	2	Returns a dynamic cursor. Similar to the adOpenKeyset cursor except that you can see records added after the Recordset is opened. It is faster than a keyset cursor. It requires maximum resources.

Value	Constant	Description
AdOpenStatic	3	Returns a static cursor. It is a fixed Recordset. You cannot see changes made by others but you can update records.

Table 5.6: Possible Values for the CursorType

■ **LockTypes**: Specifies constraints on accessing the records. The possible values for the LockType argument are shown in Table 5.7.

Value	Constant	Description
adLockReadOnly	1	The data cannot be modified when this lock type is used.
adLockPessimistic	2	Records become inaccessible to other user. The record remains locked until the Recordset object is closed.
adLockOptimistic	3	Records are locked prior to an update and unlocked soon after the update is over. Records are accessible to other users while updating.
adLockBatchOptimistic	4	Similar to Optimistic lock except that it is used for batch updates.

Table 5.7: Possible Values for the LockType Argument

■ **Options**: CommandTypeEnum constant that specifies the type of query. The possible values for this argument are, adCmdText, adCmdTable, adCmdTableDirect, adCmdStoredProc, adCmdFile, and adCmdUnknown depending on the CommandText argument.

The **Close** method of the Recordset object is used to close a Recordset.

Code Snippet 5.8 shows the opening and closing a Recordset.

```
Dim rs As ADODB.Recordset
Dim ConStr As String
Dim Con As ADODB.Connection
Dim recsaff
Dim mode
Dim loc
Dim sql As String
sql= "SELECT FirstName, LastName FROM Employee WHERE Age=25"

Private Sub ConnectToDb(mode, loc, ConStr)
    Set Con = New ADODB.Connection
```

```
      Con.ConnectionString = ConStr
      Con.mode = mode
      Con.CursorLocation = loc
      Con.Open 'Open a connection
  End Sub


  Private Sub OpenRecSet(sql As String)
      Set rs = New ADODB.Recordset
      rs.Open sql, ConStr, adOpenForwardOnly, adLockReadOnly, _
          adCmdText
      'Other lines of Code
  End Sub


  Private Sub CloseRecSet()
      rs.Close
      Set rs = Nothing
  End Sub


  Private Sub DisConDb()
      Con.Close 'Close the connection
      Set Con=Nothing
  End Sub
```

Code 5.8: Opening and Closing a Recordset

In Code 5.8, a connection to the EmpData database is established by the
ConnectToDb() procedure. rs is a Recordset object type variable. In the **OpenRecSet()**
function a Recordset is opened by executing the **rs.Open** method. The Recordset is
opened to execute a query that retrieves the first and last names of employees whose age
is 25. The query is passed as an argument to the **OpenRecSet()** function. The Recordset
is **forwardonly** and **ReadOnly**. The Recordset is then closed in the **CloseRecSet()**
function. Finally the connection is closed in the **DisConDb( )** function.

You can obtain a ForwardOnly ReadOnly Recordset by calling the Connection.Execute method. The Connection.Execute method returns only this type of Recordset. For any other type of record set, use the Recordset object.

The **MoveNext** method of the Recordset object moves the cursor to the record next to the current record. The **MovePrevious** method moves the cursor to the record previous to the current record. The **MoveFirst** method moves the cursor to the first record in the Recordset. The **MoveLast** method moves the cursor to the last record in the Recordset.

The **Update** method updates the Recordset if any modifications are made to the Recordset. To use the **Update** method, the connection mode and Recordset cursor type should support updating.

If changes are made to a Recordset using the Execute method of the connection object, then the Update method does not need to be called. The Connection.Execute method automatically updates the Recordset.

You can perform an update for a set of records in a single call to the **UpdateBatch** method of the Recordset object with the LockType set to adLockBatchOptimistic.

The Recordset object also includes a Find method for searching records. The Find method accepts three optional arguments and one mandatory argument. These arguments are as follows:

- **Search Criteria**: A string specifying the values to be searched for in the Recordset. The string may include multiple conditions.
- **SkipRecords**: Specifies the number of records to skip before beginning to search. This argument is optional.
- **SearchDirection**: Specifies the direction to search, adSearchForward or adSearchBackward. This argument is optional.
- **Start**: The record number where the search has to begin. This argument is optional and is not required if the SkipRecords argument is defined.

Once the Recordset object is opened and filled with records, the values of the fields in the records can be retrieved using a zero-based index number or by using the name of the field enclosed in double-quotes. The zero-based number represents the index of the field in the record.

Code 5.9 opens a recordset with the record of an employee, retrieves the first name and the last name from it, and displays it in the Immediate window.

```
Dim rs As ADODB.Recordset
Dim conStr As String


conStr = "Provider=microsoft.jet.OLEDB.4.0;" & _
    "Data Source=C:\EmpData.mdb"


Set rs = New ADODB.Recordset
rs.Open "select firstname, lastname from employee where d=1003"_
    , conStr, adOpenForwardOnly, adLockReadOnly


Debug.Print rs(0) & " " & rs("lastname")


rs.Close
```

Code 5.9: Retrieving Values from a Recordset

In Code snippet 5.9, the first name is retrieved using the index and the last name is retrieved using the name of the field.

The code retrieves values from a recordset with a single record. The following example demonstrates how to do the same with a recordset having multiple records. Let us consider the interface to display the names of all the employees in the Employee table of the EmpData database. Create a new project and modify the default form as shown in Figure 5.33. Name the form frmEmpNames. Set the name of the list box to display the names as lstEmpNames and the command button as cmdDisplayNames.

Figure 5.33 displays the modified form.

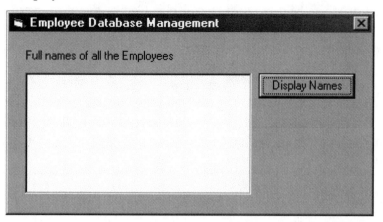

Figure 5.33: Form to Display the Names of all the Employees

Write Code 5.10 in the code window of the form frmEmpNames. The code declares a module level variable of ADODB Connection object type to store the database connection. The Form Load event is used to open the connection to the EmpData database and the Form Unload event is used to close the database connection.

```
Option Explicit
Dim dbCon As ADODB.Connection

Private Sub Form_Load()
  Set dbCon = New ADODB.Connection
  dbCon.ConnectionString = "Provider=Microsoft.Jet.OLEDB.3.51;"_
    + "Data Source=C:\EmpData.mdb"
  dbCon.Mode = adModeReadWrite
  dbCon.CursorLocation = adUseClient
  dbCon.Open
End Sub

Private Sub Form_Unload(Cancel As Integer)
  If dbCon.State = adStateOpen Then dbCon.Close
End Sub
```

Code 5.10: Opening and Closing a Connection Object

The names of the employees are retrieved from the Employee table and displayed in the list box when the user clicks the Display Names command button. Write Code 5.11 for the click event of the command button cmdDisplayNames. The code creates a new Recordset object to store the records of the employees. Notice that while opening the Recordset object, instead of providing a connection string as the previous example, the connection object dbCon is passed as an argument. The code loops through all the records in the recordset using the MoveNext method in a while loop. The loop terminates when the EOF property of the recordset is set to true. The while loop concatenates the first name and the last name of each record into a single string and adds it to the list box named lstEmpNames.

```
Private Sub cmdDisplayNames_Click()
  Dim rs As ADODB.Recordset
  Set rs = New ADODB.Recordset

  rs.Open "select firstname, lastname from employee", _
     dbCon, adOpenForwardOnly, adLockReadOnly

  While Not rs.EOF
    Me.lstEmpNames.AddItem rs("firstName") + " " + _
       rs("lastName")
    rs.MoveNext
  Wend

  rs.Close
End Sub
```

Code 5.11: Retrieving Values from a Recordset with Multiple Records

Figure 5.34 displays the form frmEmpNames during run time.

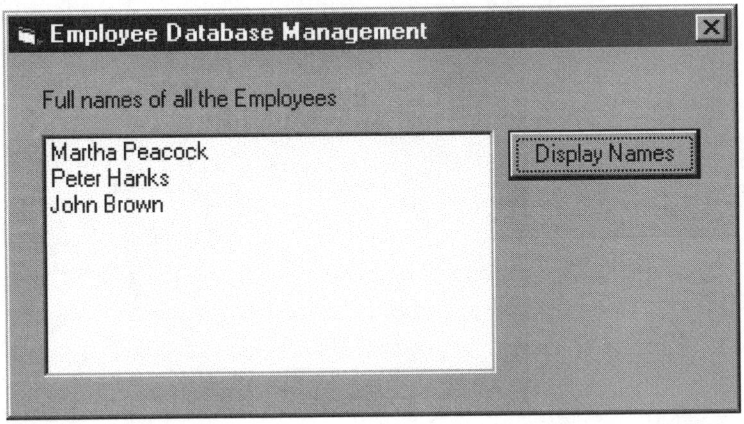

Figure 5.34: Run Time View of the Form to Display the Names of All the Employees

The Recordset object provides a **Delete** method, which can be used to delete the current record in the Recordset object. Let us reconsider the previous example of deleting an employee record and modifying the code for the click event of the command button cmdDeleteEmp given in Code 5.7. Code 5.12 is the modified form, which makes use of the Recordset object and deletes the record using its **Delete** method.

```
Private Sub cmdDeleteEmp_Click()
  If Trim(Me.txtEmpID) = "" Then
    MsgBox "Please enter a valid Employee ID", vbCritical, _
      "Employee Database Management"
  Else
    rs.Open "select * from employee where id=" & _
      Trim(Me.txtEmpID), dbCon, adOpenForwardOnly, _
        adLockOptimistic

    If rs.EOF = True And rs.BOF = True Then
        MsgBox "Record not found", vbCritical, _
        "Employee Database Management"
    Else
      If MsgBox("Are you sure to delete the record", _
          vbQuestion + vbYesNo, "Confirm Delete") = vbYes Then
```

```
        rs.Delete
        MsgBox "Record deleted", vbExclamation, _
          "Employee Database Management"
      Else

        MsgBox "Record Deletion cancelled", _
          vbExclamation, "Employee Database Management"
      End If
    End If
    If rs.State = adStateOpen Then rs.Close
  End If
End Sub
```

Code 5.12: Deleting a Record Using the Delete Method of the Recordset Object

In Code 5.12, the Recordset object is created with the record for the specified employee ID. If there is a record with the given employee ID, the Recordset object is filled with the records; otherwise it is left empty. If the recordset is empty both the BOF and the EOF property of the Recordset object is set to true. An appropriate message is displayed if there is no record for the specified employee ID. If there is a record for the given employee ID, the user is asked for the confirmation to delete the record. The record is deleted using the Delete method of the Recordset object upon the approval of the user. This shows how the Recordset and Connection objects can be used together to make more efficient programs.

Field Object

The field object is used to access the individual fields of records in a Recordset. This object is used mostly when you need to display the values of fields in a record. Field objects have a number of attributes such as type, size, range, value etc.

Field Object Properties

The most frequently used properties of the Field object are:

▓ **Name**: A string that specifies the name of the field. This is a read-only property.

▓ **Type**: Contains one of the values of the DataTypeEnum constants that specify the data type of the field.

- **Value**: Specifies the value of the field. You can modify the value of a field in a record using this property.
- **ActualSize**: A read-only property that specifies the actual size of the field.
- **Attributes**: This property is set to adFldLong if the value in the field is a Long type value, either text or binary.

Field Object Methods

The Field Object includes only two methods. The first is the **GetChunk** method that retrieves characters of a specified size. The size is passed as an argument to the method. The second method is the **AppendChunk** that appends a chunk of characters passed to it as an argument.

Let us consider an interface, which accepts the name of a table in the EmpData database and displays the field names in the table. It also displays the length and data type of the selected field and lists the data in the selected field. Since the purpose of the interface is related to the information of the fields, we need to use the ADO Field object.

Figure 5.35 displays the required interface in the design view. Create a new project and add controls to the default form as shown in Figure 5.35.

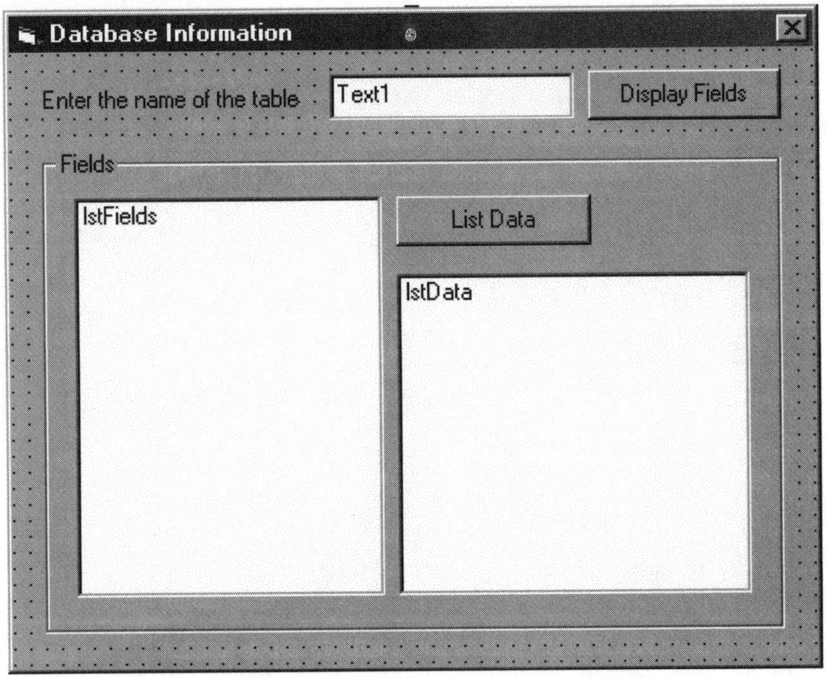

Figure 5.35: Design View of the Interface to Display Field Information in a Table

Name the form frmDBInfo. Set the name of the text box to accept the table name as txtTableName, the command button to display the fields as cmdDisplayFields, the list box to display the names of the fields as lstFields, the command button to display the data in a field as cmdListData, and the list box to display the data in a field as lstData.

Write Code 5.13 in the code window of the form frmDBInfo. The code declares two module-level variables named dbCon and rs to store the database connection and the recordset. The form load event is used to open the database connection to the EmpData database and the form unload event is used to close the connection and the recordset.

```
Option Explicit
Dim dbCon As ADODB.Connection
Dim rs As ADODB.Recordset
Private Sub Form_Load()
  Set dbCon = New ADODB.Connection
  dbCon.ConnectionString = "Provider=Microsoft.Jet.OLEDB.3.51;"_
     + "Data Source=C:\EmpData.mdb"
  dbCon.Mode = adModeReadWrite
  dbCon.CursorLocation = adUseClient
  dbCon.Open
  Set rs = New ADODB.Recordset
End Sub


Private Sub Form_Unload(Cancel As Integer)
  If rs.State = adStateOpen Then rs.Close
  If dbCon.State = adStateOpen Then dbCon.Close
End Sub
```

Code 5.13: Open and Close the Database Connection

Write Code 5.14 for the click event of the command button cmdDisplayFields. It checks whether the text box for the table name is empty. If it is not, it opens a recordset retrieving all the fields in the specified table. The code loops through all the fields in the recordset and adds the name of each of the fields to the list box lstFields. An appropriate error handler is used to avoid error resulting from incorrect table names.

```
Private Sub cmdDisplayFields_Click()
  On Error GoTo errmsg
```

```
    If Trim(Me.txtTableName) <> "" Then
       If rs.State = adStateOpen Then rs.Close
       rs.ActiveConnection = dbCon
       rs.CursorType = adOpenForwardOnly
       rs.LockType = adLockReadOnly
       rs.Open "select * from " + Trim(Me.txtTableName)
       Dim fld As ADODB.Field
       Me.lstFields.Clear
       For Each fld In rs.Fields
          Me.lstFields.AddItem fld.Name
       Next
    End If
    Exit Sub
errmsg:
    MsgBox Err.Description, vbCritical
End Sub
```

Code 5.14: Retrieve Field Names from a Recordset

Write Code 5.15 for the click event of the command button cmdListData. The code opens a recordset to retrieve the values in the selected field name in the list box lstFields. The code then adds loops through the values in the recordset and adds them to the list box lstData. It uses the **IsNull()** function to check whether the field contains a null value.

```
Private Sub cmdListData_Click()
   If Me.lstFields.ListIndex >= 0 Then
      If rs.State = adStateOpen Then rs.Close
      rs.ActiveConnection = dbCon
      rs.CursorType = adOpenForwardOnly
      rs.LockType = adLockReadOnly
      rs.Open "select " + Trim(Me.lstFields.Text) + " from " + _
         Trim(Me.txtTableName)
      Me.lstData.Clear
      While Not rs.EOF
         Me.lstData.AddItem IIf(Not IsNull(rs(0)), rs(0), "")
         rs.MoveNext
```

```
      Wend
   End If
End Sub
```

Code 5.15: Retrieve Data from the Selected Field

Figure 5.36 shows the run time view of the form displaying the data in the FirstName field of the Employee table.

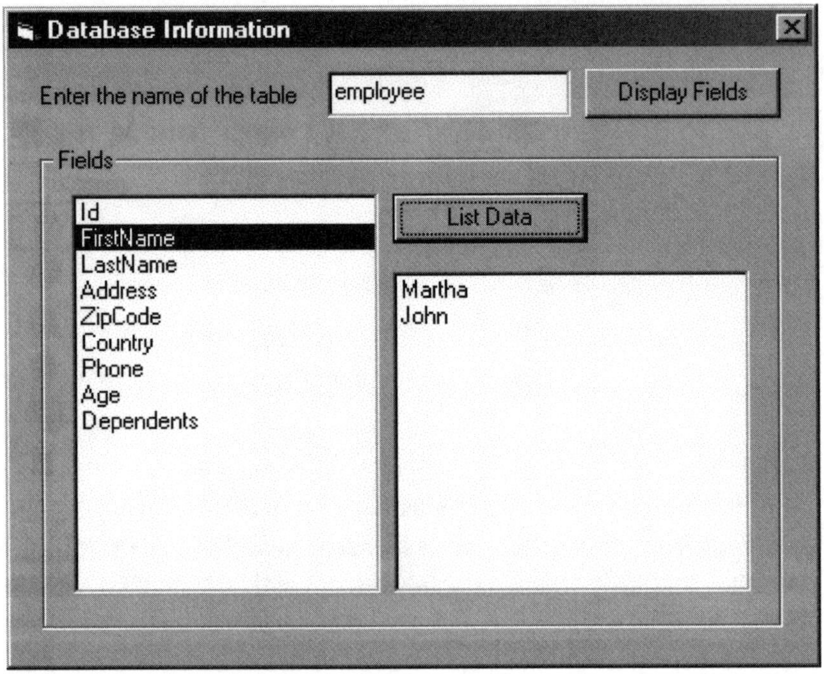

Figure 5.36: Run Time View of the Interface to Display Field Information in a Table

1. What is the name of the reference library that should be included in order to implement ADO (ActiveX Data Object) functionality in a Visual Basic project? Mention the steps to include this reference.

2. Name objects available in the ADO model. Write the code snippet to create a Connection object and open a database connection to a MS Access database named Banking.mdb that is stored in the root directory of the C drive.

3. Which ADO object do you use to access the records retrieved by a SELECT statement? Write the code snippet to create such an object and store all the records retrieved from a table named Clients. Assume that the table is in the same database mentioned in question 2.

4. How will you check if there is a record in a Recordset object or if it is an empty Recordset?

5. Point out the error in the following SELECT statement and explain the reason.

```
SELECT * FROM Employee HAVING country LIKE 'USA'
```

Case Study

The following section covers creating the database in MS Access. The design of the database was finalized at the initial stage of the development of the Library Management System in Chapter 2 "User Interface Models and Design Processes." This section will also add functionality related to the ADO model in the project.

1. Based on the structure being finalized for the database, the actual tables are designed for the database. The database will contain four tables, Books, Categories, Members, and BookIssue. The following tables list the structures of these tables.

Structure of the Books Table 5.8:

Column Name	Date Type and Size	Description
ISBN	Text – 15 characters	ISBN number of the book – set as primary key
BookName	Text – 50 characters	Name of the book
Author	Text – 50 characters	Name of the author
Price	Currency	Price of the book
Publication	Text – 50 characters	Name of the publication
CategoryID	Number – Long Integer	Category ID of the book
Availability	Yes/No	Availability status – set the Format to True/False

Table 5.8: Structure of Book Table for Case Study

Structure of Categories Table 5.9:

Column Name	Date Type and Size	Description
CategoryID	AutoNumber – Long Integer	Category ID – primary key
CategoryName	Text – 50 characters	Name of the category

Table 5.9: Structure of Categories Table for Case Study

Structure of the Members Table 5.10:

Column Name	Date Type and Size	Description
RegNo	AutoNumber – Long Integer	Registration number of the member – primary key
FirstName	Text – 20 characters	First name of the member
LastName	Text – 20 characters	Last name of the member
Address	Text – 100 characters	Address of the member
City	Text – 30 characters	Name of the city
Country	Text – 20 characters	Name of the country
Phone	Text – 20 characters	Phone number of the member

Table 5.10: Structure of Members Table for Case Study

Structure of BookIssue Table 5.11:

Column Name	Date Type and Size	Description
ISBN	Text – 15 characters	ISBN number of the book being issued – primary key
RegNo	Number – Long Integer	Registration number of the member issue to – primary key
IssueDate	Date/Time	Date of issue
ReturnDate	Date/Time	Estimated date of return
ReturnedOn	Date/Time	Actual date of return

Table 5.11: Structure of BookIssue Table for Case Study

2. Start MS Access and create a blank database with the name LibraryMgmt.mdb. Create the database in the same folder as that of the Library Management System project.

3. Create the tables named Books, Categories, Members, and BookIssue as per the structures given in the preceding tables.

4. Open the VB project named LibraryMgmt.

5. Add a module to the project by selecting **Project → Add Module** on the menu bar. Set the name of the module as modMain. This module will be used to provide a public variable to store the connection string to the above

database. The module will also initialize the database connection for the database and provide a starting procedure for the project.

6. Add the reference of Microsoft ActiveX Data Objects 2.0 Library in the project by selecting **Project → Reference** from the menu bar.

7. Add Code 5.16 to the module named modMain. The code declares two public variables named dbCon and strConString to store the ADO database connection and the connection string of the database. It also defines a procedure named Main that assigns the connection string to the variable, creates an ADO Connection object, and opens the connection for the given connection string. Finally it displays the MDI form frmMain. The public variable named strConString will be used throughout the project whenever a connection string to the database will be required, as given in Code 5.16.

```
Option Explicit
Public dbCon As ADODB.Connection
Public strConString As String
Public Sub Main()
  strConString = "Provider=Microsoft.Jet.OLEDB.4.0;Data Source="
+ App.Path + "\LibraryMgmt.mdb"


  Set dbCon = New ADODB.Connection
  dbCon.Open strConString
  frmMain.Show
End Sub
```

Code 5.16: Sample Code for ADO Database Connection

8. Select **Project → LibraryMgmt** Properties from the menu bar to display the project properties dialog box, as shown below, and select Sub Main as the Startup Object of the project, as shown in Figure 5.37.

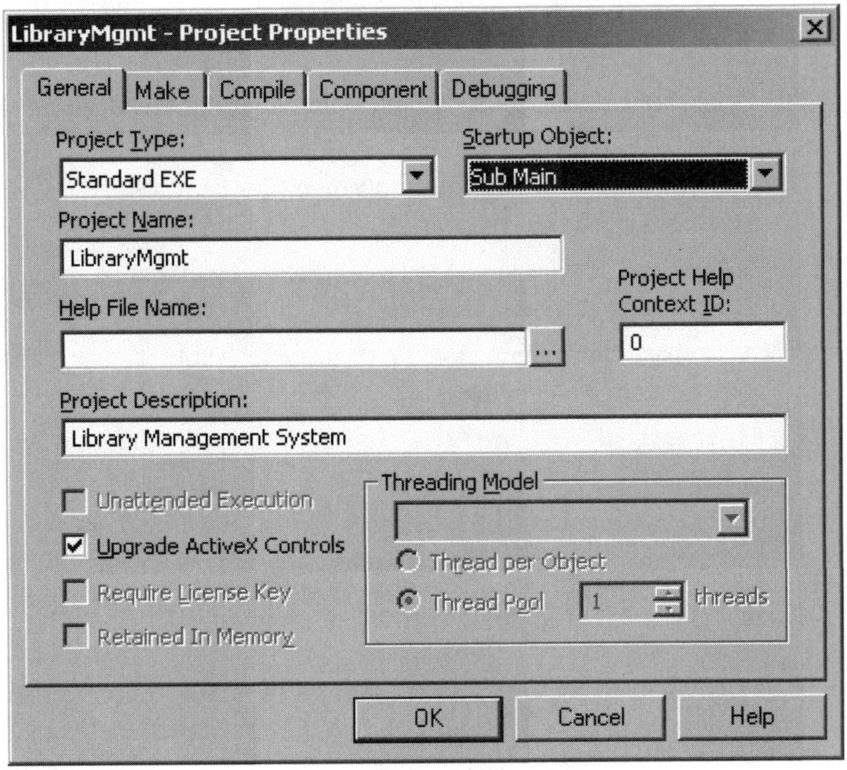

Figure 5.37: Project Properties

9. Save the project.

Summary

- A database is a collection of related data stored in one place, and accessed by multiple users.

- Databases enforce standards, maintain integrity, provide security, and reduce inconsistencies and redundancy of data.

- Databases are preferred over sequential files because they provide the features of random and indexed file storage.

- In databases, data is stored in tables. Each row of a table represents a record of the database and each column represents fields within records.

- A database can contain more than one table. Tables can be created from scratch or derived from existing tables.

- Databases enforce constraints such as primary keys, foreign keys, and indexes for secure and efficient functioning.

- An index is a column of values that is used to mark records in a database table. Indexes make it easy to search and sort records in a database.

- A primary key is a field that uniquely identifies each row or record in a database table.

- Database providers provide an interface for software to access database. Three main database providers are OLE DB, ODBC, and JDBC.

- Retrieval, insertion, deletion and updating operations are performed to make use of the data stored in databases.

- Operations that affect the state of the database are carried out as transactions. Transactions either complete successfully or fail.

- When transactions fail the state of the database is rolled back to its initial state before the transaction occurred.

- SQL is a specialized language that includes commands called queries to access and modify a database.

- The SELECT statement retrieves data from a table.

- The INSERT statement adds data to a table.

- The DELETE statement deletes records from a table.

- The UPDATE statement modifies values in a table.

- The JOIN operator joins the records in two tables on a common field.

- Databases can be created using Visual Basic's Visual Data Manager.

- Visual Data Manager has a very user friendly GUI that facilitates quick, efficient, and easy creation of databases.

- Databases can also be created explicitly outside Visual Basic in Access, Exchange, or other such database software.

- Databases can be manipulated by creating queries in Visual Data Manager. You can see the results of the query instantly.

- A more versatile way to access and modify databases is to use the ADO.

- ADO is particularly suitable for large-scale, Web-based, client/server applications.

- Five main objects comprising ADO are: Connection object, Recordset object, Field object, Command object, and Error object.

- The Connection object establishes a connection to a database. This object forms the foundations for all other objects to operate.

- A connection object is instantiated using the New operator to allocate memory to a variable of type ADODB.Connection.

- A Connection object has properties such as Connection mode, Cursor location, and Connection string.

- The Connection string property specifies the name of the provider, source, database, user Id, and password.

- The mode property specifies the access permissions for the database. By default, a connection is opened in read only mode.

- The Cursor location property decides how a Recordset can be traversed.

- The Connection object has a number of methods. The Open method opens a connection and the close method closes a connection.

- The Execute method of the Connection object executes an SQL query and returns a Recordset containing the result of the query.

- A Recordset object opens a Recordset, which is a subset of records from the database.

- A Recordset object is instantiated by using the New operator to allocate memory to a variable of type ADODB.Recordset.

- The records in a Recordset are retrieved based on the result of an SQL query.

- A Recordset object has properties such as Cursortype and locktype.

- The CursorType property specifies the type of cursor that is used to traverse a Recordset.

- The LockType property defines the way in which a Recordset can be accessed for updating, deletions, and insertions.

- A Recordset object has a set of methods. The Open method opens a Recordset and the Close method closes a Recordset.

- The Update method of the Recordset objects updates a Recordset if any changes are made to the records contained in the Recordset.

- The MoveNext, MovePrevious, MoveFirst, and MoveLast method of the Recordset object move the cursor to the next record, previous record, first record, and last record.

- The Find method of the Recordset object is used to search for records in a Recordset.

- A Recordset can also be sorted on one or more fields. The sort property of the Recordset object sets the field(s) on which the Recordset is sorted.

- The field object is used to access the field of records in a Recordset. You can access names, values, and attributes of the fields of the records.

References

- http://www.library.itt-tech.edu/periodicals.asp> DATABASE JOURNAL (Accessed on Aug. 12, 2004)
- http://www.library.itt-tech.edu/periodicals.asp> MSDN Magazine (Accessed on Aug. 12, 2004)

Homework Exercises

1.   What is a primary key? What is its importance?

2.   How does the Visual Data Manager help in rapid development of applications?

3.   What is SQL? Write SQL queries to do the following:

   a.   Retrieve the records of all the employees residing in the UK from the Employee table discussed in the chapter.

   b.   Update the salaries of employees earning $10,000 to $15,000 in the Company table discussed in the chapter.

   c.   Select the values updated in the Company table and insert them into the Employee table.

   d.   Retrieve the Ids of all the employees who reside in the UK and earn less than $15,000.

4.   What is the Connection String property of the Connection object used for?

5.   How is the CursorType property of the Recordset object used?

6.   The Error object includes properties that contain information about errors that occur while using ADO objects. If you want your software to conform to the principles of good interface design, then you must present detailed information about errors that occur while using the software. The three most commonly used properties of the Error object are:

   • Number: Every error has an error number specified in the Number property.

   • Source: The Source property specifies the source of the error.

   • Description: The Description property contains a description of the error.

   • Write a code snippet to handle and display errors using the Errors collection of the connection object and the Error object properties.

Lab Exercises

Exercise 1

Objective

■ Create a database in Microsoft Access with two tables in it and fill the tables with records.

Problem Statement

Create a Database for a Computer Department Library in Microsoft Access. Name the database Library.mdb. The database should have two tables, LibraryBooks and IssueInfo.

The fields for the LibraryBooks table should be as follows:

(Data Type for a field is given in brackets)

1. ISBNNo (Text)
2. BookName (Text)
3. Author (Text)
4. Price (Currency)
5. Category (Text)
6. Publisher (Text)

The primary key for the table is ISBNNo.

The fields for the IssueInfo table should be as follows:

1. SerialNo (AutoNumber)
2. BookName (Text)
3. StudentName (Text)
4. IssueDate (Date/Time)
5. ReturnDate (Date/Time)
6. IsOverdue (Yes/No)

The primary key for the table is SerialNo.

Lab Setup

Computer Requirements:

- Microsoft Windows Operating System
- Pentium III or higher processors
- 128-MB RAM
- 3-GB of hard disk space
- CD-ROM drives
- Floppy disk drives
- LAN connections
- Visual Basic 6.0
- Microsoft Access 2000

Procedure

1. Open Microsoft Access from the Start Menu in the computer.
2. Select **File → New** from the Main Menu.
3. The Microsoft Access dialog Box appears. Select **Blank Database** and click **OK**.

4. The File New Database dialog box appears. In the ComboBox labeled FileName, enter Library as the database name. Click the **Create** button to create the database. The Database window appears, as shown in Figure 5.38.

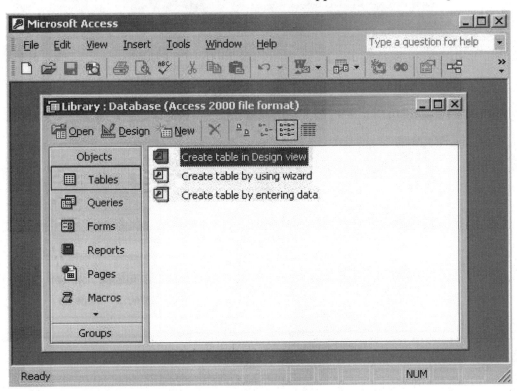

Figure 5.38: Database Window

5. Double-click the option **Create table in Design view**. A new window opens with the caption "Table1: Table." Enter the field names and data types as given in the question for the table LibraryBooks. Right-click on the field ISBNNo and select primary key in the resulting menu.

6. Close the window for Table1. A dialog box appears asking if you want to save the table. Click **Yes** and save the table as LibraryBooks.

7. Repeat steps 6 and 7 to create the table IssueInfo. Set SerialNo as the primary key.

8. In the main window, double-click the table **LibraryBooks**. Fill up the table LibraryBooks with sample values as shown in Figure 5.39.

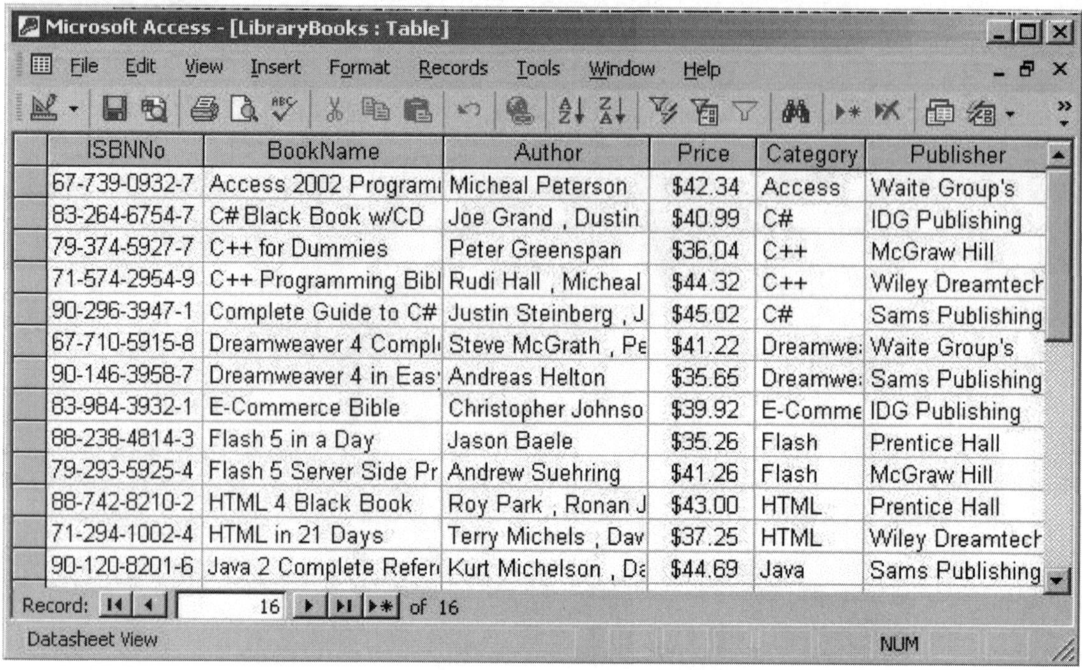

ISBNNo	BookName	Author	Price	Category	Publisher
67-739-0932-7	Access 2002 Program	Micheal Peterson	$42.34	Access	Waite Group's
83-264-6754-7	C# Black Book w/CD	Joe Grand , Dustin	$40.99	C#	IDG Publishing
79-374-5927-7	C++ for Dummies	Peter Greenspan	$36.04	C++	McGraw Hill
71-574-2954-9	C++ Programming Bibl	Rudi Hall , Micheal	$44.32	C++	Wiley Dreamtech
90-296-3947-1	Complete Guide to C#	Justin Steinberg , J	$45.02	C#	Sams Publishing
67-710-5915-8	Dreamweaver 4 Compl	Steve McGrath , Pe	$41.22	Dreamwe	Waite Group's
90-146-3958-7	Dreamweaver 4 in Eas	Andreas Helton	$35.65	Dreamwe	Sams Publishing
83-984-3932-1	E-Commerce Bible	Christopher Johnso	$39.92	E-Comme	IDG Publishing
88-238-4814-3	Flash 5 in a Day	Jason Baele	$35.26	Flash	Prentice Hall
79-293-5925-4	Flash 5 Server Side Pr	Andrew Suehring	$41.26	Flash	McGraw Hill
88-742-8210-2	HTML 4 Black Book	Roy Park , Ronan J	$43.00	HTML	Prentice Hall
71-294-1002-4	HTML in 21 Days	Terry Michels , Dav	$37.25	HTML	Wiley Dreamtech
90-120-8201-6	Java 2 Complete Refer	Kurt Michelson , Da	$44.69	Java	Sams Publishing

Record: |◄ ◄ | 16 | ► ►| ►* | of 16

Datasheet View   NUM

Figure 5.39: LibraryBooks Table with Sample Values

9. Fill up the table IssueInfo with sample values as shown in Figure 5.40.

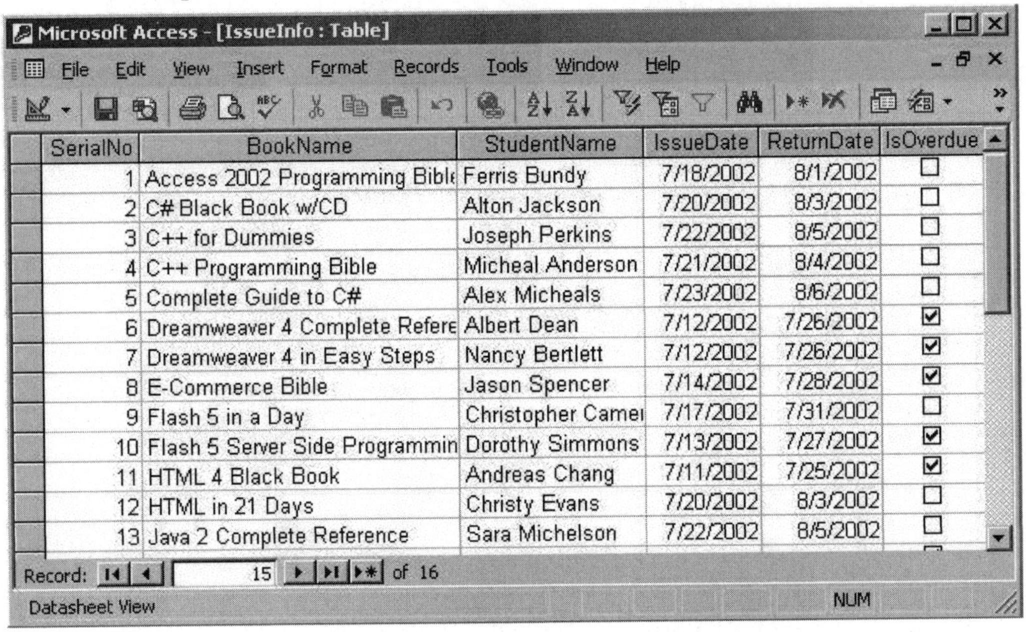

SerialNo	BookName	StudentName	IssueDate	ReturnDate	IsOverdue
1	Access 2002 Programming Bibl	Ferris Bundy	7/18/2002	8/1/2002	☐
2	C# Black Book w/CD	Alton Jackson	7/20/2002	8/3/2002	☐
3	C++ for Dummies	Joseph Perkins	7/22/2002	8/5/2002	☐
4	C++ Programming Bible	Micheal Anderson	7/21/2002	8/4/2002	☐
5	Complete Guide to C#	Alex Micheals	7/23/2002	8/6/2002	☐
6	Dreamweaver 4 Complete Refere	Albert Dean	7/12/2002	7/26/2002	☑
7	Dreamweaver 4 in Easy Steps	Nancy Bertlett	7/12/2002	7/26/2002	☑
8	E-Commerce Bible	Jason Spencer	7/14/2002	7/28/2002	☑
9	Flash 5 in a Day	Christopher Camei	7/17/2002	7/31/2002	☐
10	Flash 5 Server Side Programmin	Dorothy Simmons	7/13/2002	7/27/2002	☑
11	HTML 4 Black Book	Andreas Chang	7/11/2002	7/25/2002	☑
12	HTML in 21 Days	Christy Evans	7/20/2002	8/3/2002	☐
13	Java 2 Complete Reference	Sara Michelson	7/22/2002	8/5/2002	☐

Figure 5.40: IssueInfo Table with Sample Values

10. Save both the tables and close the database.

Conclusion/Observation

1. The LibraryBooks table should contain multiple records for the same author, multiple records for the same publisher, and multiple records for the same category.
2. The IssueInfo table should contain records showing multiple issues to the same student, and appropriate numbers of overdue and returned books.
3. There should be no instance where a certain book is issued more than once on the same date.

Lab Activity Checklist

S. No.	Tasks	Completed	
		Yes	No
1.	Database created with the proper name		
2.	Tables added to the database with proper names		
3.	Fields in the tables added according to the specified data types mentioned in the Problem Statement		
4.	Primary key properly set in both the two tables per requirement		
5.	Sample records added to the tables		

Exercise 2

Objective

■ Create a form using a CommandButton and a ListBox control, providing a basic interface between the user and the data stored in the database created in the previous exercise. The connectivity to the database will be provided through ADO.

Problem Statement

Create a form named frmLibraryBooks as shown in Figure 5.41. Add a command button to run an SQL query on the table LibraryBooks and a ListBox control to display the results of the query. The query should return a Recordset object containing the Price and BookName of all the books present in the LibraryBooks table, as shown in Figure 5.41.

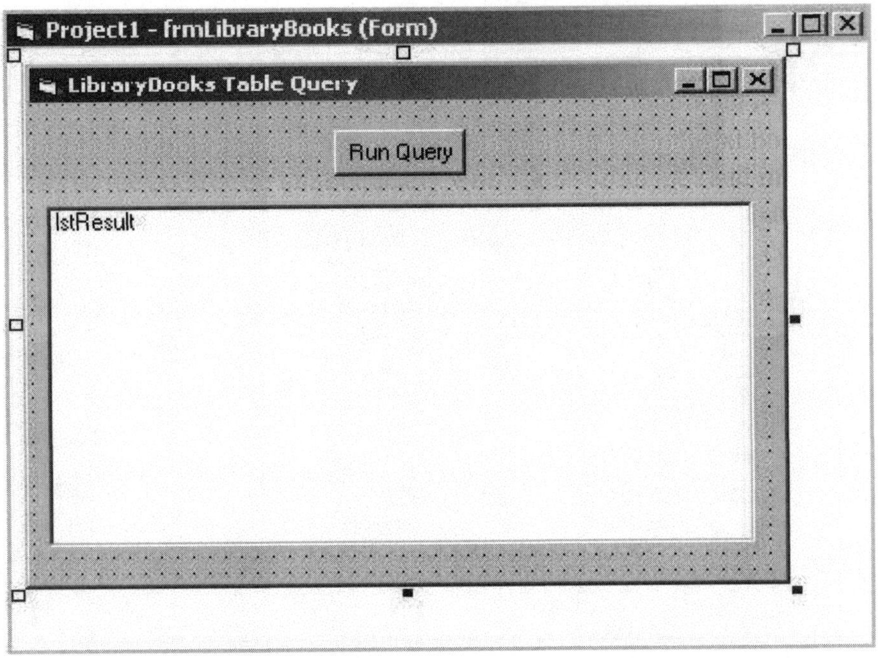

Figure 5.41 Sample Form for Exercise 2

Lab Setup

Computer Requirements:

- Microsoft Windows Operating System
- Pentium III or higher processors
- 128-MB RAM
- 3-GB of hard disk space
- CD-ROM drives
- Floppy disk drives
- LAN connections
- Visual Basic 6.0
- Microsoft Access 2000

Procedure

1. Open a new project and add a form named frmLibraryBooks. Set its caption to "LibraryBooks Table Query."

2. Add a CommandButton control named cmdRun. This button will run the query on the database.

3. Add a ListBox control named lstResult.

4. In the General Declarations section, add Code 5.17:

```
Dim rsResult As ADODB.Recordset
Dim cnnLibrary As ADODB.Connection
Dim cnnString As String
Dim newQuery As String
Dim rowcontent As String
Dim mode
Dim loc
Dim cursortype
Dim locktype
```

Code 5.17: Example of General Declaration

5. In the form's Load event, add Code 5.18. The code sets the value for the connection string, connection mode, and the location of the cursor. It then invokes a procedure named ConnectToDb() to open the database connection.

```
Private Sub Form_Load()
 cnnString = "Provider=microsoft.jet.OLEDB.4.0;" _
   & "Data Source=C:\Library.mdb"
 mode = adModeReadWrite
 loc = adUseClient


 ConnectToDb mode, loc, cnnString
End Sub
```

Code 5.18: Code for Load Event

6. In the cmdRun button's Click event, add Code 5.19. The code constructs the SQL query to retrieve the book name and the price of all the books from the LibraryBooks table and calls the procedure named OpenRecSet to open a recordset for the query. The code also adds the values in the recordset in the list box named lstResult using a while loop.

```
Private Sub cmdRun_Click()
 newQuery = "SELECT BookName, Price FROM LibraryBooks"
 locktype = adLockOptimistic
 cursortype = adOpenDynamic
 OpenRecSet newQuery, cnnString, cursortype, locktype


 While Not rsResult.EOF
      lstResult.AddItem "$" & (rsResult("Price") & " " & _
   rsResult("BookName"))
      rsResult.MoveNext
 Wend
End Sub
```

Code 5.19: Code for Command Button's Click Event

7.   Add Code 5.20 to open and close connections to the database. The code defines two procedures namely ConnectToDb() and DisConDB() to open and close the database connection respectively.

```
Private Sub ConnectToDb(mode, loc, cnnString)
    Set cnnLibrary = New ADODB.Connection
    With cnnLibrary
        .ConnectionString = cnnString
        .mode = mode
        .CursorLocation = loc
        .Open
    End With
 End Sub
Private Sub DisConDB()
 cnnLibrary.Close
 Set cnnLibrary = Nothing
End Sub
```

Code 5.20: Code to Open and Close the Database Connection

8.   Add Code 5.21 for the form's Unload event which calls the DisConDb() procedure to close the database.

```
Private Sub Form_UnLoad(Cancel As Integer)
 DisConDb
End Sub
```

Code 5.21: Form's Unload Event

9.   Add Code 5.22 to open and close the Recordset object.

```
Private Sub OpenRecSet(newQuery As String, cnnString, _
                       cursortype, locktype)
 On Error GoTo dberr
 Set rsResult = New ADODB.Recordset
 rsResult.Open newQuery, cnnString, cursortype, locktype,_
    adCmdText
 dberr:
End Sub
```

```
Private Sub CloseRecSet()
 rsResult.Close
 Set rsResult = Nothing
End Sub
```

Code 5.22: Open and Close the Recordset Object

10.   The Figure 5.42 shows the output of the application after clicking the Run button.

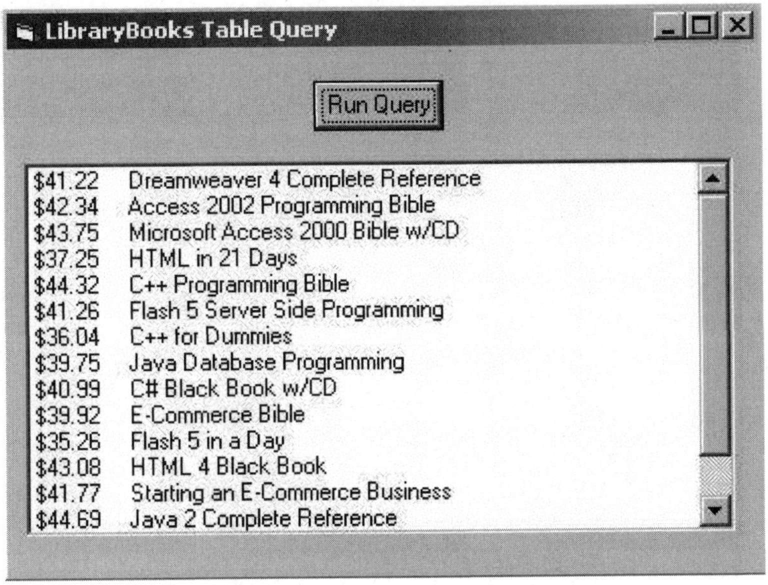

Figure 5.42: Output of the Application

Conclusion/Observation

1.   The form loads and displays a command button and an empty list box.

2.   Clicking the Run command button adds the name of all the books prefixed with the respective prices.

3.   Click the Run button twice. If it adds the same values once again at the end of the list box, enhance the program to prevent this, so that the list box does not display repeated values.

Lab Activity Checklist

S. No.	Tasks	Completed	
		Yes	No
1.	Appearance of the GUI resembles the one shown in the Problem Statement		
2.	Proper reference included in the project to implement ADO		
3.	Connection object opened and closed in proper locations		
4.	Appropriate code written for the Run command button		

Exercise 3

Objective

- To enhance the program in the previous exercise so that a query, similar to the one used in the previous example, is specified during run time instead of making it fixed in the code.

Problem Statement

Create the form shown in the following figure. The multi-line TextBox labeled "Enter Query" should take the query given below from the user and run it to output the result in the ListBox. (You can modify the code to display any query results. Exercise 4 provides such a case.) The Command button should remain disabled as long as there is no text in the TextBox. Enable it only when the textbox is not blank.

1. Write a query to display the Price and BookName for books in the
    LibraryBooks table, order the list by price, and display only those books
    whose price is between $36 and $42, as shown in Figure 5.43.

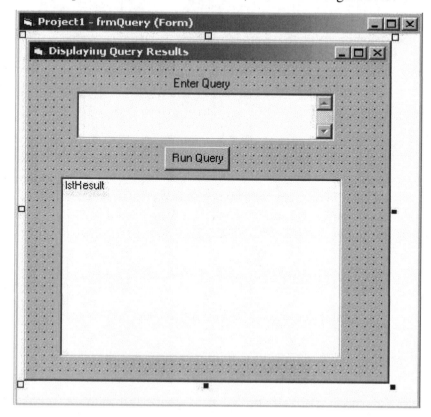

Figure 5.43: Query Result Form

Lab Setup

Computer Requirements:

- Microsoft Windows Operating System
- Pentium III or higher processors
- 128-MB RAM
- 3-GB of hard disk space
- CD-ROM drives
- Floppy disk drives
- LAN connections

- Visual Basic 6.0
- Microsoft Access 2000

Procedure

1.   Open a new project and add a form named frmQuery. Set its caption to "Displaying Query Results."

2.   Add a TextBox control named txtQuery which takes the SQL query from the user. Set its Multi-line property to True.

3.   Label the text box with a caption "Enter Query."

4.   Add a CommandButton control named cmdRun. This button will run the query on the database.

5.   Add a ListBox control named lstResult to display the query results.

6.   Add Code 5.23 in the Code Editor.

```
Dim rsResult As ADODB.Recordset
Dim cnnLibrary As ADODB.Connection
Dim cnnString As String
Dim newQuery As String
Dim mode, loc, cursortype, locktype

Private Sub ConnectToDb(mode, loc, cnnString)
    Set cnnLibrary = New ADODB.Connection
    With cnnLibrary
        .ConnectionString = cnnString
        .mode = mode
        .CursorLocation = loc
        .Open
    End With
End Sub
Private Sub DisConDb()
  cnnLibrary.Close
  Set cnnLibrary = Nothing
End Sub
Private Sub cmdRun_Click()
  On Error GoTo dberr
```

```
        lstResult.Clear
        newQuery = txtQuery.Text
        OpenRecSet newQuery, cnnString, cursortype, locktype

        lstResult.Visible = True
        While Not rsResult.EOF
            lstResult.AddItem "$" & (rsResult("Price") & " " & _
        rsResult("BookName"))
            rsResult.MoveNext
    Wend
        CloseRecSet
    dberr:
End Sub


Private Sub Form_Load()
  cmdRun.Enabled = False
  cnnString = "Provider=microsoft.jet.OLEDB.4.0;" _
      & "Data Source=library.mdb"

  mode = adModeReadWrite
  loc = adUseClient
  ConnectToDb mode, loc, cnnString
  cursortype = adOpenForwardOnly
  locktype = adLockReadOnly
End Sub


Private Sub Form_UnLoad(Cancel As Integer)
  DisConDb
End Sub
Private Sub OpenRecSet(newQuery As String, cnnString, _
                            cursortype, locktype)
  Set rsResult = New ADODB.Recordset
  rsResult.Open newQuery, cnnString, cursortype, locktype, _
      adCmdText
End Sub
```

```
Private Sub CloseRecSet()
 rsResult.Close
 Set rsResult = Nothing
End Sub


Private Sub txtQuery_Change()
    If Len(txtQuery.Text) > 0 Then
        cmdRun.Enabled = True
    Else
        cmdRun.Enabled = False
    End If
End Sub
```

Code 5.23: Code to Complete the Query

Query 1

```
SELECT Price, BookName FROM LibraryBooks
WHERE Price > 36 AND Price < 42
ORDER BY Price
```

Figure 5.44 shows the output of Code 5.23.

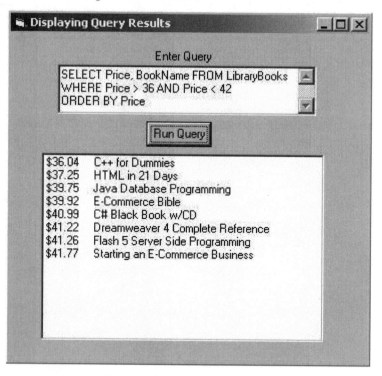

Figure 5.44: Output of Code 5.23.

Conclusion/Observation

1. The form loads and displays a command button, an empty text box, and an empty list box.

2. The Run command button is initially disabled. It is enabled only if there is text (query) to be executed.

3. Observe the output if the Run command button is clicked once by entering "SELECT * FROM LibraryBooks" in the text box and once by entering "SELECT author FROM LibraryBooks." If there is an error, find the cause. The next exercise could be helpful in finding the error.

Lab Activity Checklist

S. No.	Tasks	Completed	
		Yes	No
1.	The GUI resembles the one shown in the Problem Statement		
2.	Proper reference is included in the project to implement ADO		
3.	Connection object is opened and closed in proper locations		
4.	Appropriate code written for the controls per requirement		

Lab Exercises

Exercise 4

Objective

◾ To create an interface that can accept a SELECT statement from the user, execute it, and display the results of the SELECT statement using TextBox controls. The interface also provides navigation buttons to navigate through the records in the retrieved Recordset. The interface should change during run time according to the fields specified in the query.

Problem Statement

1. Create the form shown in the figure below. The form should display the results from any custom query entered by the user on the tables LibraryBooks and IssueInfo.

2. When the form is displayed initially, it should only display the TextBox and the CommandButton labeled "Run Query."

3. The frame should be invisible (adjust the height of the form accordingly).

4. The CommandButton should be disabled when there is no text in the TextBox and should be enabled if it contains data.

5. After the user presses the CommandButton, run the custom query on the database "Library.mdb."

6. Make the frame visible along with all the labels and the CommandButtons present in the frame.

7. The labels and TextBox controls in the frame should be control arrays.

8. The labels should display the Field names of the Recordset object and the TextBoxes should display the field values.

9. Add two CommandButtons with caption "Previous" and "Next" to navigate through the records in the Recordset. Check for BOF and EOF conditions.

10. Make sure that only those field names and values are displayed on the frame that correspond to the query entered by the user. The rest of the controls should be invisible, as shown in Figure 5.45.

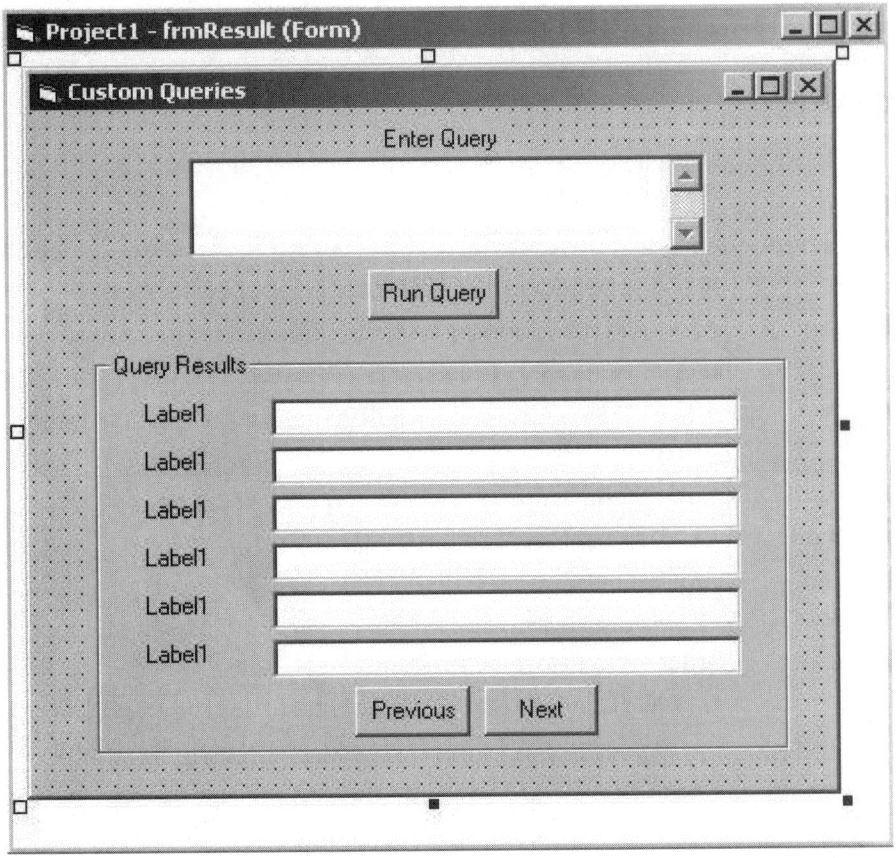

Figure 5.45: Custom Query Form

Lab Setup

Computer Requirements:

- Microsoft Windows Operating System
- Pentium III or higher processors
- 128-MB RAM
- 3-GB of hard disk space
- CD-ROM drives

- Floppy disk drives
- LAN connections
- Visual Basic 6.0
- Microsoft Access 2000

Procedure

1. Open a new project and set the name of the form to frmResult. Set its caption to "Custom Queries."
2. Include proper reference in the project to use the ADO objects.
3. Add a Label control named lblQuery and set its caption to "Enter Query."
4. Add a Text Box control named txtQuery. Set its Multi-Line property to true and the ScrollBars property to 2-Vertical.
5. Add a Command Button cmdRun and set its Caption property to "Run Query."
6. Add a frame named fraResult and set its Caption property to "Query Results."
7. Add a control array of labels named lblResult having six Label controls, to the above frame.
8. Add a control array of text boxes named txtResult having six TextBox controls, to the frame fraResult.
9. Add two Command Button controls named cmdNext and cmdPrev to the frame, which will be used to navigate through the records in the recordset.
10. Enter Code 5.24 in the Code Editor.

```
Dim rsResult As New ADODB.Recordset
Dim cnnLibrary As ADODB.Connection
Dim cnnString As String
Dim newQuery As String
Dim rowcontent As String
Dim mode
Dim loc
Dim cursortype
Dim locktype
Dim colnum As Integer
Private Sub ConnectToDb(mode, loc, cnnString)
    Set cnnLibrary = New ADODB.Connection
```

```
    With cnnLibrary
        .ConnectionString = cnnString
        .mode = mode
        .CursorLocation = loc
        .Open
    End With
End Sub

Private Sub DisConDb()
 cnnLibrary.Close
 Set cnnLibrary = Nothing
End Sub

Private Sub cmdNext_Click()
 If rsResult.EOF Then
        rsResult.MoveFirst
 Else
        rsResult.MoveNext
 End If

 If Not rsResult.EOF Then
        For colnum = 0 To rsResult.Fields.Count - 1
            txtResult(colnum).Text = rsResult.Fields(colnum).Value
        Next
 End If
End Sub

Private Sub cmdPrev_Click()
 If rsResult.BOF Then
        rsResult.MoveLast
 Else
 rsResult.MovePrevious
 End If
 If Not rsResult.BOF Then
        For colnum = 0 To rsResult.Fields.Count - 1
```

```
                txtResult(colnum).Text = rsResult.Fields(colnum).Value
        Next
  End If
End Sub


Private Sub cmdRun_Click()
  On Error GoTo dberr

  newQuery = txtQuery.Text
  OpenRecSet newQuery, cnnString, cursortype, locktype

  fraResult.Visible = True
  If Height < 5000 Then
        frmResult.Height = Height + fraResult.Height + 300
  End If

  For i = 0 To rsResult.Fields.Count - 1
        txtResult(i).Visible = True
        lblResult(i).Visible = True
  Next

  For colnum = 0 To rsResult.Fields.Count - 1
        lblResult(colnum).Caption = rsResult.Fields(colnum).Name
  Next

  If Not rsResult.EOF Then
        For colnum = 0 To rsResult.Fields.Count - 1
           txtResult(colnum).Text = rsResult.Fields(colnum).Value
        Next
  End If
  dberr:
End Sub
Private Sub Form_Load()
  Height = 2100
  cmdRun.Enabled = False
```

```
    cnnString = "Provider=microsoft.jet.OLEDB.4.0;" _
      & "Data Source=library.mdb"

   mode = adModeReadWrite
   loc = adUseClient
   ConnectToDb mode, loc, cnnString
   cursortype = adOpenDynamic
   locktype = adLockOptimistic

   fraResult.Visible = False
   For i = 0 To txtResult.Count - 1
        txtResult(i).Visible = False
        lblResult(i).Visible = False
   Next
End Sub


Private Sub Form_UnLoad(Cancel As Integer)
  DisConDb
End Sub
Private Sub OpenRecSet(newQuery As String, cnnString, _
                        cursortype, locktype)
  If rsResult.State = adStateOpen Then CloseRecSet
  Set rsResult = New ADODB.Recordset
  rsResult.Open newQuery, cnnString, cursortype, locktype,_
    adCmdText
End Sub


Private Sub CloseRecSet()
  rsResult.Close
  Set rsResult = Nothing
End Sub


Private Sub txtQuery_Change()
    If Len(txtQuery.Text) > 0 Then
        cmdRun.Enabled = True
```

```
    Else
        cmdRun.Enabled = False
    End If
End Sub
```

Code 5.24 Code for Custom Query Form

The preceding code initially declares various module level variables to be used in the module.

■ The ConnectToDb() procedure accepts the connection mode, cursor location, and the connection string to open a database connection using the connection object cnnLibrary.

■ The DisConDb procedure closes the database connection.

■ The click event of the command button cmdNext is used to move forward through the Recordset object rsResult. At the end of the Recordset (EOF) it moves to the first record in the Recordset. It loops through the fields in the Recordset object and fills the text boxes with the values in the fields. The Click event of the Command button cmdPrev performs almost the same task as that of cmdNext except that it is used to move backwards through the Recordset. At the beginning of the Recordset (BOF) it moves to the last record in the Recordset. The Click event of the Command button cmdRun is used to open the Recordset based on the query entered in the text box txtQuery. It displays the appropriate number of text boxes to display the fields retrieved in the query and fills them with the values in the first record in the Recordset.

■ The Form Load event is used to perform the initialization tasks like constructing the connection string and calling the ConnectToDb procedure to open the connection, assigning the values for the properties of the Recordset to the appropriate variables, and hiding the text boxes as they are displayed only when a query is executed.

■ The Form Unload event is used to call the DisConDb procedure to close the database connection.

■ The OpenRecSet procedure accepts the query string, connection string CursorType and the LockType of the Recordset and opens the Recordset for the specified query. The CloseRecSet procedure is used to close the Recordset object and make the Recordset variable empty.

■ The command button cmdRun should be enabled only if there is text in the text box txtQuery. This is achieved by implementing the Change event of the text box txtQuery where the command button is enabled only when the length of the text in the text box is more than zero and disabled when it is not.

11.   Save and run the project.

Conclusion/Observation

1.   Initially the frame fraResult is not visible. The frame is visible only when a certain query is executed.

2.   The number of Text Boxes displayed in the result is the same as that of the fields in the Recordset. The other Text Boxes are kept invisible.

3.   The given example works only when the executed query has fields less than or equal to six. It fails if the number of fields is greater than six. This can be handled if the program can load new Text Box controls dynamically during run time depending upon the number of fields in the retrieved Recordset.

Lab Activity Checklist

S. No.	Tasks	Completed	
		Yes	No
1.	The form is designed resembling the one shown in the Problem Statement		
2.	Proper reference is added to the project to use ADO objects		
3.	The Connection object is opened and closed in proper locations		
4.	Write appropriate code for the various controls in the form		
5.	Use the Recordset's Fields collection in loops to access the fields of the Recordset		

Exercise 5

Objective

■ Construct SQL statements to retrieve records from tables based on certain criteria.

Problem Statement

Construct SQL queries for the following statements:

1. Display all the fields from the **LibraryBooks** table ordered by author's name.

2. Delete entries from the table **IssueInfo** for those students whose books are not overdue.

3. Display the Name of student, BookName, and Category of books for all the overdue books. (Hint: Use JOIN)

4. Display the student name, book name, price of the book, and a new field showing the number of days the student has possessed the book, for all overdue books.

5. Display the total number of books which are overdue and which are not. (HINT: use GROUP BY)

Lab Setup

Computer Requirements:

■ Microsoft Windows Operating System

■ Pentium III or higher processors

■ 128-MB RAM

■ 3-GB of hard disk space

■ CD-ROM drives

■ Floppy disk drives

■ LAN connections

■ Visual Basic 6.0

■ Microsoft Access 2000

Procedure

Query1

```
SELECT * FROM LibraryBooks ORDER BY Author
```

Query2

```
DELETE
FROM IssueInfo
WHERE IsOverdue = NO
```

Query3

```
SELECT IssueInfo,StudentName, IssueInfo.BookName,
LibraryBooks.Category
FROM IssueInfo
INNER JOIN LibraryBooks
ON LibraryBooks.BookName = IssueInfo.BookName
WHERE IsOverdue = YES
```

Query4

```
SELECT IssueInfo.StudentName, IssueInfo.BookName,
       (ReturnDate - IssueDate) AS DaysKept,LibraryBooks.Price
FROM IssueInfo
INNER JOIN LibraryBooks
ON LibraryBooks.BookName = IssueInfo.BookName
WHERE IsOverdue = YES
```

Query5

```
SELECT IsOverdue, COUNT(*) FROM IssueInfo GROUP BY IsOverdue
```

Conclusion/Observation

1. The constructed queries can be checked by using the MS Access query window in SQL view. Open the Library database and create a new query in design view. Select **View→SQL** from the menu bar to enter the query to check. The entered query can be executed by selecting **Query→Run** from the menu bar. You can even save the query for further use.

2. View the design view of the queries, especially those involving joins, to have a graphical view of the query.

Lab Activity Checklist

S. No.	Tasks	Completed	
		Yes	No
1.	Correctness of the statements		
2.	Correctness of the clauses used in the SELECT statement, for instance if HAVING is being used without GROUP BY, etc.		
3.	Using proper table alias during joins		

Project

1.   Create a blank database named EmpInfo.mdb in the same folder as that of the EmpInfo project.

2.   Create three tables for the structures given below:

Structure of the Departments table:

Column Name	Data Type and Size	Description
DeptNo	AutoNumber – Long Integer	Department number – set as primary key
DeptName	Text – 30 characters	Name of the department

Structure of the Employees table:

Column Name	Data Type and Size	Description
EmpCode	AutoNumber – Long Integer	Employee Code – set as primary key
FirstName	Text – 20 characters	First Name of the employee
LastName	Text – 20 characters	Last Name of the employee
DateOfJoining	Date/Time	Joining Date of the employee
DeptNo	Number – Long Integer	Department number of the employee
Grade	Text – 1 character	Grade of the employee

Structure of the Grades table:

Column Name	Date Type and Size	Description
Grade	Text – 1 character	Grade – set as primary key
BasicSalary	Currency	Basic salary of the grade

3.   Enter the following records in the Departments table in MS Access.

DeptNo	DeptName
1	Administration
2	Marketing
3	Finance
4	Research
5	Store

4.   Enter the following records in the Grades table in MS Access.

Grade	BasicSalary
A	$ 15,000.00
B	$ 12,000.00
C	$ 10,000.00
D	$ 7,500.00
E	$ 6,500.00

5.   Open the VB project named EmpInfo.

6.   Add a module named modMain to the project. Declare a String type public variable named strConString to store the connection string pointing to the database created in question 1. Declare a public ADODB Connection object named dbCon. Include the reference of the appropriate library to use ADODB objects in the project. Provide a sub-procedure called Main in the module that assigns the connection string to the variable strConString. The sub-procedure opens an ADODB connection with the connection object dbCon. The Main method should also display the form frmMain. Set this Main method as the startup object of the project.

7.   Save the project.

Using Advanced ActiveX Controls with Databases

6

The intrinsic control set in Microsoft Visual Basic possesses several limitations when used with databases. This chapter explains these limitations and how they can be overcome using data-aware ActiveX controls. The chapter presents the techniques of using the data-bound ActiveX controls. The main ActiveX controls explained are the DataList, DataCombo, DataGrid and the Microsoft Hierarchical FlexGrid controls. The chapter also covers the Data Environment Designer, the Create command, and Connection objects.

At the end of this chapter, you will be able to:

- Evaluate situations when you need to use ActiveX controls in applications.
- Explain the meaning of Data-Bound ActiveX Controls.
- Apply the concept of data-bound controls in databases.
- Explain the operation of DataList and DataCombo controls.
- Compare the differences between DataList and DataCombo controls.
- Set up the DataGrid Control to display database contents.
- Create simple applications using DataGrid controls.
- Use DataCombo and DataList controls in DataGrid applications.
- Explain techniques for using the Microsoft Hierarchical FlexGrid control.
- Apply the features of Data Environment Designer to create hierarchical recordsets.
- Create applications using Data Environment Designer and the Hierarchical FlexGrid.
- Modify databases using data-bound ActiveX controls.

6.1 ActiveX Controls in Databases

Microsoft Visual Basic provides a rich set of ActiveX Controls to create a variety of applications. Visual Basic's intrinsic control set has a few limitations for database programming. These limitations are easily circumvented by using data-aware ActiveX controls. The most commonly used data-bound ActiveX controls are:

- DataList
- DataCombo
- DataGrid
- Microsoft Hierarchical FlexGrid

ActiveX controls, known as Object Linking and Embedding (OLE) controls, are powerful, fast, and lightweight. They extend Microsoft's Component Object Model (COM) technology. These controls simplify database maintenance, handling, and manipulation. It is possible to create complete database-driven applications in design view with minimal code because the user can set most of the control properties interactively at design time.

Data-bound ActiveX controls can integrate with databases, that is, they can bind to specific fields in a database table. They can directly edit, view, and manipulate data in tables, providing a simpler and cleaner interface for database management. One of the biggest advantages of these data-bound controls is that they display data automatically and provide for data validation.

The DataList and DataCombo controls are similar in function to the DBList and DBCombo controls except that they are data-bound. The DataGrid control provides a spreadsheet-like display and can be bound to a Recordset object or ADO Data Control. The DataGrid control allows direct editing of data within it.

The Microsoft Hierarchical FlexGrid (MSHFlexGrid) is a new ActiveX control introduced in Visual Basic 6.0. It can display hierarchical data sets from different tables in a database. It is not possible to edit data in the MSHFlexGrid directly. It provides features such as word-wrap, automatic filling of data, dynamic rearrangement of rows and columns, and many other facilities. A unique feature is that it displays both text and images in the cells.

6.1.1 Data-Bound ActiveX Controls

 Explain the concept of data-bound and data-aware ActiveX controls.

ActiveX controls like the DataList, the DataCombo, the DataGrid, and the Hierarchical FlexGrid are data-bound controls. These controls can be associated with an ActiveX Data Object (ADO), Data Control, or DataEnvironment objects to display or edit data in the data set. These ActiveX controls are data-aware, and you cannot use them without a data source. Unlike other data-bound controls (like the ListBox), you cannot use them to display regular data. Table 6.1 lists the Data-Bound ActiveX controls in alphabetical order.

Data-Bound ActiveX Controls
DataCombo
DataGrid
DataList
DataRepeater
DateTimePicker
Hierarchical FlexGrid
ImageCombo
MaskedEdit
MonthView
MSChart
MSFlexGrid
RichTextBox

Table 6.1: Data-Bound ActiveX Controls

Data-aware controls that can display multiple rows simultaneously, for example, the DataCombo, need to set some or all of the following data properties:

- BoundColumn
- DataField

- DataMember
- DataSource
- ListField
- RowMember
- RowSource

Figure 6.1 shows the data properties of a DataCombo control. The **Name** property of this control is set to dbcLocation.

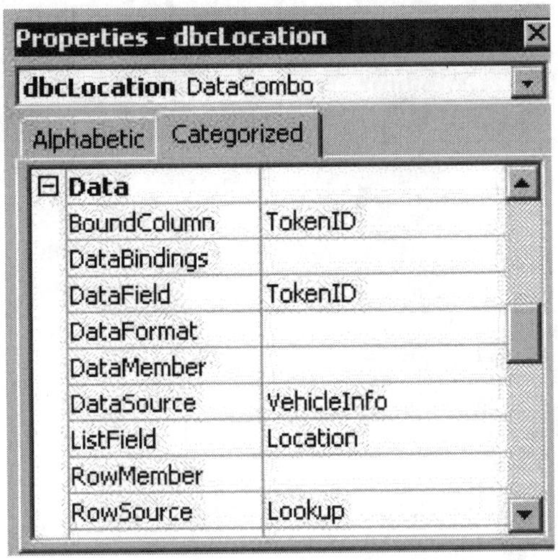

Properties - dbcLocation

dbcLocation DataCombo

Alphabetic | Categorized

⊟ **Data**	
BoundColumn	TokenID
DataBindings	
DataField	TokenID
DataFormat	
DataMember	
DataSource	VehicleInfo
ListField	Location
RowMember	
RowSource	Lookup

Figure 6.1: Properties of the DataCombo Control

6.1.2 Creating a Sample Database

 Create a database that will be used in the sample application of this chapter.

This chapter explains the design of two sample applications using ActiveX controls. The first application uses the DataList, the DataCombo, and the DataGrid controls and the second application uses the Hierarchical FlexGrid control with a DataEnvironment. Both these applications use a database named "parking.mdb" consisting of two tables **Lookup** and **VehicleInfo**. The database is created using Microsoft Access 2000.

To create the database, perform the following steps:

1. Open Microsoft Access 2000.

2. Select **File → New** from the menu and create a blank Access database with the name "parking.mdb" in the root directory.

   A window, as shown in Figure 6.2 appears.

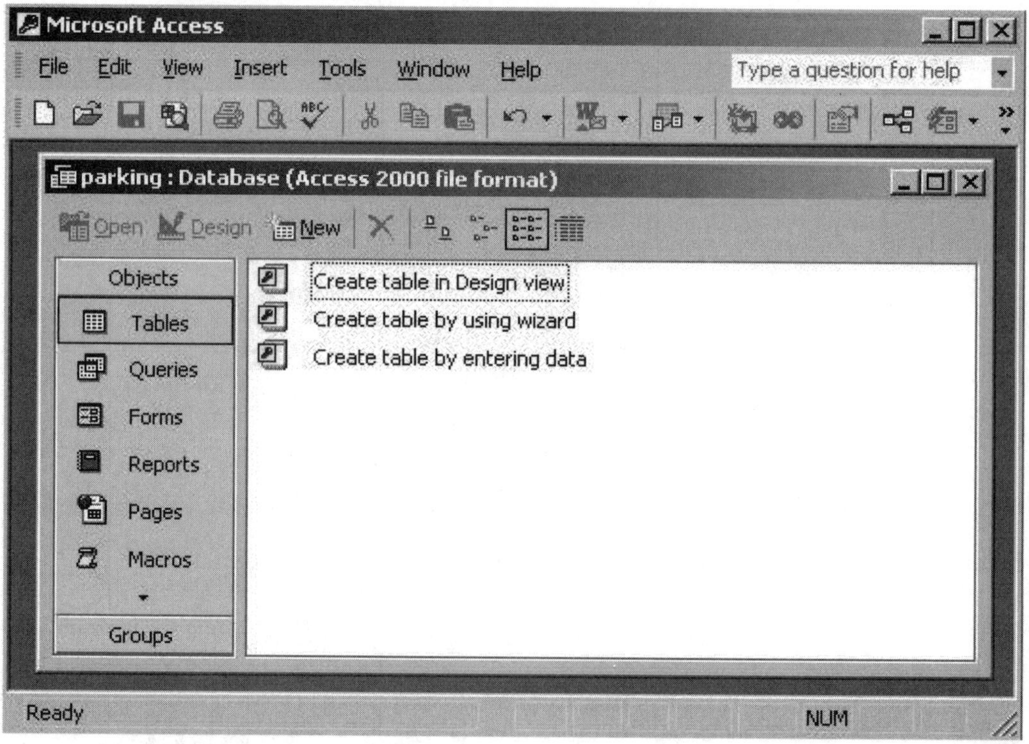

Figure 6.2: Creating the parking.mdb Database in Microsoft Access

3. Double-click the option **Create table in Design view** and enter the data from Table 6.2.

Field Name	Data Type	Description
TokenID	Number	Primary Key for the Lookup table which maps to the location
Location	Text	Location of a vehicle (Floor and Row)

Table 6.2: Field Entries for the Table Lookup

4. Select **Yes** as the option for the field labeled "Indexed". Figure 6.3 shows the snapshot for the table Lookup.

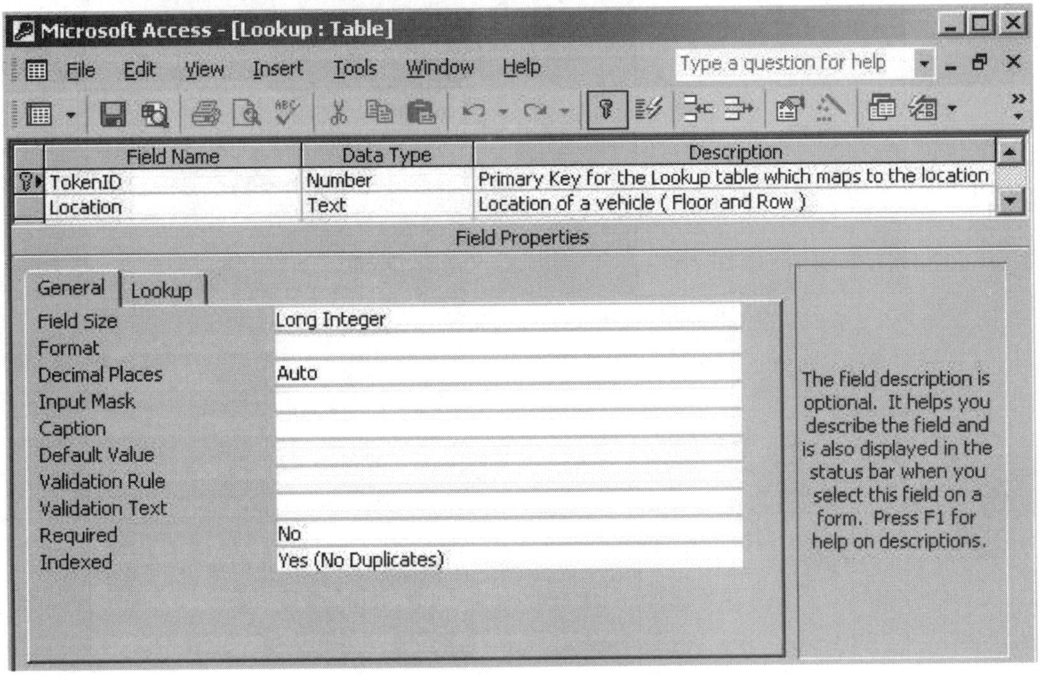

Figure 6.3: Lookup Table

5. Right-click the field **TokenID** and make it a primary key.

6. Close the Design-view window. A dialog box appears asking you to save the table. Save the table with the name **Lookup**.

7. Repeat Step 3 to create another table in the design view. Enter the details as given in Table 6.3.

Field Name	Data Type	Description
VehicleNo	Text	Primary key is the Registration number of vehicle and State
TokenID	Number	Foreign key which is used to map to the Lookup table
OwnerName	Text	Name of vehicle owner

Table 6.3: Field Entries for the Table VehicleInfo

Figure 6.4 shows the table "VehicleInfo".

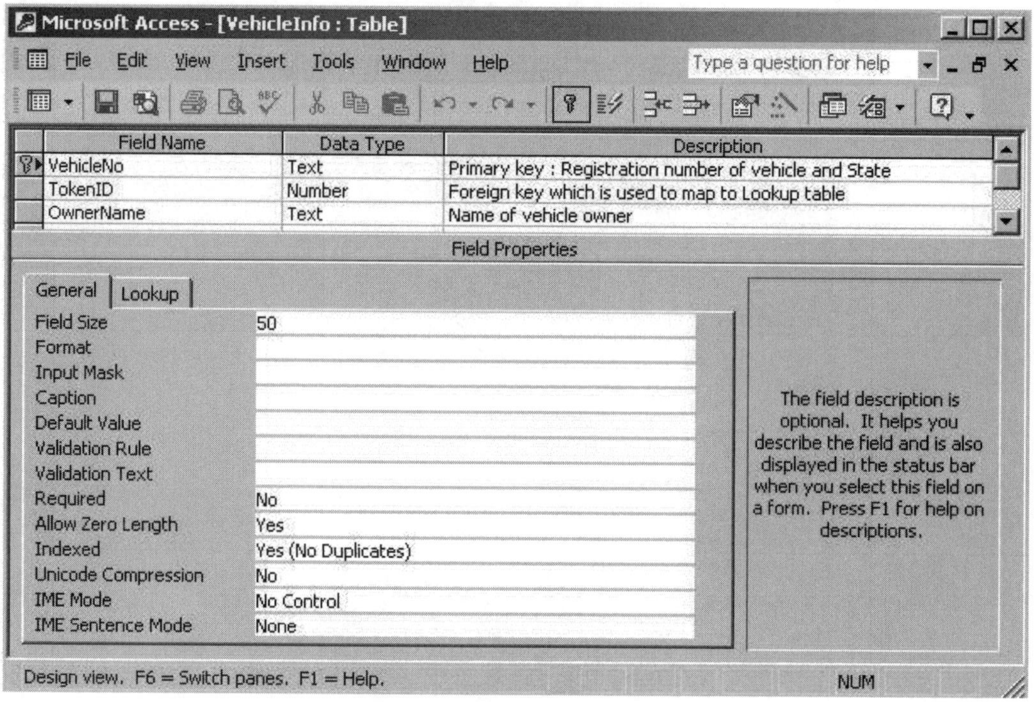

Figure 6.4: VehicleInfo Table

8.   Make the **VehicleNo** field a primary key. Close the Design view window, and
        save the table as **VehicleInfo**.

9.　Double-click on the **Lookup** table to open it. Add the sample data as shown in Figure 6.5 to the table.

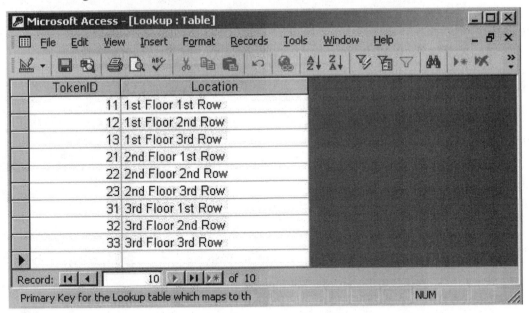

Figure 6.5: Sample Data for the Lookup Table

10. Similarly, double-click the table **VehicleInfo** and fill in the fields VehicleNo, TokenID, and OwnerName with the sample data as shown in Figure 6.6.

VehicleNo	TokenID	OwnerName
142-DFA (WA)	23	Amanda Callaghan
1609-EG (VA)	31	Claire Thomson
296-XDF (TN)	22	Nancy Maltz
617-GTQ (WA)	32	Jim Wilson
6S-8982 (WV)	12	Mario Gerla
762-WCS (NJ)	22	Michael Hugh
AFV-5050 (NY)	32	Marlene Graham
ASZ-3219 (SC)	31	Jim Arthur
BPL-260 (VT)	11	Andrew Chang
DFL-9483 (PA)	23	Kyle Bush
JVA-9330 (NC)	31	Dorothy Smith
SXG-32W (TX)	31	Josh Broch
TX-443C (TX)	22	Linda Jackson
WS-370 (RI)	23	Adrian Perrig
ZSW-9420 (VA)	13	George White

Figure 6.6: Sample Data for the VehicleInfo Table

11. Save the database and close Microsoft Access.

To create the database, you can also use the Microsoft Visual Data Manager that comes with Visual Basic, as explained in Chapter 5 "Working with Databases."

Database Description

All the sample applications using ActiveX controls use the parking database. The table "Lookup" is a **Lookup** table used to map the TokenID field to the Location field. The relation is self-explanatory. The primary key in the table is TokenID whose values are unique.

In the table **VehicleInfo**, we have three fields, VehicleNo, TokenID, and OwnerName. The TokenID field maps to the TokenID field of the **Lookup** table. VehicleNo is the primary key, which is also unique.

The two tables represent a many-to-one relationship, as the same location may have several vehicles. The ActiveX controls use the **Lookup** table to map the many-to-one relationship and are essentially read-only. Any changes to the **Lookup** table should be manual. The controls perform all the data manipulations on the VehicleInfo table. The ActiveX controls map data between the tables and display them in a very efficient and flexible way. The limitations of Visual Basic's intrinsic controls have been overcome.

ADODC Control

In the previous chapter you learned about ADO connection, Recordset, and Field objects and the issue of connectivity to data retrieved by these objects. The ADODC or ADO Data Control provides a medium for connectivity of data between data-bound controls.

To add an ADODC control to a form, you must first ensure that it appears in the Toolbox. To select the ADODC control, right-click the Toolbox and select **Components**. A **Components** dialog box opens as shown in Figure 6.7. From the Controls tab, select Microsoft ADO Data Control 6.0 (OLE DB) to add ADODC to your toolbox.

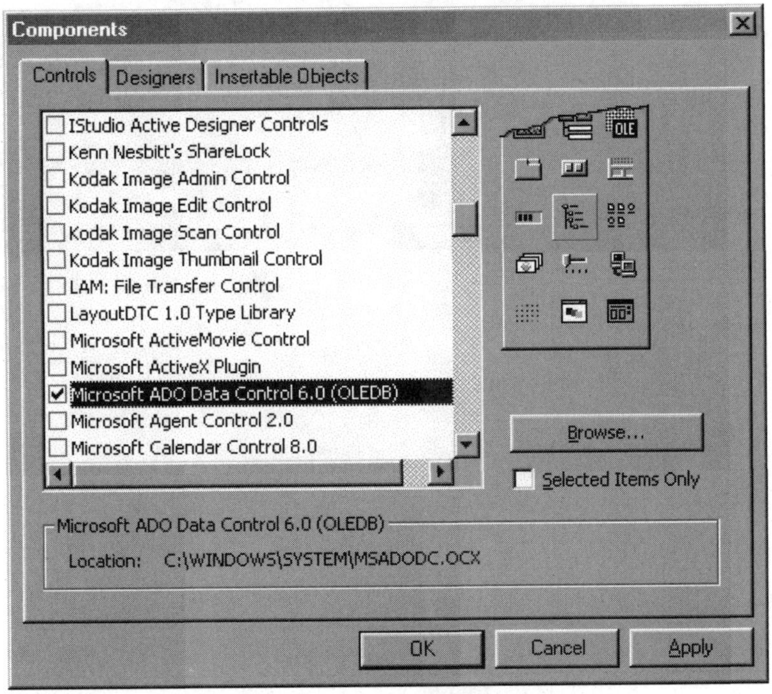

Figure 6.7: Components Dialog Box

ADODC connects to a database using a connection string object. To use ADODC, drag the control onto a form and set its properties as follows:

1. Click on the **ConnectionString** property. A **Property Pages** dialog box is displayed as shown in Figure 6.8. The first two options on this property page are used when you want to connect to an external data source. The last option is used for an internal data source, such as the Access database designed in the previous section.

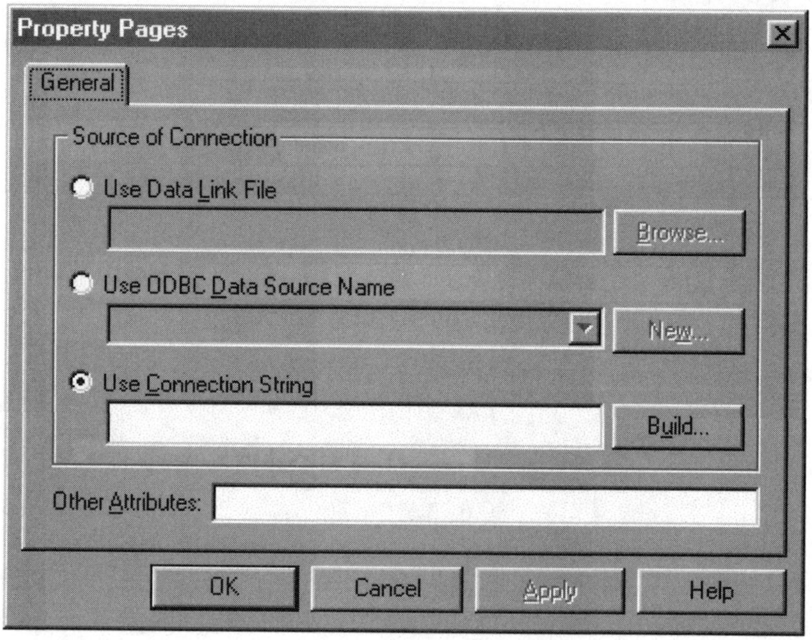

Figure 6.8: Property Pages of an ADODC Control

2. Click on the **Build** button next to the Use Connection String option. A Data Link Properties dialog box opens, as shown in Figure 6.9. Select the **Microsoft Jet 4.0 OLE DB Provider** from the Provider tab and click the **Next** button.

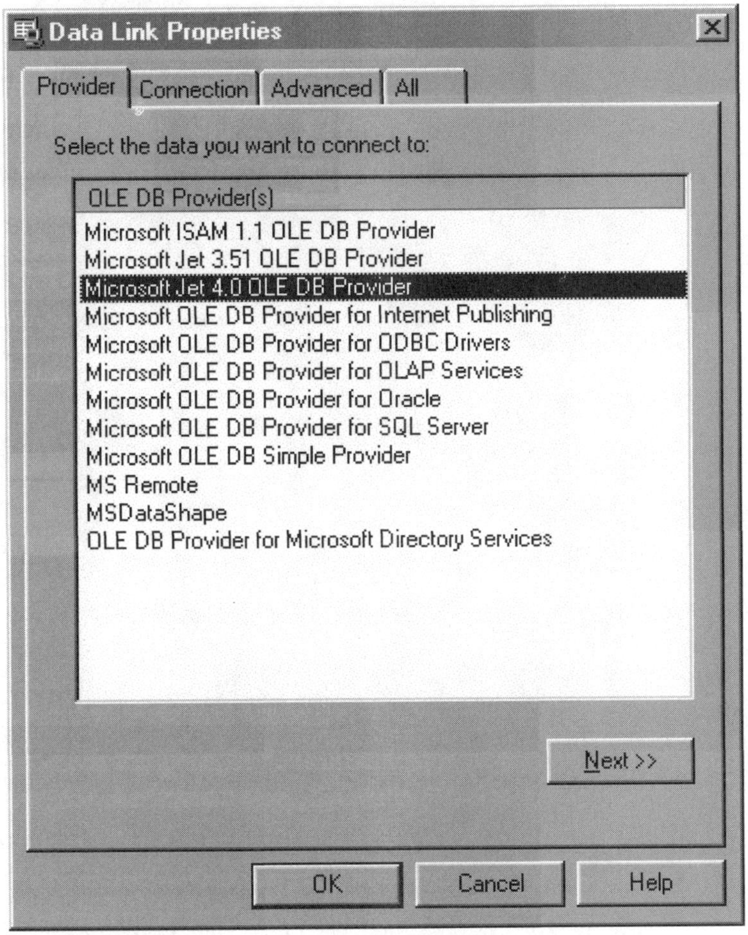

Figure 6.9: Data Link Properties Dialog Box

3.   The Connection tab is displayed, as shown in Figure 6.10. Enter a database name or click the button next to this field to select a database name. Click **OK**.

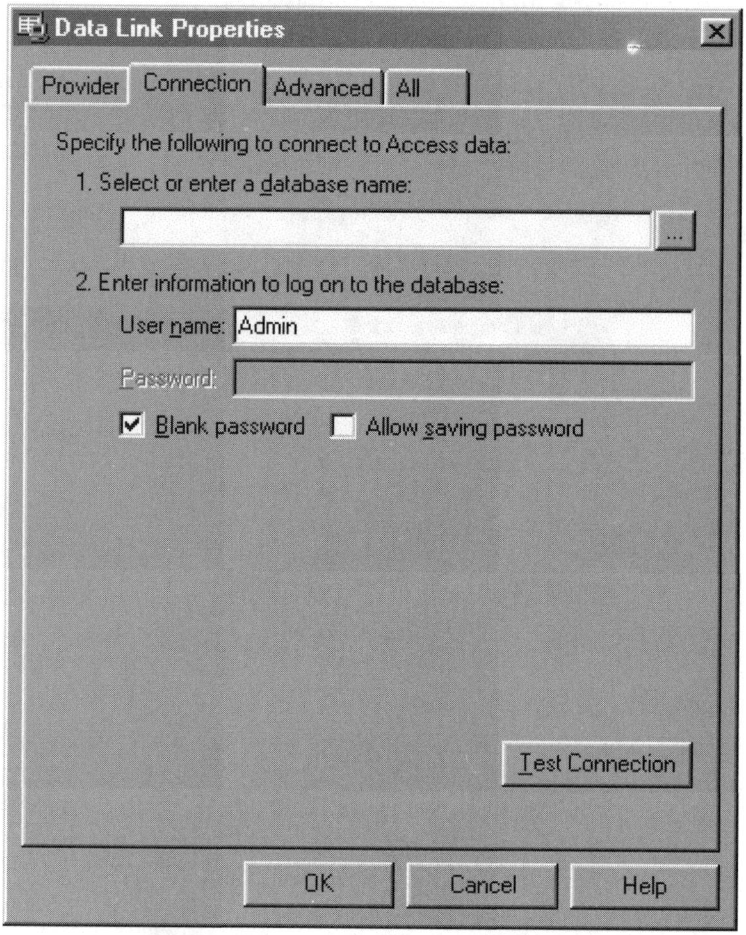

Figure 6.10: Connection Tab of the Data Link Properties Dialog Box

4. The **Property page** dialog box opens with the value of the Connection String set in the field, as shown in Figure 6.11. Click **OK** to close this dialog box.

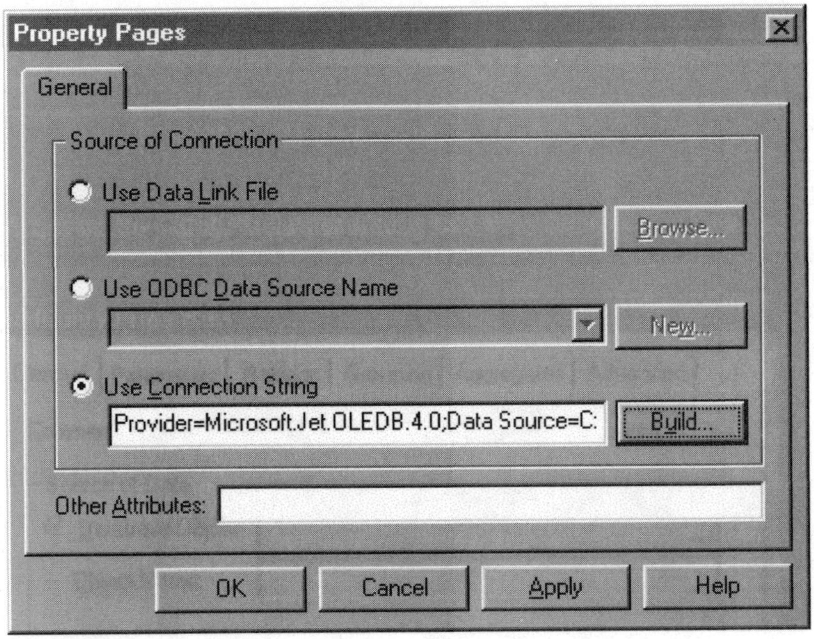

Figure 6.11: Property Page of the ADODC Control with the Connection String Property Set

5. Next, click on the **RecordSource** property to select a recordset or table from which data is accessed. A RecordSource Property Pages opens, as shown in Figure 6.12. Select the adCmdTable option from the **Command Type** list and select the name of the table in the Table or Stored procedure list. The RecordSource property will be set to this table.

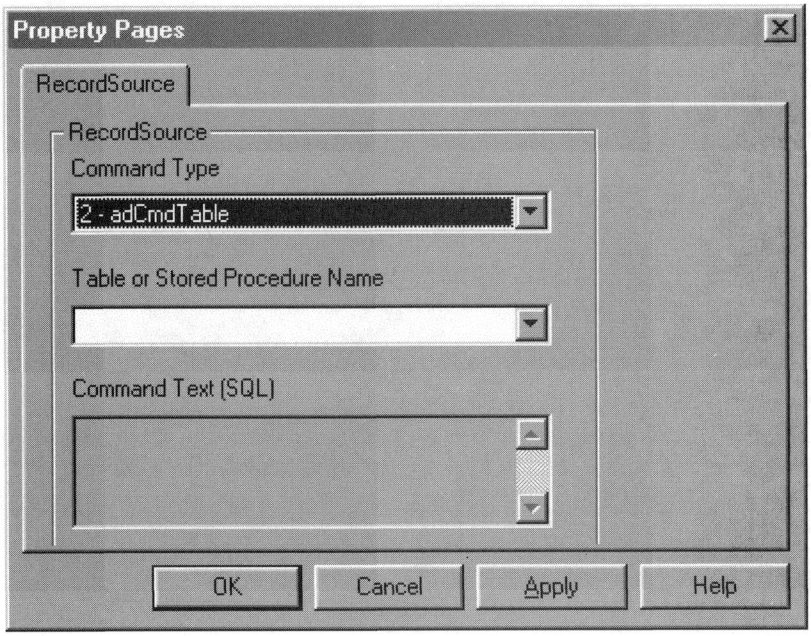

Figure 6.12: RecordSource Property Pages

6. To bind the other controls to the ADODC control, set the **DataSource** property of that control to the name of the ADODC control and its **Data Field** property to a field in the table (such as a text box).

ADODC controls are much easier to use, therefore it is used in the code listings in this chapter with all the other controls.

Practice Questions

1. Explain the difference between a data control and a data-bound control.

2. What is the advantage of using the ADODC control?

3. List the properties that need to be set for Data-Bound control so that they can display multiple rows of data simultaneously.

4. Compare the DBList control and the DataList control.

5. How can you avoid hard coding the path of a database in your programs?

6.2 Using the DataList and DataCombo Controls

The DataList and DataCombo controls are the most common ActiveX controls and are present in nearly every database application using ActiveX controls. They are optimized to work with ActiveX Data Objects. These controls are automatically populated with data from the field mentioned in the **ListField** property of the control. You can also switch data sources dynamically, and display data from different ADO Data Controls by coding.

These two controls have a unique feature: they can access two separate tables from a single database and relate data between their fields. This feature makes them very useful in situations where data from one field in a particular table looks up data from another table. Two data sources are required in such a lookup mechanism. They can be two separate ADODC or a DataEnvironment object. To add these controls to your toolbox, you have to add the MSDATLST.OCX file to your project. Follow these steps to add these controls to the toolbox.

1.   Select **Project → Components** from the menu.

2.   Select **Microsoft DataList Controls 6.0** (OLEDB) from the Controls tab of the Components dialog box and click **OK**.

Figure 6.13 shows the Components dialog box to add the controls to the Toolbox.

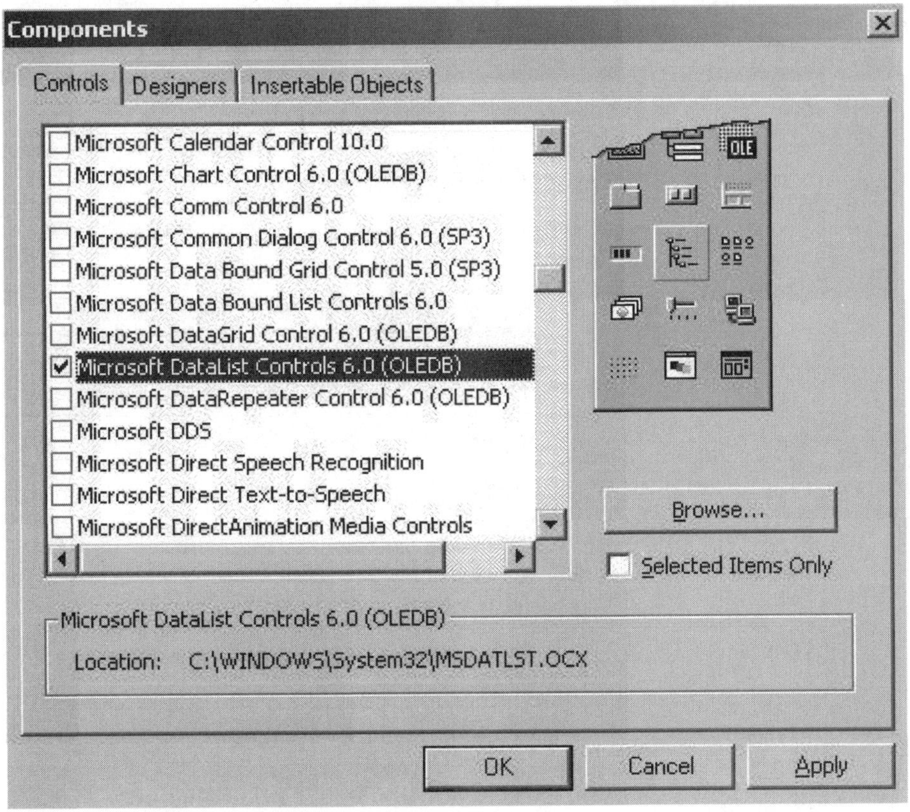

Figure 6.13: Adding the DataList Controls to the Toolbox

6.2.1 Using the DataList Control

 Explain the usage of the DataList ActiveX control.

The DataList control is similar to the ListBox control, but its rows are the values of a field in a database or a query result. Code for the DBList control and DataList control are compatible, but for any new development, you should use the DataList control. It automatically fills with data from the attached data source. You can also update a field in a related table of another data source by relating the tables by their foreign keys.

Common DataList Properties

Table 6.4 lists the common properties of the DataList and DataCombo control.

Property	Description
BoundColumn	Returns or sets the name of the source field in a Recordset object used to supply a data value to another control.
BoundText	Returns or sets the value of the data field named in the BoundColumn property.
CausesValidation	Returns or sets whether validation occurs on the control that lost focus.
DataChanged	Returns or sets a value indicating that data in a control has changed by some process other than by retrieving data from the current record.
DataField	Returns or sets a value that binds a control to a field in the current record.
DataMember	Returns or sets a value that describes the DataMember for a data connection.
DataSource	Sets a value that specifies the Data control through which the current control is bound to a database.
Enabled	Returns or sets a value that determines whether an object can respond to user-generated events.
IntegralHeight	Returns or sets a value that indicates whether a control displays partial items. Sizes the control to display an exact number of complete rows.
ListField	Returns or sets the name of the field in the Recordset object used to fill a control's list portion.
MatchEntry	Returns or sets a value indicating how a control performs a search based on user input.
MatchedWithList	Returns a value that determines if the contents of the BoundText property match one of the records in the list portion of the control.
RowMember	Returns or sets a data member name for RowSource.
RowSource	Returns or sets a data source for list items.
SelectedItem	Returns a value containing a bookmark for the selected record in a control.
VisibleCount	Returns a value indicating the number of visible items in a control.

Table 6.4: Important Properties of DataList and DataCombo Controls

Connecting a DataList to a Database

You need to have an ADODC control and a DataList control in your form. The ADODC control provides the data to the DataList. The procedure to connect the DataList to the ADODC control is as follows:

1. Open a new project and name it Datalist.vbp.

2. Select **Project → Components** and add the DataList and ADODC controls to the project.

3. Add a DataList control from the toolbox and name it dblVehInfo.

4. Add an ADODC control from the toolbox and name it adoVehInfo.

5. Set the following properties of the two controls as shown in Table 6.5 and Table 6.6.

Property	Setting
Name	AdoVehInfo
Caption	VehicleInfo
ConnectionString	Provider=Microsoft.Jet.OLEDB.4.0;Data Source =C:\parking.mdb;Persist Security Info=False
CommandType	2-adCmdTable
RecordSource	VehicleInfo

Table 6.5: Property Settings for adoVehInfo Control

Property	Setting
Name	DblVehInfo
RowSource	AdoVehInfo
ListField	OwnerName
BoundColumn	OwnerName

Table 6.6: Property Settings for dblVehInfo Control

6. Run the application by pressing **F5**.

The sample output is shown in Figure 6.14.

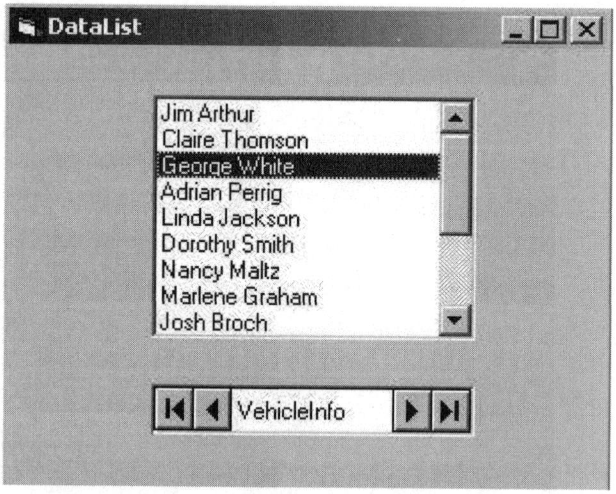

Figure 6.14: Linking a DataList to a Database

To connect a DataList to an ADODC control in code, use Code 6.1.

```
Private Sub Form_Load()

    Dim CnnStr As String 'Connection String

    CnnStr = "Provider=microsoft.jet.OLEDB.4.0;" & _
        "Data Source= C:\parking.mdb;" & _
        "Persist Security Info=False"

    With AdoVehInfo
        .ConnectionString = CnnStr 'connection string of ADODC
      .CommandType = adCmdTable 'display results from a table
        .RecordSource = VehicleInfo 'name of table to display
    End With
    Set dblVehInfo.RowSource = adoVehInfo.Recordset
    dblVehInfo.ListField = VehicleNo
End Sub
```

Code 6.1: Linking a DataList to a Database

In Code 6.1, the ADODC control adoVehInfo is connected to the database "parking.mdb" at run time. The code is added to the form's **Load** event. CnnStr is the connection string used to connect to the database. By setting the ConnectionString, CommandType, and RecordSource properties of the ADODC adoVehInfo, the control is set to display data from the table VehicleInfo in the database.

The DataList control's **RowSource** property is set to display the data from the recordset of the ADO Data Control adoVehInfo. This is done by assigning the RowSource to adoVehInfo.Recordset. Finally, the ListField property is set to display the field VehicleNo in the VehicleInfo table.

6.2.2 Using the DataCombo Control

 Explain the usage of DataCombo ActiveX control.

The DataCombo control is like the intrinsic ComboBox control but is data-bound. It has a Style property that provides a drop-down list and an optional text box for data entry. The rows of the control fill automatically with values from the field in the ListField property. The DataCombo and the DBCombo control are code-compatible, but for any future development in Visual Basic, you should use the DataCombo control.

Table 6.7 lists some of the extra properties in DataCombo control not present in the DataList control.

Property	Description
SelLength	Returns/sets the number of characters selected.
SelStart	Returns/sets the starting point of text selected.
SelText	Returns/sets the string containing the currently selected text.
Style	Returns/sets a value that determines the type of control and the behavior of its list box portion.

Table 6.7: Extra Properties of the DataCombo

The following data properties are important to the DataCombo control:

- **BoundColumn**: This is the column in the Recordset used for lookup.
- **DataField**: This is the field in the DataSource Recordset used as a lookup value.
- **DataMember**: This field is not required to be set if the data source is an ADODC. When the data source is a DataEnvironment object, you should set the value of this field to the command object that retrieves rows from a database.
- **DataSource**: It is either the name of an ADODC or a DataEnvironment object that contains the lookup field.
- **ListField**: This field fills up the DataCombo control.
- **RowMember**: This field is not required if the data source is an ADODC. If the data source is a DataEnvironment object, you should set it to the command object specified in the RowSource property.
- **RowSource**: It is either the name of an ADODC or a DataEnvironment object that fills up the DataCombo control.

Figure 6.15 shows how the DataCombo control links two different data controls. It displays the Location field from one control (Lookup) and updates the TokenID field of another control (VehicleInfo).

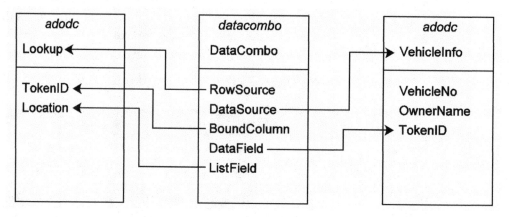

Figure 6.15: Relating Two Data Sources with a DataCombo Control

Connecting a DataCombo to a Database

You need to have two ADODC controls and a DataCombo control in your form to utilize the Lookup feature of the DataCombo control. The first ADODC control provides the data to the DataCombo for Lookup purposes and is listed as the RowSource. The second ADODC control is attached as the DataSource and its

DataField is directly manipulated by the DataCombo control. This is shown in Code 6.2.

```
Private Sub Form_Load()

Dim CnnStr As String

CnnStr = "Provider=microsoft.jet.OLEDB.4.0;" & _
         "Data Source= D:\parking.mdb;" & _
         "Persist Security Info=False"

'Set properties for ADODC adoVehInfo
With AdoVehInfo
    .ConnectionString = CnnStr
    .CommandType = adCmdTable
    .RecordSource = "VehicleInfo"
End With

'Set properties for ADODC adoLookup
With adoLookup
    .ConnectionString = CnnStr
    .CommandType = adCmdTable
    .RecordSource = "Lookup"
End With

'Set properties for DataCombo control dbcLocation
With dbcLocation
    Set .DataSource = AdoVehInfo.Recordset
    Set .RowSource =  adoLookup.Recordset
    .ListField = "Location"
    .BoundColumn = "TokenID"
    .DataField = "TokenID"
End With
End Sub
```

Code 6.2: Linking a DataCombo to a Database

In Code 6.2, the ADODC control AdoVehInfo is connected to the database "parking.mdb" during the program's execution. CnnStr is the connection string used to connect to the database. By setting the ConnectionString, CommandType, and RecordSource properties of the ADODC AdoVehInfo, the control is linked to the table VehicleInfo in the database.

The DataCombo control's **RowSource** property is set to display the data from the recordset of the ADO data control adoLookup. The DataSource is set to the ADO data control AdlVehInfo. The ListField property is set to display the field Location in the Lookup table. The field modified in the VehicleInfo table is the TokenID, and the DataField is set to this field. Finally, the BoundColumn is set to TokenID as it is the key that relates the two tables.

6.2.3 Creating a Sample Application Using DataCombo and DataList

 Explain the features of the DataList and DataCombo ActiveX controls by developing a sample application.

You have to create a sample database application using the DataList and DataCombo controls, which barely requires any code. The motive is to understand the implementation of these controls to develop a rapid database application.

Design Procedure

1. Select **File → New** from the main menu and select **Standard EXE** from the "New Project" dialog box.

2. Select **Project → Components** and from the Controls tab select **Microsoft ADO Data Control 6.0 (OLEDB)** and **Microsoft DataList Controls 6.0 (OLEDB)**, as shown in Figure 6.16.

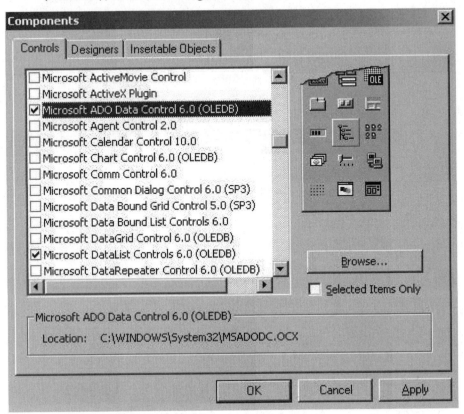

Figure 6.16: Selecting the ADO Data and the DataList Controls

3. The general toolbox contains the ADODC, DataList, and the DataCombo controls. You can use them in the form by double-clicking on them in the toolbox.

4. Add two ADODC controls and rename them as **LookUp** and **VehicleInfo**, one for each table in the parking database. Set the **Visible** property of **LookUp** to **False**.

5. Select **Microsoft Jet 4.0 OLEDB** provider from the Provider tab.

6. In the Connections tab, enter the path where you stored the database "parking.mdb". Enter Admin as the Username and select Blank password.

Click **Test Connection** and ensure that the connection is established successfully.

7.   Repeat steps 5, 6, and 7 for the VehicleInfo ADODC control.

8.   Select the RecordSource property of the **LookUp** ADODC control and enter the following values: adCmdTable for Command Type and Lookup for Table or Stored procedure name.

9.   Add a DataCombo control and set its Style property to 1-dbcSimpleCombo. Set the data properties as shown in Table 6.8. The sample is shown in Figure 6.17.

Property	Setting
Name	DbcLocation
RowSource	Lookup
ListField	Location
BoundColumn	TokenID
DataSource	VehicleInfo
DataField	TokenID
Style	1-dbcSimpleCombo

Table 6.8: Property Settings for dbcLocation

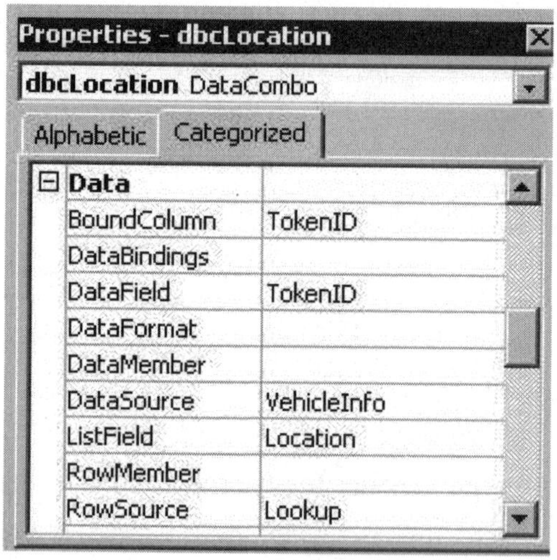

Figure 6.17: Property Settings for dbcLocation DataCombo

10. Add a DataList control and set the data properties, as shown in Table 6.9. A sample is shown in Figure 6.18.

Property	Setting
Name	DblRegNo
RowSource	VehicleInfo
ListField	VehicleNo
BoundColumn	TokenID

Table 6.9: Property Settings for dblRegNo DataList

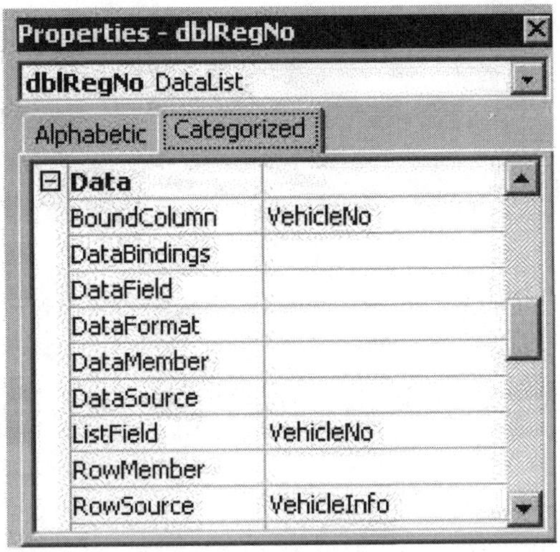

Figure 6.18: Property Settings for dblRegNo DataList

11. Add three textboxes and label them **Owner**, **VehicleNo**, and **TokenNo**.

12. Set the DataSource property of the three textboxes to **VehicleInfo** and set their DataField property to fields OwnerName, VehicleNo, and TokenId of the table VehicleInfo.

13. Set the Locked property of the textbox labeled TokenNo to True to prevent direct editing of the TokenId field.

The form should look like Figure 6.19.

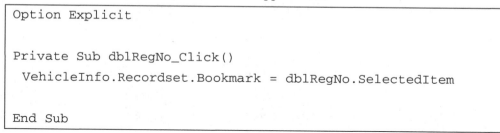

Figure 6.19: Snapshot of the Form

14.   Enter the Code 6.3 to finish the application.

```
Option Explicit


Private Sub dblRegNo_Click()
  VehicleInfo.Recordset.Bookmark = dblRegNo.SelectedItem


End Sub
```

Code 6.3: Code for Demo Application

In Code 6.3, the subroutine **dblRegNo_Click** ( ) sets the bookmark of the Recordset object of the VehicleInfo ADODC to the item that has been selected in the DataList.

As you have set all the properties of the controls at design time, no more code is required for the application.

Now you are ready to run the application. Save the project and press **F5**. The output should look like Figure 6.20.

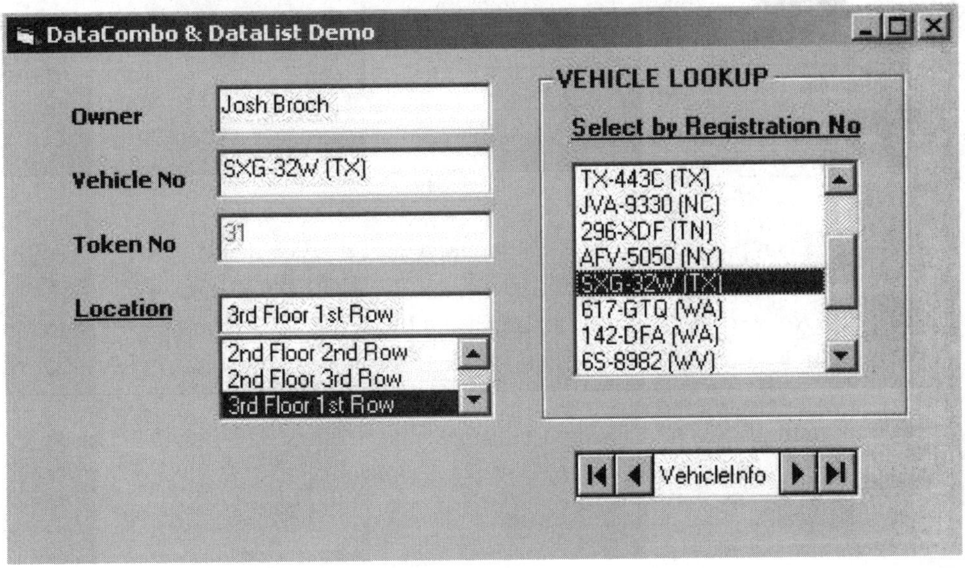

Figure 6.20: Output of the Demo Application

6.2.4 Running the Sample Application

Analyze the run-time features of the sample application.

The sample application you have developed makes use of all the important properties of the DataList and DataCombo controls. You can browse through the DataList values with the help of arrow keys or the mouse pointer and all four textboxes on the left side of the application update automatically. Make the LookUp ADODC control invisible, as it is not required on the screen. The next application demonstrating the DataGrid control would use the LookUp ADODC control.

The DataCombo control has the optional edit box, which can be used to type new values for location. The DataCombo control makes use of two tables. It displays the field Location of the table Lookup but does not make any changes to the table. The change it makes is to the field TokenID of the VehicleInfo table. Thus instead of displaying the field TokenID of the VehicleInfo table, it maps that value to the Lookup table and displays the Location field, which makes more sense than the TokenID.

6.2.5 Linking a DataCombo Control to a DataGrid

 Explain how to link a DataList or DataCombo to a DataGrid control.

You can program a DataList or DataCombo control to display the results of an SQL query in a DataGrid. On selecting a value from the DataCombo control, you can display the rows from the database matching the query. For example, if you want to list the vehicles parked on the second floor's first row, Code 6.4 displays the rows matching the SQL query in a DataGrid control. The DataGrid control displays all the rows of data matching the DataCombo controls value. Refer to the next section on DataGrid to see how to add a DataGrid control to your project.

```
Private Sub dbcLocation_Click()

    Dim Query As String
    Query = "SELECT * FROM VehicleInfo WHERE TokenID = " & _
            dbcLocation.BoundText

 'adoVehInfo is the name of the ADODC control whose
 'Data Source is the database "parking.mdb"

    adoVehInfo.RecordSource = Query
    adoVehInfo.Refresh

 'dgdVehInfo is the name of the DataGrid control
    Set dgdVehInfo.DataSource = adoVehInfo
    dgdVehInfo.ClearFields       ' clears the field layout
    dgdVehInfo.ReBind            ' reinitializes grid from source
table

End Sub
```

Code 6.4: Linking a DataCombo to a DataGrid Control

In Code 6.4, the DataCombo control dbcLocation's **Click** event is coded. The DataCombo displays the Location field as its contents. Query is a string that holds the query to the database table. The query selects the records, which match the presently selected TokenID in the DataCombo. The result of this query is stored in the Recordset by the ADODC control adoVehInfo when you assign the RecordSource property of the ADODC to the query string. By assigning the DataSource of the DataGrid to the ADODC adoVehInfo, you set it to the Recordset. Finally, to display the records, you clear the fields of the DataGrid and rebind it to the new DataSource.

Practice Questions

1. Explain the difference between a data control and a data-bound control.

2. How can you add the ActiveX controls discussed in the chapter to your toolbox?

3. Which controls can be data-bound?

4. How would you use a DataList control or a DataCombo control to link to another table to display all of the possible selections for a field taken from the other table?

5. What properties of the recordset are used for navigation?

6. How do the DataList and DataCombo controls enhance the functioning of the user interface?

6.3 Using the DataGrid Control

The DataGrid control maps records and fields from a Recordset object on a grid consisting of rows and columns. It is similar to the DBGrid control except that it is always data-bound. The control allows the user to edit the grid-fields directly and supports the addition and deletion of rows in the Recordset object. On setting the DataSource property of the DataGrid control to an ADODC control, the grid automatically fills with rows from the data control's Recordset object along with the column headers.

To add the control to your toolbox, you have to add the MSDATGRD.OCX file to your project. Figure 6.21 shows how to add the DataGrid control to the current project. The procedure is as follows:

1.   Select **Project** → **Components**. The components dialog box appears.

2.   Select **Microsoft DataGrid Control 6.0 (OLEDB)** from the Controls tab, as Shown in Figure 6.21.

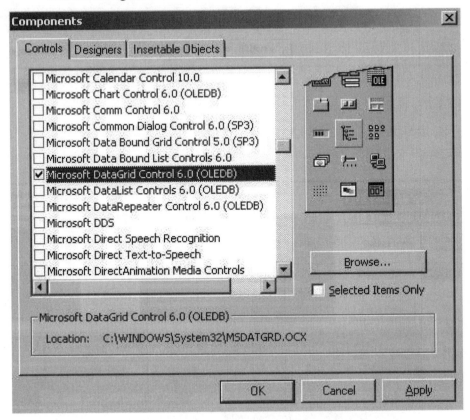

Figure 6.21: Adding the DataGrid Control

6.3.1 DataGrid Properties

 Explain the features of DataGrid control.

The DataGrid control can display 32,767 columns and an indefinite number of rows (limited only by the amount of system memory). You can edit the DataGrid cells interactively on the control. The cells can hold a variety of data types, but not linked or imbedded objects. The DataGrid control also features a word-wrap facility where the text in a cell spreads over multiple lines if it exceeds the column width. The Bookmark property provides access to data in the current row of the grid. Table 6.10 lists some of the important properties of the DataGrid control along with their description.

Property	Description
AllowAddNew	Enables interactive record addition
AllowDelete	Enables interactive record deletion
AllowUpdate	Enables or disables record updatability
Bookmark	Accesses data in the current row
Col	Sets/returns the current column number
Columns	Contains a collection of grid columns (allows addition, removal, and count)
DataMember	Specifies the source of grid data in context of a DataEnvironment
DataSource	Specifies the source of grid data (Data Control or DataEnvironment)
EditActive	Returns status or enters/exits the cell editor (Boolean)
Index	Returns/sets the number identifying a control in a control array
RecordSelectors	Shows/hides selection panel at the left border
RightToLeft	Controls whether text displays left-to-right or right-to-left
Row	Specifies display line of current data row
SelBookmarks	Contains a collection of selected row bookmarks
SelText	Sets/returns the selected text
VisibleCols	Returns the number of visible columns in the grid
VisibleRows	Returns the number of visible rows in the grid

Table 6.10: Important Properties of DataGrid Control

6.3.2 Including DataGrid in the Sample Application

 Demonstrate how the DataGrid control enhances a sample application.

You can extend the sample application developed in the earlier section to include the DataGrid control. This greatly enhances the usefulness of the application, as direct editing of database content is possible through the DataGrid control.

Open the application created in the previous section and follow these steps to add further functionality to it through the DataGrid control.

1. Select **Project → Components** and add the DataGrid control, as shown in Figure 6.16.

2. Change the **Style** property of the DataCombo control to dbcDropdownCombo.

3. Add two DataGrid controls, one each for the **Lookup** and **VehicleInfo** table.

4. Set the DataSource property of the first DataGrid to VehicleInfo and the second DataGrid to **Lookup**.

5. Right-click both the DataGrid controls one-by-one and click the option **Retrieve Fields**.

6.   Right-click the DataGrid and click **Properties**. You see the **Property Pages** dialog box similar to the one shown in Figure 6.22. Set the values of any of the given options as needed. The default values display all the columns of the table in the DataGrid.

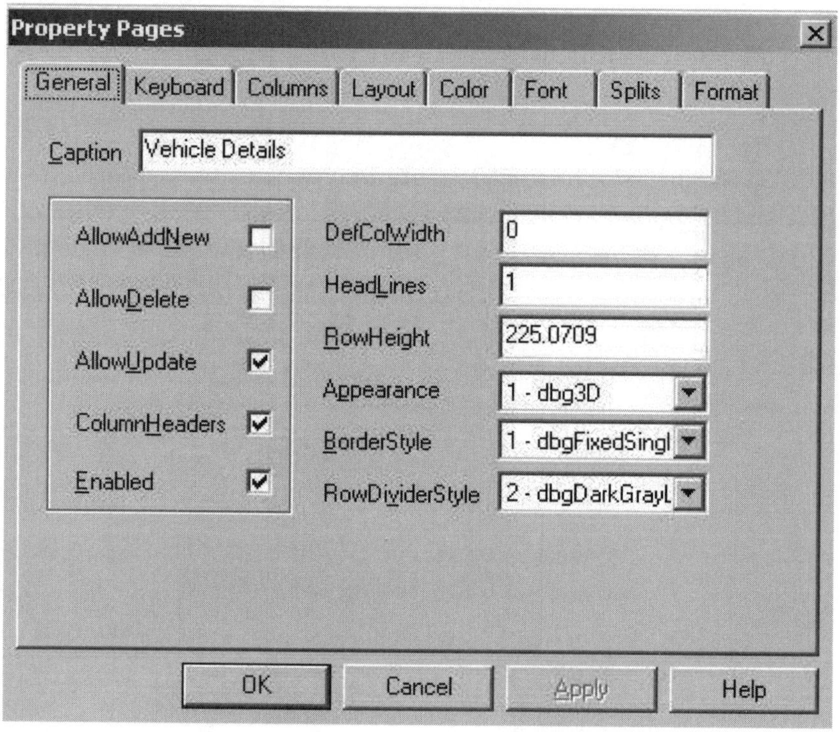

Figure 6.22: Property Pages of the DataGrid Control

7.   Add four command buttons: **cmdAdd**, **cmdUpdate**, **cmdDelete**, and **cmdCancel**.

The form should look similar to the one in Figure 6.23.

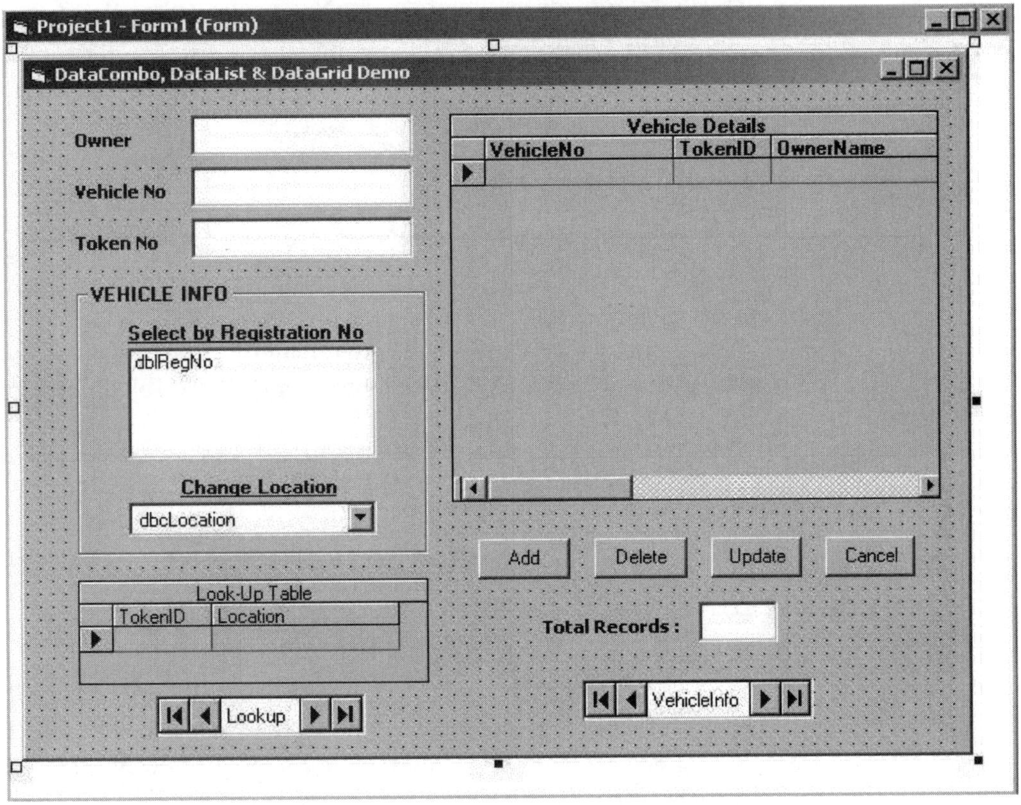

Figure 6.23: Form After Adding the DataGrid Control

The design part of the application is complete. Now you have to code the subroutines to give full functionality to the application.

8.   In the General Declarations portion of your code, add the lines shown in Code 6.5.

```
Option Explicit
Dim b_onAdd As Boolean
```

Code 6.5: General Declarations

In Code 6.5, the variable **b_onAdd** is a Boolean variable that is set to **True** whenever the **Add** button is pressed. It is used by the **click** event procedures of the buttons named **Add**, **Cancel**, and **Delete**.

9. Add a subroutine named **disableBtn**. This function disables the **Add** and **Delete** buttons by setting their Enabled property to False. Code 6.6 shows this function.

```
Private Sub disableBtn()
    cmdAdd.Enabled = False
    cmdDelete.Enabled = False
End Sub
```

Code 6.6: Function disableBtn( )

10. Add a Sub named **enableBtn**. This function enables the Add and Delete buttons after cancel or update by setting their **Enabled** property to **True**. Code 6.7 shows this function.

```
Private Sub enableBtn()
    cmdAdd.Enabled = True
    cmdDelete.Enabled = True
End Sub
```

Code 6.7: Function enableBtn( )

11. Add code for the Click event of the Add button (named **cmdAdd**). This code adds a new record at the end of the Recordset of the **VehicleInfo** data control by using the AddNew procedure of the Recordset. Code 6.8 shows the **Click** event for cmdAdd button.

```
Private Sub cmdAdd_Click()
    b_onAdd = True
    disableBtn
    VehicleInfo.Recordset.AddNew
End Sub
```

Code 6.8: Click Event for cmdAdd

12. Add code for the Cancel button's (named **cmdCancel**) Click event. This function cancels the update of a record. It checks whether a new record is being added or not, and if it is, it sets the b_onAdd flag to **False** and enables the Add and Delete buttons. It uses the CancelUpdate procedure of the Recordset of the VehicleInfo data control.

Code 6.9 shows the Click event for the cmdCancel button.

```
Private Sub cmdCancel_Click()
    If b_onAdd Then
        b_onAdd = False
        enableBtn
    End If
    VehicleInfo.Recordset.CancelUpdate
End Sub
```

Code 6.9: Click Event for cmdCancel

13.   Add code for the Click event of the Delete button **cmdDelete**. It prompts the user for confirmation by showing a message box. The reply is stored in the integer variable **response**. On a positive reply, it deletes the current record by using the Delete procedure of the Recordset and moves to the first record. The textbox displaying the total number of records is updated by using the RecordCount method. Code 6.10 shows the Click event for the cmdDelete button.

```
Private Sub cmdDelete_Click()
    Dim response As Integer
    response = MsgBox("Are you sure you want to delete this _
        record?", vbOKCancel, "Delete record for " & _
        txtName.Text)

    If response = vbOK Then
        VehicleInfo.Recordset.Delete
        VehicleInfo.Recordset.MoveFirst
        txtTotRec.Text = VehicleInfo.Recordset.RecordCount
    End If
End Sub
```

Code 6.10: Click Event for cmdDelete

14.   Add code for the Update button's (named **cmdUpdate**) Click event. It enables the Add and Delete button if they are disabled, by checking whether the Boolean variable b_onAdd is True. Then it updates the current record using the Update method. It also updates the total record count that is

displayed in the txtTotRec textbox. Code 6.11 shows the Click event for the cmdUpdate button.

```
Private Sub cmdUpdate_Click()
    If b_onAdd Then
        b_onAdd = False
        enableBtn
    End If
    VehicleInfo.Recordset.Update
    txtTotRec.Text = VehicleInfo.Recordset.RecordCount
End Sub
```

Code 6.11: Click Event for cmdUpdate

15.   Add code for the DataList control's (named **dblRegNo**) Click event to bookmark the selected item. This moves the marker to that item in the DataGrid and the user can edit that particular record. Code 6.12 shows the Click event of the dblRegNo control.

```
Private Sub dblRegNo_Click()
    VehicleInfo.Recordset.Bookmark = dblRegNo.SelectedItem
End Sub
```

Code 6.12: Click Event for DataList dblRegNo

16.   Finally, add the code for the Form's Load event. It displays the total number of records currently in the table in a textbox named txtTotRec and sets the button flag variable b_onAdd to False. Code 6.13 shows the Load event of the form.

```
Private Sub Form_Load()
    b_onAdd = False
    txtTotRec.Text = VehicleInfo.Recordset.RecordCount
End Sub
```

Code 6.13: Load Event of the Form Named Form

17.   Code 6.14 gives the complete source code of the application.

```vb
Option Explicit
Dim b_onAdd As Boolean


Private Sub disableBtn()
    cmdAdd.Enabled = False
    cmdDelete.Enabled = False
End Sub


Private Sub enableBtn()
    cmdAdd.Enabled = True
    cmdDelete.Enabled = True
End Sub


Private Sub cmdAdd_Click()
    b_onAdd = True
    disableBtn
    VehicleInfo.Recordset.AddNew
End Sub


Private Sub cmdCancel_Click()
    If b_onAdd Then
        b_onAdd = False
        enableBtn
    End If
    VehicleInfo.Recordset.CancelUpdate
End Sub


Private Sub cmdDelete_Click()
Dim response As Integer
        response = MsgBox("Are you sure you want to delete _
        this record?", vbOKCancel, "Delete record for " & _
        txtName.Text)

        If response = vbOK Then
```

```
                        VehicleInfo.Recordset.Delete
                        VehicleInfo.Recordset.MoveFirst
                        txtTotRec.Text = VehicleInfo.Recordset.RecordCount
            End If
End Sub


Private Sub cmdUpdate_Click()
    If b_onAdd Then
        b_onAdd = False
        enableBtn
    End If
    VehicleInfo.Recordset.Update
    txtTotRec.Text = VehicleInfo.Recordset.RecordCount
End Sub


Private Sub dblRegNo_Click()
    VehicleInfo.Recordset.Bookmark = dblRegNo.SelectedItem
End Sub


Private Sub Form_Load()
    b_onAdd = False
    txtTotRec.Text = VehicleInfo.Recordset.RecordCount
End Sub
```

Code 6.14: Listing for Application Using DataGrid Control

Save the project and form in a new folder, without overwriting the original application. On running the application, you should see output similar to Figure 6.24.

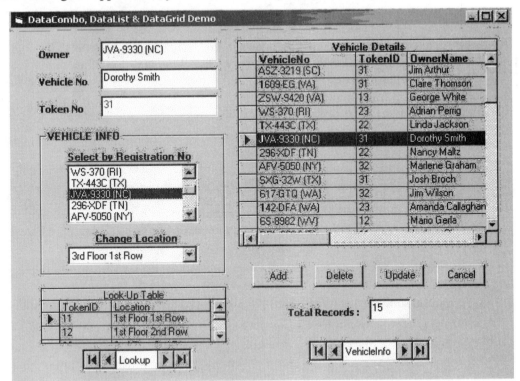

Figure 6.24: Run Time View of the Demo Application Using DataGrid

6.3.3 Running the Application

Analyze the run time properties of the Demo application.

The DataGrid lets you edit, delete, and add new records directly to the database. On pressing the Add button, you can enter a new record by editing the new data in the grid itself or by filling in the textboxes. To allocate a location to the vehicle, use the drop-down combo box because the TokenID is not directly editable. The Delete button deletes the current record from the database after getting a positive confirmation. After adding a new record, press Update to update the row count and the database. The Delete button and the Cancel button are disabled during the addition of a new record. You may cancel the addition of a new record by pressing the Cancel button.

 You need to add error handlers in the procedure cmdCancel_Click( ) to avoid crashing the application when you cancel the addition of an empty record. A simple workaround can be to add the line "cmdCancel.Enabled = False" in the disableBtn( ) method.

6.3.4 Changing Data Properties at Run Time

 Explain the methods of changing the data source and filling up a DataGrid at run time.

At run time, you can reset the DataSource property to a different data source.

For example, if you have two ADO Data Controls, Lookup and VehicleInfo, each connected to the two tables Lookup and VehicleInfo, you can reset the DataSource from one ADO Data control to another. Follow these steps to do the same:

1. Open a new project from the **File → New** menu.
2. Add two ADODC controls and a DataGrid control named dgdVehInfo, like the ones given in the demo application. You may copy the ADODC controls and the DataGrid linked to VehicleInfo from the form in the sample application.
3. Add a command button and name it CmdCaption.
4. By executing the code given in Code 6.15, you can change the table displayed in the DataGrid at run time.

```
Option Explicit
Dim lookup_on As Boolean


Private Sub CmdCaption_Click()
    If lookup_on Then
        Set dgdVehInfo.DataSource = VehicleInfo
        CmdCaption.Caption = "Lookup table"
```

```
            lookup_on = False
    Else
            Set dgdVehInfo.DataSource = Lookup
            CmdCaption.Caption = "VehicleInfo table"
            lookup_on = True
    End If


End Sub


Private Sub Form_Load()
    lookup_on = False
End Sub
```

Code 6.15: Changing the DataSource Property at Run Time

In the form's Load event, the lookup_on Boolean variable is initialized to False.

CmdCaption is a command button which can be clicked to change the display in the DataGrid. In the button's Click procedure, code is added to change the DataSource of the DataGrid dgdVehInfo at run time.

On clicking the button, the DataSource is changed to the Lookup table if initially the VehicleInfo table was displayed, and the Caption of the button is changed to "VehicleInfo Table". Clicking again on the button changes the DataSource to VehicleInfo and sets the caption to "Lookup Table".

To fill a DataGrid named dgdVehInfo with data from an ADODC control named Adodc1 at run time, you need to set the DataSource property of the DataGrid control in code. Code 6.16 displays how to fill a DataGrid at run time with records returned by an SQL query. This fills the DataGrid control with the VehicleNo and OwnerName fields from the table VehicleInfo.

```
Private Sub FillGrid()

    Dim Con As String
    Con_str = "Provider=Microsoft.Jet.OLEDB.4.0;" & _
        "Data Source=I:\parking.mdb;" & _
        "Persist Security Info=False"


    Dim QueryStr As String
```

```
QueryStr = "SELECT VehicleNo, OwnerName FROM VehicleInfo"


With Adodc1
    .ConnectionString = Con_str
    .RecordSource = QueryStr
End With
Set dgdVehInfo.DataSource = Adodc1


End Sub
```

Code 6.16: Filling up a DataGrid Control at Run Time

In Code 6.16, the procedure FillGrid defines a string variable Con, which is used to provide the connection string to the ADODC control. The string QueryStr holds the query which retrieves the two fields VehicleNo and OwnerName from the Table VehicleInfo. The ADODC control Adodc1's properties ConnectionString and RecordSource are set to the values of Con and QueryStr respectively. Finally, the DataSource property of the DataGrid dgdVehInfo is set to the ADODC control. On executing the procedure from a command button, the DataGrid displays the query results from the table VehicleInfo.

Practice Questions

1. List the important properties of the DataGrid control.
2. Which is the most important feature of a DataGrid that distinguishes it from DataList and DataCombo?
3. Compare the DataGrid control to the DataList and DataCombo controls.
4. Discuss how the AllowAddNew, AllowDelete, AllowEdit properties enhance the usage of the DataGrid control.

6.4 Using the Hierarchical FlexGrid Control

The Microsoft Hierarchical FlexGrid control is the latest grid control offered by Microsoft in Visual Basic 6.0. It is a tool designed to display hierarchical data. The MSHFlexGrid control is similar in certain ways to the DataGrid control, but is more secure as its cells are read-only. It lets you easily display relationships between related records in different tables in databases. The MSHFlexGrid control makes displaying hierarchical data easy as it supports cascading relationships among tables.

To add the control to your toolbox, you have to add the MSHFLXGD.OCX file to your project. Follow these steps to include Hierarchical FlexGrid Control in the toolbox:

1.   Select **Project → Components**.

2.   Select **Microsoft Hierarchical FlexGrid Control 6.0 (OLEDB)** from the Controls tab. Figure 6.25 shows how to add the MSHFlexGrid control to your project.

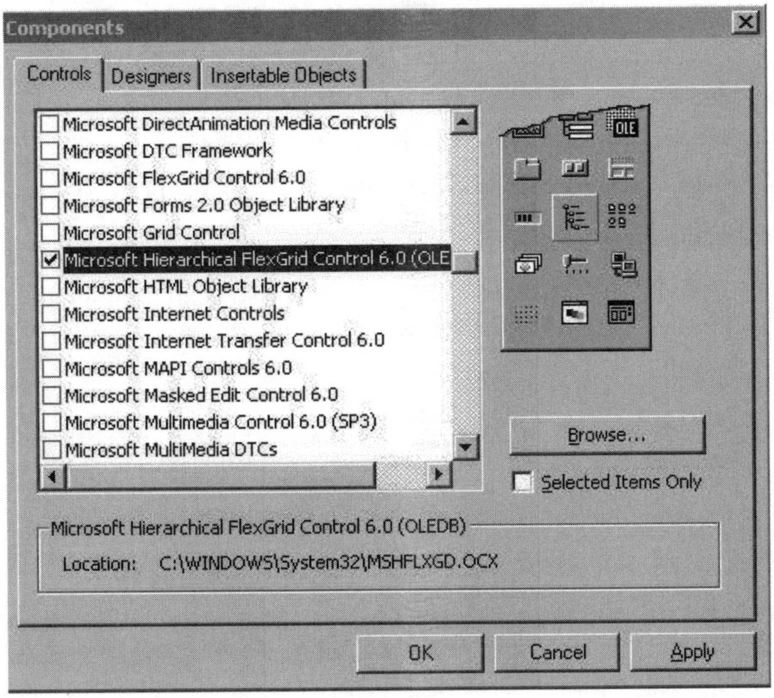

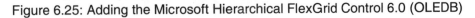

Figure 6.25: Adding the Microsoft Hierarchical FlexGrid Control 6.0 (OLEDB)

6.4.1 Features and Properties of MSHFlexGrid Control

 Explain the features and properties of MSHFlexGrid control.

MSHFlexGrid control supports the following features:

- Displaying hierarchical data sets from different tables.
- Displaying data in read-only mode, preventing data corruption.
- Allowing text as well as images in grid cells.
- Code-compatibility with the Data Bound Grid (DBGrid) control.
- Changing cell content at run time.
- Filling the grid automatically with rows from a table when the DataSource property is set to a Data Control.
- Dynamic rearrangement of rows and columns in the grid.
- Data binding when the DataSource property is set to a DataEnvironment object and the DataMember is set to a command object.
- Word-wrap facility for text in grid cells.
- Regrouping of data automatically after adjustment in columns.

 Though the MSHFlexGrid is read-only, you can program the EnterCell and LeaveCell events to enable direct editing of the grid cells.

Table 6.11 lists some of the important properties of the MSHFlexGrid control.

Property	Description
AllowBigSelection	Returns or sets whether clicking on a column or row header selects the entire column or row.
AllowUserResizing	Returns or sets whether the user can resize rows and columns with the mouse.
BandDisplay	Returns or sets the band display style.
BandLevel	Returns the band number for the current cell.
Bands	Returns the number of bands.
CellAlignment	Returns or sets the alignment of data in a cell or range of selected cells. Not available at design time.
CellPicture	Returns or sets an image that displays in the current cell or in a range of cells.
CellType	Returns the type of the current cell.
Clip	Returns or sets the contents of the cells in a selected region of a Hierarchical FlexGrid. Not available at design time.
Col	Returns or sets the active cell in a Hierarchical FlexGrid. Not available at design time.
ColAlignment	Returns or sets the alignment of data in a column.
DataField	Returns the name of the field bound to the specified column.
DataMember	Returns or sets the data member for the control.
DataSource	Returns or sets the data source for the control.
FocusRect	Determines whether the Hierarchical FlexGrid control should draw a focus rectangle around the current cell.
MergeCells	Groups cells with the same contents in a single cell spanning multiple rows or columns.
Recordset	Binds the Hierarchical FlexGrid to an ADO Recordset. Not available at design time.
RowExpanded	Returns or sets the expand and collapse state of the current row in the current band.
SelectionMode	Returns or sets whether a Hierarchical FlexGrid should allow regular cell selection, selection by rows, or selection by columns.

Sort	Sorts selected rows according to specified criteria.
TopRow	Returns or sets the uppermost row displayed in the Hierarchical FlexGrid. Not available at design time.
WordWrap	Wraps text within a cell to multiple lines.

Table 6.11: Important Properties of Hierarchical FlexGrid Control

Table 6.12 lists some of the important methods of the MSHFlexGrid control.

Property	Description
AddItem	Adds a new row to a Hierarchical FlexGrid control at run time.
BandColIndex	Returns the column index for a column number.
Clear	Clears all text, pictures, and cell formatting of the MSHFlexGrid.
ClearStructure	Clears information about the order and name of columns displayed.
CollapseAll	Collapses all rows in a specified band or all bands.
ExpandAll	Expands all rows in a specified band or all bands.
Refresh	Forces a complete repaint of a form or control.
RemoveItem	Removes a row from a Hierarchical FlexGrid control at run time.

Table 6.12: Important Methods of Hierarchical FlexGrid Control

6.4.2 Using the Data Environment Designer

 Explain the steps in creating hierarchical recordsets using the Data Environment Designer.

The Data Environment Designer creates ADO objects at design-time. It is similar to the UserConnection designer (used to create RDO or Remote Data objects) to a certain extent, but is much more versatile. It provides an interactive environment to create hierarchies between objects by creating Connection and Command objects. It can also include groupings and aggregates. After creating the objects in the DataEnvironment, you can drag and drop the objects on the form to create data-bound controls and fields automatically. It also removes the need of adding several instances of ADO Data Controls for the same tables in every form that requires accessing those tables. With the

Data Environment Designer, you can create command objects that are accessed globally by every form in your project.

To add a DataEnvironment object to your Visual Basic project, you have to add a reference to the Data Environment Designer. The method of adding a DataEnvironment object is:

1.   Select **Project → Components** from the main menu.

2.   On the Designers tab, select **Data Environment**, as shown in Figure 6.26.

3.   Click **OK**. A reference to the Data Environment Designer is added to the project.

4.   Select **Project → Add Data Environment** to add a DataEnvironment object to the current project.

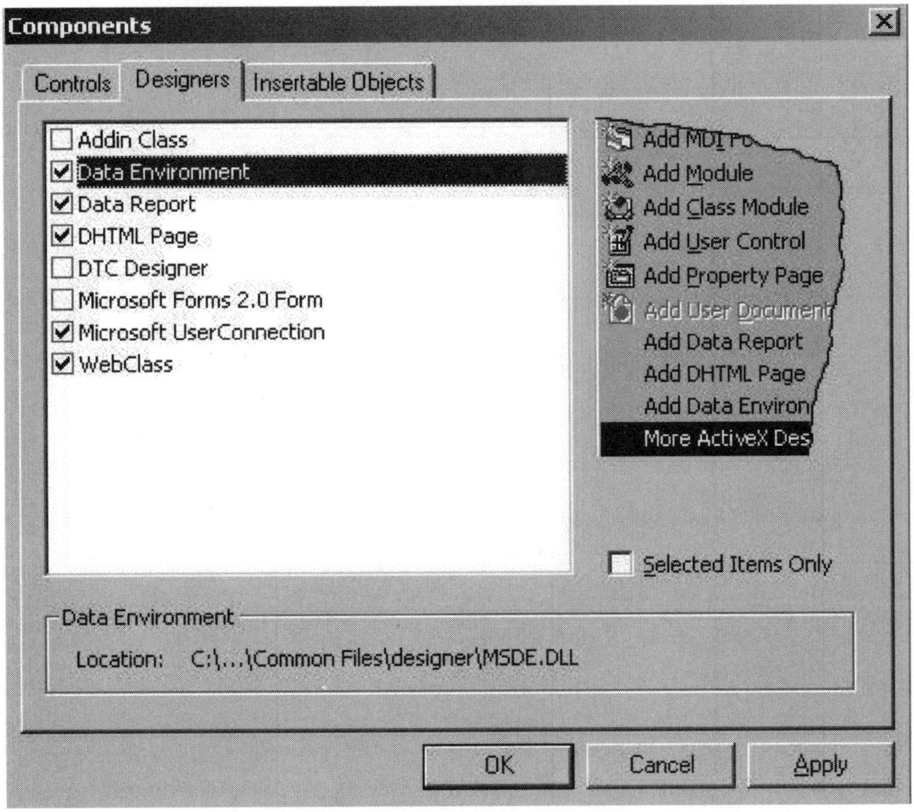

Figure 6.26: Adding a Data Environment Designer

5. The DataEnvironment window opens, as shown in Figure 6.27. You can also see a Designers folder in the Projects window that consists of the DataEnvironment1 object.

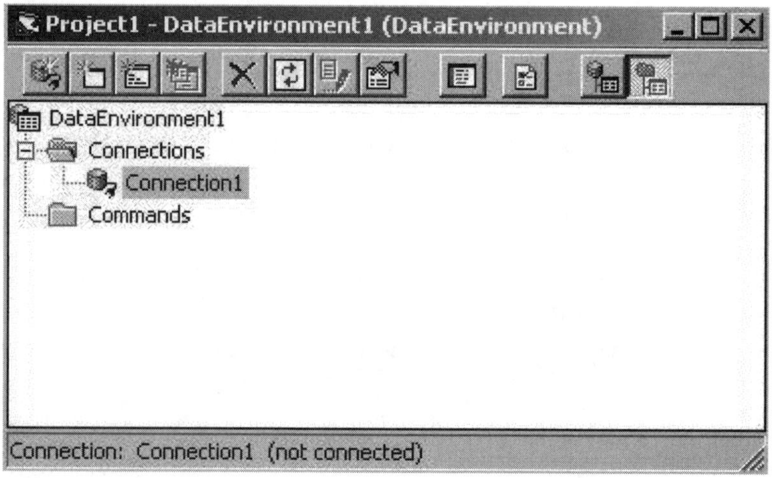

![Project1 - DataEnvironment1 window showing DataEnvironment1 with Connections folder containing Connection1, and Commands folder. Status bar reads "Connection: Connection1 (not connected)".]

Figure 6.27: Data Environment Window

6.4.3 Connection and Command Objects

 Explain the Connection and Command objects.

The Connection object specifies the physical database file, access permissions, and OLEDB provider used for data access.

Follow these steps to add a Connection to the Data Environment:

1. Right-click on the **Data Environment** icon in the DataEnvironment window and select **Add Connection**.

2. Rename the Connection in the Properties window to a name relevant to the project, such as conLookup.

3. Right-click on the icon for the connection you have created and select **Properties**.

4. The Data Link Properties dialog box appears.

5. Set the OLEDB provider name, Database name, and Access permissions.

6. Click the **Test Connection** button to test the connection.

The Command object specifies how to access data from the database. The source of the data may be a stored procedure, view, table, or an SQL statement. It is similar to the RecordSource property of the ADODC. You can declare relations between objects, groupings, and aggregates in the Command objects. It creates a Recordset object that can be used to access data.

Follow these steps to add a command to the Data Environment:

1. Right-click the **Data Environment** icon in the Data Environment window and select **Add Command**.

2. Rename the Command in the Properties window to a name relevant to the project, such as comLookup.

3. Right-click on the icon for the command you have created and select **Properties**.

4. The Command Properties dialog box appears.

5. You can see six tabs: General, Parameters, Relation, Grouping, Aggregates, and Advanced.

6. From the General tab, you can select the Connection, Table, and Object name.

7. The Relation tab is required only for child commands.

8. You can create Groupings and Aggregates from the respective tabs.

If you use the Data Environment Designer instead of an ADO Data Control, you have to add navigation buttons separately.

Portability of Project

When you select the Connection string for the connection object, the path is hard-bound to the program, which might lead to errors during run time if the database file is moved to another location. This can be avoided by coding the ConnectionString in the DataEnvironment's Initialize event.

Open the source code for the DataEnvironment that you have included in your project and add the lines shown in Code 6.17.

```
Option Explicit


Private Sub DataEnvironment_Initialize()
     'conPark is the name of the connection
     conPark.ConnectionString =
"Provider=Microsoft.Jet.OLEDB.4.0;" & _
          "Persist Security Info=False; Data Source=" & _
          App.Path & "\parking.mdb;"
End Sub
```

Code 6.17: Initialize Event for DataEnvironment

In Code 6.17, code for the connection string to the database is added to the DataEnvironment's Initialize event. App.Path is used instead of using the full path to the database file. App.Path specifies the path of the application and as such the above code would work only if the database file is stored in the same folder as that of the application.

You can code only the Initialize and Terminate events of the Data Environment.

6.4.4 Developing a Sample Application Using MSHFlexGrid Control

 Demonstrate how the MSHFlexGrid Control works using a sample application.

You will be developing a sample application using the Hierarchical FlexGrid control and the Data Environment Designer. The database is the same as the one used for the previous applications.

Follow these steps to create the application:

1. Create a new project and save it in a new folder named "Flex".

2. Select **Project → Components** from the main menu.

3. Add the Microsoft Hierarchical FlexGrid Control 6.0 (OLEDB) from the **Controls** tab, as shown in Figure 6.25.

4. On the **Designers** tab, select Data Environment, as shown in Figure 6.26.

5. Click **OK**. A reference to the Data Environment Designer is added to the project.

6. Select **Project → Add Data Environment** to add a DataEnvironment object to the current project.

7. Rename the object with the default name of DataEnvironment1.

8. Right-click the Connection1 icon and click **Properties**. On the Provider tab, select **Microsoft Jet 4.0 OLEDB provider**. On the Connections tab, select the database "parking.mdb". Enter Admin as username and Blank password.

10. Right-click the **DataEnvironment** icon and select **Add Command**.

11. This adds a new command named Command1 to the project. Right-click the **Command1** icon and select **Properties**.

12. On the General tab, select Lookup as the command name, Connection1 as connection, Table as Database object, and Lookup as Object Name.

Figure 6.28 shows the properties of the Lookup command object.

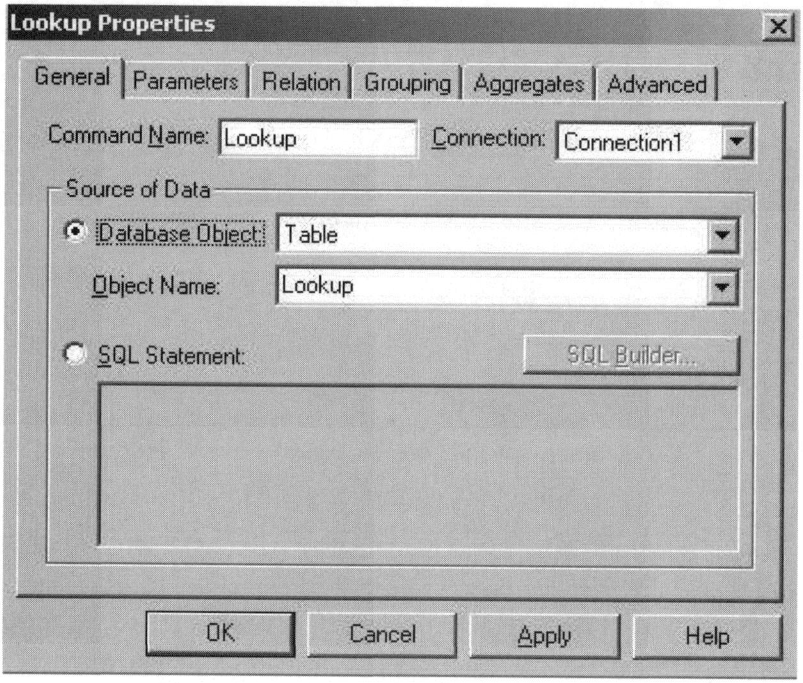

Figure 6.28: Properties of Command Object Lookup

13. Right-click the **Lookup** command and select **Add Child Command**.

14. Rename the new child command object VehicleInfo.

15. Right-click the **VehicleInfo** command and select **Properties**.

16. In the General tab, enter **Table** as the Database object and VehicleInfo as Object Name.

17. In the **Relation** tab, under Relation Definition, select TokenID from both the combo boxes and click on the Add button.

Figure 6.29 shows the relation properties of the VehicleInfo command object.

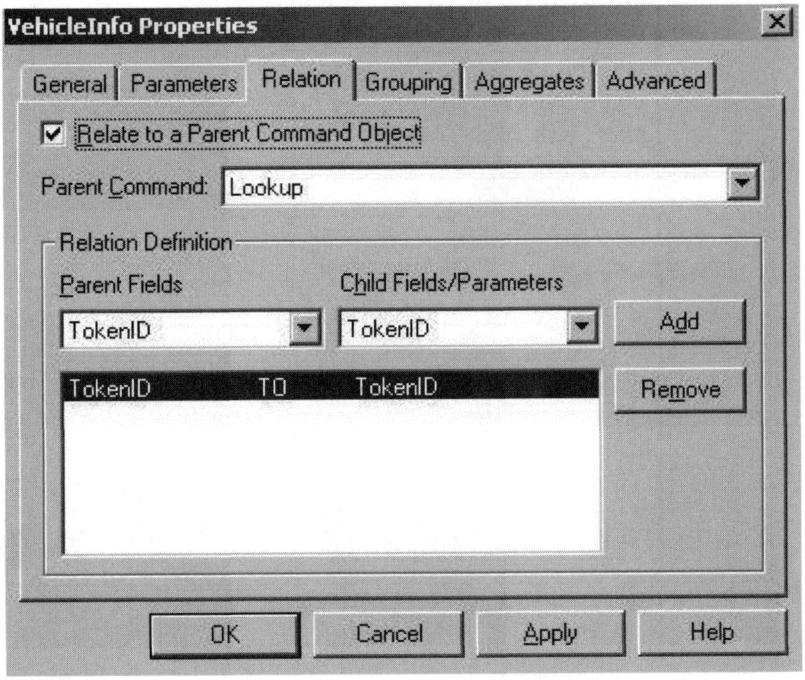

Figure 6.29: Relation Properties of Command Object VehicleInfo

18. Click **OK**. Your DataEnvironment window should look like the one shown in Figure 6.30.

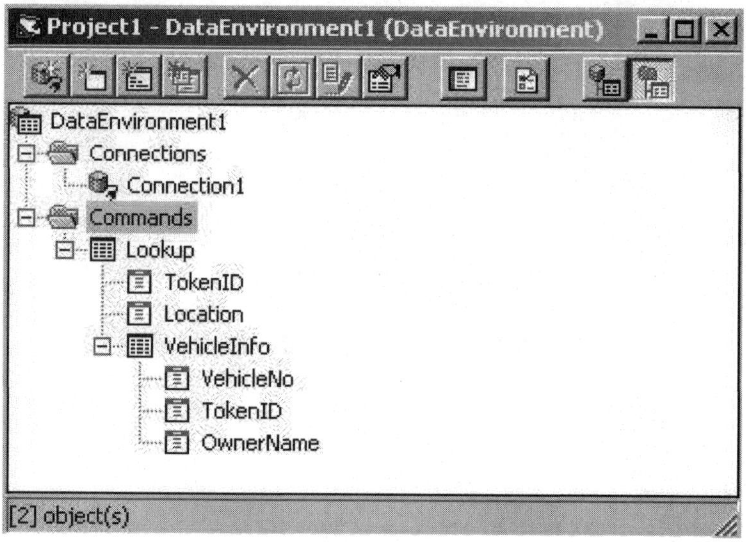

Figure 6.30: DataEnviornment Window

19. Add a Hierarchical FlexGrid and name it FlexDataDes.

20. Set its DataSource property to DataEnvironment1 and DataMember to Lookup.

21. Right-click the **FlexDataDes** control and select **Retrieve Structure**.

22. Again, right-click the **FlexDataDes** control and select **Properties**.

23.   In the Bands tab, select **Band1** (VehicleInfo) and uncheck the TokenID field, as shown in Figure 6.31.

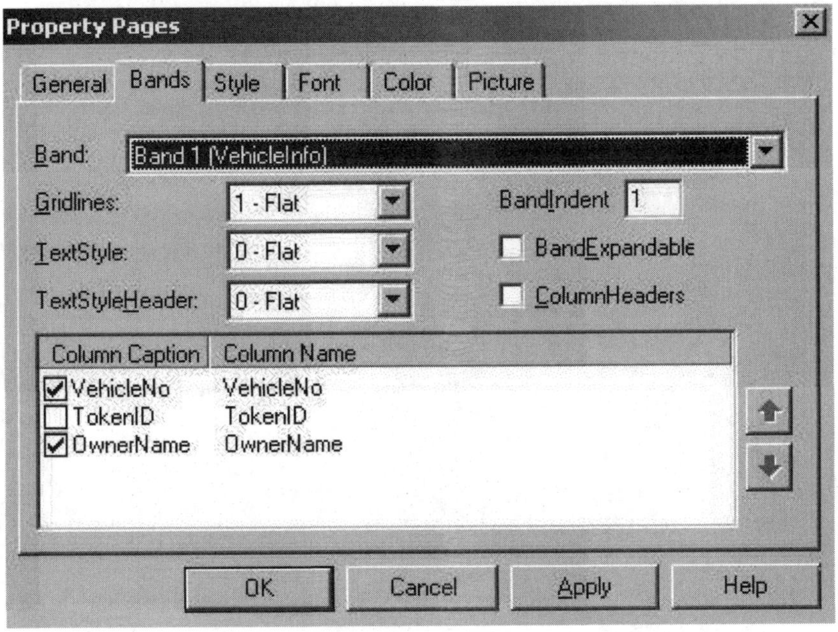

Figure 6.31: Properties of FlexDataDes

24.   Click **OK** to apply the changes and close the Property Pages of the Hierarchical FlexGrid control.

25.   Right-click the **DataEnvironment1** icon in the DataEnvironment window and add a new command object. Rename it as QueryCmd.

Right-click the **QueryCmd** command icon and click **Properties**. Select SQL Statement as Source of Data and enter the query shown in Code 6.18 in the textbox (refer to Figure 6.32). The query selects the Location and TokenID fields from the Lookup table.

```
SELECT Location, TokenID FROM Lookup
```

Code 6.18: SQL Query to Retrieve Fields from LookUp

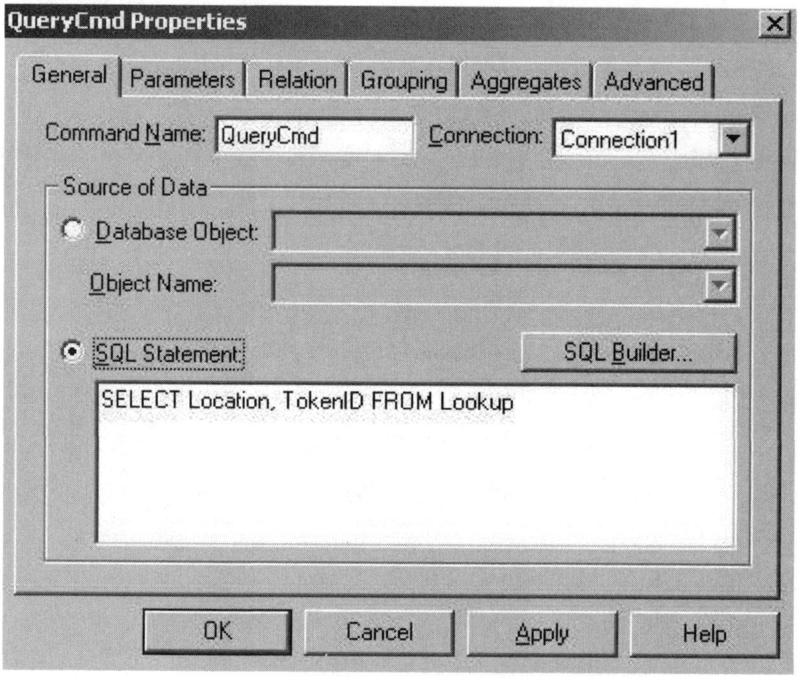

Figure 6.32: Properties of QueryCmd

26.   Click **OK**.

27.   Right-click the **QueryCmd** command icon and select Add Child Command. Rename the child command ChildQuery.

28. Right-click the **ChildQuery** command and click **Properties**. Select SQL Statement as Source of Data and enter the query shown in Code 6.19 in the textbox.

```
SELECT TokenID, VehicleNo, OwnerName FROM VehicleInfo ORDER BY
TokenID
```

Code 6.19: SQL Query to Retrieve Fields from VehicleInfo

Figure 6.33 shows the ChildProperties dialog box with Select SQL Statement as Source of Data.

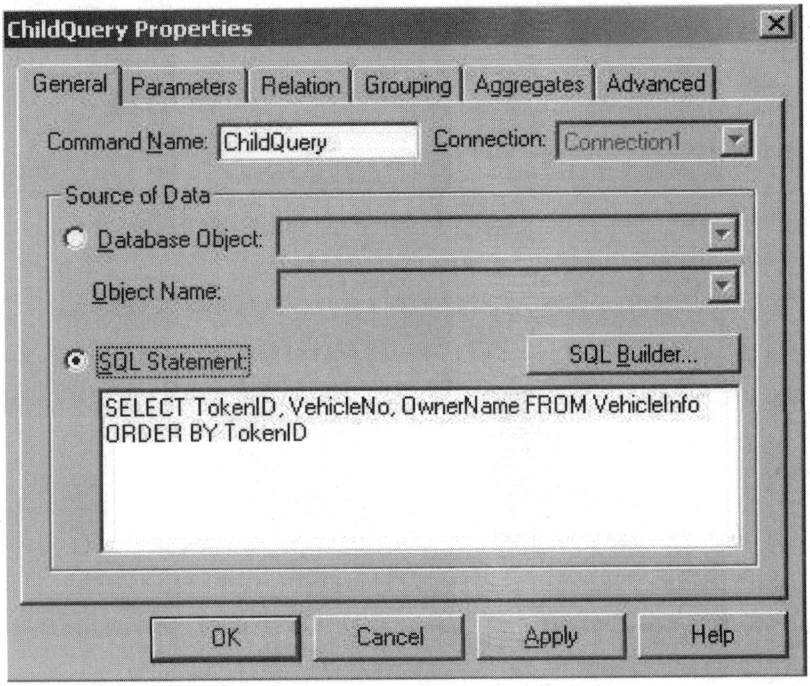

Figure 6.33: Properties of ChildQuery

29. This query selects the TokenID, VehicleNo, and OwnerName fields from the VehicleInfo table and orders the results by TokenID field.

30. Add the relation definition TokenID to TokenID in the **Relation** tab as shown in Figure 6.34 and click **OK**.

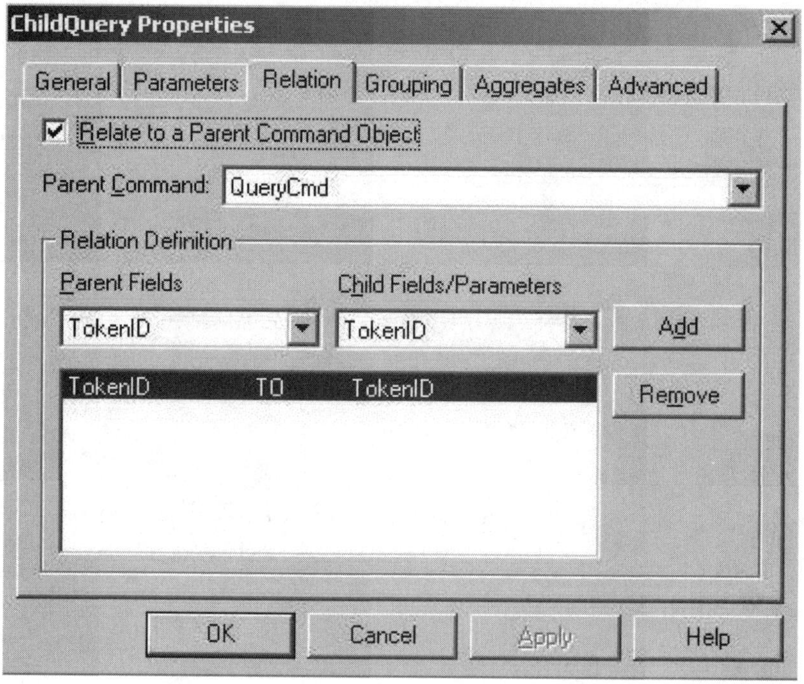

Figure 6.34: Relation Between ChildQuery and QueryCmd

31.   Your Data Environment window should look like Figure 6.35.

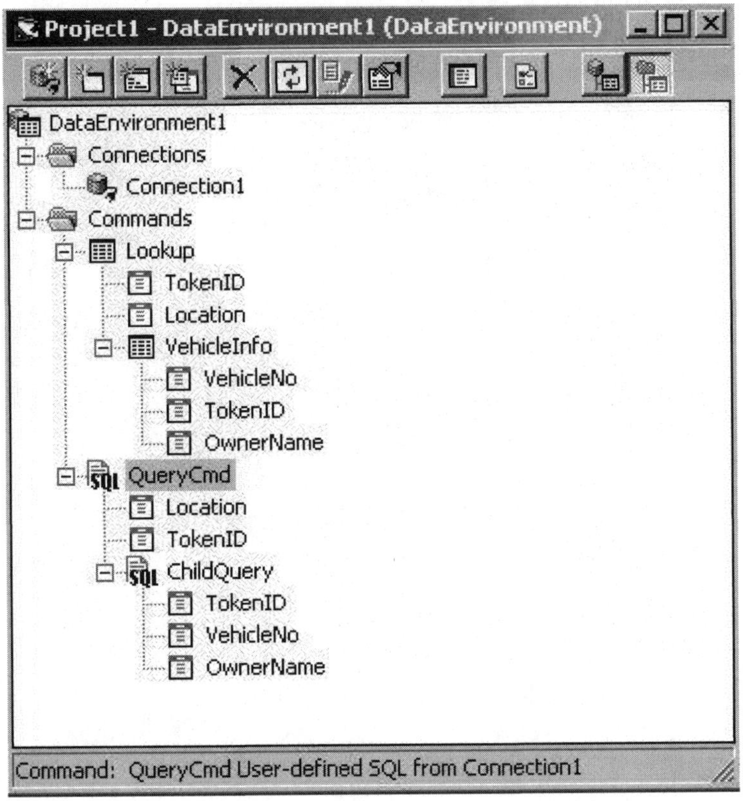

Figure 6.35: Data Environment Window

32.   Drag the QueryCmd icon from the window and drop it on the project form.
         This automatically creates two new textboxes labeled Location and TokenID
         and a Hierarchical FlexGrid control with the appropriate DataSource,
         DataMember, and DataField properties set.

33.   Add four command buttons and name them CmdBeginning, CmdEnd,
         CmdPrevious, and CmdNext. These buttons are for the navigation of the
         flexQuery control created in Step 25.

34.   Add two command buttons and name them ColExpBtn and ClearGrid1.

35.   Add a textbox and name it txtCurPos. Label it Current Position and set its text property to "Row 1, Col 1". Your application should look like Figure 6.36.

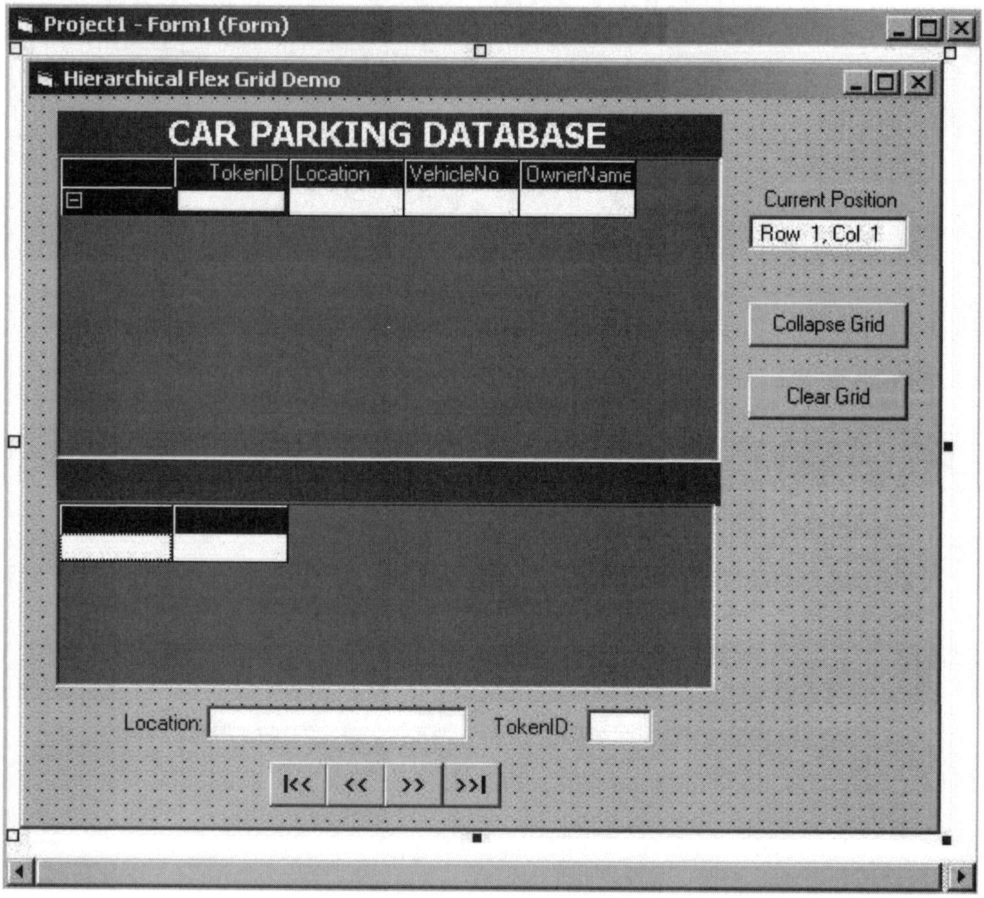

Figure 6.36: Form for the Hierarchical FlexGrid Demo

36.   Add Code 6.20 for the ColExpBtn's Click event. It calls the **ExpandCollapseGrid()** procedure, which expands or collapses the Hierarchical FlexGrid.

```
Private Sub ColExpBtn_Click()
    ExpandCollapseGrid FlexDataDes
End Sub
```

Code 6.20: Click Event for ColExpBtn Button

37.   Add Code 6.21 for the **ExpandCollapseGrid()** procedure, which collapses or expands the grid and changes the button's caption according to its state. It accepts an argument for an object of type MSHFlexGrid. Collapsed is a Boolean variable, which determines whether the Hierarchical FlexGrid is in a collapsed or expanded state. It calls the methods ExpandAll and CollapseAll according to the state of the Grid.

```
Private Sub ExpandCollapseGrid(HFGrid As MSHFlexGrid, _
                               Static Collapsed As Boolean)
   If Collapsed Then
      HFGrid.ExpandAll
      ColExpBtn.Caption = "Collapse Grid"
      Collapsed = False
   Else
      HFGrid.CollapseAll
      ColExpBtn.Caption = "Expand Grid"
      Collapsed = True
   End If
End Sub
```

Code 6.21: ExpandCollapseGrid( ) Function

38.   In the **Form Load** event, add code for the initialization for the variable collapse. On calling the procedure **ExpandCollapseGrid()**, the static variable Collapsed is initialized to the correct state of the Hierarchical FlexGrid. Code 6.22 shows the **Load** event of the form.

```
Private Sub Form_Load()
   ExpandCollapseGrid FlexDataDes
   'initializes the static variable Collapse
End Sub
```

Code 6.22: Load Event

39.   In the CmdBeginning button's **Click** event, add the Code 6.23.

```
Private Sub CmdBeginning_Click()
   DataEnvironment1.rsQueryCmd.MoveFirst
End Sub
```

Code 6.23: Click Event for Button CmdBeginning

The rsQueryCmd is the recordset that is automatically created by the DataEnvironment for its parent command object QuertyCmd. The access of the rsQueryCmd recordset is similar to the access of the recordset object created by the ADO Data Control. MoveFirst points to the first record in the recordset.

In the CmdEnd **Click** event, add the Code 6.24 to point to the Last record in the recordset.

```
Private Sub CmdEnd_Click()
    DataEnvironment1.rsQueryCmd.MoveLast
End Sub
```

Code 6.24: Event for CommandButton CmdEnd

40.   Add Code 6.25 to the CmdPrevious Click event to move to the previous record.

```
Private Sub CmdPrevious_Click()
    If DataEnvironment1.rsQueryCmd.BOF Then
        'do nothing
    Else
        DataEnvironment1.rsQueryCmd.MovePrevious
    End If
End Sub
```

Code 6.25: Click Event for CommandButton CmdPrevious

Code 6.25, shows that if the control is already at the beginning record, the procedure does nothing. Otherwise, it moves to the previous record in the recordset object by executing the MovePrevious procedure.

41.   Finally, add Code 6.26 to the CmdNext **Click** event.

```
Private Sub CmdNext_Click()
    If DataEnvironment1.rsQueryCmd.EOF Then
        'do nothing
    Else
        DataEnvironment1.rsQueryCmd.MoveNext
    End If
End Sub
```

Code 6.26: Click Event for the CommandButton CmdNext

In Code 6.26, when the control is displaying the last record, pressing the CmdNext button does nothing. Otherwise it moves to the next record.

42.   The complete code listing is given in Code 6.27.

```
Option Explicit


Private Sub ColExpBtn_Click()
   ExpandCollapseGrid FlexDataDes
End Sub


Private Sub ExpandCollapseGrid(HFGrid As MSHFlexGrid, _
                              Static Collapsed As Boolean)
   If Collapsed Then
      HFGrid.ExpandAll
      ColExpBtn.Caption = "Collapse Grid"
      Collapsed = False
   Else
      HFGrid.CollapseAll
      ColExpBtn.Caption = "Expand Grid"
      Collapsed = True
   End If
End Sub


Private Sub ClearGrid1_Click()
    FlexDataDes.Clear
End Sub


Private Sub Form_Load()
    ExpandCollapseGrid FlexDataDes
    'initializes the static variable Collapse
End Sub


Private Sub FlexDataDes_Click()
    CurPos.Text = " Row " & Str(FlexDataDes.Row) & _
                  ", Col " & Str(FlexDataDes.Col)
End Sub
```

```
Private Sub CmdBeginning_Click()
    DataEnvironment1.rsQueryCmd.MoveFirst
End Sub


Private Sub CmdEnd_Click()
    DataEnvironment1.rsQueryCmd.MoveLast
End Sub


Private Sub CmdPrevious_Click()
    If DataEnvironment1.rsQueryCmd.BOF Then
        'do nothing
    Else
        DataEnvironment1.rsQueryCmd.MovePrevious
    End If
End Sub


Private Sub CmdNext_Click()
    If DataEnvironment1.rsQueryCmd.EOF Then
        'do nothing
    Else
        DataEnvironment1.rsQueryCmd.MoveNext
    End If
End Sub
```

Code 6.27: Code for the Hierarchical FlexGrid Application

43.   Run the application by pressing **F5**.

Figure 6.37 shows the run time view of the application.

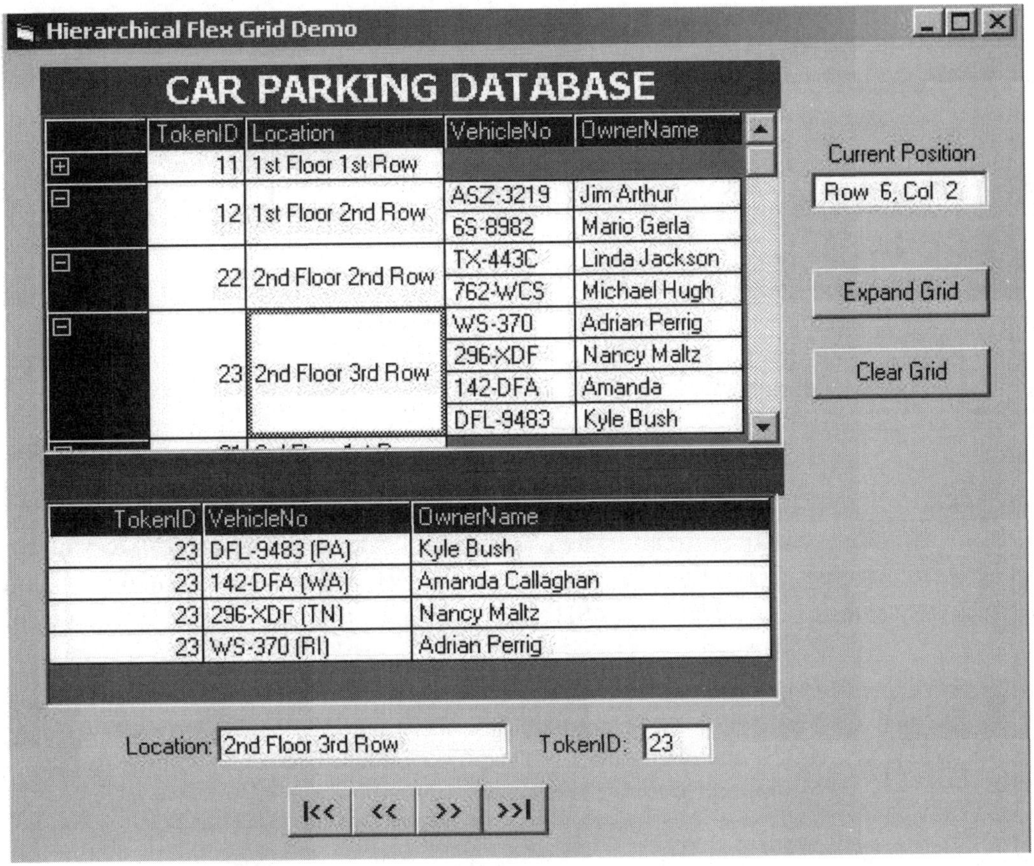

Figure 6.37: Run Time View of the Demo Application

The first Hierarchical FlexGrid named FlexDataDes displays hierarchical records retrieved by the Lookup object. You can see all the sub-records for each value of TokenID. The Clear method clears the grid. You can also collapse or expand the grid by executing the **ExpandCollapseGrid()** routine, which takes an object of type MSHFlexGrid as an argument. The ExpandAll and CollapseAll methods do the necessary work.

The second Hierarchical FlexGrid named flexQuery displays data from the ChildQuery command and the textboxes display data from the QueryCmd command. You can browse through records in the VehicleInfo table by clicking on the navigation buttons. Whenever you create a parent command with the Data Environment Designer, it automatically creates a Recordset object by prefixing the object name with "rs." For example, if you have a parent command named QueryCmd, you automatically have access to a Recordset object named rsQueryCmd, which you can refer to in your code. The navigation buttons use the methods MovePrevious, MoveNext, MoveFirst, and MoveLast of a Recordset object to navigate.

6.4.5 Creating a Hierarchical Recordset Using a SHAPE Command

Explain the steps involved in creating a hierarchical Recordset using a SHAPE command.

You can also create a hierarchical Recordset in code using a SHAPE command as the RecordSource for an ADO Data Control. MSDataShape provider, which is a part of ActiveX Data Objects, implements the SHAPE command. The Data Environment Designer also generates SHAPE commands to create hierarchies between Recordsets.

You can create relational hierarchies with the Data Environment Designer and right-click the parent command and select Hierarchy Info. This displays the SHAPE command for the relation.

A simple syntax of the SHAPE command is shown in Code 6.28.

```
SHAPE {<parent command> | <another SHAPE command>} AS <alias>
APPEND ({ <child command> | <another SHAPE command>} AS <alias>)
RELATE (<parent field> TO <child field> AS <alias>)
```
Code 6.28: Syntax of the SHAPE Command

Follow these steps to use the SHAPE command to create a Hierarchical Recordset:

1.   Open a new project and save it as "ShapeDemo".

2.   Add a MSHFlexGrid control and name it Flex1.

3.   Add an ADO Data Control and name it Adodc1.

4. Add the code given in Code 6.29 to the **Form Load** event. After the definition of the **Form Load** event, we provide the definition of a procedure named Create_Shape that is called from the **Form Load** event.

```
Private Sub Create_Shape ()

    Dim ConnectStr As String
    ConnectStr = "Provider=MSDataShape.1;" & _
    "Persist Security Info=False;" & _
    "Data Source= App.Path & "parking.mdb;" & _
    "User ID=Admin;" & _
    "Connect Timeout=15; Data Provider=MSDASQL"

    Dim ShapeStr As String
    ShapeStr = "SHAPE {SELECT Location, TokenID" & _
        " FROM Lookup} AS Lookup APPEND " & _
        " ({SELECT TokenID, VehicleNo, OwnerName " & _
        " FROM VehicleInfo} AS " & _
        " VehicleInfo RELATE TokenID TO TokenID) " & _
        " AS VehicleInfo"

    With Adodc1
        .ConnectionString = ConnectStr
        .RecordSource = ShapeStr
    End With
    Set Flex1.DataSource = Adodc1

End Sub
```

Code 6.29: Creating a Hierarchical Recordset Using Shape

Create_Shape is a procedure, which is called to display a hierarchical Recordset object created by a SHAPE command. ConnectStr is a string variable used to provide the connection string to the ADO data control. The main feature of this example is that the RecordSource of the ADODC control is not an SQL query or a table, but is a SHAPE command.

In the connection string, the provider is named MSDataShape.1, and the Data Provider is MSDASQL.

In the SHAPE command, which is stored in the string variable ShapeStr, the fields of table Lookup (which is the parent table) and the fields of the table VehicleInfo (which is the child table) are related by the field TokenID. This creates a hierarchical Recordset. The ADODC control is provided with the connection string and the SHAPE command and finally the DataSource of the Hierarchical FlexGrid Flex1 is set to the ADODC named Adodc1.

6.4.6 Scanning Through Hierarchical Recordsets

 Explain how to scan through hierarchical recordsets.

In case of hierarchical Recordsets, some fields are themselves Recordsets. To scan through such Recordsets, you need to scan the rows recursively. This scans through all the subfields that are themselves Recordsets.

Using the **While ... Wend** loop, you can scan through the Recordsets of a hierarchical Recordset object. Code 6.30 shows how to scan through the Recordset returned by the Shape command and display two sub-recordsets per Recordset.

```
Private Sub ScanRS()
    Dim CONXN As New ADODB.Connection
    Dim RS As New ADODB.Recordset
    Dim RSVehicle_Info As New ADODB.Recordset

    CONXN.Provider = "MSDataShape.1"
    CONXN.Open "Data Source=parking;" & _
            "User ID=Admin; Password=;" & _
            "Connect Timeout=15; Data Provider=MSDASQL"

    RS.StayInSync = True
    RS.Open "SHAPE {SELECT Location, TokenID FROM Lookup}" & _
        "AS Lookup APPEND" & _
```

```
          "({SELECT TokenID,VehicleNo,OwnerName FROM _
              VehicleInfo}" & "AS VehicleInfo" & _
          "RELATE TokenID TO TokenID AS VehicleInfo"), CONXN


     Set RSVehicle_Info = RS("VehicleInfo").Value

     While Not RS.EOF
         Debug.Print RS("Location"), RS("TokenID"), _
                     RS("VehicleNo"), RS("OwnerName")

         While Not RSVehicle_Info.EOF
           Debug.Print RSVehicle_Info(0), RSVehicle_Info(1)
             RSVehicle_Info.MoveNext
         Wend
         RS.MoveNext
     Wend

End Sub
```

Code 6.30: Scanning Through a Hierarchical Recordset

In Code 6.30, a Sub name ScanRS is written which displays the technique of scanning through the hierarchical Recordset. The output can be forwarded to any other control by replacing the Debug.Print statement by some control's display field.

CONXN is a new connection object that is used to open a connection to the database.

RS and RSVehicle_Info are two Recordsets used to hold the rows from the tables Lookup and VehicleInfo respectively.

The connection provider is given as MSDataShape.1 and a connection is opened to the database. The Recordset RS is set to hold the values returned by the SHAPE command by the Open command.

The recordset RSVehicle_Info is set to the value of the Recordset RS's VehicleInfo alias.

Now the two **While** loops scan through the hierarchical Recordsets. The outer **While** loop scans through the Recordsets returned by the parent command, whereas the inner **While** loop returns the individual Recordsets which are themselves contained in the

parent Recordsets. The final result is that every record is displayed from the **Lookup** command and whenever a record has a child record, it is also displayed. The example displays only two child Recordsets, which you can change to the maximum number of child records that are present in the parent Recordset.

Practice Questions

1. List and define the options for the Command Type property available for an ADO Data Control and for a Data Environment Command object.
2. What properties of the recordset are used for navigation?
3. How is SQL used in a Data Environment?
4. What is data shaping?
5. What is a hierarchical Recordset? When would it be useful to define one?

Case Study

This section adds data-bound controls to the forms in the Library Management System and provides an efficient way to manipulate the data stored in the database. It makes use of the ADO connection object created in the previous chapter to execute certain SQL commands. This section performs the most significant coding task in developing the Library Management System, as this is the stage where data will actually flow between the client's machine and the back end database.

1.   Open the VB project named LibraryMgmt.

2.   Open the form named frmBooks and add an ADODB control to the first tab of
      the Tabbed Dialog control. Set the following properties for the ADODB
      control as given in Table 6.13.

Property	Value
Name	adoCategories
Caption	Categories
Visible	False

Table 6.13: Properties and Values for ADODB Control

3.   Add a Label control named lblCategory to the first tab. Make its caption as
      Category.

4.   Add a DataCombo control named dbcCategory to the first tab. Set its
      RowSource property as adoCategories and type in the ListField property as
      CategoryName and the BoundColumn property as CategoryID.

5.   Add a command button control named cmdNewCategory next to the
      DataCombo control. Set the caption of the command button as &New
      Category.

Figure 6.38 shows the appearance of the form after adding these new controls.

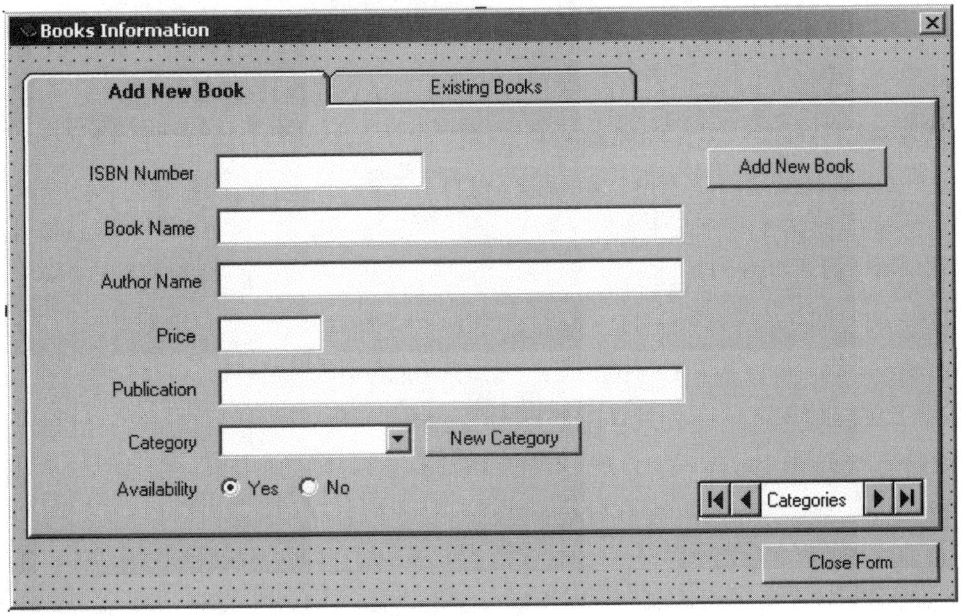

Figure 6.38: Books Information Form with Added Controls in Add New Book Tab

6.   Activate the second tab in the form frmBooks. Add controls to the tab as shown in Figure 6.39.

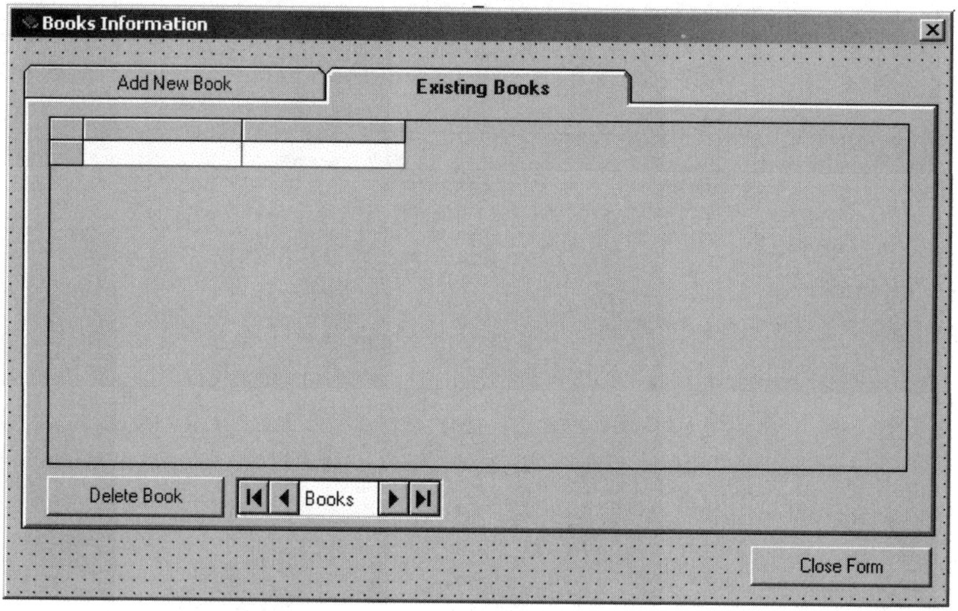

Figure 6.39: Books Information Form with Added Controls in Existing Books Tab

7. Set the properties of the controls in the second tab of the form as given in Table 6.14:

Control Type	Property	Value
ADODC control	Name	adoBooks
	Caption	Books
	Visible	False
DataGrid control	Name	dbgBooks
	DataSource	adoBooks
	AllowAddNew	False
	AllowDelete	False
	AllowUpdate	False
Command Button control	Name	cmdDeleteBook
	Caption	Delete Book

Table 6.14: Properties and Values for Controls in Existing Books Tab

8. Modify the code for the **Form Load** event of the form frmBooks as given in Code 6.31. The additional code in the procedure sets the various properties of the ADODC controls in the form connecting them to the appropriate tables in the database.

```
Private Sub Form_Load()
  Me.Left = 120
  Me.Top = 120
  Me.tabBooks.Tab = 0
  Me.optAvailability(0).Value = True
  With Me.adoBooks
    .ConnectionString = strConString
    .CommandType = adCmdTable
    .RecordSource = "Books"
    .Refresh
  End With
  With Me.adoCategories
    .ConnectionString = strConString
    .CommandType = adCmdTable
```

```
    .RecordSource = "Categories"
    .Refresh
  End With
End Sub
```

9.   In the code window of the form frmBooks, add Code 6.32 for the **Click** event
           of the command button cmdAddBook. It adds a new record to the Books table
           using the methods and properties of the ADODC control named adoBooks.
           Finally it updates the ADODC control so that the added record is displayed in
           the DataGrid control in the second tab of the tabbed dialog control.

```
Private Sub cmdAddBook_Click()
  If IsValidData = False Then
    Exit Sub
  End If
  If MsgBox("Are you sure to add the specified book", _
        vbQuestion + vbYesNo, "Add Book") = vbYes Then

    On Error GoTo errmsg
    With Me.adoBooks.Recordset
      .AddNew
      .Fields(0) = Trim(Me.txtISBN)
      .Fields(1) = Trim(Me.txtBookName)
      .Fields(2) = Trim(Me.txtAuthorName)
      .Fields(3) = CCur(Val(Me.txtPrice))
      .Fields(4) = Trim(Me.txtPublication)
      .Fields(5) = Trim(Me.dbcCategory.BoundText)
      .Fields(6) = IIf(Me.optAvailability(0).Value, True, False)
      .Update
    End With

    MsgBox "Record successfully added", vbExclamation, "Add
    Book"
    If Me.adoBooks.Recordset.State = adStateOpen Then
      Me.adoBooks.Recordset.Requery
```

```
      End If
      Me.adoBooks.Refresh
      Reset
   End If
   Exit Sub
errmsg:
   MsgBox Err.Description, vbCritical, "ERROR"
End Sub
```

Code 6.32: Code for the Click Event of Command Button cmdAddBook

10.   Add Code 6.33 for the **Click** event of the command button cmdDeleteBook.
       The code deletes the currently selected record in the DataGrid control, if the
       user approves to do so.

```
Private Sub cmdDeleteBook_Click()
   If Me.adoBooks.Recordset.RecordCount > 0 Then
      Dim strMsg As String
      strMsg = "Are you sure to delete the following book"
      strMsg = strMsg + vbNewLine + vbNewLine
      strMsg = strMsg + "ISBN : " &
Me.adoBooks.Recordset.Fields(0)
      strMsg = strMsg + vbNewLine
      strMsg = strMsg + "Book Name : " &
Me.adoBooks.Recordset.Fields(1)
      If MsgBox(strMsg, vbQuestion + vbYesNo, "Confirm Delete") =
vbYes
      Then
         On Error Resume Next
         Me.adoBooks.Recordset.Delete adAffectCurrent
      End If
   End If
End Sub
```

Code 6.33: Code for the Click Event of the Command Button cmdDeleteBook

11.   Add Code 6.34 for the **Click** event of the command button cmdNewCategory.
       It accepts the name of the new category through an input box and adds a

record for the new category in the Categories table. The addition of the record is done through the ADODC control named adoCategories that is connected to the Categories table. Adding the record to the Categories table updates the list of the DataCombo control linked to concerned ADODC control.

```
Private Sub cmdNewCategory_Click()
  Dim strCategory As String
  strCategory = InputBox("Enter New category name", "Add New
Book")
  If Trim(strCategory) <> "" Then
    Me.adoCategories.Recordset.AddNew "CategoryName",
strCategory
    Me.adoCategories.Recordset.Update
    Me.adoCategories.Refresh
    Me.dbcCategory.Text = strCategory
  End If
End Sub
```

Code 6.34: Code for the Click Event of the Command Button cmdNewCategory

12. Add Code 6.35 at the end of the function named IsValidData to provide validation of the data specified in the DataCombo named dbcCategory.

```
If Trim(Me.dbcCategory.BoundText) = "" Then
    MsgBox "Category Name cannot be blank", vbCritical, "Input
Error"
    Me.dbcCategory.SetFocus
    IsValidData = False
    Exit Function
  End If
```

Code 6.35: Code to Validate Data in the Combo Box dbcCategory

13. Open the form frmIssueBook and modify the form by adding the additional controls as shown in Figure 6.40.

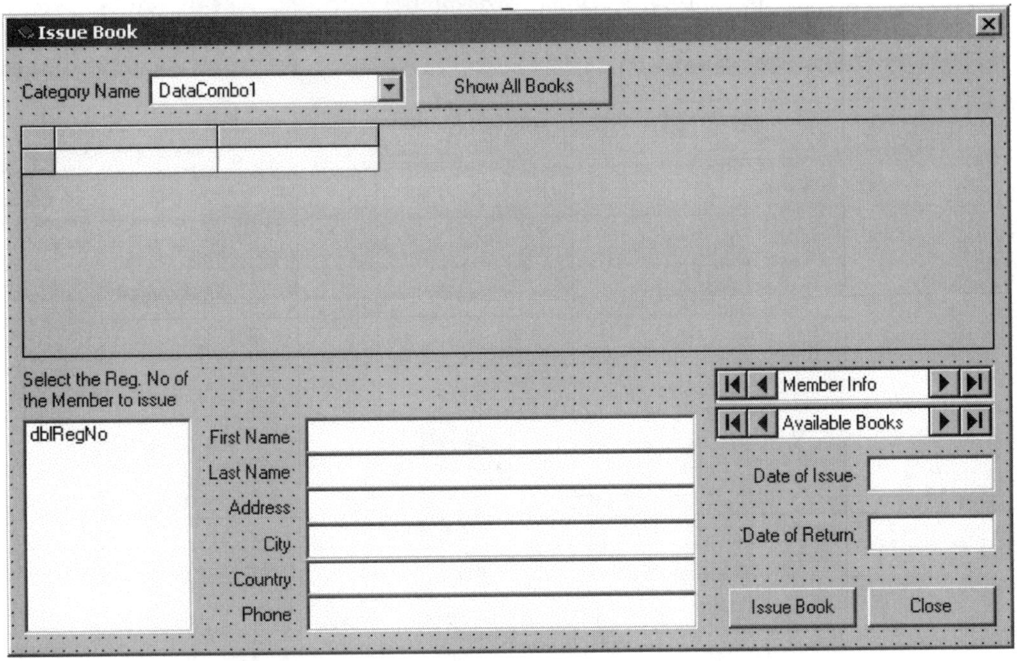

Figure 6.40: Issue Book Form with Added Controls

14. Set the properties of the newly added controls of the form as given in Table 6.15.

Control Type	Property	Value
ADODC control	Name	adoMemberInfo
	Caption	Member Info
	Visible	False
ADODC control	Name	adoBooks
	Caption	Available Books
	Visible	False
DataGrid control	Name	DbgBooks
	DataSource	adoBooks
	AllowAddNew	False

	AllowDelete	False
	AllowUpdate	False
DataCombo control	Name	DbcCategory
DataList control	Name	DblRegNo
	RowSource	adoMemberInfo
	ListField	RegNo
	BoundColumn	RegNo
Label control	Name	lblCategory
	Caption	Category Name
Label control	Name	lblRegNos
	Caption	Select the Reg. No of the Member to issue
	WordWrap	True
CommandButton control	Name	cmdShowAll
	Caption	Show All Books

Table 6.15: Details of Properties for the Newly Added Controls of the Form

15. Modify the code for the **Form Load** event of the form frmIssueBooks as given in Code 6.36. It sets the properties of the ADODC controls namely adoMemberInfo and adoBooks.

```
Private Sub Form_Load()
  Me.Top = 120
  Me.Left = 120
  Me.txtIssueDate = Date
  Me.txtReturnDate = Date + 7

  Me.adoBooks.ConnectionString = strConString
  Me.adoBooks.CommandType = adCmdText
  Me.adoBooks.RecordSource = "SELECT * FROM Books WHERE _
    Availability=true"
  Me.adoBooks.Refresh
```

```
   Me.adoMemberInfo.ConnectionString = strConString
 Me.adoMemberInfo.CommandType = adCmdTable
 Me.adoMemberInfo.RecordSource = "Members"
 Me.adoMemberInfo.Refresh
End Sub
```

Code 6.36: Modified Code for the Form Load Event of the Form frmIssueBooks

16.　　　Add Code 6.37 for the **Click** event of the DataCombo control named
dbcCategory. It sets the filter of the Recordset based on the category being
selected.

```
Private Sub dbcCategory_Click(Area As Integer)
  On Error Resume Next
  Me.adoBooks.Recordset.Filter = "CategoryID=" & _
      Me.dbcCategory.BoundText
End Sub
```

Code 6.37: Code for the Click Event of the DataCombo Control dbcCategory

17.　　　Add Code 6.38 for the **Click** event of the command button cmdShowAll,
which clears the filter in the Recordset and retrieves all the records from the
Books table.

```
Private Sub cmdShowAll_Click()
  Me.dbcCategory.Text = ""
  Me.adoBooks.Recordset.Filter = ""
  Me.adoBooks.Recordset.Requery
End Sub
```

Code 6.38: Code for the Click Event of the Command Button cmdShowAll

18.　　　Set the following properties of the TextBox controls as given in Table 6.16 in
the form to bind them with the respective fields in the Members table.

Name of the Text Box	DataSourse Property	DataField Property
txtFirstName	adoMemberInfo	FirstName
txtLastName	adoMemberInfo	LastName
txtAddress	adoMemberInfo	Address

txtCity	adoMemberInfo	City
txtCountry	adoMemberInfo	Country
txtPhone	adoMemberInfo	Phone
txtFirstName	adoMemberInfo	FirstName

Table 6.16: Details of Properties for the TextBox Controls

19.   Add Code 6.39 for the **Click** event of the DataList control dblRegNo. The code sets the bookmark of the Recordset based on the selected registration number. This in turn updates the values in the above text boxes that are bound to the fields in the Members table.

```
Private Sub dblRegNo_Click()
  If Me.adoMemberInfo.Recordset.RecordCount > 0 Then
    Me.adoMemberInfo.Recordset.Bookmark =
Me.dblRegNo.SelectedItem
    End If
End Sub
```

Code 6.39: Code for the Click Event of the DataList Control dblRegNo

20.   Add Code 6.40 for the **Click** event of the command button cmdIssueBook. It first checks if the member already has a book issued in his name. If yes, the issue is cancelled. If not, it adds a new record in the BookIssue table storing the details of the issue and marks the issued book as not available in the Books table.

```
Private Sub cmdIssueBook_Click()
  If Me.adoBooks.Recordset.RecordCount > 0 And _
        Me.adoMemberInfo.Recordset.RecordCount > 0 Then
        Dim strSQL As String
    strSQL = "SELECT * FROM bookissue WHERE regno="
    strSQL = strSQL & Me.adoMemberInfo.Recordset("regno")
    strSQL = strSQL & " AND returnedon IS NULL"

    Dim rs As ADODB.Recordset
    Set rs = New ADODB.Recordset
    rs.Open strSQL, dbCon, adOpenForwardOnly, adLockReadOnly
```

```vb
    If Not (rs.EOF = True And rs.BOF = True) Then
        MsgBox rs(0) + " already issued to this member",
vbCritical
        If rs.State = adStateOpen Then rs.Close
        Exit Sub
    End If
    If rs.State = adStateOpen Then rs.Close
    Dim strMsg As String
    strMsg = "Are you sure to make the following issue:"
    strMsg = strMsg + vbNewLine + vbNewLine
    strMsg = strMsg + "Book Name: " +
Me.adoBooks.Recordset("BookName")
    strMsg = strMsg + vbNewLine + vbNewLine + "Member Name: "
    strMsg = strMsg + Me.adoMemberInfo.Recordset("FirstName")
    strMsg = strMsg + " " +
Me.adoMemberInfo.Recordset("LastName")

    If MsgBox(strMsg, vbQuestion + vbYesNo, "Confirm Issue") =
vbYes
    Then
        strSQL = "INSERT INTO BookIssue VALUES("
        strSQL = strSQL & "'" & Me.adoBooks.Recordset("isbn") &
"',"
        strSQL = strSQL & Me.adoMemberInfo.Recordset("regno") &
","
        strSQL = strSQL & "#" & CDate(Me.txtIssueDate) & "#,"
        strSQL = strSQL & "#" & CDate(Me.txtReturnDate) & "#,"
        strSQL = strSQL & "NULL)"
        dbCon.Execute strSQL
        Me.adoBooks.Recordset("availability") = False
        Me.adoBooks.Recordset.Update
        Me.adoBooks.Recordset.Requery
    End If
  End If
End Sub
```

Code 6.40: Code for the Click Event of the Command Button cmdIssueBook

21.   Add another form to the project. This form will be used to accept the information about the return of an issued book. Set the properties of the form as given in Table 6.17.

Property	Value
Name	frmBookReturn
Caption	Book Return
BorderStyle	Fixed Single
MDIChild	True

Table 6.17: Properties and Values for the Newly Added Form

22.   Add controls to the form frmBookReturn as shown in Figure 6.41.

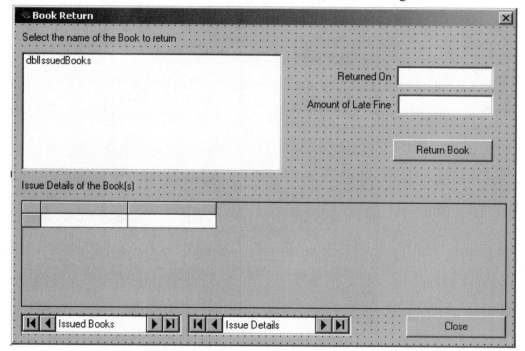

Figure 6.41: Form frmBookReturn with Added Controls

23.   Set the properties of the controls in the form as given in Table 6.18.

Control Type	Property	Value
ADODC control	Name	adoIssuedBooks
	Caption	Issued Books
	Visible	False
ADODC control	Name	adoIssueDetails
	Caption	Issue Details
	Visible	False
DataGrid control	Name	dbgIssueDetails
	DataSource	adoIssueDetails
	AllowAddNew	False
	AllowDelete	False
	AllowUpdate	False
DataList control	Name	dblIssuedBooks
	RowSource	adoIssuedBooks
	ListField	BookName
	BoundColumn	ISBN
Label control	Name	lblIssuedBook
	Caption	Select the name of the Book to return
Label control	Name	lblIssueDetails
	Caption	Issue Details of the Books
Label control	Name	lblReturnedOn
	Caption	Returned On
Label control	Name	lblLateFine
	Caption	Amount of Late Fine
TextBox control	Name	txtReturnedOn
	Locked	True
TextBox control	Name	txtLateFine

	Locked	True
Command Button control	Name	cmdReturn
	Caption	Return Book
Command Button control	Name	cmdClose
	Caption	Close

Table 6.18: Details of Properties for the Form frmBookReturn

24.   Add Code 6.41 for the **Form Load** event of the form frmBookReturn.

```
Private Sub Form_Load()
  Me.Top = 120
  Me.Left = 120
  Me.txtReturnedOn = Date

  Me.adoIssuedBooks.ConnectionString = strConString
  Me.adoIssuedBooks.CommandType = adCmdText
  Me.adoIssuedBooks.RecordSource = _
      "SELECT * FROM Books WHERE Availability=False"
  Me.adoIssuedBooks.Refresh

  Me.adoIssueDetails.ConnectionString = strConString
  Me.adoIssueDetails.CommandType = adCmdText
  Me.adoIssueDetails.RecordSource = _
      "SELECT * FROM BookIssue WHERE ReturnedOn IS NULL"
  Me.adoIssueDetails.Refresh
End Sub
```

Code 6.41: Code for the Form Load Event of the Form frmBookReturn

25.   Add Code 6.42 for the **Click** event of the command button cmdClose.

```
Private Sub cmdClose_Click()
  Unload Me
End Sub
```

Code 6.42: Code for the Click Event of the Command Button cmdClose

26.   Add Code 6.43 for the **Click** event of the DataList control dblIssuedBooks. It filters the Recordset of the ADODC control adoIssuedDetails to retrieve only the records related to the selected book name.

```
Private Sub dblIssuedBooks_Click()
  If Me.adoIssuedBooks.Recordset.RecordCount > 0 Then
    Me.adoIssuedBooks.Recordset.Bookmark = _
        Me.dblIssuedBooks.SelectedItem
    Me.adoIssueDetails.Recordset.Filter = "ISBN='" + _
        Me.adoIssuedBooks.Recordset("ISBN") + "'"
  End If
End Sub
```

Code 6.43: Code for the Click Event of the DataList Control dblIssuedBooks

27.   Add Code 6.44 for the **Click** event of the DataGrid control dbgIssueDetails. The code calculates the number of extra days, if any, in returning the book and fills the text box with late fees at the rate of $5 per day for each extra day.

```
Private Sub dbgIssueDetails_Click()
  If Me.adoIssueDetails.Recordset.RecordCount > 0 Then
    Dim extraDays As Long
    extraDays = CDate(Me.txtReturnedOn) - _
        CDate(Me.adoIssueDetails.Recordset("ReturnDate"))

    Me.txtLateFine = FormatCurrency(extraDays * 5)
  End If
End Sub
```

Code 6.44: Code for the Click Event of the DataList Control dbgIssueDetails

28.   Add Code 6.45 for the **Click** event of the command button cmdReturn. The code updates the BookIssue table with the actual date of return for the selected book. It also updates the table Books setting the availability field for the returned books as True.

```
Private Sub cmdReturn_Click()
  If Me.adoIssueDetails.Recordset.RecordCount > 0 Then
    Dim strMsg As String
    strMsg = "Are you sure to perform the following return:"
```

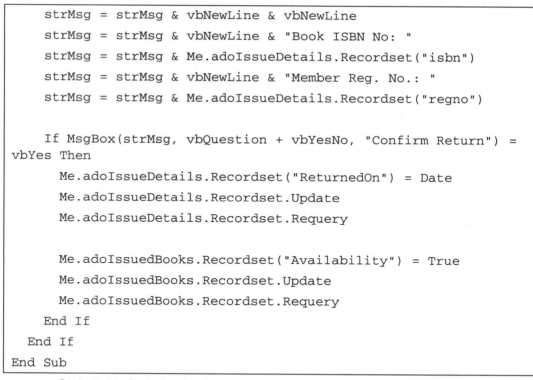

```
        strMsg = strMsg & vbNewLine & vbNewLine
        strMsg = strMsg & vbNewLine & "Book ISBN No: "
        strMsg = strMsg & Me.adoIssueDetails.Recordset("isbn")
        strMsg = strMsg & vbNewLine & "Member Reg. No.: "
        strMsg = strMsg & Me.adoIssueDetails.Recordset("regno")

        If MsgBox(strMsg, vbQuestion + vbYesNo, "Confirm Return") =
vbYes Then
            Me.adoIssueDetails.Recordset("ReturnedOn") = Date
            Me.adoIssueDetails.Recordset.Update
            Me.adoIssueDetails.Recordset.Requery

            Me.adoIssuedBooks.Recordset("Availability") = True
            Me.adoIssuedBooks.Recordset.Update
            Me.adoIssuedBooks.Recordset.Requery
        End If
    End If
End Sub
```

Code 6.45: Code for the Click Event of the Command Button cmdReturn

29.   Save the project.

Summary

- ActiveX controls make database programming easy and simple. Most of the properties can be set during design time so much less code is required.

- The most commonly used ActiveX controls in databases are:
  - DataList
  - DataCombo
  - DataGrid
  - Microsoft Hierarchical FlexGrid

- Data-bound ActiveX controls cannot function without a data source.

- When a data source is provided to a data-bound control at design time, it is automatically populated with data.

- DataList and DataCombo controls can work with two different data sources, functioning as lookup tables.

- The DataList and DataCombo controls are similar to the DBList and DBCombo controls, but they display data only from an OLEDB data source.

- The DataCombo control has an optional text box that can be used to directly enter data to the DataField.

- The five important data properties of DataList and DataCombo are:
  - BoundColumn
  - DataField
  - DataSource
  - ListField
  - RowSource

- The DataGrid control can automatically display data from the tables of a database and directly edit data records.

- DataGrid can be used with the DataList and DataCombo controls to display selective data from databases. The DataList or DataCombo can be used to display the selection criteria.

- A DataGrid's data source can be changed at run time to display different results.

- Hierarchical FlexGrid control can display hierarchical relations between various tables in a database. It can display text as well as images in the cells. Though the

Hierarchical FlexGrid is read-only, it can be programmed to receive data by coding the EnterCell and LeaveCell events.

■ The Data Environment Designer can store Command and Connection objects, which can be accessed by all the forms in a project. This removes the repetition of ADODC controls in every form which require a data source. Moreover the DataEnvironment generates SHAPE commands, which can display hierarchical recordsets.

References

- http://www.library.itt-tech.edu/periodicals.asp > FindArticles.com (Accessed on Aug. 12, 2004)
- http://www.library.itt-tech.edu/periodicals.asp > MSDN Magazine (Accessed on Aug. 12, 2004)

Homework Exercises

1. Explain the difference between a data control and a data-bound control.

2. How can you add the various ActiveX controls discussed in the chapter to your toolbox?

3. Which controls can be data-bound?

4. How would you use a DataList control or a DataCombo control to link to a table to display all the possible selections for a field taken from another table?

5. List and define the options for the Command Type property available for an ADO data control and for a Data Environment Command object.

6. What properties of the recordset are used so that a user can navigate through its data?

7. How is SQL used in a Data Environment?

8. What is data shaping?

9. What is a hierarchical recordset? When would it be useful to create one?

Lab Exercises

Exercise 1

Objective

■ Create a form with DataList and ADODC controls used to retrieve records from a database.

Problem Statement

Create a form with a DataList control displaying the names of patients in the Patient table residing in the patient database. The DataList control should obtain data from an ADODC control. On clicking an entry in the DataList, the textboxes should display all the correct entries corresponding to the patient. The textbox for the PatientID should not be editable.

■ Create a database in MS Access named patients.mdb.

■ Create two tables, Doctor and Patient.

■ Add two fields to the Doctor table—docID (Number) and docName (Text).

■ Add four fields to the Patient table—PatientID (Number), docID (Number), Name (Text), and visitDate (Date/Time).

■ Fill the databases with the sample data provided.

Lab Setup

Computer Requirements:

■ Microsoft Windows Operating System

■ Pentium III or higher processors

■ 128-MB RAM

■ 3-GB of hard disk space

■ CD-ROM drives

■ Floppy disk drives

■ Visual Basic 6.0

■ Microsoft Access

Procedure

1. Open a new project and name it prjPatients.
2. Rename the form frmPatients.
3. Click on **Project → Components** and add the Microsoft ADO Data Control and Microsoft DataList Controls.
4. Add an ADODC control and set the following properties:

Property	Value
Name	adoPatients
Caption	Patients
CommandType	adCmdTable
ConnectionString	Provider=Microsoft.Jet.OLEDB.4.0;Data Source=C:\patients.mdb;Persist Security Info=False
RecordSource	Patient

5. Add a DataList control and set the following properties:

Property	Value
Name	dblPatients
BoundColumn	Name
ListField	Name
RowSource	adoPatients

6. Add four textboxes and set the following properties:

Property	Value
Name	txtName
Text	<Leave Blank>
DataSource	adoPatients
DataField	Name

Property	Value
Name	txtDate
Text	<Leave Blank>
DataSource	adoPatients
DataField	VisitDate

Property	Value
Name	txtID
Text	<Leave Blank>
DataSource	adoPatients
DataField	PatientID
Enabled	False

Property	Value
Name	txtDoc
Text	<Leave Blank>
DataSource	adoPatients
DataField	DocID

7.   Label the textboxes with the fieldnames they display.

8.　　　The form should look like the following figure.

9.　　　Open the form's code window and add the code given below.

```
Private Sub dblPatients_Click()
    adoPatients.Recordset.Bookmark = dblPatients.SelectedItem
End Sub
```

10. Run the application. Sample output is shown in the following figure.

Conclusion/Observation

1. The form appears with all the names of the patients in the DataList control.

2. The text boxes are initially blank. They are filled with the details of each patient selected in the DataList.

3. The records in the Patient table can also be navigated using the navigation buttons of the ADODC control

Lab Activity Checklist

S. No.	Tasks	Completed	
		Yes	No
1.	ADODC control used		
2.	DataList control used		
3.	Appropriate code provided to perform the task		

Exercise 2

Objective

■ Create a form using two ADODC controls in a form for two tables, to retrieve the records of one table and related data from another table.

Problem Statement

Create a form with a DataList control displaying the names of patients in the Patients table and a DataCombo control displaying the name of the doctor treating the patient. On clicking the DataList, the DataCombo should display corresponding data.

The DataCombo control should display data from an ADODC control connected to the Doctor table and modify data from another ADODC control connected to the Patients table. Create three data-bound textboxes displaying the Name, Date of Visit, and Patient ID of the selected record. On clicking an entry in the DataList, the textboxes should display all the correct entries corresponding to the patient. The DataCombo should display the name of the doctor treating the patient whose docID matches the docID in the Doctor table.

Lab Setup

Computer Requirements:

■ Microsoft Windows Operating System

■ Pentium III or higher processors

■ 128-MB RAM

■ 3-GB of hard disk space

■ CD-ROM drives

■ Floppy disk drives

■ Visual Basic 6.0

■ Microsoft Access

Procedure

1. Open a new project and name it prjPatients2.

2. Rename the form frmPatients2.

3. Click on **Project → Components** and add the Microsoft ADO Data Control and Microsoft DataList Controls.

4. Add an ADODC control and set the following properties:

Property	Value
Name	adoPatients
Caption	Patients
CommandType	adCmdTable
ConnectionString	Provider=Microsoft.Jet.OLEDB.4.0;Data Source=C:\patients.mdb;Persist Security Info=False
RecordSource	Patient

5. Add another ADODC control and set the following properties:

Property	Value
Name	adoDoctor
Caption	Doctor
CommandType	adCmdTable
ConnectionString	Provider=Microsoft.Jet.OLEDB.4.0;Data Source=C:\patients.mdb;Persist Security Info=False
RecordSource	Doctor

6. Add a DataList control and set the following properties:

Property	Value
Name	dblPatients
BoundColumn	Name
ListField	Name
RowSource	adoPatients

7.   Add a DataCombo control and set the following properties:

Property	Value
Name	dbcPatients
BoundColumn	DocID
ListField	docName
RowSource	adoDoctor
DataField	DocID
DataSource	adoPatients
Style	dbcDropDownCombo

8.   Add three textboxes and set the following properties:

Property	Value
Name	txtName
Text	<Leave Blank>
DataSource	adoPatients
DataField	Name

Property	Value
Name	txtDate
Text	<Leave Blank>
DataSource	adoPatients
DataField	VisitDate

Property	Value
Name	txtID
Text	<Leave Blank>
DataSource	adoPatients
DataField	PatientID
Enabled	False

9. Label the textboxes with the fieldnames they display.

10. The form should look like the following figure.

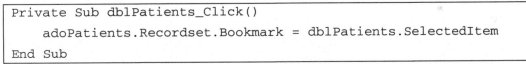

11. Open the form's code window and add the code given below:

```
Private Sub dblPatients_Click()
    adoPatients.Recordset.Bookmark = dblPatients.SelectedItem
End Sub
```

12. Run the application. The sample output is shown in the following figure.

Conclusion/Observation

1. The form is displayed with the names of the patients in the DataList control.
2. The three text boxes display the details of the patients.
3. When the user clicks on the name of a patient in the DataList, the DataCombo displays the name of the doctor associated with the selected patient.

Lab Activity Checklist

S. No.	Tasks	Completed	
		Yes	**No**
1.	Two ADODC controls added for two different tables		
2.	DataList and DataCombo controls used		
3.	The DataCombo bound to the two ADODC controls		
4.	Appropriate code is provided to perform the task		

Exercise 3

Objective

- Use a DataGrid control to display data stored in a database and provide the ability to sort the data during run time.

Problem Statement

Create a form with a DataGrid control displaying data from the patient database. The data properties of the DataGrid should be set during run time. The ADODC control from which the DataGrid gets the records should be provided a connection string and an SQL query which returns the PatientID, Name, and visitDate fields from the Patient table in the database.

Add buttons to sort the three fields in the DataGrid. The connection properties of the ADODC should be set during run time. The user should be able to add and delete records directly from the DataGrid.

Lab Setup

Computer Requirements:

- Microsoft Windows Operating System
- Pentium III or higher processors
- 128-MB RAM
- 3-GB of hard disk space
- CD-ROM drives
- Floppy disk drives
- Visual Basic 6.0
- Microsoft Access

Procedure

1. Open a new project and name it prjPatients3.
2. Rename the form frmPatients3.
3. Click on **Project → Components** and add the Microsoft ADO Data Control and Microsoft DataGrid Control.

4.   Add an ADODC control and set the following properties:

Property	Value
Name	adoPatients
Caption	Patients

5.   Add a DataGrid control and set the following properties:

Property	Value
Name	dgdPatients
Caption	Patients Information

6.   Add three command buttons and name them cmdID, cmdSortName, and cmdSortDate.

7.   Add the following code in the code window:

Code for **Click** events of the buttons:

```
Private Sub cmdID_Click()
    adoPatients.Recordset.Sort = "patientID"
End Sub


Private Sub cmdSortDate_Click()
    adoPatients.Recordset.Sort = "visitDate"
End Sub


Private Sub cmdSortName_Click()
    adoPatients.Recordset.Sort = "Name"
End Sub
```

8.   Code for the **Form Load** event:

```
Option Explicit
Private Sub Form_Load()

Dim CnnStr As String
Dim QueryStr As String


QueryStr = "SELECT PatientID, Name, visitDate FROM Patient"


CnnStr = "Provider=microsoft.jet.OLEDB.4.0; Data Source=" & _
         App.Path & "\patients.mdb;" & _
         "Persist Security Info=False"

With adoPatients
   .ConnectionString = CnnStr
    .CommandType = adCmdText
   .RecordSource = QueryStr
End With
```

```
        Set dgdPatients.DataSource = adoPatients

        dgdPatients.AllowAddNew = True

        dgdPatients.AllowUpdate = True


End Sub
```

9.   Run the Application. The following figure shows the run time view:

Conclusion/Observation

1.   The form displays all the records in the table through the DataGrid.

2.   The user can sort the records using the command buttons provided in the form.

3.   The given code assumes the database is stored in the same location as that of the application. If it is not the same, the connection string should be specified with the proper location of the database.

Lab Activity Checklist

S. No.	Tasks	Completed	
		Yes	No
1.	ADODC control used to connect to a table in the database		
2.	DataGrid control is used to display the records		
3.	Appropriate code provided for each of the command buttons performing the sort operations		
4.	Sorting is performed based on the button being clicked. The DataGrid reflects the effect of the sort		

Exercise 4

Objective

■ Use a Hierarchical FlexGrid control with a DataEnvironment data source to display the master detail relationship between two tables in a database.

Problem Statement

Create a form with a Hierarchical FlexGrid control which displays a hierarchical relation between the two tables in the patient database. The data source of the FlexGrid should be a DataEnvironment.

Create a connection object that connects to the patient database.

Create a command object called comDoctor, which displays the docID and docName fields of the doctor table.

Create a child command of the comDoctor command, which displays the Patient name, docID, and visitDate fields in the patient table.

The commands should accept SQL queries for obtaining the recordsets. Set the proper relationship between the parent and child commands.

Lab Setup

Computer Requirements:

■ Microsoft Windows Operating System

■ Pentium III or higher processors

■ 128-MB RAM

■ 3-GB of hard disk space

■ CD-ROM drives

■ Floppy disk drives

■ Visual Basic 6.0

■ Microsoft Access

Procedure

1. Open a new project and name it prjPatients4.

2. Rename the form frmPatients4.

3. Click on **Project → Components** and add the Microsoft Hierarchical FlexGrid control.

4. Click on **Project → Add Data Environment**. This adds a new DataEnvironment to the project.

5. Set the DataEnvironment's name to dePatients.

6. Add a connection object called conPatient.

7. Right-click the **Connection** and select **Properties**. Set the provider to Microsoft Jet 4.0 OLEDB provider. On the Connections tab, select the database "patients.mdb". Enter Admin as the username and blank as the password.

8. Right-click the **DataEnvironment** icon and select **Add Command**.

9. Rename the command to comDoctor. Right-click the command icon and select **Properties**.

10. On the **General** tab, select **Doctor** as the command name, conPatient as connection, and enter the SQL query.

```
SELECT docID, docName FROM Doctor
```

11. Right-click the **comDoctor** command and select **Add Child** Command.

12. Rename the new child command object comPatient.

13. Right-click the **comPatient** command and select **Properties**.

14. In the **General** tab, enter the following SQL statement:

```
SELECT Name AS PatientName, docID, visitDate FROM Patient
```

15. In the **Relation** tab, under Relation Definition, select docID from both the combo boxes, and click on the **Add** button. Your DataEnvironment window should look the following figure:

16. Add a Hierarchical FlexGrid control to the project.

17. Set the following properties of the Hierarchical FlexGrid:

Property	Value
Name	flexPatient
AllowUserResizing	flexResizeColumns
DataSource	dePatients
DataMember	comDoctor

18. Right-click the FlexGrid, select **Properties**, go to the Bands tab. In the Band 1 band, unset the display of the docID field. This does not display the docID field again in the FlexGrid.

19. Run the application. The output should be similar to the following figure.

Patients Info

	docID	docName	PatientName	visitDate
⊟	1	Dr. S. Brey	Linda Jackson	1/25/2003
			Jim Wilson	3/21/2003
⊟	2	Dr. Andrew White	Claire Thomson	3/15/2003
			George White	3/19/2003
			Andrew Chang	2/1/2003
			Michael Hugh	4/15/2003
⊞	5	Dr. D. Franks		
⊞	6	Dr. Sam Roberts		
⊟	3	Dr. A. Hussain	Adrian Perrig	3/6/2003
			Dorothy Smith	2/23/2003
			Kyle Bush	1/12/2003
⊟	4	Dr. Catherine Wills	Josh Broch	3/22/2003
			Amanda Callaghan	1/12/2003
			Mario Gerla	3/2/2003

Conclusion/Observation

1. Hierarchical FlexGrid control provides the ability to view the records. In order to edit the records using Hierarchical FlexGrid, additional code should be written.

Lab Activity Checklist

S. No.	Tasks	Completed	
		Yes	No
1.	DataEnvironment object used		
2.	Hierarchical FlexGrid control used		
3.	Two command objects created in the DataEnvironment using parent-child relationship between them		

Project

1.   Open the VB project named EmpInfo.

2.   Open the form frmAddEmp created in Chapter 3 "Working with Forms and Controls" and add two ADODC controls named adoDept and adoGrades. These ADODC controls should not be visible during run time. Add two DataCombo controls named dbcDept and dbcGrade. The dbcGrade control should display the Department names in the list through the adoDept control and bound to the DeptNo column. The dbcGrade control should display the Grades in the list through the adoGrades control and bound to the Grade column. In the Form Load event initialize the adoDept and the adoGrades control with the connection string stored in the public variable declared in the module and connect to the tables Departments and Grades, respectively. Modify the IsValidData function in the form to include the validation for the text in the dbcDept and dbcGrade controls. Write the code for the click event of the Add button to insert a record in the Employees table with the values specified in the form. The record should be added only if the IsValidData function returns a True value. Use the insert SQL statement through the dbCon object to insert the new record. The form should resemble the following figure in the design view:

3.   Open the form frmEditEmp created in Chapter 3 "Working with Forms and Controls" and add two ADODC controls named adoDept and adoGrades. These ADODC controls should not be visible during run time. Add two DataCombo controls named dbcDept and dbcGrade. The dbcGrade control should display the department names in the list using the adoDept control as the RowSource and should be bound to the column DeptNo. The dbcGrade control should display the Grades in the list using the adoGrades control as the row source and should be bound to the column Grade. Add a DataGrid control named dbgEmployee and align the control at the top of the form. The form should resemble the following figure in the design view:

4.   Add a Data Environment to the project with the name DataEnvironment1. Create a connection object named Connection1. Set the properties of the connection object to connection the database file EmpInfo.mdb. Create two command objects named Employee and EditEmployee in the data environment. The two command objects should be created on the table named Employees. The command object named Employee should be created as

read-only and the command object EditEmployee should have an optimistic lock type.

5. Save the project.

Classes and Collections

7

This chapter covers the basic concepts of classes and collections in Microsoft Visual Basic. It presents the benefits of object-oriented programming and demonstrates how class modules provide the necessary features to implement object-oriented programming. It explains the property procedures, methods, and events of classes. Further, it explains the Public, Private, and Friend access specifiers. Finally, it explains how to create classes and collections using the Class Builder Wizard.

At the end of this chapter, you will be able to:

- Explain the concept of classes.
- Create user-defined data types.
- Explain objects.
- Explain the process of encapsulation.
- Explain the use of properties and methods in classes.
- Explain the concepts of access scope of a class.
- Explain the steps to use the Class Wizard in Visual Basic.
- Explain the concept of collections.

7.1 Introduction to Object-Oriented Programming

7.2 Modules and Class Modules

7.3 Collections

7.1 Introduction to Object-Oriented Programming

A procedural programming language, like Visual Basic, is a powerful software development tool but has some limitations. The main problem with procedural languages is that they do not model real world problems. Procedural languages emphasize logic and try to fit the problem into their domain. Programs written in procedural languages put paramount importance on the code and its flow, so the data on which the code operates is considered secondary.

In the real world, however, data is most important. Everything is an object, and there is a purpose for its existence and behavior. This thought gave rise to a new paradigm called object-oriented programming.

Object-oriented programming organizes the program around "objects" rather than "actions" and data rather than logic. Object-oriented programming takes the view that what we really care about are the objects we want to manipulate rather than the logic required to manipulate them.

The programmer with an object-oriented approach concentrates more on identifying the potential objects and defining their behavior and interaction rather than simply dividing the problem into functions operating upon the data.

7.1.1 Classes

 Explain the concept of classes.

Classes contain data and functions and introduce user-defined data types into a program. User-defined data types are composed of a set of basic data types. They encapsulate the characteristics of each of the data type included in them to define a new data type. This new data type, called a class, is used in the same way as other basic data types. The instances of a class are called its objects.

User-defined data types are developed using the **class** or **Type** keywords. The **class** keyword is used to create a user-defined data type that allows us to combine data and functions that operate upon data in one entity. Generally, the data is hidden from the user and functions provide the interface to use that data.

For simplicity, data types defined with these keywords are called class declarations. They may be considered as distinct concepts in different languages.

All the controls in the Visual Basic toolbox are actually classes, from which the objects used in the forms are derived.

Customizing Form Classes

All the controls in Visual Basic are modeled as classes. When you place any control on a form, Visual Basic creates a new object based on the characteristics of that class. The technical term for this process is *instantiation*.

Each object has the same underlying properties related to the class. At the same time, each control can be customized by giving its properties different values.

For example, each TextBox control that you place on a form has identical properties such as text, height, and width. However, each property can be given a different value for a different text box. For instance, one text box may have its **text** property set to "Hello" and another may have its **text** property set to "World". This is possible because all text boxes are instances or objects of the same class type. The basic functionality of each text box object is the same, as determined by the text box class.

7.1.2 Objects

Explain the concept of objects.

When you create applications in Visual Basic using controls, you actually program objects. Programmers use objects by manipulating their properties, methods, and events. Each object is an interface that lies between the user and the object's code. This interface ensures that the object's code and its data are safe from any misuse from the user's end. For example, when you place a text box in your form, you set its properties to display single line text, and set its font as Times New Roman. You include code for responding to user events such as the **KeyDown** event, and include other methods to operate on the text box. The interface of this control would include its properties, methods, and events. You can bring the functionality of this control to your application, without knowing anything about the code that implements the control.

Applications communicate with objects through the properties and methods that they expose and the events raised by user input or other actions. Restricting access to the code of a control (or any other object) is not just a strict rule. It serves as a practical purpose. It prohibits developers from breaking the control by "enhancing" it. Once users learn what they can do with a TextBox control, they can handle any text box in any kind of application. This consistency in the user interface is a fundamental characteristic of Microsoft Windows, and objects are designed to enforce this consistency.

Objects interact with each other. As a result, when placed together in a form, they cooperate with each other, and ensure smooth running of the application.

Built-in Objects

Two useful built-in objects are the Screen and the Printer objects, which represent the monitor and the default printer in use. You can use these objects to find out the properties of the monitor (such as its resolution or the fonts that it can display) and the printer. The Screen object has a **Fonts** property, which returns the names of the fonts that can be displayed on the screen.

The Printer object also has a **Fonts** property. The fonts included for the printer may not be the same as the ones included for the Screen object.

The Printer object is similar to the Screen object and supports many of the same properties and methods. The Screen and Printer objects demonstrate encapsulation. The implementation details are hidden from the developers, who are free to focus on their application and not on the specifics of the various display adapters or printer models.

The DateTime object is another built-in object that is very useful for time and date-related information. You can display time and date in different formats using the properties and methods of this object.

Another useful object is the Math object that includes various built in mathematical functions. Functions such as **Rnd** (used for generating random numbers) are used vastly in game software. Other functions such as **Round, Sin, Tan and Log** are of prime importance in calculations. Visual Basic includes several other objects that provide efficient and quick functionality.

7.1.3 Encapsulation

 Explain some features of Object-Oriented programming.

Hiding the inner workings of an object is called *encapsulation*. For instance, the TextBox object encapsulates complicated operations, such as the breaking of multiple lines and the insertion of new characters. These are low level details that you do not have to be concerned with. Instead, you can concentrate on your application, its user interface, and its operation. In this chapter, we discuss Visual Basic objects and techniques for working with these objects. Objects encapsulate complicated operations into a black box, which you can access through its user interface.

Encapsulation is the most important feature of Object-Oriented programming. Encapsulation is the ability to wrap code and data in a single unit that can be accessed by a well-defined interface. Developers can carry the functionality of an object to their applications and manipulate it through this interface, but they cannot enhance or break the object, because they cannot alter the code or make it perform unwanted operations.

Encapsulation is often said to hide unnecessary details from the user. For example, data in a Microsoft Access database are stored in a file, with the extension .mdb. This file, however, has a complicated structure, and you never access it directly. Instead, you specify the records you are interested in and use ADO controls to retrieve them as discussed in Chapters 5 and 6. Information is presented in the form of rows and columns, which are easy to understand, visualize, and work with. The database file contains data, index files, pointers, and all kinds of complex internal data that you do not want to deal with. The ADO interface extracts and/or saves the desired information to the database. The ADO thus provides only the functional features and hides the complex details of implementation from the user.

 The operating system itself is another object, which encapsulates an incredible amount of functionality. You can adjust certain characteristics of the operating system with the applications provided in the Control Panel or even through the Registry.

1. What do the Screen and Printer objects demonstrate?
2. What are the main characteristics of classes?
3. What is the concept used in encapsulation?
4. What are the differences between procedural and object-oriented languages?
5. How are objects represented in Visual Basic?

7.2 Modules and Class Modules

In Visual Basic, modules are structures that store variables and code that other components of the application can access. They contain all the global variables and procedures in an application.

Suppose you have a function, **DisplayDate()**, that displays the current date in a particular format. You may want to call this function from many forms to display the date. One way is to define it in each form and call it repeatedly. However, this is not a clean method of programming. A better way would be to define it in a place from where it is accessible to all the forms and then call it when desired.

As an example, consider a variable **UserName**. You may want this variable in many forms to know the user's name. Avoid declaring it in all the forms. Instead, declare it in a place where it is accessible to all the other forms.

Here is where modules are beneficial. The procedures or functions being defined and the variables declared in a module are accessible to all other components of the application. There is no need of defining (and declaring) the code (and variables) in all the forms separately.

Figure 7.1 depicts this example. Form A, Form B, and Form C all need to display the current date and user name. For this they are defining the function DisplayDate() and variable **UserName** separately in their respective code. This wastes memory space and is inefficient.

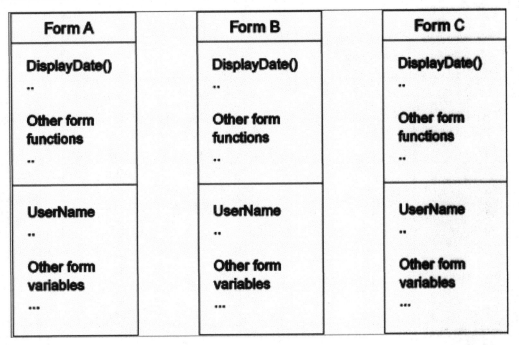

Figure 7.1: Form A, B, and C Each Using Identical Functions for Achieving the Same Functionality

Modules are used to solve this problem. A module provides an interface through which Visual Basic forms or other modules can exchange information.

Figure 7.2 shows the use of modules in the example of Figure 7.1.

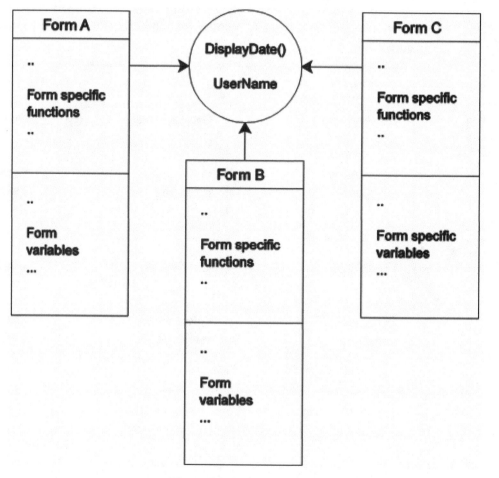

Figure 7.2: Using Modules

In Visual Basic, module files have an extension .bas. Code 7.1 uses a module containing functions to be used for two forms. The module contains a function to display the current date and time on the two forms.

To create the application:

1.   Open a Standard Exe project named DT. Add two forms named FormA and FormB to the project. Add an MDI Form to the project and set the MDIChild properties of FormA and FormB to true.

2.   Add a Module named DispDate to the project.

3. Add a Label control to each of the forms. Set the caption of the Label control (named lblCap) for FormA to "Date and Time Zone A" and "Date and Time Zone B" for the Label control (namedlblCap) in FormB.

4. Add six command buttons to FormA named cmdsd, cmdsdt, cmdsm, cmdsy, cmdshow, and cmdtime. Add another Label named lblDate.

5. Add a Timer control to FormA and FormB both. Figure 7.3 shows the design view of FormA.

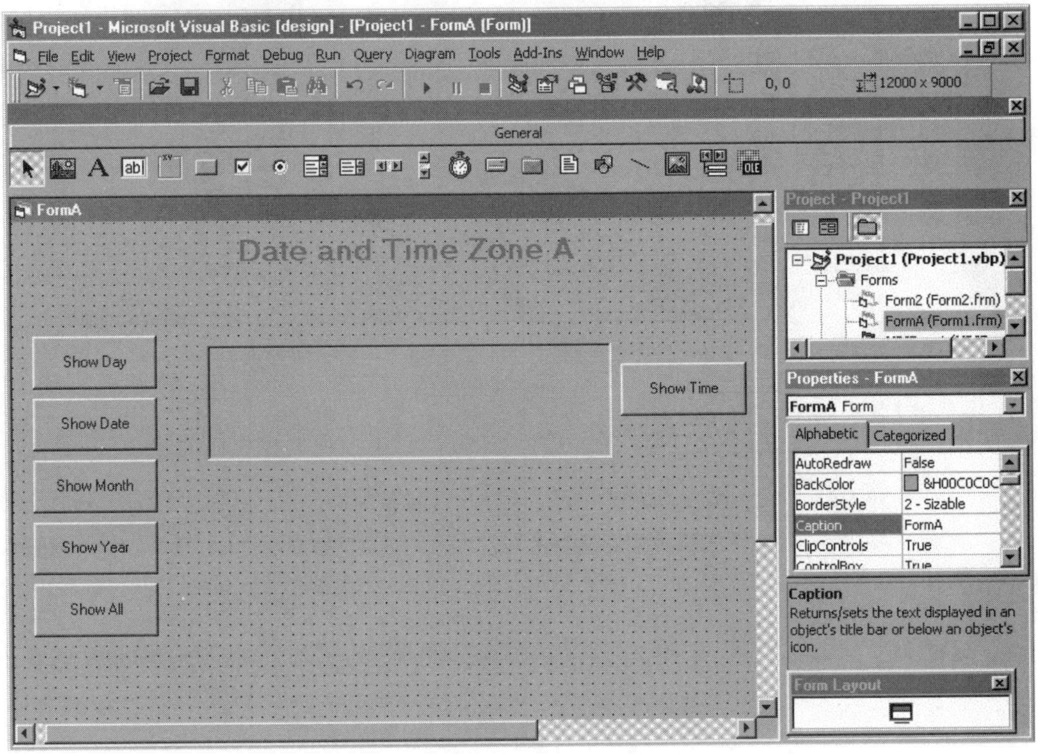

Figure 7.3: Design View of FormA

6.   Add four labels to FormB named lbldm, lbldt, lbldy, and lbltd. Figure 7.4 shows FormB in design view.

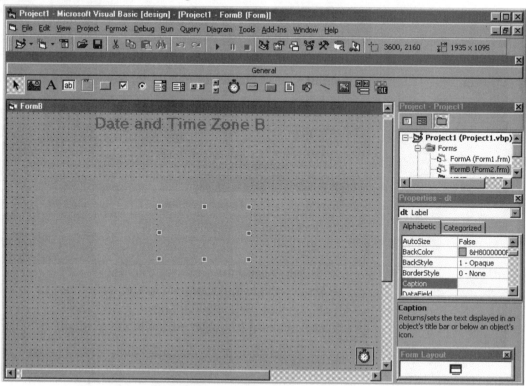

Figure 7.4: Design View of FormB

7.   Add a Menu to the MDI form as shown in Figure 7.5.

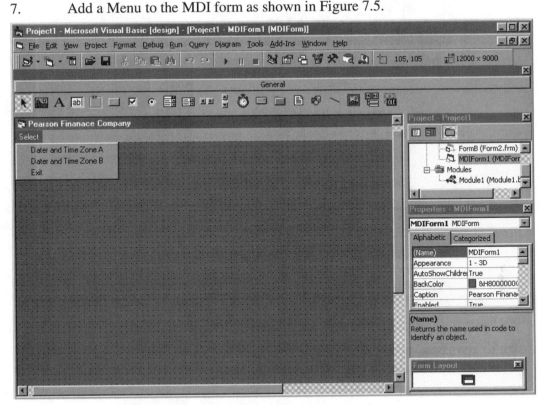

Figure 7.5: Design View of the MDIForm

8.   Add Code 7.1 to the Module named DispDate. This code contains five global variables that are used to store the formatted time, day, date, month, and year. The sub DisplayDate() uses the Now property of the DateTime object to retrieve the current date and time.

```
Global strm
     Global strdt
     Global stry
     Global timestr
     Global strd


Public Sub DisplayDate()
     Dim Today As Variant
     Today = Now
```

```
        strd = Format(Today,  "dddd")
        strdt = Format(Today,  "d")
        strm = Format(Today,  "mmmm")
        stry = Format(Today,  "yyyy")
        timestr = Format(Today,  "h:mm:ss")
End Sub
```

Code 7.1: DisplayDate() Function

9.   Add Code 7.2 to the Click events of the menu options on the MDIForm. When the "Data and Time Zone A" option is clicked FormA is shown and FormB is unloaded. When the "Data and Time Zone B" option is clicked FormB is shown and FormA is unloaded. The exit option causes the application to terminate.

```
Private Sub dta_Click()
    Unload FormB
    FormA.show
End Sub


Private Sub dtb_Click()
    Unload FormA
    FormB.show
End Sub


Private Sub ex_Click()
   End
End Sub
```

Code 7.2: Click Events of the Menu Options in the MDIForm

10.   Add Code 7.3 to the Click events of the command buttons on FormA, Load Event of FormA, and the Timer Event of Timer control. The Load Event calls the DisplayDate() function. Each of the click events displays the associated information in the lblDate label. The timer Event is used to show continually changing system time in the label.

```
Private Sub Form_Load()
   DisplayDate
```

```
End Sub
Private Sub cmdsd_Click() 'to display day
    Timer1.Enabled = False
    lblDate.Visible = True
    lblDate.Caption = "The day is " + strd
End Sub


Private Sub cmdsdt_Click() 'to display date
    Timer1.Enabled = False
    lblDate.Visible = True
    lblDate.Caption = "The date is " + strdt
End Sub


Private Sub cmdshow_Click() 'to display the complete date
    Timer1.Enabled = False
    lblDate.Caption = strd + " " + strdt + "  " + strm + "  " _
    + stry
End Sub


Private Sub cmdsm_Click() 'to display the month
    Timer1.Enabled = False
    lblDate.Visible = True
    lblDate.Caption = "The month is " + strm
End Sub


Private Sub cmdsy_Click() 'to display the year
    Timer1.Enabled = False
    lblDate.Visible = True
    lblDate.Caption = "The year is " + stry
End Sub


Private Sub cmdtime_Click() 'to display the time
    Timer1.Enabled = True
    lblDate.Visible = True
    lblDate.Caption = timestr
```

```
End Sub

Private Sub Timer1_Timer()
   ht = Int(Timer / 3600)
   mt = Int((Timer / 3600 - ht) * 60)
   st = Int((((Timer / 3600 - ht) * 60) - mt) * 60)
   lblDate = ht & " : " & mt & " : " & st
End Sub
```

Code 7.3: Click Events of the Command Buttons on FormA and Load Event of FormA

11.   The run time view of FormA is shown in Figure 7.6.

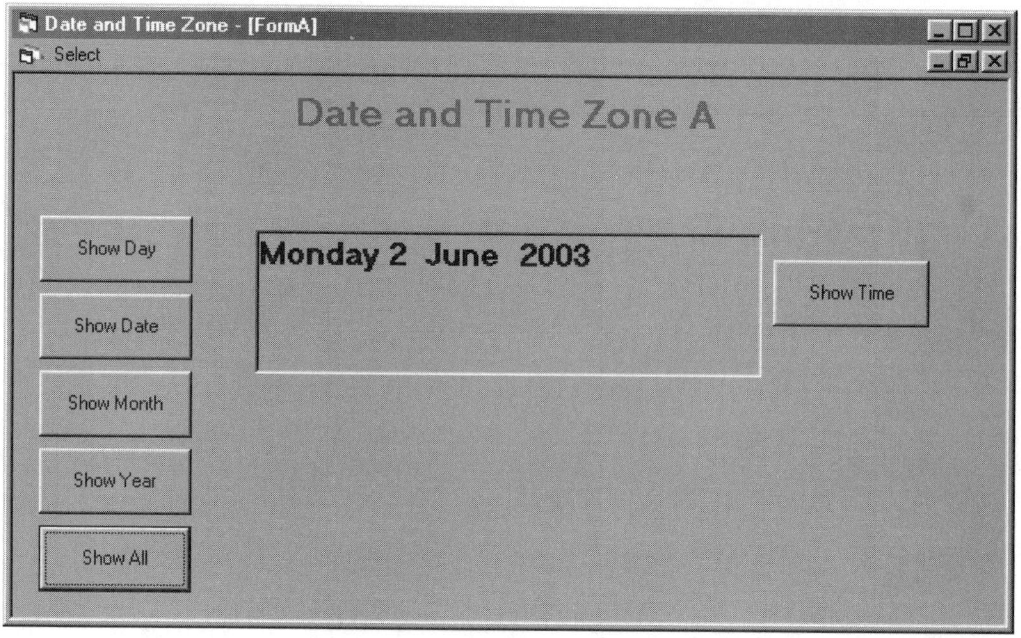

Figure 7.6: Run Time View of FormA

12.   Add Code 7.4 to the Load event of FormB. This form uses the same
        DisplayDate() function of the module DispDate as used by FormA and
        displays the information in a different format.

```
Private Sub Form_Load()
   DisplayDate
```

```
   lbltd.Caption = strd + "              " + timestr
   lbldt.Caption = strdt
   lbldm.Caption = strm
   lbldy.Caption = stry
End Sub


Private Sub Timer1_Timer()
   ht = Int(Timer / 3600)
   mt = Int((Timer / 3600 - ht) * 60)
   st = Int((((Timer / 3600 - ht) * 60) - mt) * 60)
    t = ht & " : " & mt & " : " & st
    lbltd.Caption = strd + "                " + t
End Sub
```

Code 7.4: Load Event of FormA and Timer Event

13.   The run time view of FormB is shown in Figure 7.7.

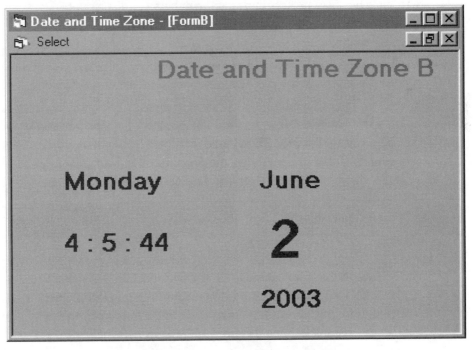

Figure 7.7: Run Time View of FormB

The preceding example demonstrates how to define the common functions or procedures in a module that can be shared among other forms or modules.

7.2.1 Modules and Class Modules

 Compare modules and class modules in Visual Basic.

Class modules serve more or less the same purpose as modules. They combine the generic concept of classes and the functionality of modules, encapsulating them in one unit. The data and procedures defined in class modules are not accessible to other applications unless you want them to be. Once created, they act as a single unit, exposing only the functionality through the functions and procedures defined in them. These procedures and functions encapsulate the implementation details. Once written, you can distribute them among as many projects as you want. You can use the procedures provided by the class modules, without worrying about how they are written. They also protect their data members from accidental or intentional modifications by encapsulating them completely.

In most trivial cases where you want to use a few global variables and procedures, modules are a good choice. However, if you need the same global variables and procedures across many projects, you should create class modules.

When you refer to a module's variables and procedures, you do not need to prefix them by the module name. However, not using a module name can cause confusion if you use the same variable or procedure name in a form from where you call module variables or procedures. Unlike the modules, the procedures and functions defined in the class modules cannot be used directly. Before accessing the procedures and the functions in a certain class module, the class should be instantiated. A class is said to be instantiated when we create an object from the class. The object is the physical representation of the class. The procedures and functions are accessed through the object of the class. This is done by prefixing the name of the procedure or the function with the name of the object.

Class modules have an extension .cls. Class modules are generally used while creating ActiveX EXE or ActiveX DLL components. When implemented as DLLs, they are loaded in the same address space as the application. However, when implemented as EXEs, they are loaded in a different address space. Thus, it runs as a separate process. However, class modules can also be included in normal Visual Basic projects in order to have an object-oriented approach to fulfill application requirements, as shown in Table 7.1.

Modules	Class Modules
Modules are structures that contain data and/or procedures.	Class modules are structures that encapsulate data and procedures, providing abstraction and hiding data from the other applications.
To access an element of a module, it does not need to be prefixed by the module name.	To access an element of a class module, it has to be prefixed by the class name or the name of an object for the class.
It can cause confusion if a module member has the same name as the member of the calling module.	No conflicting situations can ever arise with class modules, since the members of a class module are always prefixed with the name of the class or the name of an object of the class.
Modules are not implemented as DLLs or EXEs.	Class modules are generally implemented as ActiveX DLLs or ActiveX EXEs.
Modules have an extension .bas.	Class modules have an extension .cls.

Table 7.1: Comparison Between Modules and Class Modules

7.2.2 Access Scope of a Class

 Explain the access scope of classes.

Class modules may contain variables and/or procedures or functions. These may or may not be accessible to other components of the project or across projects. It depends upon the access specifier prefixed before them. Access specifiers define the visibility of the procedures, functions or properties defined within the class. Access specifiers are keywords that specify whether other applications can use the variable or procedure.

There are three levels of accessibility:

■ Only within the class module

■ Within the class module and other applications in the same project

■ Within the class module as well as other applications, but not necessarily in the same project

These correspond to the access specifiers:

- Private
- Public
- Friend

Private Specifier

If a variable or a procedure is private, its scope is limited to the module in which it is defined. Thus, a private variable is only accessible within the class module. Similarly, if a procedure is private, only other procedures in the same class module can call this procedure. Code 7.5 shows the use of a private specifier.

```
Private Sum as Integer
    Private Function CalculateSum () as Integer
    Sum = 10
    . .
End Function
```

Code 7.5: Using the Private Specifier

In code 7.5, the variable **Sum** and the function **CalculateSum** are available only to the other members of the same class module. Private procedures cannot be called from outside the class. They simply assist in building cleaner code in the class itself.

Public Specifier

If a variable or procedure is declared as **Public**, it can be accessed from code, outside of the class. Such variables or procedures are "public" to the outside world, that is, other applications can access them. This is the broadest scope. Public procedures are often called methods of the class. Code 7.6 shows the use of the **Public** specifier.

Consider the following code snippet in a class module ClsFinance.

```
Public Interest as Integer
Public Function CalculateInterest () as Integer
    . .
    . .
End Function
```

Code 7.6: Using the Public Specifier

Other applications can access the function after creating an object for the class ClsFinance. The syntax of accessing a function in a class is:

```
<object name>.<function name>
```

Friend Specifier

The **Friend** members can be accessed from anywhere in the project but not from outside. It implies that they are public with respect to other components of the same project, but private across the projects. Only functions and sub-procedures are declared as **Friend**. Variables cannot be declared as **Friend**. They can be either Private or Public. Code 7.7 shows the use of a Friend specifier.

```
Private Sum as Integer
    Friend Function CalculateSum () as Integer
    Sum = 10
      . .
End Function
```

Code 7.7: Using the Friend Specifier

In Code 7.7 the variable **Sum** is available only to the other members of the same class module. However, the function **CalculateSum()** can be accessed from anywhere in the project.

 Explain how to implement and use classes in Visual Basic.

To incorporate classes in Visual Basic, follow these steps:

1.   Open a new standard Exe project. Set its name to **clsDemo**.

2.   Right-click in the **Project Explorer** window and select **Add → Class Module** from the pop-up menu that appears, as shown in Figure 7.8.

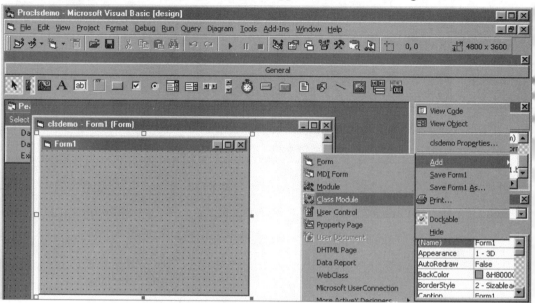

Figure 7.8: Adding a Class Module to a Project

3. The **Class Module** Dialog box opens. Select Class Module from the dialog box and click **Open**. A class module code window opens, as shown in Figure 7.9. Set the name of the class module to CDemo.

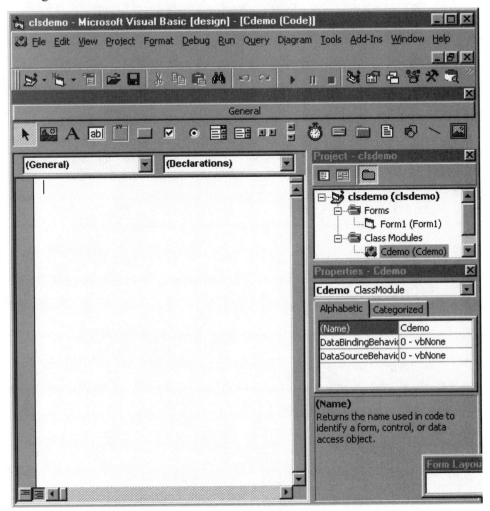

Figure 7.9: Class Module CDemo Added to the Project

4. Define the required class properties and property procedures.

5. Define the required class methods and/or subs.

6. Respond to **Terminate** and **Initialize** class events if required. You can also define your own events for the class.

7. Provide documentation to the class if desired.

Adding Property Procedures to the Class Module

At its root, a property is merely a variable which holds the property's value. For each property you create, you will have a module-level variable and Property procedures. Property procedures are code which runs when a property gets a new value or when the value is retrieved. There are two ways to define properties in class modules.

The simpler of the two methods is to declare public variables that are accessible outside the class. However, this method violates the basic concepts of object-oriented programming.

User-defined types cannot be declared as public in class modules. Hence, the above method cannot be used to define properties of user-defined types.

The second method is to define private variables and use them as the properties. Visual Basic provides special procedures called Property Procedures to access these variables. These variables specify some properties of the class. There are two property procedures:

■ Property Let

■ Property Get

Property Let procedures are used to set the value of the property (class variable). Property Get procedures are used to read the value of the property (class variable).

They are defined in Code 7.8.

```
Public Property Let <Procedure name> (<Value> As <Data Type>)
    <Class Variable> = <Value>
    End Property
Public Property Get <Procedure name> As <Data Type>
     Var = <Class Variable>
End Property
```

Code 7.8: Using the Let and Get Property Procedures

Only the property procedures will directly use the class variables and not any outside code. The data type of properties can be any of the basic data types or even user-defined data types. Property procedures may include other lines of code for computations, initializations, or other manipulations.

Sometimes the class may have read-only properties. In that case, you can omit the Property Let procedures. Another way could be to raise an error trappable by the application and then act accordingly.

You can create property procedures by selecting the Tools→Add procedure option from the main menu.

Defining class properties using property procedures are preferred to public variables because of the following benefits:

1. They are based on the principles of object-oriented programming. You can encapsulate variables and the code associated with modifying them or validating them in one unit.

2. Property procedures enable you to declare variables whose value cannot be modified (read-only properties). This is achieved through defining properties that do not have the Property Let procedures.

3. They make the code more efficient and easy to modify. For instance, you may want to change the value or validation process of a property. You can do so by simply modifying the code in the property procedures. No other code will require any changes.

   Code 7.9 shows the property procedures and properties for a class named CResult. This class contains functions to calculate averages in five subjects of students.

```
Private Average As Double
Public grade As String
Private m_eng As Single
Private m_math As Single
Private m_sc As Single
Private m_plogy As Single


Public Property Get English() As Single
        English = m_eng
End Property
```

```
Public Property Let English(ByVal vNewValue As Single)
    m_eng = vNewValue
End Property
Public Property Get Maths() As Single
    Maths = m_math
End Property

Public Property Let Maths(ByVal vNewValue As Single)
    m_math = vNewValue
End Property

Public Property Get Scn() As Single
    Scn = m_sc
End Property
Public Property Let Scn(ByVal vNewValue As Single)
    m_sc = vNewValue
End Property

Public Property Get psch() As Single
    psch = m_plogy
End Property

Public Property Let psch(ByVal vNewValue As Single)
    m_plogy = vNewValue
End Property
```

Code 7.9: Property Procedures of CResult Class

In the preceding code, the private variables **m_eng, m_math, m_plogy, and m_sc** are properties for which public property procedures are declared. The **Let** and **Get** procedures allow the values of the properties to be accessed outside the class.

Adding Methods to Class Modules

Methods encompass the functionality provided by the class. They perform various tasks. The implementation of the method is hidden from the code that accesses the method. A method can be declared as public or private depending on the functionality required from it. If a method returns a value it is declared as a **Function**. Otherwise it is declared as a **Sub**.

Properties that are declared as **Private** can only be accessed though methods. Methods can use the properties by referring to the name of the property procedure associated with the property and not the private variable name.

The CResult class can perform calculations using the method shown in Code 7.10.

```
Public Function Calc() As Double
    Average = (English + Maths + psch + Scn) / 4
    If (Average >= 75) Then
    grade = "A"
Else
    If (Average < 75) And (Average > 60) Then
    grade = "B"
Else
      grade = "C"
    End If
End If
    Calc = Average
End Function
```

Code 7.10: Methods of the CResult Class

In code 7.10 the **calc()** function is declared as public and can be accessed outside the class. It calculates the average and the grade based on the marks of each subject.

Using Class Events

Class modules have two built-in events, **Initialize** and **Terminate**. The **Initialize** events can be used for various initializations, such as file opening and other such purposes. The Terminate event may be used for clean-up activities, such as closing files or database connections. Students familiar with Object-Oriented programming in C++ may rightly relate these two events to the constructor and destructor functions of C++.

Every time an object is created, the Initialize event of the class is generated. The code contained in this event is the first code to be executed. Similarly every time a reference to an object terminates, the Terminate event is generated.

The Terminate event may be used for error handling before objects are destroyed.

You can include your own events in a class. To include an event you first need to declare it and then raise it. You can declare an event in the same way you declare a method. For instance, you can include an event in the CResult class that is generated whenever a user tries to enter negative marks for a student.

```
Public Event Invalid()
```

The RaiseEvent statement is used to raise an event. For instance the Invalid() event can be raised as:

```
RaiseEvent Invalid
```

The code that uses the class is responsible for responding to this event if it is raised.

Event declarations can include a list of parameters. However, they cannot have named and optional parameters. Also, they cannot return a value.

Using Enumerations

Enumerations provide a convenient way to work with sets of related constants and to associate constant values with names. For example, you can declare an enumeration for a set of integer constants associated with the days of the week, then use the names of the days in code rather than their integer values.

You create an enumeration by declaring an enumeration type with the Enum statement in the Declarations section of a standard module or a public class module. By default, the first constant in an enumeration is initialized to the value 0, and subsequent constants are initialized to the value of one more than the previous constant.

Creating an Object of the Class

After creating a class you can use the methods, properties, and events of the class by creating an object of the class as follows:

```
Dim obj_name As New Class_Name

or

Dim obj_name As Class_Name
Set obj_name = New Class_Name
```

The obj_name is the name of the object and Class_Name is the name of the class. You can then use this object to access all the public methods, events, and properties (public) or property procedures (for private properties) of the class as:

```
<obj_name>.<Class_member>
```

where, Class_member can be any accessible property, event, or method. The object name and the class name are separated by a period (.).

For a class named Bank, the following code snippet in Code 7.11 declares an object for the class and invokes the AddClient() method of the class on the declared object.

```
. . .
Dim objBank as Bank
Set objBank = New Bank
objBank.AddClient
. . .
```

Code 7.11: Creating an Object for the Class Named Bank

Let us consider an interface that accepts the scores secured by a student in four subjects, English, Mathematics, Science, and Psychology, and calculates the average score and the grade of the student. Let us implement the interface by using a class to perform the required calculations.

Create a new project and add controls to the form as shown in Figure 7.10.

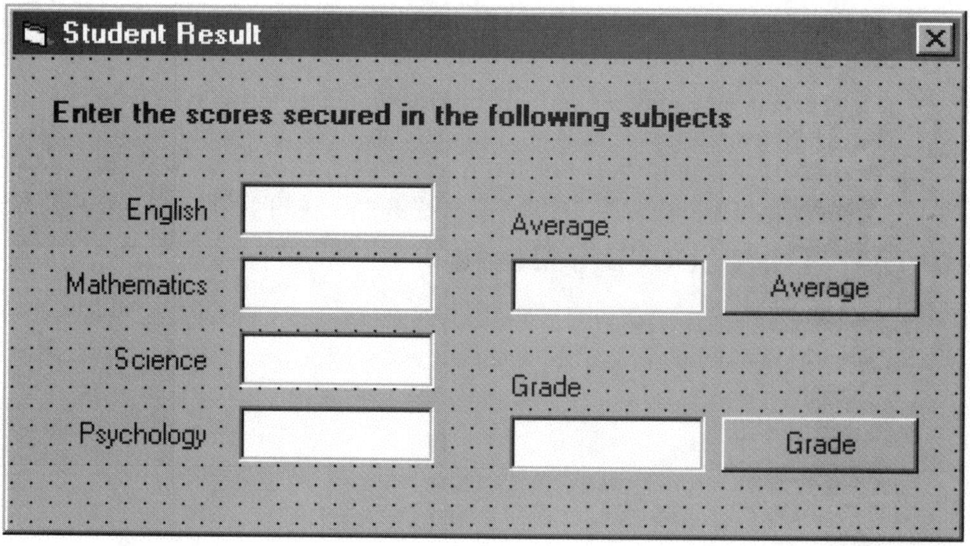

Figure 7.10: Form to Accept Scores Secured and Calculate the Average and Grade

Name the form frmResult. Set the names of the TextBox controls to accept the scores for the four subjects as txtEnglish, txtMaths, txtScience, and txtPsychology. Set the MaxLength property of these Text Boxes to 3, as the maximum score in each subject is 100. Set the name of the Text Box to display the average score as txtAverage and the Text Box to display the grade as txtGrade. Set the names of the command buttons to calculate the average and grade as cmdAverage and cmdGrade.

Add a class module named clsScores and add Code 7.12 to the class module.refer to code is missing.

```
Option Explicit


Private intEnglish As Integer
Private intMaths As Integer
Private intScience As Integer
Private intPsychology As Integer
Public Property Let psychology(ByVal vData As Integer)
        intPsychology = vData
```

```
End Property


Public Property Get psychology() As Integer
        psychology = intPsychology
End Property


Public Property Let science(ByVal vData As Integer)
        intScience = vData
End Property


Public Property Get science() As Integer
        science = intScience
End Property


Public Property Let maths(ByVal vData As Integer)
        intMaths = vData
End Property


Public Property Get maths() As Integer
        maths = intMaths
End Property


Public Property Let english(ByVal vData As Integer)
        intEnglish = vData
End Property


Public Property Get english() As Integer
        english = intEnglish
End Property
```

Code 7.12: Class Module of the Class Named clsScores

The Code 7.12 defines the property procedures for four properties of the class that are used to store the scores of each subjects. The following section provides the other necessary functions to the class.

Code 7.13 defines the two functions named CalcAvg() and GetGrade(), which calculate the average score and find the grade based on the average secured. It also defines a function named IsValidData(), which checks whether the entered scores for the individual subject is valid or not. If any subject has been specified with a score that is more than 100, it returns False. Otherwise it approves the validity of the data by returning True.

```
Public Function CalcAvg() As Integer
     CalcAvg = (intMaths + intEnglish + intScience +__
intPsychology) / 4
End Function


Public Function GetGrade() As String
    Dim intAvg As Integer
    intAvg = CalcAvg
    If intAvg >= 75 Then
    GetGrade = "A"
    ElseIf intAvg >= 60 Then
     GetGrade = "B"
Else
    GetGrade = "C"
  End If
End Function


Public Function IsValidData() As Boolean
    If intEnglish > 100 Or intMaths > 100 Or _ intScience > 100
Or intPsychology > 100
  Then
    IsValidData = False
Else
    IsValidData = True
  End If
End Function
```

Code 7.13: Functions Included in the Class clsScores

At this point the class is complete with all its properties and the necessary code to perform the required tasks. Let us now provide the functionality to the form frmResult. The first thing to do is to declare an object of the class clsScores. To do so, add the following code in the General Declaration section in the code window of the form frmResult.

```
Option Explicit
Dim objScores As clsScores
```

The preceding object is a variable of the type clsScores. Before using this variable, we must allocate memory to it, which is done by the following code. Here the **Form Load** event is used so that the task is performed as soon as the form loads in the memory.

```
Private Sub Form_Load()
Set objScores = New clsScores
End Sub
```

Code 7.14 prevents the Text Boxes from accepting non-numeric values. This is achieved by implementing the KeyPress event of each of the TextBox controls. This enhances the interface by preventing the user from specifying any incorrect value for the scores, which might lead to incorrect calculation of the result.

```
Private Sub txtEnglish_KeyPress(KeyAscii As Integer)
    If Not IsNumeric(Chr(KeyAscii)) And KeyAscii <> vbKeyBack
Then
       KeyAscii = 0
  End If
End Sub


Private Sub txtMaths_KeyPress(KeyAscii As Integer)
    If Not IsNumeric(Chr(KeyAscii)) And KeyAscii <> vbKeyBack
Then
       KeyAscii = 0
  End If
End Sub
Private Sub txtPhychology_KeyPress(KeyAscii As Integer)
   If Not IsNumeric(Chr(KeyAscii)) And KeyAscii <> vbKeyBack
Then
     KeyAscii = 0
   End If
End Sub
```

```
Private Sub txtScience_KeyPress(KeyAscii As Integer)
    If Not IsNumeric(Chr(KeyAscii)) And KeyAscii <> vbKeyBack
Then
    KeyAscii = 0
    End If
End Sub
```

Code 7.14: Code to Prevent Acceptance of Non-Numeric Values in the Text Boxes for Scores

Code 7.15 implements the Click event of the two command buttons to find the average score and the grade by invoking the appropriate methods of the class and displaying them in the respective text boxes. Notice that the properties of the object objScores are first initialized by the appropriate scores in the subjects. The code also invokes the IsValidData function of the class to ensure that the scores being entered for the subjects are valid. If the scores are found to be valid, the average and the grade is displayed in the respective text boxes, otherwise an error message is displayed.

```
Private Sub cmdAverage_Click()
    Me.txtAverage = ""
    With objScores
    .english = Val(Me.txtEnglish)
    .maths = Val(Me.txtMaths)
    .science = Val(Me.txtScience)
    .psychology = Val(Me.txtPhychology)
    End With
If objScores.IsValidData Then
    Me.txtAverage = objScores.CalcAvg
Else
    MsgBox "Score must be less than or equal to 100", _
vbCritical, "Student Scores"
    End If
End Sub
Private Sub cmdGrade_Click()
    Me.txtGrade = ""
    With objScores
    .english = Val(Me.txtEnglish)
```

```
    .maths = Val(Me.txtMaths)
    .science = Val(Me.txtScience)
    .psychology = Val(Me.txtPhychology)
End With
If objScores.IsValidData Then
    Me.txtGrade = objScores.GetGrade
Else
    MsgBox "Score must be less than or equal to 100", _
vbCritical, "Student Scores"
    End If
End Sub
```

Code 7.15: Code for the Command Buttons in the Form

Save the project and run the application.

Figure 7.11 shows the run time view of the application displaying the average and the grade for a given set of scores.

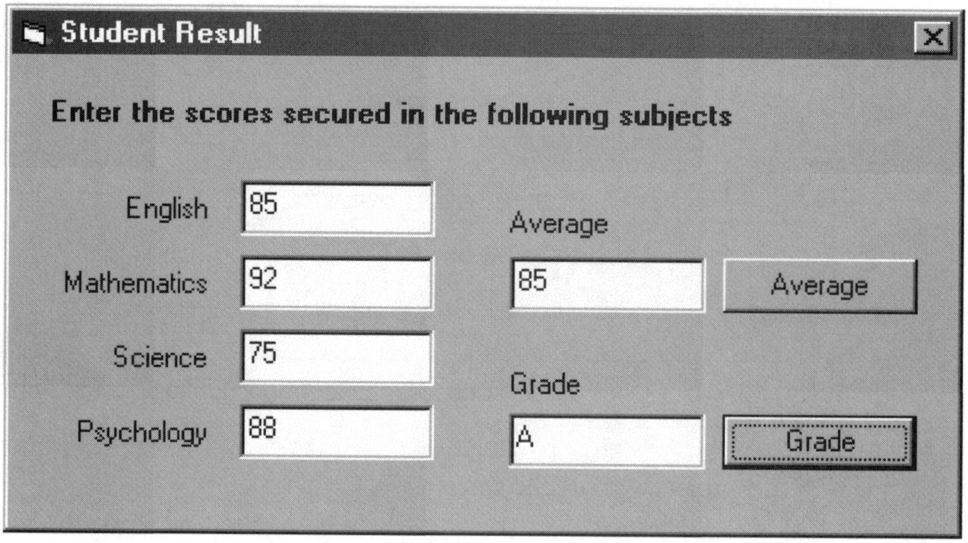

Student Result ☒

Enter the scores secured in the following subjects

English	85	Average
Mathematics	92	85	Average
Science	75	Grade
Psychology	88	A	Grade

Figure 7.11: Run Time View of the Form frmResult

Code 7.16 on p. 7.47 demonstrates how to implement classes in the applications. Notice that the form does not do any kind of calculations. It just uses the class and its methods. The application is separated into two parts—the GUI and the logic to perform the task. In larger applications, classes are used to separate the presentation (GUI) from the business logic so that the changes to one will not affect the other.

7.2.3 Using Class Builder Wizard

 Explain the steps to use Class Builder Wizard.

Visual Basic Professional and Enterprise Editions come with a Visual Basic Class Builder utility. This utility uses menu options and dialog boxes to walk you through the process of creating a class. With this utility, you can create any class or collection class. You can define all of the Properties, Methods, Events, and Enumerations. This utility then generates the code for the defined class. Start a new project before trying the Class Builder wizard.

To build a collection class using the Class Builder Wizard, perform the following steps:

1. Select **File → New Project**. The **New Project** dialog box will be displayed.

2. Select the **Class Builder Utility**. The Class Builder utility opens.

3. Click the **Add New Class** button on the toolbar or select **New** option from the File menu to add a class. The Class Module Builder dialog box is displayed as shown in Figure 7.12.

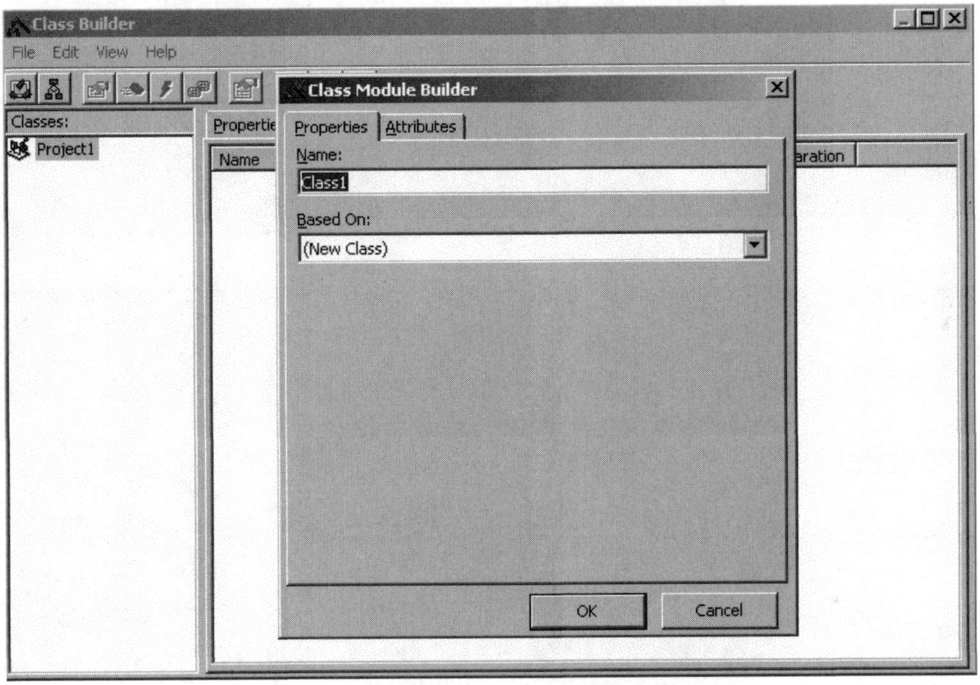

Figure 7.12: Class Module Builder Dialog Box

4. Enter the name and other attributes of the class in the Class Module Builder.

5. In order to add properties to the class, click on **File→New→Property**. The Property Builder dialog box appears as shown in Figure 7.13. Specify the name, data type, and the access declaration of the property to add, and click **OK**.

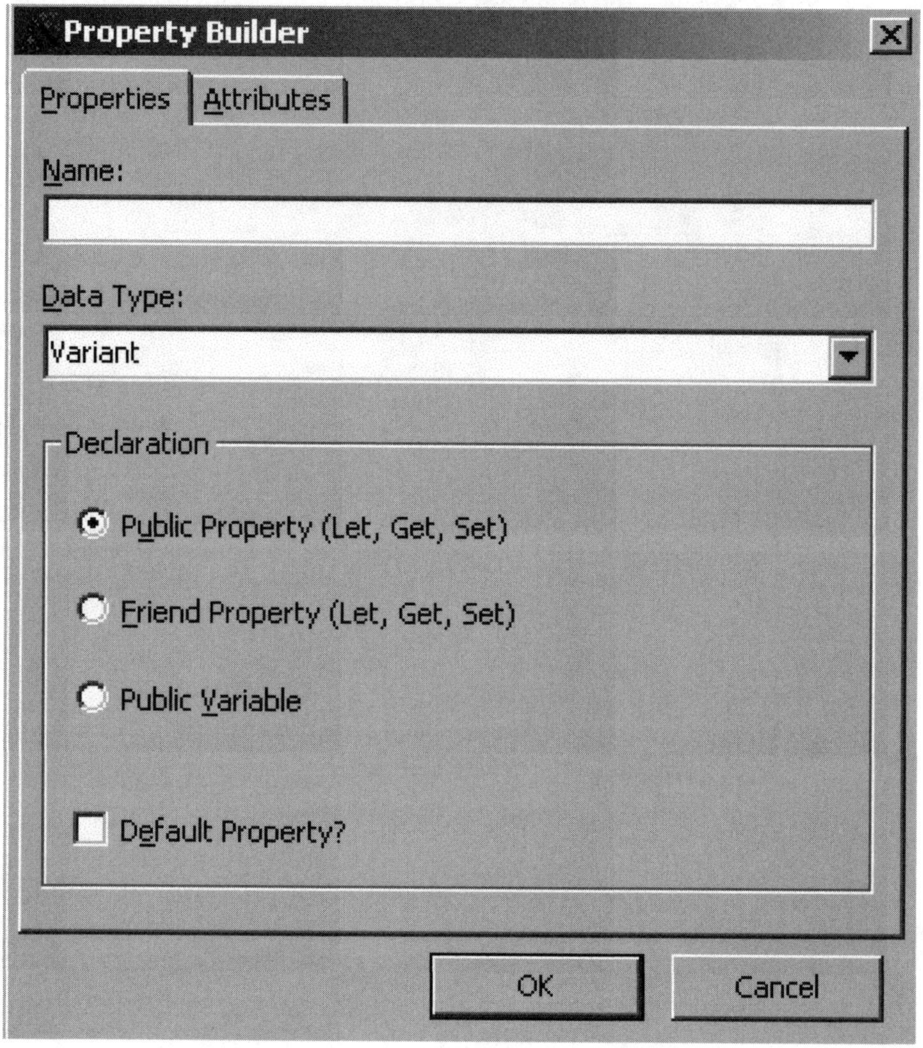

Figure 7.13: Property Builder Dialog Box

6.   In order to add methods to the class, click on **File→New→Method**. The Method Builder dialog box appears, as shown in Figure 7.14. Specify the name, data type, and access declaration of the method to add and click **OK**.

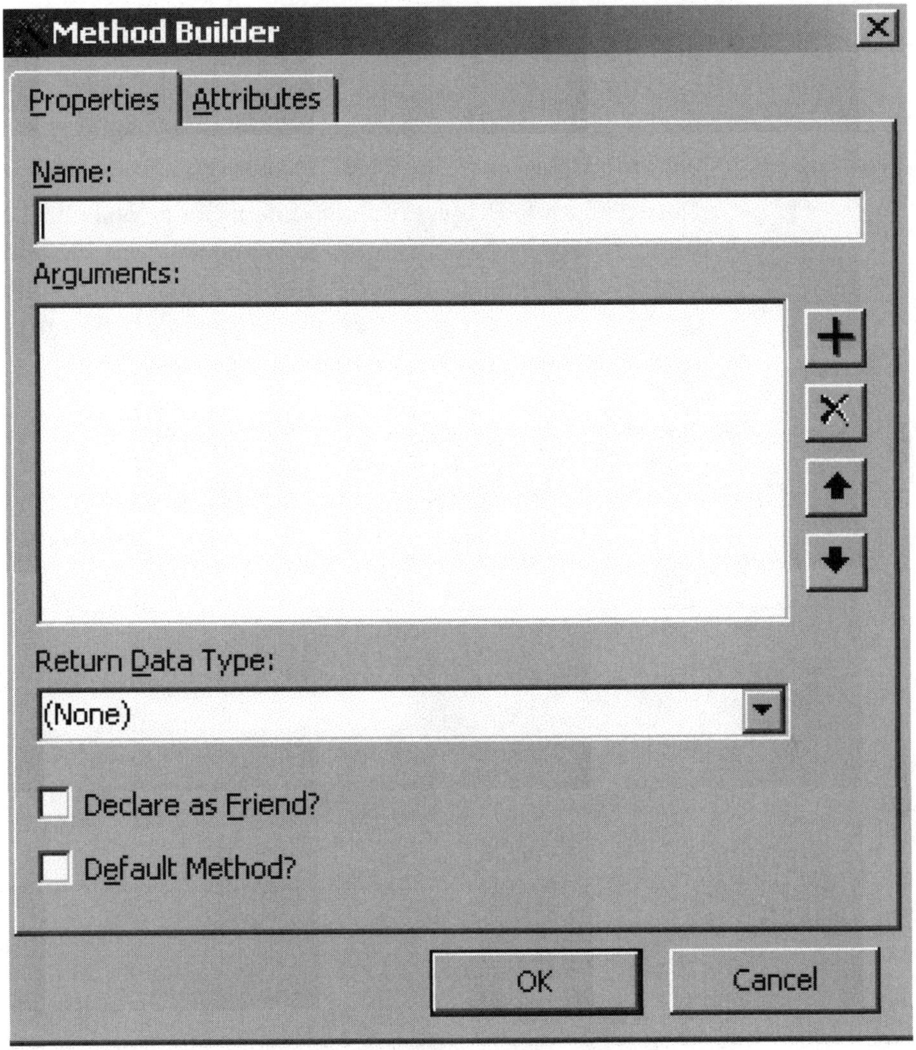

Figure 7.14: Method Builder Dialog Box

7.   Follow steps 6 and 7 to add events and **Enums** to your class.

8.   Select the project in the Class Builder dialog box and add a **Collection** to the project, using the Add New Collection button on the toolbar or the New option in the File menu.

9.   A **Collection Builder** dialog box appears. Enter the name and other attributes of the collection. Be sure to identify it as a collection of objects from the class created in step 4.

10.   Add properties, methods, events, and Enums to the collection class. As you identify the class as a collection, the Add, Remove, Item, Count, and NewEnum wrapper properties and methods are already defined for you. Use the buttons in the Class Builder dialog box toolbar to add any additional properties, methods, events, and Enums required by your application.

11.   Choose **Update Project** from the File menu to generate the code. The Class Builder Utility generates all the basic codes for the Properties procedures, events, and Enums except for the methods for all the class(es). In the module for the Collection(s), it will add all the Add, Remove methods and the Count, Item, and NewEnum property procedures.

You can access the Class Builder Wizard in a number of ways in Visual Basic. You can select the Add Class Module from the Project menu, and then choose the Visual Basic Class Builder template from the Add Class Module template gallery that appears.

Practice Questions

1. What is the difference between a module and class module in Visual Basic?

2. List the access scope of a class.

3. What properties and methods are available to classes in Visual Basic?

4. List the two property procedures in Visual Basic.

5. How can you provide read-only properties to a class?

6. What is the advantage of using properties over public variables?

7. Discuss Class Builder Utility in terms of Rapid Application Development in Visual Basic.

7.3 Collections

Collections are ordered groups of items that are considered as sets. The items of a collection can be of any data type. A collection itself is an object, so it can be created and referenced anywhere in the application just like any other object. To ensure encapsulation, however, a collection is normally created in a class defined specifically for managing the collection, called a *collection class*. Defining a collection within a collection class encapsulates the collection and keeps the collection private, so no other code can modify it unintentionally or incorrectly.

Just as Property procedures provide public exposure to private properties, public wrapper methods can provide public exposure to a private collection. Wrapper methods get their name because they provide a public wrapper around the private collection's methods. When an application needs to access a collection, the application can't use the collection's Add, Remove, and Item methods directly; rather, the application uses the Add, Remove, and Item wrapper methods provided in the collection class. These wrapper methods in the collection class then call the collection's methods.

Think of the collection class as a way to manage your own private collection. Suppose you have a collection of Star Trek action figures at home. Because your collection is private, no one else has direct access to it. If someone wants to add an action figure to your collection, they have to give the object to you and then you add it to your collection. If someone wants to remove an action figure from your collection, you have to remove it for them. If someone wants to use one of your action figures, they have to request it from you.

Visual Basic 6 provides an alternative to the Collection object called the Dictionary object. A dictionary holds two sets of information, a unique key and a value associated with the key, so you can use the key to retrieve an item. The key can be any data type except Variant, but it should usually be an integer or a string. The item can be any data type.

You add the dictionary object references by opening the project references from the Project menu and adding the Microsoft Scripting Run Time. Figure 7.15 should help you out with this.

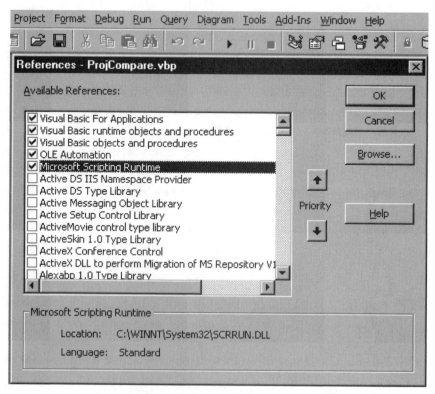

Figure 7.15: Microsoft Scripting Run Time Reference

The next step would be to define and declare the dictionary object.

```
Dim Dict1 As Dictionary
```

The next step is to create the dictionary and populate it with keys and items.

```
'Create a dictionary instance
Set Dict1 = New Dictionary
With Dict1
'Set compare mode
.CompareMode = BinaryCompare
'Add items to the dictionary
.Add 1, "Item 1"
.Add 2, "Item 2"
.Add 3, "Item 3"
End With
```

We now have a dictionary object that holds three rows with key values 1 to 3 and their associated item values. The Compare Mode sets and returns the comparison mode for comparing string keys in a Dictionary object. The values can be vbBinaryCompare, vbTextCompare, or vbDatabaseCompare. Remember to set the Compare Mode before you add any data to the dictionary otherwise you will get an error.

So now we have a dictionary object, containing some data ready to be accessed. Lets take a look at a couple of methods we have available to look up keys and items within a dictionary object.

The Exists method is used to find a specific key in the dictionary object. Say for example that you want to find out if an object contains a key with a value of 1999. We use the following syntax to get either a true or false.

```
Dim bReturnValue As Boolean
bReturnValue = Dict1.Exists(1999)
```

In this case, it will return False.

If you wish to get the item of a specific key, use the Items method, which has the following syntax:

```
Dim vItemValue As Variant
vItemValue = Dict1.Item(3)
```

In this case "Item 3" will be returned to you.

You can add a collection class to a project whenever the project needs to manage a collection of objects. The collection class can manage a set of objects from the same class or different types of objects. For example, you could define a collection of tasks to define the items on a to do list. Or, you could define a collection to track all open child forms in an MDI application or all objects required for one form. You could also define a "dirty objects" collection to hold any object that was changed by the user.

Before developing a collection class, you need to define what the collection class will contain. Determine what type of objects will be stored in the collection and whether the collection will be limited to objects of a specific type or objects of any type.

Once you know what will be in the collection, you can start the code for the collection class. A collection class is implemented using a class module.

Consider an example to summarize the concepts of classes and collections: an application that helps the user to maintain a list of birthdays of his/her friends. The application maintains the list with the help of a class named Buddy and a collection class named BirthdayList, which is based on the Buddy class. Follow the following steps to create the class and the collection:

1. Create a new project named prjBirthdayList.

2. Name the default form frmBuddyList.

3. Click **Add-Ins→Class Builder** Utility from the menu bar.

4. Click **File→New→Class** from the menu bar of the Class Builder Utility.

5. Set the name of the class as Buddy. Click **OK**.

6. Select the name of the above class in the Class Builder Utility and click **File→New→Property** from the menu bar. Set the name of the property as FirstName, data type as String, and access declaration as Public. Click **OK**.

7. Follow the above step to add two more properties to the class, namely LastName of String type and Birthday of Date data type.

8. Select the name of the project in the Class Builder Utility and click **File→New→Collection** from the menu bar.

9.   In the resulting dialog box, set the name of the collection as BirthdayList and select the name of the Buddy class in the Existing Class list, as shown in Figure 7.16.

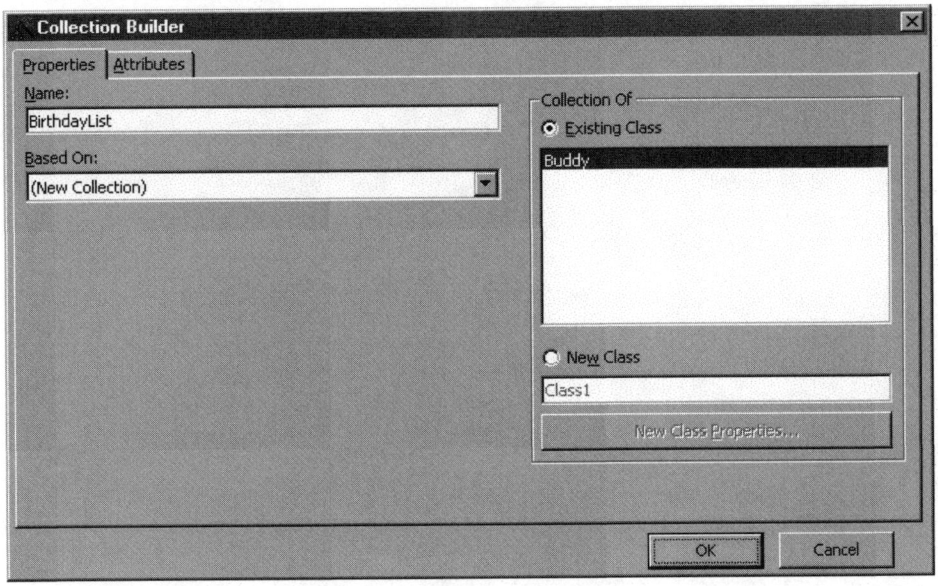

Figure 7.16: Creating a Collection Class Based on the Buddy Class

10. Click **OK**. The Class Builder Utility should resemble the Figure 7.17.

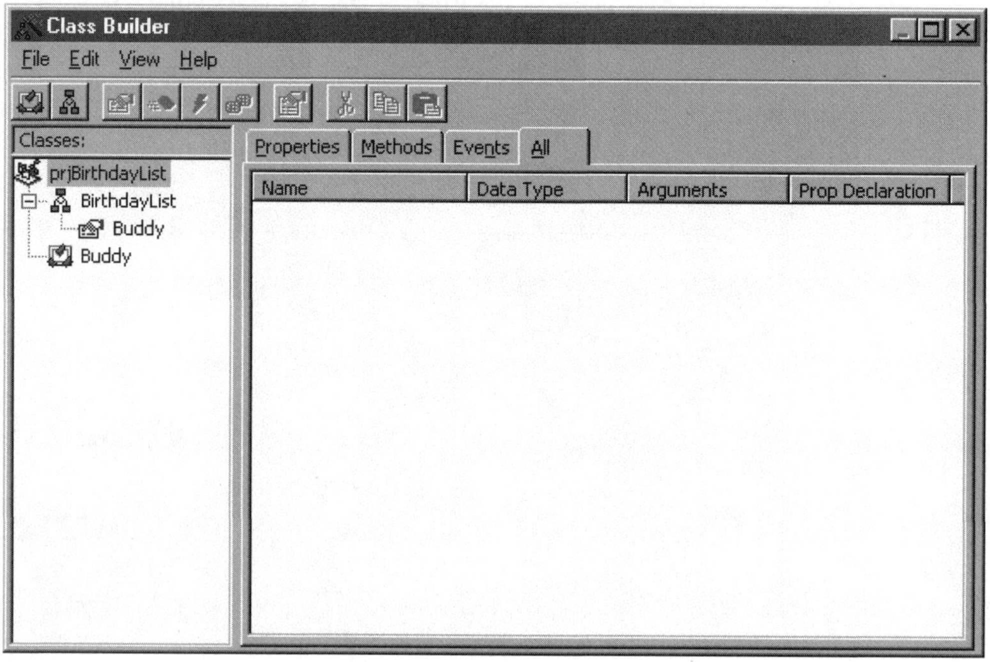

Figure 7.17: Class Builder Showing the Created Collection and Class

The Buddy class will be used to hold the information of the friends and the collection BirthdayList will be used to store objects of the class Buddy.

11. Click **File→Update** Project from the menu bar and close the Class Builder Utility. Two class modules are added to the project, one for the Buddy class and the other form the BirthdayList collection.

12. Activate the form frmBuddyList and add controls to the form as shown in Figure 7.18.

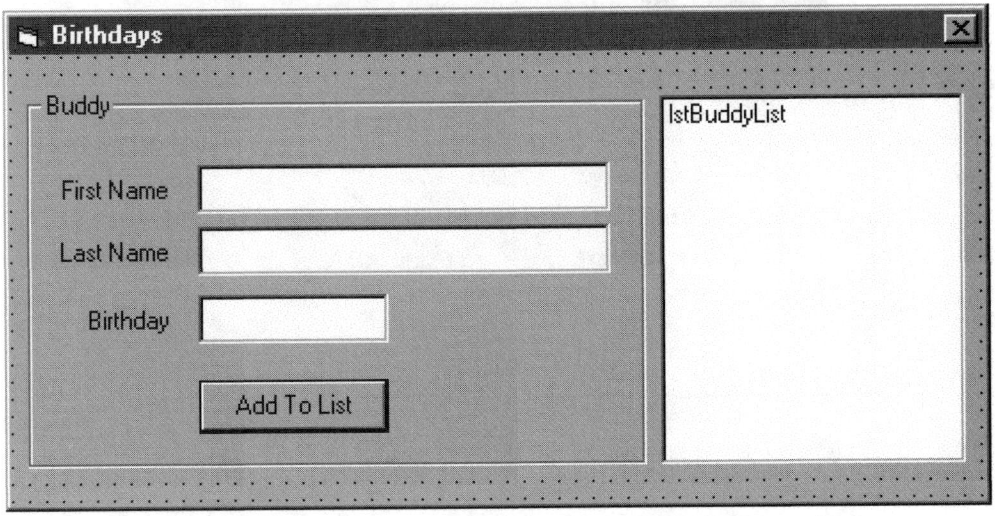

Figure 7.18: Design View of the Form frmBuddyList

Set the names of the text boxes for first name, last name, and birthday as txtFirstName, txtLastName, and txtBirthday. Set the name of the command button as cmdAddToList and the name of the list box as lstBuddyList. The text boxes will be used to accept the details of a friend and the command button will be used to add the specified friend to the list. The list box will display the names of all the friends present in the collection.

13. Open the code window of the form frmBuddyList and add the following Code 7.16 to the general declaration section.

```
Option Explicit
  Dim objBuddyList As BirthdayList
  Dim objBuddy As Buddy


Private Sub Form_Load()
      Set objBuddyList = New BirthdayList
End Sub
```

Code 7.16: Code to Create Objects of the Collection Class and Initialize the Collection Object

Code 7.16 declares two objects for the Buddy class and the BirthdayList collection. The Form Load event is used to initialize the collection object. This collection object will hold all the objects of the Buddy class.

14.   Add Code 7.17 to populate the list box named lstBuddyList with the names of the friends in the collection object.

```
Public Sub PopulateList()
      Me.lstBuddyList.Clear
      For Each objBuddy In objBuddyList
      Me.lstBuddyList.AddItem objBuddy.FirstName + " " + _
         objBuddy.LastName
      Next
End Sub
```

Code 7.17: Using the Collection Object to Populate the List Box in the Form

The preceding code loops through all the objects in the objBuddyList collection and retrieves the first name and the last name of all the objects in the collection. These names are then added to the list box named lstBuddyList.

15.   Add Code 7.18 for the Click event of the command button cmdAddToList. This will check if the supplied values in the three text boxes are valid. If the values are valid, the code adds the values to the objBuddyList collection object. Since the collection was created on the basis of the class Buddy, these values will be stored in the collection object as an object of the buddy class.

```
Private Sub cmdAddToList_Click()
    If Trim(Me.txtFirstName) = "" Then
    MsgBox "Invalid First Name", vbCritical, "Birthdays"
        Me.txtFirstName.SetFocus
    Exit Sub
End If
If Trim(Me.txtLastName) = "" Then
      MsgBox "Invalid Last Name", vbCritical, "Birthdays"
        Me.txtLastName.SetFocus
    Exit Sub
End If
If Not IsDate(Me.txtBirthday) Then
      MsgBox "Invalid date of birth", vbCritical, "Birthdays"
```

```
Me.txtBirthday.SetFocus
Exit Sub
End If
  objBuddyList.Add Trim(Me.txtFirstName), _
Trim(Me.txtLastName), CDate(Me.txtBirthday)
    PopulateList
    Me.txtBirthday = ""
    Me.txtFirstName = ""
    Me.txtLastName = ""
    Me.txtFirstName.SetFocus
End Sub
```

Code 7.18: Using the BuddyList Collection to Add an Object of the Buddy Class

The preceding code calls the PopulateList procedure to display the full name of the added buddy in the list box.

16. Add Code 7.19 to the Double-click event of the list box. The code retrieves the Buddy object from the collection based on the item being double-clicked on the list. Here it used the Item property of the collection class, which returns an object of the Buddy class. The code then displays the information from the retrieved Buddy object, using the properties of the Buddy object.

```
Private Sub lstBuddyList_DblClick()
If Me.lstBuddyList.ListIndex >= 0 Then
    Set objBuddy = objBuddyList.Item(Me.lstBuddyList.ListIndex _
+ 1)
    Dim strMsg As String
    strMsg = objBuddy.FirstName + " " + objBuddy.LastName
    strMsg = strMsg + vbNewLine + vbNewLine
    strMsg = strMsg + "Birthday: "
    strMsg = strMsg & Format(objBuddy.Birthday, "mmm dd, yyyy")
    MsgBox strMsg, vbExclamation, "Birthdays"
  End If
End Sub
```

Code 7.19: Implementing the Double-Click Event of the List Box

17. Save and run the project. Add sample data and double-click on an item in the list box. Figure 7.19 shows a run time view of the application.

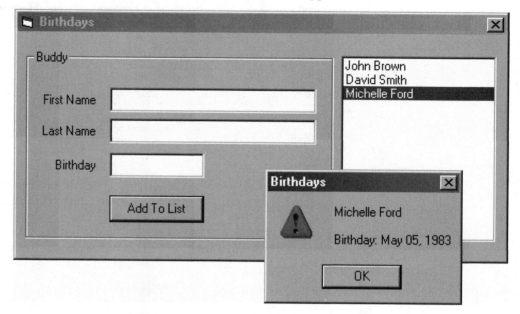

Figure 7.19: Run Time View for Code 7.20

This example demonstrates how to use classes to implement the object-oriented approach and how collections can store objects of a certain class. The preceding example can be further enhanced to include database connectivity through ADO as explained in Chapter 5 "Working with Databases" to enable the user to store the information in a database.

Practice Questions

1. Define a collection. Compare collections to arrays.
2. What is the need for a collection? State the relation between a class and a collection.
3. What are the default methods and properties added to a collection, created using the Class Builder Utility?
4. Mention a real-life example where you can implement the concept of a collection.

1.   Open the VB project named LibraryMgmt.

2.   Add a Data Environment object named DataEnvironment1 to the project by selecting **Project → Add Data Environment** from the menu bar. This DataEnvironment object will be used to store a Connection object to the concerned database and a few Command objects to handle the tables in the database.

3. Set the properties of the connection object named Connection1 in the Data Environment to connect to the LibraryMgmt.mdb file, as shown in Figure 7.20.

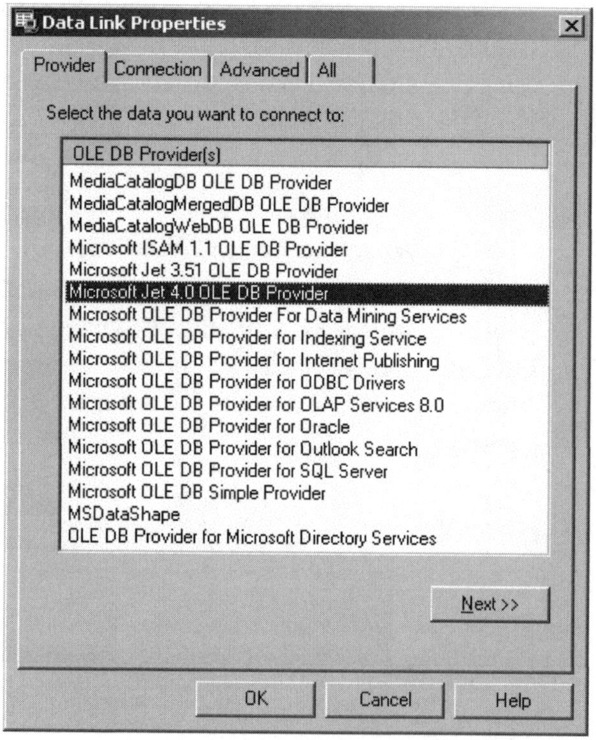

Figure 7.20: Data Link Properties Dialog Box

4. Add four Command objects to the connection object with the properties given in Table 7.2. These Command objects will be used as the record source for data bound controls in the forms.

Object Name	Property	Value
Members	Connection	Connection1
	Database Object	Table
	Database Object Name	Members
	LockType	Optimistic
ModifyMembers	Connection	Connection1
	Database Object	Table

Object Name	Property	Value
	LockType	Optimistic
SearchMember	Connection	Connection1
	Database Object	Table
	Database Object Name	Members
	LockType	Read Only
Categories	Connection	Connection1
	Database Object	Table
	Database Object Name	Categories
	LockType	Read Only

Table 7.2: Details of Command Objects

5.   Open the form named frmModifyMember and add a DataGrid control to the form with the following properties as given in Table 7.3.

Property	Value
Name	dbgMembers
Align	Align Top
DataSource	DataEnvironment1
DataMember	ModifyMembers
AllowAddNew	False
AllowUpdate	False
AllowDelete	False

Table 7.3: DataGrid Control Properties and Its Values

Figure 7.21 shows the design view of the form after adding the DataGrid control.

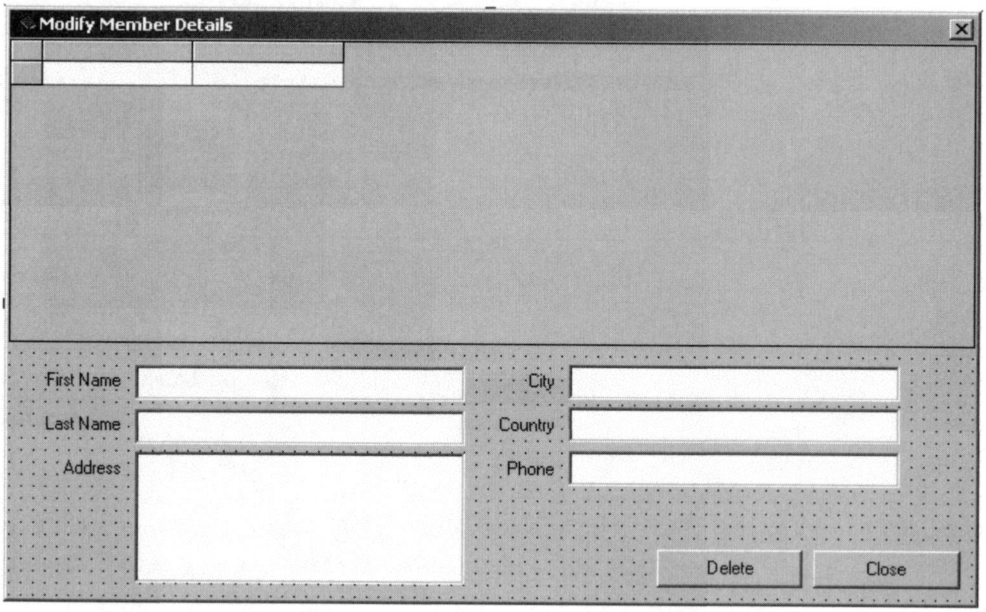

Figure 7.21: Form Design View with DataGrid Control

6. Modify the code for the **Form Load** event of the form as given in Code 7.20. The code executes the Requery method of the Recordset for the ModifyMembers command in DataEnvironment1 to retrieve the updated records from the underlying table.

```
Private Sub Form_Load()
                Me.Top = 120
Me.Left = 120
            DataEnvironment1.rsModifyMembers.Requery
End Sub
```

Code 7.20: Sample Code for Form Load Event

7. Add the following code for the Unload event of the form. The code closes the Recordset related to the ModifyMembers command in DataEnvironment1.

```
Private Sub Form_Unload(Cancel As Integer)
DataEnvironment1.rsModifyMembers.Close
End Sub
```

8. Set the following TextBox control properties, as given in Table 7.4. Then, bind the TextBox controls in the form with the respective fields in the Members table.

Name of the Text Box	DataSource Property	DataMember Property	DataField Property
txtFirstName	DataEnvironment1	ModifyMembers	FirstName
txtLastName	DataEnvironment1	ModifyMembers	LastName
txtAddress	DataEnvironment1	ModifyMembers	Address
txtCity	DataEnvironment1	ModifyMembers	City
txtCountry	DataEnvironment1	ModifyMembers	Country
txtPhone	DataEnvironment1	ModifyMembers	Phone

Table 7.4: TextBox Control Properties

9. Add Code 7.21 for the **Validate** event of the text boxes. The **Validate** event is fired when the focus is transferred to another control. This event is used to validate the data entered in the text boxes. Since the text boxes are bound to the fields in the table, the user can directly change the values in the table by editing the contents of the text boxes. If the user changes the value in a text field and moves to another record or another control in the form, the underlying table is updated with the new value being specified in the text box. This might create some problem in ensuring a valid record in the table, as someone might delete the value in a certain field. Thus, there should be some validation before the user transfers the focus from the text box to another control or moves to another record. This can be achieved by implementing the Validate event of the control. The Validate event is provided by almost all the controls other than the TextBox controls. The Validate event procedure provides a Cancel argument which can be used to prevent the transfer of focus from the control if the value specified is not valid.

```
Private Sub txtFirstName_Validate(Cancel As Boolean)
If DataEnvironment1.rsModifyMembers.RecordCount > 0 Then
If Trim(Me.txtFirstName) = "" Then
    MsgBox "First Name cannot be blank", vbCritical, "Input
    Error"
    Cancel = True
End If
  End If
```

```vb
End Sub
Private Sub txtLastName_Validate(Cancel As Boolean)
If DataEnvironment1.rsModifyMembers.RecordCount > 0 Then
If Trim(Me.txtLastName) = "" Then
        MsgBox "Last Name cannot be blank", vbCritical, "Input
          Error"
        Cancel = True
      End If
    End If
End Sub


Private Sub txtAddress_Validate(Cancel As Boolean)
    If DataEnvironment1.rsModifyMembers.RecordCount > 0 Then
If Trim(Me.txtAddress) = "" Then
                    MsgBox "Address cannot be blank", vbCritical,
          "Input Error"
                    Cancel = True
    End If
  End If
End Sub


Private Sub txtCity_Validate(Cancel As Boolean)
    If DataEnvironment1.rsModifyMembers.RecordCount > 0 Then
      If Trim(Me.txtCity) = "" Then
        MsgBox "City name cannot be blank", vbCritical, "Input
          Error"
        Cancel = True
      End If
    End If
End Sub


Private Sub txtCountry_Validate(Cancel As Boolean)
    If DataEnvironment1.rsModifyMembers.RecordCount > 0 Then
      If Trim(Me.txtCountry) = "" Then
        MsgBox "Country name cannot be blank", vbCritical, "Input
          Error"
```

```
        Cancel = True
      End If
   End If
End Sub
```

Code 7.21: Code for the Validate Event

10. Add Code 7.22 for the **Click** event of the command button **cmdDelete**. It is used to delete the current record of the Members table, using the Delete method of the Recordset object.

```
Private Sub cmdDelete_Click()
  If Trim(Me.txtFirstName) <> "" Then
    If MsgBox("Are you sure to delete the selected record", _
         vbQuestion + vbYesNo, "Confirm Delete") = vbYes Then

      On Error Resume Next
      DataEnvironment1.rsModifyMembers.Delete adAffectCurrent
    End If
  End If
End Sub
```

Code 7.22: Code for the Click Event

11. Open the form named frmSearchMember and change the height property of the form to 6765.

12. Add a Frame control to the form named frmSearchResult with the Caption property set to Search Result.

13. Add a DataGrid control to display the result of the search. Set the properties of the DataGrid control as given in Table 7.5:

Property	Value
Name	DbgSearchResult
DataSource	DataEnvironment1
DataMember	SearchMember
AllowAddNew	False

AllowUpdate	False
AllowDelete	False

Table 7.5: DataGrid Control Properties

14.   Add Code 7.23 for the Click event of the command button cmdSearch. It uses the Filter property of the Recordset object to filter the required records based on the criteria specified by the user. The Filter property is used to specify the search condition based on which records will be searched in the recordset object. The condition is specified in the format <Fieldname>=<Value>. The following code calls the GetCondition function to get the search condition and applies the filter on the recordset object. It also changes the size of the form to hide and unhide the frame displaying the result of the search.

```
Private Sub cmdSearch_Click()
  On Error GoTo errmsg
  Dim strFilterString As String
  strFilterString = GetCondition
  If strFilterString <> "" Then
    DataEnvironment1.rsSearchMember.Filter = strFilterString
    Me.Height = 6765
  Else
    Me.Height = 3150
  End If
  Exit Sub
errmsg:
  MsgBox Err.Description
End Sub
```

Code 7.23: Code for the Click Event

15.   Add the function named GetCondition() as given Code 7.24 which is used by the **cmdSearch** command button. The function returns a string containing the search criteria based on the values being specified by the user in the criteria.

```
Private Function GetCondition() As String
  Dim strCondition As String
  Dim x As Byte
```

```
For x = 0 To 2
   If Trim(Me.txtValue(x)) <> "" Then

     If Me.cboFieldName(x).Text <> "RegNo" Then
       strCondition = strCondition + Me.cboFieldName(x).Text +
       " like "
       strCondition = strCondition + "'" + Trim(Me.txtValue(x))
       + "'"
     Else
       strCondition = strCondition + Me.cboFieldName(x).Text +
       "="
       strCondition = strCondition & Val(Me.txtValue(x))
     End If
     If x < 2 Then
       If Me.cboOperator(x).Text = "AND" Then
         strCondition = strCondition + " AND "
       Else
         strCondition = strCondition + " OR "
       End If
     End If
   End If
 Next
 strCondition = Trim(strCondition)
 If strCondition <> "" Then
   If Right(strCondition, 3) = "AND" Then
     strCondition = Mid(strCondition, 1, Len(strCondition) - 4)
   ElseIf Right(strCondition, 2) = "OR" Then
     strCondition = Mid(strCondition, 1, Len(strCondition) - 3)
   End If
 End If
 GetCondition = Trim(strCondition)
End Function
```

Code 7.24: Code for the GetCondition() Function

16. Open the form named frmAddMember and set the following properties of the TextBox controls as given in Table 7.6 in the form to bind them with the respective fields in the Members table.

Name of the Text Box	DataSource Property	DataMember Property	DataField Property
txtFirstName	DataEnvironment1	Members	FirstName
txtLastName	DataEnvironment1	Members	LastName
txtAddress	DataEnvironment1	Members	Address
txtCity	DataEnvironment1	Members	City
txtCountry	DataEnvironment1	Members	Country
txtPhone	DataEnvironment1	Members	Phone

Table 7.6: TextBox Control Properties

17. Modify the code for the Form Load event of the form frmAddMember. The additional line in the procedure creates a new record in the Recordset of the Members command in DataEnvironment1. As the text boxes are bound to the fields in the Members table, the user can enter the respective values to construct the new record for the new member. Use Code 7.25.

```
Private Sub Form_Load()
  DataEnvironment1.rsMembers.AddNew
  Me.Top = 120
  Me.Left = 120
End Sub
```

Code 7.25: Code for the Form Load Event

18. Add the following form, as given in Code 7.26 for the Click event of the command button cmdAddMember. It uses the Update method of the Recordset object to update the new record of the underlying table. If the user seeks to add another record to the table, the code creates another new record in the Recordset.

```
Private Sub cmdAddMember_Click()
  If Not IsValidData Then
    Exit Sub
```

```
  End If
    DataEnvironment1.rsMembers.Update
    MsgBox "Record successfully added", vbExclamation, "Add
Member"

    If MsgBox("Do you want to add another member", _
          vbQuestion + vbYesNo, "Add Member") = vbYes Then

      DataEnvironment1.rsMembers.AddNew
    Else
      Unload Me
    End If
End Sub
```

Code 7.26: Code for the Click Event of the Command Button

19. Add the following code for the Unload event of the form. It cancels the creation of the new record which was initiated during the Load event of the form or through the Click event of the cmdAddMember command button.

```
Private Sub Form_Unload(Cancel As Integer)
DataEnvironment1.rsMembers.CancelUpdate
End Sub
```

20. In the following code, window of the Data Environment, add the following code for the Initialize event of DateEnvironment1. The code initializes the Connection object with the connection string which is used throughout the project. This enables the connection object to be initialized with the appropriate connection string at run time.

```
Private Sub DataEnvironment_Initialize()
Connection1.Open strConString
End Sub
```

21. Open the form frmMain and add Code 7.27 for the **Click** event of the menu items to display the remaining forms.

```
Private Sub mnuBookReturn_Click()
  frmBookReturn.Show
  frmBookReturn.SetFocus
End Sub
```

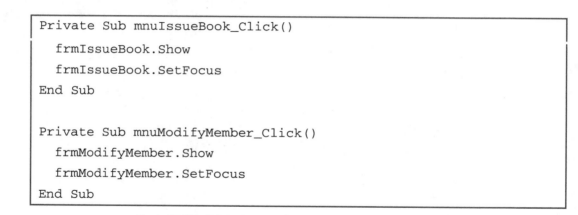

```
Private Sub mnuIssueBook_Click()
    frmIssueBook.Show
    frmIssueBook.SetFocus
End Sub


Private Sub mnuModifyMember_Click()
    frmModifyMember.Show
    frmModifyMember.SetFocus
End Sub
```

Code 7.27: Code for the Click Event of the Menu Items

22.   Save and run the project.

Summary

■ Classes contain data and functions and introduce user-defined types into a program.

■ All the controls on the Visual Basic Toolbox are actually classes, from which the objects you use on your forms are derived.

■ When you place any control on a form, Visual Basic creates a new object based on that class.

■ Each object has an interface between the user and the object's code and its data.

■ Two useful built-in objects are the Screen and Printer objects, which represent the monitor and the current printer.

■ Encapsulation is the ability to wrap code and data in a single unit that can be accessed by a well-defined interface.

■ Visual Basic Professional and Enterprise Editions come with a Visual Basic Class Builder utility. This utility uses menu options and dialog boxes to walk you through the process of creating a class.

■ Collections are ordered groups of items that are considered sets. The items of a collection can be of any data type.

■ Visual Basic 6 provides an alternative to the Collection object called the Dictionary object.

References

- http://www.library.itt-tech.edu/periodicals.asp > FindArticles.com (Accessed on Aug. 12, 2004)
- http://www.library.itt-tech.edu/periodicals.asp > MSDN Magazine (Accessed on Aug. 12, 2004)

Homework Exercises

1.   What is data hiding with respect to encapsulation in Visual Basic?
2.   What are access scopes of classes in Visual Basic?
3.   How are properties defined in Visual Basic classes?
4.   How are methods defined in Visual Basic classes?
5.   What is the basic difference between the module and class module?
6.   What is the extension of the class modules in Visual Basic?
7.   What is the extension of the modules in Visual Basic?
8.   What is encapsulation?
9.   What are objects and how are they used in Visual Basic?

Lab Exercises

Exercise 1

Objective

- To access a database by using class and collection.

Problem Statement

Access a dictionary database to display the meaning of words entered by the user.

Lab Setup

Computer Requirements:

- Microsoft Windows Operating System
- Pentium III or higher processors
- 128-MB RAM
- 3-GB of hard disk space
- CD-ROM drives
- Floppy disk drives
- LAN connections
- Visual Basic 6.0
- Microsoft Access

Procedure

1. Create a new Standard Exe project and add a form to it. Add two text boxes to the form, one for the word input by the user and the other for the meaning that is displayed. Add a command button with the caption "show meaning." The form is shown in Design View in Figure 7.22.

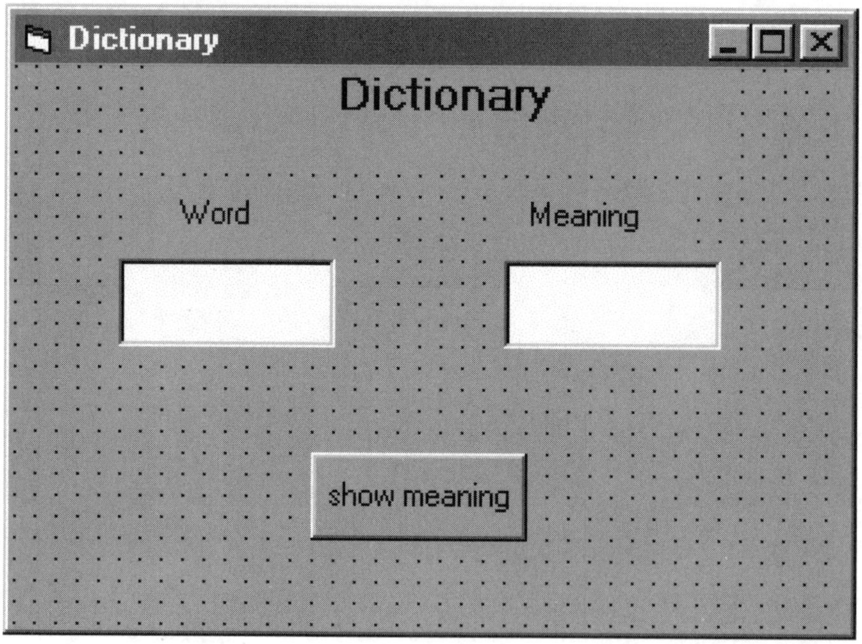

Figure 7.22: Form Design View for Exercise 1

2. Add a class module to the project that contains the required functions. Add Code 7.28 to the class module.

```
Private m_word As String
Private ConStr As String
Private m_mean As String
Private Con As ADODB.Connection


Public Function ConnectToDb()
    Set Con = New ADODB.Connection    'Establish a new
connection
```

```
        Con.ConnectionString =
"Provider=microsoft.jet.OLEDB.4.0;" _
        & "Data Source=C:\db2.mdb"
    Con.Mode = adModeRead
    Con.CursorLocation = adUseClient
    Con.Open   'Open a connection
End Function


Public Sub DisConDb()
    Con.Close 'Close the connection
    Set Con = Nothing
End Sub


Public Sub ret_word()
    Dim flag As Integer
    Dim str12 As String
    Dim F As Field
    Dim rs As New ADODB.Recordset
    Dim sql As String
    Dim allowed As Integer

    sql = "select * from wordlist"
    flag = 0
    allowed = 0
    rs.Open sql, Con.ConnectionString

    While (Not rs.EOF And flag <> 1)
        For Each F In rs.Fields
            If F.Name = "Word" And allowed = 0 Then
                str12 = F.Value
                If StrComp(str12, word) = 0 Then
                    allowed = 1
                End If
            End If
            If F.Name = "Meaning" And allowed = 1 Then
```

```
                    meaning = F.Value
                    flag = 1
                End If
            Next
            rs.MoveNext
        Wend
        If flag = 0 Then
            meaning = ""
        End If


        rs.Close
    End Sub


    Public Property Get word() As String
        word = m_word
    End Property


    Public Property Let word(ByVal vNewValue As String)
        m_word = vNewValue
    End Property


    Public Property Get meaning() As String
        meaning = m_mean
    End Property


    Public Property Let meaning(ByVal vNewValue As String)
        m_mean = vNewValue
    End Property
```

Code 7.28: Code for Exercise 1

Add Code 7.29 to the Click event of the command button on the form.

```
Private Sub Command1_Click()
    Dim var As New Class1
    var.word = Text1.Text
```

```
    var.ConnectToDb
    var.ret_word
    Text2.Text = var.meaning
    If (Text2.Text = "") Then
        MsgBox "Word Not Found"
    End If
    var.DisConDb
End Sub
```

Code 7.29: Code for Click Event of Command1 for Exercise1

The run time view of the application is shown in Figure 7.23.

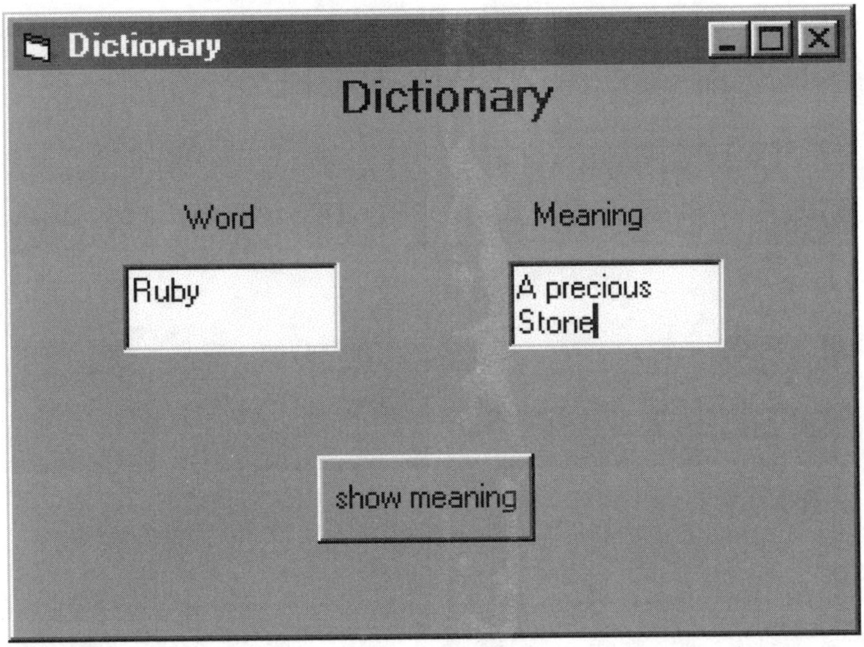

Figure 7.23: Run Time View for Code 7.31

Conclusion/Observation

The students get a better idea of the usage of class modules with databases in real-time applications.

Lab Activity Checklist

S. No.	Tasks	Completed	
		Yes	No
1.	Form added to the project		
2.	Class module added to the project		
3.	Access specifier correctly assigned		
4.	Property procedures included		
5.	Methods included for database connection, disconnecting, and retrieval		

Exercise 2

Objective

- To access the ParkingDB database by using classes and collections.

Problem Statement

Retrieve the data in the parkingdb.mdb database using classes and collections. The parkingdb.mdb database is discussed in Chapter 6 "Using Advanced ActiveX Controls with Databases." Create classes to represent the LookUp and Vehicle entity in the database and create a collection to represent the one-to-many relation between the two entities. Create a parent collection to store all the LookUp objects. The entire database related activity should be handled in the class and collection, not in the form. Figure 7.24 shows the run time view of the form.

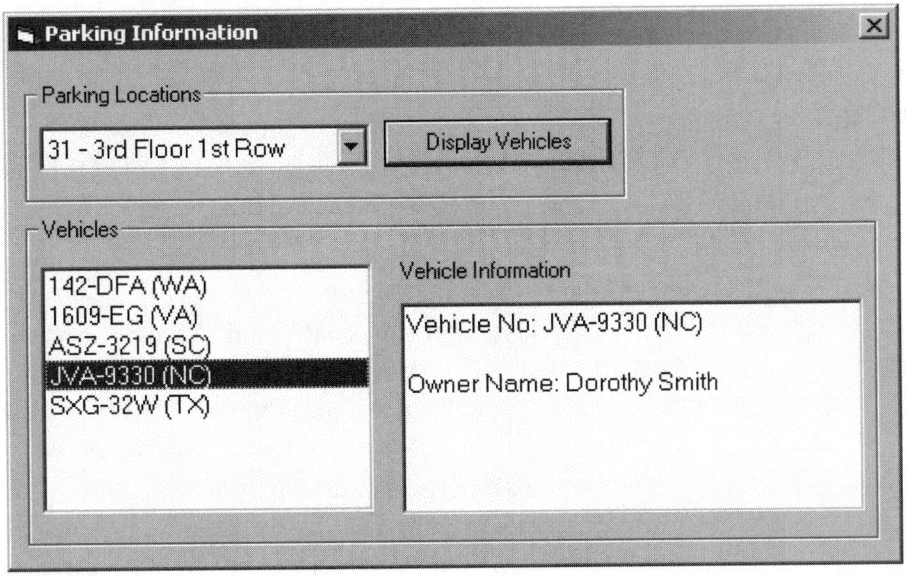

Figure 7.24: Run Time View for Exercise 2

The Locations combo box displays the Token ID and the name of all the available locations. The Display Vehicles command button lists all the vehicles parked in the specified location. The Vehicle Information text box displays the information of the vehicle being selected in the list box. (HINT: There will be two classes for the LookUp and the VehicleInfo tables. The LookUp class will contain a collection of several

Vehicle objects. The parent collection will contain the objects of all the LookUp objects).

Lab Setup

Computer Requirements:

- Microsoft Windows Operating System
- Pentium III or higher processors
- 128-MB RAM
- 3-GB of hard disk space
- CD-ROM drives
- Floppy disk drives
- LAN connections
- Visual Basic 6.0
- Microsoft Access

Procedure

Create a new project and add the **Microsoft ActiveX Data Objects 2.0 Library** reference by selecting Project→References on the menu bar. Then, perform the following steps:

1. Invoke the Class Builder Utility.

2. Create two classes named LookUp and Vehicle. Add two properties namely TokenID of integer type and Location of string type to the LookUp class. Add three properties, TokenID of integer type, VehicleNo of string type, and OwnerName of string type to the class Vehicle.

3. Select the LookUp class in the Class Builder Utility and click **File→New→Collection** to create a collection as a member of the LookUp class. This collection will be used to hold all the objects of the Vehicle class that are related to a certain LookUp object. Name the new collection as VehicleCollection and select the name of the Vehicle class in the Existing Class list as shown in Figure 7.25.

Click **OK** to add the collection.

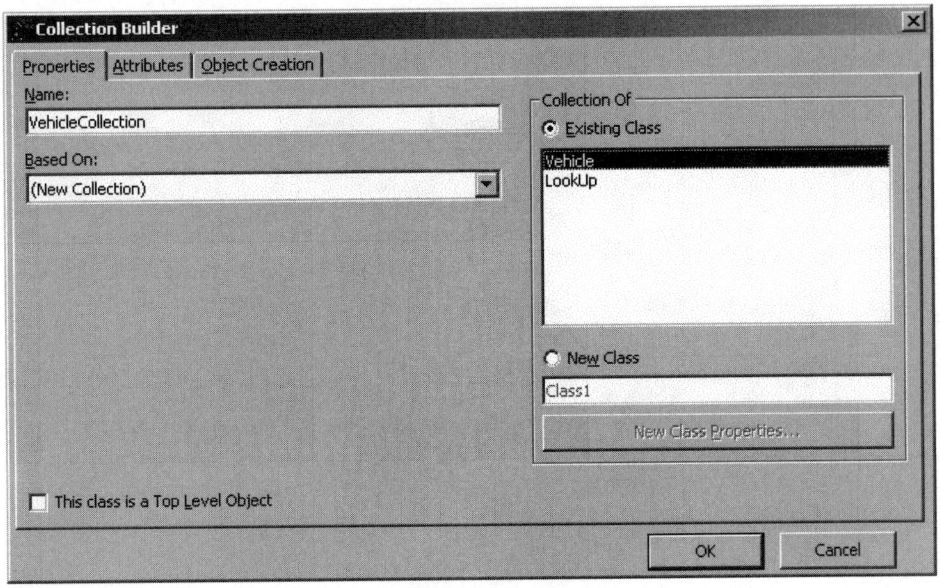

Figure 7.25: Collection Builder Utility

4.   Select the name of the project in the Class Builder Utility and click **File→New→Collection** to create the parent collection which will hold all the objects of the LookUp objects. Name the new collection LookUpCollection and select the name of the LookUp class to indicate that the new collection is to be created based on the LookUp class. Click **OK** to add the collection.

5.   Click **File→Update** Project to add the class modules for each of the preceding classes and collections to the project.

6.   Modify the code of the LookUpCollection class module as given in Code 7.30.

```
Option Explicit
Private dbCon As ADODB.Connection
Private mCol As Collection


Public Function Add(TokenID As Integer, Location As String, _
    VehicleCollection As VehicleCollection, _
    Optional sKey As String) As LookUp
```

```
     Dim objNewMember As LookUp
   Set objNewMember = New LookUp
   objNewMember.TokenID = TokenID
   objNewMember.Location = Location
   Set objNewMember.VehicleCollection = VehicleCollection
   If Len(sKey) = 0 Then
     mCol.Add objNewMember
   Else
   mCol.Add objNewMember, sKey
   End If

   Set Add = objNewMember
   Set objNewMember = Nothing
End Function

Public Property Get Item(vntIndexKey As Variant) As LookUp
   Set Item = mCol(vntIndexKey)
End Property

Public Property Get Count() As Long
   Count = mCol.Count
End Property

Public Sub Remove(vntIndexKey As Variant)
   mCol.Remove vntIndexKey
End Sub

Public Property Get NewEnum() As IUnknown
   Set NewEnum = mCol.[_NewEnum]
End Property

Private Sub Class_Initialize()
   Set mCol = New Collection
   Set dbCon = New ADODB.Connection
   dbCon.Open "Provider=Microsoft.Jet.OLEDB.4.0;" & _
```

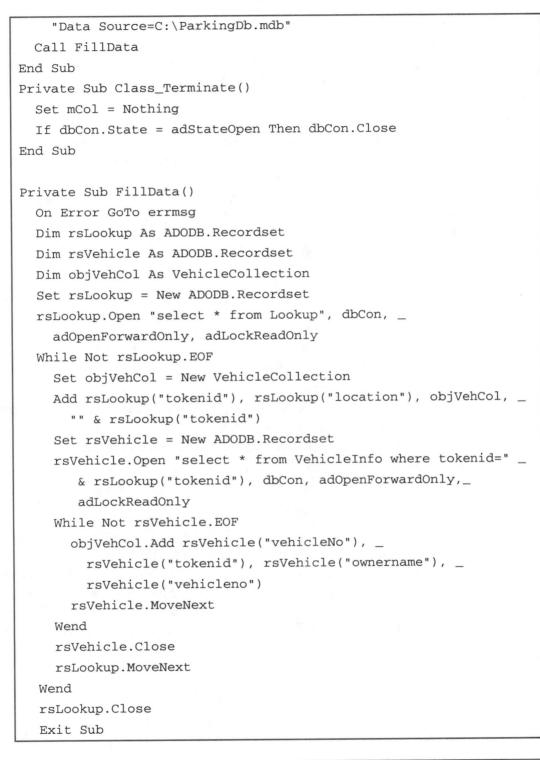

```
            "Data Source=C:\ParkingDb.mdb"
    Call FillData
End Sub
Private Sub Class_Terminate()
    Set mCol = Nothing
    If dbCon.State = adStateOpen Then dbCon.Close
End Sub


Private Sub FillData()
    On Error GoTo errmsg
    Dim rsLookup As ADODB.Recordset
    Dim rsVehicle As ADODB.Recordset
    Dim objVehCol As VehicleCollection
    Set rsLookup = New ADODB.Recordset
    rsLookup.Open "select * from Lookup", dbCon, _
        adOpenForwardOnly, adLockReadOnly
    While Not rsLookup.EOF
        Set objVehCol = New VehicleCollection
        Add rsLookup("tokenid"), rsLookup("location"), objVehCol, _
            "" & rsLookup("tokenid")
        Set rsVehicle = New ADODB.Recordset
        rsVehicle.Open "select * from VehicleInfo where tokenid=" _
            & rsLookup("tokenid"), dbCon, adOpenForwardOnly,_
            adLockReadOnly
        While Not rsVehicle.EOF
            objVehCol.Add rsVehicle("vehicleNo"), _
                rsVehicle("tokenid"), rsVehicle("ownername"), _
                rsVehicle("vehicleno")
            rsVehicle.MoveNext
        Wend
        rsVehicle.Close
        rsLookup.MoveNext
    Wend
    rsLookup.Close
    Exit Sub
```

```
errmsg:
  MsgBox "ERROR!" + Err.Description, vbCritical, "ERROR"
End Sub
```

Code 7.30: Code for the LookUpCollection Class Module

The general declaration section of the above code declares an object of AODB.Connection to store the database connection. The Class_Initialize event procedure is used to initialize the database connection. The Class_Terminate event procedure is used to close the database connection. A private procedure named FillData is used to populate the internal collection mcol with the data from the two tables in the ParkingDB database. This collection holds all the LookUp objects created for each of the records in the LookUp table. These LookUp objects in turn will hold a collection for all the Vehicle objects created for each of the related records in the VehicleInfo table. Thus, the parent collection object will indirectly contain all the records from both the tables in the database.

7.   The code modules for the other class and collection remain the same as if they were generated by the Class Builder Utility. Open the default form in the project and name it frmMain.

8.   Add the controls to the form as shown in the Problem Statement. Name the combo box to display the location cboLocation, the command button cmdDisplayVehicles, the list box to display the vehicles lstVehicle, and the text box to display the vehicle information txtVehicleInfo.

9.   Declare the following two module level objects for the LookUpCollection and VehicleCollection in the general declaration section of the form frmMain.

        ```
        Dim objLookUpCol As LookUpCollection
        Dim objVehicleCol As VehicleCollection
        ```

10.   Add Code 7.31 for the Load event of the form. The code initializes the objLookUpCol. This will raise the Class_Initialize event of the collection for the objLookUpCol object and populate the collection with the records in the tables as discussed above. The code also retrieves the LookUp objects from the collection and adds the token Id and the location name of each of these objects to the combo box cboLocation.

```
Private Sub Form_Load()
  Set objLookUpCol = New LookUpCollection
  Dim objLookUp As LookUp
```

```
    Set objLookUp = New LookUp
    For Each objLookUp In objLookUpCol
      Me.cboLocation.AddItem objLookUp.TokenID & _
        " - " & objLookUp.Location
    Next
    If Me.cboLocation.ListCount > 0 Then
      Me.cboLocation.ListIndex = 0
    End If
End Sub
```

Code 7.31: Code for the Form Load Event

11.   Add Code 7.32 for the Click event of the combo box cboLocation. It clears
       the list box for the vehicles and the text box for the vehicle information, when
       the user clicks on an item in the combo box.

```
Private Sub cboLocation_Click()
  Me.lstVehicle.Clear
  Me.txtVehicleInfo = ""
End Sub
```

Code 7.32: Code for the Click Event of the Combo Box cboLocation

12.   Add Code 7.33 for the Click event of the command button
       cmdDisplayVehicles. It retrieves the VehicleCollection object for the selected
       location and populates the list with the vehicle number of each Vehicle object
       in the collection.

```
Private Sub cmdDisplayVehicles_Click()
  Dim objLookUp As LookUp
  Set objLookUp = objLookUpCol.Item("" & _
    Val(Me.cboLocation.Text))
  Set objVehicleCol = objLookUp.VehicleCollection
  Dim objVehicle As Vehicle
  For Each objVehicle In objVehicleCol
    Me.lstVehicle.AddItem objVehicle.VehicleNo
  Next
```

```
End Sub
```

Code 7.33: Code for the Click Event of Command Button cmdDisplayVehicles

13.   Add Code 7.34 for the Click event of the list box lstVehicle. It retrieves the Vehicle object from the VehicleCollection based on the selected vehicle number and displays the information of the vehicle in the text box txtVehicleInfo.

```
Private Sub lstVehicle_Click()
  If Me.lstVehicle.ListIndex >= 0 Then
    Dim objVehicle As Vehicle
    Set objVehicle = objVehicleCol.Item(Me.lstVehicle.Text)
    Dim strInfo As String
    strInfo = "Vehicle No: " & objVehicle.VehicleNo
    strInfo = strInfo + vbNewLine + vbNewLine
    strInfo = strInfo + "Owner Name: " & objVehicle.OwnerName

    Me.txtVehicleInfo = strInfo
  End If
End Sub
```

Code 7.34: Code for the Click Event of the List Box lstVehicle

14.   Finally the Form Unload event is implemented to clear the contents of the objLookUpCol object. This triggers the Class_Terminate event of the collection class and closes the database connection.

```
Private Sub Form_Unload(Cancel As Integer)
Set objLookUpCol = Nothing
End Sub
```

15.   Save and run the project.

Conclusion/Observation

In this exercise, you learned how to create classes and collections in Visual Basic.

Lab Activity Checklist

S. No.	Tasks	Completed	
		Yes	No
1.	Classes and collections used		
2.	Class Builder used for creating classes		
3.	Features of Object-Oriented programming employed to the fullest		

Project

1.   Open the VB project named EmpInfo.

2.   Open the form frmEditEmp. Set the DataSource of the DataGrid dbgEmployee and the two DataCombo controls as DataEnvironment1 and the DataMember as EditEmployee. The DataField of the DataCombo dbcDept should be DeptNo and that for dbcGrade should be Grade. Write the code for the click event of the command button cmdDeleteEmp to delete the current employee record, using the Data Environment object DataEnvironment1. The deletion should take place only if the user approves of doing so. For the command button cmdUpdate, write the code to move the record pointer of the recordset in the command EditEmployee to the first record. (HINT: This is done as moving to record pointer makes the current record to be updated in the database). Implement the Form Load event to initialize the adoDept and the adoGrades control with the appropriate connection strings and connect to the tables Departments and Grades respectively. The connection string should be specified using the public variable declared in the module modMain.

3.   Open the form named frmSearchEmp. Add an ADODC control named adoEmp which should not be visible during run time. Add a DataGrid control named dbgEmployee as read-only and set the data source as adoEmp.

The form should resemble Figure 7.26 at design time.

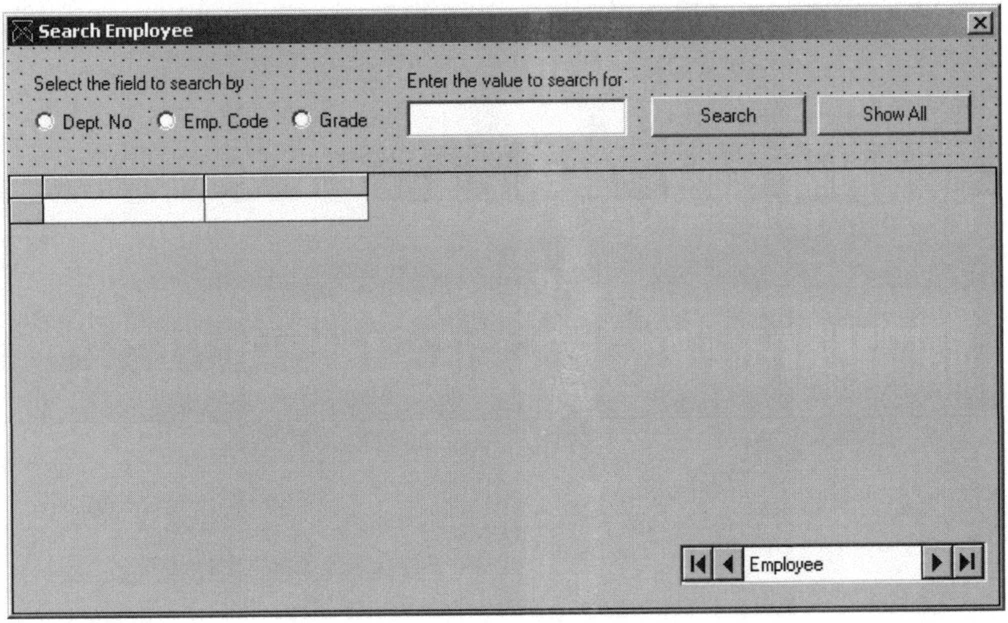

Figure 7.26: Form Design View

4.   In the Form Load event, initialize the adoEmp control with the appropriate connection string, using the public variable declared in the module modMain and connect to the table Employees. Define a function named GetCondition which will return the search condition as a string, depending on the field being selected to search and the value being specified to search for. Write the code for the click event of the command button cmdSearch which will filter the recordset of the adoEmp control to display the required records in the DataGrid control. Use the GetCondition function to retrieve the search condition. Write the code for the command button named cmdShowAll which will remove the filter from the recordset and display all the records in the DataGrid control.

5.   In the code window for the DataEnvironment, implement the Initialize event of DataEnvironment1 to open the connection object named Connection1 with the appropriate connection string. Use the public variable declared in the module modMain to specify the connection string.

6.   Save and run the project.

Distributing VB Applications

8

This chapter provides step-by-step instructions on how to create the installation package of applications developed in Visual Basic, using the Package and Deployment Wizard. It also explains how to deploy an installation package on the local computer, remote computer, and Web servers.

At the end of this chapter, you will be able to:

- Install the Package and Deployment Wizard.
- Run the Package and Deployment Wizard.
- Explain the tasks performed by the Package and Deployment Wizard.
- Explain the files that you need to distribute as a part of the setup package.
- Create a disk-based installation package.
- Deploy an installation package on physical media, such as floppy disks and CD-ROMs.
- Deploy an installation package on the network.
- Deploy an installation package over the Internet.
- Manage the scripts created by the Package and Deployment Wizard.

8.1 Introduction to the Package and Deployment Wizard

After creating, debugging, and testing your Visual Basic program, you need to create a setup package and distribute your program. This enables end users to install and run the program on their computers. Visual Basic provides the Package and Deployment Wizard to create a setup of your program. The type of setup package you create depends on the way you want to distribute the application. The three ways in which you can distribute your application are:

- On the network
- On physical media, such as CD-ROMs and floppy disks
- In files that you can download from the Internet

8.1.1 Installing and Running the Package and Deployment Wizard

- Install the Package and Deployment Wizard.
- Run the Package and Deployment Wizard.

The Package and Deployment Wizard is installed by default as part of the Visual Studio 6.0 package. You can also install the Package and Deployment Wizard separately.

Figure 8.1, shows the Visual Studio 6.0 Enterprise dialog box that appears when you select the custom installation option while installing Visual Studio 6.0.

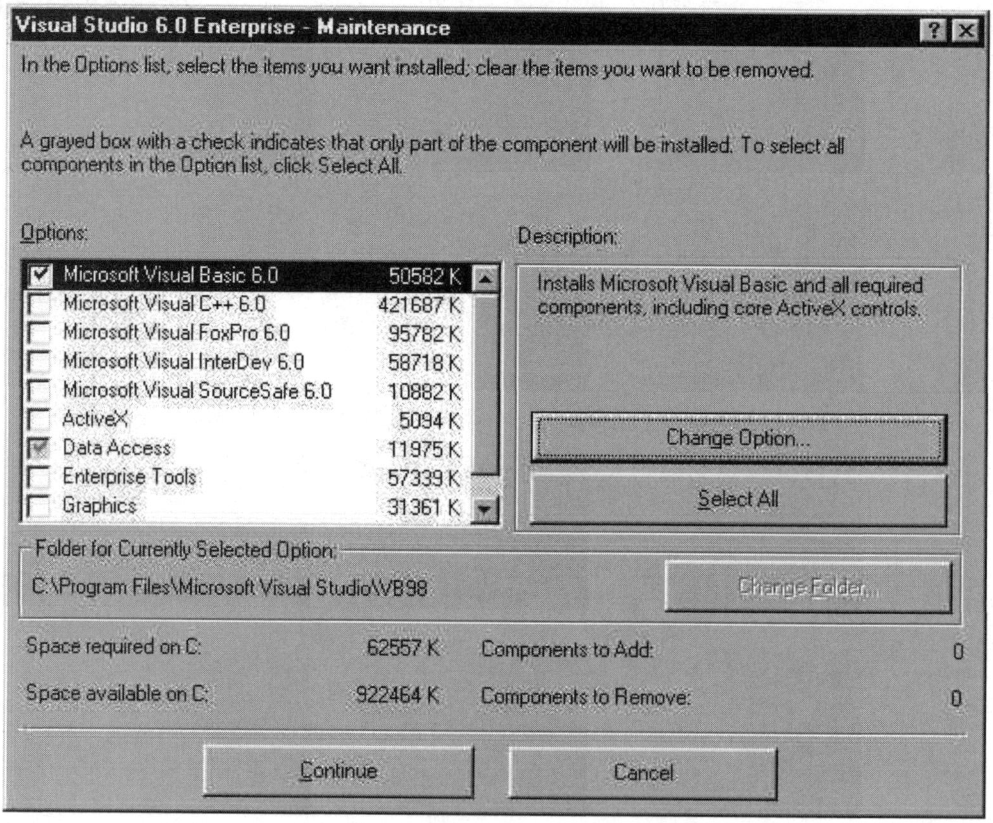

Figure 8.1: Visual Studio 6.0 Enterprise - Maintenance Dialog Box

In Figure 8.1, when you select the Microsoft Visual Basic 6.0 option and click the **Change Option** button, the Visual Studio 6.0 Enterprise—Microsoft Visual Basic 6.0 dialog box appears.

Figure 8.2 shows the tools installed as a part of Visual Basic 6.0.

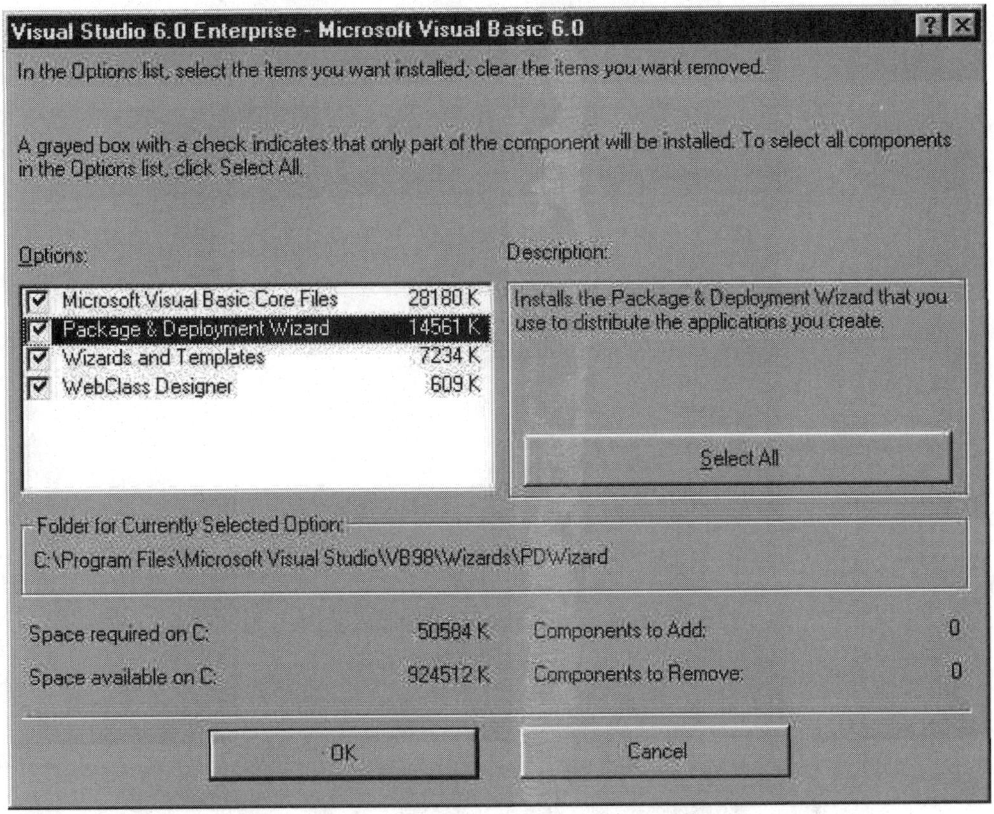

Figure 8.2: List of Visual Basic 6.0 Component List for Installation

In Figure 8.2, you can select the Package and Deployment Wizard as a tool to package and deploy programs and projects that you create in Visual Basic.

You can run the Package and Deployment Wizard as a stand-alone application or as a part of the Visual Basic Add-ins.

To run the Package and Deployment Wizard as a stand-alone application:

1.   Select **Start → Programs → Microsoft Visual Studio 6.0 → Microsoft Visual Studio 6.0 Tools → Package and Deployment Wizard**.

To run the Package and Deployment Wizard as a Visual Basic Add-in:

2.   Load the wizard using the Add-In Manager dialog box.

3.   Use the Add-in menu to run the Package and Deployment Wizard.

4. Select **Add-Ins** → **Add-In Manager** to display the **Add-In Manager** dialog box.

Figure 8.3 shows the Add-In Manager dialog box.

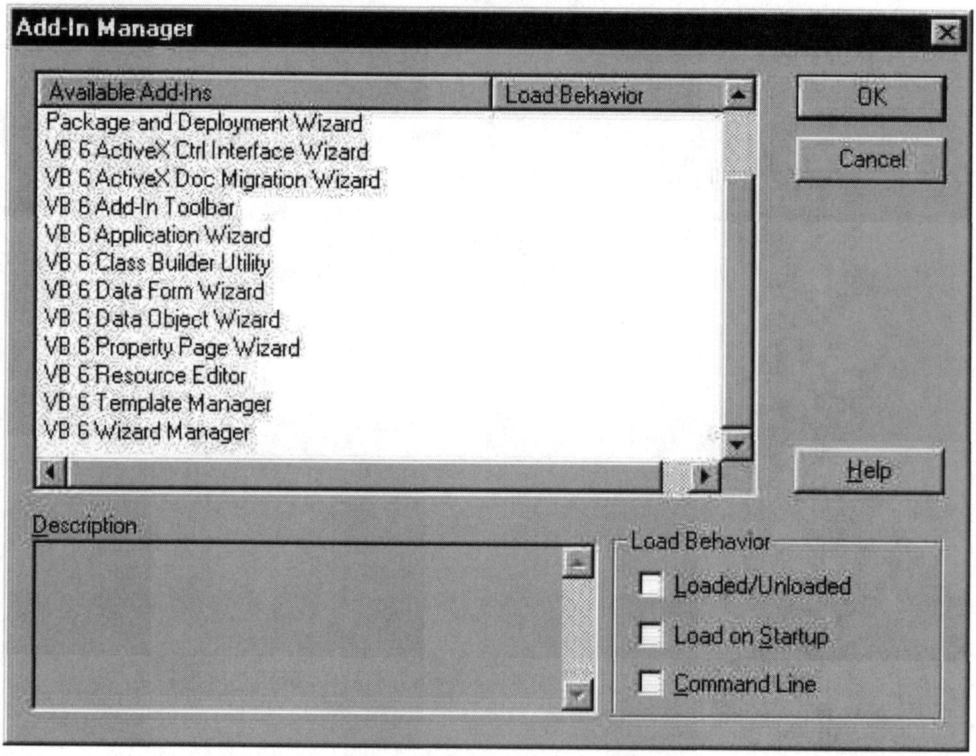

Figure 8.3: Add-In Manager Dialog Box

To run the Package and Deployment Wizard as Visual Basic add-in:

1. Select the Package and Deployment Wizard from the Available Add-Ins list.

2. Select the **Loaded/Unloaded** check box. Figure 8.4 shows the Package and Deployment Wizard loaded as an add-in.

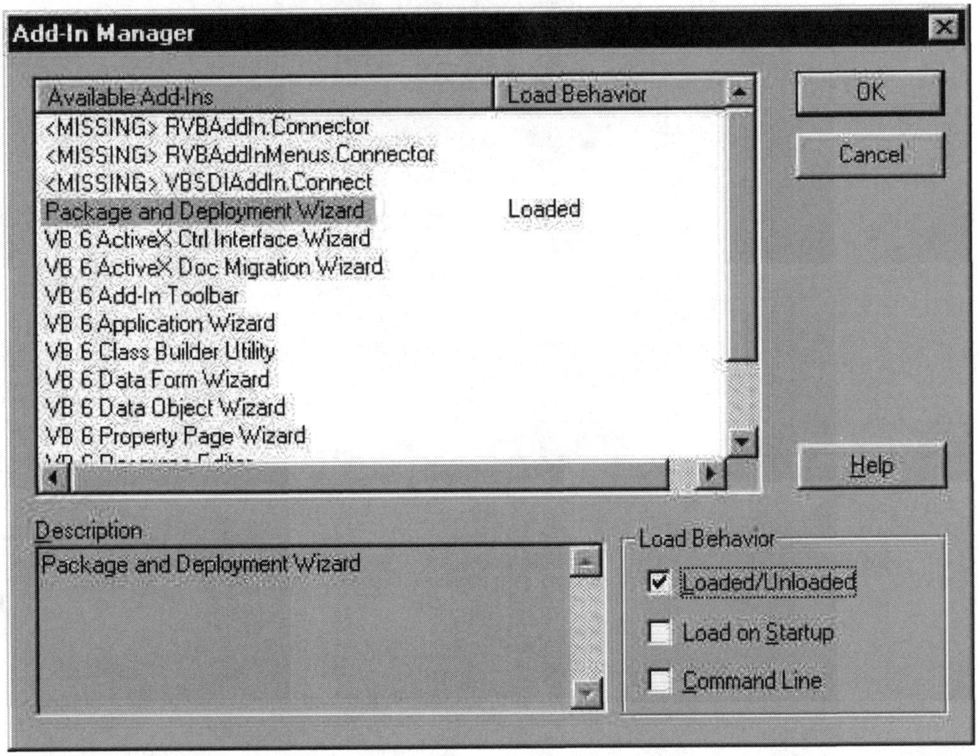

Figure 8.4: Package and Deployment Wizard Loaded as an Add-In

3. Click **OK** to close the Add-In Manager dialog box.

4.   The Package and Deployment Wizard is now available as a Visual Basic Add-in, which you can run by selecting **Add-Ins → Package and Deployment wizard**, as shown in Figure 8.5.

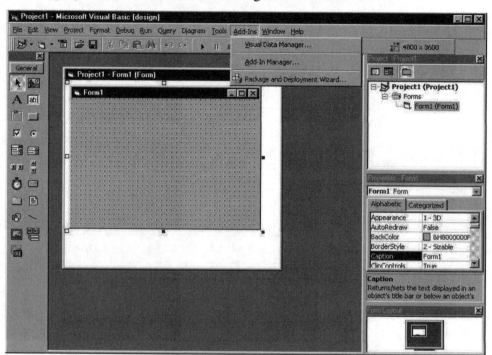

Figure 8.5: Add-Ins Menu

8.1.2 Tasks Performed by the Package and Deployment Wizard

Explain the tasks performed by the Package and Deployment Wizard.

The Package and Deployment Wizard performs the tasks necessary to create an installation package for your Visual Basic program. The Package and Deployment Wizard:

■   Determines the files to be distributed with the Visual Basic program, such as the VB libraries, DLL files, help files, and database files.

- Creates a setup program that enables end users to copy and install the Visual Basic project on their computers.
- Compresses the files to be included with the package. This reduces the size of the installation package to be stored on floppy disks or downloaded from the Internet.
- Creates the installation floppy disks, CD-ROMs, or files that you can download.
- Creates a dependency file that lists all files included in the installation package and the location where these files would be stored on the computer of the end user as a part of the package.

After creating the setup program and the installation files using the Package and Deployment Wizard, test the installation process on another computer to ensure that the project is successfully installed.

Practice Questions

1. Specify the three ways in which you can distribute your application.
2. How can you select the most appropriate method of distribution for your application?
3. What is a dependency file?
4. What is the purpose of a setup program?
5. Besides the stand-alone method, what is the other way in which you can run the Package and Deployment Wizard?

8.2 Packaging an Application

The first step that you perform as a part of the Package and Deployment Wizard is to create a package that includes the setup files and other application files. The three types of packages that you can create using the Package and Deployment Wizard are:

- Disk-based installation packages
- Network-based installation packages
- Web-based installation packages

The same process packages all three types. During the packaging process, the Package and Deployment Wizard determines the set of files to be distributed as a part of the installation package.

8.2.1 Files to be Distributed with the Installation Package

 Explain the files that you need to distribute as a part of the setup package.

The first step in creating an installation package using the Package and Deployment Wizard is to identify the files to be distributed as a part of the package. There are three main types of files that are required to run and distribute an installation package. These files are:

- Run time files
- Setup files
- Application-specific files

Run Time Files

Run time files are files needed to run all applications created in Visual Basic. These run time files are:

- Msvbvm60.dll
- Stdole2.tlb
- Oleaut32.dll

- Olepro32.dll
- Comcat.dll
- Asyncfilt.dll
- Ctl3d32.dll

These run time files are needed if you are creating a disk-based or a network-based installation package. To create a Web-based installation package, the Package and Deployment Wizard includes only the msvbvm60.dll run time file. This is because the wizard assumes that any computer capable of downloading files from the Internet would already have the rest of the run time files.

Setup Files

Setup files are files needed to set up the packaged application on the computer of the end user. The setup files included with the package are:

- Setup.exe: Performs all preinstallation steps on the computer of the end user. The setup.exe file installs the required .DLL and run time files without which the installation cannot proceed.

- Setup1.exe: Installs the project that you create in Visual Basic. This is the main setup file to install the application.

- Setup.lst: Text file that contains a list of all files included as a part of the package and the instructions of how to install the package on the computer of the end user.

- St6unst.exe: File that enables the end user to remove the package from the computer.

The Package and Deployment Wizard creates the setup files only as a part of disk-based and network-based installation. For Web-based installation, these files are not needed.

Application-Specific Files

Application-specific files are files needed for the application to run, such as database files, executable files, and ActiveX controls. These files are also known as dependency files because the application is dependent on these files to run.

8.2.2 Creating an Installation Package

 Create a disk-based installation package.

To create an installation package:

1. Select **Start → Programs → Microsoft Visual Studio 6.0 → Microsoft Visual Studio 6.0 Tools → Package and Deployment Wizard**. The Package and Deployment Wizard opens, as shown in Figure 8.6.

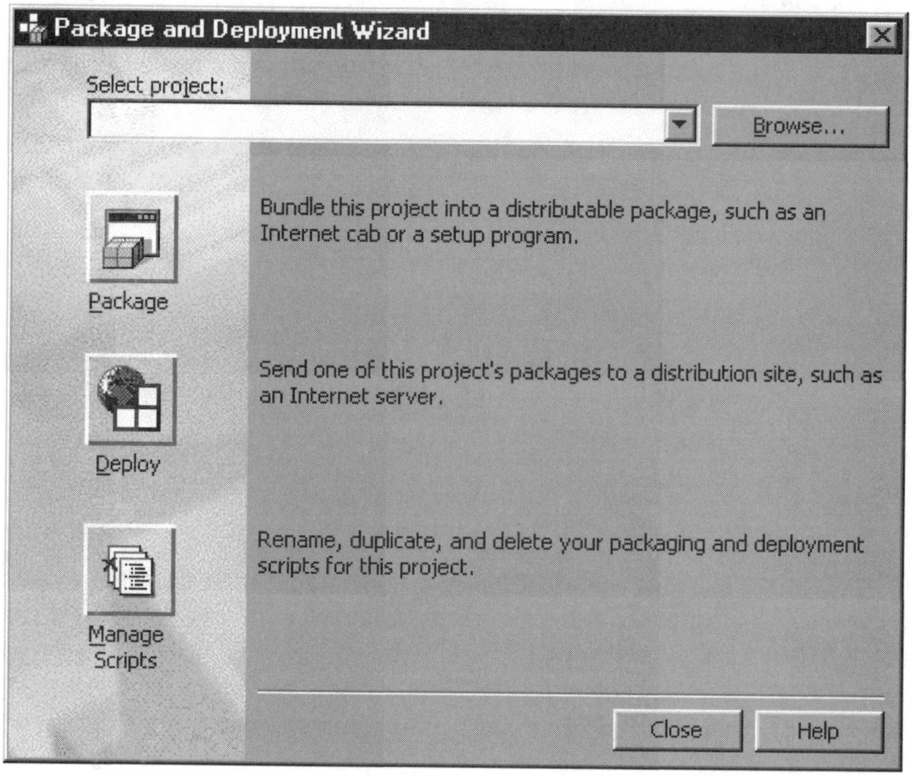

Figure 8.6: Package and Deployment Wizard

2. Click the Browse button, and select the project file that you need to package.

Figure 8.7 shows the selected Car Parking project.

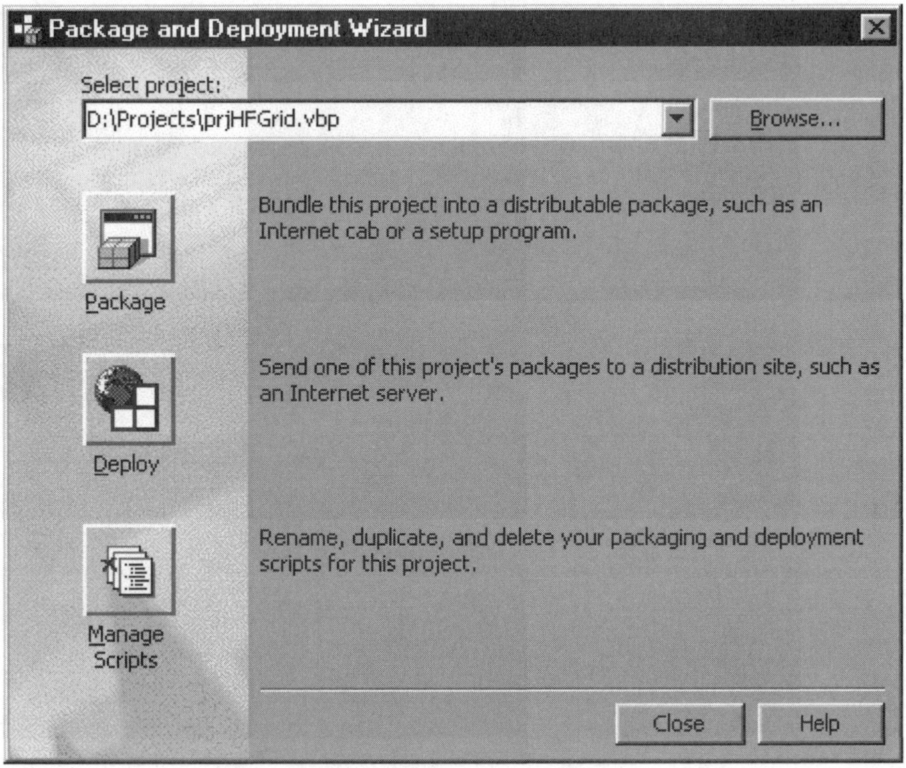

Figure 8.7: Visual Basic Project to Be Packaged

3.   Click the **Package** button to start the packaging process. If the wizard prompts
       for the compilation of the project, select **Compile**. The Package and
       Deployment Wizard determines the files to be included in the package. The
       wizard displays the Package Type dialog box where you select the type of
       package you need to create.

Figure 8.8 shows the Package Type dialog box.

![Package and Deployment Wizard - Package Type dialog box showing "Choose the type of package you want to create." with Package type list containing "Standard Setup Package" (highlighted) and "Dependency File", and a Description reading "Use to create a package that will be installed by a setup.exe program." Buttons: Help, Cancel, < Back, Next >, Finish.]

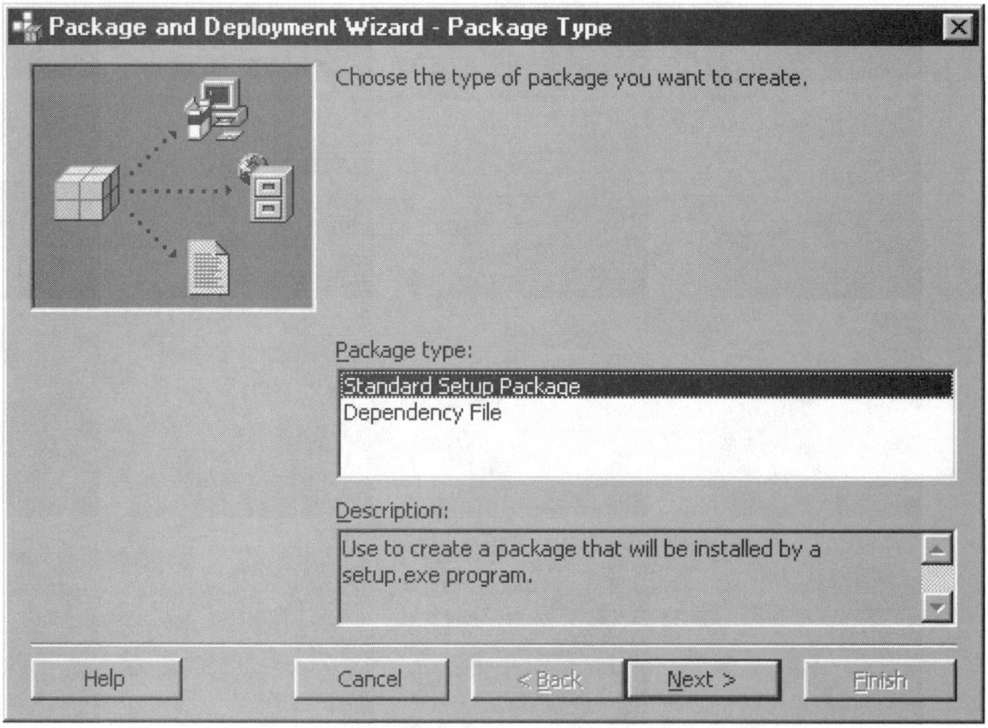

Figure 8.8: Package Type Dialog Box

4. Select the Standard Setup Package from the Package type list, and click **Next**. This creates a package with a setup.exe program that the end user uses to install the package.

Selecting the Dependency File option in the Package Type dialog box creates a file that stores information about all run time files required for the setup.

Figure 8.9 shows the Package Folder dialog box that appears when you select a package type and click **Next**. In this dialog box, you select the destination folder where you want the package to be assembled.

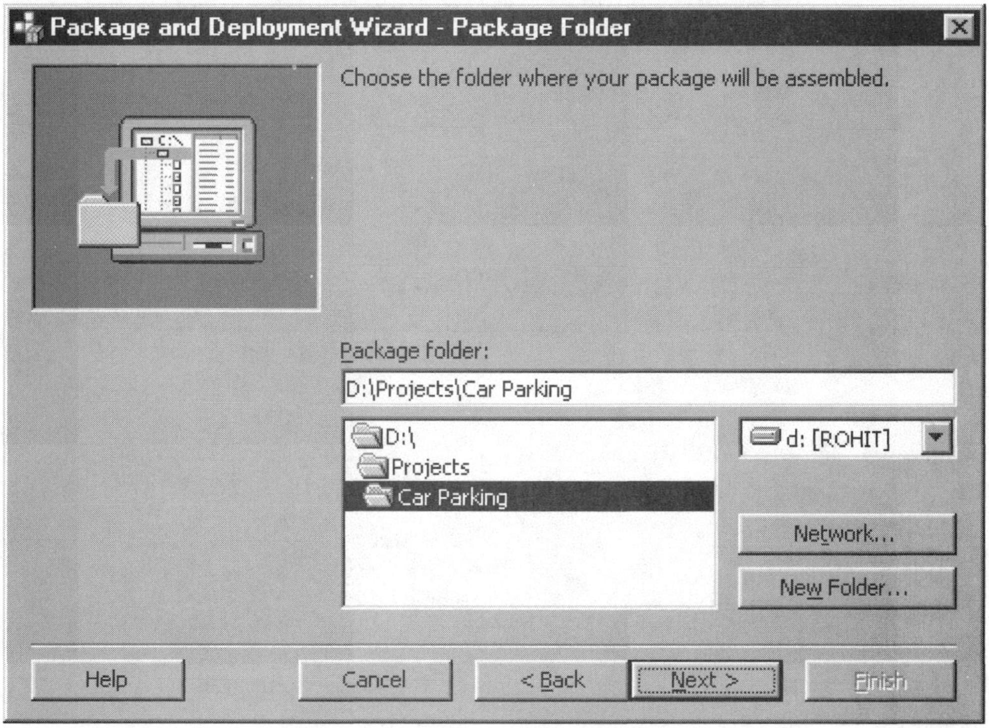

Figure 8.9: Package Folder Dialog Box

5.   Select the folder in which you want to assemble the package, and click **Next**. The **Included Files** dialog box, which shows the list of files to be included in your package, appears.

Figure 8.10 shows the **Included Files** dialog box.

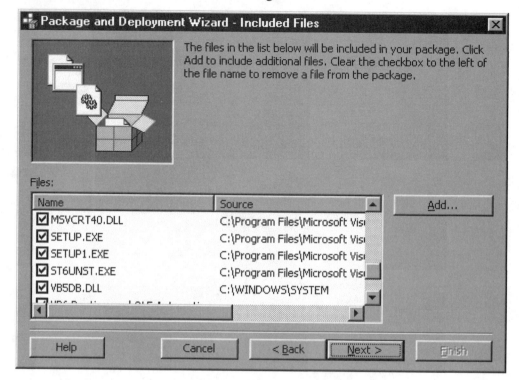

Figure 8.10: Included Files Dialog Box

 You can add more files to your installation package, such as data files, by clicking the Add button and selecting the files in the Included Files dialog box.

6.   Click **Next** in the **Included Files** dialog box. The **Cab Options** dialog box that enables you to select whether to create a single cab file or multiple cab files for the package appears. A cab file or a *cabinet* file is a type of compressed file created by the Package and Deployment Wizard. A cab file can contain multiple files needed for the installation package. To distribute your application on floppy disks, select the multiple cab files option and select the 1.44 MB option from the Cab size drop-down list.

File size may or may not be an issue when creating an installation package. For example, a high-speed connection can probably handle large cab files for a Web-based installation process. On the other hand, smaller files may be needed because of dial-up bandwidth restrictions or other hardware requirements.

Figure 8.11 shows the Cab Options dialog box.

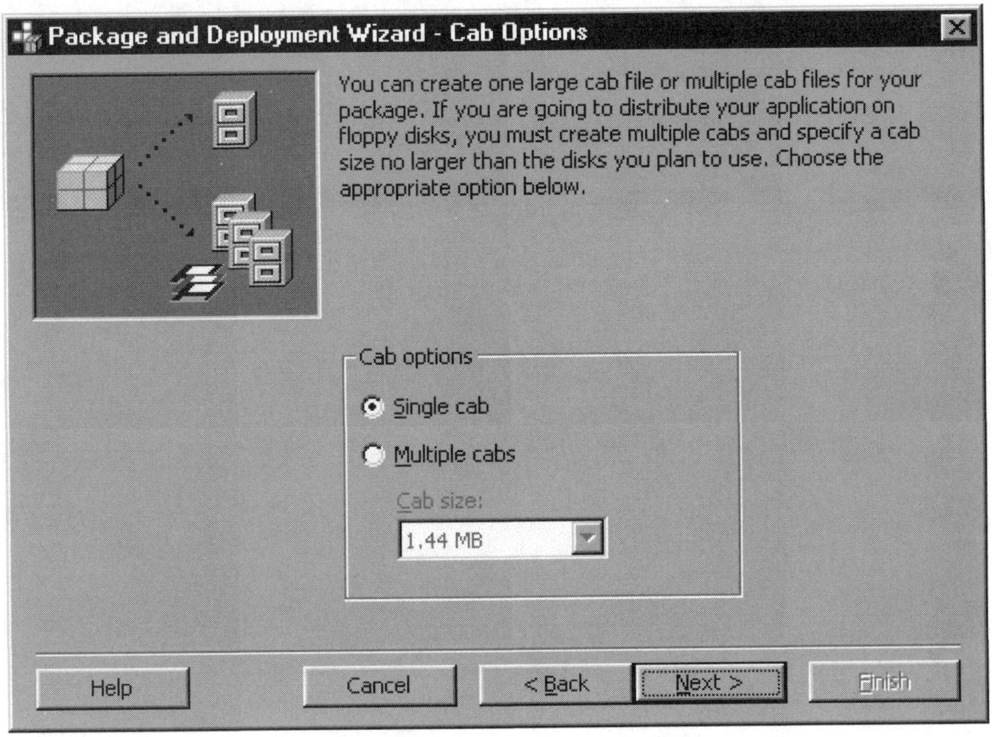

Package and Deployment Wizard - Cab Options

You can create one large cab file or multiple cab files for your package. If you are going to distribute your application on floppy disks, you must create multiple cabs and specify a cab size no larger than the disks you plan to use. Choose the appropriate option below.

Cab options
- ◉ Single cab
- ○ Multiple cabs

Cab size:
1.44 MB

| Help | Cancel | < Back | Next > | Finish |

Figure 8.11: Cab Options Dialog Box

7.   Select the Single cab option, and click **Next**. The Installation Title dialog box, where you specify a title for the application, appears. The setup program displays this title during the installation process on the computer of the end user.

Figure 8.12 shows the Installation Title dialog box.

![Package and Deployment Wizard - Installation Title dialog box. Enter the title to be displayed when the setup program is run. Installation title: Project1. Buttons: Help, Cancel, < Back, Next >, Finish]

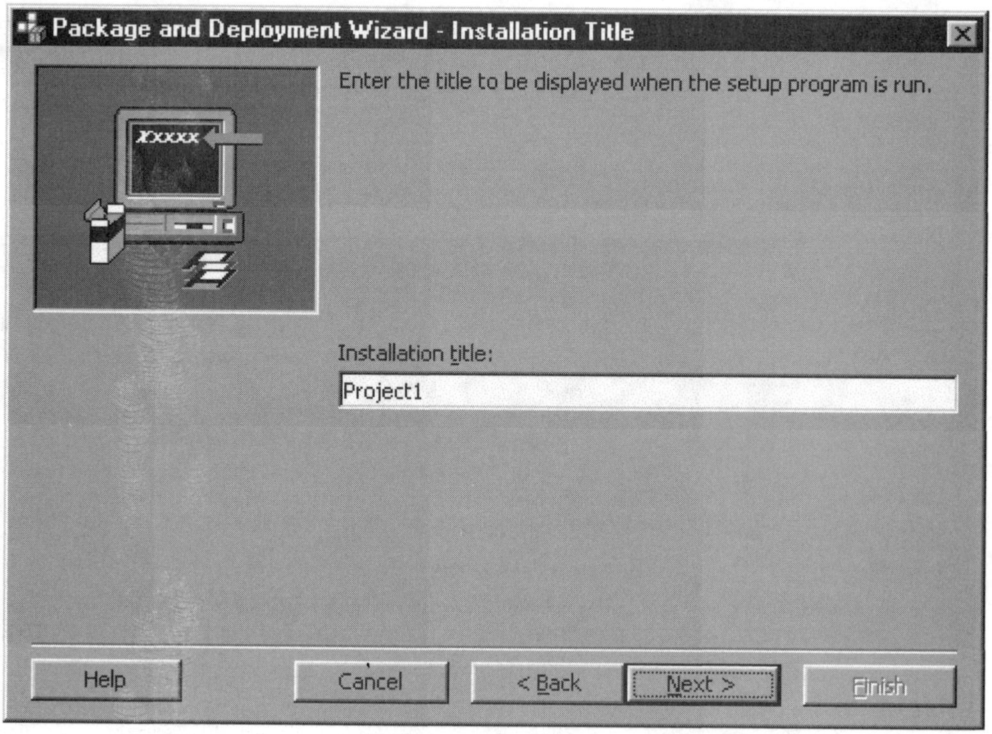

Figure 8.12: Installation Title Dialog Box

8.   Enter Car Parking Application in the Installation title text box, and click **Next**.
        The Start Menu Items dialog box that enables you to specify the items and
        groups that the setup program should add on the Start menu appears.

 By default the setup program creates one group with a single item on the Programs
menu by the name of your installation title. You can add or remove the groups or
items as required.

Figure 8.13 shows the Start Menu Items dialog box.

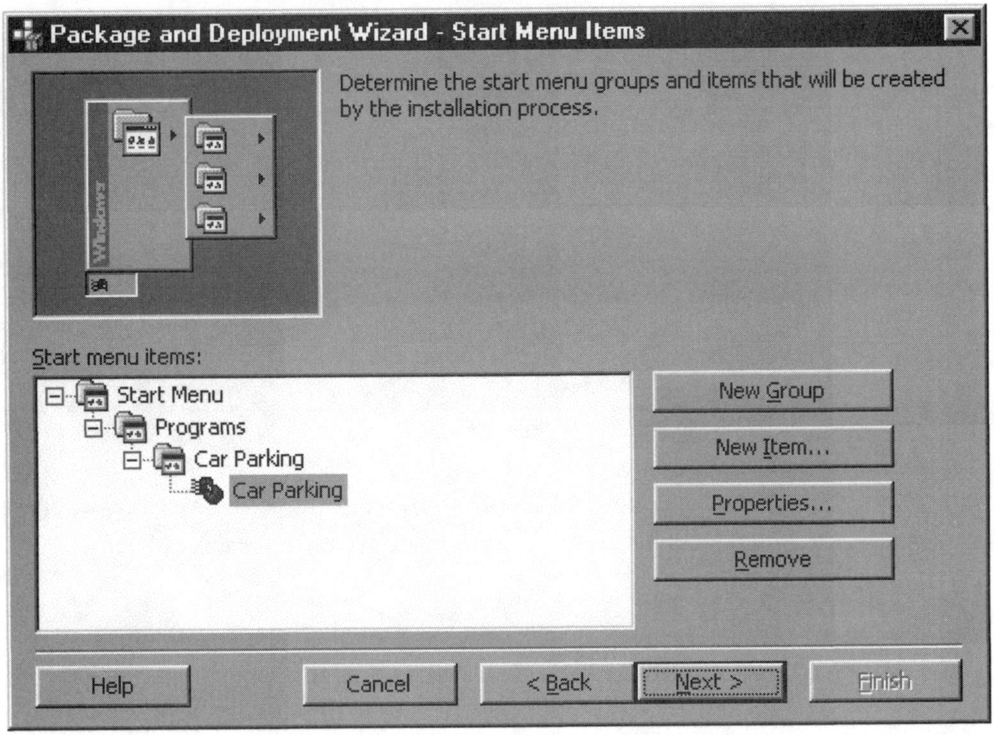

Figure 8.13: Start Menu Items Dialog Box

9.   Click **Next** in the Start Menu Items dialog box to accept the default group and item. The Install Location dialog box that displays the locations where each file of the installation package would be saved when the end user installs the program appears.

Figure 8.14 shows the Install Locations dialog box.

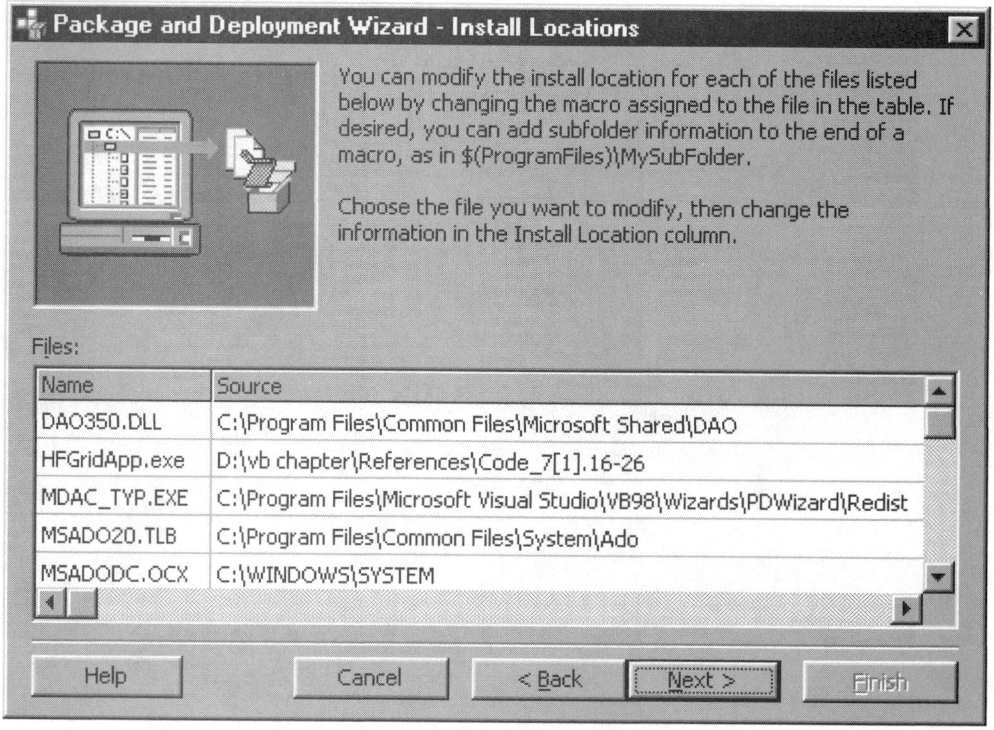

Figure 8.14: Install Locations Dialog Box

10. Click **Next** in the Install Location dialog box to accept the default locations specified by the Package and Deployment Wizard. The Shared Files dialog box that enables you to specify whether any file of the setup package can be shared by multiple programs appears. You typically share ActiveX controls that you create as a part of your application.

Figure 8.15 shows the Shared Files dialog box.

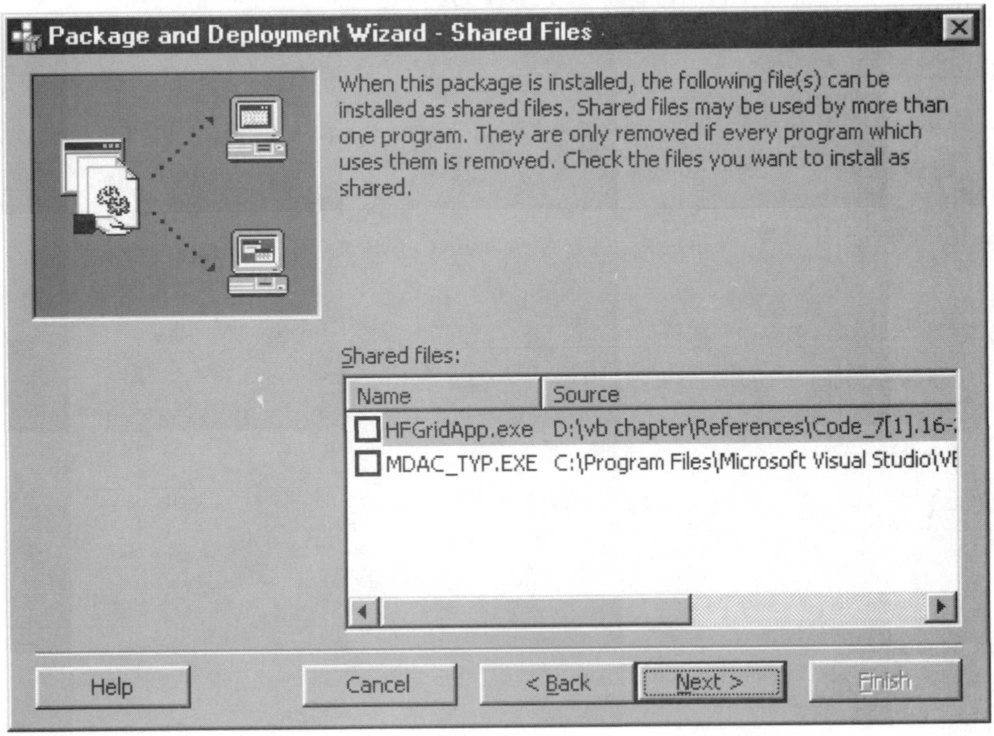

Figure 8.15: Shared Files Dialog Box

11. Click **Next** in the Shared Files dialog box. The Finished dialog box appears. Specify the setup script name in this box. The setup script saves all the settings from the previous dialog boxes while packaging a Visual Basic program. You can use this script to recreate the installation routine whenever required. Specify the name of the setup script as Car Parking Script in the Script name text box, and click the Finish button. The Package and Deployment Wizard starts creating the cab files and packaging your program.

After the Package and Deployment Wizard completes creating the package, it returns to the first page of the Package and Deployment Wizard.

1. Specify the three main types of files required to run and distribute an installation package.

2. State why it is preferable to create multiple CAB files rather than a single CAB file for a Web-based installation package.

3. Identify the run time file that the Package and Deployment Wizard includes in a Web-based installation package.

4. Identify the setup file that enables an end user to remove the package from the computer.

5. Identify the type of installation package for which the Package and Deployment Wizard does not create setup files.

8.3 Deploying an Application

After creating an installation package, the next step in the Packaging and Deployment process is to distribute or deploy the package. The deployment process depends on the distribution media, which can be CD-ROMs, floppy disks, networks, or the Internet.

8.3.1 Disk-Based Deployment

 Deploy an installation package over physical media, such as floppy disks and CD-ROMs.

To deploy the package over floppy disks and CD-ROMs:

1.   Click the **Deploy** button on the Package and Deployment Wizard. The Package to Deploy dialog box appears where you select the package that you need to deploy.

Figure 8.16 shows the Package to Deploy dialog box.

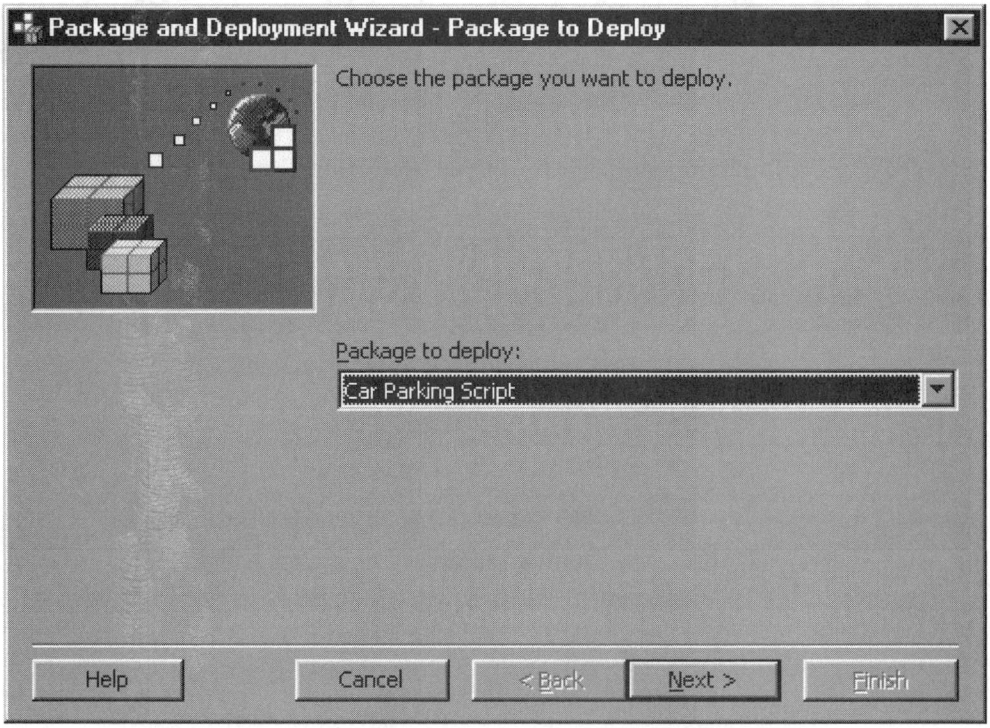

Figure 8.16: Package to Deploy Dialog Box

2. Click **Next** to accept the default selection. The Deployment Method dialog
    box appears. You select the method for deploying the package.

Figure 8.17 shows the Deployment Method dialog box.

Package and Deployment Wizard - Deployment Method ⊠

Choose the type of deployment you want to perform.

Deployment method:

Floppy Disks
Folder
Web Publishing

Description:

Use to distribute a package to multiple floppy disks.

| Help | | Cancel | < Back | Next > | Finish |

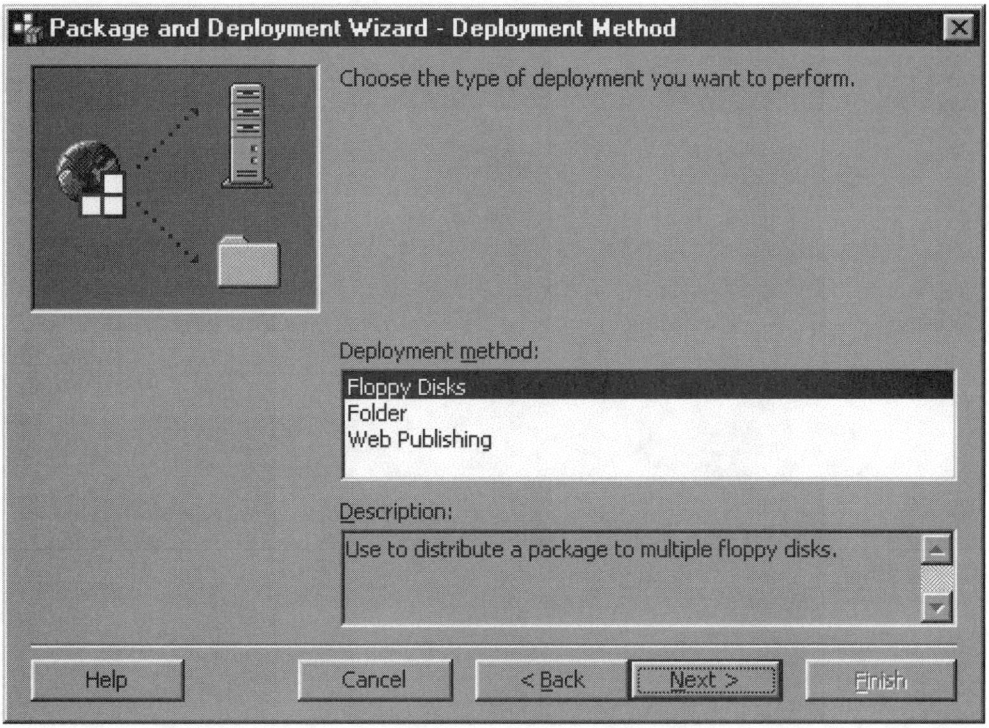

Figure 8.17: Deployment Method Dialog Box

 The Floppy Disks option in the Deployment Method list box is available only if you select the multiple cab option of 1.44 MB or less while packaging the application.

3.   Select the Floppy Disks option from the Deployment method list, and click **Next**. The Floppy Drive dialog box, where you select the floppy disk drive to deploy the package appears. The dialog box also provides the option to format the floppy disks before copying files.

Figure 8.18 shows the Floppy Drive dialog box.

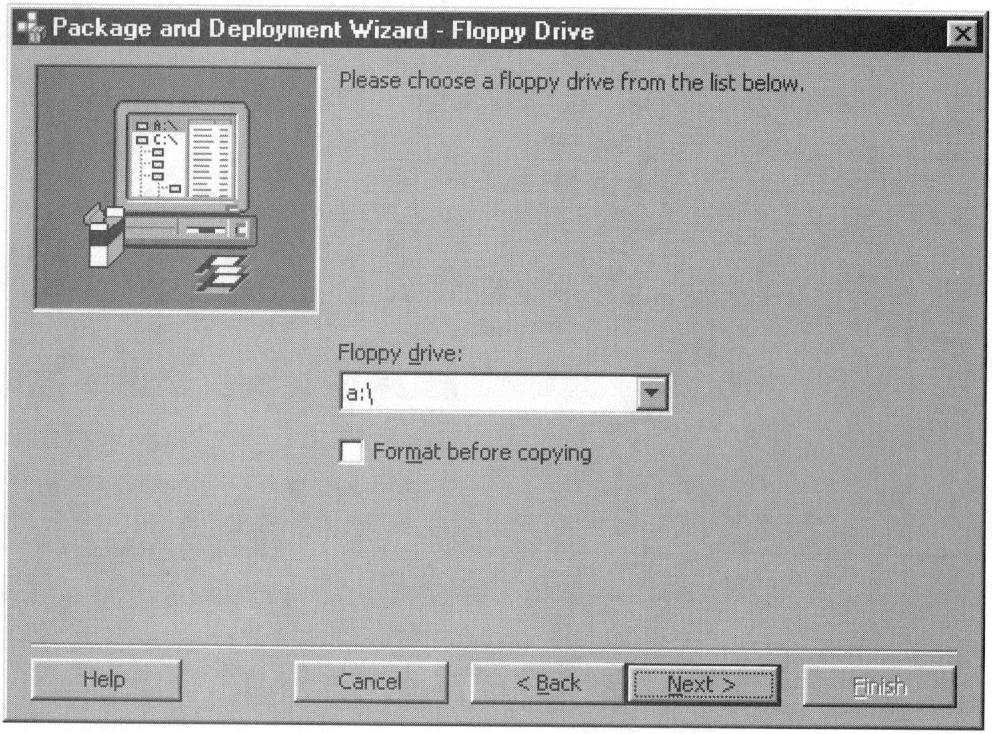

Figure 8.18: Floppy Drive Dialog Box

4. Select the floppy disk drive from the Floppy drive drop-down list, and click **Next**. The Finished dialog box, which is the final screen of the deployment process, appears.

Figure 8.19 shows the Finished dialog box.

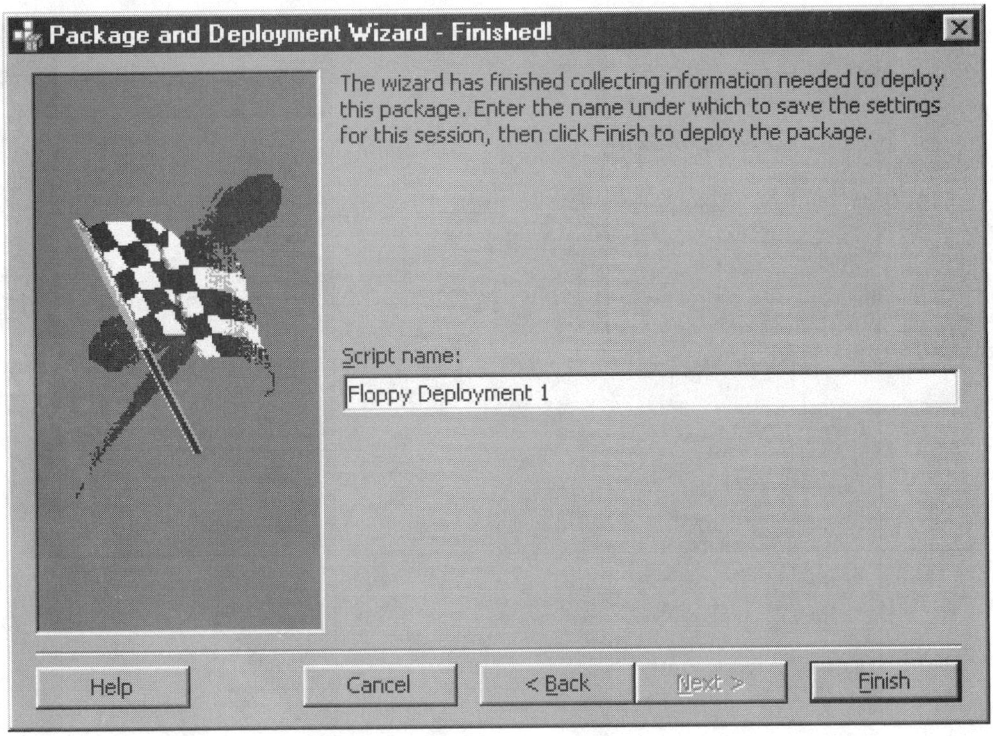

Figure 8.19: Finished Dialog Box

5. Specify Car Parking deploy in the Script name text box, and click **Finish**. The deployment settings for the Car Parking package are saved in this script. The Package and Deployment Wizard start the deployment process by prompting you to insert the floppy disk in the floppy drive.

Figure 8.20 shows the message box that prompts for the floppy disk.

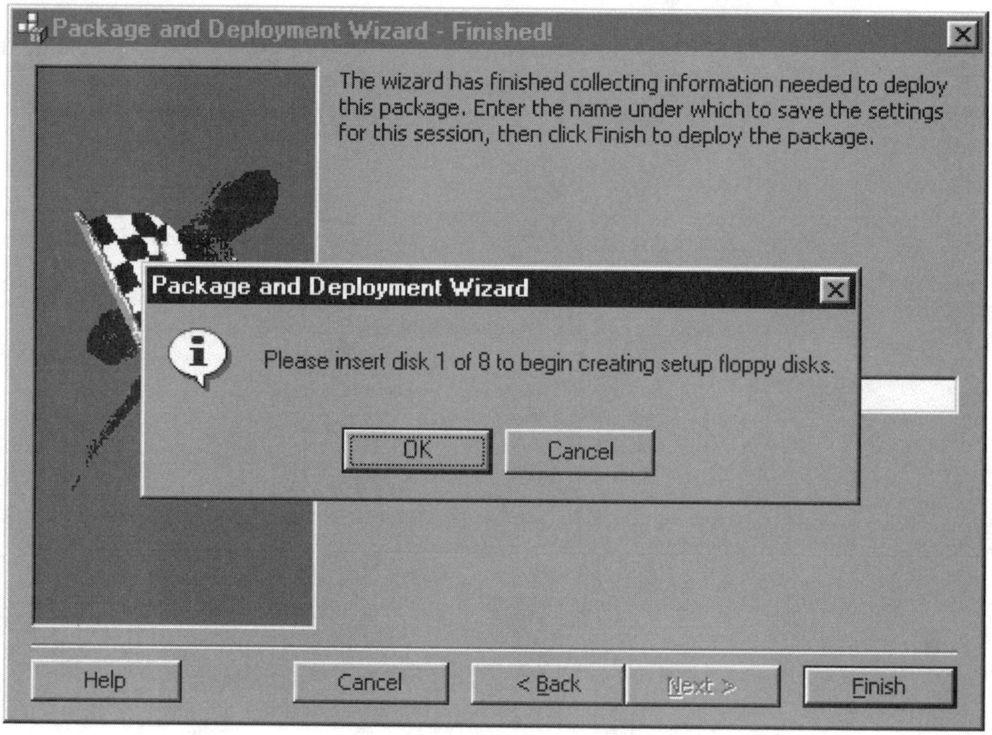

Figure 8.20: Prompting for the Floppy Disk

8.3.2 Network-Based Deployment

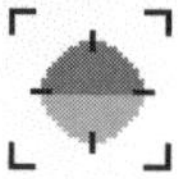

Deploy an installation package on the network.

In a network-based deployment, the installation package is deployed on the network from where it is accessible to all client computers on the network. It enables the end users to run the setup process from the client computer on the network and saves the time required to run the setup process separately using floppy disks.

To deploy the Car Parking installation package on the network:

1. Click the Deploy button on the Package and Deployment Wizard. The Package to Deploy dialog box where you select the package that you need to deploy appears.

2. Select the Car Parking package, and click **Next**. The Deployment Method dialog box where you select the method for deploying the package appears.

3. Select the Folder option from the Deployment methods list, and click **Next**. The Folder dialog box where you select the location on the network to deploy the installation package appears, as shown in Figure 8.21.

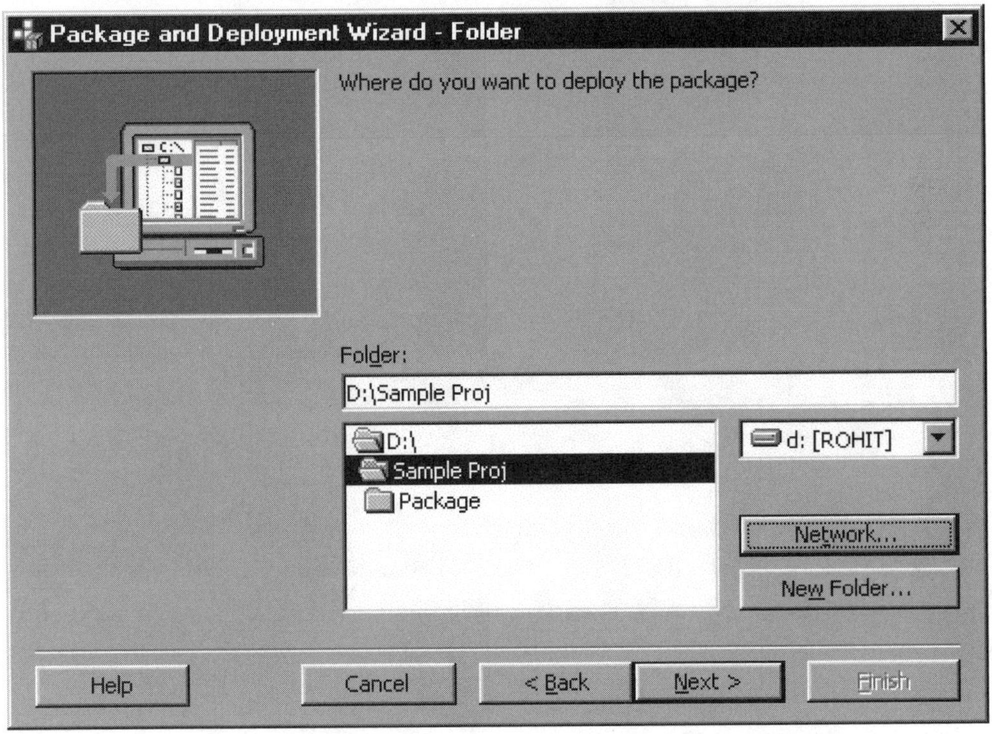

Figure 8.21: Folder Dialog Box

4. Click the **Network** button in the Folder dialog box to open the Browse for Folder dialog box. You use this dialog box to select the computer on the network where you want to deploy the package.

Figure 8.22 shows the Browse for Folder dialog box.

Browse for Folder

Network Folder

- Network Neighborhood
  - Entire Network

ROHIT]

work...

Folder...

OK   Cancel

Help   Finish

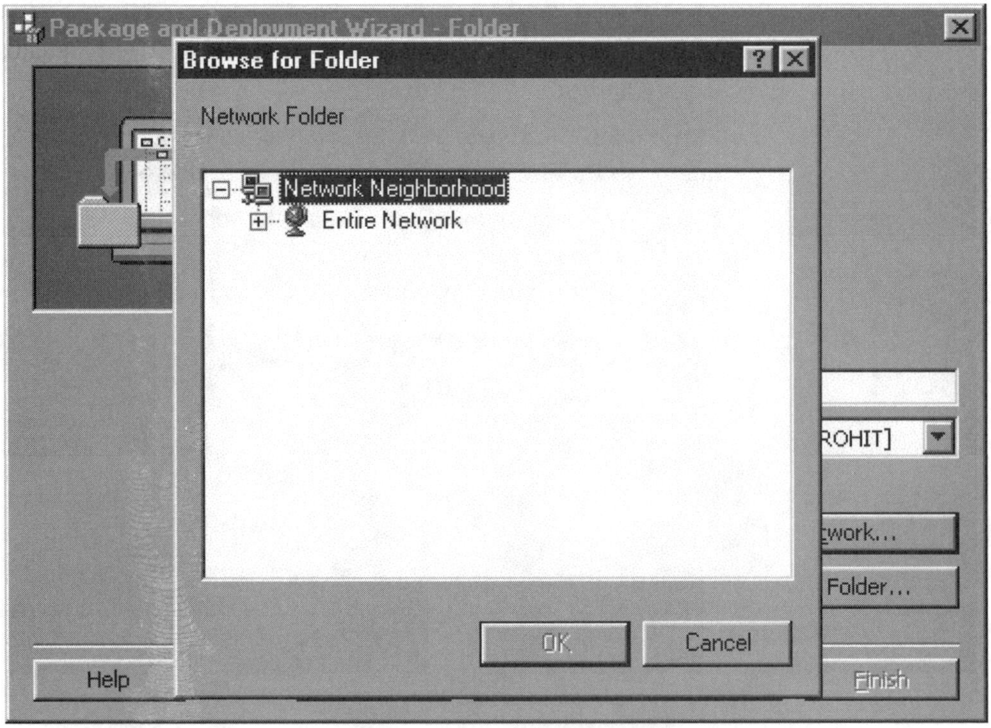

Figure 8.22: Browse for Folder Dialog Box

5. Select the computer and the folder on the network where you want to deploy the package. Click **OK**. You return to the Folder dialog box.

6. Click **Next** in the Folder dialog box. The Finished dialog box appears. Specify the script name for storing the deployment settings. Click **Finish** to deploy the package in the specified shared folder on the network.

8.3.3 Web-Based Deployment

Deploy an installation package on the Internet.

In the Web-based deployment method, the Package and Deployment Wizard deploys the package on the Internet. Multiple Cabinet (.cab) files are created using this method.

This enables end users to download and install the package from remote locations. Another advantage of the Web-based deployment method is that it enables you to instantly provide the latest version of the package or any other updates to end users.

To deploy the package on the Internet:

1.   Click the **Deploy** button on the Package and Deployment Wizard.

2.   Select the Car Parking package. Click **Next** in the Package to Deploy dialog box.

3.   Select the Web Publishing option from the Deployment method list in the Deployment Method dialog box. Click **Next**. The Items to Deploy dialog box where you select the files that you want to deploy on the Internet appears. The list of files includes the setup.exe, setup.lst, and cab files of the package. Figure 8.23 shows the Items to Deploy dialog box.

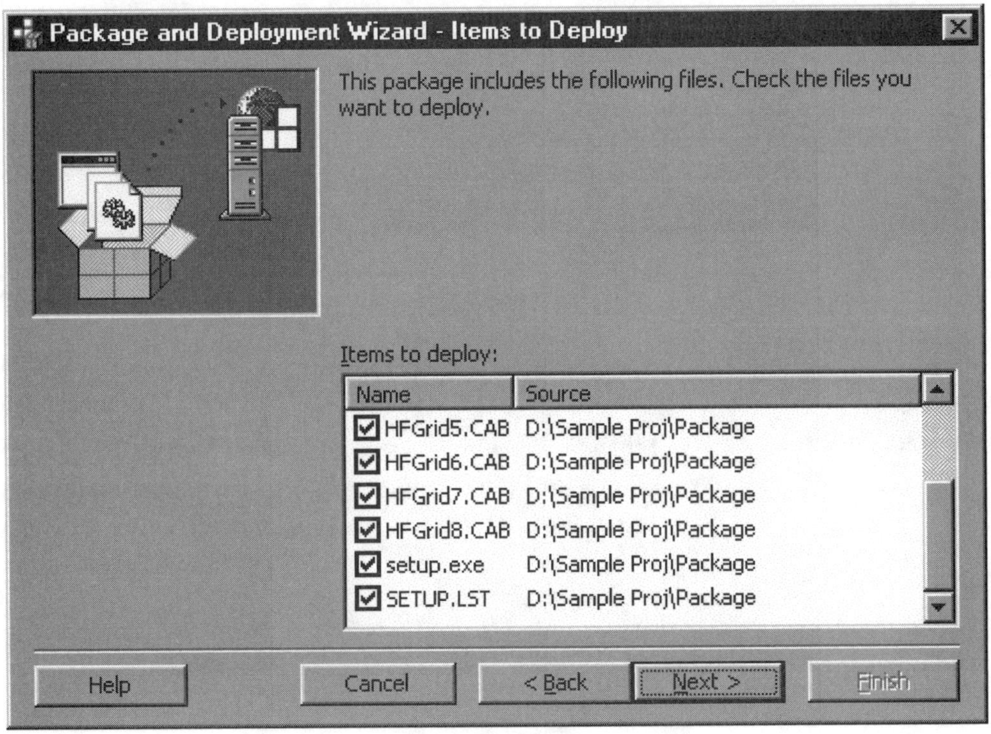

Figure 8.23: Items to Deploy Dialog Box

4.   Click **Next** to accept the default file selection. The Additional Items to Deploy dialog box appears. You can select the additional files that you want to

deploy, such as Web pages or graphic files from this dialog box. Figure 8.24 shows the Additional Items to Deploy dialog box.

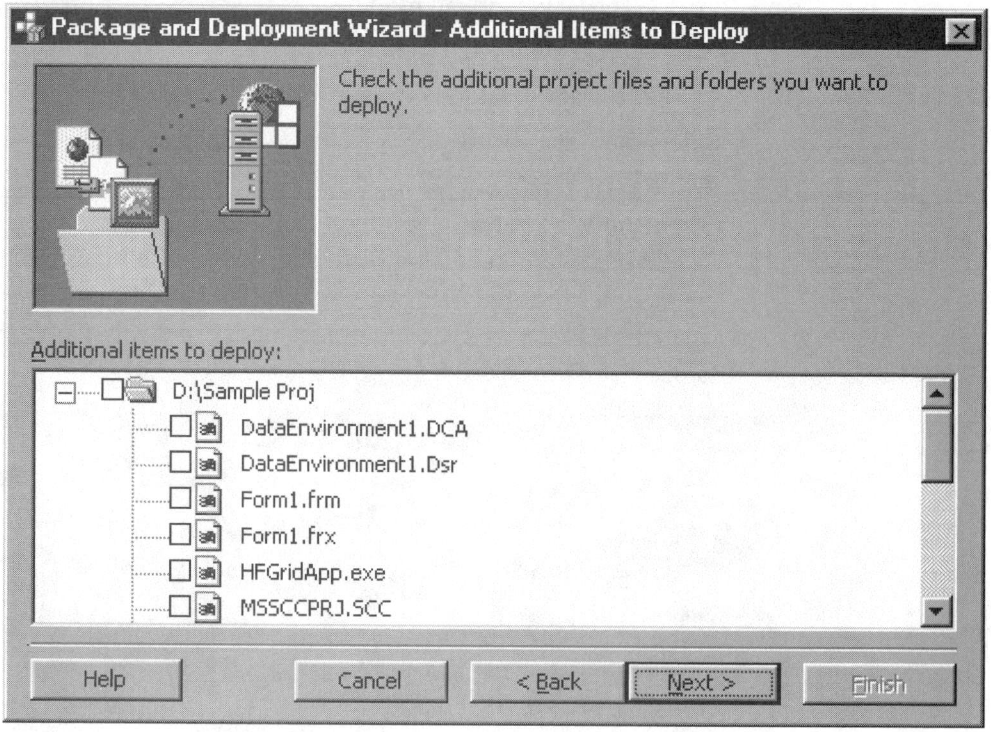

Figure 8.24: Additional Items to Deploy Dialog Box

5.   Select the relevant check boxes to select additional files to deploy. Click **Next**. The Web Publishing Site dialog box where you specify the URL of the Web site to deploy the application appears. In addition, you select the Web publishing protocol for file transfer. You can select either HTTP post or FTP as the publishing protocol.

Figure 8.25 shows the Web Publishing Site dialog box.

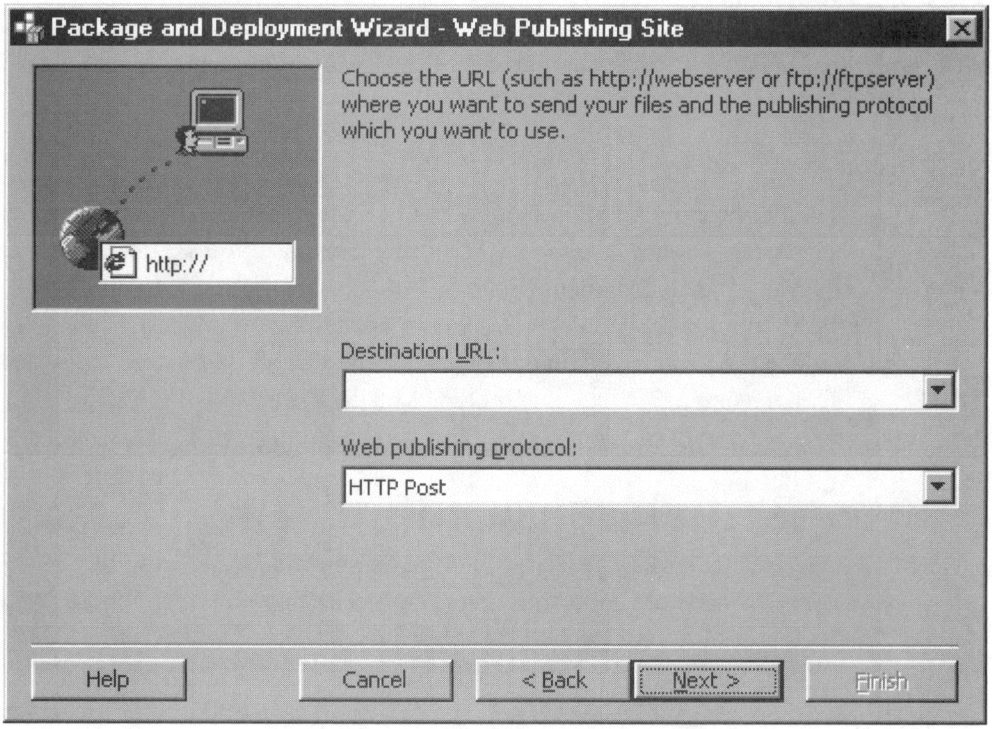

Figure 8.25: Web Publishing Site Dialog Box

6.   Specify www.carparkingproject.com in the Destination URL text box, and click **Next**. The Finished dialog box where you specify the name of the script that stores the deployment settings appears.

7.   Specify the name of the deployment script and click **Finish** to deploy the installation package to the specified URL on the Web.

During the Web-based deployment process, you may be prompted to specify the user name and password of the Web server where you are deploying files.

8.3.4 Managing Scripts

 Manage the scripts created by the Package and Deployment Wizard.

The Package and Deployment Wizard creates a separate script for the packaging and deploying process. These scripts store the settings you selected while running the Package and Deployment Process. You can use the script to apply these settings again while running the Package and Deployment Wizard on similar projects. This helps reduce time and maintain consistency. You can view, rename, copy, and delete the scripts using the Package and Deployment Wizard.

To rename the Car Parking script for the deployment process of the Car Parking application:

1. Click the **Manage Scripts** button on the Package and Deployment Wizard. The Manage Script dialog box appears. This dialog box enables you to rename, copy, and delete the packaging and deployment scripts.

Figure 8.26 shows the Manage Scripts dialog box.

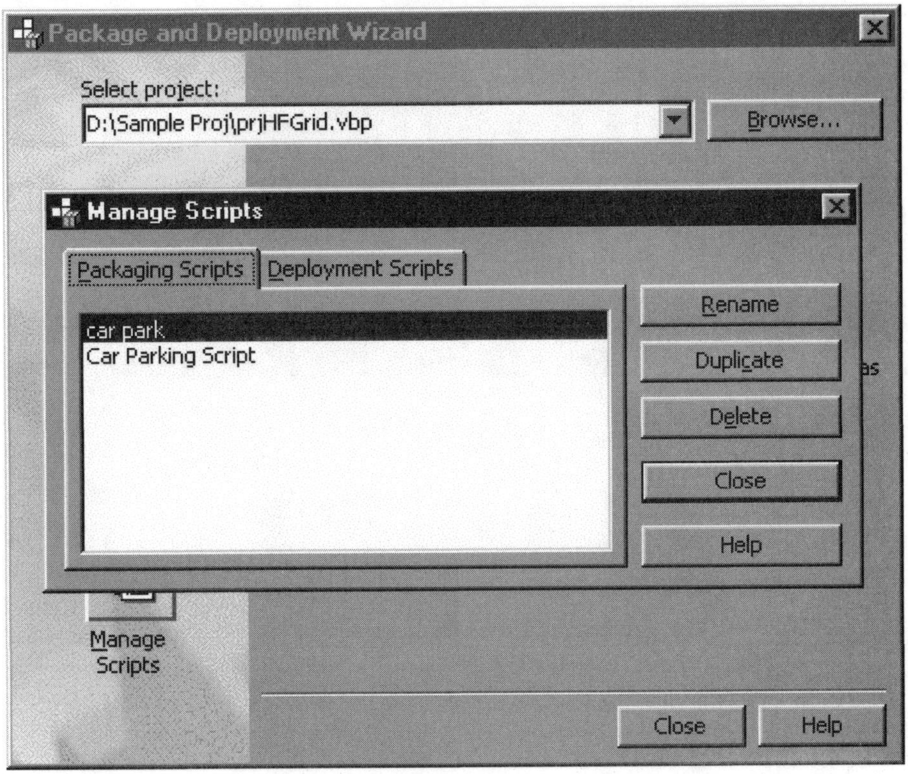

Figure 8.26: Manage Scripts Dialog Box

2. Select the Deployment Scripts tab in the Manage Scripts dialog box, as shown in Figure 8.27.

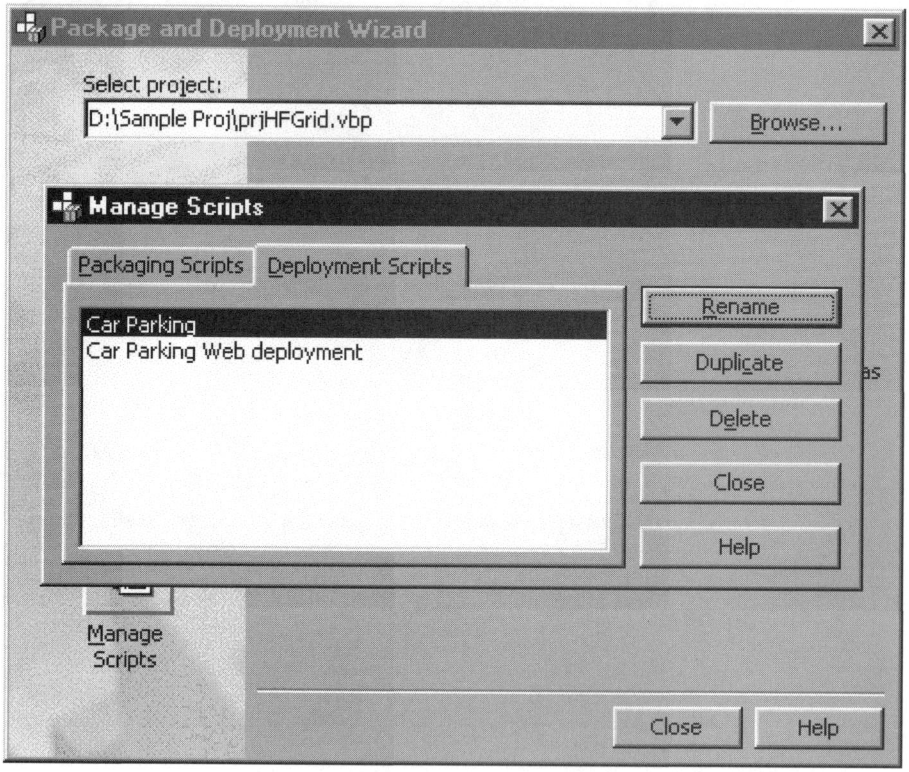

Package and Deployment Wizard

Select project:

D:\Sample Proj\prjHFGrid.vbp   ▼   Browse...

Manage Scripts

Packaging Scripts | Deployment Scripts

Car Parking
Car Parking Web deployment

Rename
Duplicate
Delete
Close
Help

Manage
Scripts

Close   Help

Figure 8.27: Deployment Scripts Tab

3. Click the **Rename** button to rename the Car Parking deployment script.

4. Type Car Parking Floppy Deployment as the name of the script, and click **OK**.

5. Click **Close** in the Manage Scripts dialog box.

If you delete a packaging script, the Package and Deployment Wizard would not be able to deploy that package. You need to repackage the script to deploy it using the Package and Deployment Wizard.

1. What are the different types of deployment provided by the Package and Deployment Wizard? Mention the features of each of them.

2. Which deployment method is not made available by the Package and Deployment Wizard when you select the single cab option while creating an installation package? Why?

3. Specify the publishing protocol that the Package and Deployment Wizard provides for the Web-based deployment.

4. What is a script?

5. What are the advantages of having a Managing Scripts option in the Package and Deployment Wizard?

Case Study

Having finished with writing the code of the Library Management System in the previous section, this section creates and deploys the Installation package for the application. This is the last step of the entire design and development phase of the system where the application will be made available to the client for implementation.

1.   Open the LibraryMgmt project.

2.   Select Package and Deployment Wizard from the Add-Ins menu on the menu bar. The Package and Deployment Wizard dialog box appears, as shown in Figure 8.28:

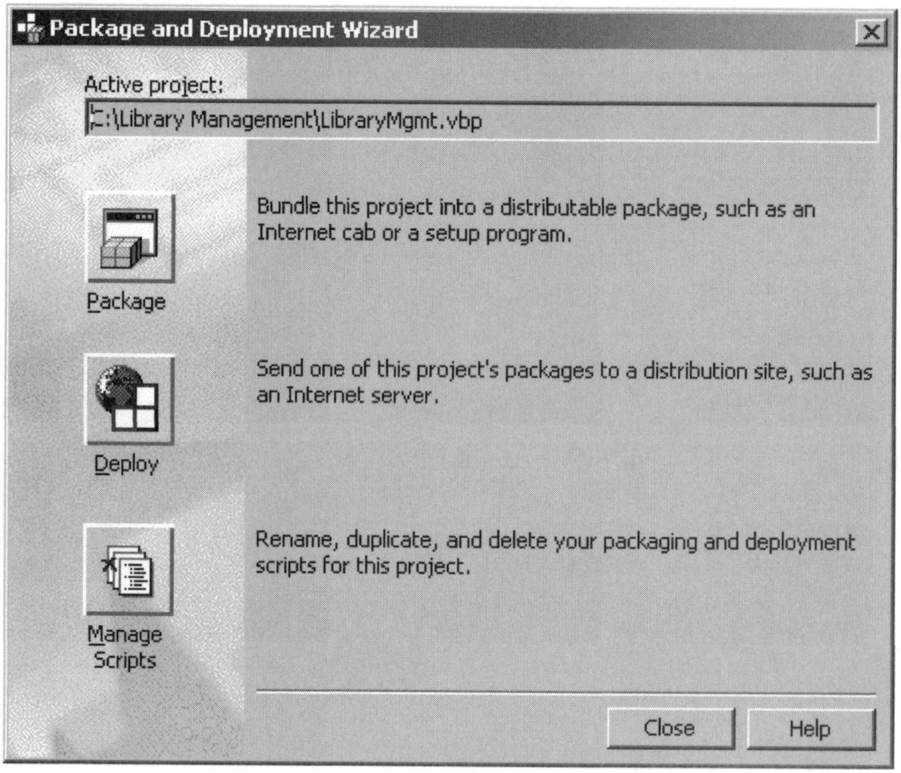

Figure 8.28: Package and Development Wizard

3.   Click the Package button to start the creation of the Installation package. If the wizard displays the following pop-up box prompting compilation of the project, select the Compile button, as shown in Figure 8.29.

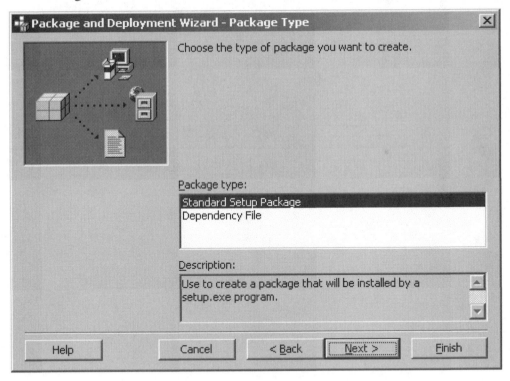

Figure 8.29: Pop-up Box Prompting Compilation

4.   Select the Standard Setup Package in the Package Type dialog box, as shown in Figure 8.30.

Figure 8.30: Package and Development Wizard Dialog Box

5.   Click **Next.** The Package Folder dialog box appears. Choose the folder location, and click **Next**. If the folder does not exist, the wizard asks to create the specified folder, as shown in Figure 8.31.

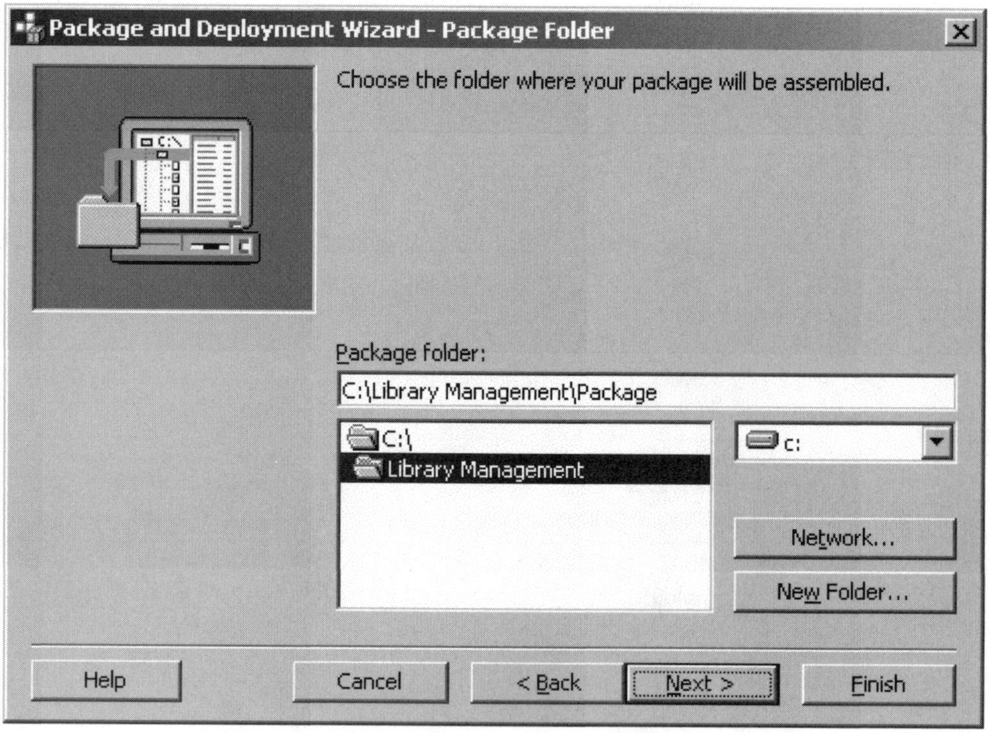

Figure 8.31: Package Folder Dialog Box

6.   Click **Yes.** The Included Files dialog box that displays the list of files to be included in the installation package appears. Click the **Add** button to add the LibraryMgmt.mdb database file to the package. Figure 8.32 shows the Included Files dialog box after adding the database file. Click **Next** after adding the file.

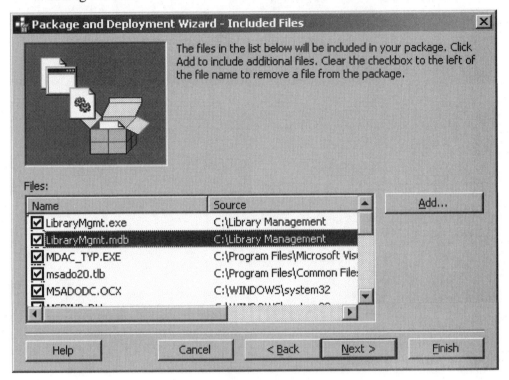

Figure 8.32: Included File Dialog Box

7. Select Multiple Cabs option with the cab size of 1.44 MB in the Cab Options dialog box, as shown in Figure 8.33. Click **Next**.

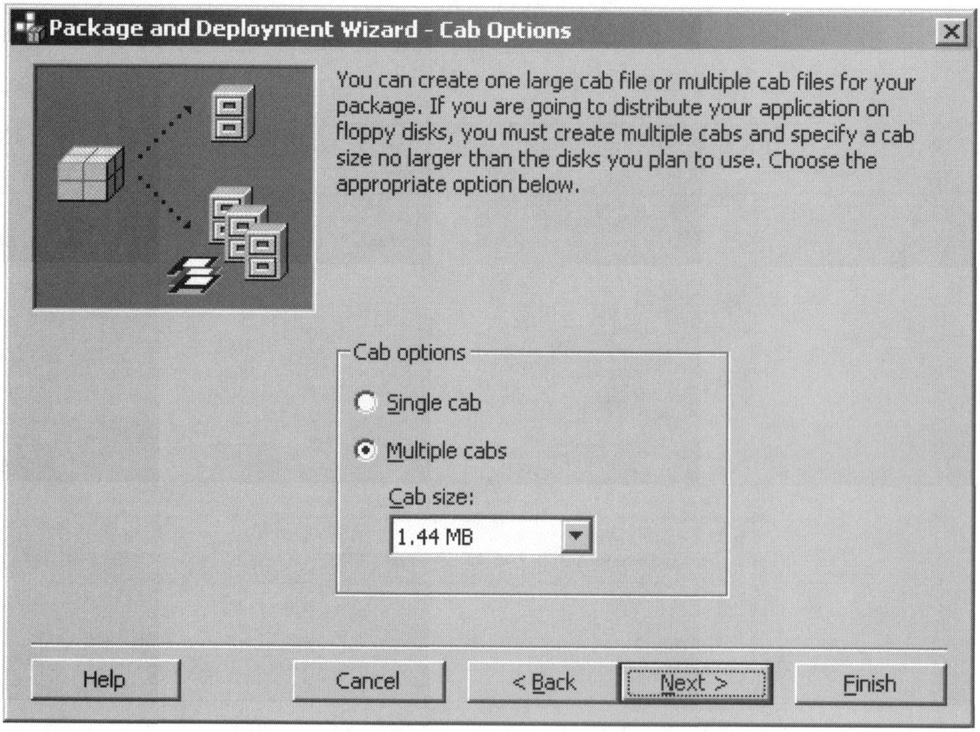

Figure 8.33: Cab Options Dialog Box

8.   The Installation Title dialog box appears, as shown in Figure 8.34. Specify the title as Library Management, and click **Next**.

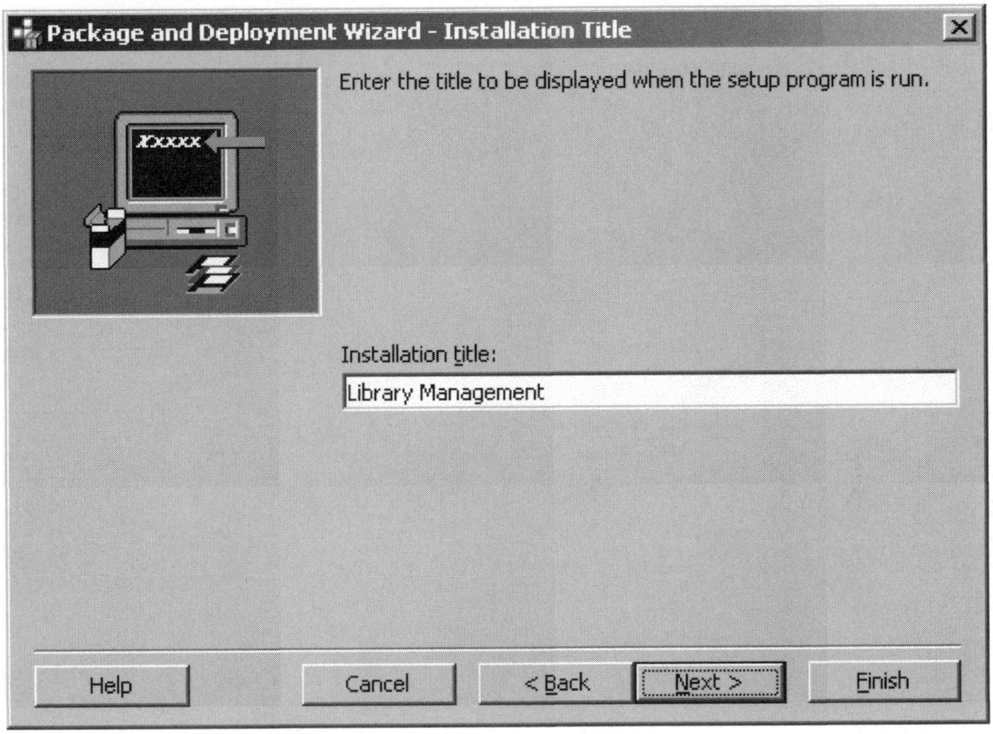

Figure 8.34: Installation Title Dialog Box

9.   The Start Menu Item dialog box appears. Specify the Start Menu Items, as shown in Figure 8.35. Click **Next** to accept the default specification.

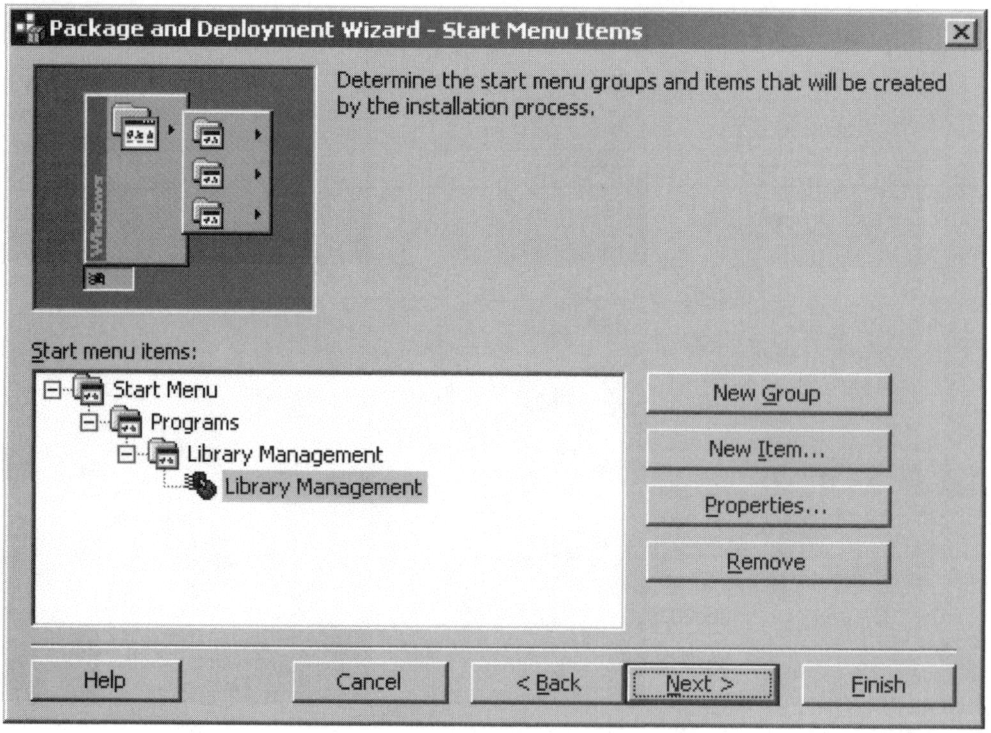

Figure 8.35: Start Menu Item Dialog Box

10.   The Install Locations dialog box that lists the files in the installation package and their respective install locations appears, as shown in Figure 8.36. Ensure that the database file named LibraryMgmt.mdb has the install location as the application path. Click **Next**.

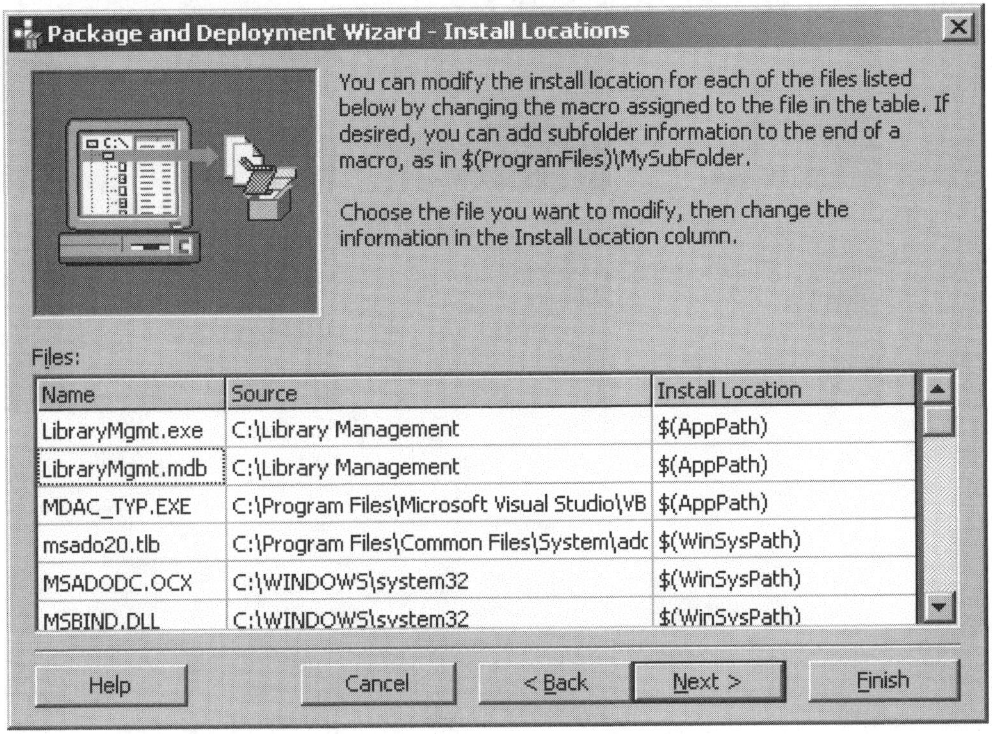

Name	Source	Install Location
LibraryMgmt.exe	C:\Library Management	$(AppPath)
LibraryMgmt.mdb	C:\Library Management	$(AppPath)
MDAC_TYP.EXE	C:\Program Files\Microsoft Visual Studio\VB	$(AppPath)
msado20.tlb	C:\Program Files\Common Files\System\adc	$(WinSysPath)
MSADODC.OCX	C:\WINDOWS\system32	$(WinSysPath)
MSBIND.DLL	C:\WINDOWS\system32	$(WinSysPath)

Figure 8.36: Install Location Dialog Box

11.   The Shared Files dialog box where you specify shared files, if any, appears as shown in Figure 8.37. None of the files in the Library application is to be used as shared. Therefore, click **Next**.

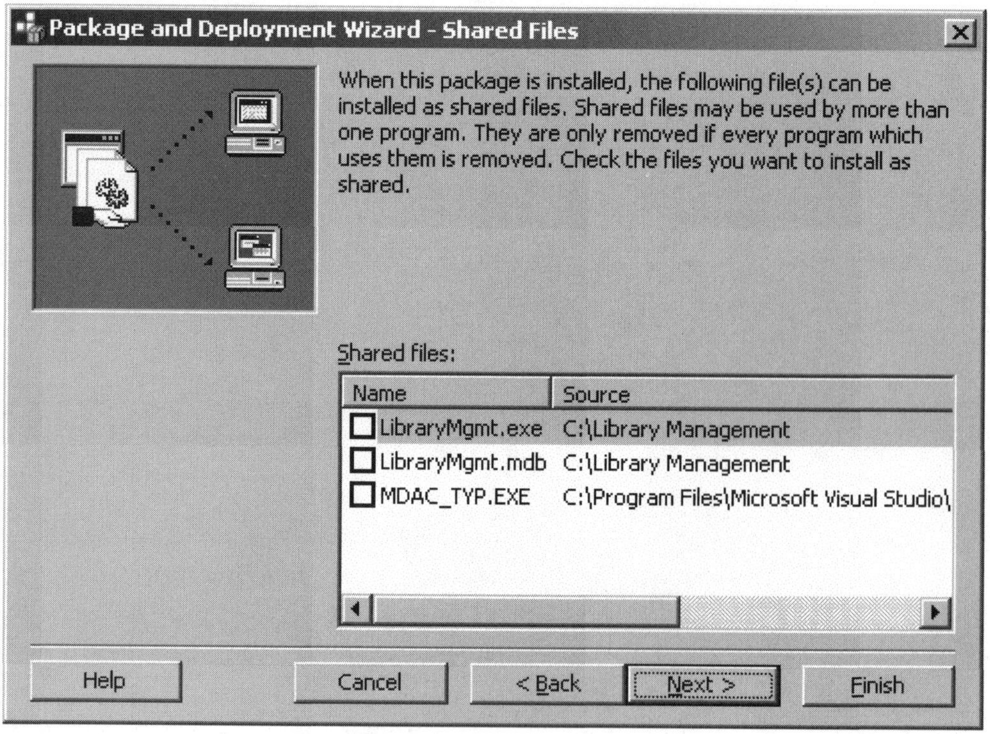

Figure 8.37: Shared Files Dialog Box

12. Specify the name of the script as Library Management Package in the final step of the wizard shown in Figure 8.38. Click **Finish** to create the Installation package. The wizard finishes the task displaying a report of the task being performed.

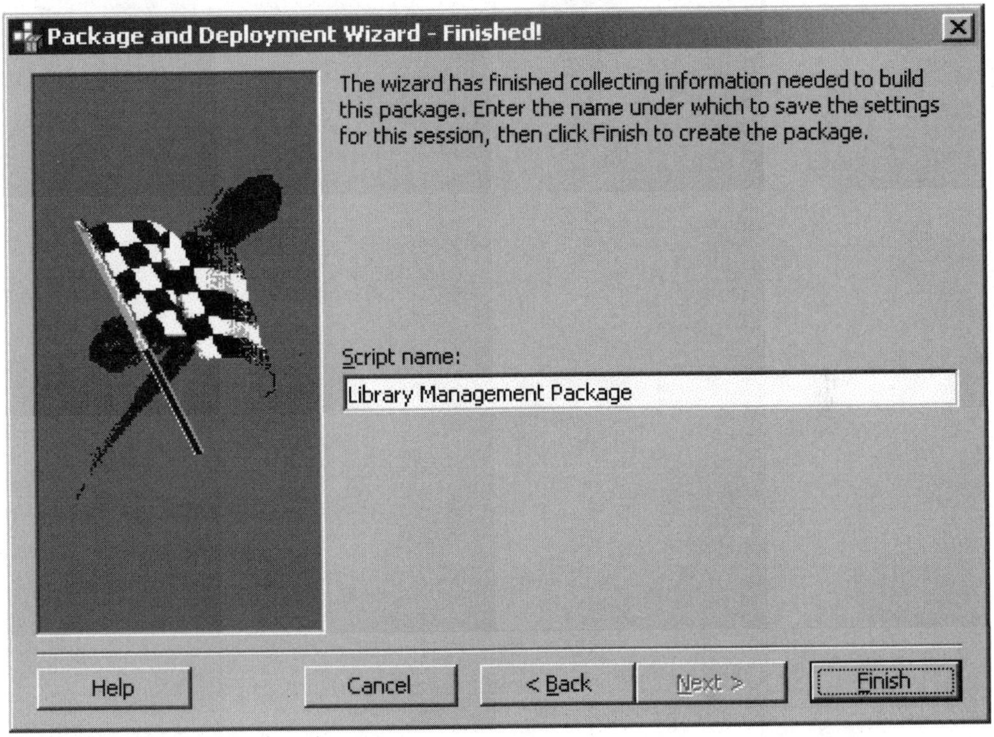

Figure 8.38: Script Name Dialog Box

13. Click **Close** to return to the initial dialog box of the Package and Deployment Wizard.

14. Click the **Deploy** button to deploy the installation package.

15. Specify the name of the Deployment script as Library Management Folder Deployment in the first step of deployment, as shown in Figure 8.39.

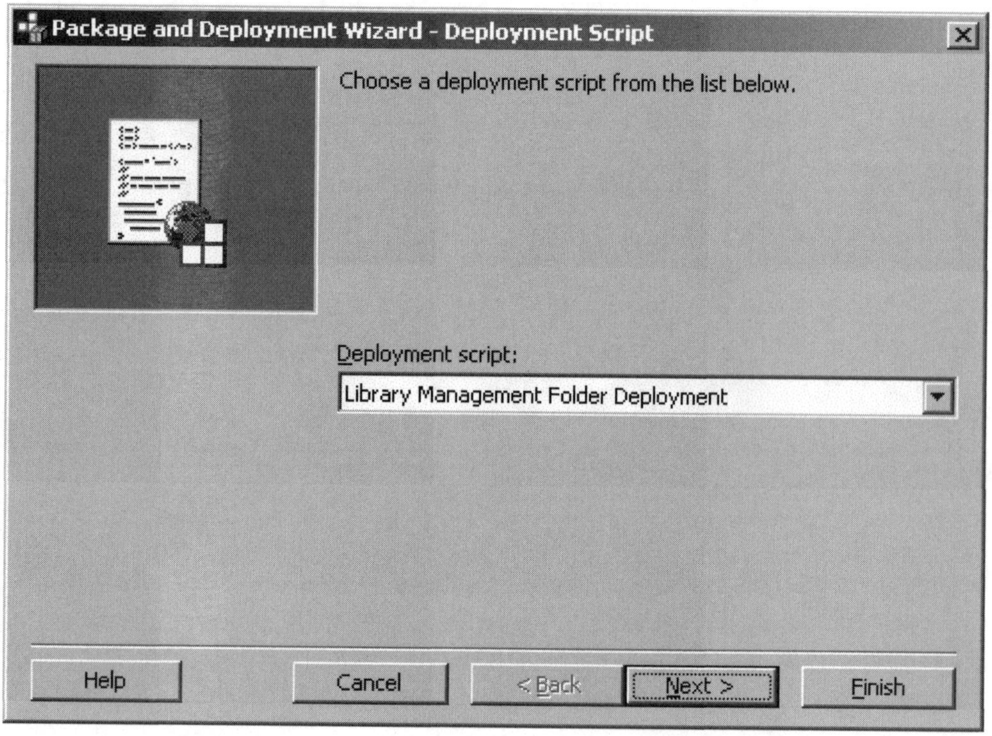

Figure 8.39: Deployment Script Dialog Box

16.   Click **Next**. The Package to Deploy dialog box appears, as shown in Figure 8.40. Select the package created in step 12. Click **Next**.

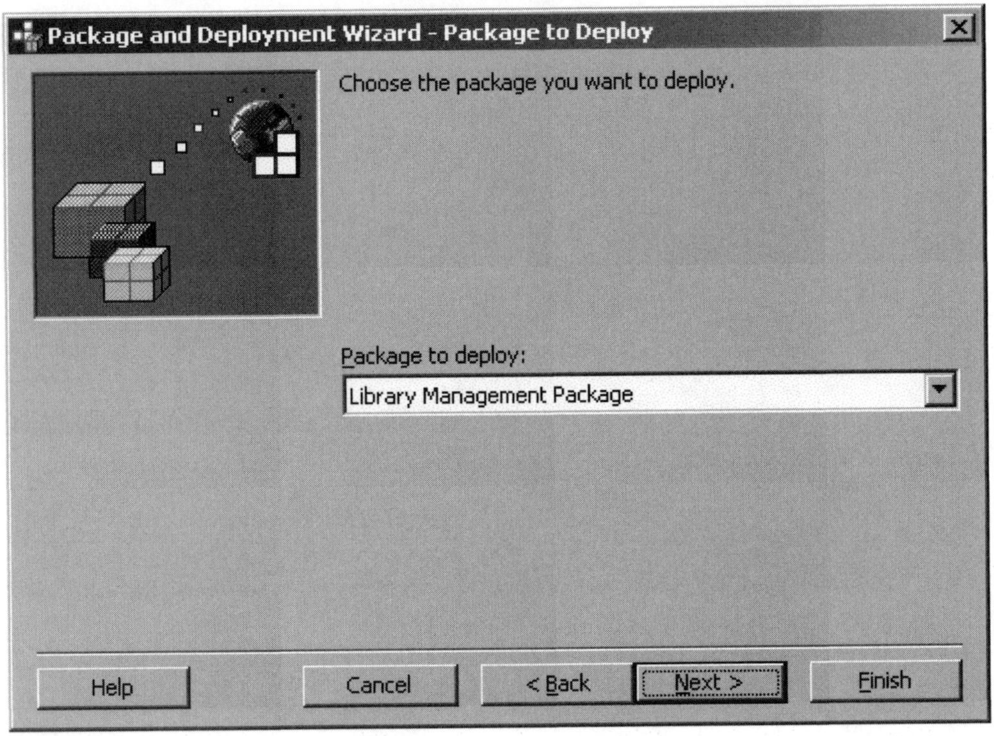

Figure 8.40: Package to Deploy Dialog Box

17. Select Folder as the Deployment method in the Deployment Method dialog box shown in Figure 8.41, and click **Next**.

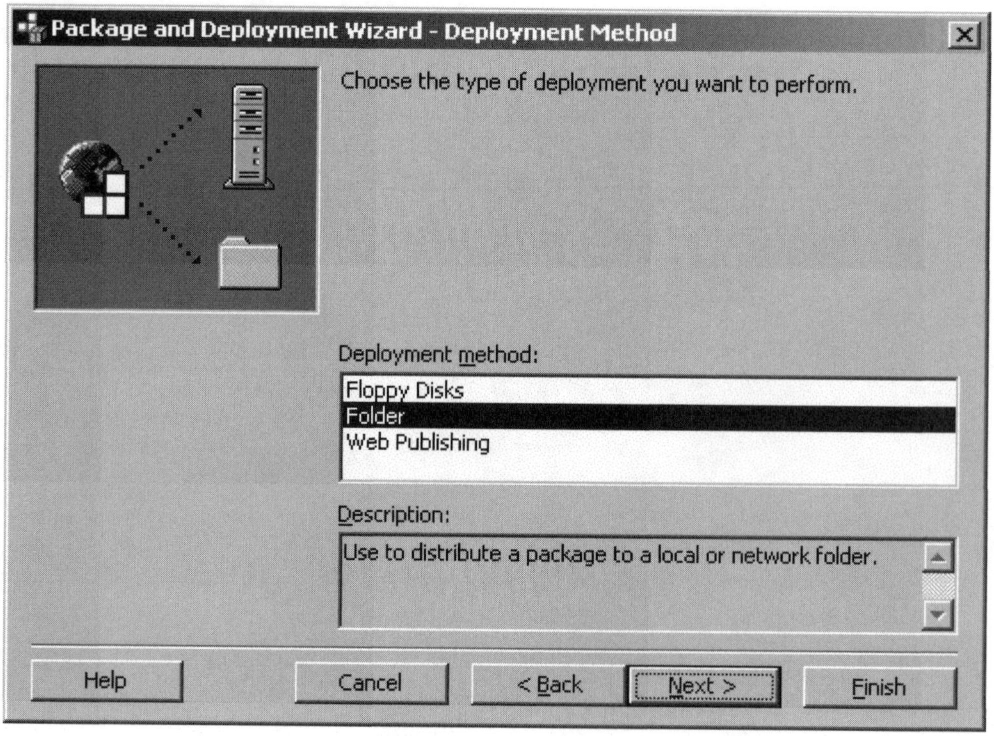

Figure 8.41: Deployment Method Dialog Box

18.   Specify the Deployment Folder, as shown in Figure 8.42. You can specify a folder in the same computer or on any remote computer on the network.

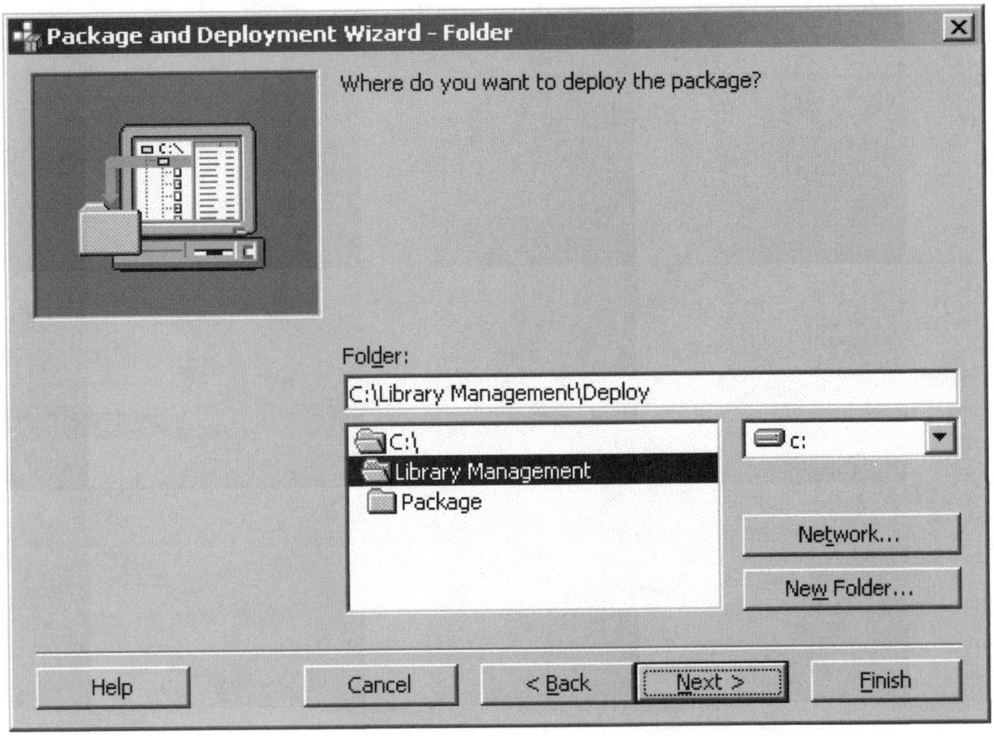

Figure 8.42: Folder Dialog Box

19. Specify the name of the deployment script as Library Management Folder Deployment, as shown in Figure 8.43, and click **Next**. The wizard displays a report of the task being performed.

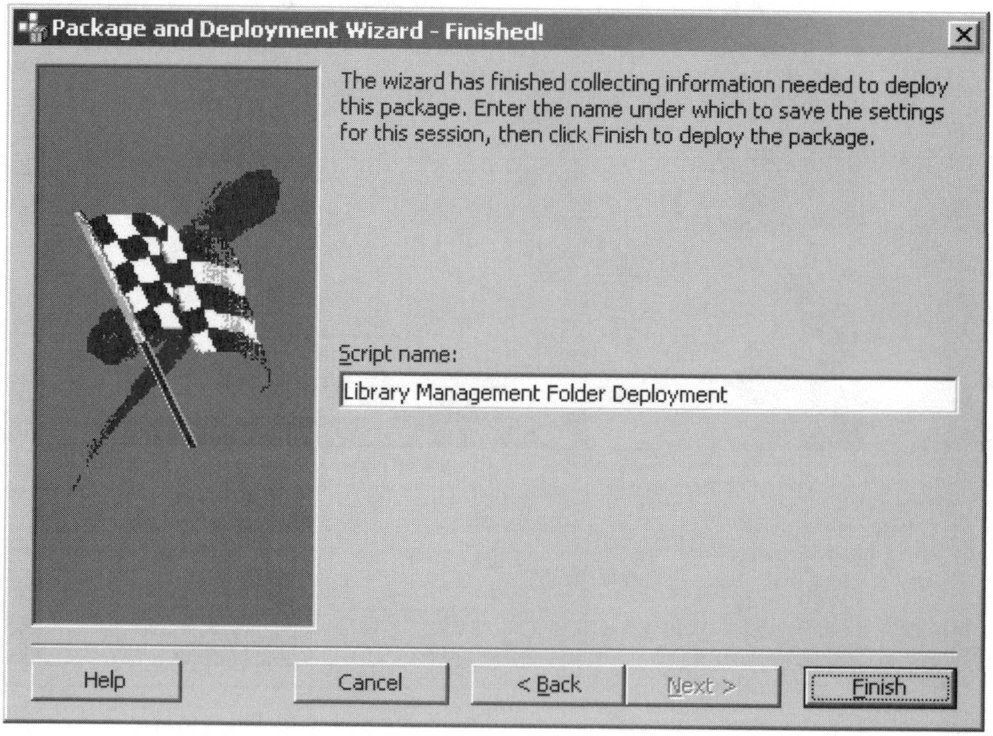

Figure 8.43: Script Name Dialog Box to Finish Deployment

20. Click **Close** to return to the initial dialog box of the Package and Deployment Wizard.

21. Click **Close** again to close the Package and Deployment Wizard.

22. Check the Installation package by running the Setup.exe program from the installation package folder or the deployment folder.

Summary

- The three ways in which you can distribute your application are:
  - On the network
  - On physical media, such as CD-ROMs and floppy disks
  - In files that you can download from the Internet
- You can run the Package and Deployment Wizard as a stand-alone application or as a part of the Visual Basic Add-ins.
- The tasks performed by the Package and Deployment Wizard are:
  - Determines the files to be distributed
  - Creates a setup program
  - Compresses the files to be included with the package
  - Creates installation files
  - Creates a dependency file
- The three types of packages that you can create using the Package and Deployment Wizard are:
  - Disk-based installation packages
  - Network-based installation packages
  - Web-based installation packages
- The three main types of files required to run and distribute an installation package are:
  - Run time files
  - Setup files
  - Application-specific files
- The setup files included with the package are:
  - Setup.exe
  - Setup1.exe
  - Setup.lst
  - St6unst.exe
- A cab file or a cabinet file is a type of compressed file created by the Package and Deployment Wizard.

- A cab file can contain multiple files needed for the installation package.

- In a network-based deployment, the installation package is deployed over the network from where it is accessible to all client computers on the network.

- In the Web-based deployment method, the Package and Deployment Wizard deploys the package over the Internet. This enables the end users to download and install the package from remote locations over the Internet.

- The Package and Deployment Wizard creates a script that stores the settings that you selected while running the Package and Deployment Process.

- You can use a script to apply these settings again while running the Package and Deployment Wizard on similar projects.

- If you delete a packaging script, the Package and Deployment Wizard cannot deploy that package. You need to repackage the script to deploy it using the Package and Deployment Wizard.

References

- http://www.library.itt-tech.edu/periodicals.asp > FindArticles.com (Accessed on Aug. 12, 2004)
- http://www.library.itt-tech.edu/periodicals.asp > MSDN Magazine (Accessed on Aug. 12, 2004)

Homework Exercises

1.   What is the difference between a network-based and a Web-based deployment process?

2.   Specify the two ways by which you can run the Package and Deployment Wizard.

3.   Specify the tasks performed by the Package and Deployment Wizard.

4.   What are the advantages of packaging an application?

Lab Exercises

Exercise 1

Objective

■ To use the Package and Deployment Wizard to create an installer for an application.

Problem Statement

You have created an Employee Time Sheet project that enables the employees of your organization to log the time spent in daily activities. You need to package and distribute your project to all employees of your organization. Identify the type of deployment process that you would use for this purpose and use the Package and Deployment Wizard to package and deploy the project.

Lab Setup

Computer Requirements:

■ The Microsoft Windows operating system

■ Pentium III or higher processors

■ 128-MB RAM

■ 3-GB of hard disk space

■ A CD-ROM drive

■ A floppy disk drive

■ A LAN connection

■ Visual Basic 6.0

Procedure

You need to use the network-based deployment process to distribute the Employee Time Sheet project over the network to all employees of the organization. The employees need to install the project from a central location on the network. The steps to package and deploy the Employee Time Sheet project are:

1. Select **Start → Programs → Microsoft Visual Studio 6.0 → Microsoft Visual Studio 6.0 Tools → Package and Deployment Wizard**. The Package and Deployment Wizard opens, as shown in Figure 8.44.

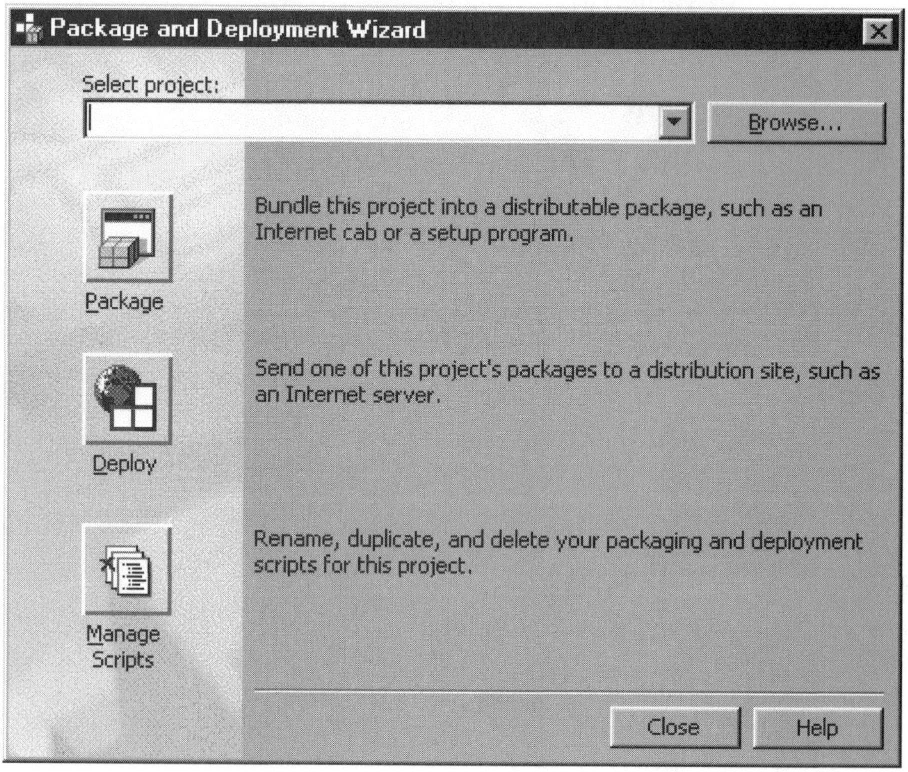

Figure 8.44: Package and Deployment Wizard

2. Click the **Browse** button, and select the Employee Time Sheet project to be packaged. The selected project is displayed in the Select Project list box.

3.   Click the **Package** button. The Package Type dialog box appears, as shown in Figure 8.45.

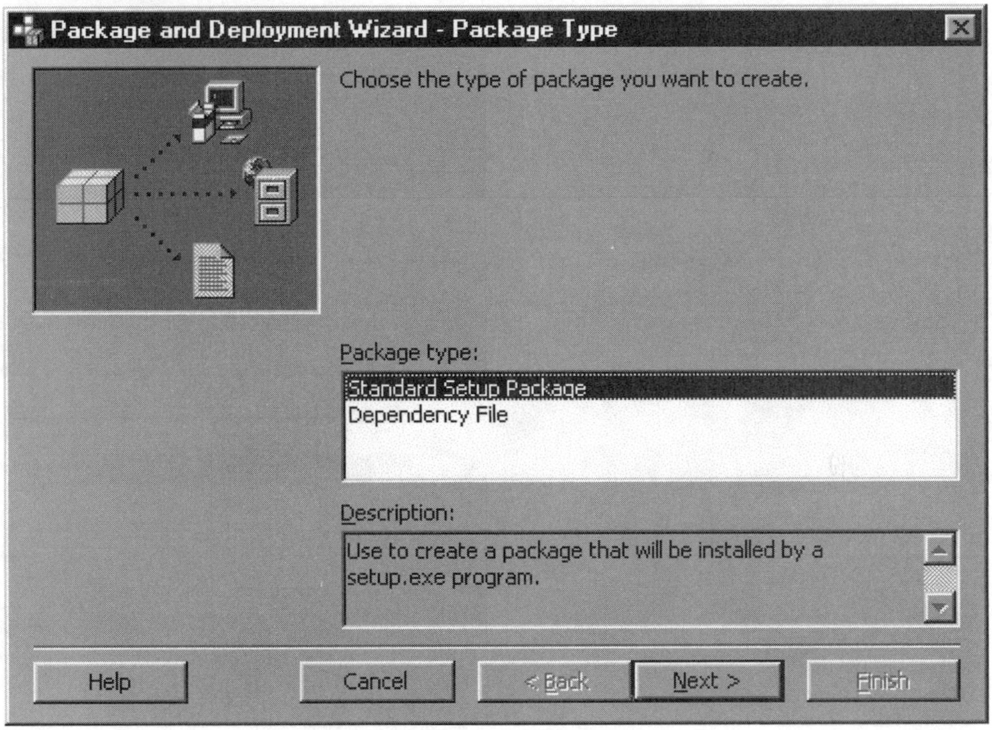

Figure 8.45: Package Type Dialog Box

4. Select the Standard Setup Package option from the Package type list, and click **Next**. The Package Folder dialog box appears, as shown in Figure 8.46.

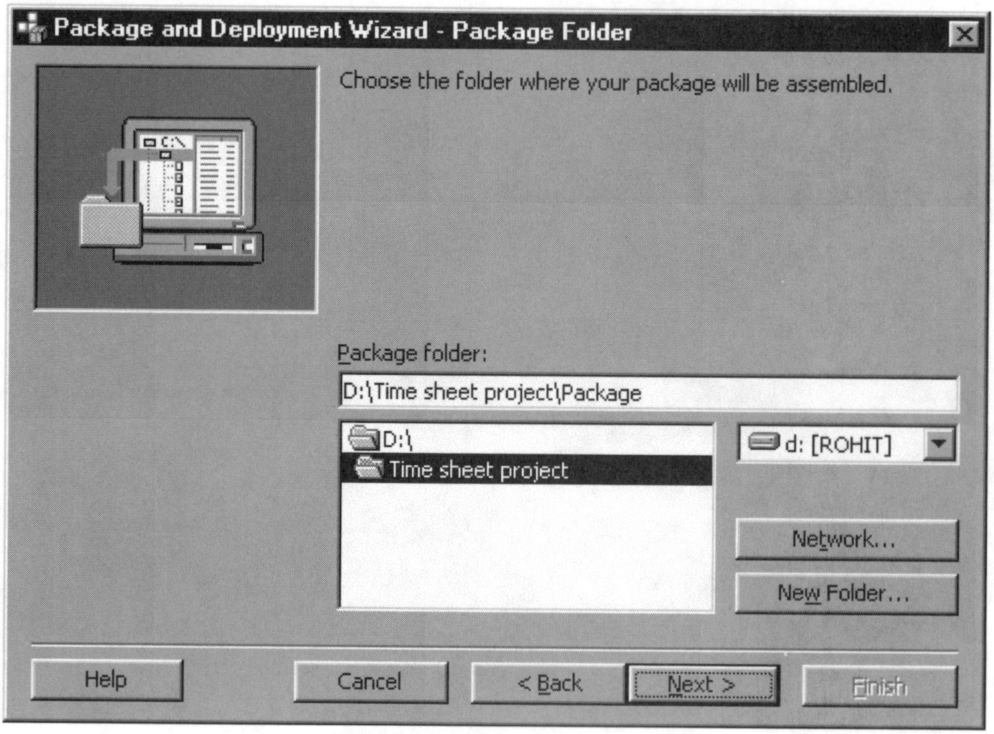

Figure 8.46: Package Folder Dialog Box

5. Select the folder on the local computer where you want to save the package, and click **Next**. The DAO Drivers dialog box appears, as shown in Figure 8.47.

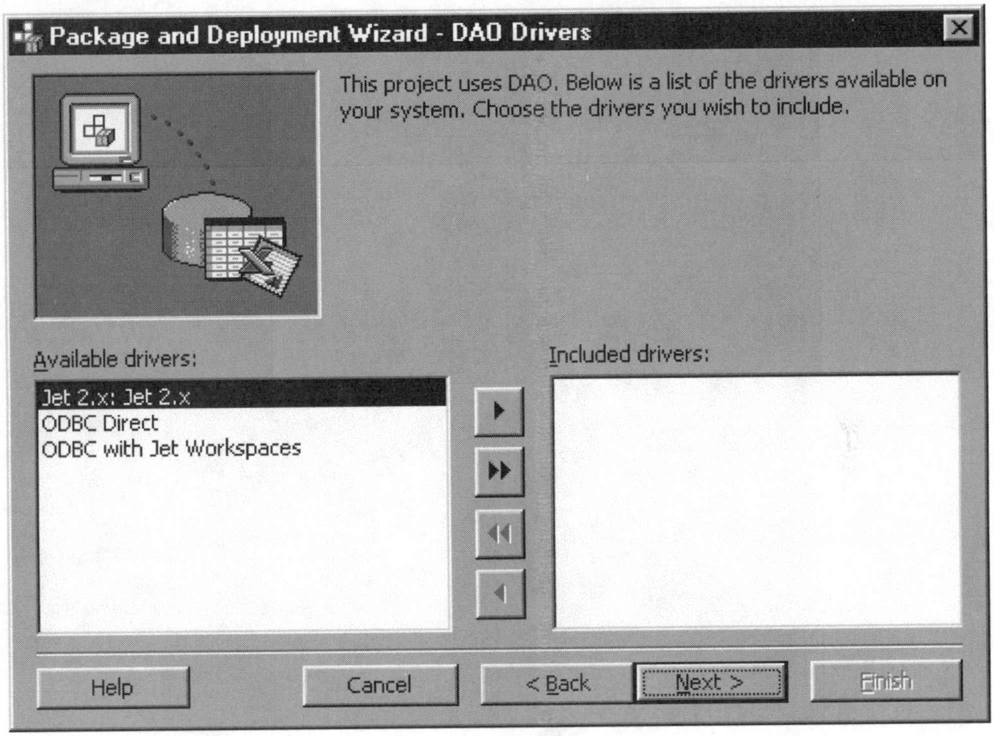

Figure 8.47: DAO Drivers Dialog Box

6. Select the ODBC with Jet Workspace driver, and click the right arrow button to include it with the package.

7. Click **Next** in the DAO Drivers dialog box.

8.   Click **Next** in the Included Files dialog box to accept the default set of files included in the package. The Cab Options dialog box appears, as shown in Figure 8.48.

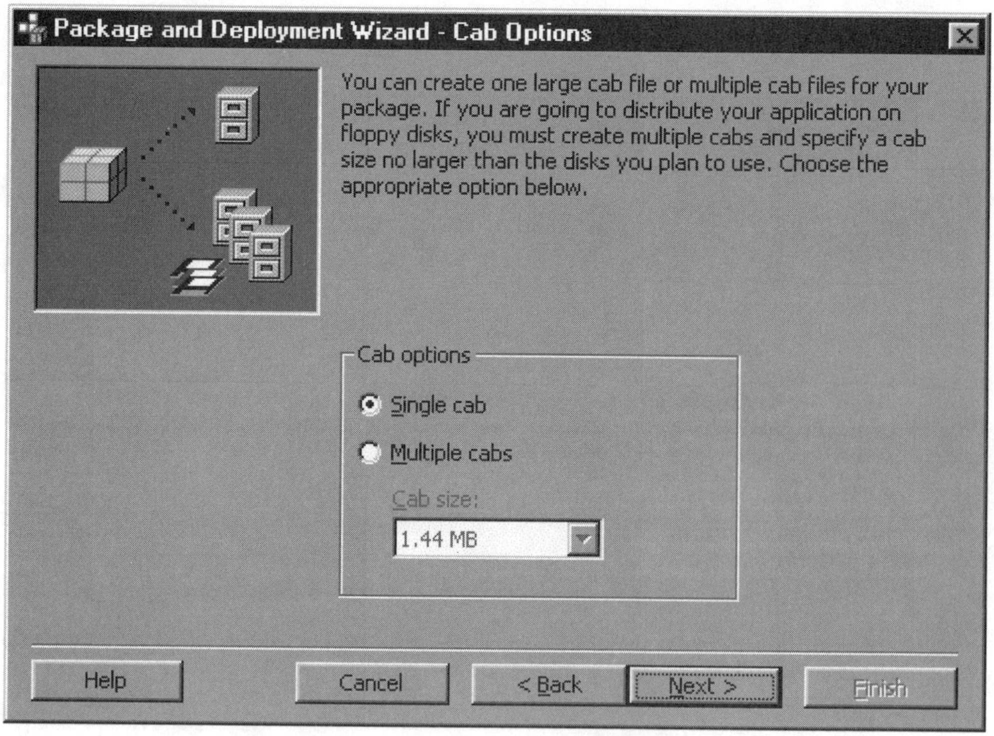

Figure 8.48: Cab Option Dialog Box

9. Select the Single cab option in the Cab Options dialog box, and click **Next**. The Installation Title dialog box appears, as shown in Figure 8.49.

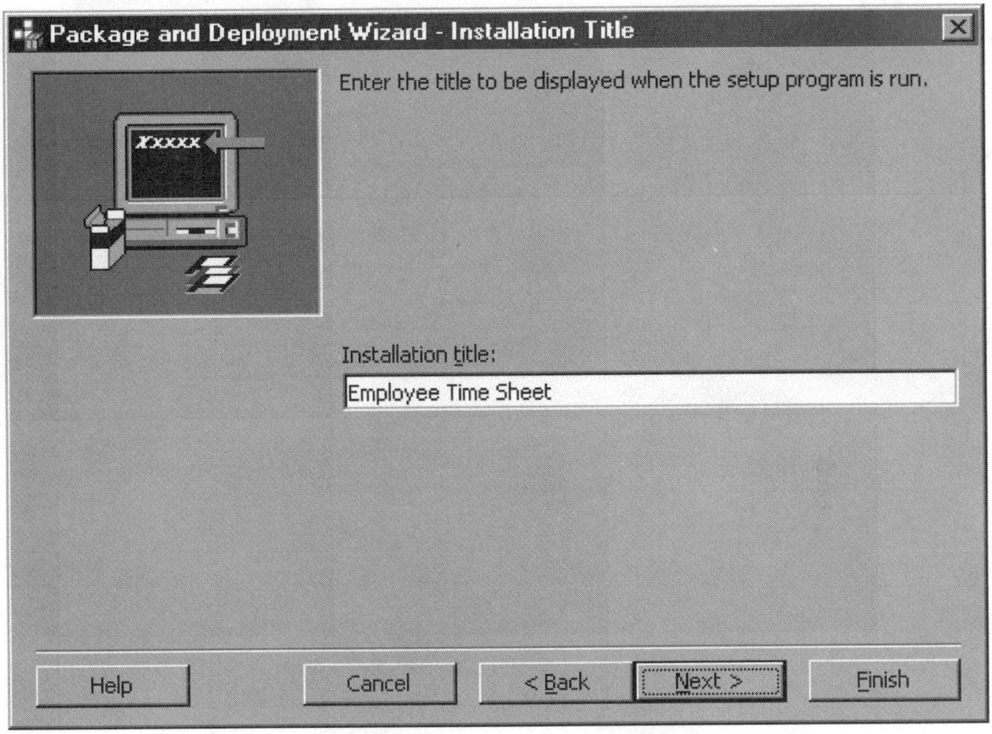

Figure 8.49: Installation Title Dialog Box

10. Specify Employee Time Sheet in the Installation title text box, and click **Next**. The Start Menu Items dialog box appears, as shown in Figure 8.50

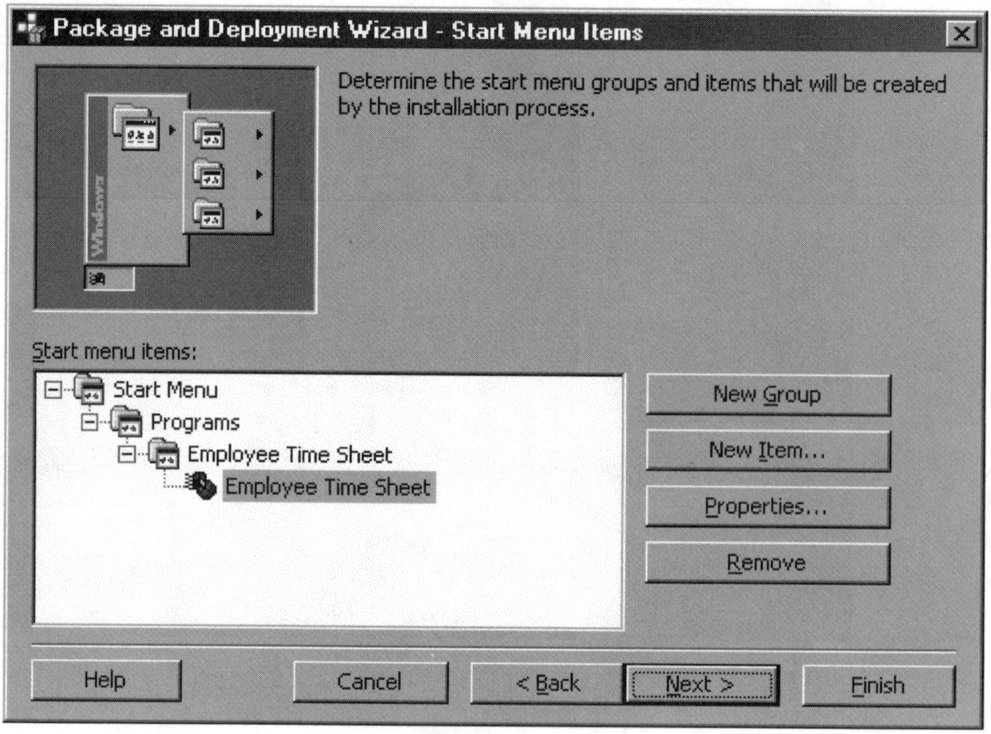

Figure 8.50: Start Menu Items Dialog Box

11. Click **Next** in the Start Menu Items dialog box to accept the default selection. The Install Locations dialog box appears, as shown in Figure 8.51.

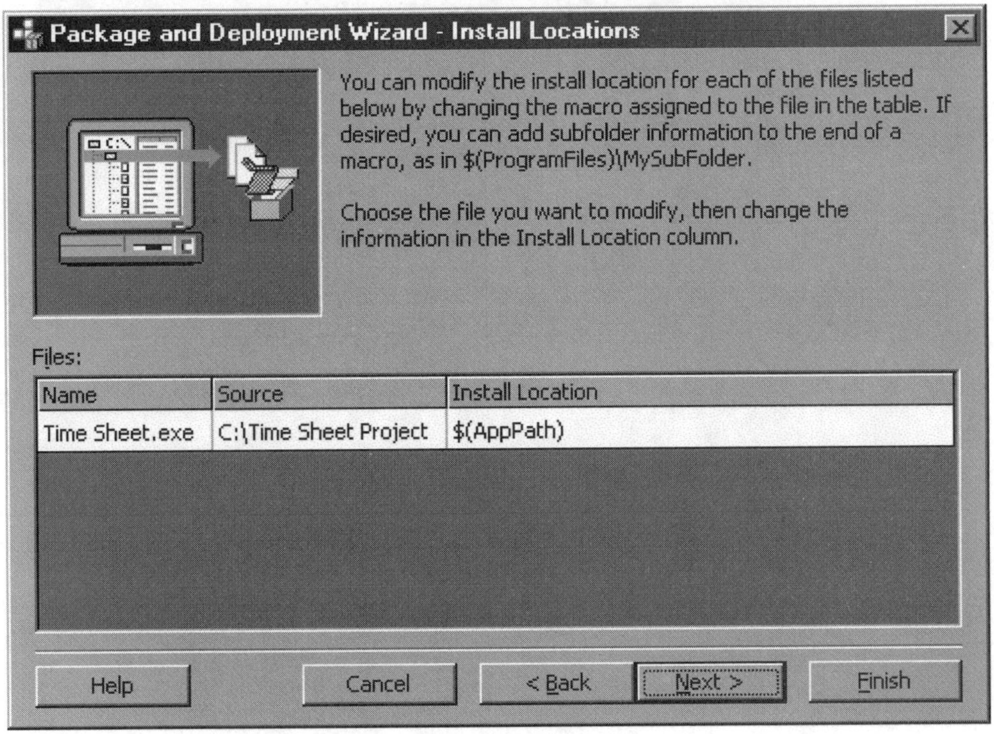

Figure 8.51: Install Locations Dialog Box

12. Click **Next** in the Install Locations dialog box to verify and accept the locations where the package files should be saved.

13.   Click **Next** in the Shared Files dialog box, as shown in Figure 8.52.

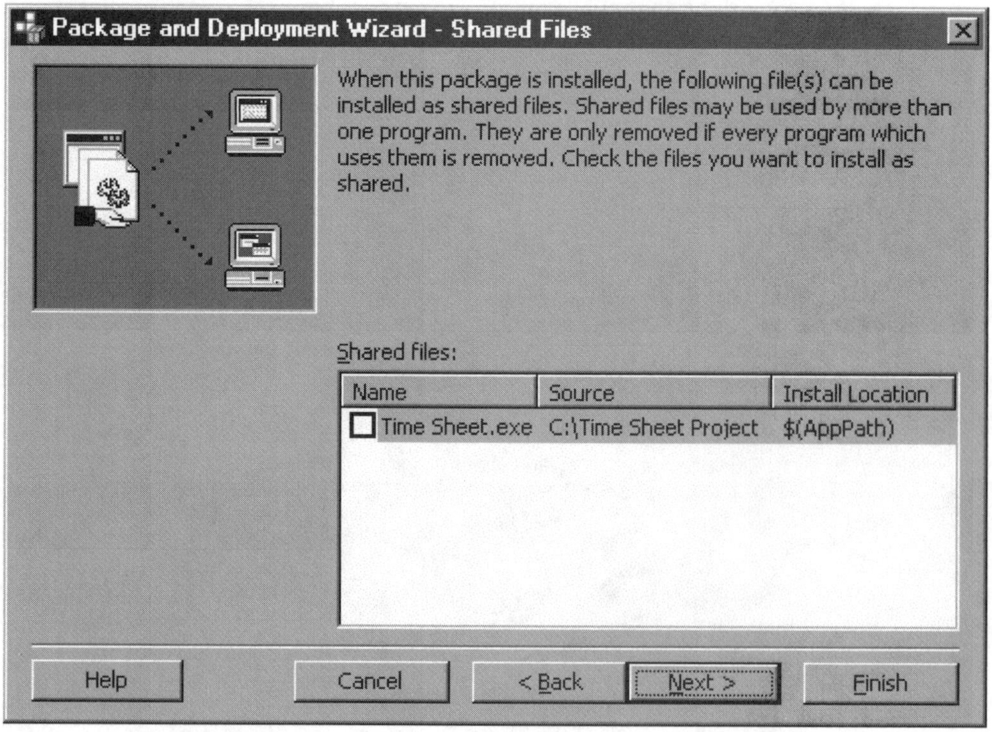

Figure 8.52: Shared Files Dialog Box

14.   Enter Time Sheet in the Script name text box on the Final screen of the Package and Deployment Wizard.

15.   Click **Finish** to complete the packaging process. The Package and Deployment Wizard page appears.

16.   Click the **Deploy** button on the Package and Deployment Wizard page to start the deployment process after packaging the Employee Time Sheet project. The Package to Deploy dialog box appears, as shown in Figure 8.53.

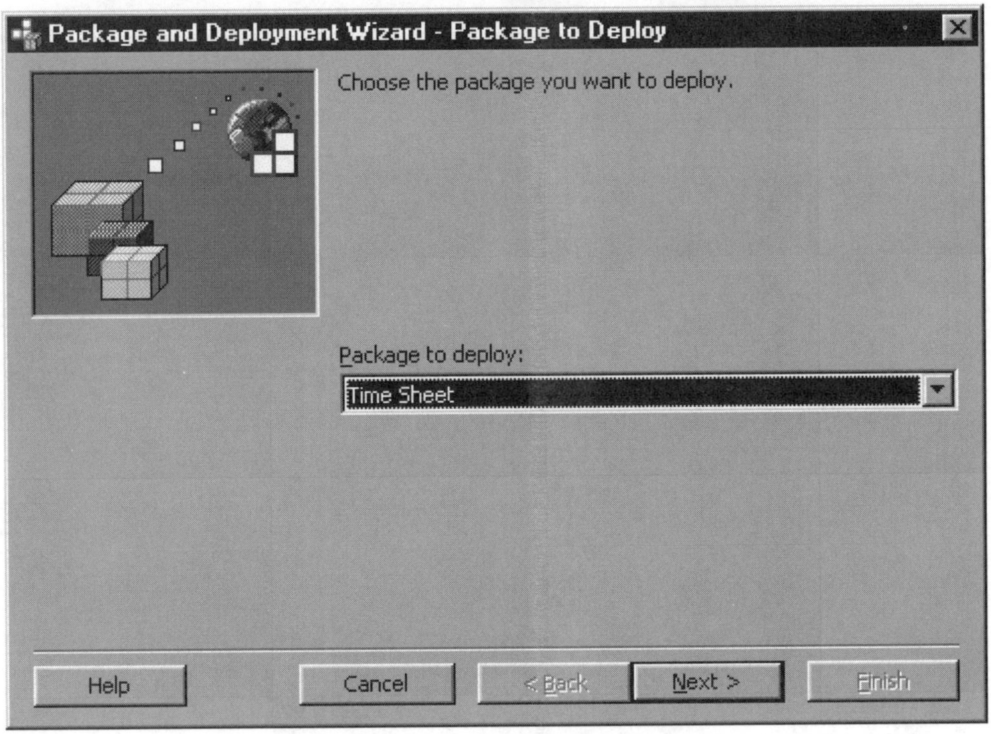

Figure 8.53: Package to Deploy Dialog Box

17.   Select the Time Sheet package from the Package to deploy the drop-down list, and click **Next**. The Deployment Method dialog box appears, as shown in Figure 8.54.

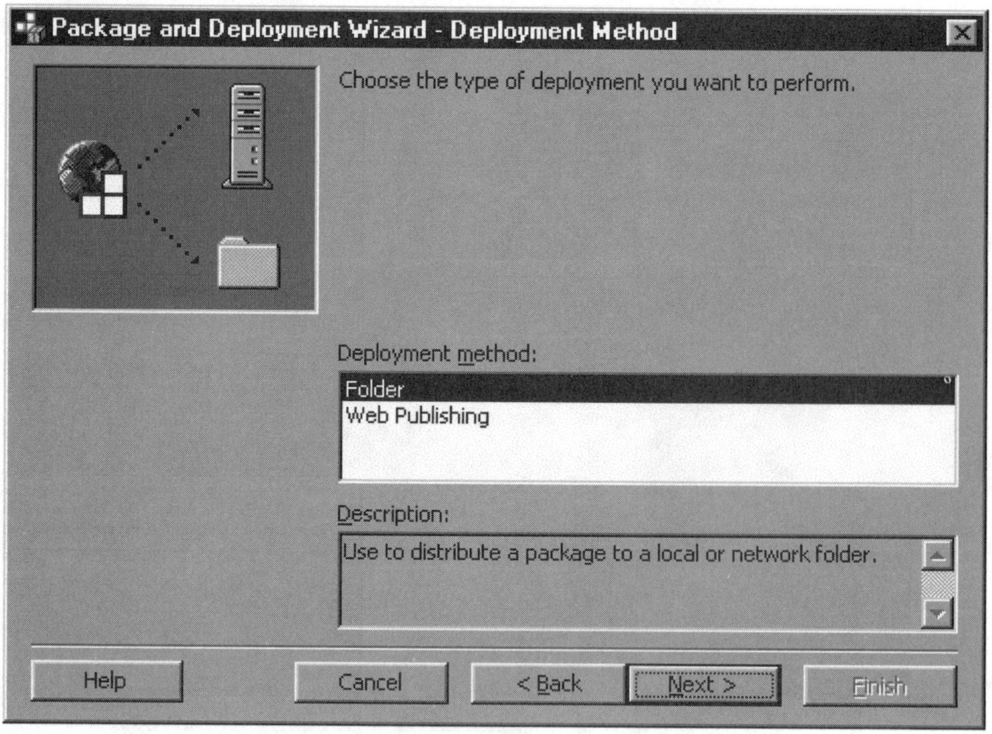

Figure 8.54: Deployment Method Dialog Box

18.   Select the Folder option from the Deployment method list box, and click **Next**. The Folder dialog box appears.

19.   Click the **Network** button in the Folder dialog box. The Browse for Folder dialog box appears, as shown in Figure 8.55.

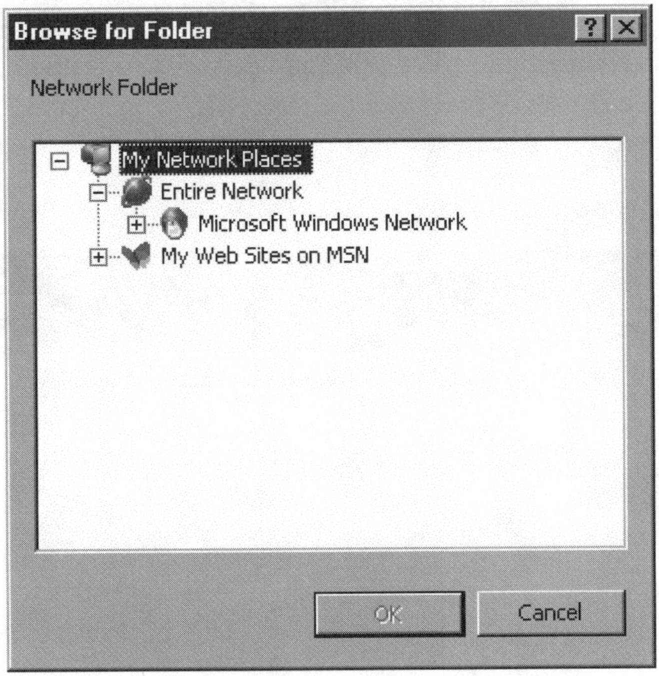

Figure 8.55: Browser for Folder Dialog Box

20.   Select the shared folder on the network server where you want to deploy the Time Sheet package, and click **OK**.

21.   Click **Next** in the Folder dialog box.

22.   Specify the script name for the deployment process, and click **Finish** to deploy the package in the specific network location from where employees can access the installation package and install the Employee Time Sheet project on their computer.

23.   Access the Time Sheet installation package on the network server from a client computer on the network and install the project to check whether or not it is successfully installed.

Conclusion/Observation

The packaging and deployment is done as the final step after the application is tested successfully. After the installation package is created and deployed, the application can be installed in the computer of the end user by running setup.exe in the deployed folder. If the application performs properly after being installed, the packaging and deployment is successful.

Lab Activity Checklist

S. No.	Tasks	Completed	
		Yes	No
1.	The installation package is created.		
2.	The installation package is properly deployed.		

Exercise 2

Objective

■ To use the Package and Deployment Wizard to create an installer for an application that uses an MS Access database.

Problem Statement

Create a VB project named EmpInfo, and add the following form named frmMain to the project.

Figure 8.56 shows the design view of the form:

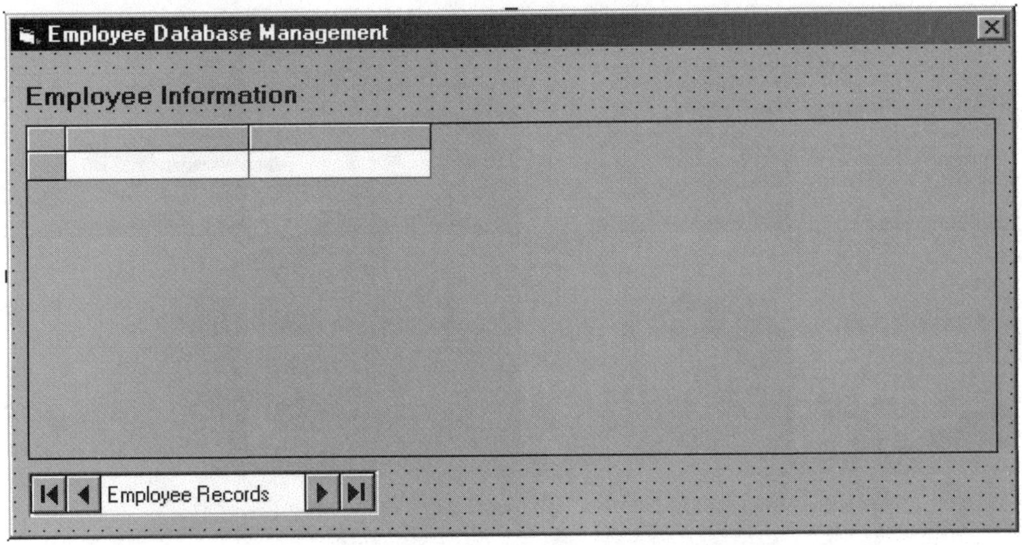

Figure 8.56: Design View of the Form frmMain

The above form contains a DataGrid control named dgdEmp and an ADODC control named adoEmp. The properties of the ADODC and the DataGrid control should be set in run time. Save the project. Create a MS Access database named EmpDB.mdb in the same location as the application. Create a table named Employees in the database with the following structure:

Column Name	Data Type and Size
EmployeeID	AutoNumber
LastName	Text – 20 characters
FirstName	Text – 10 characters
BirthDate	Date/Time
HireDate	Date/Time
Address	Text – 60 characters
City	Text – 15 characters
Country	Text – 15 characters
HomePhone	Text – 24 characters

Add some sample records to the table. Write the following code for the Form Load event of the form, frmMain.

```
Private Sub Form_Load()
  Me.adoEmp.ConnectionString =
"Provider=Microsoft.Jet.OLEDB.4.0;" + _
    "Data Source=" + App.Path + "\EmpDB.mdb"
  Me.adoEmp.CommandType = adCmdTable
  Me.adoEmp.RecordSource = "Employees"
  Set Me.dgdEmp.DataSource = Me.adoEmp
End Sub
```

Figure 8.57 shows the run time view of the application:

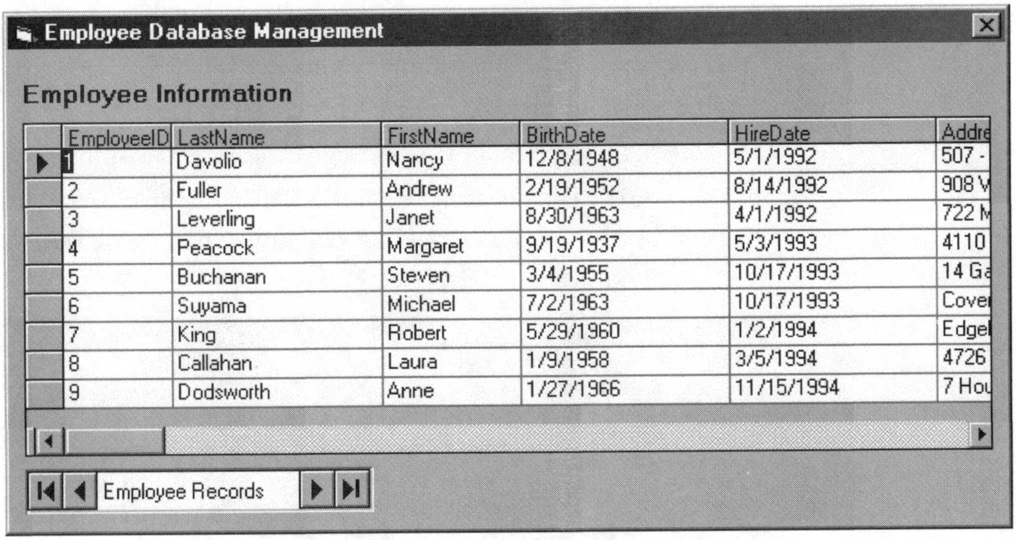

Figure 8.57: Run Time View of the Application

Create the installation package for the above application, and include the database so that the application performs the same on any computer on which the application is installed.

Lab Setup

Computer Requirements:

- ▣ The Microsoft Windows operating system
- ▣ Pentium III or higher processors
- ▣ 128-MB RAM
- ▣ 3-GB of hard disk space
- ▣ A CD-ROM drive
- ▣ A floppy disk drive
- ▣ A LAN connection
- ▣ Visual Basic 6.0

Procedure

1. Create the database and the VB project. Refer to previous chapters for creating a database and creating forms in VB.

2. Add the given code to the Form Load event of the form.

3. Ensure that the database is in the same folder as that of the project.

4. Select **Start → Programs → Microsoft Visual Studio 6.0 → Microsoft Visual Studio 6.0 Tools → Package and Deployment Wizard**. The Package and Deployment Wizard opens, as shown in Figure 8.58.

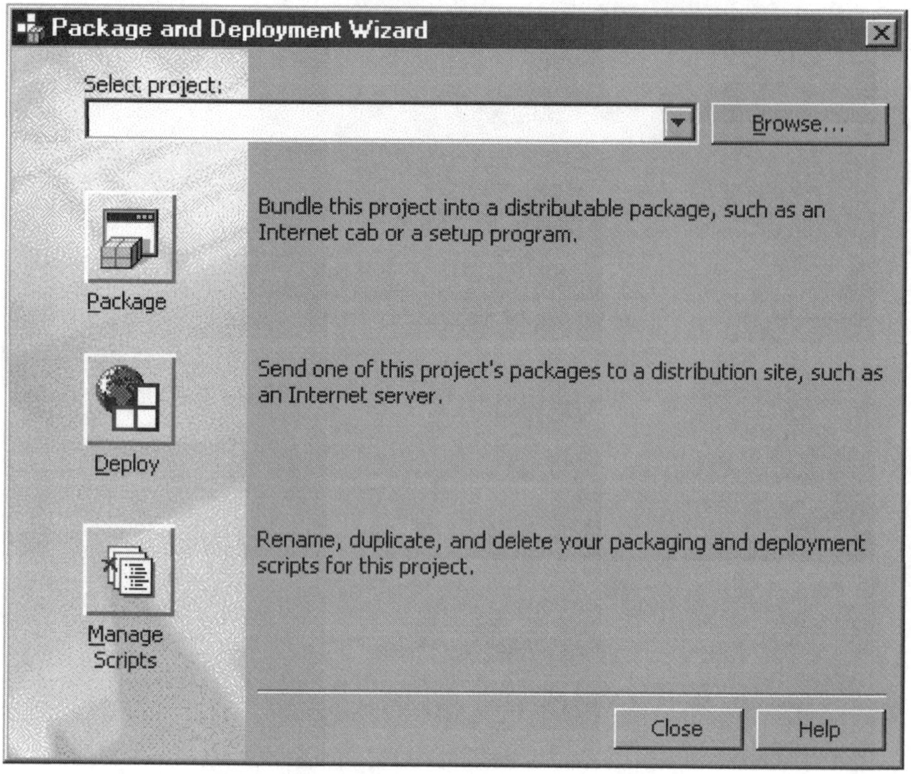

Figure 8.58: Package and Deployment Wizard

5. Select the name of the project by clicking the Browse button, and click the **Package** button to start the packaging of the specified project.

6.   Select **Compile** if the wizard asks for compilation of the project. The Package Type dialog box appears, as shown in Figure 8.59.

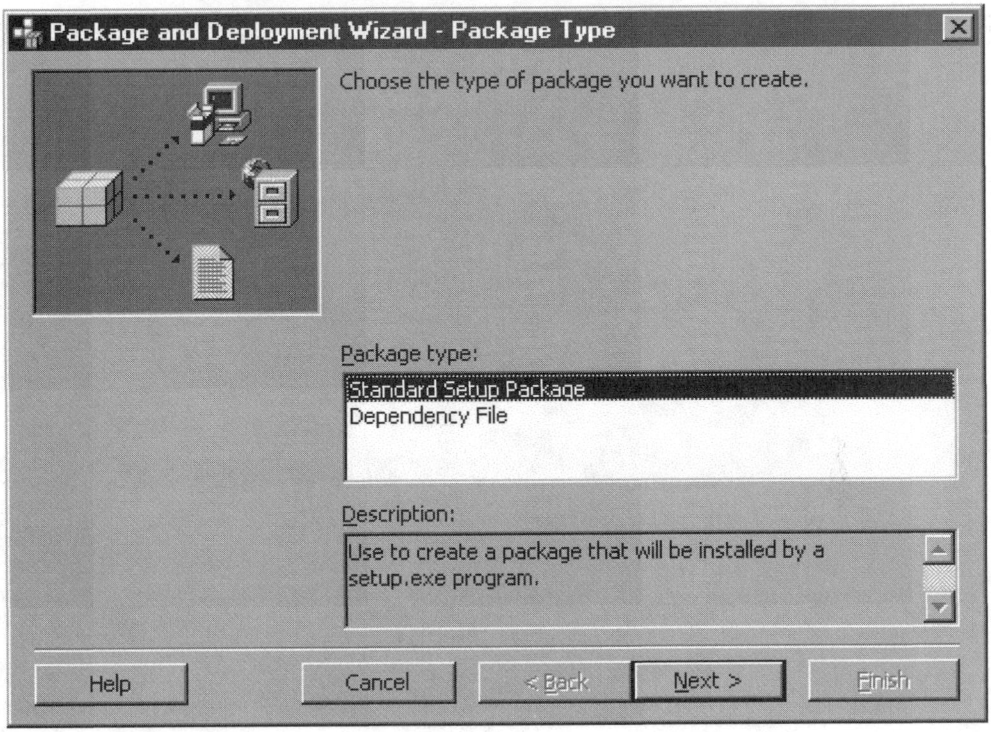

Figure 8.59: Package Type Dialog Box

7. Select Standard Setup Package as the type of the package, and click **Next**. The Package folder dialog box appears, as shown in Figure 8.60 below.

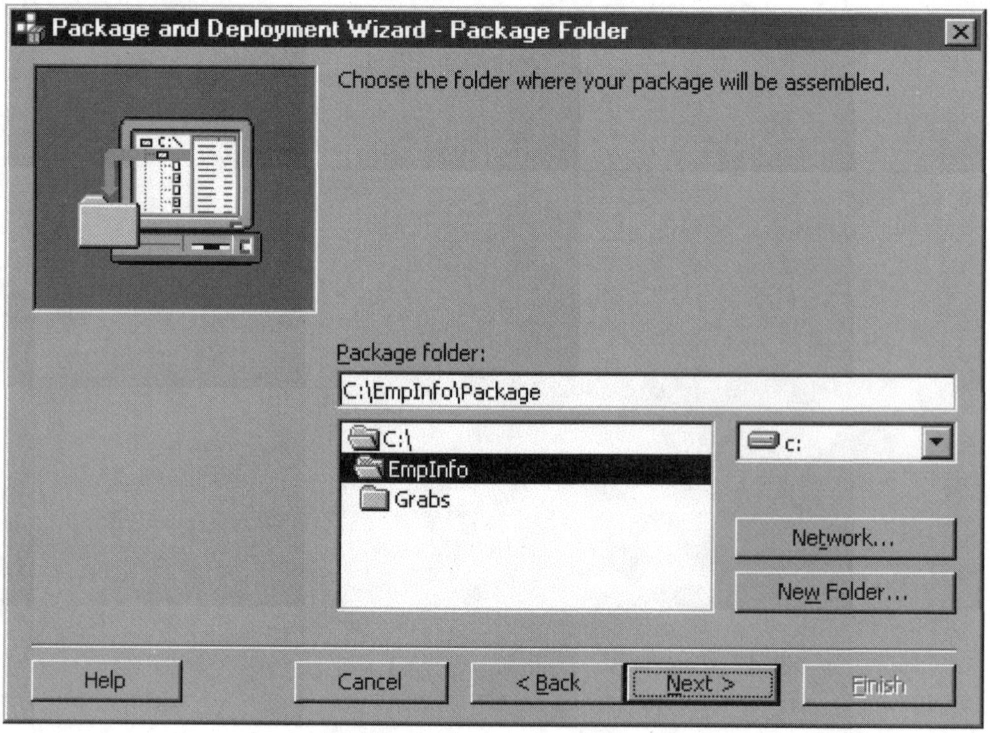

Figure 8.60: Package Folder Dialog Box

8. Click **Next** in the Package folder dialog box. The Included Files dialog box appears, as shown in the Figure 8.61:

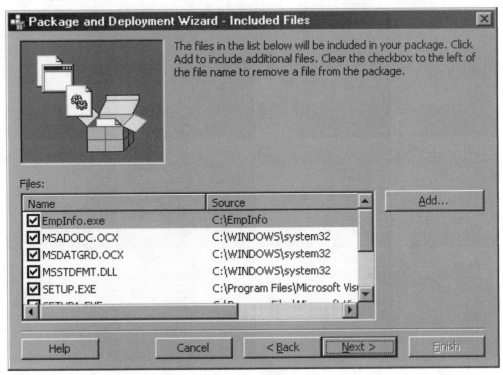

Figure 8.61: Included Files Dialog Box

9. Click the **Add** button to add the database file to the installation package. Figure 8.62 shows the Included Files dialog box after adding the database file, EmpDB.mdb.

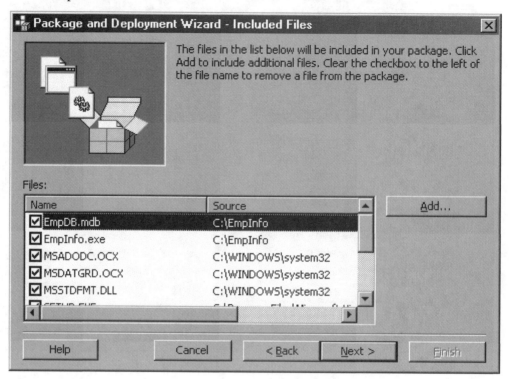

Figure 8.62: Included Files Dialog Box

10. Click **Next**. The Cab Options dialog box appears, as shown in Figure 8.63:

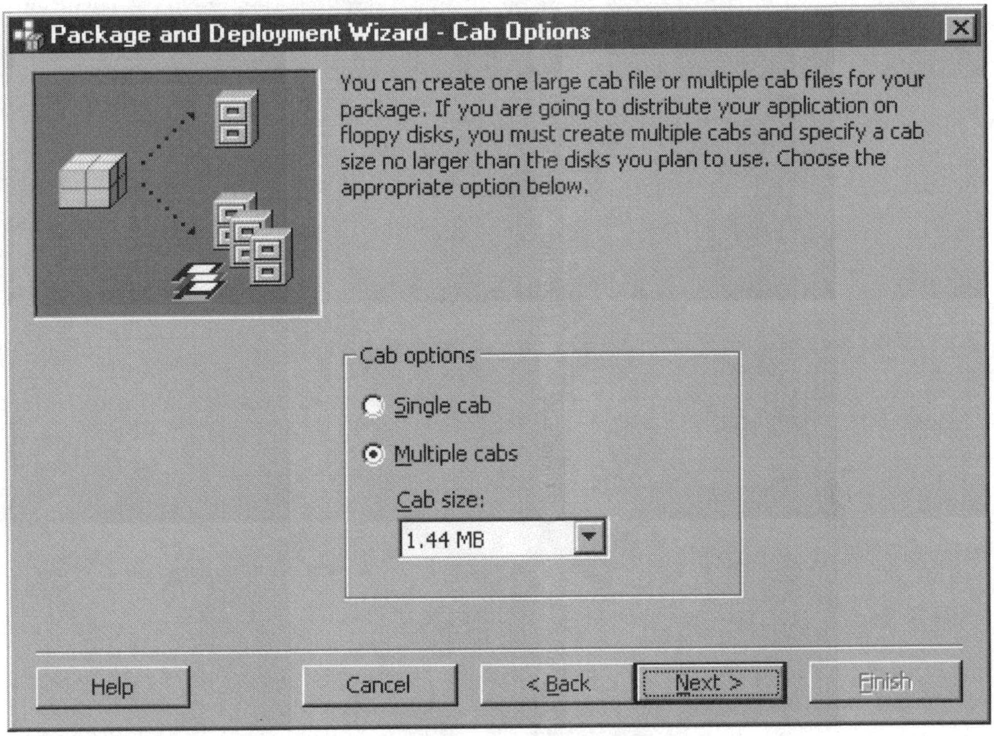

Figure 8.63: Cab Options Dialog Box

11. Select the Multiple cabs option and Cab size as 1.44 MB. Click **Next** to proceed. The Installation Title dialog box appears, as shown in Figure 8.64.

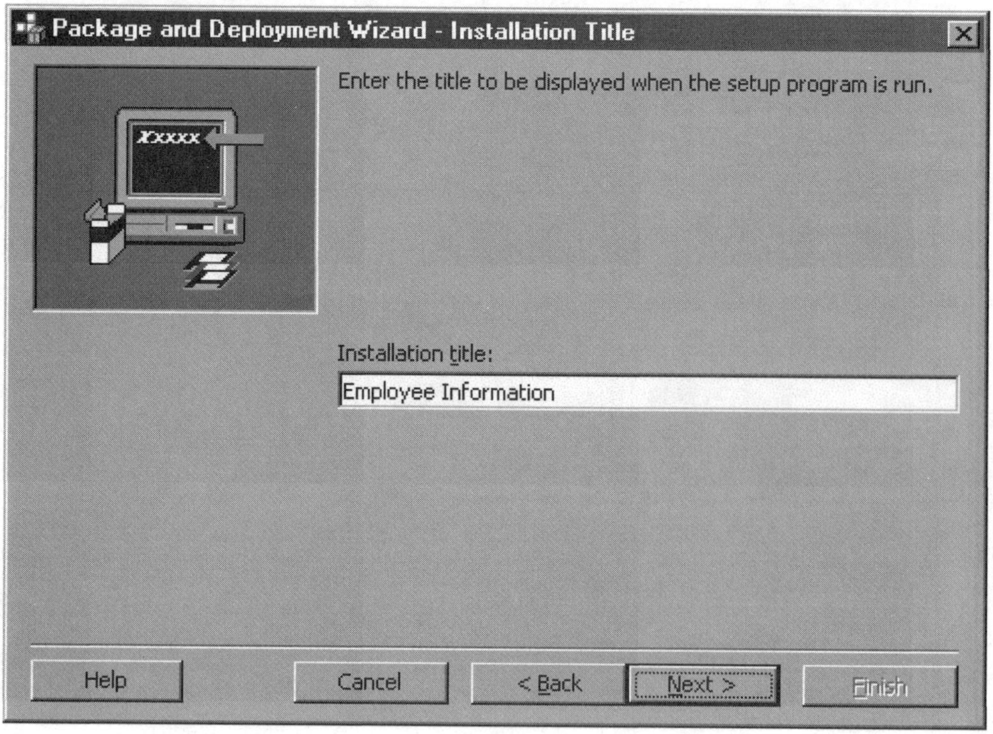

Figure 8.64: Installation Title Dialog Box

12. Enter Employee Information as the Installation Title, and click **Next**. The Start Menu Items dialog box appears, as shown in Figure 8.65.

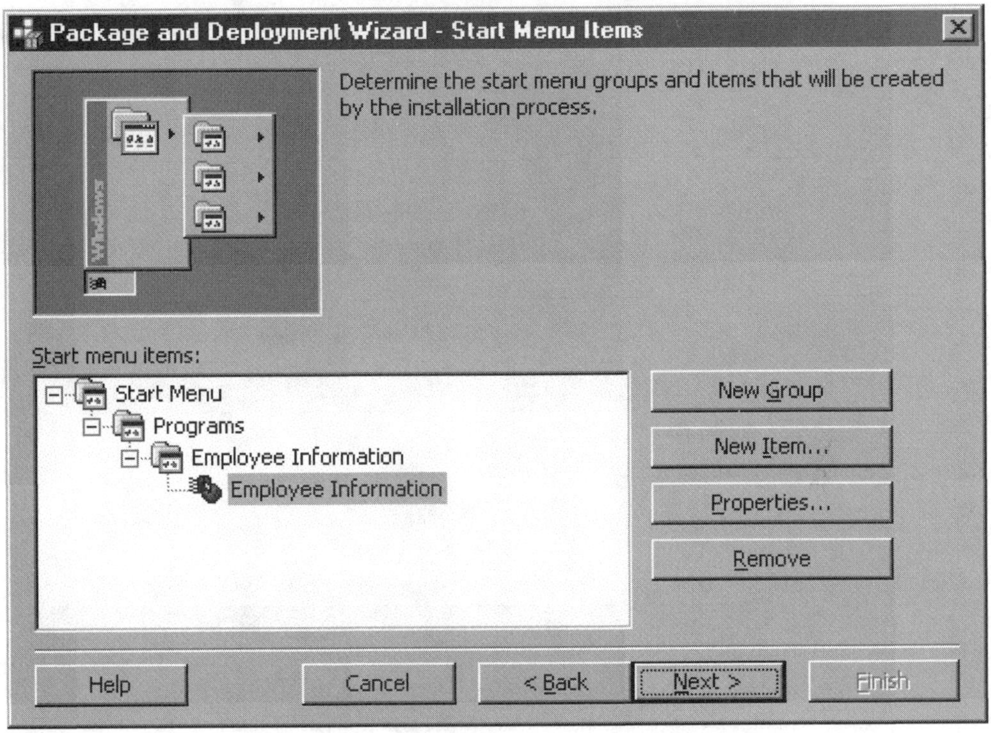

Figure 8.65: Start Menu Items Dialog Box

13.   Click **Next**. The Install Locations dialog box appears, as shown in Figure 8.66.

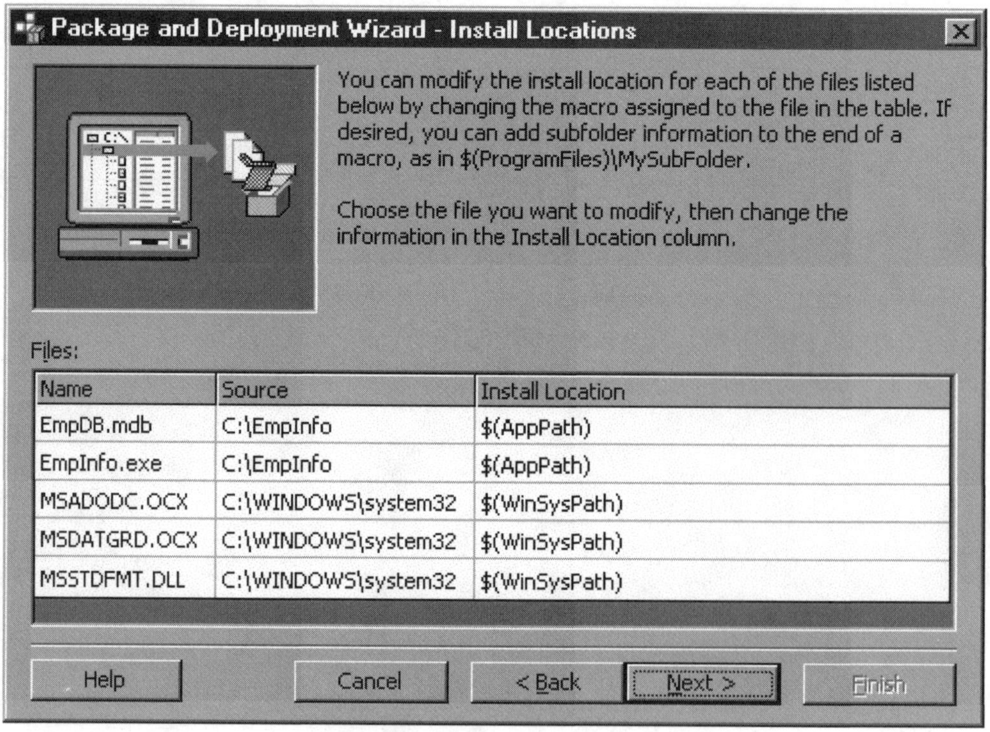

Figure 8.66: Install Location Dialog Box

14. Ensure that the Install Location of the database file is set to the application path denoted by $(AppPath). Click **Next** to proceed to the Shared Files dialog box, as shown in Figure 8.67.

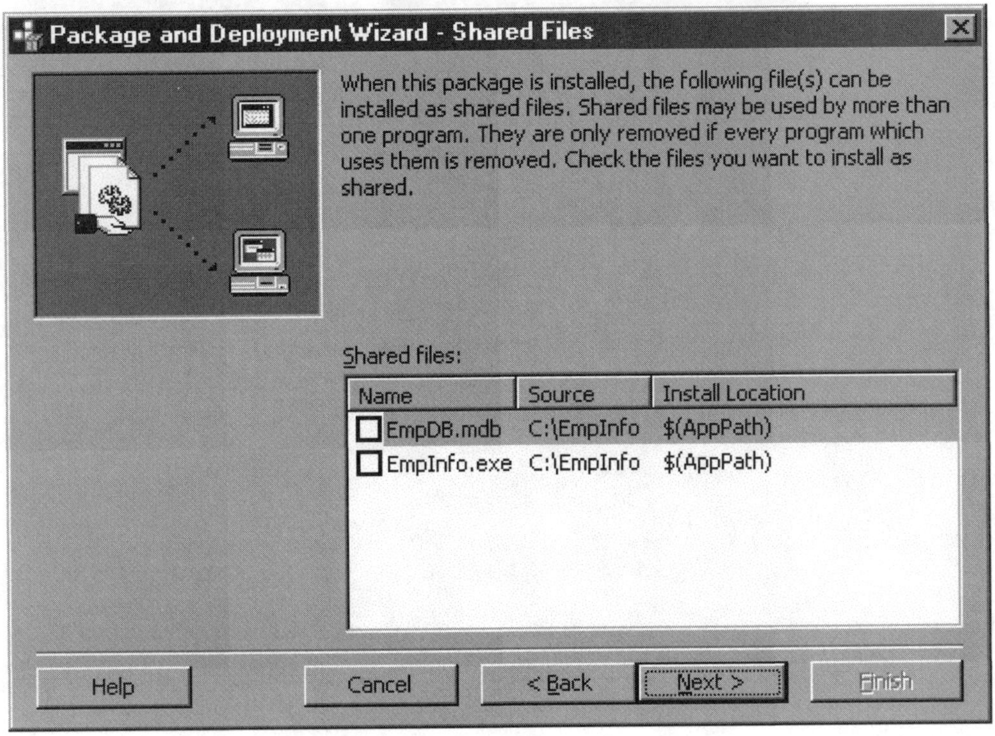

Figure 8.67: Shared Files Dialog Box

15.   Click **Next**. Specify the script name as Emp Info package, and click **Finish** to build the package with the given specifications Figure 8.68 shows.

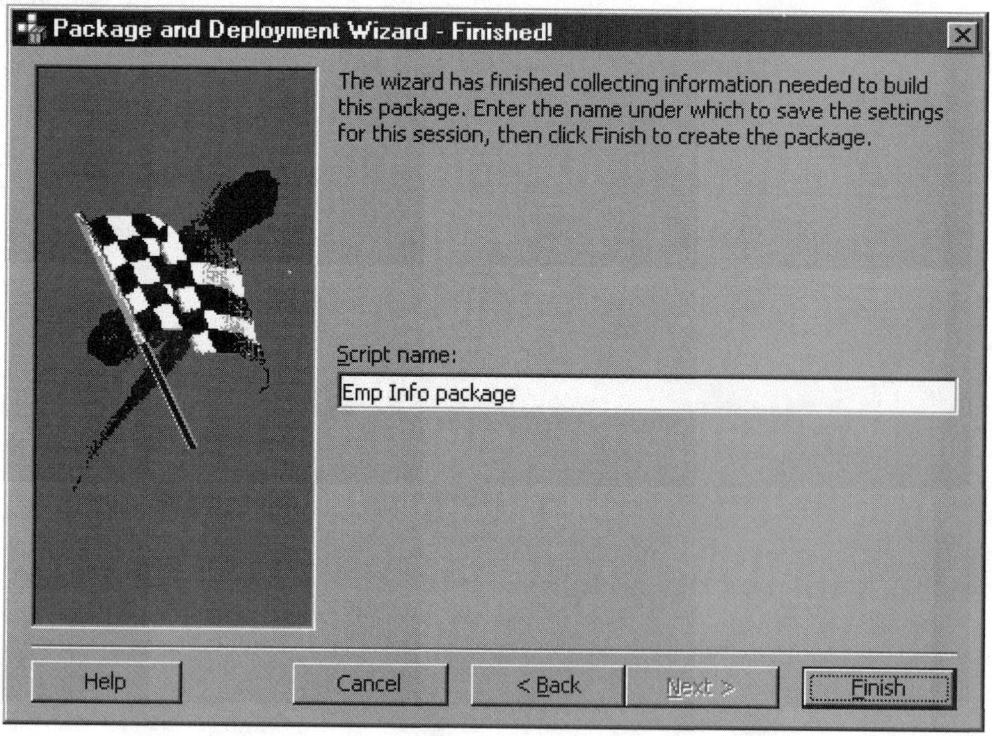

Figure 8.68: Script Name Dialog Box

Conclusion/Observation

In the above procedure, the most significant step is step 9 where the database file is added to the installation package. The next important step is step 14 where the database file is specified to be installed in the same location as that of the application. This enables the application to connect to the appropriate database at run time as it is done in the load event of the form, frmMain. After the package is being created, the application is ready to be deployed and installed in any location.

Lab Activity Checklist

S. No.	Tasks	Completed	
		Yes	No
1.	The installation package is created.		
2.	The database file is added to the installation package and the install location is specified as the application path.		

Project

1. Create the Installation package for the EmpInfo project created in previous chapters.

2. Deploy the installation package in a folder of another computer on the network.

Glossary

A

Abstraction: Refers to abstraction of complicated operations by hiding the details.

ActiveX controls: Controls, which are developed using ActiveX technology, and can be added to applications to provide extra functionality to applications.

ADO: ADO or ActiveX Data Objects provides a platform to access and manipulate databases in a simple, quick, and easy way. ADO is based on COM technology and is particularly apt for Client/Server, and other Web-based applications.

C

Child window: The windows that are displayed from the main window in an MDI application.

Class: A user-defined data type that binds together code and data.

Collections: Ordered groups of items that are considered as sets. The items of a collection can be of any data type. A collection itself is an object. Therefore, it can be created and referenced anywhere in the application just like any other object. However, to ensure encapsulation a collection is normally created in a class defined specifically for managing the collection, called a *collection class.*

D

Data-Bound: Visual Basic controls, which can display data from a data control like ADODC.

DataCombo: A data-bound ActiveX control similar to DBCombo, which can display data obtained from a data source in a combo box. It has an optional textbox to enter data.

DataEnvironment: A container object consisting of Command and Connection objects; generally used to create hierarchical recordsets from a database.

DataGrid: Another ActiveX control that displays data from a data source in a fashion similar to a spreadsheet. DataGrid can directly edit, add, and delete records.

DataList: A data-bound ActiveX control similar to DBList, which can display data obtained from a data source in a listed manner.

E

Encapsulation: Hiding the inner workings of an object is called *encapsulation.*

F

Foreign Key: A field that is included in more than one table, in order to jointly operate on the tables. The foreign key is lifted from one table and included in other tables so that the tables have a common column.

Friend Specifier: "Friend" members can be accessed from anywhere in the project but not from outside.

H

Hierarchical FlexGrid: A new data-bound ActiveX control, which can display hierarchical recordsets in bands. It can display data from a DataEnvironment or an ADODC control.

J

JDBC: Java Database Connectivity is Java's new database provider, which works in Java language. Its most important feature is its ability for cross-platform operation.

M

MDI Application: An application that consists of many document windows, which can be opened simultaneously at any point in time.

O

ODBC: Open Database Connectivity is the oldest and one of the most widely used database providers that interfaces with a range of databases.

OLE DB: Object Linking and Embedding Database is Microsoft's new database provider that is especially suitable for Client/Server and other Web based applications. It has full support for ODBC.

P

Parent Window: The main window from which other windows are displayed in an MDI application.

Primary Key: A field that has a non-null value for every record and uniquely identifies each record.

Private Specifier: An access specifier that hides the properties and methods of a class from other code samples.

Properties: Variables defined in a class that describes attributes of the objects of that class.

Property Procedures: Procedures that are used for accessing private properties outside the class.

Public Specifier: An access specifier that allows the properties and methods of a class to be accessed by the other code outside the class.

S

SDI Application: An application that contains a single document window, which can be opened at any point in time.

Shape: An ADO language having syntax similar to SQL. Shape creates a hierarchical Recordset when joining tables, instead of returning multiple rows of the matching fields. It is an efficient alternative to the SQL Join.

SQL: Structured Query Language is a language for writing specialized commands called queries that access a database and retrieve or modify the data stored in it.

Bibliography

- Connell, John. 2000. Beginning Visual Basic 6 Database Programming. Wrox Press, Ltd. Birmingham, UK.

- Getz, Ken and Mike Gilbert. 2000. Visual Basic Language Developer's Handbook. Sybex. Alameda, CA 94501.

- Koop, Ed, Anne Prince, and Joel Murach. 1999. Murach's Visual Basic 6. Murach. Fresno, California 93711-2765.

- Petroutsos, Evangelos. 1998. Mastering Visual basic 6. Sybex. Alameda, CA 94501.

- Petroutsos, Evangelos. 2000. Mastering Database Programming with Visual Basic 6. Sybex. Alameda, CA 94501.

- Petroutsos, Evangelos, and Kevin Hough. 1999. Visual Basic 6 Developer's Handbook. Sybex. Alameda, CA 94501.

- Thayer, Rob. 1999. Visual Basic 6 Unleashed, Professional Reference Edition. Sams. Indiapolis, IN.

- Thompson, Kevin, and Deanna Dicken. 2002. Learn SQL in a Weekend. Premier Press. Boston, MA 02210.

- Wright, Peter. 2000. Beginning Visual Basic 6. Wrox Press, Ltd. Birmingham, UK.

Index

I

Index, 3.65, 3.87, 3.104, 3.109, 3.114, 4.56, 4.59, 4.70, 4.71, 4.73, 4.74, 5.7, 5.22, 5.23, 6.36

Initialize() Event, 3.26

INSERT Statement, 5.32, 5.76

Installation Title, 8.18, 8.64

Interface Style, 3.1, 3.98

Internet Connectivity Dialog Box, 4.31

Introduction Dialog Box, 4.26

J

JOIN Operator, 5.35, 5.76

L

Label Control, 2.28, 3.43, 3.44, 3.50, 3.51, 3.97, 3.104, 3.114, 3.117, 3.123, 3.131, 4.49, 4.56, 4.59, 5.102, 6.77, 6.84, 6.89, 7.11

Line Control, 3.1, 3.68, 3.71, 3.97

ListBox Control, 3.53, 3.124, 5.87, 5.88, 5.95, 6.19

Load() Event, 3.28

M

MDI, 3.14, 3.17, 3.20, 4.1, 4.24, 4.39, 4.40, 4.41, 4.42, 4.43, 4.44, 4.45, 4.46, 4.47, 4.50, 4.51, 4.62, 4.65, 4.77, 4.78, 4.79, 4.80, 4.81, 4.84, 4.85, 4.86, 5.74, 7.10, 7.13, 7.43

MDI Child Form, 3.14, 3.20, 4.42, 4.77, 4.79

MDI Parent Form, 3.14, 4.42, 4.77, 4.78, 4.80

Menu Bar, 2.16, 4.85

Menu Item, 4.72

Menus, 1.11, 4.1, 4.3, 4.4, 4.27, 4.28

Menus Dialog Box, 4.27

Microsoft Access, 2.17, 4.71, 4.79, 5.1, 5.3, 5.5, 5.11, 5.12, 5.24, 5.25, 5.28, 5.48, 5.81, 5.82, 5.88, 5.95, 5.102, 5.108, 6.5, 6.6, 6.10, 6.97, 6.102, 6.107, 6.112, 7.6, 7.67, 7.74

Microsoft Multimedia Control, 3.1, 3.79, 3.121

Modules, 7.1, 7.8, 7.9, 7.10, 7.18, 7.19

Move Method, 3.19, 3.28

Multiple Document Interface, 3.17, 4.1, 4.24, 4.41, 4.62

N

Network Button, 8.29, 8.69

O

Object-Oriented Programming, 7.1, 7.3

Objects, 2.6, 5.45, 6.54, 7.4, 7.5, 7.6, 7.47, 7.53

OptionButton Control, 3.1, 3.48, 3.49, 3.50, 3.75, 3.104, 3.105, 3.117

U

V

W